A-Z SURREY

CONTENTS

REFERENCE

Motorway	M3
Primary Route	A31
Tunnel	
A Road	A22
B Road	B2236
Dual Carriageway	
One-way Street	
Traffic flow on A Roads is also indicated by a heavy line on the driver's left.	
Road Under Construction	
Opening dates are correct at the time of publication.	
Proposed Road	
Junction Names (London Area)	SUNBURY CROSS
Restricted Access	
Pedestrianized Road	
Track & Footpath	
Residential Walkway	
London Low Emission Zone	
For information contact Transport for London (www.tfl.gov.uk/roadusers/lez)	
Railway Stations:	Level Crossing / Tunnel
National Rail Network	
Overground	
Underground	
Heritage	
London Tramlink	Stop / Tunnel
The boarding of Tramlink trams at stops may be limited to a single direction, indicated by the arrow.	
Built-up Area	STATION / VIEW
Local Authority Boundary	
National Park Boundary	
Posttown & London Postal District Boundaries	
Postcode Boundary (within Posttown)	

Map Continuation	86
Large Scale Town Centre	203
Airport	
Car Park (selected)	P
Church or Chapel	†
Fire Station	
Hospital	H
House Numbers (A & B Roads only)	69 / 60
Information Centre	i
National Grid Reference	520
Park & Ride	Artington P+R
Police Station	▲
Post Office	★
Safety Camera with Speed Limit	30 Fixed Speed Limit / V Variable Speed Limit
Fixed cameras and long term road works cameras. Symbols do not indicate camera direction.	
Toilet:	
without facilities for the Disabled	
with facilities for the Disabled	
Disabled use only	
Viewpoint	
Educational Establishment	
Hospital or Healthcare Building	
Industrial Building	
Leisure or Recreational Facility	
Place of Interest	
Public Building	
Shopping Centre or Market	
Other Selected Buildings	

SCALE

Map Pages 4-199	Map Pages 200-203
1:19,000 3⅓ inches (8.47cm) to 1 mile 5.26cm to 1km	1:9,051 7 inches (17.78cm) to 1 mile 11.05cm to 1km
0 ¼ ½ ¾ Mile	0 ⅛ ¼ ⅜ Mile
0 250 500 750 Metres 1 Kilometre	0 100 200 300 400 500 Metres

Copyright of Geographers' A-Z Map Company Limited

Fairfield Road, Borough Green, Sevenoaks, Kent TN15 8PP
Telephone: 01732 781000 (Enquiries & Trade Sales)
01732 783422 (Retail Sales)
www.az.co.uk
Copyright © Geographers' A-Z Map Co. Ltd.
Edition 7 2013

Ordnance Survey®

This product includes mapping data licensed from Ordnance Survey® with the permission of the Controller of Her Majesty's Stationery Office.
© Crown Copyright 2013. All rights reserved. Licence number 100017302
Safety camera information supplied by www.PocketGPSWorld.com
Speed Camera Location Database Copyright 2013 © PocketGPSWorld.com

Every possible care has been taken to ensure that, to the best of our knowledge, the information contained in this atlas is accurate at the date of publication. However, we cannot warrant that our work is entirely error free and whilst we would be grateful to learn of any inaccuracies, we do not accept any responsibility for loss or damage resulting from reliance on information contained within this publication.

2 KEY TO MAP PAGES

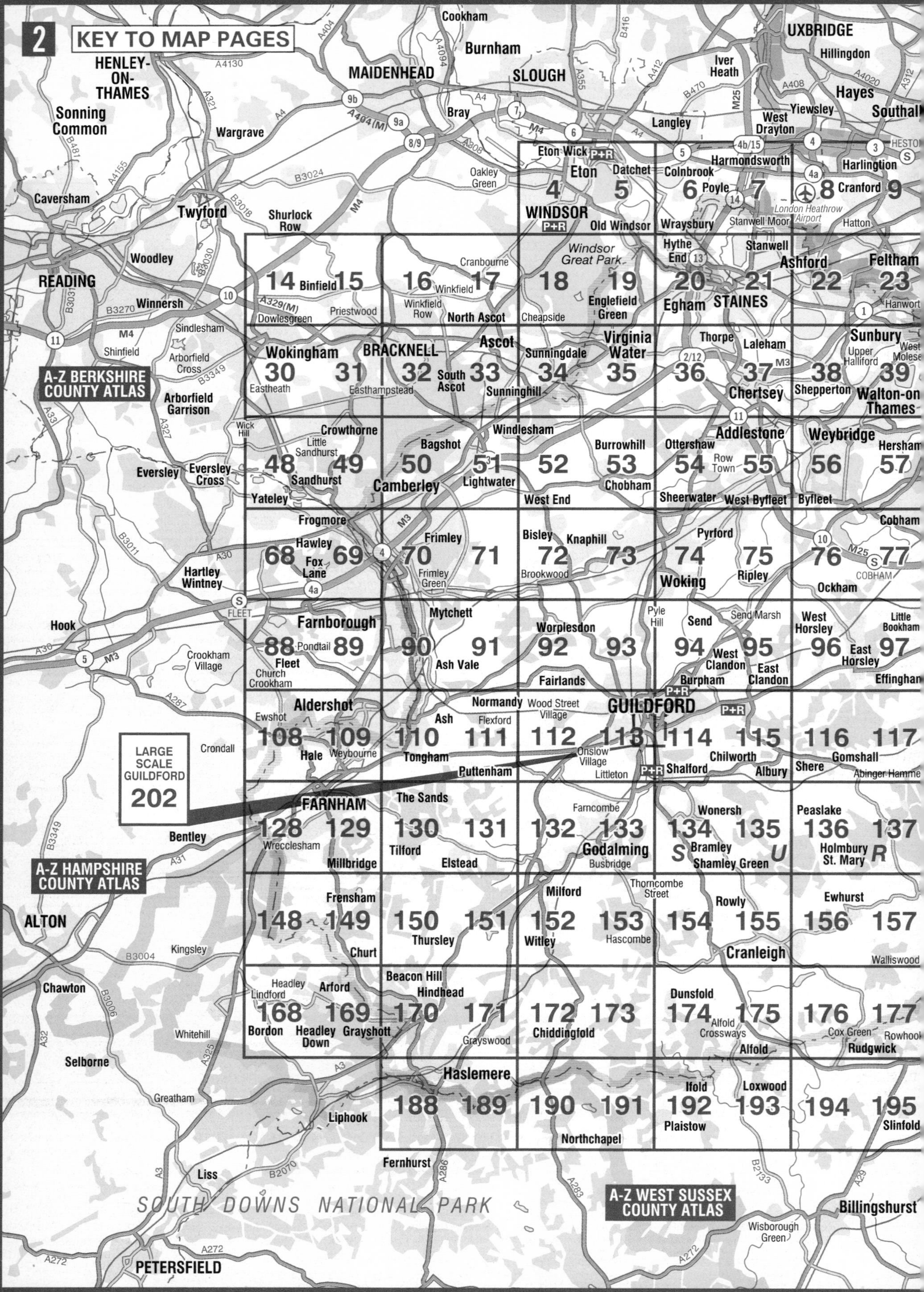

HENLEY-ON-THAMES

Sonning Common

Wargrave

Woodley

READING

Winnersh

Caversham

Twyford

Shurlock Row

Shinfield

M4

Sindlesham

Arborfield Cross

Arborfield Garrison

Eversley

Eversley Cross

Hook

Hartley Wintney

Crookham Village

Fleet

ALTON

Kingsley

Chawton

Whitehill

Selborne

Greatham

Liss

PETERSFIELD

Cookham

Burnham

MAIDENHEAD

SLOUGH

UXBRIDGE

Hillingdon

Iver Heath

Hayes

West Drayton

Yiewsley

Southal

Bray

Langley

Oakley Green

Cranbourne

Winkfield

Winkfield Row

North Ascot

Eton Wick

Eton

Datchet

Colnbrook

Poyle

Harmondsworth

Harlington

Cranford

HESTO

WINDSOR

Old Windsor

Wraysbury

Stanwell Moor

London Heathrow Airport

Hatton

Windsor Great Park

Hythe End

Stanwell

Ashford

Feltham

Egham

STAINES

Hanworth

A-Z Berkshire County Atlas

Map grid

14 Binfield	15	16	Winkfield	17	18 Cheapside	19 Englefield Green	20	21	22	23

Dowlesgreen · Priestwood · Winkfield Row

Wokingham 30 / 31 · BRACKNELL 32 · South Ascot 33 · Sunningdale 34 · Virginia Water 35 · Thorpe 36 · Laleham 37 · Sunbury 38 · Upper Halliford · West Molesey 39

Eastheath · Easthampstead · Sunninghill · Chertsey · Shepperton · Walton-on-Thames

Crowthorne 48 / 49 · Little Sandhurst · Bagshot 50 / 51 · Windlesham 52 · Burrowhill 53 · Ottershaw 54 · Row Town · Addlestone 55 · Weybridge 56 · Hersham 57

Wick Hill · Sandhurst · Camberley · Lightwater · West End · Chobham · Sheerwater · West Byfleet · Byfleet

Yateley

Frogmore 68 / 69 · Frimley 70 / 71 · Bisley 72 · Knaphill 73 · Pyrford 74 · Ripley 75 · Cobham 76 / 77

Hawley · Fox Lane · Frimley Green · Brookwood · Woking · Ockham · COBHAM

Farnborough 88 / 89 · Mytchett 90 / 91 · Worplesdon 92 / 93 · Send 94 / 95 · West Horsley 96 · East Horsley 97

Pondtail · Fleet · Church Crookham · Ash Vale · Fairlands · Pyle Hill · Send Marsh · West Clandon · East Clandon · Little Bookham · Effingham · Burpham

Aldershot 108 / 109 · Ash 110 / 111 · GUILDFORD 112 / 113 / 114 / 115 · 116 / 117

Ewshot · Hale · Weybourne · Normandy · Flexford · Wood Street Village · Onslow Village · Littleton · Chilworth · Shalford · Albury · Shere · Gomshall · Abinger Hamme

LARGE SCALE GUILDFORD 202

Crondall

Bentley

A-Z Hampshire County Atlas

FARNHAM 128 / 129 · The Sands 130 / 131 · 132 / 133 · Wonersh 134 / 135 · Peaslake 136 / 137

Wrecclesham · Tilford · Elstead · Farncombe · Godalming · Busbridge · Bramley · Shamley Green · Holmbury St. Mary · Rowhook

Millbridge

Frensham 148 / 149 · Thursley 150 / 151 · Milford 152 · Witley 153 · Hascombe 154 · Rowly 155 · Ewhurst 156 / 157

Churt · Cranleigh · Walliswood

Beacon Hill 168 / 169 · Hindhead 170 / 171 · 172 / 173 · Dunsfold 174 / 175 · 176 / 177

Headley · Lindford · Arford · Grayshott · Grayswood · Chiddingfold · Alfold Crossways · Alfold · Cox Green · Rudgwick

Bordon · Headley Down

Haslemere 188 / 189 · 190 / 191 · Ifold 192 · Loxwood 193 · 194 / 195

Liphook · Northchapel · Plaistow · Slinfold

Fernhurst

SOUTH DOWNS NATIONAL PARK

A-Z West Sussex County Atlas

Billingshurst

Wisborough Green

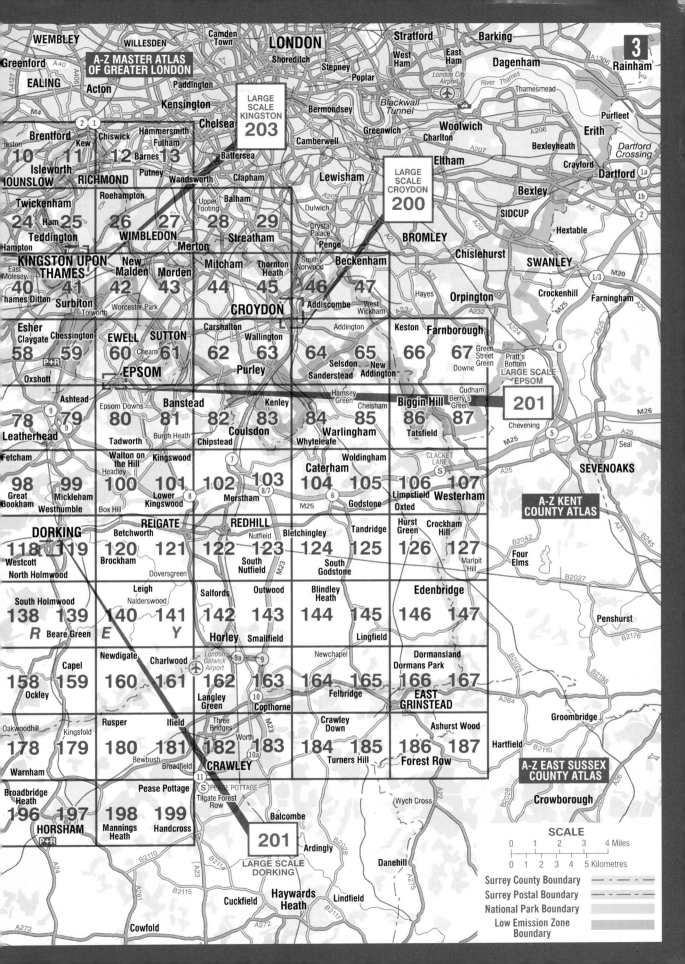

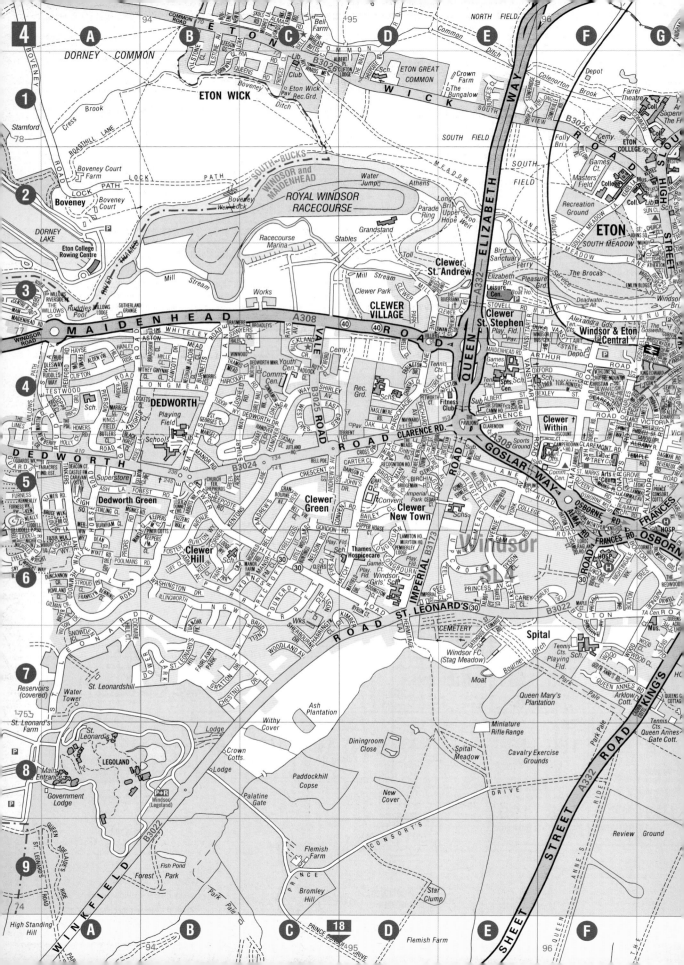

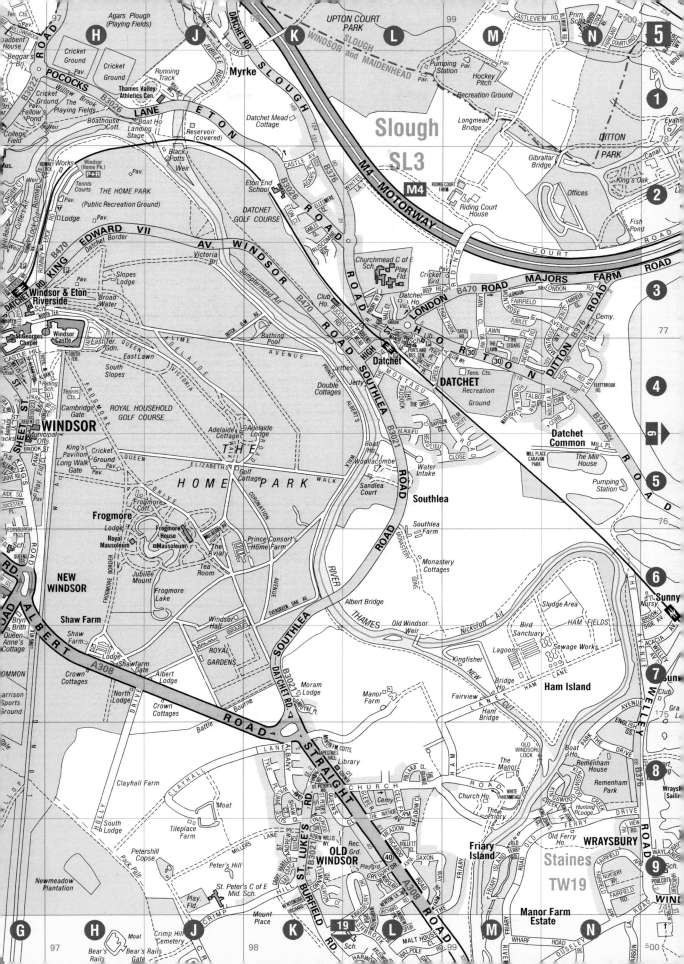

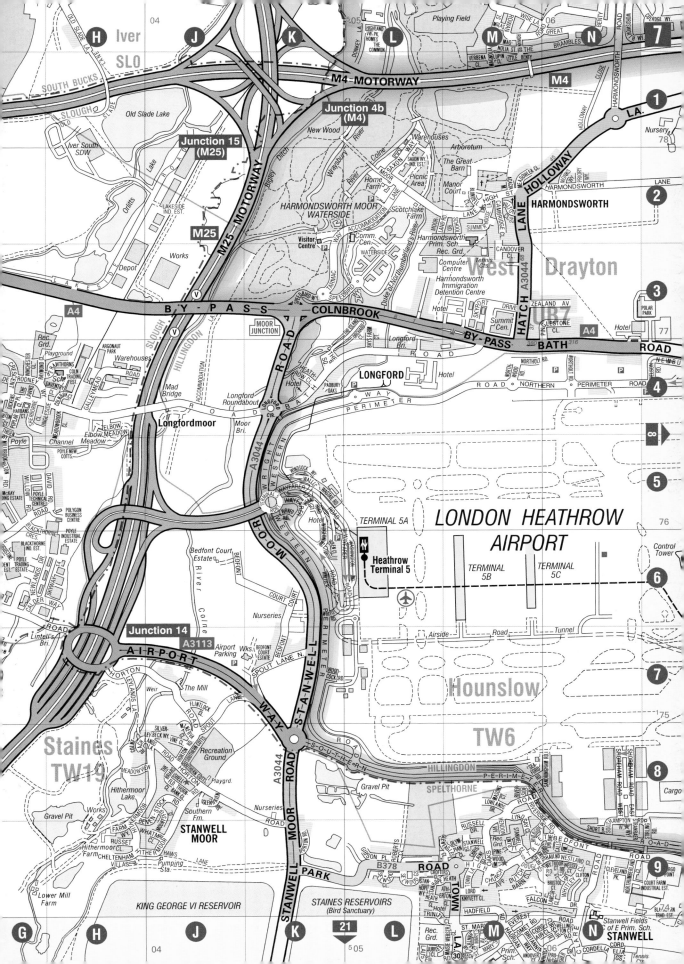

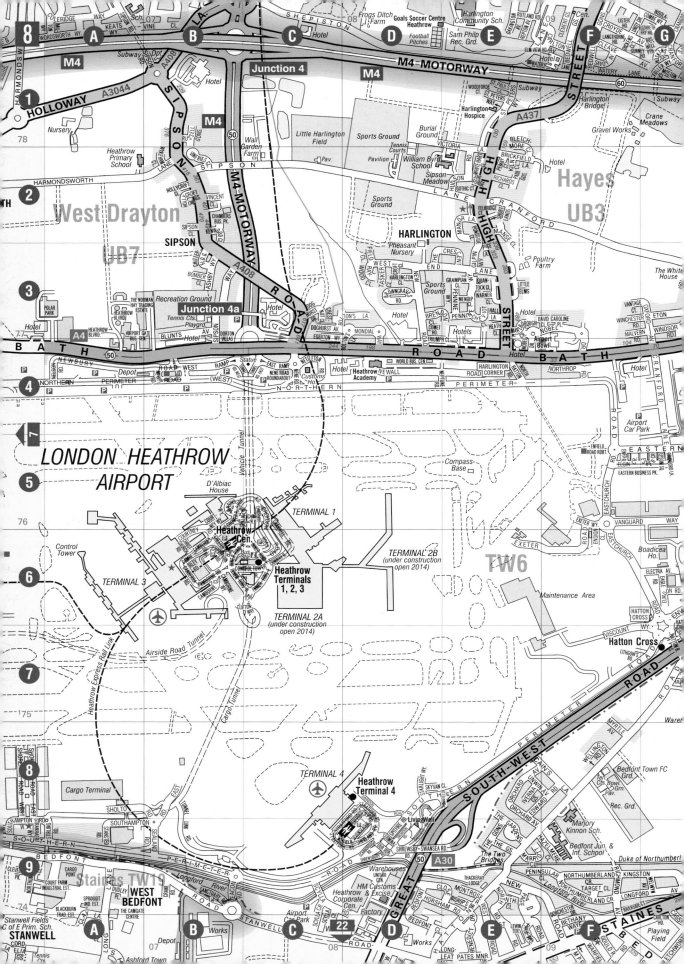

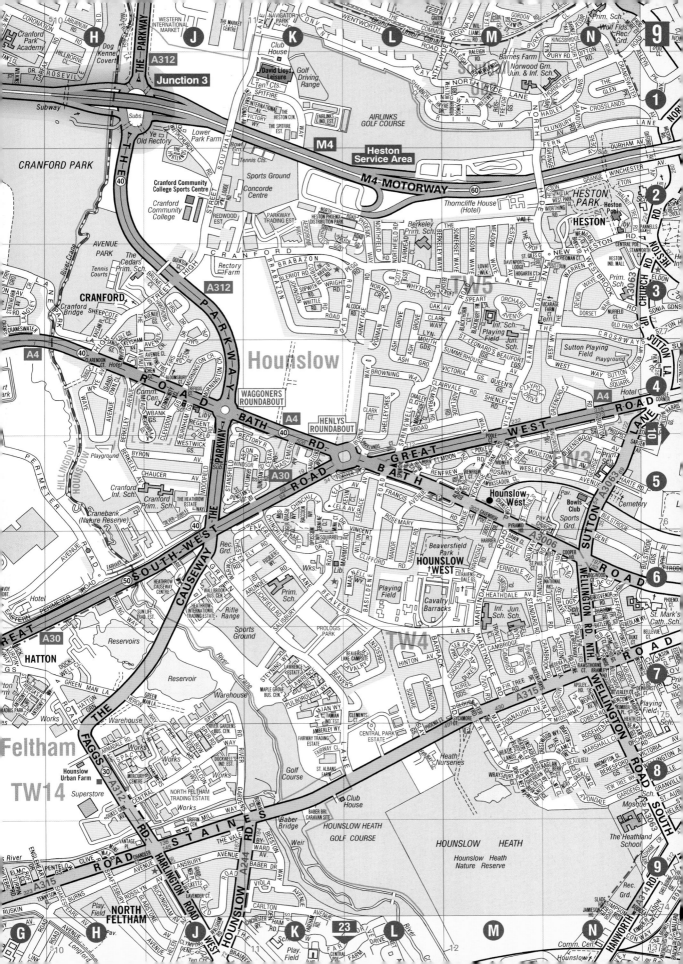

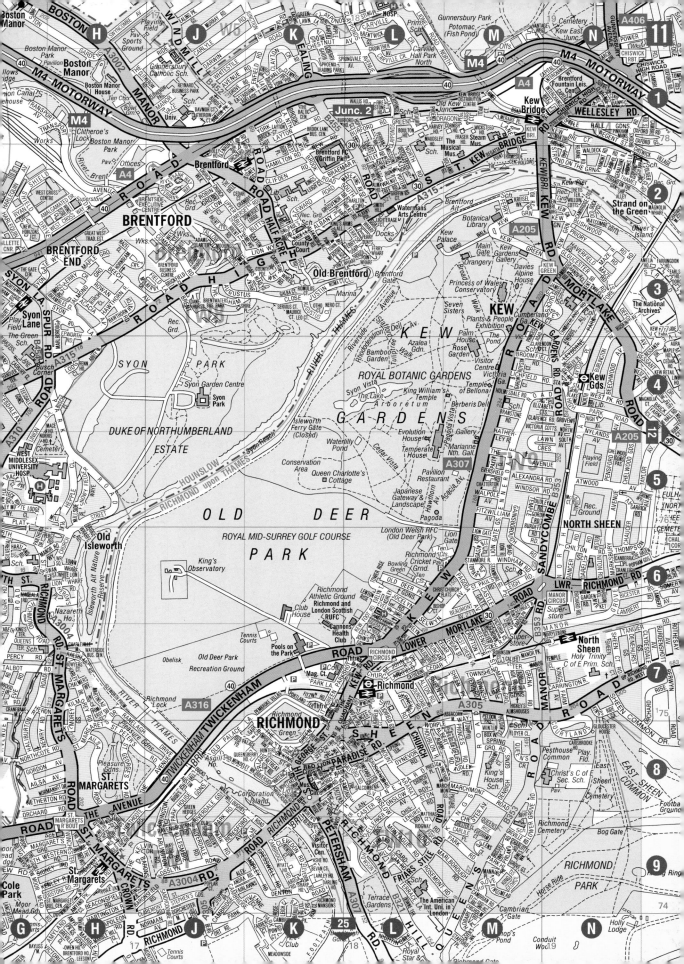

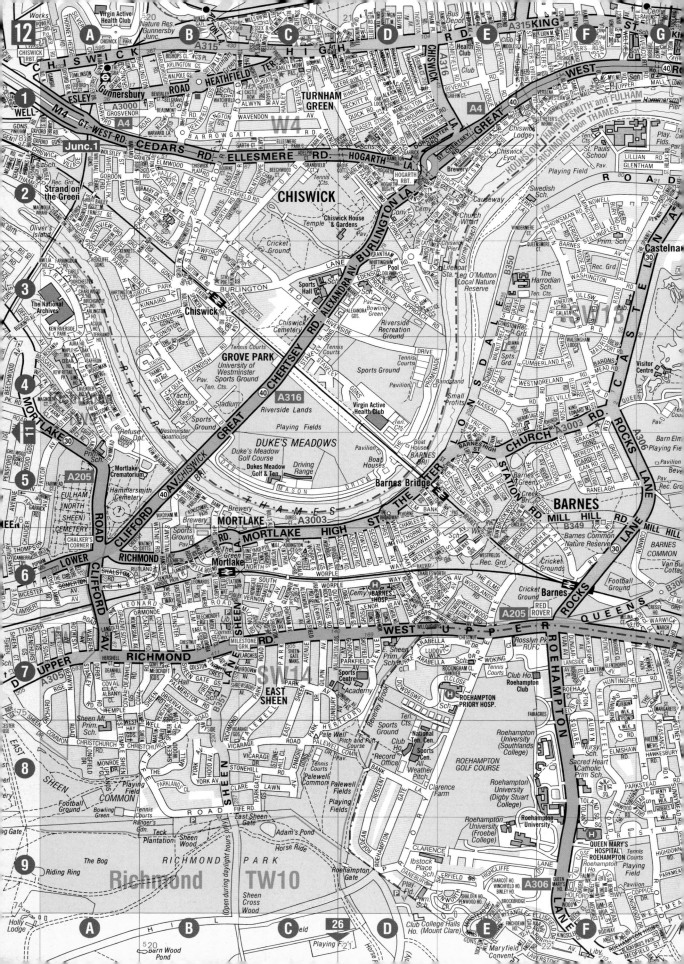

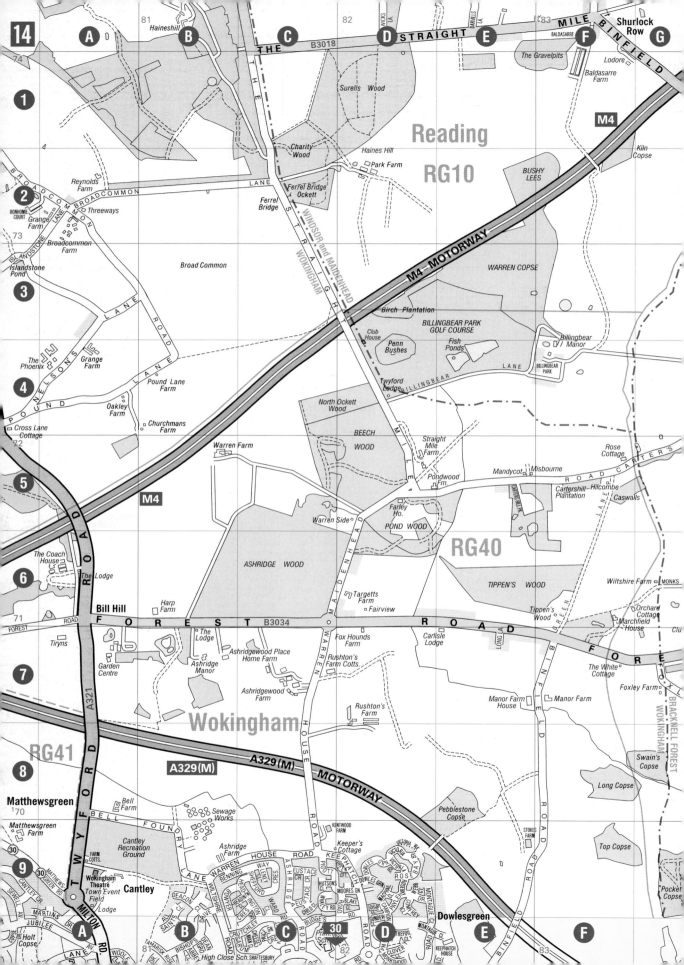

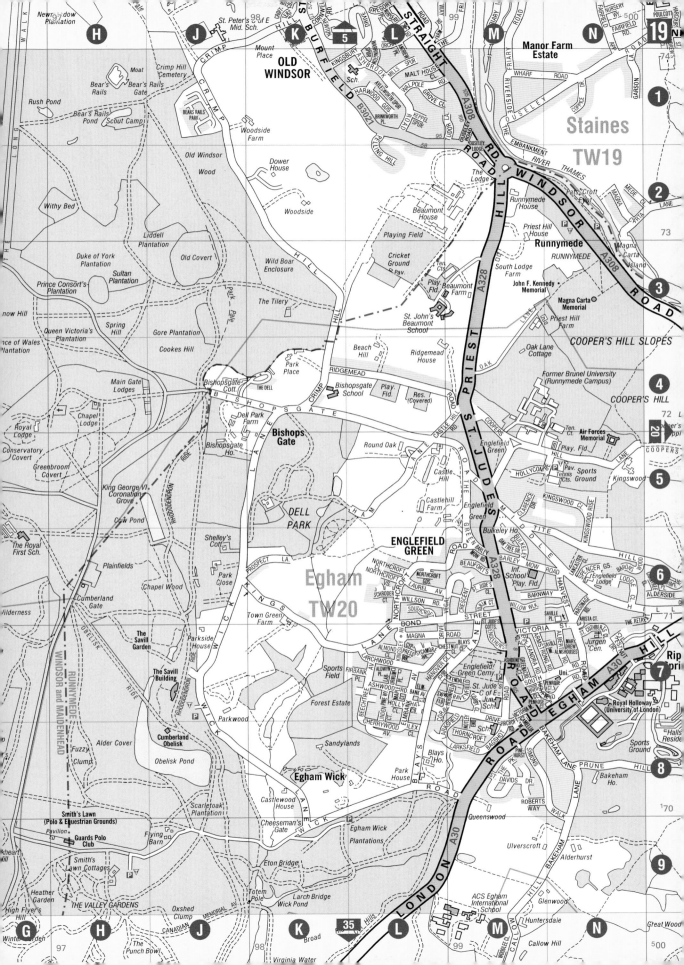

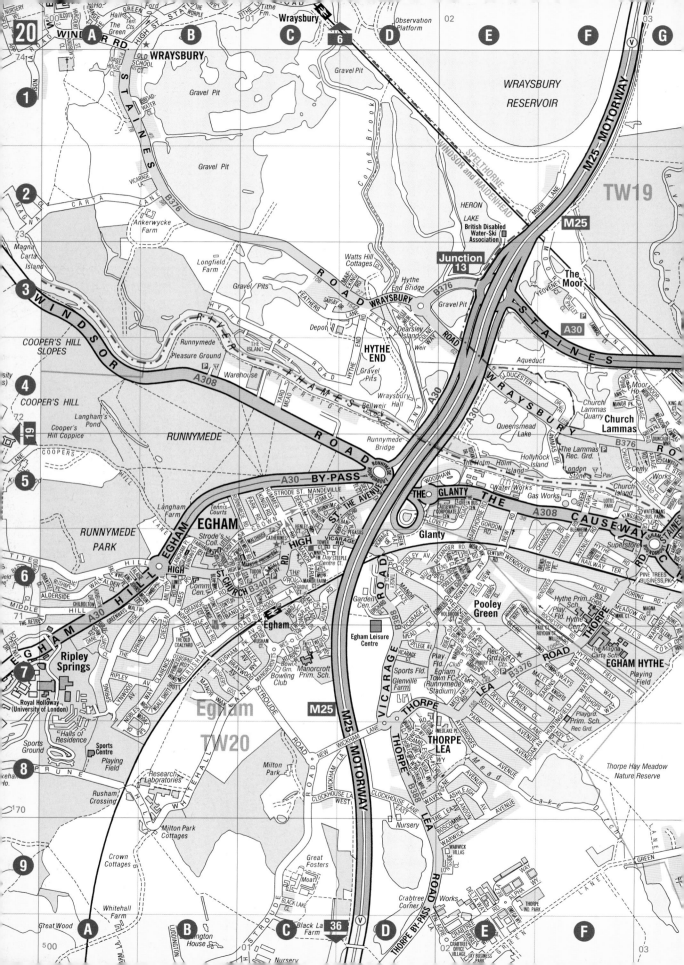

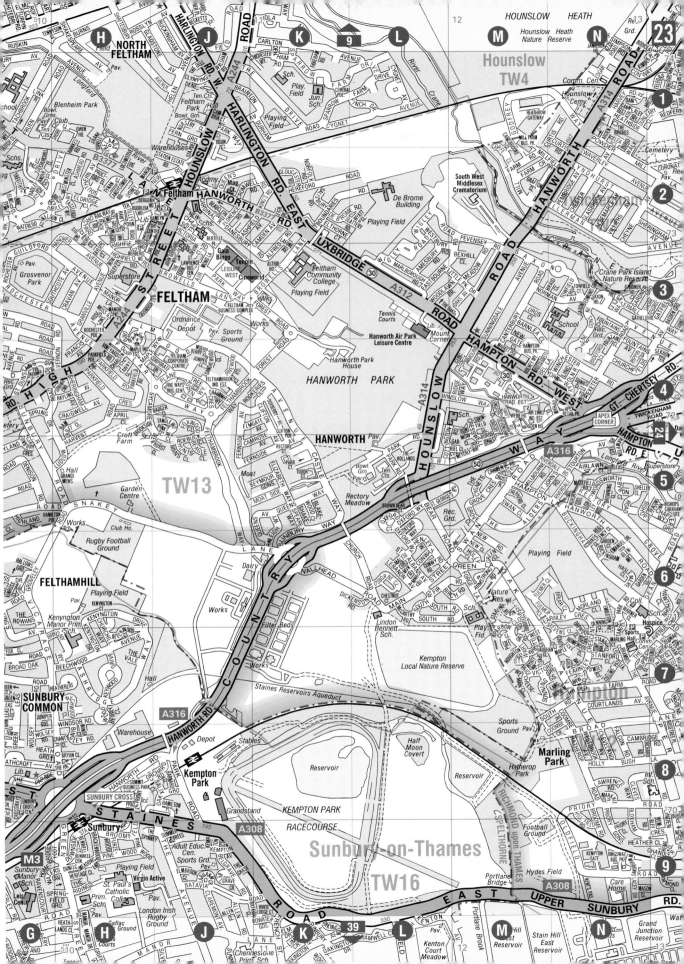

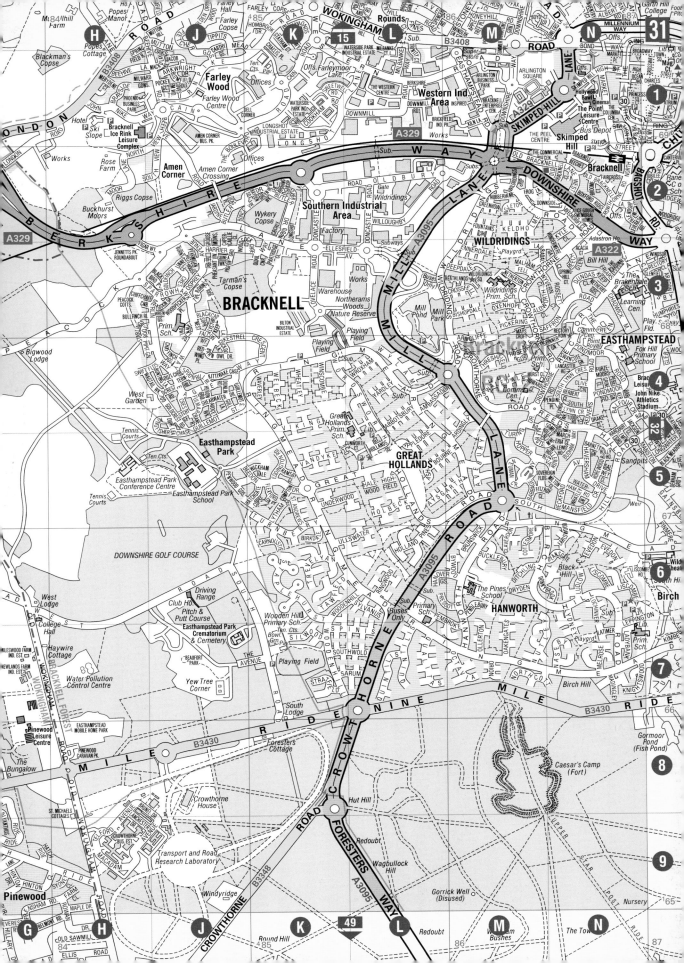

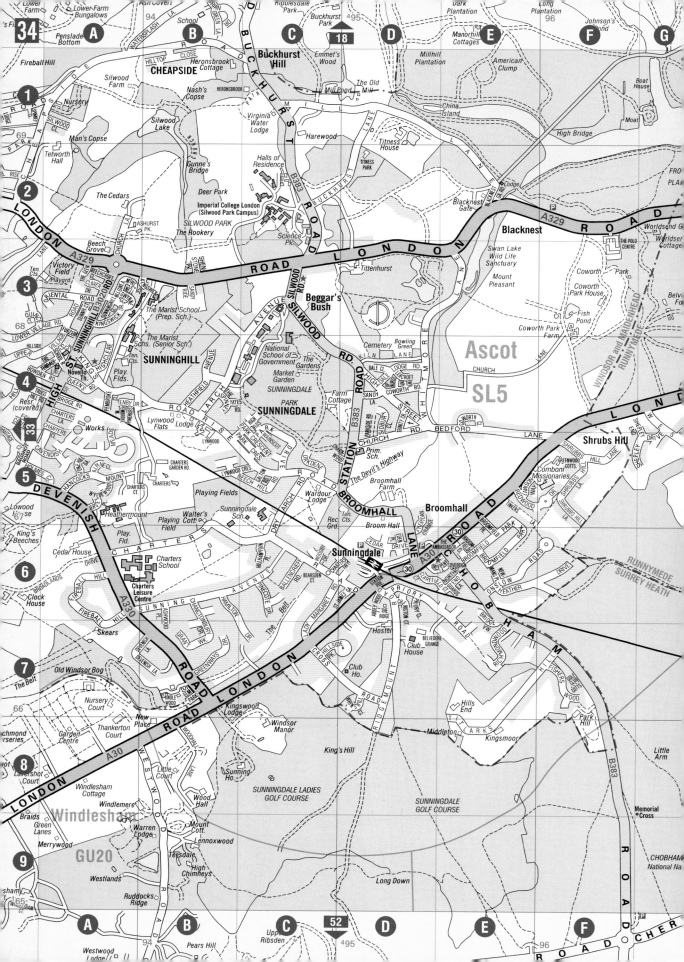

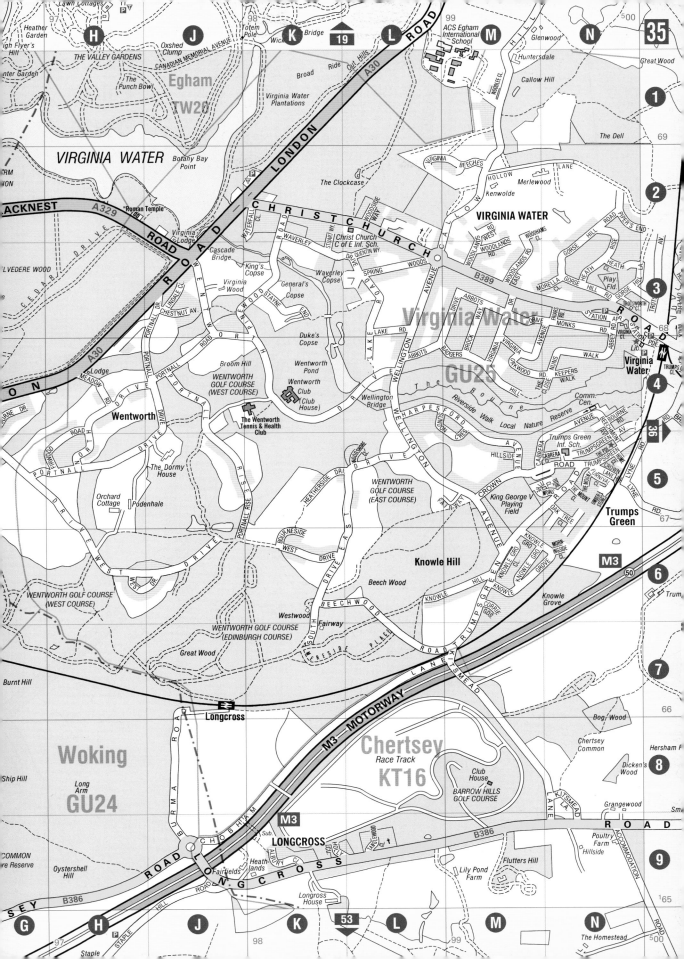

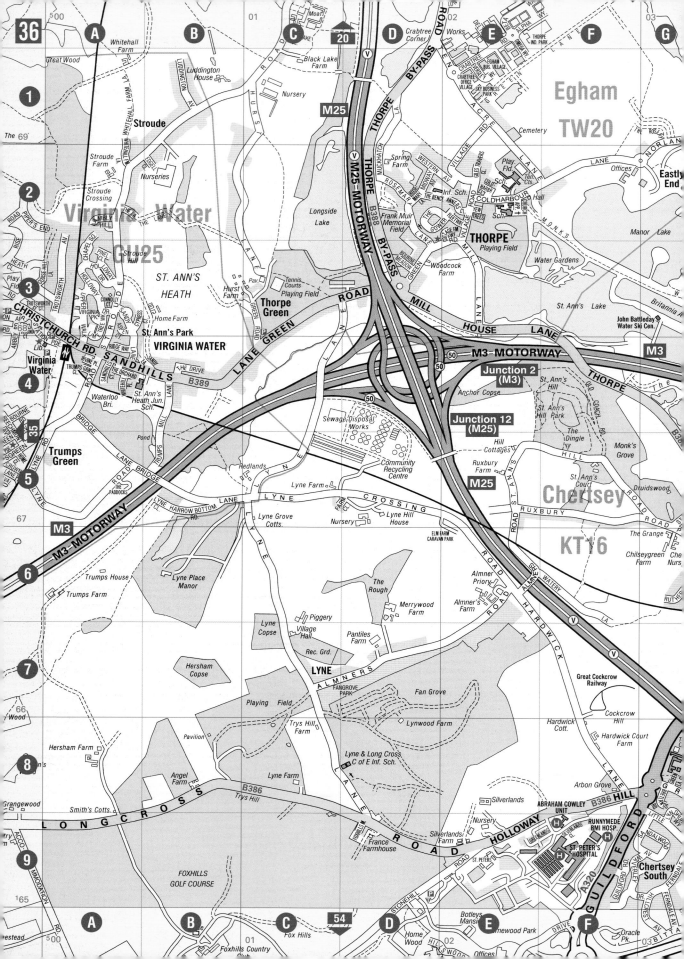

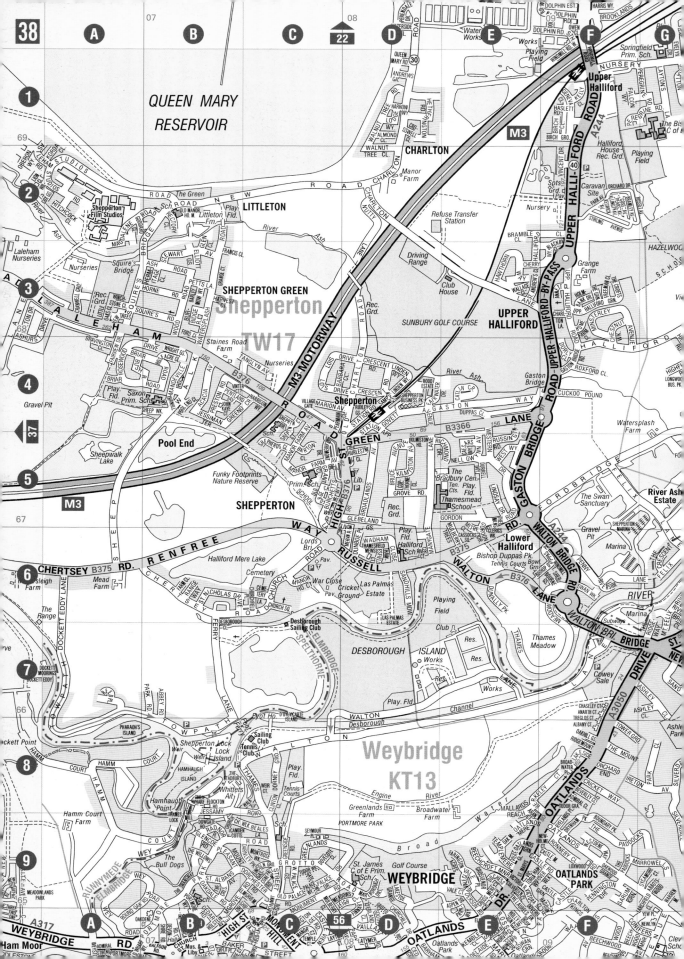

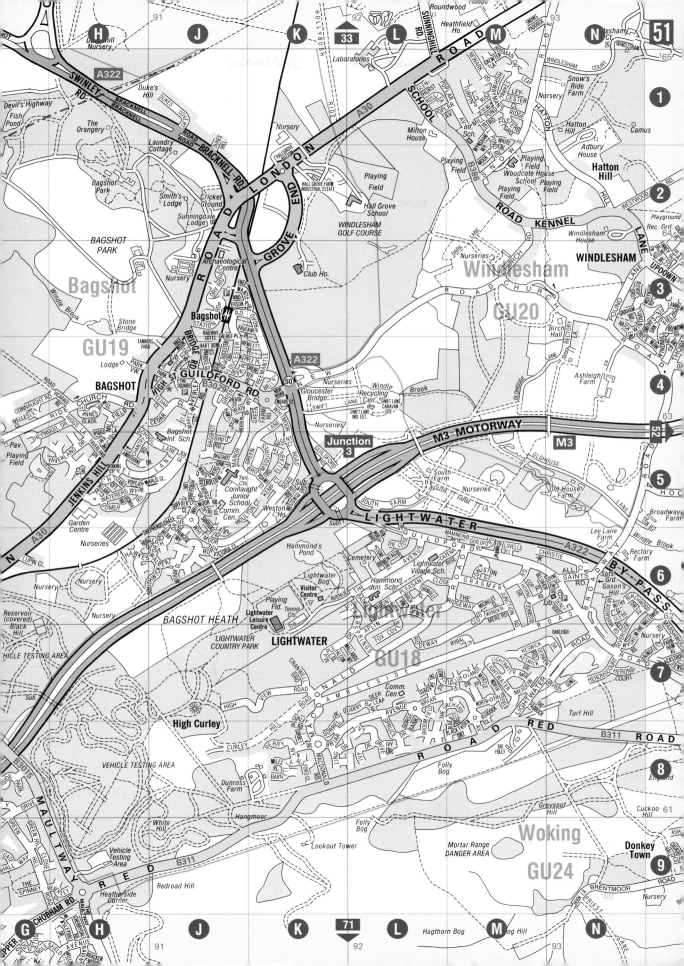

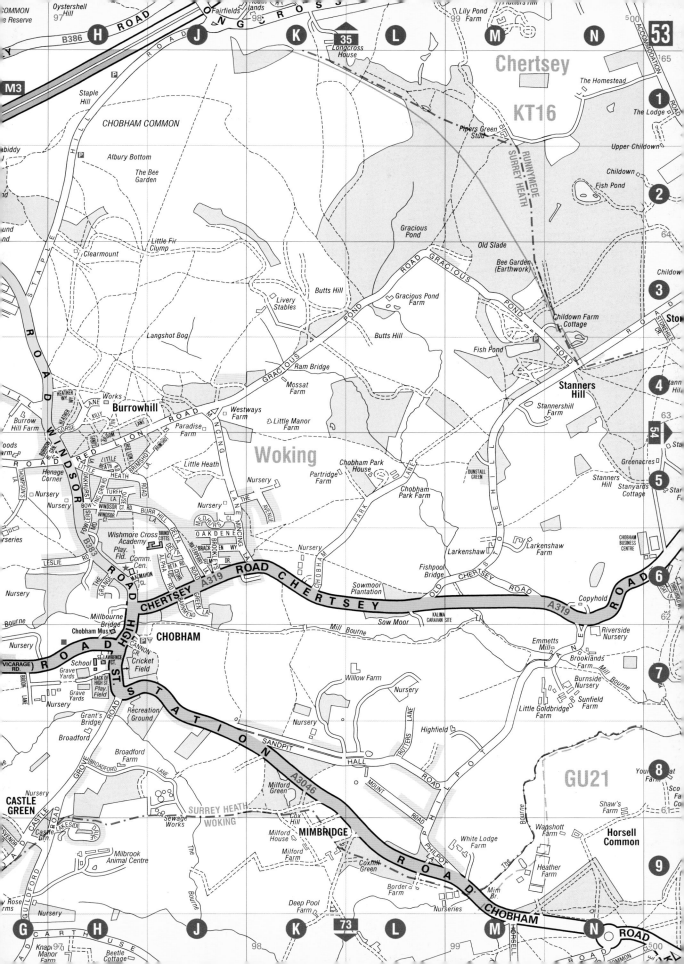

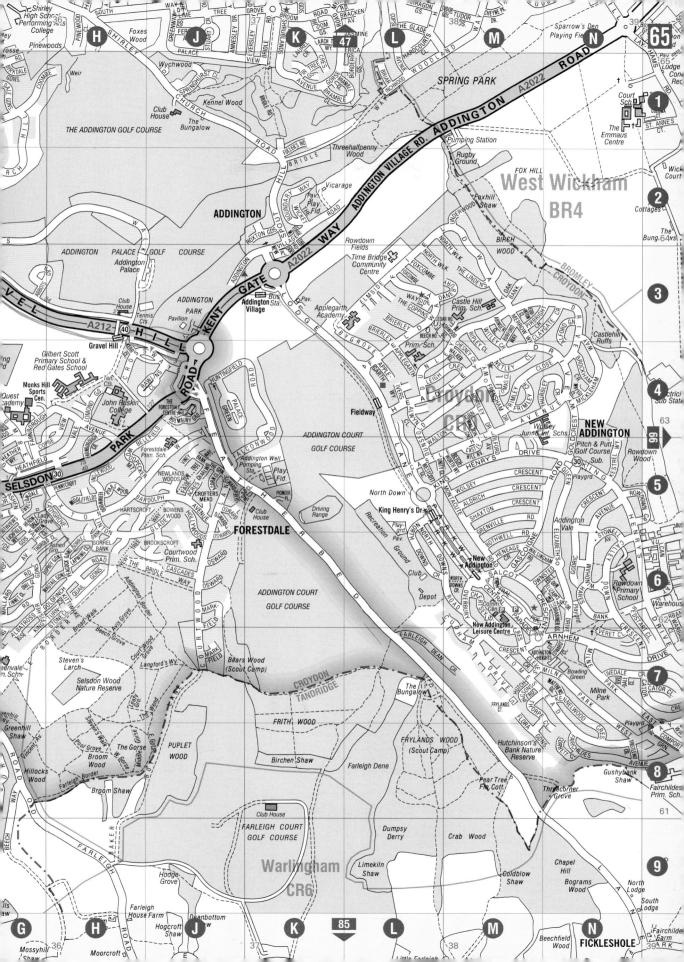

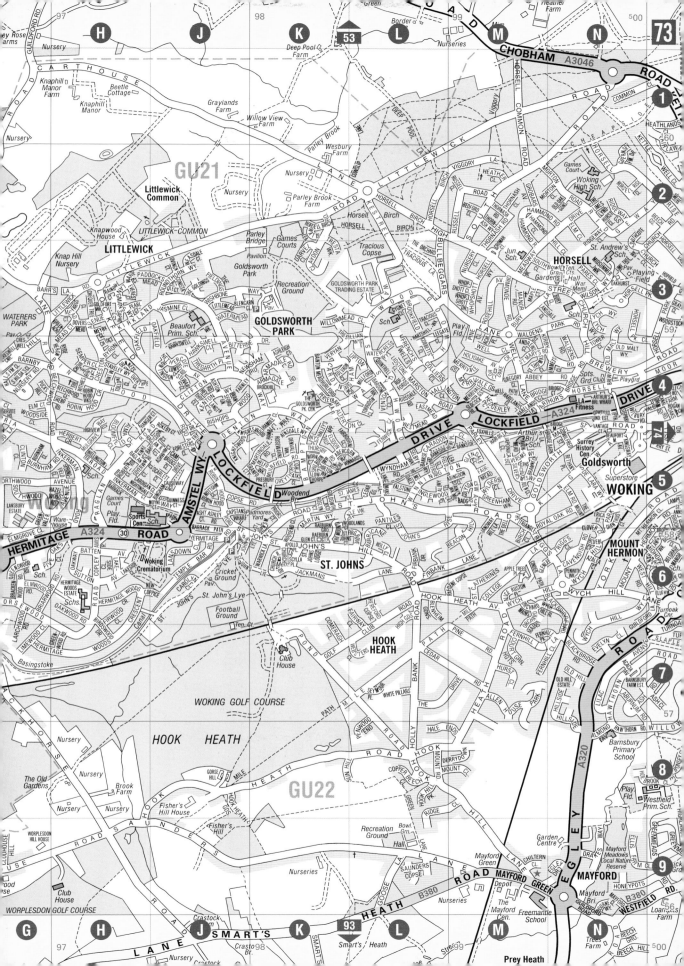

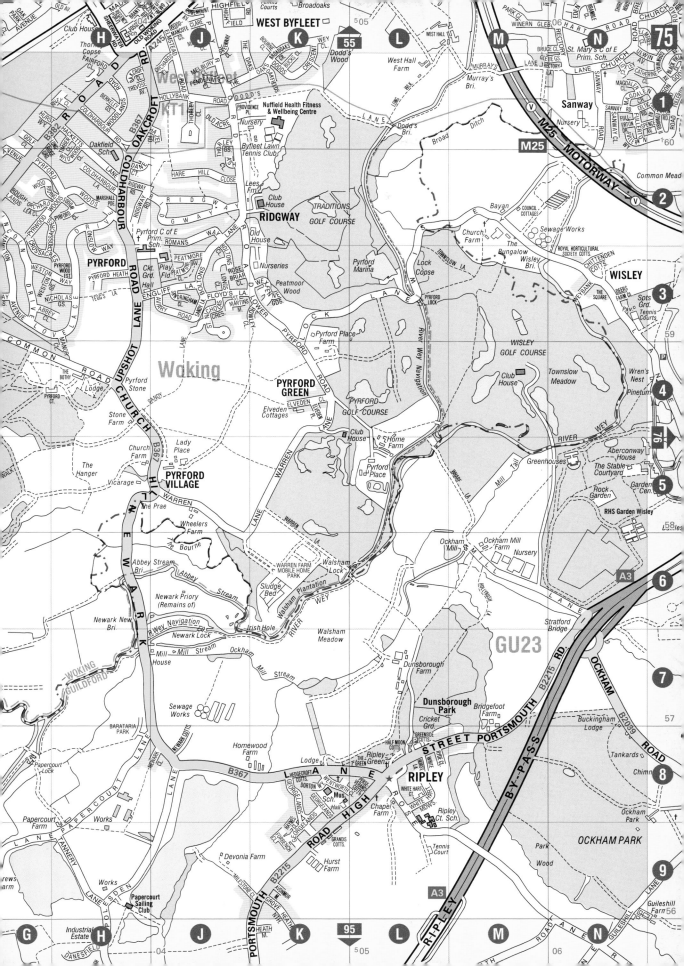

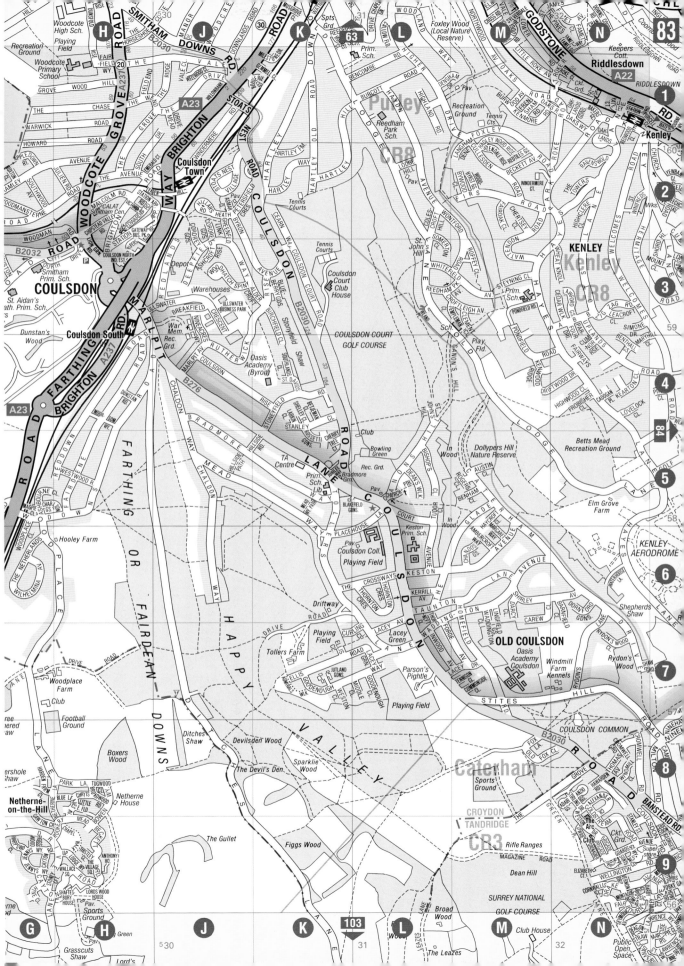

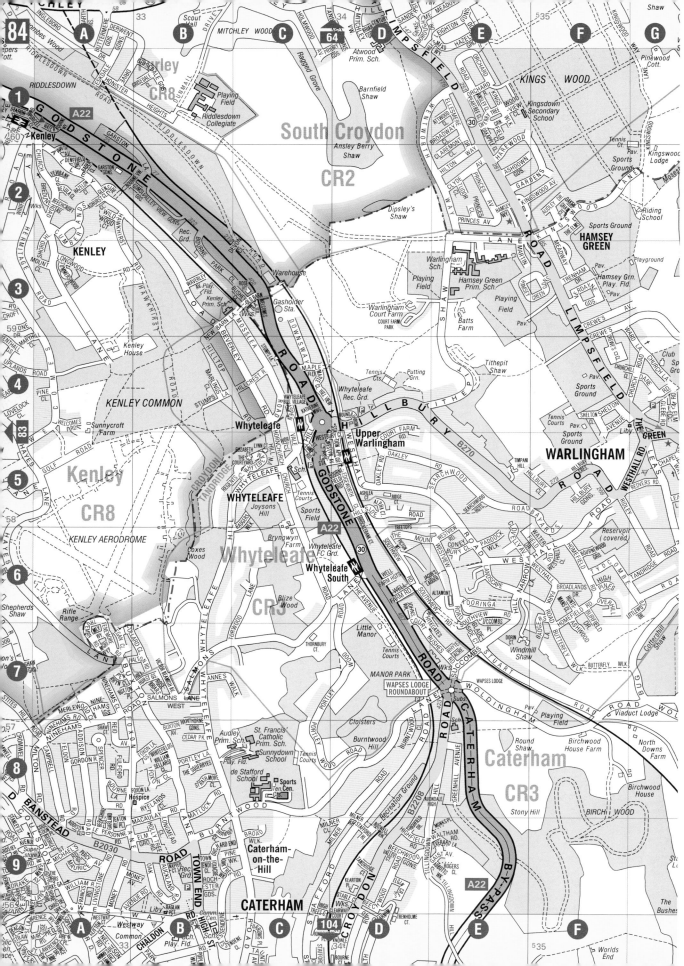

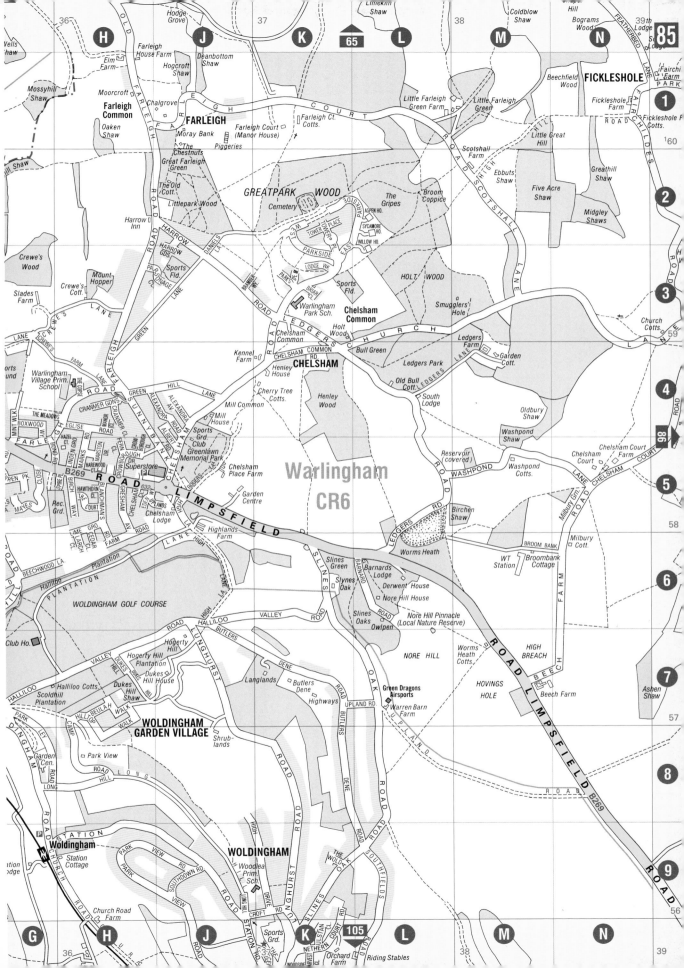

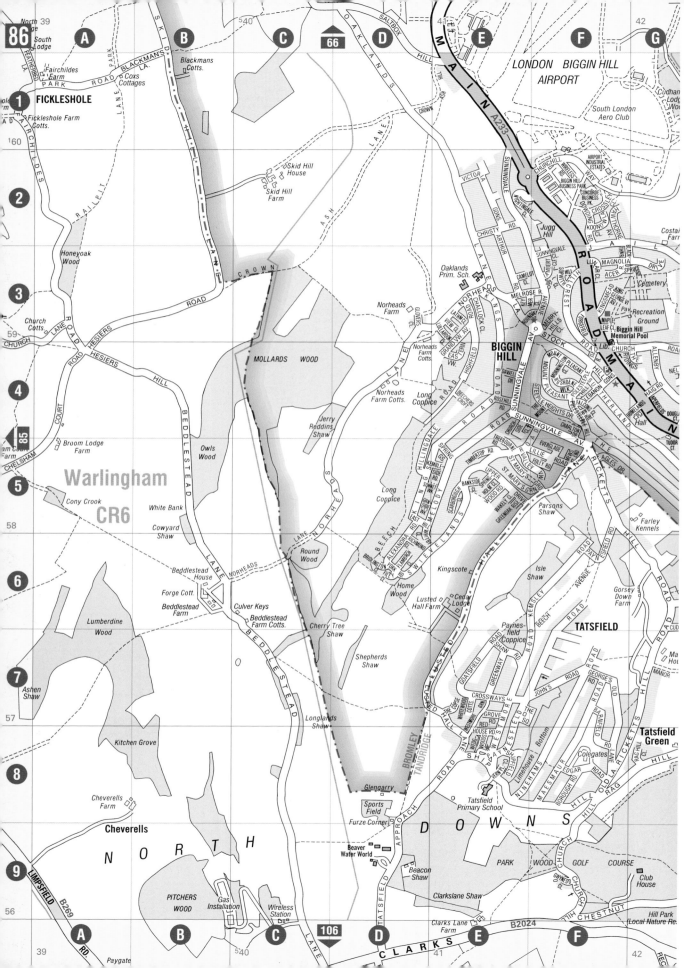

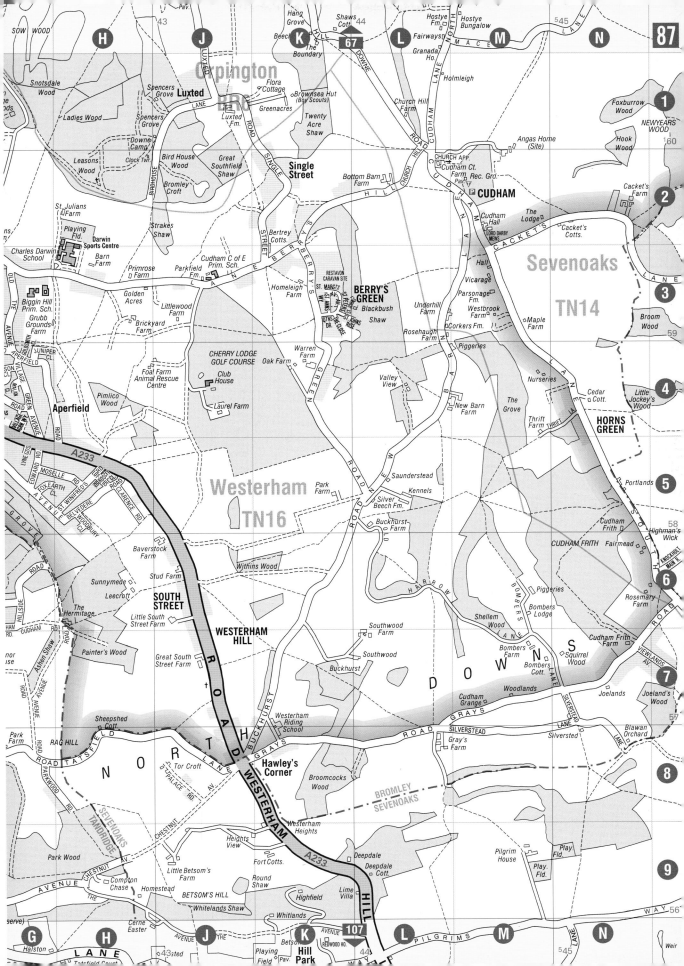

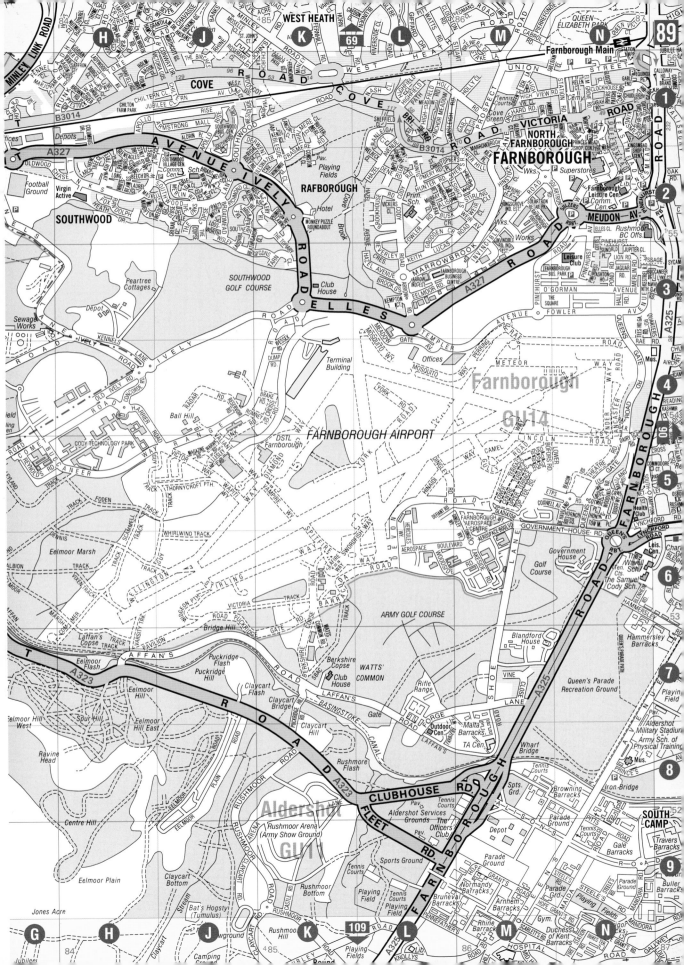

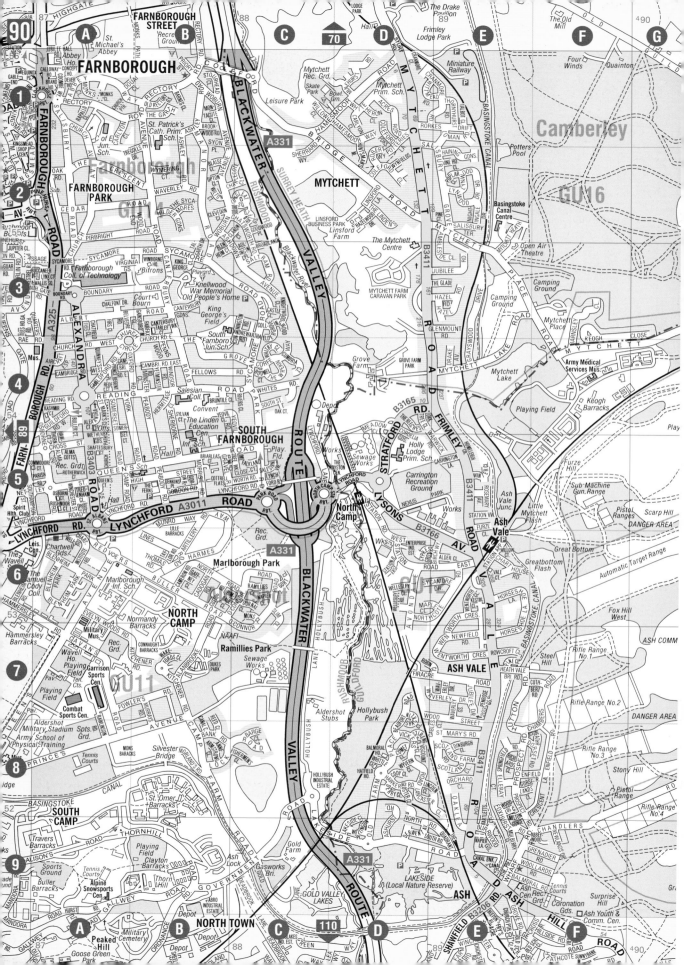

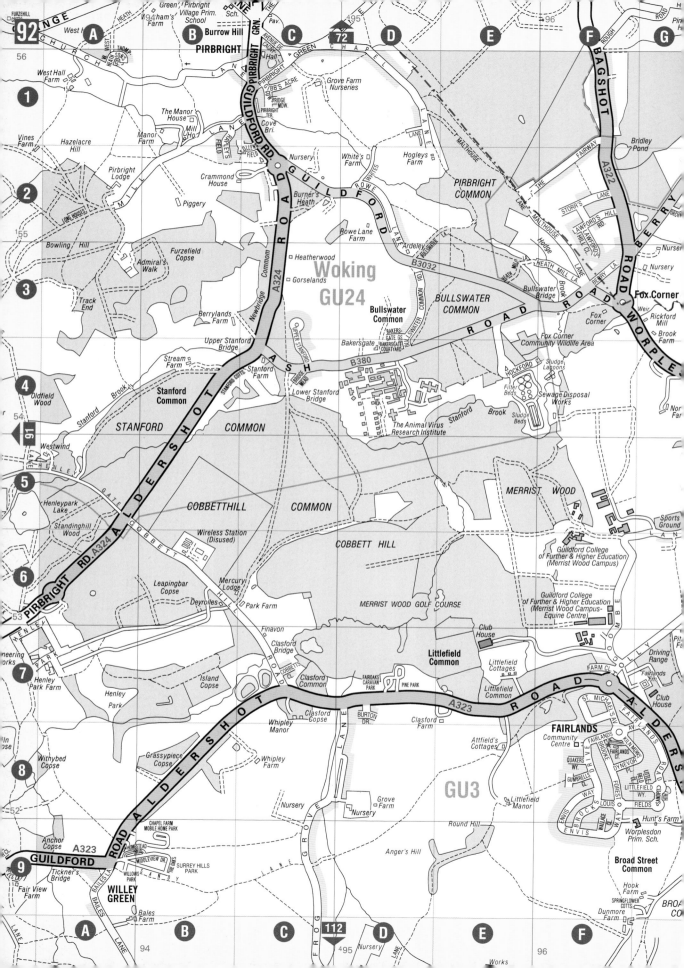

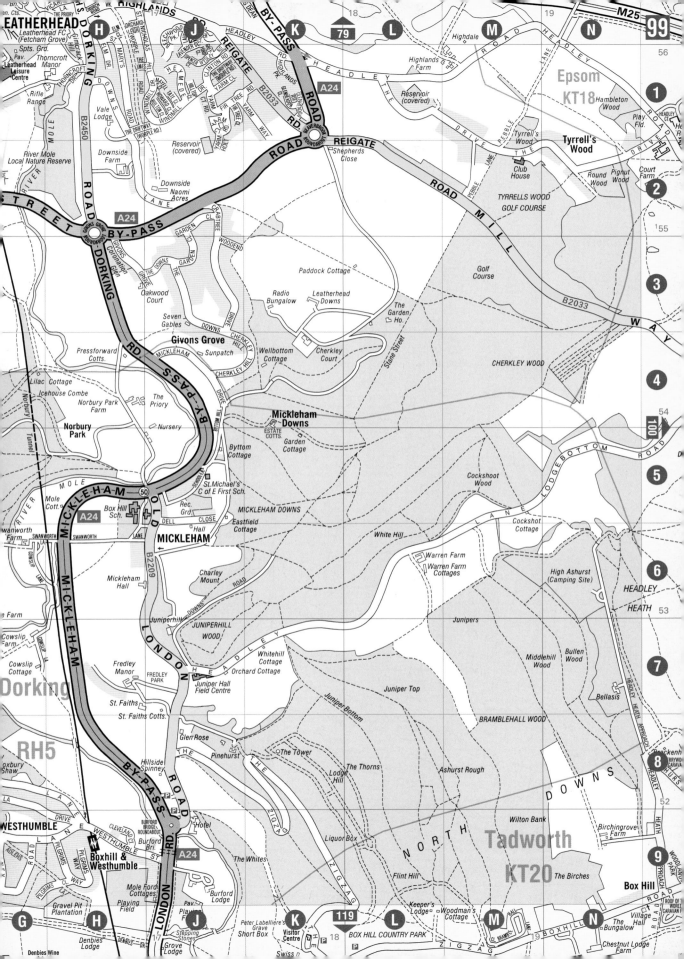

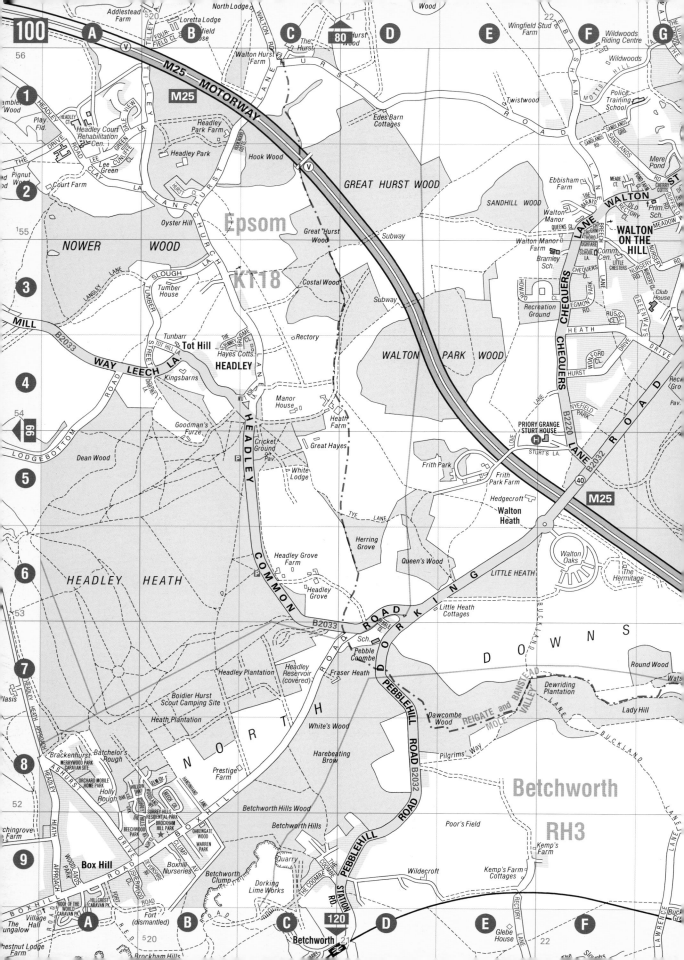

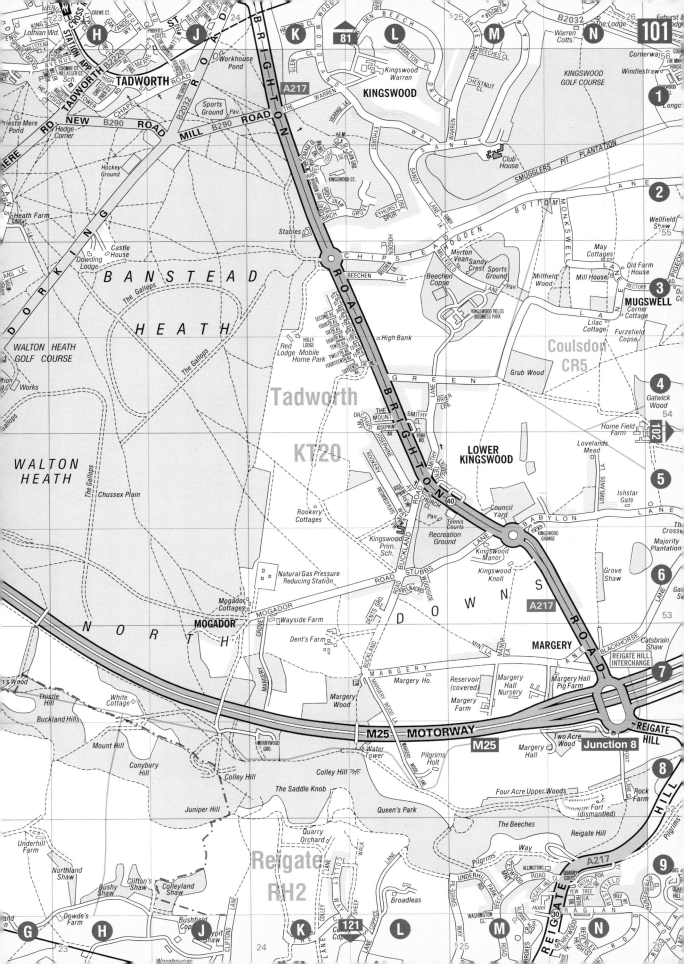

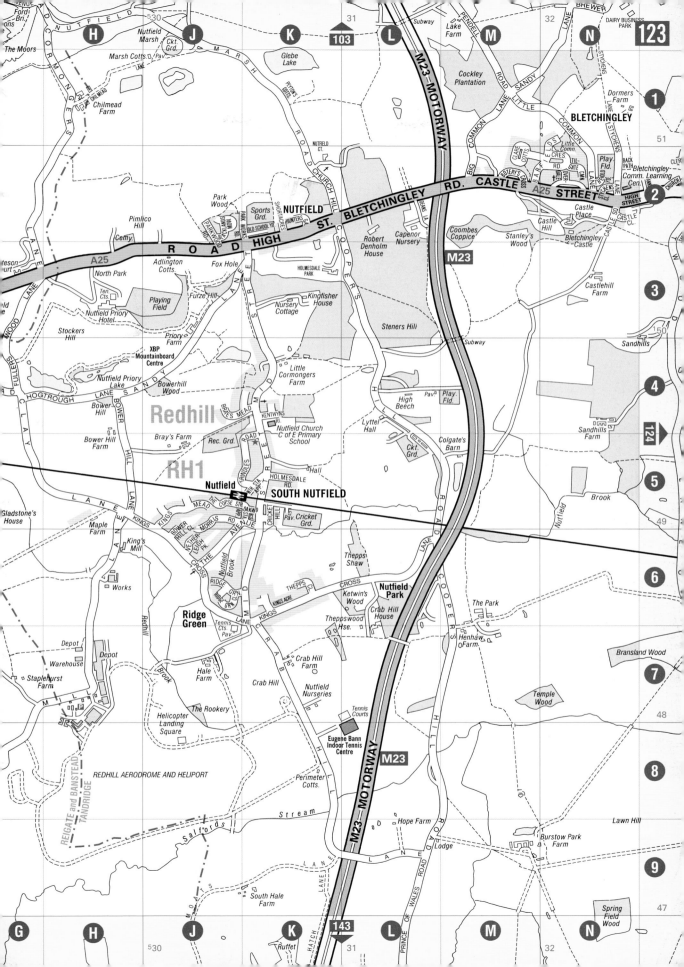

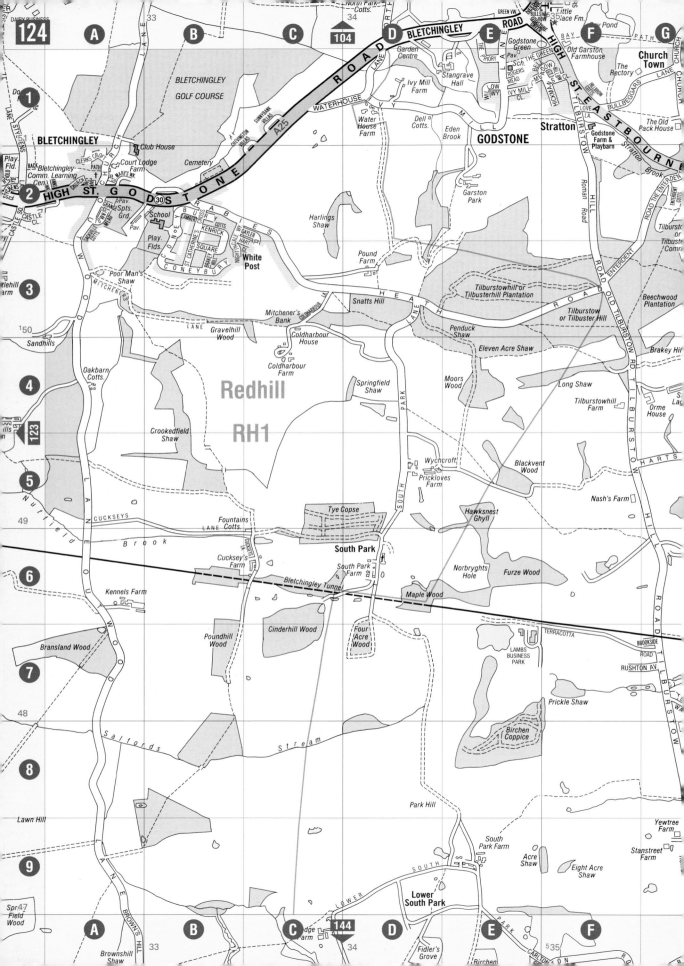

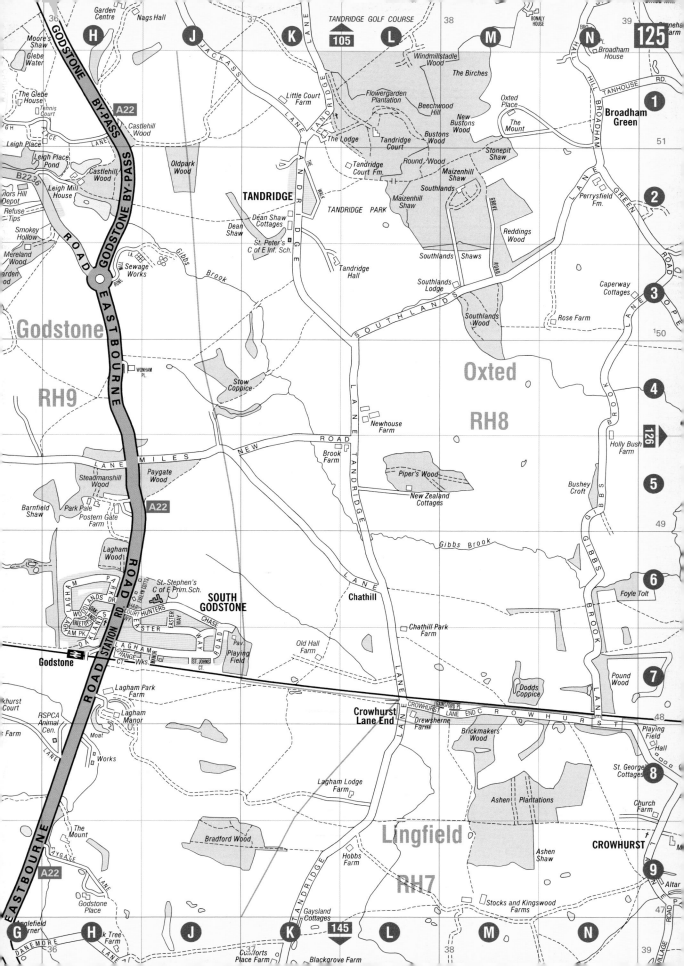

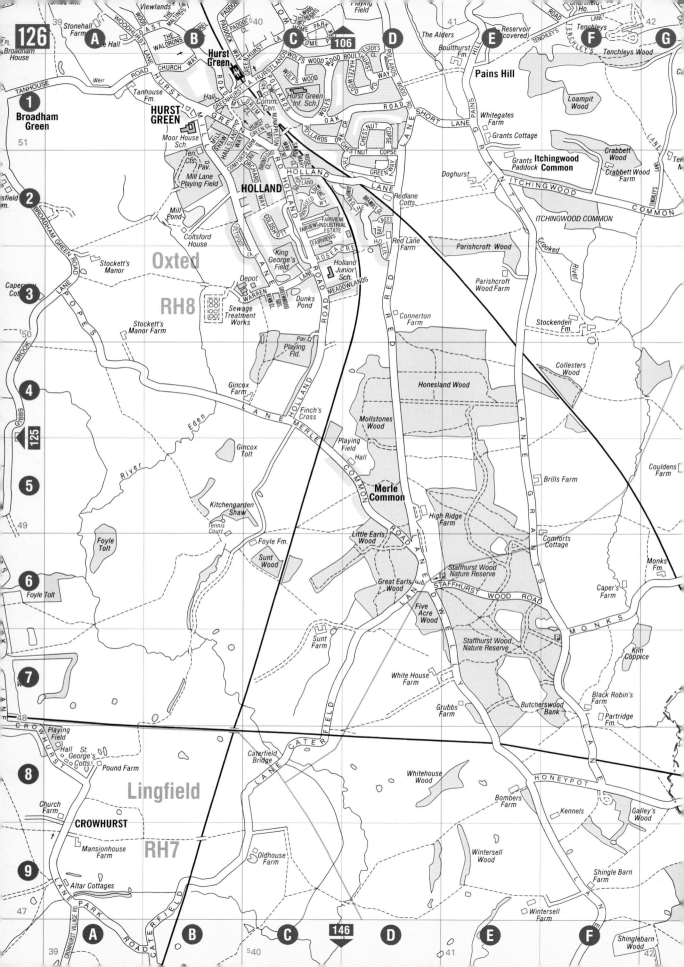

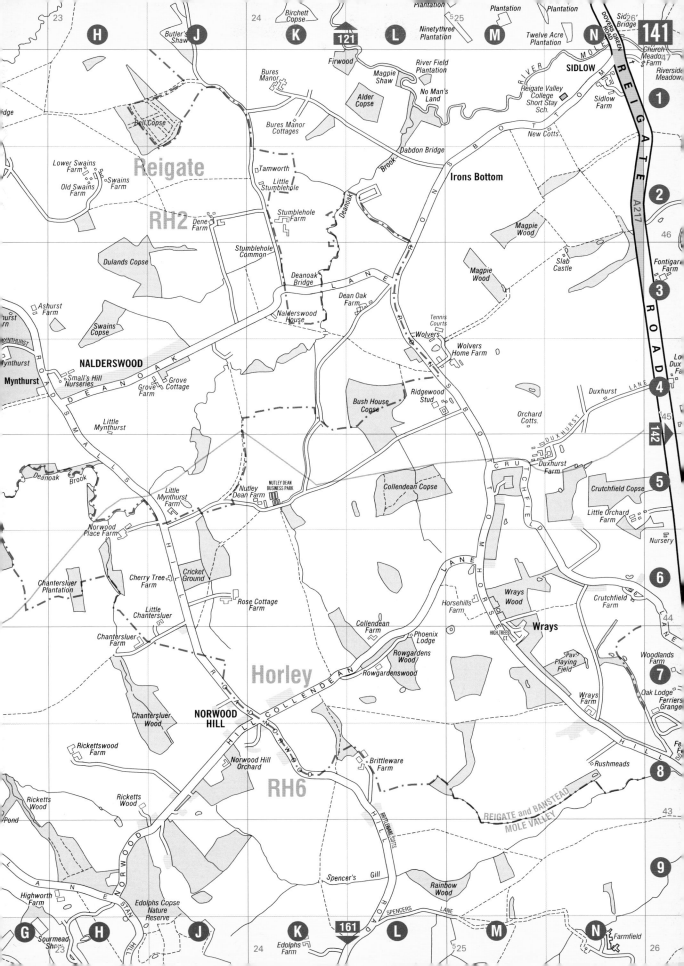

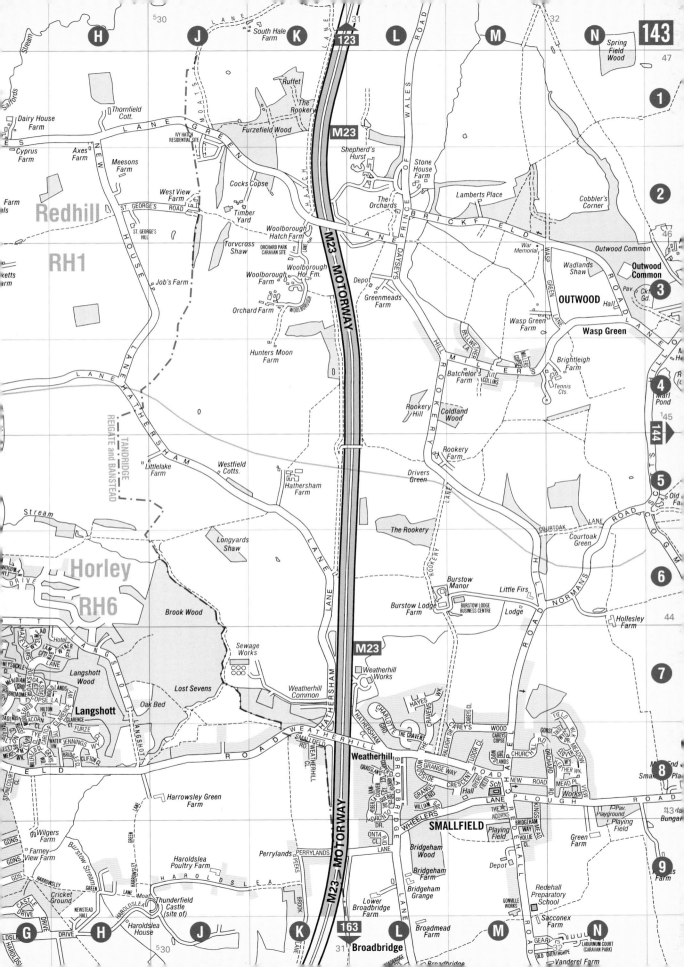

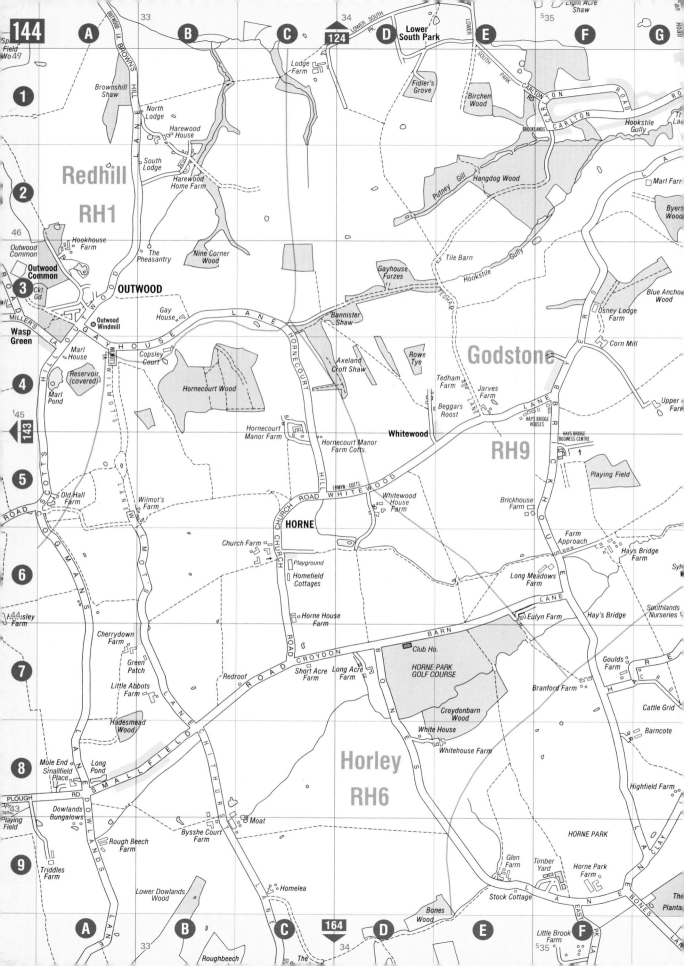

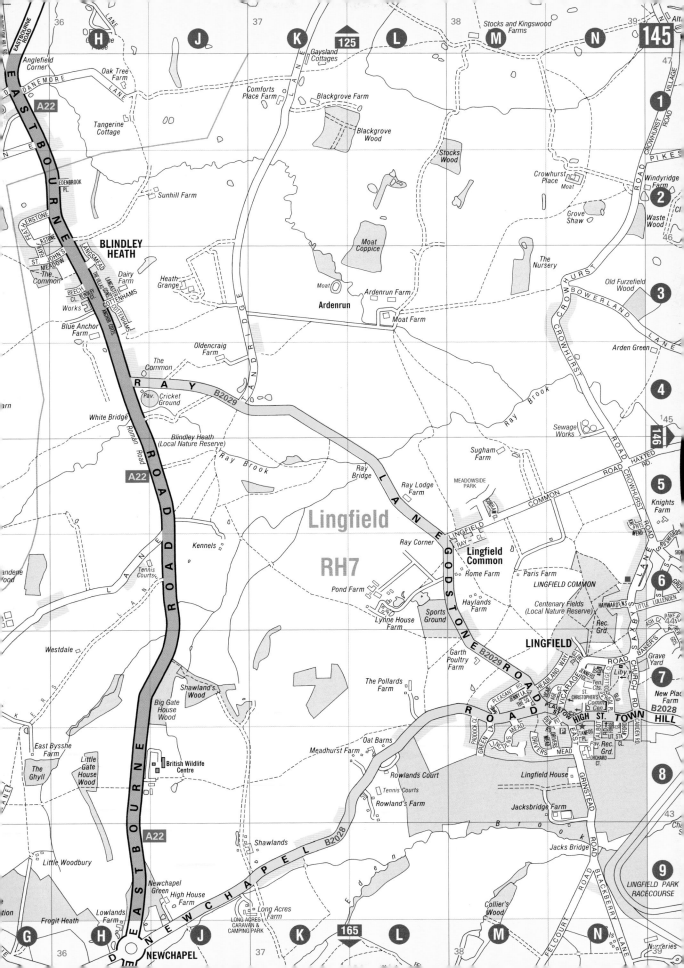

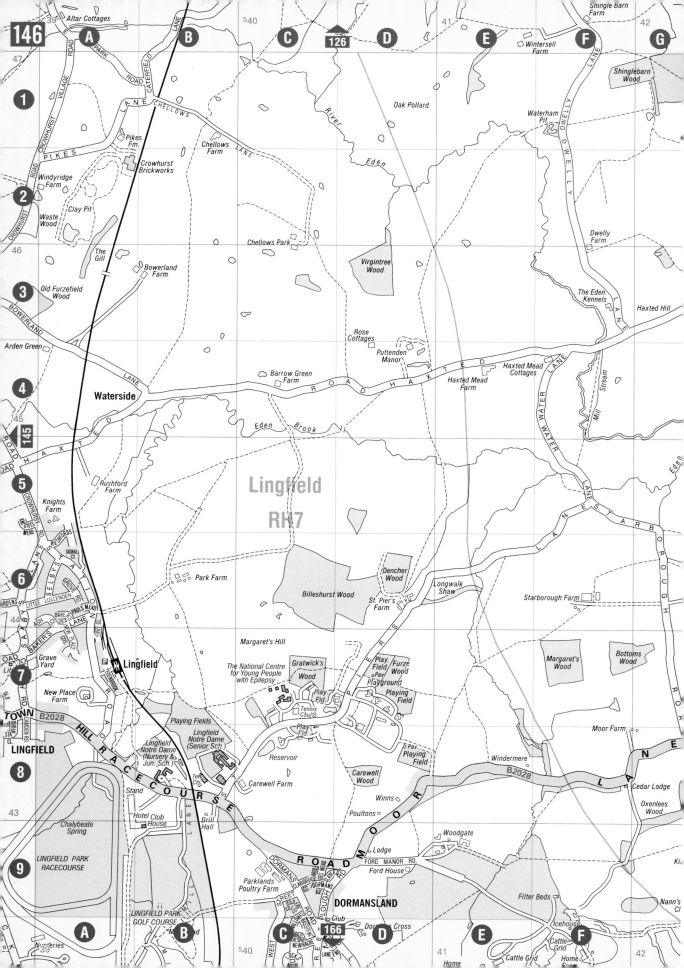

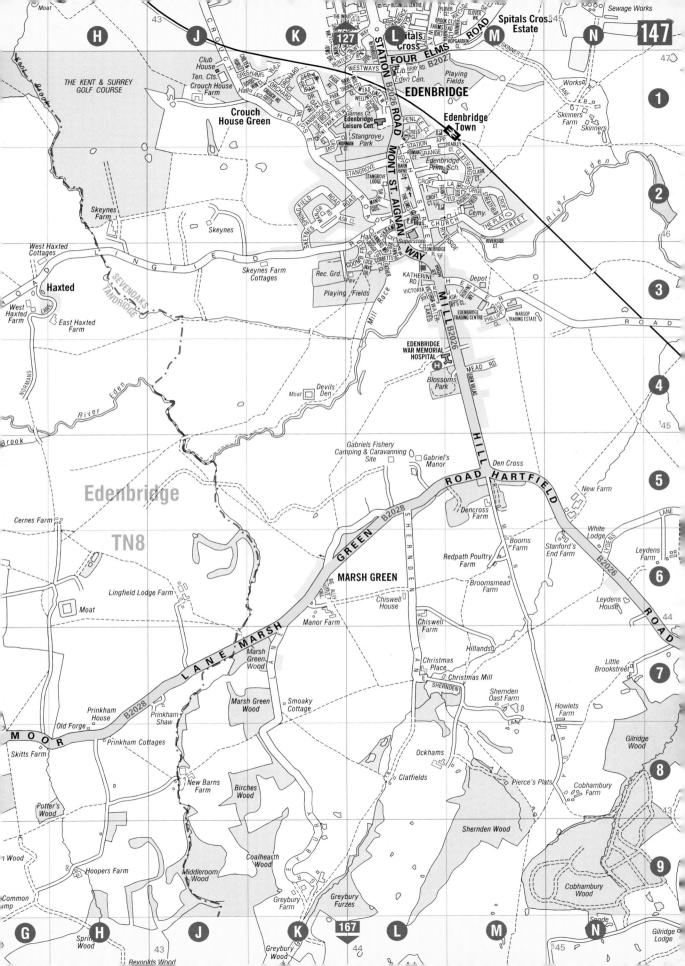

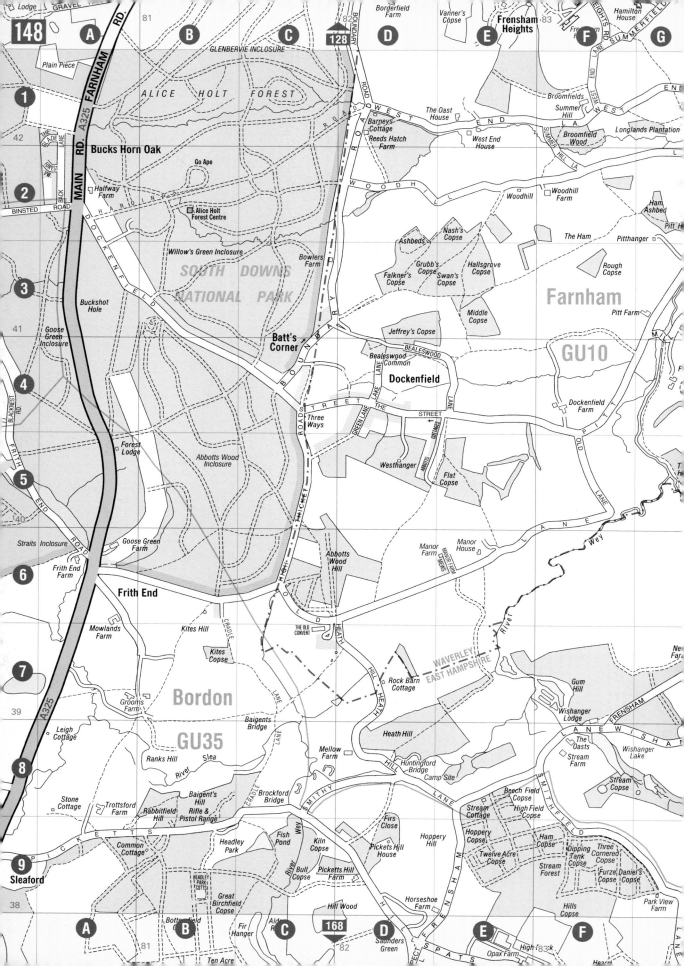

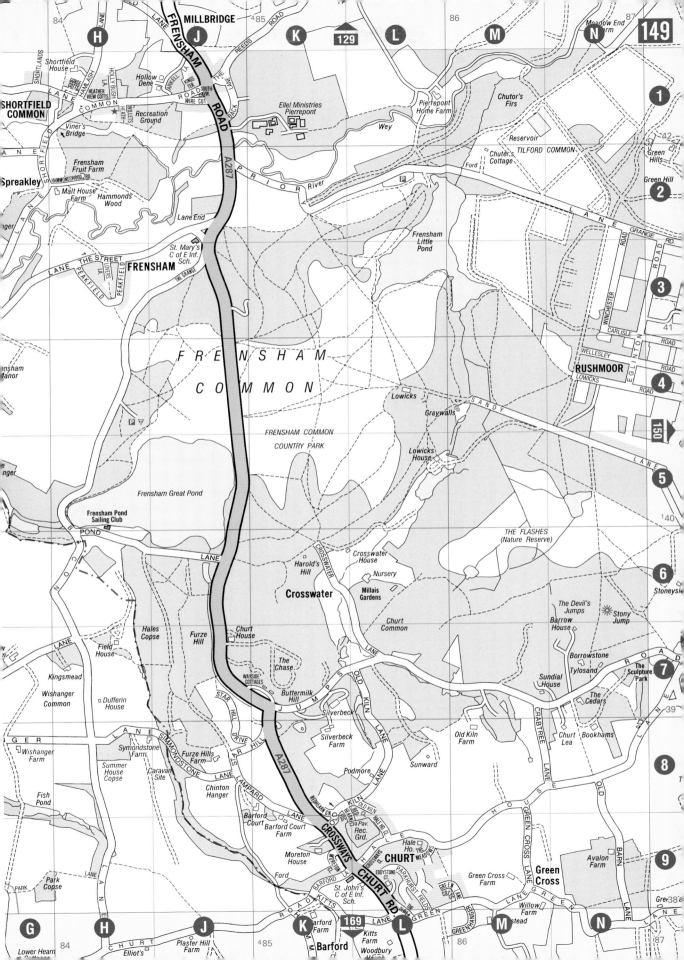

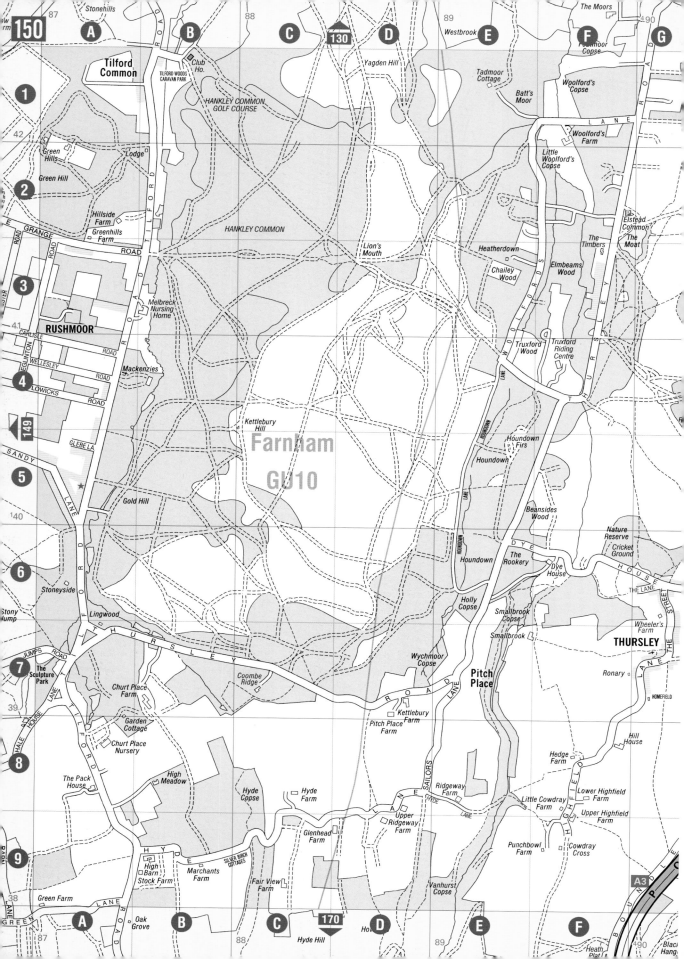

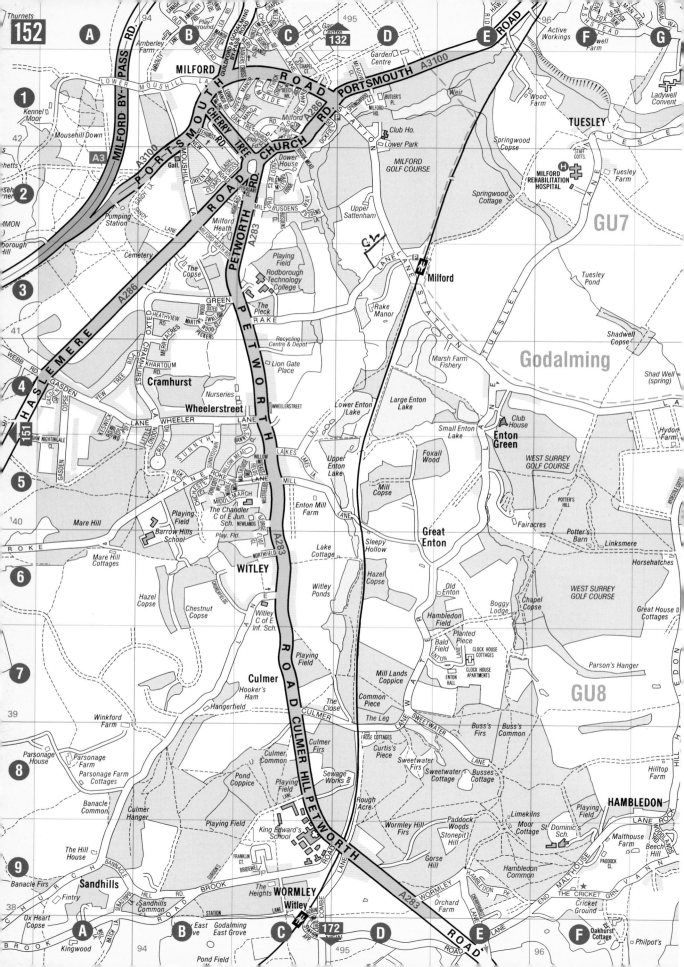

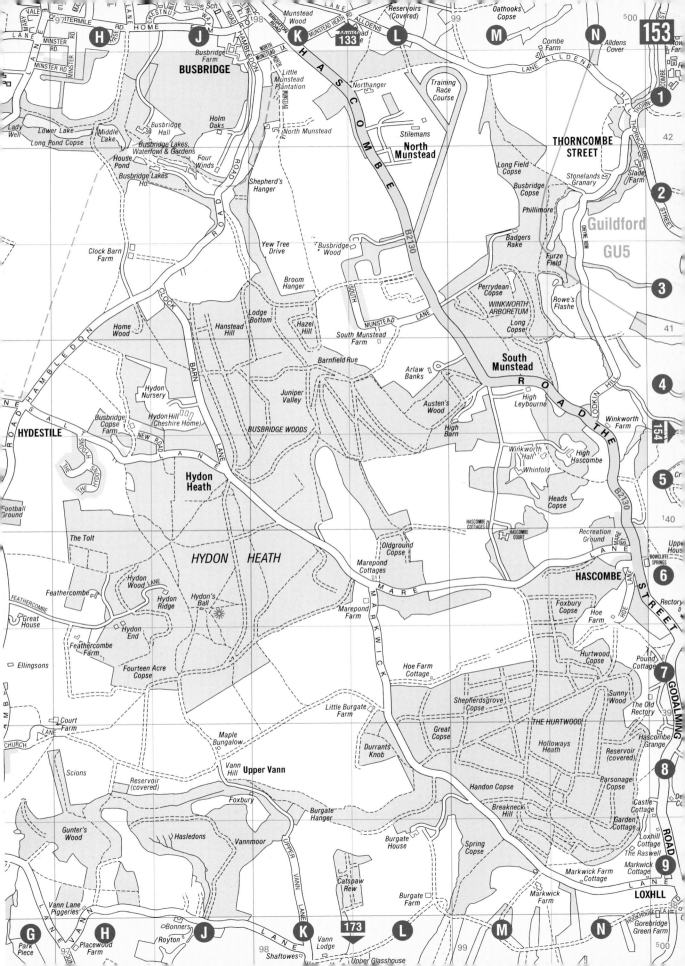

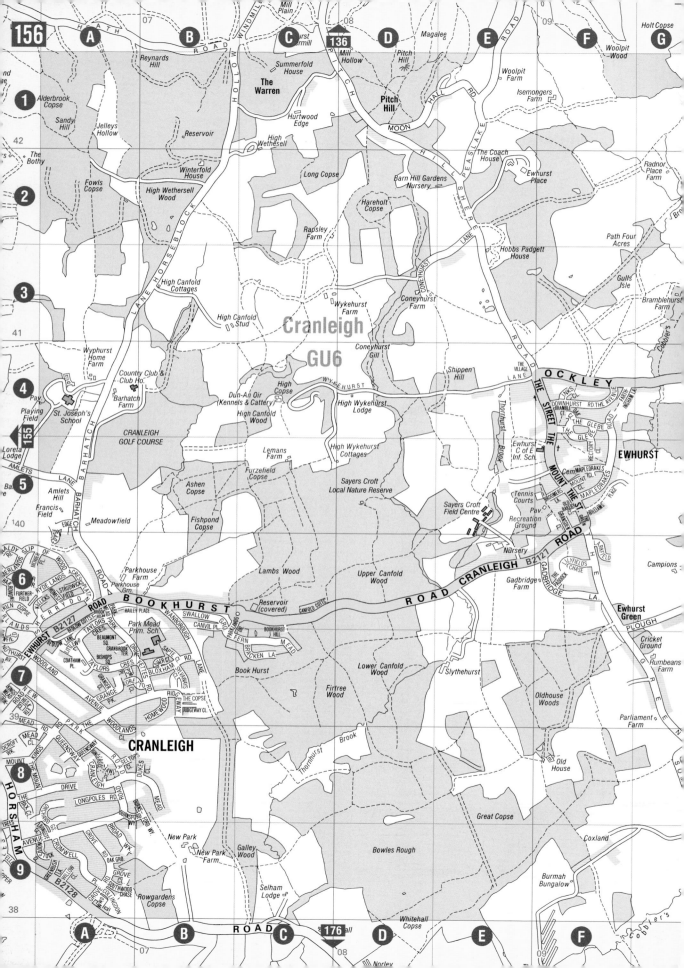

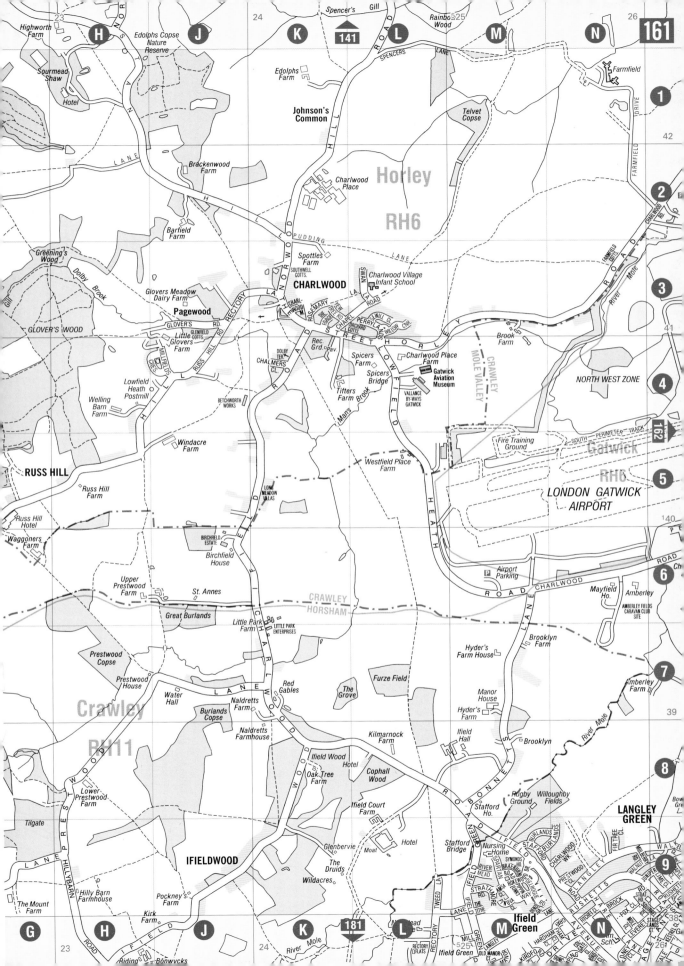

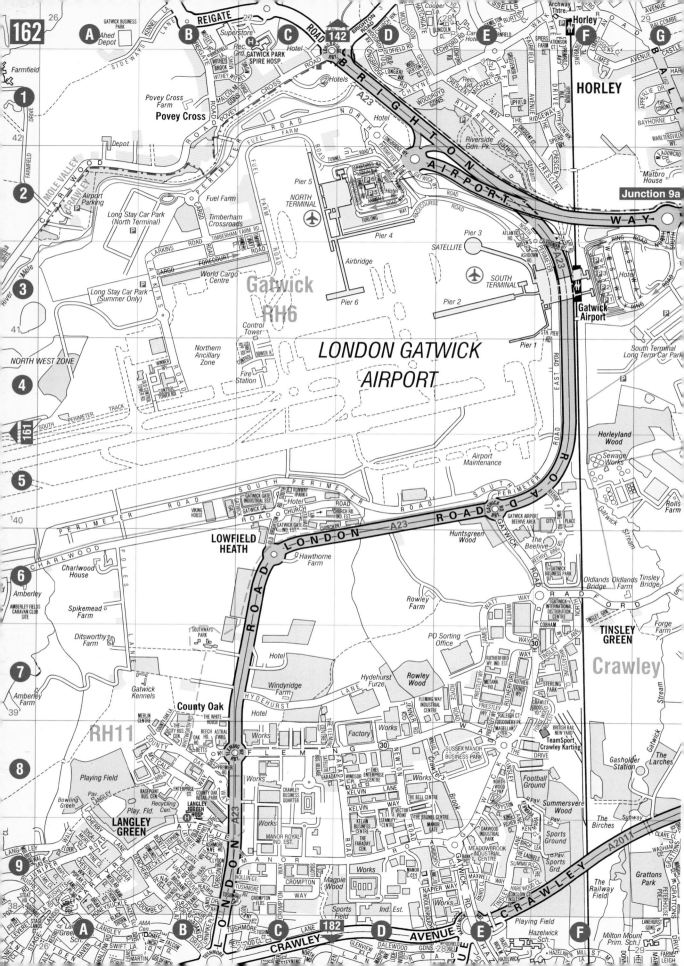

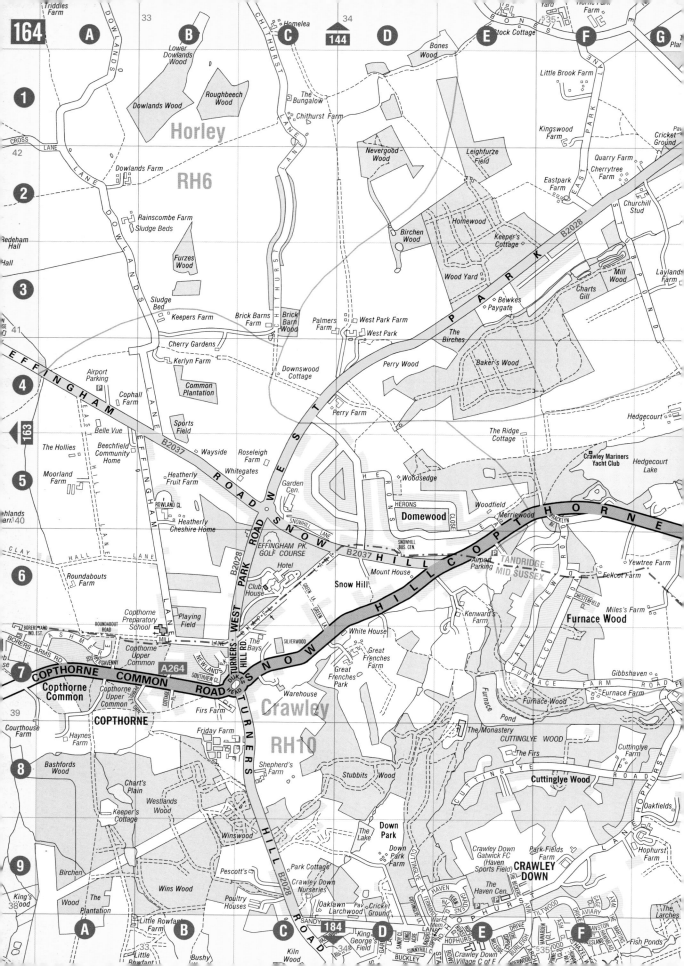

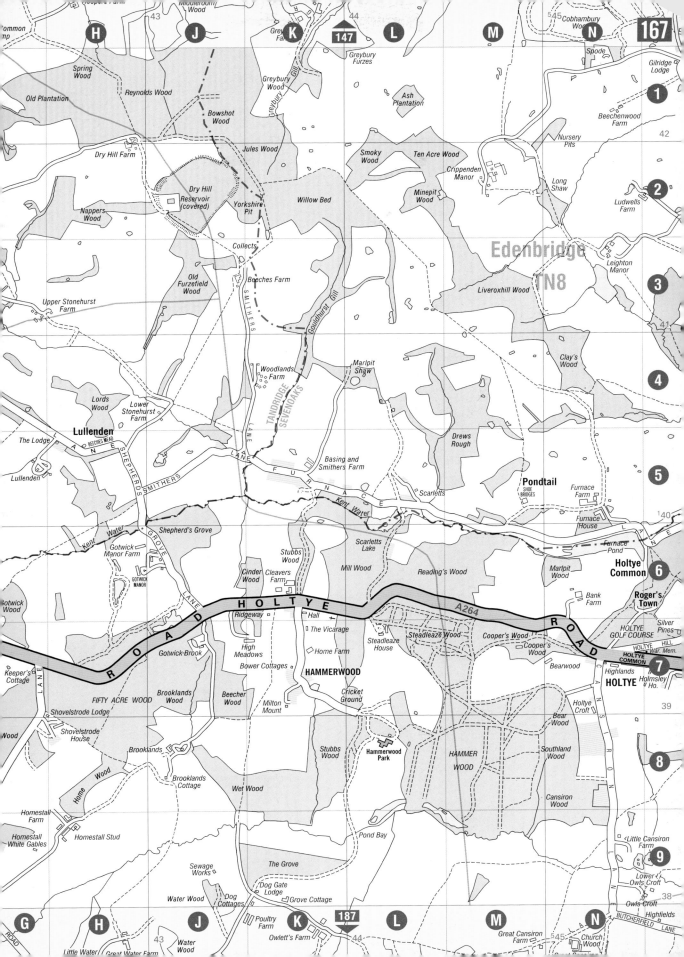

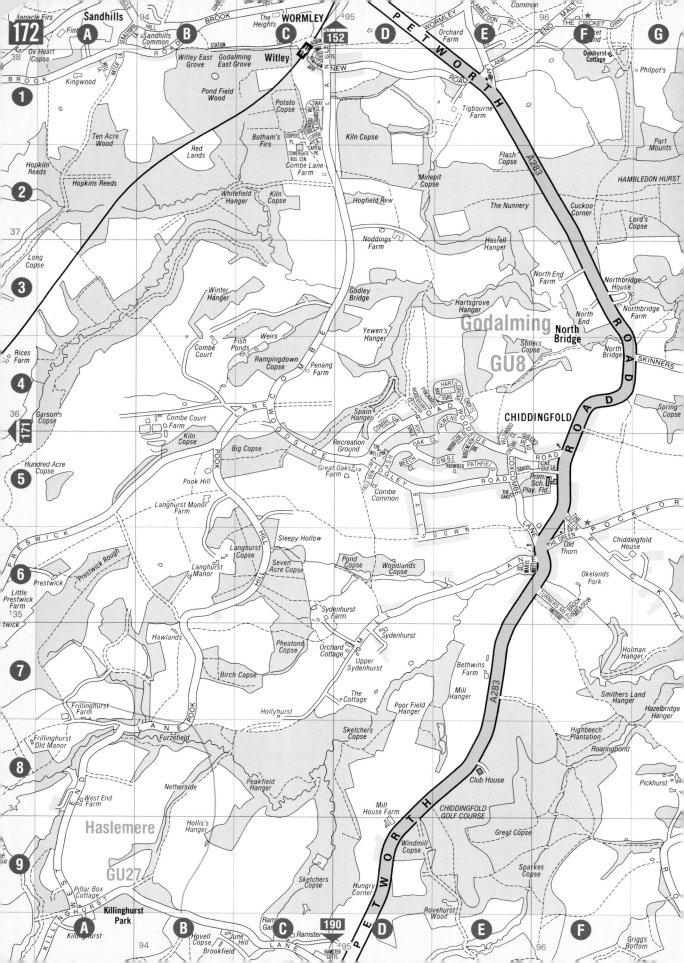

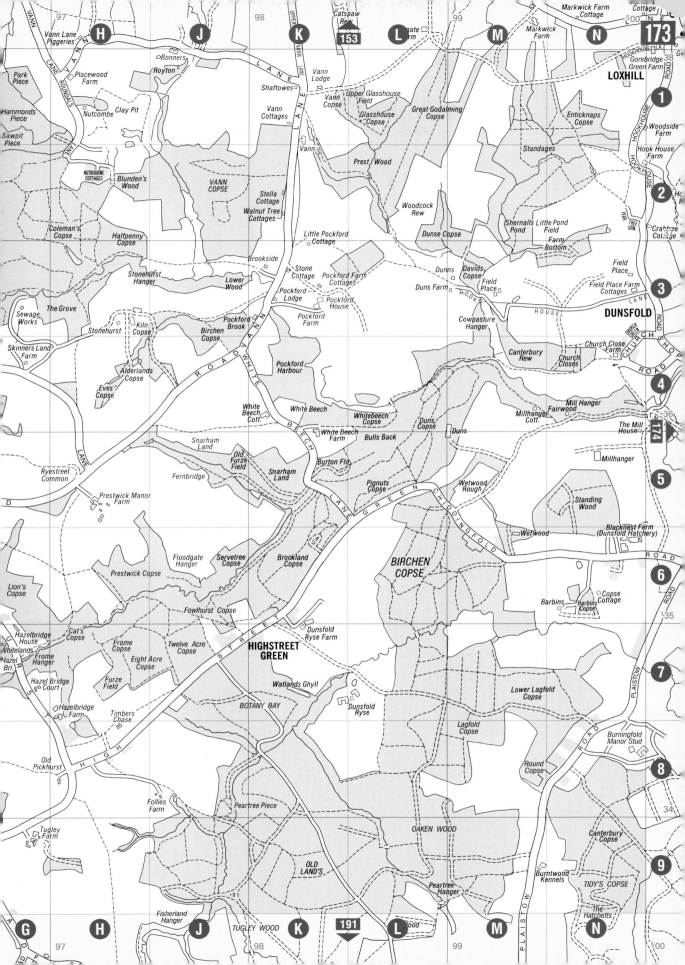

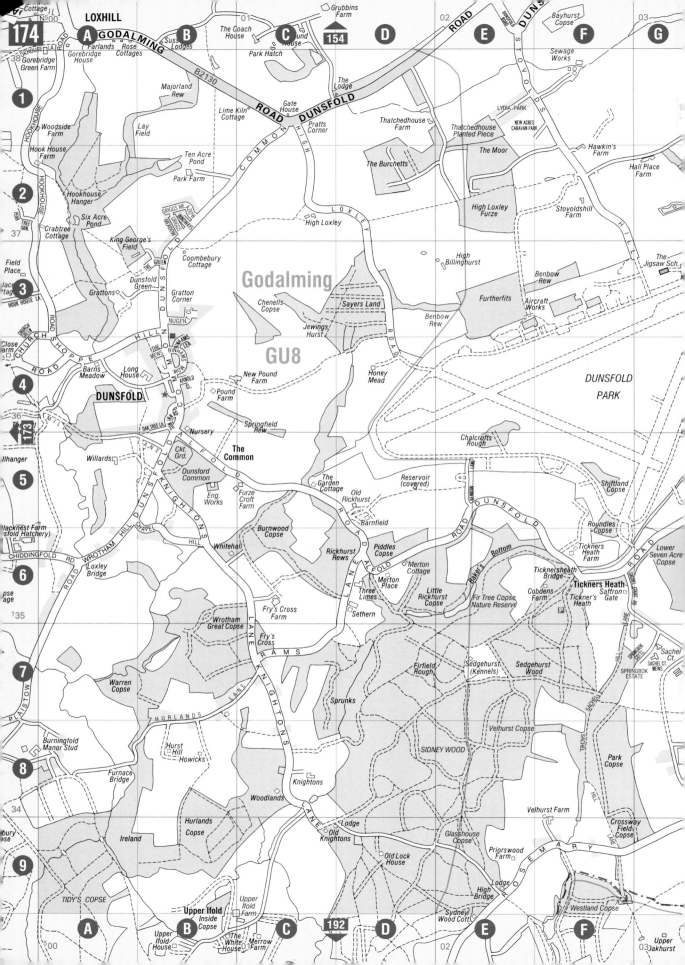

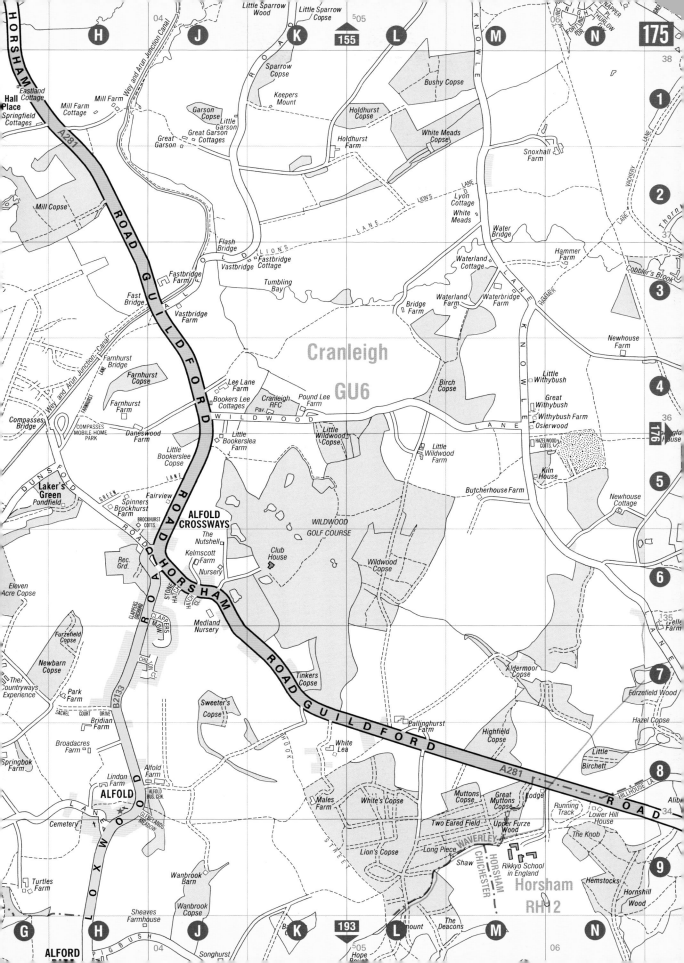

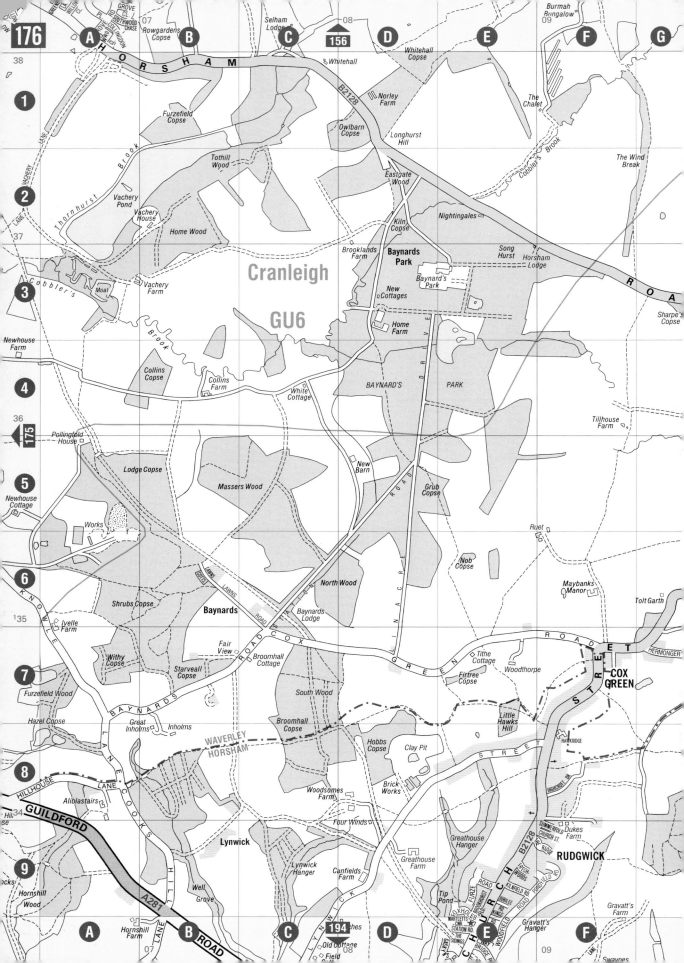

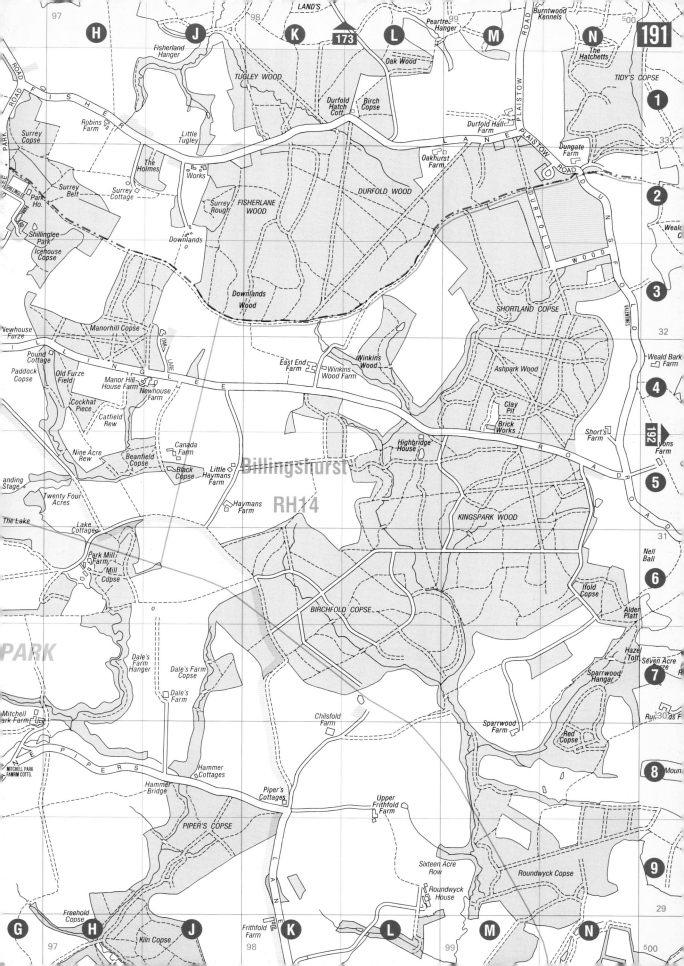

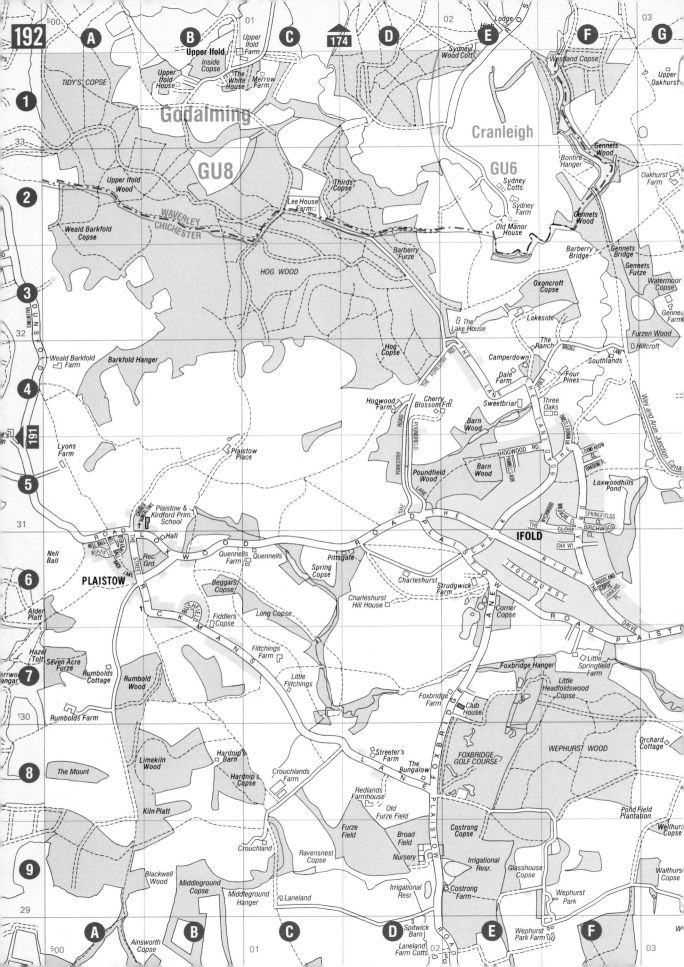

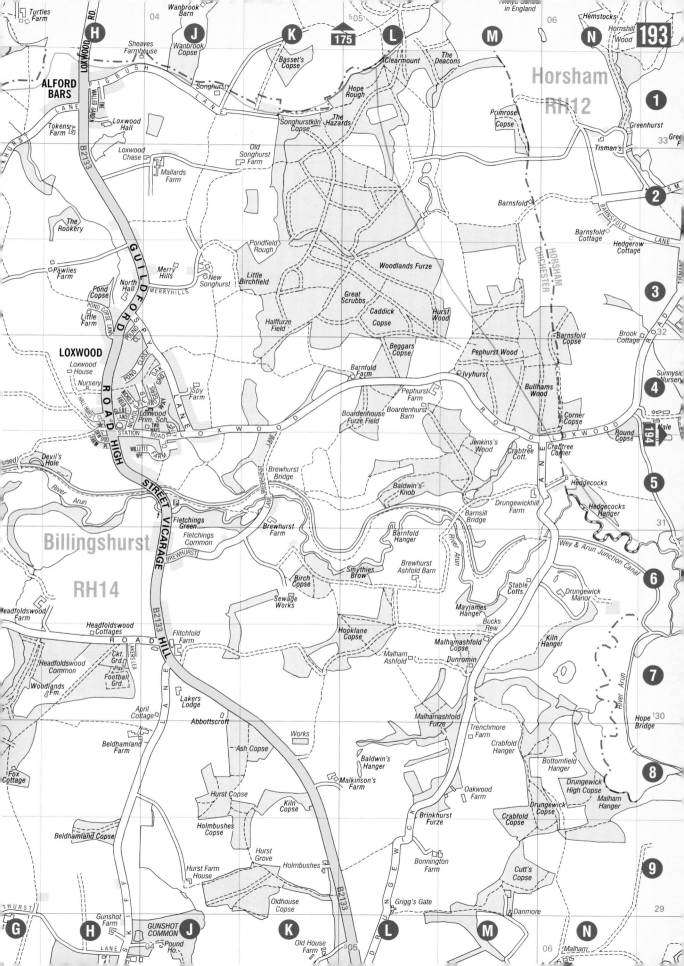

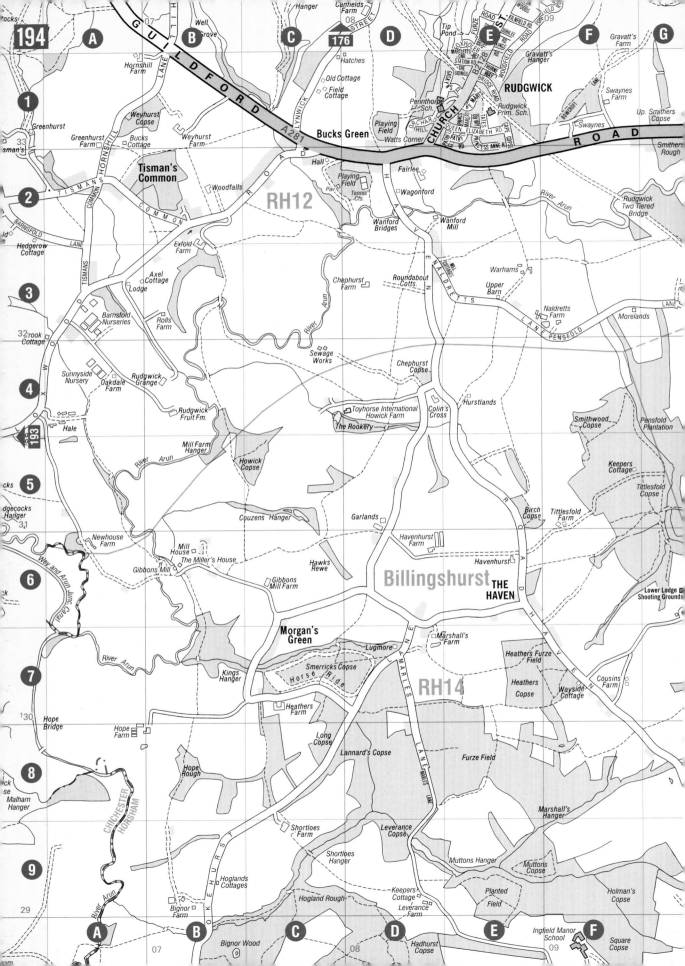

Stan : Stanwell
Stan M : Stanwell Moor
Sto D : Stoke D'Abernon
Sunb : Sunbury
S'dale : Sunningdale
S'hill : Sunninghill
Surb : Surbiton
Sut : Sutton
Sut G : Sutton Green
Tad : Tadworth
Tand : Tandridge
Tats : Tatsfield
Tat C : Tattenham Corner
Tedd : Teddington
T Dit : Thames Ditton
T Have : The Haven
T Hea : Thornton Heath
Thor : Thorpe
Thur : Thursley
Til : Tilford
T'sey : Titsey
Tong : Tongham
Turn H : Turners Hill
Twick : Twickenham
Twy : Twyford
Up Hale : Upper Hale
Up Hart : Upper Hartfield
V Wat : Virginia Water
Wad : Waddon
W'ton : Wallington
W'wood : Walliswood
Wal T : Walton-on-Thames
Wal H : Walton on the Hill
Wan : Wanborough
Warf : Warfield
Warl : Warlingham
Warnh : Warnham
W By : West Byfleet
W Cla : West Clandon
W Dray : West Drayton
W End : West End
W Hoa : West Hoathly
W Hors : West Horsley
W Mole : West Molesey
W Wick : West Wickham
Westc : Westcott
Weste : Westerham
Westh : Westhumble
Weybo : Weybourne
Weybr : Weybridge
White : Whitehill
Whit V : Whiteley Village
Whitt : Whitton
Whyte : Whyteleafe
Windl : Windlesham
W'sor : Windsor
Wink : Winkfield
Wink R : Winkfield Row
Win : Winnersh
W Grn : Wisborough Green
Wis : Wisley
Wit : Witley
Wok : Woking
W'ham : Wokingham
Wold : Woldingham
Wone : Wonersh
Wood : Woodham
Wood V : Wood Street Village
W Pk : Worcester Park
Worm : Wormley
Worp : Worplesdon
Worth : Worth
Wott : Wotton
Wray : Wraysbury
Wrec : Wrecclesham
W Cros : Wych Cross
Yate : Yateley

A

AARON'S HILL . . . 7E 132
Aaron's Hill GU7: Godal . . . 7E 132
Abbess Cl. SW2 . . . 2M 29
Abbetts La. GU15: Camb . . . 3N 69
Abbey Bus. Pk.
GU9: Farnh . . . 3M 129
Abbey Chase KT16: Chert . . . 6K 37
Abbey Cl. GU6: Cranl . . . 8H 155
GU22: Pyr . . . 3G 75
RG12: Brac . . . 4B 32
RG40: W'ham . . . 1B 30
Abbey Ct. GU9: Farnh . . . 1H 129
GU15: Camb . . . 1B 70
KT16: Chert . . . 6K 37
TW12: Hamp . . . 8A 24
TW18: Lale . . . 3L 37
Abbeydore Cl. GU35: Head . . . 4D 168
Abbey Dr. SW17 . . . 6E 28
TW18: Lale . . . 2L 37
Abbeyfield *GU1: Guil* . . . *4B 114*
(off Lwr. Edgeborough Rd.)
Abbeyfield Cl. CR4: Mit . . . 1C 44
Abbey Gdns. KT16: Chert . . . 5J 37
TW15: Ashf . . . 6C 22
W6 . . . 2K 13
Abbey Grn. KT16: Chert . . . 5J 37
Abbey Ind. Est. CR4: Mit . . . 4D 44
Abbey Mdws. KT16: Chert . . . 6L 37
Abbey M. RH19: Ash W . . . 3H 187
TW7: Isle . . . 4H 11
TW18: Lale . . . 3L 37
Abbey Mill Bus. Pk.
GU7: Eash . . . 7B 132
Abbey Moor Golf Course . . . 9J 37
Abbey Pde. *SW19* . . . *8A 28*
(off Merton High St.)
Abbey Pl. KT16: Chert . . . 2J 37
RG42: Warf . . . 6A 16
Abbey Rd.
CR0: Croy . . . 4A 200 (9M 45)
CR2: Sels . . . 6G 64
GU21: Wok . . . 4M 73
GU25: V Wat . . . 4N 35
KT16: Chert . . . 6K 37
SW19 . . . 8A 28
TW17: Shep . . . 7B 38
Abbey St. GU9: Farnh . . . 1H 129
Abbey Wlk. KT8: W Mole . . . 2B 40
Abbey Way GU14: Farnb . . . 1A 90
Abbey Wood SL5: S'dale . . . 6D 34
Abbeywood GU12: Ash V . . . 9F 90
Abbot Cl. KT14: Byf . . . 6M 55
TW18: Stain . . . 8M 21
Abbot Rd.
GU1: Guil . . . 7D 202 (5N 113)
Abbots Av. KT19: Eps . . . 7N 59
Abbotsbury RG12: Brac . . . 4L 31
Abbotsbury Ct. RH13: Hors . . . 5L 197
Abbotsbury Rd. SM4: Mord . . . 4N 43
Abbots Cl. GU2: Guil . . . 6H 113
GU51: Fleet . . . 4B 88
Abbots Dr. GU25: V Wat . . . 4L 35
Abbotsfield Rd.
RH11: Ifield . . . 4J 181
Abbotsford Cl. GU22: Wok . . . 4C 74
Abbots Grn. CR0: A'ton . . . 3G 65
Abbots Hospital GU1: Guil . . . 5D 202
Abbots La. CR8: Ken . . . 3N 83
Abbotsleigh Cl. SM2: Sut . . . 4N 61
Abbotsleigh Rd. SW16 . . . 5G 28
Abbotsmede Cl. TW1: Twick . . . 3F 24
Abbots Pk. SW2 . . . 2L 29
Abbot's Ride GU9: Farnh . . . 3K 129
Abbots Ri. RH1: Red . . . 1E 122
Abbotstone Rd. SW15 . . . 6H 13
Abbots Wlk. SL4: W'sor . . . 5B 4
Abbots Way BR3: Beck . . . 4H 47
GU1: Guil . . . 2F 114
KT16: Chert . . . 6H 37
ABBOTSWOOD . . . 1B 114
Abbotswood GU1: Guil . . . 1B 114
KT13: Weybr . . . 9G 38
Abbotswood Cl. GU1: Guil . . . 9B 94
Abbotswood Dr.
KT13: Weybr . . . 6E 56
Abbotswood Rd. SW16 . . . 4H 29
Abbott Av. SW20 . . . 9J 27
Abbott Cl. TW12: Hamp . . . 7M 23
Abbotts Cotts. GU10: Dock . . . 5D 148
Abbotts Mead TW10: Ham . . . 5K 25
Abbotts Rd. CR4: Mit . . . 3G 45
SM3: Chea . . . 1K 61
Abbott's Tilt KT12: Hers . . . 9M 39
Abbotts Wlk. CR3: Cate . . . 9E 84
Abelia Cl. GU24: W End . . . 9B 52
Abell Ct. KT15: Addl . . . 2K 55
Abercairn Rd. SW16 . . . 8G 28
Aberconway Rd. SM4: Mord . . . 3N 43
Abercorn Cl. CR2: Sels . . . 9G 64
Abercorn Ho. GU17: Haw . . . 5K 69
Abercorn M. TW10: Rich . . . 7M 11
Abercorn Way GU21: Wok . . . 5K 73
Aberdare Cl. BR4: W Wick . . . 8M 47
Aberdeen Rd.
CR0: Croy . . . 7C 200 (1N 63)
Aberdeen Ter. GU26: G'hott . . . 5B 170
Aberfoyle Rd. SW16 . . . 7H 29
(not continuous)
Abergavenny Gdns.
RH10: Copt . . . 7A 164
Abingdon *W14* . . . *1L 13*
(off Kensington Village)
Abingdon Cl. GU21: Wok . . . 5M 73
KT4: W Pk . . . 9G 43
RG12: Brac . . . 4C 32
SW19 . . . 7A 28
Abingdon Ct. GU22: Wok . . . 5B 74
Abingdon Rd. GU47: Sandh . . . 7H 49
SW16 . . . 9J 29
Abinger Av. SM2: Chea . . . 5H 61
ABINGER BOTTOM . . . 5N 137
Abinger Cl. CR0: N Add . . . 3M 65
RH5: Nth H . . . 9J 119
SM6: W'ton . . . 2J 63
ABINGER COMMON . . . 3L 137
Abinger Comn. Rd.
RH5: A Com . . . 4M 137
Abinger Ct. *SM6: W'ton* . . . *2J 63*
(off Abinger Cl.)
Abinger Dr. RH1: Red . . . 5C 122
Abinger Gdns. TW7: Isle . . . 6E 10
ABINGER HAMMER . . . 9G 116
Abinger Keep *RH6: Horl* . . . *7G 142*
(off Langshott La.)
Abinger La.
RH5: A Com, A Ham . . . 9J 117
Abinger Rd.
RH5: Cold, Holm M, Ockl
. . . 9A 138
Abinger Way GU4: B'ham . . . 7D 94
Aboyne Dr. SW20 . . . 1F 42
Aboyne Rd. SW17 . . . 4B 28
Abrahams Rd. RH11: Craw . . . 8M 181
Abro Ind. Est. GU11: Alde . . . 9B 90
Abury La. RG12: Brac . . . 5E 32
Acacia Av. GU22: Wok . . . 7N 73
GU47: Owls . . . 6J 49
TW8: Brent . . . 3H 11
TW17: Shep . . . 4B 38
TW19: Wray . . . 7A 6
Acacia Cl. KT15: Wood . . . 6H 55
SE20 . . . 1D 46
Acacia Ct. RG12: Brac . . . 3N 31
Acacia Dr. KT15: Wood . . . 6H 55
SM3: Sut . . . 7L 43
SM7: Ban . . . 1J 81
Acacia Gdns. BR4: W Wick . . . 8M 47
Acacia Gro. KT3: N Mal . . . 2C 42
Acacia M. UB7: Harm . . . 2M 7
Acacia Rd. BR3: Beck . . . 2J 47
CR4: Mit . . . 1E 44
GU1: Guil . . . 2C 202 (3N 113)
SW16 . . . 9J 29
TW12: Hamp . . . 7A 24
TW18: Stain . . . 6K 21
Academy Cl. GU15: Camb . . . 7C 50
Academy Gdns. CR0: Croy . . . 7C 46
Academy Ga. GU15: Camb . . . 9N 49
Academy Ho. RG40: W'ham . . . 1A 30
Academy Pl. GU47: Coll T . . . 8K 49
TW7: Isle . . . 4E 10
Access Bus. Pk. KT14: Byf . . . 7M 55
Accommodation La.
UB7: Harm . . . 2L 7
UB7: L'ford . . . 4J 7
Accommodation Rd.
KT16: L'cross . . . 9N 35
KT17: Ewe . . . 2F 60
AC Court KT7: T Dit . . . 5G 40
Ace Pde. KT9: Ches . . . 9L 41
Acer Cl. KT19: Eps . . . 5B 60
RG42: Warf . . . 9E 16
Acer Dr. GU24: W End . . . 9C 52
Acer Rd. TN16: B Hil . . . 3F 86
Aces Ct. TW3: Houn . . . 5C 10
Acfold Rd. SW6 . . . 4N 13
Acheulian Cl. GU9: Farnh . . . 4H 129
Achilles Pl. GU21: Wok . . . 4M 73
Ackmar Rd. SW6 . . . 4M 13
Ackrells Mead GU47: Sandh . . . 6E 48
Acorn Av. GU16: Frim G . . . 9D 70
Acorn Cl. RH6: Horl . . . 7G 143
RH19: E Grin . . . 1A 186
SL3: Lang . . . 1D 6
SM7: Ban . . . 2K 81
TW12: Hamp . . . 7B 24
Acorn Dr. RG40: W'ham . . . 1B 30
Acorn Gdns. SE19 . . . 1C 46
Acorn Gro. GU22: Wok . . . 8A 74
KT20: K'wood . . . 2L 101
UB3: Harl . . . 3G 9
Acorn Keep GU9: Heath E . . . 4J 109
Acorn M. GU14: Farnb . . . 7M 69
Acorn Rd. GU17: B'water . . . 1G 69
Acorns RH13: Hors . . . 4N 197
Acorns, The RH6: Smallf . . . 8M 143
RH11: Craw . . . 8N 181
Acorns Way KT10: Esh . . . 2C 58
Acorn Way BR3: Beck . . . 4M 47
BR6: Farnb . . . 1K 67
Acqua Ho. TW9: Kew . . . 3A 12
Acre La. SM5: Cars . . . 1E 62
SM6: W'ton . . . 1E 62
Acre Pas. SL4: W'sor . . . 4G 4
Acre Rd.
KT2: K Tham . . . 1K 203 (9L 25)
SW19 . . . 7B 28
Acres Gdns. KT20: Tad . . . 6J 81
Acres Platt GU6: Cranl . . . 6A 156
Acropolis Ho.
KT1: K Tham . . . 5L 203
Acton La. W4 . . . 1B 12
Acuba Rd. SW18 . . . 3N 27
Adair Cl. SE25 . . . 2E 46
Adair Gdns. CR3: Cate . . . 8N 83
Adair Wlk. GU24: B'wood . . . 8M 71
Adams Cl. KT5: Surb . . . 5M 41
Adams Cft. GU24: B'wood . . . 7N 71
Adams Dr. GU51: Fleet . . . 4C 88
Adams M. SW17 . . . 3D 28
Adamson Ct. RH11: Craw . . . 8N 181
Adamson Way BR3: Beck . . . 4M 47
Adams Pk. Rd. GU9: Farnh . . . 8J 109
Adams Quarter TW8: Brent . . . 3J 11
Adams Rd. BR3: Beck . . . 4H 47
Adams Wlk.
KT1: K Tham . . . 3J 203 (1L 41)
Adams Way CR0: Croy . . . 5C 46
SE25 . . . 4E 46
Adam Wlk. SW6 . . . 3H 13
Adare Wlk. SW16 . . . 4K 29
Adastra Way SM6: W'ton . . . 3J 63
ADDINGTON . . . 2K 65
Addington Bus. Cen.
CR0: N Add . . . 6A 66
Addington Cl. SL4: W'sor . . . 6D 4
Addington Ct. SW14 . . . 6C 12
Addington Court Golf Course
. . . 5K 65
Addington Golf Course, The . . . 1J 65
Addington Hgts.
CR0: N Add . . . 7M 65
Addington Palace Golf Course
. . . 3H 65
Addington Rd. BR4: W Wick . . . 1M 65
CR0: Croy . . . 7L 45
CR2: Sande, Sels . . . 7D 64
Addington Village Rd.
CR0: A'ton . . . 3J 65
(not continuous)
Addington Village Stop
(London Tramlink) . . . 3K 65
ADDISCOMBE . . . 7D 46
Addiscombe Av. CR0: Croy . . . 7D 46
Addiscombe Ct. Rd.
CR0: Croy . . . 7B 46
Addiscombe Gro.
CR0: Croy . . . 3E 200 (8B 46)
Addiscombe Rd.
CR0: Croy . . . 3E 200 (8A 46)
(not continuous)
RG45: Crowt . . . 3H 49
Addiscombe Stop
(London Tramlink) . . . 7D 46
Addison Av. TW3: Houn . . . 4C 10
Addison Cl. CR3: Cate . . . 9A 84
Addison Ct. GU1: Guil . . . 5B 114
Addison Gdns.
KT5: Surb . . . 8M 203 (3M 41)
Addison Pl. SE25 . . . 3D 46
Addison Rd. CR3: Cate . . . 8A 84
GU1: Guil . . . 5F 202 (5A 114)
GU16: Frim . . . 6C 70
GU21: Wok . . . 4B 74
SE25 . . . 3D 46
TW11: Tedd . . . 7H 25
Addisons Cl. CR0: Croy . . . 8J 47
ADDLESTONE . . . 1K 55
Addlestone Ho. KT15: Addl . . . 9K 37
Addlestone Leisure Cen. . . . 1J 55
ADDLESTONE MOOR . . . 8K 37
Addlestone Moor KT15: Addl . . . 8L 37
Addlestone Pk. KT15: Addl . . . 2K 55
Addlestone Rd.
KT13: Weybr . . . 1N 55
KT15: Addl . . . 1N 55
Addlestone Station (Rail) . . . 1M 55
Adecroft Way KT8: W Mole . . . 2C 40
Adela Av. KT3: N Mal . . . 4G 42
Adela Ho. *W6* . . . *1H 13*
(off Queen Caroline St.)
Adelaide Cl. RH11: Craw . . . 9B 162
RH12: Hors . . . 4M 197
Adelaide Pl. KT13: Weybr . . . 1E 56
Adelaide Rd.
KT6: Surb . . . 8J 203 (4L 41)
KT12: Wal T . . . 9H 39
SL4: W'sor . . . 4J 5
SW18 . . . 8M 13
TW5: Hest . . . 4M 9
TW9: Rich . . . 7M 11
TW11: Tedd . . . 7F 24
TW15: Ashf . . . 6M 21
Adelaide Sq. SL4: W'sor . . . 5G 5
Adelaide Ter. TW8: Brent . . . 1K 11
Adelina M. SW12 . . . 2H 29
Adelphi Cl. RH10: Craw . . . 5H 183
Adelphi Ct. W4 . . . 2C 12
Adelphi Rd.
KT17: Eps . . . 6K 201 (9C 60)
Adeney Cl. W6 . . . 2J 13
Adlers La. RH5: Westh . . . 9G 99
Adlington Pl. GU14: Farnb . . . 3C 90
Admark Ho. KT18: Eps . . . 2A 80
Admiral Cl. KT13: Weybr . . . 8F 38
Admiral Ct. SM5: Cars . . . 7C 44
Admiral Ho. TW11: Tedd . . . 5G 25
Admiral Kepple Ct. SL5: Asc . . . 8J 17
Admiral M. SW19 . . . 8A 28
Admiral Rd. RH11: Craw . . . 6M 181
Admiral's Bri. La.
RH19: E Grin . . . 7M 185
Admirals Ct. GU1: Guil . . . 2D 114
Admirals Rd. GU24: Pirb . . . 4K 91
KT22: Fetc . . . 4D 98
KT23: Book . . . 6C 98
Admiral Stirling Ct.
KT13: Weybr . . . 1A 56
Admirals Wlk. CR5: Coul . . . 7K 83
RH5: Ran C . . . 8B 98
Admiralty Rd. TW11: Tedd . . . 7F 24
Admiralty Way GU15: Camb . . . 2L 69
TW11: Tedd . . . 7F 24
Admiral Way GU7: Godal . . . 9G 132
Adrian Ct. RH11: Craw . . . 8N 181
Adrian M. SW10 . . . 2N 13
Advance Rd. SE27 . . . 5N 29
Adversane Ct. *RH12: Hors* . . . *4K 197*
(off Blenheim Rd.)
Aerodrome Way TW5: Hest . . . 2K 9
Aerospace Blvd.
GU14: Farnb . . . 6L 89
AFC Wimbledon . . . 2N 41
Agar Cl. KT6: Surb . . . 8M 41
Agar Cres. RG42: Brac . . . 8N 15
Agar Ho. KT1: K Tham . . . 6J 203
Agars Pl. SL3: Dat . . . 2K 5
Agate La. RH12: Hors . . . 3L 197
Agates La. KT21: Asht . . . 5K 79
Agevin Ct. GU51: Fleet . . . 2A 88
Agincourt SL5: Asc . . . 2N 33
Agnes Scott Ct.
KT13: Weybr . . . *9C 38*
(off Palace Dr.)
Agraria Rd. GU2: Guil . . . 4L 113
Agua Ho. KT16: Chert . . . 6L 37
Ailsa Av. TW1: Twick . . . 8G 11
Ailsa Cl. RH11: Craw . . . 6N 181
Ailsa Rd. TW1: Twick . . . 8H 11
Ainger Cl. GU12: Alde . . . 1B 110
Ainsdale Way GU21: Wok . . . 5K 73
Ainslie Wlk. SW12 . . . 1F 28
Ainsworth Rd.
CR0: Croy . . . 2A 200 (7M 45)
Aintree Cl. SL3: Poy . . . 4G 6
Aintree Est. *SW6* . . . *3K 13*
(off Aintree St.)
Aintree Rd. RH10: Craw . . . 5E 182
Aintree St. SW6 . . . 3K 13
Airbourne Ho. *SM6: W'ton* . . . *1G 62*
(off Maldon Rd.)
Aircraft Esplanade
GU14: Farnb . . . 4A 90
Airedale Av. W4 . . . 1E 12
Airedale Av. Sth. W4 . . . 1E 12
Airedale Rd. SW12 . . . 1D 28
Air Forces Memorial . . . 5N 19
Airlinks Golf Course . . . 1K 9
Air Links Ind. Est.
TW13: Hanw . . . 4M 23
Airlinks Ind. Est. TW5: C'ford . . . 1K 9
Air Pk. Way TW13: Felt . . . 3J 23
Airport Bowl . . . 4F 8
Airport Gate Bus. Cen.
UB7: Sip . . . 3A 8
Airport Ind. Est.
TN16: B Hil . . . 2F 86
Airport Way RH6: Gatw . . . 2E 162
TW19: Stan M . . . 7H 7
Air Sea M. TW2: Twick . . . 3D 24
Aisgill Av. W14 . . . 1L 13
(not continuous)
Aisne Rd. GU16: Deep . . . 5J 71
Aissele Pl. KT10: Esh . . . 1B 58
Aitken Cl. CR4: Mit . . . 6D 44
Aitken Ho. GU27: Hasl . . . 1G 189
Aitman Dr. TW8: Brent . . . 1N 11
Aits Vw. KT8: W Mole . . . 2B 40
Akabusi Cl. CR0: Croy . . . 5D 46
Akehurst Cl. RH10: Copt . . . 7L 163
Akehurst St. SW15 . . . 9F 12
Akerman Rd. KT6: Surb . . . 5J 41
Alamein Rd. GU11: Alde . . . 2N 109
Alanbrooke Cl. GU21: Knap . . . 5F 72
Alanbrooke Rd. GU11: Alde . . . 7B 90
Alan Hilton Ct. *KT16: Otter* . . . *3F 54*
(off Cheshire Cl.)
Alan Rd. SW19 . . . 6K 27
Alan Turing Rd. GU2: Guil . . . 3G 113
Albain Cres. TW15: Ashf . . . 3N 21
Alba M. SW18 . . . 3M 27
Albany Cl. GU51: Fleet . . . 5C 88
KT10: Esh . . . 5A 58
RH2: Reig . . . 9M 101
SW14 . . . 7A 12
Albany Ct. GU16: Camb . . . 5A 70
GU51: Fleet . . . 4C 88
KT13: Weybr . . . 1C 56
(Hillcrest)
KT13: Weybr . . . 8F 38
(Oakhill Gdns.)
TW15: Ashf . . . 8D 22
TW20: Egh . . . 6D 20
Albany Cres. KT10: Clay . . . 3E 58
Albany M. KT2: K Tham . . . 7K 25
SM1: Sut . . . 2N 61
Albany Pde. TW8: Brent . . . 2L 11
Albany Pk. GU16: Camb . . . 5N 69
SL3: Coln . . . 4F 6
Albany Pk. Ind. Est.
GU16: Camb . . . 5A 70
Albany Pk. Rd.
KT2: K Tham . . . 7K 25
KT22: Leat . . . 6G 78
Albany Pas. TW10: Rich . . . 8L 11
Albany Pl. TW8: Brent . . . 2K 11
TW20: Egh . . . 5D 20
Albany Reach KT7: T Dit . . . 4F 40
Albany Rd. GU51: Fleet . . . 5B 88
KT3: N Mal . . . 3C 42
KT12: Hers . . . 1L 57
RH11: Craw . . . 3N 181
SL4: O Win . . . 8K 5
SL4: W'sor . . . 5G 4
SW19 . . . 6N 27
TW8: Brent . . . 2K 11
TW10: Rich . . . 8M 11
Albany Ter. *TW10: Rich* . . . *8M 11*
(off Albany Pas.)
Albany Way TW18: Stain . . . 7M 21
Albatross Gdns. CR2: Sels . . . 7G 65
Albemarle SW19 . . . 3J 27
Albemarle Av. TW2: Whitt . . . 2N 23
Albemarle Gdns.
KT3: N Mal . . . 3C 42
Albemarle Pk. BR3: Beck . . . 1L 47
Albemarle Rd. BR3: Beck . . . 1M 47
Alben Rd. RG42: Bin . . . 6H 15
Alberta Av. SM1: Sut . . . 1K 61
Alberta Dr. RH6: Smallf . . . 8L 143
Albert Av. KT16: Chert . . . 2J 37
Albert Carr Gdns. SW16 . . . 6J 29
Albert Crane Ct.
RH11: Craw . . . 1M 181
Albert Dr. GU21: Wok . . . 2E 74
SW19 . . . 3K 27
TW18: Stain . . . 6H 21
Albert Gro. SW20 . . . 9J 27
Albertine Cl. KT17: Eps D . . . 3G 81
Albert Mans. CR0: Croy . . . 1E 200
Albert M. RH1: Red . . . 6E 122
Albert Pl. SL4: E Wic . . . 1D 4

Albert Rd.—Amen Corner

Albert Rd. CR4: Mit 2D 44
CR6: Warl 4J 85
GU11: Alde 2N 109
GU14: Farnb 3A 90
GU15: Camb 1A 70
GU19: Bag 6J 51
KT1: K Tham 3L 203 (1M 41)
KT3: N Mal 3E 42
KT15: Addl 9M 37
KT17: Eps 7M 201 (9E 60)
KT21: Asht 5M 79
RG40: W'ham 3A 30
RG42: Brac 9N 15
RG45: Crowt 2G 49
RH1: Mers 7G 102
RH6: Horl 7E 142
SE25 3D 46
SL4: O Win, W'sor 6G 5
SM1: Sut 2B 62
TW1: Twick 2F 24
TW3: Houn 7A 10
TW10: Rich 8L 11
TW11: Tedd 7F 24
TW12: H Hill 6C 24
TW15: Ashf 6A 22
TW20: Eng G 7N 19
Albert Rd. Nth. RH2: Reig 2L 121
Albert St. GU51: Fleet 5A 88
SL4: W'sor 4E 4
Albert Ter. *W6 1F 12*
(off Beavor La.)
Albert Wlk. RG45: Crowt 2G 49
Albery Cl. RH12: Hors 4H 197
Albion Cl. RH10: Craw 4H 183
Albion Cotts. RH5: Holm M 5K 137
Albion Ct. SM2: Sut 4B 62
W6 1G 13
(off Albion Pl.)
Albion Ho. GU21: Wok 4B 74
Albion M. W6 1G 13
Albion Pl. SL4: W'sor 5D 4
W6 1G 13
Albion Rd. GU47: Sandh 8G 49
KT2: K Tham 9B 26
RH2: Reig 4A 122
SM2: Sut 3B 62
TW2: Twick 2E 24
TW3: Houn 7A 10
Albion St.
CR0: Croy 1A 200 (7M 45)
Albion Way RH12: Hors 6H 197
TN8: Eden 8K 127
Albon Ho. *SW18 9N 13*
(off Neville Gill Cl.)
ALBURY 8K 115
Albury Av. SM2: Chea 5H 61
TW7: Isle 3F 10
Albury Cl. KT16: L'cross 9K 35
KT19: Eps 5A 60
TW12: Hamp 7B 24
Albury Cotts. GU12: Ash 2G 111
Albury Ct. CR0: Croy 7B 200
CR4: Mit 1B 44
SM1: Sut 1A 62
ALBURY HEATH 1N 135
Albury Ho. GU1: Guil 5B 114
Albury Keep *RH6: Horl 8F 142*
(off Langshott La.)
Albury Pk. GU5: Alb 8N 115
Albury Pl. RH1: Mers 7G 103
Albury Rd. GU1: Guil 4B 114
KT9: Ches 2L 59
KT12: Hers 3F 56
RH1: Mers 7G 102
Alcester Ct. SM6: W'ton 1F 62
Alcester Rd. SM6: W'ton 1F 62
Alcock Cl. SM6: W'ton 4H 63
Alcock Rd. TW5: Hest 3L 9
Alcocks Cl. KT20: Tad 7K 81
Alcocks La.
KT20: K'wood, Tad 8K 81
Alcorn Cl. SM3: Sut 8M 43
Alcot Cl. RG45: Crowt 3G 48
Alcott Cl. TW14: Felt 2G 22
Alden Ct.
CR0: Croy 4F 200 (9B 46)
Aldenham Ter. RG12: Brac 5A 32
Aldenholme KT13: Weybr 3F 56
Alden Vw. SL4: W'sor 4A 4
Alderbrook Cl.
RG45: Crowt 3D 48
Alderbrook Farm Cotts.
GU6: Cranl 3M 155
Alderbrook Rd. GU6: Cranl 2K 155
SW12 1F 28
Alderbury Rd. SW13 2F 12
Alder Cl. GU12: Ash V 6E 90
RH10: Craw D 1E 184
TW20: Eng G 6A 20
Aldercombe La. CR3: Cate 5B 104
Alder Copse RH12: Hors 8F 196
Alder Cft. CR5: Coul 3K 83
Alder Gro. GU46: Yate 1B 68
Aldergrove Gdns.
TW3: Houn 5M 9
Alder Lodge SW6 4H 13
Alderman Ho. *GU11: Alde 3M 109*
(off Grosvenor Rd.)
Alderman Judge Mall
KT1: K Tham 4J 203
Alderman Willey Cl.
RG41: W'ham 2A 30
Alderney Av. TW5: Hest, Isle 3B 10
Alder Rd. GU35: Head D 3G 168
SW14 6C 12
Alders, The BR4: W Wick 7L 47
GU9: B Lea 6N 109
KT14: W By 8L 55
SW16 5G 29
TW5: Hest 2N 9
TW13: Hanw 5M 23
Alders Av. RH19: E Grin 7N 165
Aldersbrook Dr.
KT2: K Tham 7M 25
Aldersey Rd. GU1: Guil 3B 114
Alders Gro. KT8: E Mol 4D 40
ALDERSHOT 2M 109
Aldershot Lodge
GU11: Alde 4A 110
Aldershot Military Mus. 7A 90
Aldershot Pk. 5B 110
Aldershot Pools & Lido 5B 110
Aldershot Rd. GU2: Guil 7G 92
GU3: Guil, Norm, Worp 8B 92
GU12: Ash 3C 110
GU24: Pirb 5A 92
GU51: Fleet 5B 88
GU52: Chu C 1A 108
Aldershot Station (Rail) 3N 109
Aldershot Town FC 2N 109
Alderside Wlk. TW20: Eng G 6A 20
Aldersmead Av. CR0: Croy 5G 47
Alderson Cl. SL5: Asc 8G 16
Alders Rd. RH2: Reig 1N 121
ALDERSTEAD HEATH 3H 103
Alderstead Heath Caravan Site
RH1: Mers 2H 103
Alderstead La. RH1: Mers 3H 103
Alders Vw. Dr.
RH19: E Grin 7A 166
Alderton Ct. *KT8: W Mole 3N 39*
(off Walton Rd.)
Alderton Rd. CR0: Croy 6C 46
Alderville Rd. SW6 5L 13
Alderwick Dr. TW3: Houn 6D 10
Alderwood Cl. CR3: Cate 3B 104
Aldingbourne Cl.
RH11: Ifield 2L 181
Aldis M. SW17 6C 28
Aldis St. SW17 6C 28
Aldren Rd. SW17 4A 28
Aldrich Cres. CR0: N Add 5M 65
Aldrich Gdns. SM3: Chea 9L 43
Aldrich Ter. SW18 3A 28
Aldridge Pk. RG42: Wink R 7F 16
Aldridge Ri. KT3: N Mal 6D 42
Aldrington Rd. SW16 6G 29
Aldrin Pl. GU14: Cove 1J 89
Aldwick Cl. GU14: Farnb 8M 69
Aldwick Rd. CR0: Bedd 9K 45
Aldworth Cl. RG12: Brac 3M 31
Aldworth Gdns. RG45: Crowt 2F 48
Aldwych Cl. RH10: Craw 5H 183
Aldwyn Pl. TW20: Eng G 7L 19
Alexa Ct. SM2: Sut 3M 61
Alexander Cl. RG40: Finch 9A 30
TW2: Twick 3E 24
Alexander Ct. BR3: Beck 1N 47
Alexander Cres. CR3: Cate 8N 83
Alexander Fleming Rd.
GU2: Guil 4G 113
Alexander Godley Cl.
KT21: Asht 6M 79
Alexander Ho. *GU11: Alde 2N 109*
(off Station Rd.)
KT2: K Tham 2J 203
RG40: W'ham 3C 30
Alexander M. SW16 6G 29
Alexander Pl. RH8: Oxt 6A 106
Alexander Raby Mill
KT15: Addl 2N 55
(off Bourneside Rd.)
Alexander Rd. CR5: Coul 2F 82
GU11: Alde 2L 109
RH2: Reig 6M 121
TW20: Egh 6E 20
Alexanders Wlk. CR3: Cate 4C 104
Alexander Wlk. RG12: Brac 4N 31
Alexandra Av. CR6: Warl 4J 85
GU15: Camb 1M 69
SM1: Sut 9M 43
W4 3C 12
Alexandra Cl. GU47: Coll T 8K 49
KT12: Wal T 8H 39
TW15: Ashf 8E 22
TW18: Stain 7M 21
Alexandra Ct. GU14: Farnb 4A 90
RG40: W'ham 3A 30
RH10: Craw 4B 182
SL4: W'sor 5G 4
(off Alexandra Rd.)
TW3: Houn 5B 10
TW15: Ashf 7E 22
Alexandra Dr. KT5: Surb 6N 41
Alexandra Gdns.
GU21: Knap 5F 72
SM5: Cars 4E 62
TW3: Houn 5B 10
W4 3D 12
Alexandra Ho. *W6 1H 13*
(off Queen Caroline St.)
Alexandra Lodge
KT13: Weybr 1C 56
(off Monument Hill)
Alexandra Mans. *KT17: Eps 9E 60*
(off Alexandra Rd.)
Alexandra M. SW19 7L 27
Alexandra Pl. CR0: Croy 7B 46
GU1: Guil 5B 114
SE25 4A 46
Alexandra Rd.
CR0: Croy 1F 200 (7B 46)
CR4: Mit 8C 28
CR6: Warl 4J 85
GU11: Alde 2K 109
(not continuous)
GU12: Ash 3D 110
GU14: Farnb 3A 90
KT2: K Tham 8N 25
KT7: T Dit 4F 40
KT15: Addl 1M 55
(not continuous)
KT17: Eps 9E 60
SL4: W'sor 5G 4
SW14 6C 12
SW19 7L 27
TN16: B Hil 6D 86
TW1: Twick 9J 11
TW3: Houn 5B 10
TW8: Brent 2K 11
TW9: Kew 5M 11
TW15: Ashf 8E 22
TW20: Eng G 7M 19
Alexandra Sq. SM4: Mord 4M 43
Alexandra Ter.
GU1: Guil 4E 202 (4A 114)
GU11: Alde 2M 109
(off Alexandra Rd.)
Alexandra Way KT19: Eps 7N 59
ALFOLD 8H 175
ALFOLD BARS 1H 193
Alfold Bus. Cen. GU6: Alf 8J 175
ALFOLD CROSSWAYS 5J 175
Alfold Rd. GU6: Alf, Cranl 7K 155
GU8: Duns 5B 174
Alfonso Cl. GU12: Alde 4A 110
Alford Cl. GU4: B'ham 9B 94
GU47: Sandh 8F 48
Alford Grn. CR0: N Add 3N 65
Alfred Cl. RH10: Worth 4J 183
W4 1C 12
Alfred Rd. GU9: Farnh 2H 129
KT1: K Tham 6K 203 (2L 41)
SE25 4D 46
SM1: Sut 2A 62
TW13: Felt 3K 23
Alfreton Cl. SW19 4J 27
Alfriston KT5: Surb 5M 41
Alfriston Av. CR0: Croy 6J 45
Alfriston Cl. KT5: Surb 4M 41
Alfriston Rd. GU16: Deep 7G 71
Algar Cl. TW7: Isle 6G 10
Algar Rd. TW7: Isle 6G 11
Algarve Rd. SW18 2N 27
Alice Crocker Ho.
RH19: E Grin 8A 166
Alice Gilliatt Ct. *W14 2L 13*
(off Star Rd.)
Alice Gough Memorial Homes
RG12: Brac 2N 31
Alice Holt Cotts.
GU10: Holt P 9A 128
Alice Holt Forest Cen. 2B 148
Alice M. TW11: Tedd 6F 24
Alice Rd. GU11: Alde 2N 109
Alice Ruston Pl. GU22: Wok 6M 73
Alice Way TW3: Houn 7B 10
Alicia Av. RH10: Craw 3F 182
Alington Gro. SM6: W'ton 5G 63
Alison Cl. CR0: Croy 7G 46
GU14: Cove 2L 89
GU21: Wok 2A 74
Alison Dr. GU15: Camb 1D 70
Alison's Rd. GU11: Alde 8M 89
Alison Way GU11: Alde 2L 109
Alkerden Rd. W4 1D 12
Allan Cl. KT3: N Mal 4C 42
Allbrook Cl. GU19: Bag 5H 51
TW11: Tedd 6E 24
Allcard Cl. RH12: Hors 4K 197
Allcot Cl. RH11: Craw 6K 181
Allden Av. GU12: Alde 5B 110
Allden Cotts. *GU7: Godal 7E 132*
(off Aaron's Hill)
Allden Gdns. GU12: Alde 5B 110
Alldens Hill GU5: Braml 1N 153
GU8: Bus 1N 153
Alldens La. GU8: Bus 9L 133
Allder Way CR2: S Croy 4M 63
Allenby Av. CR2: S Croy 5N 63
Allenby Rd. GU15: Camb 9M 49
TN16: B Hil 4G 86
Allen Cl. CR4: Mit 9F 28
TW16: Sunb 9J 23
Allendale Cl.
GU47: Sandh 5F 48
Allenford Ho. *SW15 9E 12*
(off Tunworth Cres.)
Allen Ho. Pk. GU22: Wok 7M 73
Allen Rd. BR3: Beck 1G 46
CR0: Croy 7L 45
KT23: Book 4B 98
TW16: Sunb 9J 23
Allen's Cl. RH19: Ash W 3F 186
Allenswood SW19 2K 27
Allen Way SL3: Dat 4M 5
Allestree Rd. SW6 3K 13
Alleyn Pk. UB2: S'hall 1A 10
Allfarthing La.
SW18 9N 13 & 1A 28
Allford Ct. RH11: Craw 4M 181
Allgood Cl. SM4: Mord 5J 43
Alliance Cl. TW4: Houn 8N 9
Alliance Ct. TW15: Ashf 5D 22
Allingham Ct. GU7: Godal 4J 133
Allingham Gdns.
RH12: Hors 3A 198
Allingham Rd. RH2: Reig 6M 121
Allington Av. TW17: Shep 2F 38
Allington Cl. GU9: Farnh 9K 109
SW19 6J 27
Allington Ct. *CR0: Croy 5F 46*
(off Chart Cl.)
Allingtons RH2: Reig 9M 101
Allkins Ct. SL4: W'sor 5G 5
Alloway Cl. GU21: Wok 5L 73
All Saints Cl. RG40: W'ham 1B 30
All Saint's Ct. *TW5: Hest 4L 9*
(off Springwell Rd.)
All Saints Cres. GU14: Cove 6K 69
All Saints Dr. CR2: Sande 8C 64
All Saints Pas. SW18 8M 13
All Saints Ri. RG42: Warf 8B 16
All Saints Rd. GU18: Ligh 6N 51
SM1: Sut 9N 43
SW19 8A 28
(not continuous)
Allsmoor La. RG12: Brac 2D 32
All Souls Rd. SL5: Asc 3L 33
Allum Gro. KT20: Tad 8G 81
Allyington Way
RH10: Worth 4H 183
Allyn Cl. TW18: Stain 7H 21
Alma Cl. GU12: Alde 2B 110
GU21: Knap 4H 73
Alma Cotts. GU14: Farnb 5A 90
Alma Ct. *CR3: Cate 8N 83*
(off Coulsdon Rd.)
Alma Cres. SM1: Sut 2K 61
Alma Gdns. GU16: Deep 6H 71
Alma Ho. GU12: Alde 2B 110
TW8: Brent 2L 11
Alma La.
GU9: Heath E, Up Hale 5G 109
Alma Pl. CR7: T Hea 4L 45
Alma Rd. GU35: Head D 4H 169
KT10: Esh 7E 40
RH2: Reig 2N 121
SL4: E Wic 1C 4
SL4: W'sor 5F 4
SM5: Cars 2C 62
SW18 7N 13
Alma Sq. GU14: Farnb 5A 90
Alma Ter. SW18 1B 28
Alma Way GU9: Heath E 5J 109
Almer Rd. SW20 8F 26
Almners Rd. KT16: Lyne 7C 36
(not continuous)
Almond Av. GU22: Wok 8N 73
SM5: Cars 8D 44
Almond Cl. GU1: Guil 9N 93
GU14: Farnb 7M 69
RH11: Craw 4M 181
SL4: W'sor 5E 4
TW13: Felt 2H 23
TW17: Shep 1D 38
TW20: Eng G 7L 19
Almond Ct. GU15: Camb 8B 50
GU52: Chu C 7C 88
(off Pine Gro.)
Almond Gro. TW8: Brent 3H 11
Almond Rd. KT19: Eps 7C 60
Almond Way CR4: Mit 4H 45
Almorah Rd. TW5: Hest 4L 9
Almsgate GU3: Comp 1F 132
Alms Heath GU23: Ockh 8C 76
Almshouse La. KT9: Ches 5J 59
Almshouses *GU10: Wrec 4E 128*
(off Riverdale)
KT16: Chert 6J 37
RH4: Dork 1L 201 (4H 119)
Alnwick Gro. SM4: Mord 3N 43
Aloes, The GU51: Fleet 5C 88
Alphabet Gdns. SM5: Cars 5B 44
Alpha Ct. CR3: Whyte 5D 84
Alpha Ho. RG45: Crowt 2H 49
Alpha Pl. SM4: Mord 7J 43
Alpha Rd.
CR0: Croy 1F 200 (7B 46)
GU12: Alde 3B 110
GU22: Wok 3D 74
GU24: Chob 6J 53
KT5: Surb 5M 41
RH11: Craw 3A 182
TW11: Tedd 6D 24
Alpha Way TW20: Thor 9E 20
Alphea Cl. SW19 8C 28
Alphington Av. GU16: Frim 5C 70
Alphington Grn. GU16: Frim 5C 70
Alpine Av. KT5: Surb 8B 42
Alpine Cl.
CR0: Croy 5F 200 (9B 46)
GU14: Cove 2J 89
KT19: Ewe 2B 60
SL5: S'hill 5A 34
Alpine Rd. KT12: Wal T 6H 39
RH1: Red 9E 102
Alpine Snowsports Cen. 9A 90
Alpine Vw. SM5: Cars 2C 62
Alpine Walks RH11: Craw 4A 182
Alresford Rd. GU2: Guil 4K 113
Alric Av. KT3: N Mal 2D 42
Alsace Wlk. GU15: Camb 5N 69
Alsager *KT22: Leat 6G 79*
(off Clements Mead)
Alsford Cl. GU18: Ligh 8K 51
Alsom Av. KT4: W Pk 1F 60
Alston Cl. KT6: Surb 6H 41
Alstonfield KT10: Esh 2C 58
Alston Rd. SW17 5B 28
Altamont CR6: Warl 6E 84
Alterton Cl. GU21: Wok 4K 73
Alt Gro. SW19 8L 27
Althea St. SW6 5N 13
Althorne Rd. RH1: Red 5E 122
Althorp Rd. SW17 2D 28
Altitude Apartments
CR0: Croy 4E 200
Alton Cl. TW7: Isle 5F 10
Alton Ct. TW18: Stain 9G 21
Alton Gdns. TW2: Whitt 1D 24
Alton Ho. RH1: Red 1E 122
Alton Ride GU17: B'water 9H 49
Alton Rd. CR0: Wad 9L 45
GU10: Farnh 5B 128
GU51: Fleet 4D 88
SW15 2F 26
TW9: Rich 7L 11
Altyre Cl. BR3: Beck 4J 47
Altyre Rd.
CR0: Croy 3E 200 (8A 46)
Altyre Way BR3: Beck 4J 47
Alvernia Cl. GU7: Godal 9F 132
Alverstoke Gdns.
GU11: Alde 3K 109
Alverstone Av. SW19 3M 27
Alverstone Rd. KT3: N Mal 3E 42
Alveston Gdns. SE25 4B 46
Alvia Gdns. SM1: Sut 1A 62
Alway Av. KT19: Ewe 2C 60
Alwin Pl. GU9: Up Hale 5G 109
Alwyn Av. W4 1C 12
Alwyn Cl. CR0: N Add 4L 65
Alwyne Ct. GU21: Wok 3A 74
Alwyne Rd. SW19 7L 27
Alwyns Cl. KT16: Chert 5J 37
Alwyns La. KT16: Chert 5H 37
Amalgamated Dr.
TW8: Brent 2H 11
Amanda Ct. *TW15: Ashf 3A 22*
(off Edward Way)
Ambarrow Court
Local Nature Reserve 5E 48
Ambarrow Cres.
GU47: Sandh 6E 48
Ambarrow Farm Courtyard
GU47: Sandh 5D 48
Ambarrow La. GU47: Sandh 5C 48
Ambassador RG12: Brac 4L 31
Ambassador, The
SL5: S'dale 6E 34
Ambassador Cl. TW3: Houn 5M 9
Ambassadors Cinema
Woking 4A 74
(off Victoria Way)
Amber Ct.
CR0: Croy 1F 200 (7B 46)
GU12: Alde 2A 110
KT5: Surb 6M 41
TW18: Stain 6H 21
(off Laleham Rd.)
Ambercroft Way CR5: Coul 6M 83
Amber Gdns. GU14: Farnb 1M 89
Amber Hill GU15: Camb 2F 70
Amberley Cl. GU23: Send 3H 95
RH10: Craw 3G 183
RH12: Hors 2N 197
Amberley Ct. *RH11: Craw 7B 162*
(off County Oak La.)
Amberley Dr. KT15: Wood 6H 55
Amberley Flds. Caravan Club Site
RH11: Low H 6N 161
Amberley Gdns. KT19: Ewe 1E 60
Amberley Grange
GU11: Alde 4L 109
Amberley Gro. CR0: Croy 6C 46
Amberley La. GU8: Mil 1B 152
Amberley Pl. *SL4: W'sor 4G 4*
(off Peascod St.)
Amberley Rd. GU8: Mil 9B 132
RH12: Hors 2N 197
Amberley Way SM4: Mord 6L 43
TW4: Houn 8K 9
Amberside Cl. TW7: Isle 9D 10
Amberwood Cl. SM6: W'ton 2J 63
Amberwood Dr.
GU15: Camb 8D 50
Amberwood Ri. KT3: N Mal 5D 42
Amblecote KT11: Cob 7M 57
Ambleside GU7: Godal 6K 133
RG45: Crowt 3H 49
SW19 2K 27
Ambleside Av. BR3: Beck 4H 47
KT12: Wal T 7K 39
SW16 5H 29
Ambleside Cl. GU14: Cove 1K 89
GU16: Mytc 3E 90
RH1: Red 8F 122
RH11: Ifield 4J 181
Ambleside Cres.
GU9: Up Hale 6F 108
Ambleside Dr. TW14: Felt 2G 22
Ambleside Gdns.
CR2: Sels 5G 64
SM2: Sut 3A 62
SW16 6H 29
Ambleside Rd. GU18: Ligh 7K 51
Ambleside Way TW20: Egh 8D 20
Ambrey Way SM6: W'ton 5H 63
Ambrose Cl. BR6: Orp 1N 67
Amelia Ho. TW9: Kew 3A 12
W6 1H 13
(off Queen Caroline St.)
AMEN CORNER 2J 31
Amen Corner SW17 7D 28

Brantwood Gdns.—Broadway Ct.

Brantwood Gdns.
KT14: W By 9H 55
Brantwood Rd. CR2: S Croy 5N 63
Brasenose Dr. SW13 . . . . .2H 13
Brassey Cl. RH8: Oxt 7C 106
TW14: Felt 2H 23
Brassey Hill RH8: Oxt 8C 106
Brassey Rd. RH8: Oxt 8B 106
Brasted Cl. SM2: Sut 6M 61
Brasted Rd. TN16: Weste 4N 107
Brathway Rd. SW18 . . . . .1M 27
Brattain Ct. RG12: Brac 2B 32
Bratten Ct. CR0: Croy 5A 46
Bravington Cl. TW17: Shep 4A 38
Braxted Pk. SW16 . . . . .7K 29
Braybourne Dr. TW7: Isle 3F 10
Braybrooke Rd. RG42: Brac 8N 15
Bray Cl. RH10: Craw 5H 183
Bray Ct. SW16 . . . . .6J 29
Braycourt Av. KT12: Wal T 6J 39
Braye Cl. GU47: Sandh 6H 49
Bray Gdns. GU22: Pyr 3G 75
Bray Rd. GU2: Guil 4L 113
KT11: Sto D 3M 77
TN8: Eden 1L 147
Braywood Av. TW20: Egh 7B 20
Braziers La. RG42: Wink R 6H 17
Brazil Cl. CR0: Bedd 6J 45
Breakfield CR5: Coul 3J 83
Breamore Cl. SW15 . . . . .2F 26
Breamwater Gdns.
TW10: Ham 4H 25
Breasley Cl. SW15 . . . . .7G 13
Brecon Cl. CR4: Mit 2J 45
GU14: Cove 7J 69
KT4: W Pk 8H 43
Brecon Rd. W6 . . . . .2K 13
Brecons, The KT13: Weybr 1E 56
Bredin Ho. SW10 . . . . .3N 13
(off Coleridge Gdns.)
Bredon Rd. CR0: Croy 6C 46
Bredune CR8: Ken 2A 84
Breech, The GU47: Coll T 8K 49
Breech La. KT20: Wal H 2F 100
Breer St. SW6 . . . . .6N 13
Breezehurst Dr.
RH11: Craw 6K 181
Breezehurst Rdbt.
RH11: Craw 7M 181
Bregsells La. RH5: B Grn 7K 139
Bremer Rd. TW18: Stain 4J 21
Bremner Av. RH6: Horl 7D 142
Brenda Rd. SW17 . . . . .3D 28
Brende Gdns. KT8: W Mole 3B 40
Brendon Cl. KT10: Esh 3C 58
UB3: Harl 3D 8
Brendon Dr. KT10: Esh 3C 58
Brendon Rd. GU14: Cove 7J 69
Brenley Cl. CR4: Mit 2E 44
BRENTFORD 2K 11
Brentford Bus. Cen.
TW8: Brent 3J 11
BRENTFORD END 3H 11
Brentford FC 2K 11
Brentford Fountain Leisure Cen.
. . . . .1N 11
Brentford Ho. TW1: Twick 1H 25
Brentford Station (Rail) 2J 11
Brent Lea TW8: Brent 3J 11
Brentmoor Rd.
GU24: W End 9N 51
Brent Rd. CR2: Sels 5E 64
TW8: Brent 2J 11
Brent Side TW8: Brent 2J 11
Brentside Executive Cen.
TW8: Brent 2H 11
Brentwaters Bus. Pk.
TW8: Brent 3J 11
Brent Way TW8: Brent 3K 11
Brentwick Gdns. TW8: Brent . . .1L 11
Brentwood Ct. KT15: Addl 1K 55
Bret Harte Rd. GU16: Frim 5C 70
Bretlands Rd. KT16: Chert 8G 36
Brettgrave KT19: Eps 6B 60
Brett Ho. Cl. SW15 . . . . .1J 27
Brettingham Cl.
RH11: Craw 6K 181
Brewer Rd. RH10: Craw 5C 182
Brewers Cl. GU14: Cove 9M 69
Brewers La. TW9: Rich 8K 11
Brewer St. RH1: Blet 9N 103
Brewery La. KT14: Byf 9N 55
TW1: Twick 1F 24
Brewery Mews Cen.
TW7: Isle 6G 10
Brewery Rd. GU21: Wok 4N 73
Brewhouse La. SW15 . . . . .6K 13
Brew Ho. Rd. RH3: Brock 7B 120
Brewhurst La. RH14: Loxw 6J 193
Brewster Pl. KT1: K Tham 1B 42
Breydon Wlk. RH10: Craw 5F 182
Brian Av. CR2: Sande 8B 64
Briane Rd. KT19: Eps 6B 60
Briar Av. GU18: Ligh 8K 51
SW16 . . . . .8K 29
Briar Banks SM5: Cars 5E 62
Briar Cl. CR6: Warl 3K 85
KT14: W By 7K 55
RH11: Craw 9A 162
TN8: Eden 9M 127
TW7: Isle 8F 10
TW12: Hamp 6N 23
Briar Ct. SM3: Chea 1H 61
SW15 . . . . .7G 13
Briar Gro. CR2: Sande 9D 64
Briar Hill CR8: Pur 7J 63
Briar La. BR4: A'ton 1L 65
SM5: Cars 5E 62
Briarleas Ct. GU14: Farnb 5B 90
Briar Patch GU7: Godal 5G 133
Briar Rd. GU23: Send 2D 94
SW16 . . . . .2J 45
TW2: Twick 2E 24
TW17: Shep 4A 38
Briars, The GU12: Ash 3F 110
GU52: Chu C 7B 88
SL3: Lang 1B 6
TW19: Stan M 8J 7
Briars Cl. GU14: Cove 2J 89
Briars Ct. KT22: Oxs 1D 78
Briars Wood RH6: Horl 7G 142
Briarswood Cl. RH10: Craw . . .1H 183
Briar Wlk. KT14: W By 8J 55
SW15 . . . . .7G 13
Briar Way GU4: B'ham 8D 94
Briarwood Cl. TW13: Felt 5F 22
Briarwood Ct. KT4: W Pk 7F 42
(off The Avenue)
Briarwood Rd. GU21: Wok 6G 73
KT17: Ewe 3F 60
Briavels Ct. KT18: Eps 2D 80
Brickbat All. KT22: Leat 8H 79
Brick Farm Cl. TW9: Kew 4A 12
Brickfield Cl. TW8: Brent 3J 11
Brickfield Cotts. GU3: Flex 3A 112
GU11: Alde 4J 109
RG45: Crowt 4E 48
Brickfield Farm Gdns.
BR6: Farnb 1L 67
Brickfield La. RH6: Hookw 1B 162
UB3: Harl 2E 8
Brickfield Rd. CR7: T Hea 9M 29
RH1: Out 2L 143
SW19 . . . . .5N 27
Brickfields Country Pk. 4N 109
Brickfields Ind. Pk.
RG12: Brac 1L 31
BRICK HILL 1F 52
Brickhouse La.
RH7: Newchap 4F 144
RH9: S Gods 4F 144
Brick Kiln La. RH8: Limp 8E 106
Bricklands RH10: Craw D 2E 184
Brick La. GU51: Fleet 3A 88
Bricksbury Hill
GU9: Up Hale 5H 109
Brickwood Rd.
CR0: Croy 2F 200 (8B 46)
Brickyard Copse RH5: Ockl . . .6C 158
Brickyard La. RH5: Wott 1L 137
RH10: Craw D 1E 184
Brideake Cl. RH11: Craw 6M 181
Bridewell Cl. GU8: Worm 9C 152
Bridge Av. W6 . . . . .1H 13
Bridge Av. Mans. W6 . . . . .1H 13
(off Bridge Av.)
Bridge Barn La. GU21: Wok 5N 73
Bridge Cl. GU21: Wok 4M 73
KT12: Wal T 6G 38
KT14: Byf 8A 56
TW11: Tedd 5F 24
TW18: Stain 5G 20
Bridge Ct. GU10: Wrec 4E 128
GU21: Wok 4N 73
KT12: Wal T 7G 39
(off Bridge St.)
KT13: Weybr 1C 56
KT22: Leat 9G 79
BRIDGE END 7C 76
Bridge End GU15: Camb 2N 69
Bridge End Cl.
KT2: K Tham 2M 203 (9N 25)
Bridgefield GU9: Farnh 1J 129
Bridgefield Cl. SM7: Ban 2H 81
Bridgefield Rd. SM1: Sut 3M 61
Bridgefoot TW16: Sunb 9G 23
Bridge Gdns. KT8: E Mol 3D 40
TW15: Ashf 8D 22
Bridgeham Cl. KT13: Weybr . . .2B 56
Bridgeham Way
RH6: Smallf 9M 143
Bridgehill Cl. GU2: Guil 1K 113
Bridge Ho. CR0: Croy 4B 200
KT16: Chert 6L 37
SM2: Sut 3N 61
(off Bridge Rd.)
Bridge Ind. Est. RH6: Horl 8F 142
Bridgelands RH10: Copt 7L 163
Bridge La. GU25: V Wat 4A 36
Bridgeman Ct. SL4: W'sor 5D 4
Bridgeman Dr. SL4: W'sor 5D 4
Bridgeman Rd. TW11: Tedd 7G 24
Bridge Mead GU24: Pirb 4C 92
Bridgemead GU16: Frim 6A 70
(off Frimley High St.)
Bridge M. GU7: Godal 7H 133
GU10: Tong 5D 110
GU21: Wok 4N 73
Bridgend Rd. SW18 . . . . .7N 13
Bridge Pk. GU4: Guil 9E 94
Bridgepark SW18 . . . . .8M 13
Bridge Pl. CR0: Croy 7A 46
Bridge Retail Pk.
RG40: W'ham 3A 30
Bridge Rd. GU6: Cranl 8N 155
GU7: Godal 6H 133
GU11: Alde 4M 109
GU14: Cove 1L 89
GU15: Camb 3N 69
GU19: Bag 4J 51
Bridge Rd. GU27: Hasl 1G 189
KT8: E Mol 3D 40
KT9: Ches 2L 59
KT13: Weybr 1A 56
KT16: Chert 6K 37
KT17: Eps 8E 60
RH12: Rudg 1E 194
SL5: S'hill 4A 34
SM2: Sut 3N 61
SM6: W'ton 2F 62
TW1: Twick 9H 11
TW3: Houn, Isle 6D 10
TW7: Isle 6D 10
Bridge Row
CR0: Croy 1E 200 (7A 46)
Bridges Cl. RH6: Horl 8H 143
Bridges Ct. RH12: Hors 3M 197
Bridges La. CR0: Bedd 1J 63
Bridges Pl. RH12: Hors 7J 197
SW6 . . . . .4L 13
Bridge Sq. GU9: Farnh 1H 129
Bridges Rd. SW19 . . . . .7N 27
Bridges Rd. M. SW19 . . . . .7N 27
Bridgestone Pl.
RH13: Hors 7L 197
Bridge St.
GU1: Guil 5B 202 (4M 113)
GU7: Godal 7H 133
KT12: Wal T 7F 38
KT22: Leat 9G 79
SL3: Coln 3F 6
TW9: Rich 8K 11
TW18: Stain 5G 21
W4 . . . . .1C 12
Bridge St. Pas. GU1: Guil 5B 202
Bridge Vw. SL5: S'dale 6E 34
W6 . . . . .1H 13
Bridge Wlk. GU46: Yate 8C 48
Bridgewater GU21: Wok 3B 74
Bridgewater Ct. SL3: Lang 1C 6
Bridgewater Rd.
KT13: Weybr 3E 56
Bridgewater Ter. SL4: W'sor 4G 4
Bridgewater Way SL4: W'sor . . .4G 4
Bridge Way CR5: Chip 6C 82
KT11: Cob 9G 57
TW2: Whitt 1C 24
Bridge Wharf KT16: Chert 6L 37
Bridge Wharf Rd. TW7: Isle 6H 11
Bridgewood Rd. KT4: W Pk 1F 60
SW16 . . . . .8H 29
Bridgford St. SW18 . . . . .4A 28
Bridle Cl. GU26: G'hott 6M 169
KT1: K Tham 7H 203 (3K 41)
KT19: Ewe 2C 60
TW16: Sunb 2H 39
Bridle Ct. GU11: Alde 2K 109
Bridle End KT17: Eps 9E 60
Bridle La. KT11: Sto D 2B 78
KT22: Oxs 2B 78
TW1: Twick 9H 11
Bridle Path CR0: Bedd 9J 45
GU10: Ews 4C 108
Bridle Path, The KT17: Ewe 6H 61
Bridlepath Way TW14: Bedf 1F 22
Bridle Rd. CR0: Croy 9K 47
CR2: Sande 5D 64
KT10: Clay 3H 59
KT17: Eps 9E 60
Bridle Road, The CR8: Pur 6J 63
Bridle Way BR6: Farnb 1L 67
CR0: Croy 2K 65
RH10: Craw 2H 183
Bridle Way, The CR0: Sels 6H 65
Bridleway, The CR5: Coul 1F 82
SM6: W'ton 2G 63
Bridleway Cl. KT17: Ewe 6H 61
Bridlington Cl. TN16: B Hil 6D 86
Bridport Rd. CR7: T Hea 2L 45
Brier Lea KT20: Lwr K 4L 101
Brierley CR0: N Add 3L 65
(not continuous)
Brierley Cl. SE25 . . . . .3D 46
Brierley Rd. SW12 . . . . .3G 28
Brierly Cl. GU2: Guil 1K 113
Brier Rd. KT20: Tad 6G 81
Brigade Pl. CR3: Cate 9N 83
Briggs Cl. CR4: Mit 9F 28
Bright Hill
GU1: Guil 6D 202 (5A 114)
Brightlands Rd. RH2: Reig 1A 122
Brightman Rd. SW18 . . . . .2B 28
Brighton Cl. KT15: Addl 2L 55
Brighton Rd.
CR2: S Croy 8C 200 (2N 63)
CR5: Coul 1F 102
CR8: Pur 7L 63
GU7: Bus, Godal 7H 133
GU12: Alde 4A 110
KT6: Surb 5J 41
KT15: Addl 2L 55
KT20: K'wood, Lwr K, Tad
. . . . .8K 81
RH1: Mers 1F 102
RH1: Red 4D 122
RH1: Salf 1E 142
RH6: Gatw, Craw 1D 162
RH6: Horl 9D 142
RH10: Craw 6B 182
RH11: Craw 9A 182
RH11: Hand, Pease P 4N 199
RH13: Hors, Mann H 7K 197
RH17: Hand 5N 199
SM2: Ban, Sut 7M 61
SM7: Ban 3L 81
Brighton Ter. RH1: Red 4D 122
Brightside Av. TW18: Stain 8L 21
Brightwell Cl. CR0: Croy 7L 45
Brightwell Cres. SW17 . . . . . . .6D 28
Brightwell Pk. 1H 129
Brightwells Rd. GU9: Farnh . . .1H 129
Brigstock Rd. CR5: Coul 2F 82
CR7: T Hea 4L 45
Brimshot La. GU24: Chob 5H 53
Brimstone La. RH5: Holm 3M 139
Brind Cotts. GU24: Chob 6J 53
Brindle Cl. GU11: Alde 5N 109
Brindles, The SM7: Ban 4L 81
Brinkley KT1: K Tham 1N 41
Brinkley Rd. KT4: W Pk 8G 42
BRINKSWAY 4B 188
Brinksway GU51: Fleet 4B 88
Brinkworth Pl. SL4: O Win 1L 19
Brinn's La. GU17: B'water 1H 69
Brinsworth Cl. TW2: Twick 2D 24
Brinsworth Ho. TW2: Twick 3D 24
Brisbane Av. SW19 . . . . .9N 27
Brisbane Cl. RH11: Craw 9B 162
Briscoe M. TW2: Twick 3D 24
Briscoe Rd. SW19 . . . . .7B 28
Brisson Cl. KT10: Esh 3N 57
Bristol Cl. RH10: Craw 9H 163
SM6: W'ton 4J 63
TW4: Houn 1A 24
TW19: Stan 9N 7
Bristol Ct. TW19: Stan 9N 7
Bristol Gdns. SW15 . . . . .1H 27
Bristol Rd. SM4: Mord 4A 44
Bristow Rd. CR0: Bedd 1J 63
GU15: Camb 3N 69
TW3: Houn 6C 10
Britannia Cl. GU35: Bor 6A 168
Britannia Ct. KT2: K Tham 1H 203
Britannia Ind. Est. SL3: Poy 5G 6
Britannia La. TW2: Whitt 1C 24
Britannia Rd. KT5: Surb 6M 41
SW6 . . . . .3N 13
Britannia Way SW6 . . . . .3N 13
(off Britannia Rd.)
TW19: Stan 1M 21
British Disabled Water-Ski
Association 2E 20
British Gro. W4 . . . . .1E 12
British Gro. Pas. W4 . . . . .1E 12
British Gro. Sth. W4 . . . . .1E 12
British Rail New Yd.
RH10: Craw 8F 162
British Wildlife Cen. 8J 145
Briton Cl. CR2: Sande 7B 64
Briton Cres. CR2: Sande 7B 64
Briton Hill Rd. CR2: Sande 6B 64
Brittain Ct. GU47: Sandh 8H 49
Brittain Rd. KT12: Hers 2L 57
Britten Cl. GU12: Ash 2F 110
RH11: Craw 6L 181
RH13: Hors 4A 198
Brittenden Cl. BR6: Chels 3N 67
Brittens Cl. GU2: Guil 7K 93
Brittleware Cotts.
RH6: Charlw 8L 141
Brixton Hill SW2 . . . . .1J 29
Brixton Hill Pl. SW2 . . . . .1J 29
Broadacre TW18: Stain 6J 21
Broad Acres GU7: Godal 3H 133
Broadacres GU3: Guil 1H 113
BROADBRIDGE 1L 163
Broadbridge Cotts.
RH6: Smallf 1L 163
BROADBRIDGE HEATH 5D 196
Broadbridge Heath By-Pass
RH12: Broadb H 5C 196
Broadbridge Heath Leisure Cen.
. . . . .6D 196
Broadbridge Heath Rd.
RH12: Broadb H, Warnh
. . . . .4D 196
Broadbridge La.
RH6: Smallf 8L 143
Broadbridge Retail Pk.
RH12: Broadb H 5E 196
Broad Cl. KT12: Hers 9L 39
Broadcommon La.
RG10: Hurst 2A 14
Broadcommon Rd.
RG10: Hurst 2A 14
Broadcoombe CR2: Sels 4F 64
Broadeaves Cl. CR2: S Croy 2B 64
BROADFIELD 7N 181
Broadfield Barton
RH11: Craw 7N 181
Broadfield Cl. CR0: Wad 8K 45
KT20: Tad 7H 81
Broadfield Dr. RH11: Craw 6N 181
Broadfield Pk. 8A 182
Broadfield Pk. RH11: Craw 7B 182
Broadfield Pl. RH11: Craw 7N 181
Broadfield Rd. GU5: P'lake 2E 136
Broadfield Rdbt.
RH11: Craw 6N 181
Broadfields KT8: E Mol 5E 40
Broadfield Stadium 7A 182
BROADFORD 1N 133
Broadford La. GU24: Chob 8H 53
Broadford Pk. GU4: Chil 1N 133
Broadford Pk. Bus. Cen.
GU4: Chil 1N 133
Broadford Rd.
GU3: P'marsh 2M 133
GU4: Chil 2M 133
Broadgates Rd. SW18 . . . . .2B 28
BROAD GREEN 6M 45
Broad Grn. Av. CR0: Croy 6M 45
BROADHAM GREEN 1N 125
Broadham Grn. Rd.
RH8: Oxt 1N 125
Broadham Pl. RH8: Oxt 9N 105
Broad Ha'penny
GU10: Wrec 7F 128
Broad Highway KT11: Cob 1L 77
Broadhurst GU14: Cove 1H 89
KT21: Asht 3L 79
Broadhurst Cl. TW10: Rich 8M 11
Broadhurst Gdns.
RH2: Reig 6N 121
Broadhurst M. GU12: Alde 3A 110
Broadlands GU14: Farnb 3C 90
GU16: Frim 6D 70
RH6: Horl 7G 143
TW13: Hanw 4A 24
Broadlands Av. SW16 . . . . .3J 29
TW17: Shep 5D 38
Broadlands Bus. Campus
RH12: Hors 5J 179
Broadlands Cl. SW16 . . . . .3J 29
Broadlands Ct. RG42: Brac 9K 15
TW9: Kew 3N 11
(off Kew Gdns. Rd.)
Broadlands Dr. CR6: Warl 6F 84
SL5: Asc, S'hill 6N 33
Broadlands Way KT3: N Mal . . .5E 42
Broad La. RG12: Brac 2A 32
RH5: Leigh, Newd 7C 140
TW12: Hamp 8N 23
Broadley Grn. GU20: Windl 4A 52
Broadleys SL4: W'sor 3C 4
Broadmead GU14: Cove 2J 89
KT21: Asht 4M 79
RH1: Mers 6G 102
(off Station Rd.)
RH6: Horl 7G 143
W14 . . . . .1K 13
Broadmead Av. KT4: W Pk 6F 42
Broadmead Cl. TW12: Hamp 7A 24
Broadmead Rd. GU22: Wok 9D 74
GU23: Send 9D 74
Broadmeads GU23: Send 9D 74
BROADMOOR 3A 138
Broadmoor Est. RG45: Crowt . . .3J 49
Broad Oak TW16: Sunb 7G 23
Broadoaks KT6: Surb 8A 42
Broadoaks Cres.
KT14: W By 9K 55
Broadpool Cotts. SL5: Asc 8L 17
Broadrick Heath RG42: Warf 8B 16
Broadstone RH18: F Row 7J 187
Broad St.
GU3: Guil, Wood V 1F 112
GU24: W End 9A 52
RG40: W'ham 2B 30
TW11: Tedd 7F 24
BROAD STREET COMMON 9G 92
Broad St. Wlk.
RG40: W'ham 2B 30
(off Broad St.)
Broadview Rd. SW16 . . . . .8H 29
Broad Wlk. CR3: Cate 9C 84
CR5: Coul 1E 102
GU6: Cranl 9A 156
GU16: Frim 4C 70
KT18: Tat C 6J 81
TW5: Hest 4L 9
TW9: Kew 3M 11
Broad Walk, The KT8: E Mol . . .3F 40
Broadwalk RH10: Craw 3B 182
Broadwater Cl. GU21: Wok 8F 54
KT12: Hers 2H 57
TW19: Wray 1B 20
Broadwater Gdns.
BR6: Farnb 1K 67
Broadwater La. GU7: Godal . . .5J 133
Broadwater Pk. Golf Course
. . . . .4K 133
Broadwater Pl. KT13: Weybr . . .8F 38
Broadwater Ri. GU1: Guil 4C 114
Broadwater Rd. SW17 . . . . .5C 28
Broadwater Rd. Nth.
KT12: Hers 2G 57
Broadwater Rd. Sth.
KT12: Hers 2G 57
Broadway GU21: Knap 5E 72
RG12: Brac 1N 31
SL4: Wink 2M 17
TW18: Stain 6K 21
Broadway, The CR0: Bedd 1J 63
GU21: Wok 4B 74
GU47: Sandh 8G 49
KT7: T Dit 7E 40
KT15: N Haw 6J 55
RH10: Craw 3B 182
SM1: Sut 2A 62
SM3: Chea 3K 61
SW13 . . . . .5D 12
SW19 . . . . .7L 27
TW18: Lale 2L 37
Broadway Arc. W6 . . . . .1H 13
(off Hammersmith B'way.)
Broadway Av. CR0: Croy 4A 46
TW1: Twick 9H 11
Broadway Centre, The W6 . . . . .1H 13
Broadway Chambers W6 . . . . . .1H 13
(off Hammersmith B'way.)
Broadway Cl. CR2: Sande 1E 84
Broadway Ct. BR3: Beck 2M 47
GU21: Knap 4F 72
SW19 . . . . .7M 27

Broadway Gdns.—Bucknall Way

Broadway Gdns. CR4: Mit 3C 44
Broadway Ho. GU21: Knap 5F 72
Broadway Mans. *SW6* *3M 13*
(off Fulham Rd.)
Broadway Mkt. SW17 . . . . .5D 28
Broadway Pl. SW19 . . . . .7L 27
Broadway Rd. GU18: Ligh 6N 51
GU20: Windl 6N 51
Broadwell Ct. *TW5: Hest* *4L 9*
(off Springwell Rd.)
Broadwell Rd. GU10: Wrec . . .5E 128
Broadwood Cl. RH12: Hors . . .3N 197
Broadwood Cotts.
RH5: Cap 4L 159
Broadwood Ri.
RH11: Craw 8M 181
Broadwood Rd. CR5: Coul 8H 83
Brocas St. SL4: Eton 3G 4
Brocas Ter. SL4: Eton 3G 4
Brockbridge Ho. SW15 . . . . .9E 12
Brock Cl. GU16: Deep 6H 71
Brockdene Dr. BR2: Kes 1F 66
Brockenhurst KT8: W Mole 4N 39
Brockenhurst Av. KT4: W Pk . . .7D 42
Brockenhurst Cl. GU21: Wok . . .1B 74
Brockenhurst Dr. GU46: Yate . . .2C 68
Brockenhurst Rd. CR0: Croy . . .6E 46
GU11: Alde 4N 109
RG12: Brac 2D 32
SL5: Asc 3L 33
Brockenhurst Way SW16 . . . . . .1H 45
BROCKHAM 5A 120
Brockham Cl. SW19 . . . . .6L 27
Brockham Ct.
CR2: S Croy 8C 200 (2N 63)
RH1: Red *1F 122*
(off Goodworth Rd.)
Brockham Cres. CR0: N Add . . .4N 65
Brockham Dr. SW2 . . . . .1K 29
Brockham Grn. RH3: Brock . . .4A 120
Brockham Hill *KT20: Box H* . . .*9B 100*
(off Boxhill Rd.)
Brockham Hill Pk.
KT20: Box H 9B 100
Brockham Ho. *SW2* *1K 29*
(off Brockham Dr.)
Brockhamhurst Rd.
RH3: Betch 1N 139
Brockham Keep *RH6: Horl* *7G 142*
(off Langshott La.)
Brockham La. RH3: Brock 3N 119
BROCKHAM PARK 9B 120
Brockham Pk. Ho.
RH3: Betch 9B 120
BROCK HILL 5E 16
Brockhill GU21: Wok 4K 73
Brockhurst Cl. RH12: Hors 7F 196
Brockhurst Cotts. GU6: Alf 5H 175
Brockhurst Lodge
GU9: Wrec 4G 128
Brocklands GU46: Yate 2A 68
Brocklebank Ct.
CR3: Whyte 5D 84
Brocklebank Rd. SW18 . . . . . . .1A 28
Brocklesby Rd. SE25 . . . . .3E 46
Brockley Combe
KT13: Weybr 1E 56
Brock Rd. RH11: Craw 9N 161
Brocks Cl. GU7: Godal 6K 133
Brocks Dr. GU3: Worp 8F 92
SM3: Chea 9K 43
Brockshot Cl. TW8: Brent 1K 11
Brock Way GU25: V Wat 4M 35
Brockway Cl. GU1: Guil 2D 114
Brockwell Av. BR3: Beck 4L 47
Brockwell Park 1M 29
Brockwell Pk. Gdns. SE24 . . . . .1L 29
Brockwell Pk. Row SW2 . . . . . .1L 29
Broderick Gro. KT23: Book 4A 98
Brodie Rd.
GU1: Guil 5E 202 (4A 114)
Brodrick Rd. SW17 . . . . .3C 28
Brograve Gdns. BR3: Beck 1L 47
Broke Ct. GU4: Guil 9E 94
Broken Furlong SL4: Eton 1E 4
Brokes Cres. RH2: Reig 1M 121
Brokes Rd. RH2: Reig 1M 121
Bromford Cl. RH8: Oxt 2C 126
Bromley Environmental
Education Centre at High Elms
(BEECHE) 3M 67
Bromley Gro. BR2: Brom 1N 47
Bromley Rd. BR2: Brom 1L 47
BR3: Beck 1L 47
Bromley Tennis Cen. 1M 67
Brompton Cemetery 2N 13
Brompton Cl. GU15: Camb 8E 50
SE20 . . . . .1D 46
TW4: Houn 8N 9
Brompton Pk. Cres. SW6 . . . . . .2N 13
Brompton Vs. *SW6* *2M 13*
(off Lillie Rd.)
Bronsart Rd. SW6 . . . . .3K 13
Bronson Rd. SW20 . . . . .1J 43
Bronte Ct. RH1: Red 2E 122
Bronte Ho. SW4 . . . . .1G 29
SW17 . . . .*4B 28*
(off Grosvenor Way)
Brontes, The RH19: E Grin 9N 165
BROOK
GU5 . . . . .2N 135
GU8 . . . . .9N 151
Brook, The RH10: Craw 2B 182
Brook Av. GU9: Weybo 5L 109
SL5: Asc 2J 33
Brook Cl. GU12: Ash 1F 110
GU47: Owls 6K 49
GU51: Fleet 5B 88
KT19: Ewe 5D 60
RH4: Dork 3J 119
RH19: E Grin 9D 166
SW17 . . . . .3E 28
SW20 . . . . .2G 43
TW19: Stan 1A 22
Brook Cotts. GU46: Yate 9B 48
Brook Ct. *GU14: Cove* *9H 69*
(off Melrose Av.)
TN8: Eden 9L 127
Brook Dr. RG12: Brac 3C 32
Brooke Ct. GU16: Frim G 8D 70
Brooke Forest GU3: Worp 8F 92
Brooke Pl. RG42: Bin 6J 15
Brookers Cl. KT21: Asht 4J 79
Brookers Cnr. RG45: Crowt 2H 49
Brookers Row RG45: Crowt 1H 49
Brook Farm Rd. KT11: Cob 2L 77
Brookfield GU7: Godal 3K 133
GU21: Wok 3L 73
Brookfield Av. SM1: Sut 1B 62
Brookfield Cl. KT16: Otter 3F 54
KT21: Asht 7L 79
RH1: Red 9E 122
Brookfield Dr. RH6: Horl 6F 142
Brookfield Gdns. KT10: Clay 3F 58
Brookfield Pl. KT11: Cob 2M 77
Brookfield Rd. GU12: Alde 1C 110
Brookfields Av. CR4: Mit 4C 44
Brook Gdns. GU14: Cove 3L 89
KT2: K Tham 9B 26
SW13 . . . . .6E 12
Brook Grn. *GU24: Chob* *6J 53*
(off Chertsey Rd.)
RG42: Brac 9L 15
(not continuous)
Brook Hill GU5: Alb 3M 135
RH8: Oxt 8M 105
Brookhill Cl. RH10: Copt 7L 163
Brookhill Rd. RH10: Copt 8L 163
Brook Ho. GU6: Cranl 6A 156
GU9: Hale *6J 109*
(off Farnborough Rd.)
GU51: Fleet *4A 88*
(off Upper St.)
Brookhouse Rd. GU14: Cove . . .2L 89
Brookhurst Fld.
RH12: Rudg 9E 176
Brookhurst Rd. KT15: Addl 3K 55
Brookland Ct. RH2: Reig 1N 121
BROOKLANDS 6A 56
Brooklands GU11: Alde 3K 109
RH9: S Gods 1E 144
Brooklands, The TW7: Isle 4D 10
Brooklands Av. SW19 . . . . .3N 27
Brooklands Bus. Pk.
KT13: Weybr 7N 55
Brooklands Cl.
GU9: Heath E 5J 109
KT11: Cob 2M 77
TW16: Sunb 9F 22
Brooklands Ct. CR4: Mit 1B 44
KT1: K Tham 7H 203
KT15: N Haw 6M 55
Brooklands Dr. KT13: Weybr . . .6N 55
Brooklands Ind. Est.
KT13: Weybr 6N 55
Brooklands La. KT13: Weybr . . .3A 56
Brooklands Mus. 5A 56
Brooklands Pl. TW12: H Hill 6B 24
Brooklands Rd.
GU9: Heath E 5K 109
KT7: T Dit 7F 40
KT13: Weybr 8B 56
RH11: Craw 8A 182
Brooklands Way
GU9: Heath E 5K 109
RH1: Red 1C 122
RH19: E Grin 1N 185
Brook La. GU5: Alb 2N 135
GU23: Send 9G 74
GU24: Chob 7G 53
RH12: Fay 9B 180
Brook La. Bus. Cen.
TW8: Brent 1K 11
Brook La. Nth. TW8: Brent 1K 11
(not continuous)
Brookley Cl. GU10: Run 9A 110
Brookleys GU24: Chob 6J 53
Brookly Gdns. GU51: Fleet 3C 88
Brooklyn Av. SE25 . . . . .3E 46
Brooklyn Cl. GU22: Wok 6A 74
SM5: Cars 8C 44
Brooklyn Ct. GU22: Wok 6A 74
Brooklyn Gro. SE25 . . . . .3E 46
Brooklyn Rd. GU22: Wok 5A 74
SE25 . . . . .3E 46
Brook Mnr. RH19: E Grin 2N 185
Brook Mead GU8: Mil 2C 152
KT19: Ewe 3D 60
Brookmead CR0: Bedd 5G 45
Brookmead Ct. GU6: Cranl 8N 155
GU9: Farnh *2G 128*
(off Pengilly Rd.)
Brookmead Ind. Est.
CR0: Bedd 5G 44
Brook Mdw. GU8: Chid 6F 172
Brookmead Rd. CR0: Croy 5G 45
Brook Rd. CR7: T Hea 3N 45
GU4: Guil 1E 134
GU8: Brook, Worm 1N 171
GU15: Camb 2N 69
Brook Rd. GU19: Bag 5J 51
KT6: Surb 8L 41
RH1: Mers 7G 102
RH1: Red 4D 122
RH12: Hors 2L 197
TW1: Twick 9G 11
Brook Rd. Sth. TW8: Brent 2K 11
Brooksby Cl. GU17: B'water . . .1G 68
Brooks Cl. KT13: Weybr 6B 56
Brookscroft CR0: Sels 6J 65
BROOKSIDE 7K 17
Brookside GU4: J Wel 7N 93
GU6: Cranl 7N 155
(Ewhurst Rd.)
GU6: Cranl 9N 155
(Waverleigh Rd.)
GU9: Hale 6H 109
GU47: Sandh 8H 49
KT16: Chert 6G 37
RH5: B Grn 5M 139
RH9: S Gods 7G 124
RH10: Copt 7L 163
RH10: Craw 2D 182
RH10: Craw D 1E 184
SL3: Coln 3E 6
SM5: Cars 2E 62
Brookside Av. TW15: Ashf 6L 21
TW19: Wray 6A 6
Brookside Cl. TW13: Felt 4H 23
Brookside Cres. KT4: W Pk 7F 42
Brookside Residential Pk. Homes
GU14: Farnb 5M 69
Brookside Rural Pk.
RH12: Rudg 7G 177
Brookside Way CR0: Croy 5G 46
Brooks La. W4 . . . . .2N 11
Brooks Rd. W4 . . . . .1N 11
Brook St.
KT1: K Tham 4J 203 (1L 41)
SL4: W'sor 5G 5
Brook Trad. Estate, The
GU12: Alde 2C 110
Brook Valley RH5: Mid H 2H 139
Brookview RH10: Copt 7L 163
Brookview Rd. SW16 . . . . .6G 28
Brookville Rd. SW6 . . . . .3L 13
Brook Way KT22: Leat 5G 78
Brookwell La. GU5: Braml 1C 154
BROOKWOOD 7D 72
Brookwood RH6: Horl 7F 142
Brookwood Av. SW13 . . . . .5E 12
Brookwood Country Pk. 6F 72
Brookwood Ho. *RH6: Horl* *5F 142*
(off Skipton Way)
Brookwood Lye Rd.
GU24: B'wood 7E 72
Brookwood Pk. RH6: Horl 9F 142
Brookwood Rd. GU14: Farnb . . .1B 90
SW18 . . . . .2L 27
TW3: Houn 5B 10
Brookwood Station (Rail) 8D 72
Broom Acres GU47: Sandh 7G 49
GU52: Fleet 7A 88
Broom Bank CR6: Warl 6M 85
Broom Cl. KT10: Esh 2B 58
TW11: Tedd 8K 25
Broomcroft Cl. GU22: Pyr 3F 74
Broomcroft Dr. GU22: Pyr 2F 74
Broomdashers Rd.
RH10: Craw 2D 182
Broome Cl. GU46: Yate 8B 48
KT18: Head 4B 100
RH12: Hors 3K 197
Broome Cotts. RH4: Dork 4J 119
Broome Ct. KT20: Tad 6K 81
RG12: Brac 2N 31
Broome Hall Rd.
RH5: Cold, Ockl 9D 138
Broome Lodge *TW18: Stain* *6J 21*
(off Kingston Rd.)
Broome Rd. TW12: Hamp 8N 23
Broomers La. GU6: Ewh 5F 156
Broom Fld. GU18: Ligh 8L 51
Broomfield GU2: Guil 2H 113
GU8: Els 7J 131
RG42: Bin 9J 15
TW16: Sunb 9H 23
TW18: Stain 7J 21
Broomfield Cl. GU3: Guil 1H 113
SL5: S'dale 6E 34
Broomfield Ct. KT13: Weybr 3C 56
Broomfield Pk. RH4: Westc . . .6C 118
SL5: S'dale 5E 34
Broomfield Ride KT22: Oxs 8D 58
Broomfield Rd. BR3: Beck 2H 47
KT5: Surb 7M 41
KT15: N Haw 7K 55
TW9: Kew 4M 11
TW11: Tedd 7J 25
Broomfields KT10: Esh 2C 58
Broom Gdns. CR0: Croy 9K 47
BROOMHALL 5D 34
Broom Hall KT22: Oxs 1D 78
Broomhall End *GU21: Wok* *3A 74*
(off Broomhall La.)
Broomhall La. GU21: Wok 3A 74
SL5: S'dale 5D 34
Broomhall Rd. CR2: Sande 5A 64
GU21: Wok 3A 74
Broomhill GU10: Ews 4C 108
Broomhill Rd. GU14: Cove 9J 69
SW18 . . . . .8M 13
Broomhouse La. SW6 . . . . .5M 13
Broomhouse Rd. SW6 . . . . .5M 13
Broomhurst Ct. RH4: Dork 7H 119
Broomlands La.
RH8: Limp, T'sey 4F 106
Broom La. GU24: Chob 5H 53
Broomleaf Cnr. GU9: Farnh . . .1J 129
Broomleaf Rd. GU9: Farnh 1J 129
Broomloan La. SM1: Sut 8M 43
Broom Lock TW11: Tedd 7J 25
Broom Pk.
TW11: Tedd 1G 203 (8K 25)
Broom Rd. CR0: Croy 9K 47
TW11: Tedd 6H 25
Broom Squires GU26: Hind . . .5E 170
Broom Squires Ct.
GU27: Hasl 2E 188
Broomsquires Rd.
GU19: Bag 5K 51
Broom Water TW11: Tedd 7J 25
Broom Water W. TW11: Tedd . . .6J 25
Broom Way GU17: Haw 2K 69
KT13: Weybr 1F 56
Broomwicks Pl.
RH12: Broadb H *5E 196*
(off Sullington Mead)
Broomwood Cl. CR0: Croy 4G 47
Broomwood Way
GU10: Lwr Bou 5H 129
Broster Gdns. SE25 . . . . .2C 46
Brougham Pl.
GU9: Up Hale 5G 108
Brough Cl. KT2: K Tham 6K 25
Broughton Av. TW10: Ham 4H 25
Broughton M. GU16: Frim 5D 70
Broughton Rd. CR7: T Hea 5L 45
SW6 . . . . .5N 13
Broughton Rd. App. SW6 . . . . . .5N 13
Brow, The RH1: Red 8E 122
Browell Ho. *GU4: Guil* *2F 114*
(off Merrow St.)
Browells La. TW13: Felt 3J 23
(not continuous)
Brown Bear Ct. TW13: Hanw 5L 23
Brown Cl. SM6: W'ton 4J 63
Browne Cl. GU22: Wok 7D 74
Browngraves Rd. UB3: Harl 3D 8
Browning Av. KT4: W Pk 7G 42
SM1: Sut 1C 62
Browning Cl. GU15: Camb 2G 70
RH10: Craw 2G 182
TW12: Hamp 5N 23
Browning Copse RG12: Brac 2K 31
Browning Ct. *W14* *2L 13*
(off Turneville Rd.)
Browning Rd. KT22: Fetc 3D 98
Brownings TN8: Eden 8L 127
Brownings, The
RH19: E Grin 9M 165
Browning Way TW5: Hest 4L 9
Brownjohn Ct. RH10: Craw 2E 182
Brownlow Dr. RG42: Brac 8A 16
Brownlow Rd. CR0: Croy 1B 64
RH1: Red 3C 122
Brownrigg Cres. RG12: Brac 9C 16
Brownrigg Rd. TW15: Ashf 5B 22
Brown's Hill RH1: Out 1A 144
Browns La. KT24: Eff 5L 97
Brownsover Rd. GU14: Cove 1H 89
Brown's Rd. KT5: Surb 6M 41
Browns Wlk. GU10: Rowl 7E 128
Browns Wood RH19: E Grin 6A 166
BROX .4E 54
Broxhead Common (Nature Reserve)
. . . . .2A 168
Broxhead Farm Rd.
GU35: Lind 2A 168
Broxhead Trad. Est.
GU35: Lind 3A 168
Broxholme Cl. SE25 . . . . .3A 46
Broxholme Ho. *SW6* *4N 13*
(off Harwood Rd.)
Broxholm Rd. SE27 . . . . .4L 29
Brox La. KT15: Addl 5F 54
KT16: Otter 4E 54
Brox M. KT16: Otter 3E 54
Brox Rd. KT16: Otter 3E 54
Bruce Av. TW17: Shep 5D 38
Bruce Cl. KT14: Byf 9M 55
Bruce Dr. CR2: Sels 5G 64
Bruce Hall M. SW17 . . . . .5E 28
Bruce Rd. CR4: Mit 8E 28
SE25 . . . . .3A 46
Bruce Wlk. SL4: W'sor 5A 4
Brudenell SL4: W'sor 6C 4
Brudenell Rd. SW17 . . . . .4D 28
Brumana Cl. KT13: Weybr 3C 56
Brumfield Rd. KT19: Ewe 2B 60
Brunel Centre, The
RH10: Craw 8D 162
Brunel Cl. TW5: C'ford 3J 9
Brunel Ct. *SW13* *5E 12*
(off Westfields Av.)
Brunel Dr. RG45: Crowt 8H 31
Brunel Pl. RH10: Craw 4C 182
Brunel Wlk. TW2: Whitt 1A 24
Brunner Ct. KT16: Otter 2E 54
Brunswick RG12: Brac 6M 31
Brunswick Cl. KT7: T Dit 7F 40
KT12: Wal T 8K 39
RH10: Craw 5E 182
TW2: Twick 4D 24
Brunswick Ct. *RH10: Craw* *5E 182*
(off Brunswick Cl.)
SM1: Sut 1N 61
Brunswick Dr. GU24: B'wood . . .7A 72
Brunswick Gro. KT11: Cob 9K 57
Brunswick M. SW16 . . . . .7H 29
Brunswick Rd. GU16: Deep 8G 71
GU24: B'wood 8L 71
(not continuous)
KT2: K Tham 9N 25
SM1: Sut 1N 61
Brunswick Ter. BR3: Beck 1L 47
Bruntile Cl. GU14: Farnb 4B 90
Brushfield Way GU21: Knap 6F 72
Brushwood Rd. RH12: Hors . . .2A 198
Bruton Rd. SM4: Mord 3A 44
Bruton Way RG12: Brac 6C 32
Bryan Cl. TW16: Sunb 8H 23
Bryan's All. SW6 . . . . .5N 13
Bryanston Av. TW2: Whitt 2B 24
Bryanstone Av. GU2: Guil 8J 93
Bryanstone Cl. GU2: Guil 9J 93
GU52: Chu C 7B 88
Bryanstone Ct. SM1: Sut 9A 44
Bryanstone Gro. GU2: Guil 8J 93
Bryce Cl. RH12: Hors 3N 197
Bryce Gdns. GU11: Alde 5A 110
Bryer Pl. SL4: W'sor 6A 4
Brympton Cl. RH4: Dork 7G 119
Brynford Cl. GU21: Wok 2A 74
Bryn Rd. GU10: Wrec 4E 128
Bryony Ho. RG42: Brac 9K 15
Bryony Rd. GU1: Guil 9D 94
Bryony Way TW16: Sunb 7H 23
Buccaneer Ct. GU14: Farnb 3A 90
Buccaneer Way GU14: Farnb . . .5G 89
Buccleuch Rd. SL3: Dat 3K 5
Buchan, The GU15: Camb 7E 50
Buchanan M. GU51: Fleet 5C 88
Buchan Country Pk. 7K 181
Buchan Country Pk.
Countryside Cen. 7L 181
BUCHAN HILL 9M 181
Buchan Pk. RH11: Craw 7L 181
Buchans Lawn RH11: Craw 7N 181
Bucharest Rd. SW18 . . . . .1A 28
Buckfast Rd. SM4: Mord 3N 43
Buckham Thorns Rd.
TN16: Weste 4L 107
Buckhold Rd. SW18 . . . . .9M 13
Buckhurst Av. SM5: Cars 7C 44
Buckhurst Cl. RH1: Red 1C 122
RH19: E Grin 7M 165
Buckhurst Gro.
RG40: W'ham 3E 30
BUCKHURST HILL 9C 18
Buckhurst Hill RG12: Brac 3D 32
Buckhurst La. SL5: S'hill 2C 34
Buckhurst Mead
RH19: E Grin 6M 165
Buckhurst Rd. GU16: Frim G . . .8D 70
SL5: Asc, S'hill 9C 18
TN16: Weste 8J 87
Buckhurst Way
RH19: E Grin 7M 165
Buckingham Av. CR7: T Hea 9L 29
KT8: W Mole 1B 40
TW14: Felt 9J 9
Buckingham Cl. GU1: Guil 2B 114
TW12: Hamp 6N 23
Buckingham Ct.
RH11: Craw 7N 181
SM2: Sut 5M 61
TW18: Stain *5J 21*
(off Kingston Rd.)
Buckingham Dr.
RH19: E Grin 1C 186
Buckingham Gdns.
CR7: T Hea 1L 45
KT8: W Mole 1B 40
Buckingham Ga.
RH6: Gatw 3G 163
Buckingham Rd. CR4: Mit 3J 45
KT1: K Tham 7L 203 (3M 41)
RH5: Holm 5J 139
TW10: Ham 3K 25
TW12: Hamp 5N 23
Buckingham Way
GU16: Frim 5D 70
SM6: W'ton 5G 63
BUCKLAND 2F 120
Buckland Cl. GU14: Farnb 7A 70
Buckland Ct. RH1: Red 1F 122
Buckland Ct. Gdns.
RH3: Buckl 2F 120
Buckland Cres. SL4: W'sor 4C 4
Buckland La. KT20: Wal H 6F 100
RH3: Buckl 8F 100
Buckland Rd. BR6: Orp 1N 67
KT9: Ches 2M 59
KT20: Lwr K 7L 101
RH2: Reig 2J 121
SM2: Chea 6H 61
Bucklands Rd. TW11: Tedd 7J 25
Buckland's Wharf
KT1: K Tham 3G 203 (1K 41)
Buckland Wlk. SM4: Mord 3A 44
Buckland Way KT4: W Pk 7H 43
Bucklebury RG12: Brac 6M 31
Buckleigh Av. SW20 . . . . .2K 43
Buckleigh Rd. SW16 . . . . .7H 29
Buckle La. RG42: Warf 3M 15
Bucklers All. SW6 . . . . .2L 13
Buckler's Way SM5: Cars 9D 44
Buckles Way SM7: Ban 3K 81
Buckley La.
RH13: Hors, Mann H 9N 197
Buckley Pl. RH10: Craw D 1D 184
Buckmans Rd.
RH11: Craw 2B 182
Bucknall Way BR3: Beck 3L 47

Bucknills Cl.—Bywood Cl.

Bucknills Cl. KT18: Eps ... 1B 80
Bucks Cl. KT14: W By ... 1K 75
Bucks Copse RG41: W'ham ... 3A 30
BUCKS GREEN ... 1E 194
Buckshead Hill
RH13: Plum P ... 9E 198
BUCKS HORN OAK ... 2A 148
Buckston Browne Gdns.
BR6: Dow ... 8H 67
Buckswood Dr.
RH11: Craw ... 5M 181
Buckthorn Cl.
RG40: W'ham ... 1D 30
Buckthorns RG42: Brac ... 8K 15
Buddleia Ho. TW13: Felt ... 2H 23
Budd's All. TW1: Twick ... 8J 11
Budebury Rd. TW18: Stain ... 6J 21
Budge La. CR4: Mit ... 6D 44
Budgen Cl. RH10: Craw ... 9H 163
Budgen Dr. RH1: Red ... 9E 102
Budge's Gdns.
RG40: W'ham ... 1C 30
Budge's Rd. RG40: W'ham ... 1C 30
Budham Way RG12: Brac ... 5N 31
Buer Rd. SW6 ... 5K 13
Buff Av. SM7: Ban ... 1N 81
Buffbeards La. GU27: Hasl ... 1C 188
Buffers La. KT22: Leat ... 6G 79
Bug Hill CR3: Wold ... 7G 84
CR6: Warl, Wold ... 7G 84
Buick Ho.
KT2: K Tham ... 3M 203 (1M 41)
Bulbeggars La. RH9: Gods ... 1F 124
Bulganak Rd. CR7: T Hea ... 3N 45
Bulkeley Av. SL4: W'sor ... 6E 4
Bulkeley Cl. TW20: Eng G ... 6M 19
Bullard Cotts. GU4: W Cla ... 1H 115
Bullard Rd. TW11: Tedd ... 7E 24
Bullbeggars La. GU21: Wok ... 3L 73
BULLBROOK ... 1C 32
Bullbrook Dr. RG12: Brac ... 9C 16
Bullbrook Row RG12: Brac ... 1C 32
Buller Ct. GU14: Farnb ... 4A 90
Buller Rd. CR7: T Hea ... 1A 46
Bullers Rd. GU9: Weybo ... 6K 109
Bullfinch Cl. GU47: Coll T ... 7K 49
RH6: Horl ... 7C 142
RH12: Hors ... 1J 197
Bullfinch Ri. RG12: Brac ... 3H 31
Bullfinch Rd. CR2: Sels ... 6G 64
Bull Hill KT22: Leat ... 8G 79
Bull La. RG42: Brac ... 9N 15
Bullocks La. GU27: Hasl ... 8N 189
GU28: Hasl ... 8N 189
Bullrush Cl. CR0: Croy ... 5B 46
SM5: Cars ... 8C 44
Bull's All. SW14 ... 5C 12
Bulls Head Row RH9: Gods ... 9E 104
BULLSWATER COMMON ... 4D 92
Bullswater Comn. Rd.
GU24: Pirb ... 4D 92
Bullswater La. GU24: Pirb ... 3D 92
Bulmer Cotts.
RH5: Holm M ... 6K 137
Bulow Est. *SW6 ... 4N 13*
(off Pearscroft Rd.)
Bulrushes Farm
RH19: E Grin ... 2N 185
Bulstrode Av. TW3: Houn ... 5N 9
Bulstrode Gdns. TW3: Houn ... 6A 10
Bulstrode Rd. TW3: Houn ... 6A 10
Bunbury Way KT17: Eps D ... 3G 80
BUNCE COMMON ... 1C 140
Bunce Comn. Rd.
RH2: Leigh ... 1C 140
Bunce Dr. CR3: Cate ... 1A 104
Bunce's Cl. SL4: E Wic ... 1E 4
Bunce Vw. RG12: Brac ... 2J 31
Bunch La. GU27: Hasl ... 1E 188
Bunch Way GU27: Hasl ... 2E 188
Bundy's Way TW18: Stain ... 7H 21
Bungalow Rd. SE25 ... 3B 46
Bungalows, The
GU2: Guil ... 7J 93
SM6: W'ton ... 2F 62
SW16 ... 8F 28
Bunting Cl. CR4: Mit ... 4D 44
RH13: Hors ... 5M 197
Bunting La. RG12: Brac ... 4J 31
Buntings, The GU9: Farnh ... 3E 128
Bunyan Cl. RH11: Craw ... 6K 181
Bunyan's La. GU24: Chob ... 1F 72
Bunyard Dr. GU21: Wok ... 1E 74
Burbage Grn. RG12: Brac ... 4D 32
Burbage Rd. SE24 ... 1N 29
Burbeach Cl. RH11: Craw ... 6N 181
Burberry Cl. KT3: N Mal ... 1D 42
Burbidge Rd. TW17: Shep ... 3B 38
Burbury Woods
GU15: Camb ... 9C 50
Burcham Cl. TW12: Hamp ... 8A 24
Burchets Hollow
GU5: P'lake ... 4E 136
Burchetts Way TW17: Shep ... 5C 38
Burcote KT13: Weybr ... 3E 56
Burcote Rd. SW18 ... 1B 28
Burcott Gdns. KT15: Addl ... 3L 55
Burcott Rd. CR8: Pur ... 1L 83
Burden Cl. TW8: Brent ... 1J 11
Burdenshot Hill GU3: Worp ... 3K 93
Burdenshott Av. TW10: Rich ... 7A 12
Burdenshott Rd. GU3: Worp ... 3K 93
Burden Way GU2: Guil ... 7L 93
Burdett Av. SW20 ... 9F 26
Burdett Cl. RH10: Worth ... 4H 183
Burdett Rd. CR0: Croy ... 5A 46
TW9: Rich ... 5M 11
Burdock Cl. CR0: Croy ... 7G 47
GU18: Ligh ... 7M 51
RH11: Craw ... 7M 181
Burdon La. SM2: Chea ... 4K 61
Burdon Pk. SM2: Chea ... 5L 61
Burfield Cl. SW17 ... 5B 28
Burfield Dr. CR6: Warl ... 6F 84
Burfield Rd. SL4: O Win ... 9K 5
Burford Bri. Rdbt.
RH5: Mick ... 9J 99
Burford Cl. RG40: W'ham ... 3D 30
Burford Ho. KT17: Ewe ... 7H 61
TW8: Brent ... 1K 11
Burford La. KT17: Ewe ... 7H 61
Burford Lea GU8: Els ... 7J 131
Burford Rd. GU15: Camb ... 2N 69
KT4: W Pk ... 6E 42
RH13: Hors ... 6L 197
SM1: Sut ... 8M 43
TW8: Brent ... 1L 11
Burford Wlk. SW6 ... 3N 13
Burford Way CR0: N Add ... 3M 65
Burge Cl. GU14: Cove ... 1H 89
Burges Gro. SW13 ... 3G 13
Burgess Cl. TW13: Hanw ... 5M 23
Burgess M. SW19 ... 7N 27
Burgess Rd. SM1: Sut ... 1N 61
Burges Way TW18: Stain ... 6J 21
Burgh Cl. RH10: Craw ... 9H 163
Burgh Cft. KT17: Eps ... 2E 80
Burghead Cl. GU47: Coll T ... 8J 49
Burghfield KT17: Eps ... 2E 80
BURGH HEATH ... 6K 81
Burgh Heath Rd.
KT17: Eps, Eps D
... 8M 201 (1E 80)
Burghley Av. KT3: N Mal ... 9C 26
Burghley Hall Cl. SW19 ... 2K 27
Burghley Ho. SW19 ... 4K 27
Burghley Pl. CR4: Mit ... 4D 44
Burghley Rd. SW19 ... 5J 27
Burgh Mt. SM7: Ban ... 2L 81
Burgh Wood SM7: Ban ... 2K 81
Burgoine Quay
KT1: H Wic ... 2G 203 (9K 25)
Burgos Cl. CR0: Wad ... 3L 63
Burgoyne Rd. GU15: Camb ... 9E 50
SE25 ... 3C 46
TW16: Sunb ... 7G 22
BURHILL ... 5J 57
Burhill Golf Course ... 5H 57
Burhill Rd. KT12: Hers ... 5J 57
Burke Cl. SW15 ... 7D 12
Burket Cl. UB2: S'hall ... 1M 9
Burlands RH11: Craw ... 9M 161
Burlea Cl. KT12: Hers ... 2J 57
BURLEIGH ... 9K 17
Burleigh Av. SM6: W'ton ... 9E 44
Burleigh Cl. KT15: Addl ... 2K 55
RH10: Craw D ... 1E 184
Burleigh Ct. KT22: Leat ... 9G 79
Burleigh Gdns. GU21: Wok ... 4B 74
TW15: Ashf ... 6D 22
Burleigh La. RH10: Craw D ... 2E 184
SL5: Asc ... 9J 17
Burleigh Pk. KT11: Cob ... 8M 57
Burleigh Pl. SW15 ... 8J 13
Burleigh Rd. GU16: Frim ... 6B 70
KT15: Addl ... 2K 55
SL5: Asc ... 1J 33
SM3: Sut ... 7K 43
Burleigh Way
RH10: Craw D ... 2E 184
Burlescombe Ho. *RH1: Red ... 1E 122*
(off Burrage Rd.)
Burley Cl. RH14: Loxw ... 4J 193
SW16 ... 1H 45
Burley Orchard KT16: Chert ... 5J 37
Burleys Rd. RH10: Craw ... 3G 183
Burley Way GU17: B'water ... 5H 49
Burlingham Cl. GU4: Guil ... 1F 114
Burlings, The SL5: Asc ... 1J 33
Burlington Av. TW9: Kew ... 4N 11
Burlington Cl. TW14: Bedf ... 1E 22
Burlington Ct. GU11: Alde ... 3M 109
GU17: Haw ... 3J 69
RH1: Red ... 2D 122
(off Station Rd.)
Burlington Gdns. SW6 ... 5K 13
W4 ... 1B 12
Burlington La. W4 ... 3B 12
Burlington M. SW15 ... 8L 13
Burlington Pl. RH2: Reig ... 2M 121
SW6 ... 5K 13
Burlington Rd. CR7: T Hea ... 1N 45
KT3: N Mal ... 3E 42
SW6 ... 5K 13
TW7: Isle ... 4D 10
W4 ... 1B 12
Burlsdon Way RG12: Brac ... 9C 16
Burma Rd. GU24: Chob ... 9J 35
Burmarsh Ct. SE20 ... 1F 46
Burmester Rd. SW17 ... 4A 28
Burnaby Cres. W4 ... 2B 12
Burnaby Gdns. W4 ... 2A 12
Burnbury Rd. SW12 ... 2G 29
Burn Cl. KT15: Addl ... 1M 55
KT22: Oxs ... 2D 78
Burne-Jones Dr.
GU47: Coll T ... 9J 49
Burnell Av. TW10: Ham ... 6J 25
Burnell Rd. SM1: Sut ... 1N 61
Burnet Av. GU1: Guil ... 9D 94
Burnet Cl. GU24: W End ... 9B 52
Burnet Gro.
KT19: Eps ... 6H 201 (9B 60)
Burnetts Rd. SL4: W'sor ... 4B 4
Burney Av.
KT5: Surb ... 8M 203 (4M 41)
Burney Cl. KT22: Fetc ... 3C 98
Burney Ct. RH11: Craw ... 6M 181
Burney Ho. *KT22: Leat ... 8G 78*
(off Highbury Dr.)
Burney Rd. RH5: Westh ... 9G 99
Burnfoot Av. SW6 ... 4K 13
Burnham Cl. GU21: Knap ... 5G 73
SL4: W'sor ... 5A 4
Burnham Dr. KT4: W Pk ... 8J 43
RH2: Reig ... 2M 121
Burnham Gdns. CR0: Croy ... 6C 46
TW4: C'ford ... 4J 9
Burnham Ga.
GU1: Guil ... 2C 202 (3N 113)
Burnham Gro. RG42: Brac ... 8A 16
Burnham Mnr.
GU15: Camb ... 7E 50
Burnham Pl. RH13: Hors ... 7K 197
Burnham Rd. GU21: Knap ... 5G 73
SM4: Mord ... 3N 43
Burnhams Gro. KT19: Eps ... 7A 60
Burnhams Rd. KT23: Book ... 2M 97
Burnham St. KT2: K Tham ... 9N 25
Burnhill Rd. BR3: Beck ... 1K 47
Burnmoor Chase RG12: Brac ... 6C 32
Burnsall Cl. GU14: Farnb ... 8N 69
Burns Av. GU52: Chu C ... 7C 88
TW14: Felt ... 9H 9
Burns Cl. GU14: Farnb ... 8L 69
RH12: Hors ... 1L 197
SM5: Cars ... 5E 62
SW19 ... 7B 28
Burns Dr. SM7: Ban ... 1K 81
Burnside GU51: Fleet ... 4B 88
KT21: Asht ... 5M 79
Burnside Cl. TW1: Twick ... 9G 10
Burnside Ct. SM5: Cars ... 9E 44
Burns Rd. RH10: Craw ... 1G 182
Burns Way RH12: Fay ... 8H 181
RH19: E Grin ... 9M 165
TW5: Hest ... 5L 9
BURNTCOMMON ... 3H 95
Burnt Comn. Cl. GU23: Rip ... 3H 95
Burnt Comn. La. GU23: Rip ... 3J 95
Burnt Hill Rd.
GU10: Lwr Bou, Wrec ... 5F 128
Burnt Hill Way GU10: Wrec ... 6G 128
Burnt Ho. Gdns. RG42: Warf ... 8C 16
Burnt Ho. La. RH12: Rusp ... 2E 180
Burnthouse Ride RG12: Brac ... 3J 31
Burnthwaite Rd. SW6 ... 3L 13
Burnt Oak La. RH5: Newd ... 2D 160
Burnt Pollard La.
GU18: Ligh ... 6B 52
Burntwood Cl. CR3: Cate ... 8D 84
SW18 ... 2C 28
Burntwood Grange Rd.
SW18 ... 2B 28
Burntwood La. CR3: Cate ... 9B 84
SW17 ... 4A 28
BURPHAM ... 9D 94
Burpham La. GU4: B'ham ... 7C 94
Burrage Rd. RH1: Red ... 1F 122
Burrell, The RH4: Westc ... 6C 118
Burrell Cl. CR0: Croy ... 5H 47
Burrell Ct. RH11: Craw ... 5L 181
Burrell Rd. GU16: Frim ... 6A 70
Burrell Row BR3: Beck ... 1K 47
Burrells, The KT16: Chert ... 7K 37
Burr Hill La. GU24: Chob ... 5J 53
Burritt Rd. KT1: K Tham ... 1N 41
BURROW HILL ... 9B 72
BURROWHILL ... 5H 53
Burrow Hill Grn.
GU24: Chob ... 5G 53
Burrows Cl. GU2: Guil ... 2J 113
KT23: Book ... 2N 97
BURROWS CROSS ... 1D 136
Burrows Cross
GU5: Gom, P'lake ... 1D 136
Burrows La. GU5: Gom ... 1D 136
Burrow Wlk. SE21 ... 1N 29
Burr Rd. SW18 ... 2M 27
Burrwood Gdns.
GU12: Ash V ... 9E 90
Burstead Cl. KT11: Cob ... 8L 57
Burstock Rd. SW15 ... 7K 13
Burston Gdns.
RH19: E Grin ... 6N 165
Burston Rd. SW15 ... 8J 13
Burston Vs. *SW15 ... 8J 13*
(off St John's Av.)
BURSTOW ... 3L 163
Burstow Ent. Pk.
RH6: Smallf ... 3N 163
Burstow Golf Course ... 5L 163
Burstow Lodge Bus. Cen.
RH6: Smallf ... 6M 143
Burstow Pk. Bus. Cen.
RH6: Ship B ... 5L 163
Burstow Rd. SW20 ... 9K 27
Burtenshaw Rd. KT7: T Dit ... 6G 41
Burton Cl. CR7: T Hea ... 2A 46
GU20: Windl ... 3A 52
KT9: Ches ... 4K 59
RH6: Horl ... 9E 142
Burton Ct. KT7: T Dit ... 5G 40
SE20 ... 1F 46
Burton Dr. GU3: Worp ... 7D 92
Burton Gdns. TW5: Hest ... 4N 9
Burton Rd.
KT2: K Tham ... 1K 203 (8L 25)
Burtons Ct. RH12: Hors ... 6J 197
Burton's Rd. TW12: H Hill ... 5B 24
Burton Way SL4: W'sor ... 6B 4
Burtop Rd. Est. SW17 ... 4A 28
Burwash Rd. RH10: Craw ... 4E 182
Burway Cl. CR2: S Croy ... 3B 64
Burway Cres. KT16: Chert ... 3J 37
Burwell *KT1: K Tham ... 4M 203*
(off Excelsior Cl.)
Burwood Av. CR8: Ken ... 1M 83
Burwood Cl. GU1: Guil ... 2F 114
KT6: Surb ... 7N 41
KT12: Hers ... 3K 57
RH2: Reig ... 3B 122
Burwood Pde. *KT16: Chert ... 6J 37*
(off Guildford St.)
BURWOOD PARK
KT11 ... 8H 57
KT12 ... 2H 57
Burwood Pk. Rd.
KT12: Hers ... 1J 57
Burwood Rd. KT12: Hers ... 4F 56
Bury Cl. GU21: Wok ... 3N 73
Bury Flds.
GU2: Guil ... 7B 202 (5M 113)
Bury Gro. SM4: Mord ... 4N 43
Bury La. GU21: Wok ... 3M 73
Bury M. GU2: Guil ... 7B 202
Burys, The GU7: Godal ... 6H 133
Bury St.
GU2: Guil ... 7B 202 (5M 113)
Burywood Hill RH5: Ockl ... 3E 158
BUSBRIDGE ... 9J 133
Busbridge Lakes,
Waterfowl & Gardens ... 1H 153
Busbridge La. GU7: Godal ... 8G 133
Busby Ho. SW16 ... 5G 29
Busch Cl. TW7: Isle ... 4H 11
Busdens Cl. GU8: Mil ... 2C 152
Busdens La. GU8: Mil ... 2C 152
Busdens Way GU8: Mil ... 2C 152
Bushbury Rd.
RH3: Betch, Brock ... 8N 119
Bush Cl. KT15: Addl ... 2L 55
Bush Cotts. SW18 ... 8M 13
Bushell Cl. SW2 ... 3K 29
Bushetts Gro. RH1: Mers ... 7F 102
Bushey Cl. CR8: Ken ... 3C 84
Bushey Ct. SW20 ... 2G 43
Bushey Cft. RH8: Oxt ... 8M 105
Bushey Down SW12 ... 3F 28
Bushey La. SM1: Sut ... 1M 61
BUSHEY MEAD ... 1J 43
Bushey Rd. CR0: Croy ... 8K 47
SM1: Sut ... 1M 61
SW20 ... 2G 42
Bushey Shaw KT21: Asht ... 4H 79
Bushey Way BR3: Beck ... 5N 47
Bushfield RH14: Plais ... 6B 192
Bushfield Dr. RH1: Red ... 8E 122
Bush La. GU23: Send ... 2F 94
RH12: Hors ... 9N 179
Bushnell Rd. SW17 ... 3F 28
Bush Rd. TW9: Kew ... 2M 11
TW17: Shep ... 4A 38
Bush Wlk. RG40: W'ham ... 2B 30
Bushwood Rd. TW9: Kew ... 2N 11
Bushy Ct. *KT1: H Wic ... 9J 25*
(off Beverley Rd.)
BUSHY HILL ... 2F 114
Bushy Hill Dr. GU1: Guil ... 1D 114
Bushy Park ... 8D 24
Bushy Pk. Gdns.
TW11: Tedd ... 6D 24
Bushy Pk. Rd. TW11: Tedd ... 8H 25
(not continuous)
Bushy Rd. KT22: Fetc ... 9B 78
TW11: Tedd ... 7F 24
Business Centre, The
RG41: W'ham ... 4A 30
Business Pk. 5 KT22: Leat ... 7F 78
Business Pk. 8 KT22: Leat ... 6H 79
Business Pk. 25 RH1: Red ... 1F 122
Business Village, The
SW18 ... 8M 13
Busk Cres. GU14: Cove ... 2L 89
Butcherfield La. TN7: Hart ... 1N 187
Butchers Yd. BR6: Dow ... 7J 67
Bute Av. TW10: Ham ... 3L 25
Bute Ct. SM6: W'ton ... 2G 62
Bute Gdns. SM6: W'ton ... 2G 63
TW10: Ham ... 2L 25
Bute Gdns. W. SM6: W'ton ... 2G 62
Bute Rd. CR0: Croy ... 7L 45
SM6: W'ton ... 1G 62
Butler Dr. RG12: Brac ... 2J 31
Butler Farm Cl.
TW10: Ham ... 5K 25
Butler Rd. GU19: Bag ... 5K 51
RG45: Crowt ... 1G 48
Butlers Cl. SL4: W'sor ... 4A 4
TW4: Houn ... 6N 9
Butlers Dene Rd.
CR3: Wold ... 7J 85
Butlers Hill KT24: W Hors ... 8C 96
Butler's Pl. GU8: Mil ... 1D 152
Butlers Rd. RH13: Hors ... 4N 197
Butt Cl. GU6: Cranl ... 6N 155
Buttercup Cl. GU35: Lind ... 4B 168
RG40: W'ham ... 2E 30
Buttercup Sq. TW19: Stan ... 2M 21
Butterfield RH19: E Grin ... 7L 165
Butterfield Cl. TW1: Twick ... 9F 10
Butterfields GU15: Camb ... 2N 69
Butterfly Wlk.
CR6: Warl, Wold ... 7F 84
Butter Hill
RH4: Dork ... 3J 201 (5G 119)
SM5: Cars ... 9E 44
SM6: W'ton ... 9E 44
Buttermer Cl. GU10: Wrec ... 4D 128
Buttermere Cl.
GU14: Cove ... 1K 89
RH12: Hors ... 2A 198
SM4: Mord ... 5J 43
TW14: Felt ... 2G 22
Buttermere Ct. *GU12: Ash V ... 9D 90*
(off Lakeside Cl.)
RH10: Craw ... 5H 183
(off Grayrigg Rd.)
Buttermere Dr. GU15: Camb ... 1H 71
SW15 ... 8K 13
Buttermere Gdns. CR8: Pur ... 9A 64
RG12: Brac ... 2A 32
Buttermere Way
TW20: Egh ... 8D 20
Buttersteep Ri. SL5: Asc ... 7G 33
Butterwick W6 ... 1J 13
Butt La. GU3: Put ... 7L 111
Buttonscroft Cl. CR7: T Hea ... 2N 45
Butts, The TW8: Brent ... 2J 11
TW16: Sunb ... 2K 39
Butts Cl. RH11: Craw ... 2N 181
Butts Cotts TW13: Hanw ... 4M 23
Butts Cres. TW13: Hanw ... 4A 24
Butts La. GU7: Godal ... 7G 133
Butts Rd. GU21: Wok ... 4A 74
Buxton Av. CR3: Cate ... 8B 84
Buxton Cl. KT19: Eps ... 7A 60
Buxton Cres. SM3: Chea ... 1K 61
Buxton Dr. KT3: N Mal ... 1C 42
Buxton La. CR3: Cate ... 7A 84
Buxton Pl. CR3: Cate ... 7A 84
Buxton Rd. CR7: T Hea ... 4M 45
SW14 ... 6D 12
TW15: Ashf ... 6M 21
Byam St. SW6 ... 5N 13
Byards Cft. SW16 ... 9H 29
Byatt Wlk. TW12: Hamp ... 7M 23
Bychurch End TW11: Tedd ... 6F 24
Bycroft Way RH10: Craw ... 1F 182
Byegrove Rd. SW19 ... 7B 28
Byerley Way RH10: Craw ... 2H 183
Byers La. RH9: S Gods ... 4F 144
Byeway, The SW14 ... 6B 12
Byeways TW2: Twick ... 4B 24
Byeways, The KT5: Surb ... 4N 41
Byfeld Gdns. SW13 ... 4F 12
Byfield Rd. TW7: Isle ... 6G 10
BYFLEET ... 8N 55
Byfleet Ind. Est. KT14: Byf ... 6M 55
Byfleet & New Haw Station (Rail)
... 6M 55
Byfleet Rd. KT11: Cob ... 8B 56
KT14: Byf ... 8B 56
KT15: N Haw ... 4M 55
Byfleets La.
RH12: Broadb H, Warnh
... 2D 196
Byfleet Technical Cen.
KT14: Byf ... 7M 55
Bygrove CR0: N Add ... 3L 65
Byland Cl. SM4: Mord ... 6A 44
Bylands GU22: Wok ... 6C 74
Byne Rd. SM5: Cars ... 8C 44
Bynes Rd. CR2: S Croy ... 4A 64
By-Pass Rd. KT22: Leat ... 7H 79
Byrd Rd. RH11: Craw ... 6L 181
Byrefield Rd. GU2: Guil ... 9J 93
Byrne Cl. CR0: Croy ... 5N 45
Byrne Rd. SW12 ... 2F 28
Byron SL3: Lang ... 1D 6
Byron Av. CR5: Coul ... 2J 83
GU15: Camb ... 3F 70
KT3: N Mal ... 4F 42
SM1: Sut ... 1B 62
TW4: C'ford ... 5H 9
Byron Av. E. SM1: Sut ... 1B 62
Byron Cl. GU21: Knap ... 4H 73
GU46: Yate ... 2A 68
GU51: Fleet ... 5B 88
KT12: Wal T ... 7M 39
KT23: Book ... 2A 98
RH10: Craw ... 2F 182
RH12: Hors ... 2L 197
SE20 ... 2E 46
SW16 ... 7J 29
TW12: Hamp ... 5N 23
Byron Ct. SL4: W'sor ... 6D 4
Byron Dr. RG45: Crowt ... 4G 48
Byron Gdns. SM1: Sut ... 1B 62
Byron Gro. RH19: E Grin ... 1M 185
Byron Pl. KT22: Leat ... 9H 79
Byron Rd. CR2: Sels ... 6E 64
KT15: Addl ... 1N 55
Byton Rd. SW17 ... 7D 28
Byttom Hill RH5: Mick ... 4J 99
Byward Av. TW14: Felt ... 9K 9
Byway, The KT19: Ewe ... 1E 60
SM2: Sut ... 5B 62
Byways GU46: Yate ... 1A 68
Byways, The
KT21: Asht ... 5K 79
Bywood RG12: Brac ... 6M 31
Bywood Av. CR0: Croy ... 5F 46
Bywood Cl. CR8: Ken ... 2M 83
SM7: Ban ... 4L 81

Byworth Cl.—Carlton Ho.

Byworth Cl. GU9: Farnh 1E 128
Byworth Rd. GU9: Farnh 1E 128

C

Cabbage Hill RG42: Warf 6L 15
Cabbage Hill La. RG42: Bin 5K 15
Cabbell Pl. KT15: Addl 1L 55
Cabell Rd. GU2: Guil 2G 113
Caberfeigh Cl. RH1: Red 3B 122
Cabin Moss RG12: Brac 6C 32
Cable Ho. Ct. GU21: Wok 2A 74
Cabot Cl. CR0: Wad 9L 45
Cabrera Av. GU25: V Wat 5M 35
Cabrera Cl. GU25: V Wat 5N 35
Cabrol Rd. GU14: Farnb 9M 69
Caburn Ct. RH11: Craw 5A 182
Caburn Hgts. RH11: Craw 5A 182
Caci Ho. *W14 1L 13*
(off Kensington Village)
Cacket's La. TN14: Cud 2M 87
Cackstones, The
RH10: Craw 1H 183
Cadbury Cl. TW7: Isle 4G 11
TW16: Sunb 8F 22
Cadbury Rd. TW16: Sunb 8F 22
Caddy Cl. TW20: Egh 6C 20
Cadet Way GU52: Chu C 9C 88
Cadman Ct. *W4 1A 12*
(off Chaseley Dr.)
Cadmer Cl. KT3: N Mal 3D 42
Cadnam Cl. GU11: Alde 6A 110
Cadnam Point SW15 2G 26
Cadogan Cl. BR3: Beck 1N 47
TW11: Tedd 6E 24
Cadogan Ct. GU15: Camb 3C 70
GU51: Fleet 4A 88
SM2: Sut 3N 61
Cadogan Ho. *GU1: Guil 4B 114*
(off St Lukes Sq.)
Cadogan Pl. CR8: Ken 4N 83
Cadogan Rd. GU11: Alde 6B 90
KT6: Surb 4K 41
Caenshill Ho. KT13: Weybr 4B 56
Caenshill Pl. KT13: Weybr 4B 56
Caenshill Rd. KT13: Weybr 4B 56
Caenswood Hill
KT13: Weybr 6B 56
Caenwood Cl. KT13: Weybr 3B 56
Caen Wood Rd. KT21: Asht 5J 79
Caerleon Cl. GU26: Hind 3A 170
KT10: Clay 4H 59
Caernarvon GU16: Frim 6D 70
Caernarvon Cl. CR4: Mit 2J 45
Caesar Ct. GU11: Alde 2K 109
Caesars Camp Rd.
GU15: Camb 7D 50
Caesar's Cl. GU15: Camb 7D 50
Caesars Ct. GU9: Up Hale 6H 109
Caesars Gate RG42: Warf 8C 16
Caesars Wlk. CR4: Mit 4D 44
Caesars Way TW17: Shep 5E 38
Caffins Cl. RH10: Craw 1C 182
Cage Yd. RH2: Reig 3M 121
Caillard Rd. KT14: Byf 7N 55
Cain Rd. RG12: Brac 1J 31
Cain's La. TW14: Felt 8F 8
Cairn Cl. GU15: Camb 3F 70
Cairn Ct. KT17: Ewe 6E 60
Cairngorm Cl. TW11: Tedd 6G 24
Cairngorm Pl. GU14: Cove 7K 69
Cairns Av. SW16: Mit 2G 45
Cairo New Rd.
CR0: Croy 3A 200 (8M 45)
Caistor M. SW12 1F 28
Caistor Rd. SW12 1F 28
Caithness Dr.
KT18: Eps 8K 201 (1C 80)
Caithness Rd. CR4: Mit 8F 28
Calbourne Rd. SW12 1D 28
Calcott Pk. GU46: Yate 9B 48
Caldbeck Av. KT4: W Pk 8F 42
Caldbeck Ho. *RH11: Craw 6L 181*
(off Salvington Rd.)
Caldecote *KT1: K Tham 4M 203*
(off Excelsior Cl.)
Calder Ct. SL3: Lang 1B 6
Calderdale Cl. RH11: Craw 5N 181
Calder Rd. SM4: Mord 4A 44
Calder Way SL3: Poy 6G 7
Caldwell Ho. *SW13 3H 13*
(off Trinity Chu. Rd.)
Caldwell Rd. GU20: Windl 2A 52
Caledonian Ho.
RH10: Craw 1B 182
(off Barnfield Rd.)
Caledonian Way RH6: Gatw 3F 162
Caledonia Rd. TW19: Stan 2N 21
Caledon Pl. GU4: B'ham 9C 94
Caledon Rd. SM6: W'ton 1E 62
Calendar M. KT6: Surb 5K 41
Calfridus Way RG12: Brac 2C 32
California Cl. SM2: Sut 6M 61
California Rd. KT3: N Mal 3A 42
Callender Ct. *CR0: Croy 5N 45*
(off Harry Cl.)
Calley Down Cres.
CR0: N Add 6N 65
Callis Farm Cl. TW19: Stan 9N 7
Callisto Cl. RH11: Craw 6K 181
Calloway Ho. GU14: Farnb 1A 90
Callow Fld. CR8: Pur 9L 63
Callow Hill GU25: V Wat 2M 35
Calluna Ct. GU22: Wok 5B 74
Calluna Dr. RH10: Copt 8L 163
Calonne Rd. SW19 5J 27
Calshot Rd. TW6: Lon A 5B 8
Calshot Way GU16: Frim 7E 70
TW6: Lon A 5B 8
Calthorpe Gdns. SM1: Sut 9A 44
Calton Gdns. GU11: Alde 5A 110
Calverley Ct. KT19: Ewe 1C 60
Calverley Rd. KT17: Ewe 3F 60
Calvert Cl. GU12: Alde 3B 110
KT19: Eps 6A 60
Calvert Ct. TW9: Rich 7M 11
Calvert Cres. RH4: Dork 3H 119
Calvert Rd. KT24: Eff 6J 97
RH4: Dork 3H 119
Calvin Cl. GU15: Camb 2F 70
Calvin Wlk. RH11: Craw 6K 181
Camac Rd. TW2: Twick 2D 24
Camargue Pl. GU7: Godal 7J 133
Cambalt Rd. SW15 8J 13
Camber Cl. RH10: Craw 3G 183
CAMBERLEY 9B 50
Camberley Av. SW20 1G 42
Camberley Bus. Cen.
GU15: Camb 1M 69
Camberley Cl. SM3: Chea 9J 43
Camberley Heath Golf Course 2E 70
Camberley Indoor Bowling Club 3N 69
Camberley Rd. TW6: Lon A 6B 8
Camberley Station (Rail) 1B 70
Camberley Theatre, The 9B 50
Camberley Towers
GU15: Camb 1B 70
(off Up. Gordon Rd.)
Camborne Cl. TW6: Lon A 6B 8
Camborne Cres. *TW6: Lon A 6B 8*
(off Camborne Rd.)
Camborne M. SW18 1M 27
Camborne Rd. CR0: Croy 6D 46
SM2: Sut 4M 61
SM4: Mord 4J 43
SW18 1M 27
TW6: Lon A 6B 8
Camborne Way TW5: Hest 4A 10
TW6: Lon A 6B 8
Cambourne Wlk.
TW10: Rich 9K 11
Cambray Rd. SW12 2G 29
Cambria Cl. TW3: Houn 7A 10
Cambria Ct. TW14: Felt 1J 23
TW18: Stain 5G 20
Cambria Gdns. TW19: Stan 1N 21
(not continuous)
Cambrian Cl. GU15: Camb 1N 69
SE27 4M 29
Cambrian Rd. GU14: Cove 7J 69
TW10: Rich 9M 11
Cambrian Way RG40: Finch 8A 30
Cambria St. SW6 3N 13
Cambridge Av. KT3: N Mal 2D 42
(not continuous)
Cambridge Cl. GU21: Wok 5J 73
SW20 9G 26
TW4: Houn 7M 9
UB7: Harm 2M 7
Cambridge Cotts. TW9: Kew 2N 11
Cambridge Cres.
TW11: Tedd 6G 24
Cambridge Gdns.
KT1: K Tham 1N 41
Cambridge Gro. W6 1G 13
Cambridge Gro. Rd.
KT1: K Tham 2N 41
(not continuous)
Cambridge Ho. SL4: W'sor 4F 4
Cambridge Lodge Pk.
RH6: Horl 5E 142
Cambridge Mdws.
GU9: Farnh 2E 128
Cambridge Pk. TW1: Twick 9J 11
Cambridge Pk. Ct.
TW1: Twick 1K 25
Cambridge Pl. GU9: Farnh 1H 129
Cambridge Rd. CR4: Mit 2G 44
GU11: Alde 2L 109
GU47: Owls 6K 49
KT1: K Tham 3M 203 (1M 41)
KT2: K Tham 3M 203 (1M 41)
KT3: N Mal 3C 42
KT8: W Mole 3N 39
KT12: Wal T 5J 39
RG45: Crowt 3H 49
RH13: Hors 6K 197
SE20 2E 46
SM5: Cars 3C 62
SW13 5E 12
SW20 9F 26
TW1: Twick 9K 11
TW4: Houn 7M 9
TW9: Kew 3N 11
TW11: Tedd 5F 24
TW12: Hamp 8N 23
TW15: Ashf 8D 22
Cambridge Rd. E.
GU14: Farnb 4A 90
(not continuous)
Cambridge Rd. Nth. W4 1A 12
Cambridge Rd. Sth. W4 1A 12
Cambridge Rd. W.
GU14: Farnb 4A 90
(not continuous)
Cambridgeshire Cl.
RG42: Warf 8D 16
Cambridge Sq. *GU15: Camb 9A 50*
(off Princess Way)
RH1: Red 6E 122
Cambridge Wlk.
GU15: Camb 9A 50
Camden Av. TW13: Felt 2K 23
Camden Cotts. KT13: Weybr 9B 38
Camden Gdns. CR7: T Hea 2M 45
SM1: Sut 2N 61
Camden Rd. RH7: Ling 8N 145
SM1: Sut 2N 61
SM5: Cars 1D 62
Camden Wlk. GU51: Fleet 4D 88
Camden Way CR7: T Hea 2M 45
Cameford Ct. SW2 1J 29
Camel Gro. KT2: K Tham 6K 25
Camellia Ct. GU24: W End 9C 52
Camellia Ho. *TW13: Felt 2H 23*
(off Tilley Rd.)
Camellia La. KT5: Surb 3A 42
Camellia M. TW20: Eng G 8M 19
Camellia Pl. TW2: Whitt 1B 24
Camelot Cl. SW19 5L 27
TN16: B Hil 3E 86
Camelot Ct. RH11: Ifield 3K 181
CAMELSDALE 3D 188
Camelsdale Rd.
GU27: Hasl 3C 188
Cameron Cl. GU6: Cranl 9N 155
Cameron Pl. SW16 3L 29
Cameron Rd. CR0: Croy 5M 45
GU11: Alde 6B 90
Cameron Sq. CR4: Mit 9C 28
Camgate Centre, The
TW19: Stan 9A 8
Camilla Cl. KT23: Book 3B 98
TW16: Sunb 7G 22
Camilla Dr. RH5: Westh 8G 98
Camille Cl. SE25 2D 46
Camm Av. SL4: W'sor 6B 4
Camm Gdns.
KT1: K Tham 4M 203 (1M 41)
KT7: T Dit 6F 40
Camomile Av. CR4: Mit 9D 28
Campana Rd. SW6 4M 13
Campaspe Bus. Pk.
TW16: Sunb 4G 38
Campbell Av. GU22: Wok 8B 74
Campbell Cir. KT13: Weybr 6A 56
Campbell Cl. GU11: Alde 5A 110
GU46: Yate 9E 48
GU51: Fleet 4A 88
KT14: Byf 8M 55
SW16 5H 29
TW2: Twick 2D 24
Campbell Cres.
RH19: E Grin 9L 165
Campbell Flds. GU11: Alde 3N 109
Campbell Pl. GU16: Frim 3D 70
GU51: Fleet 4A 88
Campbell Rd. CR0: Croy 6M 45
CR3: Cate 8A 84
GU11: Alde 1M 109
KT8: E Mol 2E 40
KT13: Weybr 4B 56
RH10: Craw 5G 182
TW2: Twick 3D 24
Campden Rd. CR2: S Croy 2B 64
Campen Cl. SW19 3K 27
Camp End Rd. KT13: Weybr 8D 56
Camperdown Ho. SL4: W'sor 5F 4
Camp Farm Rd. GU11: Alde 8B 90
Camp Hill GU10: Farnh 3A 130
Camphill Ct. KT14: W By 8J 55
Camphill Ind. Est.
KT14: W By 7K 55
Camphill Rd. KT14: W By 8J 55
Campion Cl. CR0: Croy 1B 64
GU17: Haw 3L 69
GU35: Lind 5B 168
Campion Dr. KT20: Tad 7G 81
Campion Ho. RG42: Brac 9K 15
RH1: Red 9D 102
Campion Rd. RH12: Hors 3L 197
SW15 7H 13
TW7: Isle 4F 10
Campion Way
RG40: W'ham 1D 30
Camp Rd. CR3: Wold 7H 85
GU14: Farnb 5A 90
SW19 6G 26
Campus Ho. TW7: Isle 3E 10
Camp Vw. SW19 6G 27
Camrose Av. TW13: Felt 5K 23
Camrose Cl. CR0: Croy 6H 47
SM4: Mord 3M 43
Canada Av. RH1: Red 7E 122
Canada Copse GU8: Mil 9B 132
Canada Dr. RH1: Red 7E 122
Canada Rd. GU16: Deep 6H 71
KT11: Cob 9K 57
KT14: Byf 7M 55
Canadian Memorial Av.
TW20: Eng G 1J 35
Canal Bank GU12: Ash V 9E 90
KT15: Addl 3M 55
Canal Bank M. GU21: Wok 4A 74
Canal Bri. KT15: Addl 4M 55
Canal Cl. GU11: Alde 8B 90
Canal Cotts. GU12: Ash V 9E 90
Canalside RH1: Mers, Red 9F 102
Canalside Gdns. UB2: S'hall 1M 9
Canal Wlk. CR0: Croy 5B 46
Canberra Cl. GU46: Yate 7A 48
RH11: Craw 9B 162
Canberra Pl. RH12: Hors 4M 197
TW9: Rich 6N 11
Canberra Rd. TW6: Lon A 6B 8
Canbury Av.
KT2: K Tham 1L 203 (9M 25)
Canbury Bus. Cen.
KT2: K Tham 2K 203 (9L 25)
Canbury Bus. Pk.
KT2: K Tham 2K 203
Canbury Ct. KT2: K Tham 8K 25
Canbury Pk. Rd.
KT2: K Tham 2K 203 (9L 25)
Canbury Pas.
KT2: K Tham 2H 203 (9K 25)
Candleford Cl. RG12: Brac 8A 16
Candler M. TW1: Twick 1G 25
Candlerush Cl.
GU22: Wok 4D 74
Candover Cl. UB7: Harm 3M 7
Candy Cft. KT23: Book 4B 98
Canes La. GU35: Lind 4A 168
Canewdon Cl. GU22: Wok 6A 74
Canfold Cotts. GU6: Cranl 6C 156
Canford Dr. KT15: Addl 8K 37
Canford Gdns. KT3: N Mal 5D 42
Canford Pl. TW11: Tedd 7J 25
Canham Gdns. TW4: Houn 1N 23
Canham Rd. SE25 2B 46
Can Hatch KT20: Tad 5K 81
Canmore Gdns. SW16 8G 29
Canning Rd. CR0: Croy 8C 46
GU12: Alde 2B 110
Cannizaro Rd. SW19 7H 27
Cannon Cl. GU47: Coll T 7L 49
SW20 2H 43
TW12: Hamp 7B 24
Cannon Cres. GU24: Chob 7H 53
Cannon Gro. KT22: Fetc 9E 78
Cannon Hill RG12: Brac 5A 32
Cannon Hill La. SW20 4J 43
Cannon M. SL5: Asc 9F 16
Cannons Health Club
Richmond 7K 11
Cannonside KT22: Fetc 9E 78
Cannon Way KT8: W Mole 3A 40
KT22: Fetc 8E 78
Canonbury Cotts.
RH12: Rusp 3E 180
Canons Cl. CR4: Mit 3D 44
RH2: Reig 2L 121
Canon's Hill CR5: Coul, Pur 4M 83
Canons La. KT20: Tad 5K 81
Canons Leisure Cen.
Mitcham 3D 44
Canon's Wlk. CR0: Croy 9G 46
Canons Yd. RH2: Reig 6N 121
Canopus Way TW19: Stan 1N 21
Cansiron La. RH19: Ash W 3H 187
TN7: Hart 2L 187
TN8: Cow 7N 167
Cantelupe Ho.
RH19: E Grin 9B 166
(off Cantelupe Rd.)
Cantelupe M. *RH19: E Grin 9B 166*
(off Cantelupe Rd.)
Cantelupe Rd.
RH19: E Grin 9B 166
Canter, The RH10: Craw 2J 183
Canterbury Cl. KT4: W Pk 8J 43
Canterbury Ct. *CR2: S Croy 4N 63*
(off St Augustines Av.)
GU14: Farnb 3B 90
(off Canterbury Gdns.)
RH4: Dork 1J 201
TW15: Ashf 5A 22
Canterbury Gdns.
GU14: Farnb 3B 90
Canterbury Gro. SE27 5L 29
Canterbury Hall KT4: W Pk 6G 43
Canterbury Ho. CR0: Croy 1D 200
KT19: Eps 7N 59
(off Queen Alexandra's Way)
Canterbury M. KT22: Oxs 9C 58
SL4: W'sor 5D 4
Canterbury Rd. CR0: Croy 6K 45
GU2: Guil 1J 113
GU12: Ash 1E 110
GU14: Farnb 3B 90
RH10: Craw 7C 182
SM4: Mord 6N 43
TW13: Hanw 3M 23
Canterbury Wlk.
GU14: Farnb 3B 90
Canterville Pl. RG12: Brac 2A 32
CANTLEY 9A 14
Cantley Cres. RG41: W'ham 9A 14
Cantley Gdns. SE19 1C 46
Canvas Ct. GU27: Hasl 2F 188
Canvey Cl. RH11: Craw 6A 182
Canvil Pl. GU6: Cranl 6B 156
Cape Copse RH12: Rudg 1E 194
CAPEL 5J 159
Capel Av. SM6: W'ton 2K 63
Capel By-Pass
RH5: B Grn, Cap, Ockl 3H 159
Capel La. RH11: Craw 4L 181
Capel Rd.
RH12: Cap, Rusp 2M 179
Capercaillie Cl. RG12: Brac 2J 31
Capern Rd. SW18 2A 28
Capital Bus. Cen.
CR2: S Croy 4A 64
Capital Ind. Est. CR4: Mit 4D 44
Capital Interchange Way
TW8: Brent 1N 11
Capital Pk. GU8: Worm 2C 172
GU22: Wok 8D 74
Capitol, The
Horsham 6K 197
Capitol Sq.
KT17: Eps 6L 201 (9D 60)
Capper Rd. GU15: Camb 8M 49
Capricorn Cl. RH11: Craw 5K 181
Capri Rd. CR0: Croy 7C 46
Capsey Rd. RH11: Ifield 3K 181
Capstans Wharf GU21: Wok 5J 73
Captains Wlk. RH11: Craw 5A 182
Capua Ct. RH10: Craw 8G 163
Caradon Cl. GU21: Wok 5L 73
Caraway Cl. RH11: Craw 7N 181
Caraway Pl. GU2: Guil 7K 93
SM6: W'ton 9F 44
Carbery La. SL5: Asc 2M 33
Cardamom Cl. GU2: Guil 8K 93
Card Hill RH18: F Row 8H 187
Cardigan Cl. GU21: Wok 5H 73
Cardigan Rd. SW13 5F 12
SW19 7A 28
TW10: Rich 9L 11
Cardinal Av. KT2: K Tham 6L 25
SM4: Mord 5K 43
Cardinal Cl. CR2: Sande 9D 64
KT4: W Pk 1F 60
SM4: Mord 5K 43
Cardinal Cres. KT3: N Mal 1B 42
Cardinal Dr. KT12: Wal T 7L 39
Cardinal Ho. *GU14: Farnb 1A 90*
(off Jubilee Hall Rd.)
Cardinal Pl. GU22: Wok 5A 74
SW15 7J 13
Cardinal Rd. TW13: Felt 2J 23
CARDINALS, THE 5E 110
Cardinals, The *GU10: Tong 5D 110*
(off South Side)
RG12: Brac 3N 31
Cardinals Wlk. TW12: Hamp 8C 24
TW16: Sunb 7F 22
Cardingham GU21: Wok 4K 73
Cardington Sq. TW4: Houn 7L 9
Cardwell Cres. SL5: S'hill 4N 33
Cardwells Keep GU2: Guil 9K 93
Carew Cl. CR5: Coul 6M 83
Carew Ct. SM2: Sut 5N 61
Carew Manor & Dovecote 9G 45
Carew Mnr. Cotts.
SM6: Bedd 9H 45
Carew Rd. CR4: Mit 1E 44
CR7: T Hea 3M 45
SM6: W'ton 3G 63
TW15: Ashf 7D 22
Carey Cl. SL4: W'sor 6E 4
Carey Ho. RH11: Craw 3A 182
Carey Rd. RG40: W'ham 3B 30
Careys Cl. RH6: Smallf 7M 143
Careys Copse RH6: Smallf 8M 143
Carey's Wood RH6: Smallf 8M 143
Carfax RH12: Hors 6J 197
Carfax Av. GU10: Tong 4D 110
Carfax Rd. UB3: Harl 1G 9
Cargate Av. GU11: Alde 3M 109
Cargate Gro. GU11: Alde 3M 109
Cargate Hill GU11: Alde 3L 109
Cargate Ter. GU11: Alde 3L 109
Cargill Rd. SW18 2N 27
Cargo Forecourt Rd.
RH6: Gatw 3B 162
Cargo Point TW19: Stan 9A 8
Cargo Rd. RH6: Gatw 2B 162
Cargreen Pl. *SE25 3C 46*
(off Cargreen Rd.)
Cargreen Rd. SE25 3C 46
Carina Dr. RG40: W'ham 1E 30
Carisbrooke GU16: Frim 6D 70
Carisbrooke Ho. TW4: Houn 1M 23
Carisbrooke Ct. SM2: Chea 4L 61
Carisbrooke Ho.
KT2: K Tham 2J 203
TW10: Rich 8N 11
Carisbrooke Rd. CR4: Mit 3H 45
Carlcott Cl. KT12: Wal T 6J 39
Carleton Av. SM6: W'ton 5H 63
Carleton Cl. KT10: Esh 7D 40
Carlile Pl. TW10: Rich 9M 11
Carlingford Gdns. CR4: Mit 8D 28
Carlingford Rd. SM4: Mord 5J 43
Carlin Pl. GU15: Camb 2A 70
Carlinwark Dr. GU15: Camb 8D 50
Carlisle Cl. KT2: K Tham 9N 25
Carlisle M. KT2: K Tham 9N 25
Carlisle Rd. GU10: Rush 3N 149
SM1: Sut 3L 61
TW12: Hamp 8B 24
Carlisle Way SW17 6E 28
Carlos St. GU7: Godal 7H 133
Carlson Ct. SW15 7L 13
Carlton Av. CR2: S Croy 4B 64
TW14: Felt 9K 9
UB3: Harl 1F 8
Carlton Cl. GU15: Camb 3F 70
GU21: Wok 1B 74
KT9: Ches 3K 59
RH10: Craw 4C 182
Carlton Ct. RH6: Horl 6E 142
TW18: Stain 6J 21
Carlton Cres. GU52: Chu C 7C 88
SM3: Chea 1K 61
Carlton Dr. SW15 8J 13
Carlton Grn. RH1: Red 9C 102
Carlton Ho. TW3: Houn 9A 10
TW14: Felt 1G 22

Carlton Pk. Av.—Centurion Ct.

Carlton Pk. Av. SW20 1J 43
Carlton Pl. KT13: Weybr 1C 56
(off Castle Vw. Rd.)
Carlton Rd. CR2: S Croy 3A 64
GU21: Wok 1C 74
GU35: Head D 5H 169
KT3: N Mal 1D 42
KT12: Wal T 6J 39
RH1: Red 1B 122
RH2: Reig 1B 122
RH9: S Gods 1F 144
SW14 6B 12
TW16: Sunb 8G 22
Carlton Towers SM5: Cars 9D 44
Carlton Tye RH6: Horl 8G 143
Carlton Vs. SW15 8K 13
Carlton Yd. GU9: Farnh 1H 129
(off Victoria Rd.)
Carlwell St. SW17 6C 28
Carlyle Cl. KT8: W Mole 1B 40
Carlyle Ct. RG45: Crowt 2H 49
SW6 4N 13
(off Imperial Rd.)
Carlyle Ho. KT8: W Mole 4A 40
(off Down St.)
Carlyle Pl. SW15 7J 13
Carlyle Rd. CR0: Croy 8D 46
TW18: Stain 8J 21
W5 1J 11
Carlyon Cl. GU14: Farnb 1A 90
GU16: Mytc 1D 90
Carlys Cl. BR3: Beck 1G 47
Carmalt Gdns. KT12: Hers 2K 57
SW15 7H 13
Carman Wlk. RH11: Craw 8N 181
Carmarthen Cl. GU14: Farnb 7L 69
Carmel Cl. GU22: Wok 5A 74
Carmel Lodge SW6 2M 13
(off Lillie Rd.)
Carmel Way TW9: Rich 5A 12
Carmichael Ct. SW13 5E 12
(off Grove Rd.)
Carmichael M. SW18 1B 28
Carmichael Rd. SE25 4C 46
Carminia Rd. SW17 3F 28
Carnation Cl. RG45: Crowt 8G 30
Carnation Dr. RG42: Wink R 7E 16
Carnegie Cl. KT6: Surb 8M 41
Carnegie Pl. SW19 4J 27
Carnforth Cl. KT19: Ewe 3A 60
Carnforth Rd. SW16 8H 29
(not continuous)
Carnie Lodge SW17 4F 28
Carnival Pool
Wokingham 3A 30
Carnival Sq. GU51: Fleet 4A 88
Carnoustie RG12: Brac 6K 31
Carnwath Rd. SW6 6M 13
Carolina Rd. CR7: T Hea 1M 45
Caroline Cl. CR0: Croy 1B 64
SW16 4K 29
TW7: Isle 3D 10
Caroline Ct. RH11: Craw 4B 182
TW15: Ashf 7C 22
Caroline Ho. W6 1H 13
(off Queen Caroline St.)
Caroline Pl. UB3: Harl 3F 8
Caroline Rd. SW19 8L 27
Caroline Wlk. SW6 2K 13
(off Lillie Rd.)
Caroline Way GU16: Frim 5D 70
Carolyn Cl. GU21: Wok 6J 73
Carpenter Cl. KT17: Ewe 5E 60
Carpenters Ct. TW2: Twick 3E 24
Carrara Wharf SW6 6K 13
Carriage Pl. SW16 6G 29
Carrick Cl. TW7: Isle 6G 10
Carrick Ga. KT10: Esh 9C 40
Carrick La. GU46: Yate 9D 48
Carrier Bus. Pk.
RH10: Craw 2F 182
Carrigshaun KT13: Weybr 2E 56
Carrington Av. TW3: Houn 8B 10
Carrington Cl. CR0: Croy 6H 47
KT2: K Tham 6B 26
RH1: Red 2D 122
Carrington La. GU12: Ash V 5E 90
Carrington Pl. KT10: Esh 1B 58
Carrington Rd. TW10: Rich 7N 11
Carroll Av. GU1: Guil 3D 114
Carroll Cres. SL5: Asc 4K 33
Carrow Rd. KT12: Wal T 9L 39
CARSHALTON 1E 62
Carshalton Athletic 1C 62
CARSHALTON BEECHES 5C 62
Carshalton Beeches Station (Rail)
3D 62
Carshalton Gro. SM1: Sut 1B 62
Carshalton Lodge
KT13: Weybr 9E 38
(off Oatlands Dr.)
CARSHALTON ON THE HILL 4E 62
Carshalton Pk. Rd.
SM5: Cars 2D 62
Carshalton Pl. SM5: Cars 2E 62
Carshalton Rd. CR4: Mit 3E 44
GU15: Camb 6E 50
SM1: Sut 2A 62
SM5: Cars 2A 62
SM7: Ban 1D 82
Carshalton Station (Rail) 1D 62
Carslake Rd. SW15 9H 13
Carson Rd. SE21 3N 29
CARTBRIDGE 9D 74
Cartbridge Cl. GU23: Send 1D 94
Carter Cl. SL4: W'sor 5D 4
Carterdale Cotts. RH5: Cap 5J 159
Carter Rd. RH10: Craw 6H 183
SW19 7B 28
Carters Cl. GU1: Guil 8A 94
KT4: W Pk 8J 43
Carter's Cotts. RH1: Red 5C 122
Carter's Hill RG40: W'ham 5F 14
RG42: Bin 5F 14
Carters Hill Pk.
RG40: W'ham 5E 14
Carters La. GU22: Wok 7E 74
Carterslodge La.
RH17: Hand 9J 199
Cartersmead Cl. RH6: Horl 7F 142
Carters Rd. KT17: Eps 2E 80
Carters Wlk. GU9: Heath E 4J 109
Carter's Yd. SW18 8M 13
Carthona Dr. GU52: Fleet 6A 88
Carthouse Cotts. GU4: Guil 9E 94
Carthouse La. GU21: Wok 1H 73
Cart Lodge M. CR0: Croy 7B 46
Cartmel Cl. RH2: Reig 1C 122
Cartmel Gdns. SM4: Mord 4A 44
Cartwright Way SW13 3G 13
Carville Cres. TW8: Brent 1L 11
Carylls Cotts. RH12: Fay 8E 180
Cascades CR0: Sels 6J 65
Cascades Ct. SW19 8L 27
Caselden Cl. KT15: Addl 2L 55
Casewick Rd. SE27 6L 29
Casher Rd. RH10: Craw 6G 183
Cassidy Rd. SW6 3M 13
(not continuous)
Cassilis Rd. TW1: Twick 8H 11
Cassino Cl. GU11: Alde 2N 109
Cassiobury Av. TW14: Felt 1G 22
Cassland Rd. CR7: T Hea 3A 46
Cassocks Sq. TW17: Shep 6E 38
Castello Av. SW15 8H 13
CASTELNAU 2G 12
Castelnau SW13 4F 12
Castelnau Gdns. SW13 2G 13
Castelnau Mans. SW13 2G 13
(off Castelnau, not continuous)
Castelnau Row SW13 2G 12
Castle, The RH12: Hors 1L 197
Castle Av. KT17: Ewe 5F 60
SL3: Dat 2K 5
Castle Bus. Cen.
TW12: Hamp 9B 24
(off Castle M.)
Castle Cl. BR2: Brom 2N 47
GU14: Farnb 3C 90
GU15: Camb 2D 70
RH1: Blet 2N 123
RH2: Reig 7N 121
SW19 4J 27
TW16: Sunb 8F 22
Castlecombe Dr. SW19 1J 27
Castle Ct. GU9: Farnh 9G 108
Castlecraig Ct. GU47: Coll T 8J 49
Castle Dr. RH2: Reig 7M 121
RH6: Horl 1G 162
Castle Farm Caravan Site
SL4: W'sor 5A 4
Castle Fld. GU9: Farnh 9G 108
Castlefield Ct. RH2: Reig 3N 121
Castlefield Rd. RH2: Reig 3M 121
Castle Gdns. RH4: Dork 3M 119
Castlegate TW9: Rich 6M 11
CASTLE GREEN 9G 53
Castle Grn. KT13: Weybr 9F 38
Castle Gro. Rd. GU24: Chob 9G 53
Castle Hill
GU1: Guil 7C 202 (5N 113)
GU9: Farnh 9G 108
SL4: W'sor 4G 5
Castle Hill Av. CR0: N Add 5L 65
Castle Hill Local Nature Reserve
3N 59
Castle Hill Rd. TW20: Eng G 5L 19
Castle Ho. SM2: Sut 3M 61
Castlemaine Av.
CR2: S Croy 2C 64
KT17: Ewe 5G 61
Castle M. KT13: Weybr 9F 38
SW17 5C 28
TW12: Hamp 9B 24
(not continuous)
Castle of Mey Ho.
GU27: Hasl 2D 188
Castle Pde. KT17: Ewe 4F 60
Castlerigg Way
RH10: Craw 5H 183
Castle Rd. CR5: Chip 7C 82
GU11: Alde 9K 89
GU15: Camb 2C 70
GU21: Wok 1B 74
KT13: Weybr 9E 38
KT18: Eps 2A 80
RH12: Broadb H 5D 196
TW7: Isle 5F 10
Castle Row W4 1C 12
Castle Sq.
GU1: Guil 6D 202 (5N 113)
RH1: Blet 2N 123
Castle St.
GU1: Guil 6C 202 (5N 113)
GU9: Farnh 9G 109
GU52: Fleet 6A 88
KT1: K Tham 3J 203 (1L 41)
RH1: Blet 2M 123
Castleton Cl. CR0: Croy 5H 47
SM7: Ban 2M 81
Castleton Dr. SM7: Ban 2M 81
Castleton Rd. CR4: Mit 3H 45
Castletown Rd. W14 1K 13
Castle Vw. KT18: Eps 1A 80
Castle Vw. Rd. KT13: Weybr 1C 56
Castleview Rd. SL3: Lang 1M 5
Castle Wlk. RH2: Reig 3M 121
TW16: Sunb 2K 39
Castle Way KT17: Ewe 6F 60
SW19 4J 27
TW13: Hanw 5K 23
Castle Yd. TW10: Rich 8K 11
Castor Ct. GU46: Yate 8A 48
GU52: Chu C 8C 88
Caswall Cl. RG42: Bin 7H 15
Caswall Ride GU46: Yate 1D 68
Caswell Cl. GU14: Farnb 8L 69
Catalina Rd. TW6: Lon A 5C 8
Catalpa Cl. GU1: Guil 1M 113
Catena Ri. GU18: Ligh 6L 51
Caterfield La. RH7: Crow 1B 146
RH8: Oxt 8C 126
Cater Gdns. GU3: Guil 1J 113
CATERHAM 2D 104
Caterham By-Pass CR3: Cate 7E 84
Caterham Cl. GU24: Pirb 8B 72
Caterham Ct. CR3: Cate 2B 104
Caterham Dr. CR5: Coul 5M 83
CATERHAM-ON-THE-HILL 9B 84
Caterham Station (Rail) 2D 104
Caterways RH12: Hors 5G 197
Cathcart Rd. SW10 2N 13
Cathedral Cl. GU2: Guil 4L 113
Cathedral Ct. GU2: Guil 3K 113
GU14: Farnb 3N 89
(off O'Gorman Av.)
Cathedral Hill GU2: Guil 2K 113
Cathedral Hill Ind. Est.
GU2: Guil 2K 113
Cathedral Pl. GU1: Guil 2C 202
(off Markenfield Rd.)
Cathedral Vw. GU2: Guil 3J 113
Catherine Cl. KT14: Byf 1N 75
Catherine Ct. SW19 6L 27
Catherine Dr. TW9: Rich 7L 11
TW16: Sunb 7G 22
Catherine Gdns. TW3: Houn 7D 10
Catherine Howard Ct.
KT13: Weybr 9C 38
(off Old Palace Rd.)
Catherine Rd.
KT6: Surb 8G 203 (4K 41)
Catherine Wheel Rd.
TW8: Brent 3K 11
Cat Hill RH5: Ockl 7B 158
Cathill La. RH5: Ockl 7B 158
Cathles Rd. SW12 1F 28
Catlin Cres. TW17: Shep 4E 38
Catlin Gdns. RH9: Gods 8E 104
Cator Cl. CR0: N Add 7A 66
Cator Cres. CR0: N Add 7A 66
Cator La. BR3: Beck 1J 47
Cator Rd. SM5: Cars 2D 62
Cato's Hill KT10: Esh 1B 58
Cat St. TN7: C Hat, Up Hart 9N 187
CATTESHALL 6K 133
Catteshall Hatch
GU7: Godal 5K 133
Catteshall La. GU7: Godal 7H 133
Catteshall Rd. GU7: Godal 5K 133
(not continuous)
Catteshall Ter. GU7: Godal 6K 133
(off Catteshall Rd.)
Causeway RH12: Hors 7J 197
Causeway, The KT9: Ches 1L 59
KT10: Clay 4F 58
SM2: Sut 5A 62
SM5: Cars 9E 44
SW18 8N 13
SW19 6H 27
TW4: Houn 7H 9
TW11: Tedd 7F 24
TW14: Felt, Houn 7H 9
TW18: Stain 5E 20
Causeway Corporate Cen.
TW18: Stain 5E 20
Causeway Ct. GU21: Wok 5J 73
Causewayside GU27: Hasl 1H 189
(off High St.)
Cavalier Ct. KT5: Surb 5M 41
Cavalier Way RH19: E Grin 2B 186
Cavalry Ct. GU11: Alde 2K 109
Cavalry Cres. SL4: W'sor 6F 4
TW4: Houn 7L 9
Cavalry Gdns. SW15 8L 13
Cavan's Rd. GU11: Alde 7A 90
Cavell Way GU21: Knap 6F 72
KT19: Eps 7N 59
RH10: Craw 4G 182
Cavendish Av. KT3: N Mal 4F 42
Cavendish Cl. RH12: Hors 1K 197
TW16: Sunb 7G 22
Cavendish Ct. GU17: Haw 3J 69
KT13: Weybr 3D 56
KT16: Chert 7J 37
(off Victory Rd.)
SL3: Poy 4G 6
SM6: W'ton 3F 62
TW16: Sunb 7G 22
Cavendish Dr. KT10: Clay 2E 58
Cavendish Gdns.
GU52: Chu C 8A 88
RH1: Red 2E 122
Cavendish Ho. CR0: Croy 1D 200
Cavendish Meads SL5: S'hill 5A 34
Cavendish M. GU11: Alde 3M 109
Cavendish Pde. TW4: Houn 5M 9
Cavendish Pk. Caravan Site
GU47: Coll T 9K 49
Cavendish Rd. CR0: Croy 7M 45
GU11: Alde 3M 109
GU22: Wok 6N 73
GU52: Chu C 9A 88
KT3: N Mal 3E 42
KT13: Weybr 5C 56
RH1: Red 3E 122
SM2: Sut 4A 62
SW12 1G 28
SW19 8B 28
TW16: Sunb 7G 22
W4 4B 12
Cavendish Ter. TW13: Felt 3H 23
Cavendish Wlk. KT19: Eps 7A 60
Cavendish Way
BR4: W Wick 7L 47
Cavenham Cl. GU22: Wok 6A 74
Caverleigh Way
KT4: W Pk 7F 42
Cave Rd. TW10: Ham 5J 25
Caversham Av. SM3: Chea 8K 43
Caversham Ho.
KT1: K Tham 4J 203
Caversham Rd.
KT1: K Tham 3L 203 (1M 41)
Caves Farm Cl.
GU47: Sandh 7F 48
Cawcott Dr. SL4: W'sor 4B 4
Cawsey Way GU21: Wok 4A 74
Caxton Av. KT15: Addl 3J 55
Caxton Cl. RH10: Craw 6B 182
Caxton Ct. GU27: Hasl 1G 188
Caxton Gdns. GU2: Guil 2L 113
Caxton La. RH8: Limp 9G 106
Caxton M. TW8: Brent 2K 11
Caxton Ri. RH1: Red 2E 122
Caxton Rd. SW19 6A 28
Caxton Yd. GU9: Farnh 1G 129
(off The Borough)
Cayton Rd. CR5: Coul 9G 83
Cearn Way CR5: Coul 2K 83
Cecil Cl. KT9: Ches 1K 59
TW15: Ashf 8D 22
Cecil Ct. CR0: Croy 8C 46
SW10 2N 13
(off Fawcett St.)
Cecil Hepworth Playhouse, The
7G 39
(off Hepworth Way)
Cecil Mans. SW17 3E 28
Cecil Pl. CR4: Mit 4D 44
Cecil Rd. CR0: Croy 5J 45
SM1: Sut 3L 61
SW19 8N 27
TW3: Houn 5C 10
TW15: Ashf 8D 22
Cedar Av. GU17: B'water 1J 69
KT11: Cob 2K 77
TW2: Whitt 9B 10
Cedar Cl. CR6: Warl 6H 85
GU12: Alde 4C 110
GU19: Bag 4J 51
KT8: E Mol 3E 40
KT10: Esh 3N 57
KT17: Eps 1E 80
RG40: W'ham 2B 30
RH2: Reig 5A 122
RH4: Dork 3K 201 (5H 119)
RH11: Craw 9A 162
RH12: Hors 5H 197
SE21 2N 29
SM5: Cars 3D 62
SW15 5C 26
TW18: Lale 2L 37
Cedar Ct. GU27: Hasl 2F 188
KT15: Addl 1L 55
KT16: Otter 2E 54
KT22: Fetc 9G 78
SL4: W'sor 5D 4
SM2: Sut 3A 62
SW19 4J 27
TW8: Brent 2J 11
TW20: Egh 5C 20
Cedarcroft Rd. KT9: Ches 1M 59
Cedar Dr. GU51: Fleet 4D 88
KT22: Fetc 1E 98
RG42: Brac 8A 16
SL5: S'dale 6D 34
SL5: S'hill 3G 35
TN8: Eden 1K 147
Cedar Gdns. GU21: Wok 5L 73
GU24: Chob 6J 53
SM2: Sut 3A 62
Cedar Gro. GU24: Bis 2D 72
KT13: Weybr 1D 56
Cedar Hgts. TW10: Ham 2L 25
Cedar Hill KT18: Eps 3B 80
Cedar Ho. GU4: Guil 1E 114
KT22: Leat 6F 78
TW9: Kew 4A 12
TW16: Sunb 8G 22
(off Spelthorne Gro.)
Cedarland Ter. SW20 8G 27
Cedar La. GU16: Frim 6B 70
Cedar Lodge
GU27: Hasl 3J 189
RH10: Craw 5B 182
Cedar M. SW15 8J 13
Cedarne Rd. SW6 3N 13
Cedar Pk. CR3: Cate 8B 84
Cedar Pk. Gdns. SW19 6G 26
Cedar Rd.
CR0: Croy 2E 200 (8A 46)
GU14: Farnb 2A 90
GU22: Wok 7L 73
KT8: E Mol 3E 40
KT11: Cob 1J 77
KT13: Weybr 1B 56
SM2: Sut 3A 62
TW4: C'ford 5K 9
TW11: Tedd 6G 24
TW14: Bedf 2E 22
Cedars RG12: Brac 3D 32
SM7: Ban 1D 82
Cedars, The GU1: B'ham 9C 94
GU8: Mil 2B 152
GU24: Pirb 9A 72
GU51: Fleet 5C 88
KT14: Byf 8A 56
KT22: Leat 8K 79
KT23: Book 4C 98
RH2: Reig 3B 122
RH3: Brock 3N 119
SL3: Dat 4M 5
SM6: W'ton 1G 63
TW11: Tedd 7F 24
Cedars Av. CR4: Mit 3E 44
Cedars Cl. GU47: Sandh 7E 48
Cedars Ct. GU1: B'ham 9C 94
Cedars Rd. BR3: Beck 1H 47
CR0: Bedd 9J 45
KT1: H Wic 9J 25
SM4: Mord 3M 43
SW13 5F 12
W4 1B 12
Cedar Ter. TW9: Rich 7L 11
Cedar Tree Gro. SE27 6M 29
Cedar Vw. GU52: Chu C 7C 88
KT1: K Tham 6H 203
Cedarville Gdns. SW16 7K 29
Cedar Wlk. CR8: Ken 3N 83
KT10: Clay 3F 58
KT20: Tad 7K 81
Cedar Way GU1: Guil 1M 113
SL3: Lang 1A 6
TW16: Sunb 8F 22
Cedarways GU9: Farnh 4G 128
Celandine Cl. RG45: Crowt 1H 49
RH11: Craw 6N 181
Celandine Ct. GU46: Yate 8A 48
Celandine Rd. KT12: Hers 1M 57
Celery La. GU10: Wrec 6G 128
Celia Cres. TW15: Ashf 7M 21
Cell Farm Av. SL4: O Win 8L 5
Celtic Rd. KT14: Byf 1N 75
Cemetery La. TW17: Shep 6C 38
Cemetery Pales
GU24: B'wood 9C 72
Cemetery Wlk. RH17: Hand 7K 199
Centaur Ct. TW8: Brent 1L 11
Centaurs Bus. Pk. TW7: Isle 2G 10
Centenary Ct. RH1: Red 2D 122
(off Warwick Rd.)
Centenary Fields
(Local Nature Reserve)
6M 145
Central Av. KT8: W Mole 3N 39
SM6: W'ton 2J 63
TW3: Houn 7C 10
Central Ct. KT15: Addl 1L 55
Centrale Shop. Cen.
CR0: Croy 2B 200 (8N 45)
Centrale Stop (London Tramlink)
2B 200 (8N 45)
Central Gdns. SM4: Mord 4N 43
Central Hill SE19 6N 29
Central La. SL4: Wink 2M 17
Central London Golf Course 3B 28
Central Mall SW18 9N 13
(off Southside Shop. Cen.)
Central Pde. CR0: N Add 6M 65
KT6: Surb 5L 41
KT8: W Mole 3N 39
RH1: Red 2D 122
RH6: Horl 9E 142
TW5: Hest 3N 9
TW14: Felt 1K 23
Central Pk. Est. TW4: Houn 8L 9
Central Pl. SE25 4D 46
Central Rd. KT4: W Pk 7F 42
SM4: Mord 5M 43
Central School Path SW14 6B 12
Central Ter. BR3: Beck 2G 47
Central Wlk.
KT19: Eps 6J 201 (9C 60)
RG40: W'ham 2B 30
Central Way RH8: Oxt 5N 105
SL4: Wink 2M 17
SM5: Cars 4C 62
TW14: Felt 8H 9
Centre, The KT12: Wal T 7H 39
TW3: Houn 6B 10
TW13: Felt 2J 23
Centre Ct. Shop. Cen. SW19 7L 27
Centre Rd. SL4: W'sor 3A 4
Centre Sq. SW18 8M 13
(off Buckhold Rd.)
Centre Vw. Apartments
CR0: Croy 4C 200
Centrillion Point CR0: Croy 6C 200
Centrium GU22: Wok 4B 74
Centro GU15: Camb 9A 50
Centrum Bus. Pk.
GU9: Farnh 9H 109
Centurion Cl. GU47: Coll T 7J 49
Centurion Ct. SM6: W'ton 8F 44

Century Ct.—Chavecroft Ter.

Century Ct. GU21: Wok 3B 74
Century Gdns. CR2: Sande 9D 64
Century Ho. SM7: Ban 2N 81
SW15 .... 7J 13
Century Rd. TW18: Stain 6E 20
Century Way GU24: B'wood 6A 72
Cerne Rd. SM4: Mord 5A 44
Cerotus Pl. KT16: Chert 6H 37
Chadacre Rd. KT17: Ewe 3G 60
Chadhurst Cl. RH5: Nth H 8K 119
Chadwick Av. SW19 .... 7M 27
Chadwick Cl. RH11: Craw 8N 181
SW15 .... 1E 26
TW11: Tedd 7G 25
Chadwick M. RG12: Brac 3N 31
W4 .... 2A 12
Chadwick Pl. KT6: Surb 6J 41
Chadworth Way KT10: Clay 2D 58
Chaffers Mead KT21: Asht 3M 79
Chaffinch Av. CR0: Croy 5G 46
Chaffinch Bus. Pk.
BR3: Beck 3G 47
Chaffinch Cl. CR0: Croy 4G 46
GU47: Coll T 7J 49
KT6: Surb TH9N 41
RH11: Craw 1B 182
RH12: Hors 1K 197
Chaffinch Gdns. RG12: Brac 4J 31
Chaffinch Rd. BR3: Beck 1H 47
Chaffinch Way RH6: Horl 7C 142
Chailey Cl. RH11: Craw 6M 181
TW5: Hest 4L 9
Chailey Pl. KT12: Hers 1M 57
Chalcot Cl. SM2: Sut 4M 61
Chalcot M. SW16 .... 4J 29
Chalcott Gdns. KT6: Surb 7J 41
CHALDON 2L 103
Chaldon Cl. RH1: Red 5C 122
Chaldon Comn. Rd.
CR3: Cate 2N 103
Chaldon Ct. SE19 .... 1A 46
Chaldon Path CR7: T Hea 3M 45
Chaldon Rd. CR3: Cate 2A 104
RH11: Craw 8A 182
SW6 .... 3K 13
Chaldon Way CR5: Coul 4J 83
Chale Rd. SW2 .... 1J 29
Chalet Cl. TW15: Ashf 7E 22
Chalet Ct. CR7: T Hea 4N 45
Chalet Hill GU35: Bor 6A 168
Chale Wlk. SM2: Sut 5N 61
Chalfont Dr. GU14: Farnb 3A 90
Chalfont Rd. SE25 .... 2C 46
Chalford Cl. KT8: W Mole 3A 40
Chalgrove Av. SM4: Mord 4M 43
Chalgrove Rd. SM2: Sut 4B 62
Chalice Cl. SM6: W'ton 3H 63
CHALKER'S CORNER 6A 12
Chalk Hill Rd. W6 .... 1J 13
Chalk La. GU8: S'ford 3N 131
KT18: Eps, Eps D 2C 80
KT21: Asht 6M 79
KT24: E Hor 1G 116
Chalkley Cl. CR4: Mit 1D 44
Chalkmead RH1: Mers 8G 102
Chalk Paddock KT18: Eps 2C 80
Chalk Pit Cotts.
KT24: W Hors 8C 96
Chalkpit La. CR3: Wold 3M 105
KT23: Book 5N 97
RH3: Betch 2A 120
RH4: Dork 1J 201 (4G 119)
RH8: Oxt 3M 105
Chalk Pit Rd. KT18: Eps D 6B 80
SM7: Ban 4M 81
Chalkpit Ter. RH4: Dork 3G 118
Chalk Pit Way SM1: Sut 2A 62
Chalkpit Wood RH8: Oxt 5N 105
Chalk Rd. GU7: Godal 6G 133
RH14: Ifo 6E 192
Chalky La. KT9: Ches 6K 59
Challen Ct. RH12: Hors 5H 197
Challenge Ct. KT22: Leat 6H 79
TW2: Twick 1E 24
Challenge Rd. TW15: Ashf 4E 22
Challice Way SW2 .... 2K 29
Challis Pl. RG42: Brac 9K 15
Challis Rd. TW8: Brent 1K 11
Challock Cl. TN16: B Hil 3E 86
Challoner Ct. BR2: Brom 1N 47
W14 .... *1L 13*
(off Challoner St.)
Challoner Cres. W14 .... 1L 13
Challoner Mans. *W14* *1L 13*
(off Challoner St.)
Challoners Cl. KT8: E Mol 3D 40
Challoner St. W14 .... 1L 13
Chalmers Cl. RH6: Charlw 4K 161
Chalmers Rd. SM7: Ban 2B 82
TW15: Ashf 6C 22
Chalmers Rd. E. TW15: Ashf 5C 22
Chalmers Way TW1: Isle 7H 11
TW14: Felt 8J 9
Chamberlain Cres.
BR4: W Wick 7L 47
Chamberlain Gdns.
TW3: Houn 4C 10
Chamberlain Wlk.
TW13: Hanw 5M 23
Chamberlain Way KT6: Surb 6L 41
Chamber La. GU10: Farnh 3B 128
Chamberlens Garages *W6* *1G 12*
(off Dalling Rd.)
Chambers Bus. Pk. UB7: Sip 2B 8
Chambers Pl. CR2: S Croy 4A 64
Chambers Rd. GU12: Ash V 8F 90
Chambon Pl. W6 .... 1F 12
Chamomile Gdns.
GU14: Cove 9H 69
Champion Down KT24: Eff 6M 97
Champions Dr. TN8: Eden 9K 127
Champion Way GU52: Chu C 8B 88
Champney Cl. SL3: Hort 6C 6
Champneys Cl. SM2: Chea 4L 61
Chancellor Ct. GU2: Guil 4G 113
(not continuous)
Chancellor Gdns.
CR2: S Croy 5M 63
Chancellor Gro. SE21 .... 3N 29
Chancellor's Rd. W6 .... 1H 13
Chancellor's St. W6 .... 1H 13
Chancellors Wharf W6 .... 1H 13
Chancel Mans. RG42: Warf 7A 16
Chancerygate Bus. Cen.
RG41: W'ham 3A 30
Chancery La. BR3: Beck 1L 47
Chancery M. SW17 .... 3C 28
Chanctonbury Chase
RH1: Red 3E 122
Chanctonbury Dr.
SL5: S'dale 6B 34
Chanctonbury Gdns.
SM2: Sut 4N 61
Chanctonbury Way
RH11: Craw 5A 182
Chandaria Ct. CR0: Croy 3B 200
Chandler Cl. RH10: Craw 5B 182
TW12: Hamp 9A 24
Chandler Ct. RH6: Horl 8F 142
TW14: Felt 9H 9
Chandlers Cl. *GU21: Wok* *5J 73*
(off Robin Hood Rd.)
KT8: W Mole 4B 40
TW14: Felt 1G 22
Chandlers La. GU46: Yate 8B 48
Chandlers Rd. GU12: Ash V 9F 90
Chandlers Way SW2 .... 1L 29
Chandler Way RH5: Dork 7J 119
Chandon Lodge SM2: Sut 4A 62
Chandos Gdns. CR5: Coul 6M 83
Chandos Rd. TW18: Stain 6F 20
Channel Cl. TW5: Hest 4A 10
Channings GU21: Wok 2A 74
Channon Ct. KT6: Surb 8J 203
Chantilly Way KT19: Eps 6A 60
Chantlers Cl. RH19: E Grin 8M 165
Chanton Dr. KT17: Chea 6H 61
SM2: Chea, Ewe 6H 61
Chantrey Rd. RH10: Craw 6C 182
Chantry Cl. KT21: Asht 6J 79
RH6: Horl 7D 142
SL4: W'sor 4D 4
TW16: Sunb 8H 23
Chantry Cotts. GU4: Guil 9D 114
Chantry Ct. *GU16: Frim* *5B 70*
(off Church Rd.)
SM5: Cars 9C 44
Chantry Ho.
KT1: K Tham 8K 203 (3L 41)
Chantry Hurst KT18: Eps 2C 80
Chantry La. GU5: Shere 8A 116
Chantry Quarry
GU1: Guil 8D 202 (6N 113)
Chantry Rd. GU4: Guil 9D 114
GU19: Bag 5H 51
KT9: Ches 2M 59
KT16: Chert 6L 37
Chantrys, The GU9: Farnh 1E 128
Chantrys Ct. GU9: Farnh 1F 128
Chantry Vw. Rd.
GU1: Guil
.... 8D 202 & 8F 202 (6N 113)
Chantry Way CR4: Mit 2B 44
Chapel, The SW15 .... 9K 13
Chapel Av. KT15: Addl 1K 55
Chapel Cl. GU8: Mil 9C 132
Chapel Ct. GU8: Mil 1C 152
RH4: Dork 1J 201 (4G 119)
Chapel Farm Animal Trail 8G 98
Chapel Farm Mobile Home Pk.
GU3: Norm 9B 92
Chapel Flds. GU7: Godal 4G 132
Chapel Gdns. GU35: Lind 4A 168
CHAPEL GREEN 4B 30
Chapel Grn. CR8: Pur 9L 63
Chapel Gro. KT15: Addl 1K 55
KT18: Tat C 6H 81
Chapel Hill GU8: Duns 6B 174
KT24: Eff 5L 97
Chapelhouse Cl.
GU2: Guil 3H 113
Chapelier Ho. SW18 .... 7M 13
Chapel La. GU8: Mil 9C 132
GU14: Cove 6K 69
GU17: Haw 6K 69
GU19: Bag 5H 51
GU24: Pirb 9D 72
KT23: Book, Westh 6C 98
RG42: Bin 8H 15
RH4: Westc 6C 118
RH5: Westh 8E 98
RH10: Craw D 7C 164
RH18: F Row 8H 187
RH19: Ash W 3F 186
Chapel La. Works
RH4: Westc 6C 118
Chapel Mill Rd.
KT1: K Tham 6M 203 (2M 41)
Chapel Pk. Rd. KT15: Addl 1K 55
Chapel Pines GU15: Camb 8F 50
Chapel Rd. CR6: Warl 5G 84
GU10: Rowl 7D 128
GU15: Camb 1N 69
KT20: Tad 1H 101
RH1: Red 3D 122
RH6: Charlw 3K 161
RH6: Smallf 8M 143
RH8: Limp 8E 106
SE27 .... 5M 29
TW1: Twick 1H 25
TW3: Houn 6B 10
Chapel Sq. GU15: Camb 9L 49
GU25: V Wat 3A 36
Chapel St.
GU1: Guil 6C 202 (5N 113)
GU14: Farnb 8B 70
GU21: Wok 4B 74
Chapel Ter. RG42: Bin 8H 15
Chapel Vw. CR2: Sels 3F 64
Chapel Wlk.
CR0: Croy 2B 200 (8N 45)
CR5: Coul 9H 83
Chapel Way KT18: Tat C 6H 81
Chapel Yd. *SW18* *8N 13*
(off Wandsworth High St.)
Chaplain's Hill RG45: Crowt 3J 49
Chaplin Cres. TW16: Sunb 7F 22
Chaplin M. SL3: Lang 1B 6
Chapman Rd. CR0: Croy 7L 45
RH10: Craw 7G 182
Chapman's La.
RH19: E Grin 9L 165
(not continuous)
Chapman Sq. SW19 .... 3J 27
Chapter Ho. *GU14: Farnb* *1A 90*
(off Jubilee Hall Rd.)
Chapter M. SL4: W'sor 3G 5
Chapter Way SW19 .... 9B 28
TW12: Hamp 5A 24
Chara Pl. W4 .... 2C 12
Charcot Ho. SW15 .... 9E 12
Chardin Rd. W4 .... 1D 12
Chard Rd. TW6: Lon A 5C 8
Chargate Cl. KT12: Hers 3G 57
Charing Cl. BR6: Orp 1N 67
Charing Ct. BR2: Brom 1N 47
Charing Cross Sports Club 2J 13
Chariotts Pl. SL4: W'sor 4G 4
Charlbury Cl. RG12: Brac 3D 32
Charlecombe Ct.
TW18: Stain 6K 21
Charlecote Cl. GU14: Farnb 2B 90
Charles Babbage Cl.
KT9: Ches 4J 59
Charles Cobb Gdns.
CR0: Wad 2L 63
Charlesfield Rd. RH6: Horl 7D 142
Charles Haller St. SW2 .... 1L 29
Charles Harrod Ct. *SW13* *2H 13*
(off Somerville Av.)
CHARLESHILL 6E 130
Charles Hill GU10: Til 5B 130
Charles Ho. *KT16: Chert* *7H 37*
(off Sth. Guildford St.)
SL4: W'sor 4F 4
Charles Lesser Ho.
KT9: Ches 2K 59
Charles Nex M. SE21 .... 3N 29
Charles Rd. SW19 .... 9M 27
TW18: Stain 7M 21
Charles Sq. RG12: Brac 1A 32
Charles St.
CR0: Croy 4B 200 (9N 45)
GU15: Camb 9A 50
KT16: Chert 7H 37
SL4: W'sor 4F 4
SW13 .... 5D 12
TW3: Houn 5N 9
Charleston Cl. TW13: Felt 4H 23
Charleston Ct. RH10: Craw 6F 182
Charlesworth Pl. SW13 .... 6D 12
Charleville Ct. *W14* *1L 13*
(off Charleville Rd.)
Charleville Mans. *W14* *1K 13*
(off Charleville Rd., not continuous)
Charleville M. TW7: Isle 7H 11
Charleville Rd. W14 .... 1K 13
Charlmont Rd. SW17 .... 7C 28
Charlock Cl. RH11: Craw 7M 181
Charlock Way GU1: Guil 9D 94
Charlotte Cl. GU9: Heath E 4J 109
KT21: Asht 5L 79
Charlotte Ct. GU1: Guil 5B 114
KT10: Esh 2C 58
RH11: Craw *3A 182*
(off Leopold Rd.)
Charlotte Gro. RH6: Smallf 7L 143
Charlotte Ho. *W6* *1H 13*
(off Queen Caroline St.)
Charlotte M. GU14: Farnb 9B 70
KT10: Esh *1B 58*
(off Heather Pl.)
Charlotte Rd. SM6: W'ton 3G 63
SW13 .... 4E 12
Charlottes Ct. *GU14: Farnb* *5A 90*
(off Camp Rd.)
Charlotte Sq. TW10: Rich 9M 11
Charlotte Ter. *KT10: Esh* *3C 58*
(off Princess Sq.)
CHARLOTTEVILLE 5B 114
CHARLTON 2D 38
Charlton Av. KT12: Hers 1J 57
Charlton Ct. GU47: Owls 6J 49
Charlton Dr. TN16: B Hil 4F 86
Charlton Gdns. CR5: Coul 5G 83
Charlton Ho. TW8: Brent 2L 11
Charlton Kings KT13: Weybr 9F 38
Charlton La. TW17: Shep 2D 38
(not continuous)
Charlton Rd. TW17: Shep 2D 38
CHARLWOOD
RH6 .... 3K 161
RH19 .... 8N 185
Charlwood CR0: Sels 5J 65
Charlwood Cl. KT23: Book 2B 98
RH10: Copt 6L 163
Charlwood Dr. KT22: Oxs 2D 78
Charlwood Ho. TW9: Kew 3A 12
Charlwood La. RH5: Newd 5F 160
RH6: Charlw 5F 160
Charlwood M. RH6: Charlw 3K 161
Charlwood Pl. RH2: Reig 3L 121
Charlwood Rd. RH6: Gatw 2A 162
RH11: Gatw, Low H 6N 161
RH11: Ifield 7K 161
SW15 .... 7J 13
Charlwoods Bus. Cen.
RH19: E Grin 7N 165
Charlwoods Pl.
RH19: E Grin 7A 166
Charlwoods Rd.
RH19: E Grin 6A 166
Charlwood Ter. SW15 .... 7J 13
Charlwood Wlk.
RH11: Craw 9N 161
Charman Rd. RH1: Red 3C 122
Charmans Cl. RH12: Hors 3A 198
Charm Cl. RH6: Horl 7C 142
Charminster Av. SW19 .... 1M 43
Charminster Ct. KT6: Surb 6K 41
Charminster Rd. KT4: W Pk 7J 43
Charmouth Ct. TW10: Rich 8M 11
Charnwood SL5: S'dale 5C 34
Charnwood Av. SW19 .... 1M 43
Charnwood Cl. KT3: N Mal 3D 42
Charnwood Rd. SE25 .... 4A 46
Charrington Rd.
CR0: Croy 2B 200 (8N 45)
Charrington Way
RH12: Broadb H 5C 196
Chart, The 9H 107
Charta Rd. TW20: Egh 6E 20
Chart Cl. CR0: Croy 5F 46
CR4: Mit 3D 44
RH5: Dork 7K 119
Chart Downs RH5: Dork 7J 119
Charter Ct. KT3: N Mal 2D 42
Charter Cres. TW4: Houn 7M 9
CHARTERHOUSE 4F 132
Charter Ho. *SM2: Sut* *3N 61*
(off Mulgrave Rd.)
Charterhouse GU7: Godal 5E 132
Charterhouse Cl.
RG12: Brac 4C 32
Charterhouse Club 4E 132
Charterhouse Rd.
GU7: Godal 4G 132
Charterhouse School Golf Course
.... 4D 132
Charter Pl. TW18: Stain 7J 21
Charter Quay KT1: K Tham 4H 203
Charter Rd. KT1: K Tham 2A 42
Charters SL5: S'hill 5B 34
Charters Cl. SL5: S'hill 4A 34
Charters Ct. SL5: S'hill 5A 34
Charters Gdn. Ho.
SL5: S'hill 5B 34
Charters Ho. *GU11: Alde* *2N 109*
(off Sebastopol Rd.)
Charters La. SL5: S'hill 4A 34
Charters Leisure Cen. 6A 34
Charter Sq. KT1: K Tham 1A 42
Charters Rd. SL5: S'dale 6A 34
Charters Way SL5: S'dale 6C 34
Charter Wlk. *GU27: Hasl* *2G 189*
(off West St.)
Chartfield Av. SW15 .... 8G 13
Chartfield Pl. KT13: Weybr 2C 56
Chartfield Rd. RH2: Reig 4A 122
Chartfield Sq. SW15 .... 8J 13
Chart Gdns. RH5: Dork 8J 119
Chartham Gro. SE27 .... 4M 29
Chartham Pk. Golf Course 4M 165
Chartham Rd. SE25 .... 2E 46
Chart Ho. CR4: Mit 1D 44
Chart Ho. Rd. GU12: Ash V 6E 90
Chart La. RH2: Reig 3N 121
RH4: Dork 2L 201 (5H 119)
Chart La. Sth.
RH5: Dork, Nth H 7J 119
Charts Cl. GU6: Cranl 8N 155
Chart Way RH12: Hors 6J 197
Chartway RH2: Reig 2N 121
Chartwell 9N 107
Chartwell GU9: Farnh 5E 128
GU16: Frim G 9C 70
GU22: Wok *5A 74*
(off Mt. Hermon Rd.)
Chartwell Cl. CR0: Croy 7A 46
Chartwell Ct. RH4: Dork 8H 119
Chartwell Dr. BR6: Farnb 2M 67
Chartwell Gdns. GU11: Alde 6A 90
SM3: Chea 1K 61
Chartwell Lodge
RH5: Nth H 9H 119
Chartwell Pl.
KT18: Eps 8M 201 (1D 80)
SM3: Chea 1K 61
Chartwood Pl. RH4: Dork 3J 201
Charwood SW16 .... 5L 29
Charwood Rd. RG40: W'ham 2D 30
Chase, The CR5: Coul 1G 83
GU2: Guil 4K 113
GU14: Farnb 8B 70
KT20: K'wood 9M 81
KT21: Asht 5J 79
KT22: Oxs 2C 78
KT24: E Hor 4G 96
RG45: Crowt 1F 48
RH2: Reig 4B 122
RH10: Craw 4E 182
SL5: Asc 8L 17
SM6: W'ton 2J 63
SW16 .... 8K 29
SW20 .... 9K 27
TW16: Sunb 9J 23
Chase Ct. SW20 .... 1K 43
TW7: Isle 5G 10
Chase End
KT19: Eps 5K 201 (8C 60)
Chasefield Cl. GU4: B'ham 9C 94
Chasefield Rd. SW17 .... 5D 28
Chase Gdns. RG42: Bin 6H 15
TW2: Whitt 1D 24
Chase La. GU27: Hasl 4H 189
Chaseley Ct. KT13: Weybr 7F 38
Chaseley Dr. CR2: Sande 6A 64
W4 .... 1A 12
Chasemore Cl. CR4: Mit 6D 44
Chasemore Gdns. CR0: Wad 2L 63
Chasemore Ho. *SW6* *3K 13*
(off Williams Cl.)
Chase Plain GU26: Hind 8A 170
Chase Rd. GU35: Lind 4A 168
KT19: Eps 5K 201 (8C 60)
Chase Side Av. SW20 .... 9K 27
Chaseside Gdns.
KT16: Chert 6K 37
Chasewater Ct. GU11: Alde 3M 109
Chatelet Cl. RH6: Horl 7F 142
Chatfield Cl. GU14: Farnb 3A 90
Chatfield Ct. CR3: Cate 9A 84
Chatfield Dr. GU4: Guil 1E 114
Chatfield Rd.
CR0: Croy 1A 200 (7M 45)
Chatfields RH11: Craw 5N 181
Chatham Cl. SM3: Sut 6L 43
Chatham Ho. *SM6: W'ton* *2F 62*
(off Melbourne Rd.)
Chatham M. GU2: Guil 9K 93
Chatham Rd.
KT1: K Tham 3M 203 (1N 41)
CHATHILL 6L 125
Chatley Heath Semaphore Tower
.... 4E 76
Chatsfield KT17: Ewe 6F 60
Chatsworth Av. GU27: Hasl 9G 170
SW20 .... 9K 27
Chatsworth Cl. W4 .... 2B 12
Chatsworth Ct. SW16 .... 2K 45
Chatsworth Cres.
TW3: Houn 7D 10
Chatsworth Gdns.
KT3: N Mal 4E 42
Chatsworth Gro.
GU9: Up Hale 6G 108
Chatsworth Hgts.
GU15: Camb 8E 50
Chatsworth Lodge *W4* *1C 12*
(off Bourne Pl.)
Chatsworth Pk. SM7: Ban 4N 81
Chatsworth Pl. CR4: Mit 2D 44
KT22: Oxs 9D 58
TW11: Tedd 5G 24
Chatsworth Rd.
CR0: Croy 6E 200 (1A 64)
GU14: Farnb 2C 90
SM3: Chea 2J 61
W4 .... 2B 12
Chatsworth Way SE27 .... 4M 29
CHATTERN HILL 5C 22
Chattern Hill TW15: Ashf 5C 22
Chattern Rd. TW15: Ashf 5D 22
Chatterton Ct. TW9: Kew 5M 11
Chatton Row GU24: Bis 4D 72
Chaucer Av. KT13: Weybr 4B 56
RH19: E Grin 1M 185
TW4: C'ford 5J 9
TW9: Rich 6N 11
Chaucer Cl. RG40: W'ham 2E 30
SL4: W'sor 6G 4
SM7: Ban 1K 81
Chaucer Ct.
GU2: Guil 7B 202 (5M 113)
RH1: Red 9E 102
SW17 .... *4B 28*
(off Lanesborough Way)
Chaucer Gdns. SM1: Sut 9M 43
Chaucer Grn. CR0: Croy 6E 46
Chaucer Gro. GU15: Camb 1B 70
Chaucer Ho. GU1: Guil 4B 114
SM1: Sut *9M 43*
(off Chaucer Gdns.)
Chaucer Mans. *W14* *2K 13*
(off Queen's Club Gdns.)
Chaucer Rd. GU14: Farnb 8L 69
RG45: Crowt 4G 48
RH10: Craw 1F 182
SM1: Sut 1M 61
TW15: Ashf 5N 21
Chaucer Way KT15: Addl 3J 55
SW19 .... 7B 28
Chavasse Way GU14: Cove 9J 69
Chave Cft. KT18: Tat C 6H 81
Chavecroft Ter. KT18: Tat C 6H 81

Frampton Rd.—Gander Grn. Cres.

Frampton Rd. TW4: Houn 8M 9
France Hill Dr.
GU15: Camb 1A 70
Frances Ct. SE25 .....2C 46
Frances Rd. SL4: W'sor 6F 4
Franche Ct. Rd. SW17 .....4A 28
Francis Av. TW13: Felt 4H 23
Francis Barber Cl. SW16 .....6K 29
Franciscan Rd. SW17 .....6D 28
Francis Chichester Cl.
SL5: Asc 3M 33
Francis Cl. KT19: Ewe 1C 60
TW17: Shep 3B 38
Francis Ct. GU2: Guil 1L 113
KT5: Surb 8K 203
Francis Crick Rd.
GU2: Guil 4G 113
Francis Edwards Way
RH11: Craw 7K 181
Francis Gdns. RG42: Warf 8B 16
Francis Gro. SW19 .....7L 27
Francis Ho. SW10 .....3N 13
(off Coleridge Gdns.)
Francis Rd. CR0: Croy 6M 45
CR3: Cate 9A 84
SM6: W'ton 3G 63
TW4: Houn 5L 9
Francis Way GU15: Camb 2G 70
Frank Beswick Ho. SW6 .....2L 13
(off Clem Attlee Ct.)
Franklands Dr. KT15: Addl 4H 55
Franklin Cl. KT1: K Tham 2N 41
SE27 .....4M 29
Franklin Ct. GU2: Guil 3J 113
(off Derby Rd.)
GU8: Worm 9C 152
GU14: Cove 1H 89
(off Whetstone Rd.)
Franklin Cres. CR4: Mit 3G 45
Franklin Rd. RH10: Craw 4G 183
Franklin Sq. W14 .....1L 13
Franklin Way CR0: Wad 6J 45
Franklyn Cres. SL4: W'sor 6A 4
Franklyn Rd. GU7: Godal 8E 132
KT12: Wal T 5H 39
Franks Av. KT3: N Mal 3B 42
Franksfield GU5: P'lake 4F 136
Frank Soskice Ho. SW6 .....2L 13
(off Clem Attlee Ct.)
Franks Rd. GU2: Guil 9K 93
Frank Towell Ct. TW14: Felt 1H 23
Frant Fld. TN8: Eden 2L 147
Frant Rd. CR7: T Hea 4M 45
Fraser Gdns. RH4: Dork 4G 118
Fraser Ho. TW8: Brent 1M 11
Fraser Mead GU47: Coll T 9K 49
Fraser Rd. RG42: Brac 9N 15
Fraser St. W4 .....1D 12
Fraser Wlk. RH17: Hand 9N 199
Fraynes Cft. GU51: Fleet 5A 88
Frederica Ct. SW2 .....2M 29
Frederick Cl. SM1: Sut 1L 61
Frederick Gdns. CR0: Croy 5M 45
SM1: Sut 2L 61
Frederick Rd. SM1: Sut 2L 61
Frederick Sanger Rd.
GU2: Guil 4G 113
Frederick St. GU11: Alde 2M 109
Fredley Pk. RH5: Mick 7J 99
Freeborn Way RG12: Brac 9C 16
Freedown La. SM2: Sut 9N 61
Freelands Av. CR2: Sels 5G 64
Freelands Rd. KT11: Cob 1J 77
Freeman Cl. TW17: Shep 3F 38
Freeman Ct. SW16 .....1J 45
Freeman Dr. KT8: W Mole 2N 39
Freeman Rd. RH12: Warnh 9F 178
SM4: Mord 4B 44
Freemantle Rd. GU19: Bag 3J 51
Freemasons Pl. CR0: Croy 7B 46
(off Freemasons Rd.)
Freemasons Rd. CR0: Croy 7B 46
Free Prae Rd. KT16: Chert 7J 37
Freesia Dr. GU24: Bis 3D 72
Freestone Yd. SL3: Coln 3F 6
Fremantle Way
GU24: B'wood 6A 72
French Apartments, The
CR8: Pur 8L 63
Frenchaye KT15: Addl 2L 55
Frenches, The RH1: Red 1E 122
Frenches Ct. RH1: Red 1E 122
Frenches Rd. RH1: Red 1E 122
French Gdns. GU17: Haw 2J 69
KT11: Cob 1K 77
Frenchlands Ga.
KT24: E Hor 5F 96
French La.
GU8: Bow G, Thur 6K 151
French St. TN16: Weste 6N 107
TW16: Sunb 1K 39
French's Wells GU21: Wok 4L 73
FRENSHAM 3H 149
Frensham RG12: Brac 5B 32
Frensham Av. GU51: Fleet 4D 88
Frensham Cl. GU46: Yate 9A 48
Frensham Common Country Pk.
.....4K 149
Frensham Ct. GU10: Wrec 7G 128
SW19 .....2B 44
Frensham Dr. CR0: N Add 4M 65
SW15 .....4E 26
FRENSHAM HEIGHTS 9F 128
Frensham Hgts. Rd.
GU10: Rowl 9F 128
Frensham La. GU10: Churt 7F 148
GU35: Churt, Head 1D 168
GU35: Head, Lind 3B 168
Frensham Pond Sailing Club
.....5H 149
Frensham Rd. CR8: Ken 1M 83
GU9: Farnh 3H 129
GU10: Fren, Lwr Bou 3H 129
RG45: Crowt 1G 49
Frensham Va.
GU10: Lwr Bou 7G 129
Frensham Way
KT17: Eps D 3H 81
Freshborough Ct. GU1: Guil 4B 114
Freshfield Bank
RH18: F Row 7G 187
Freshfield Cl. RH10: Craw 4E 182
Freshfield Flats
KT20: Lwr K 5L 101
Freshfields CR0: Croy 7J 47
Freshford St. SW18 .....4A 28
Freshmount Gdns.
KT19: Eps 7A 60
Freshwater Cl. SW17 .....7E 28
Freshwater Pde.
RH12: Hors 6H 197
(off Bishopric)
Freshwater Rd. SW17 .....7E 28
Freshwood Cl. BR3: Beck 1L 47
Freshwood Dr. GU46: Yate 2C 68
Freshwoods RH12: Rudg 9E 176
Freshwood Way SM6: W'ton 5F 62
Frewin Rd. SW18 .....2B 28
Friar M. SE27 .....4M 29
Friars Av. SW15 .....4E 26
Friars Ct. SM6: W'ton 1F 62
Friars Cft. GU4: Guil 9E 94
Friars Fld. GU9: Farnh 9G 108
Friar's Ga. GU2: Guil 5K 113
Friars Keep RG12: Brac 3N 31
Friars La. TW9: Rich 8K 11
Friars Orchard KT22: Fetc 8D 78
Friars Ri. GU22: Wok 5C 74
Friars Rd. GU25: V Wat 3N 35
Friars Rookery RH10: Craw 3D 182
Friars Stile Pl. TW10: Rich 9L 11
Friars Stile Rd. TW10: Rich 9L 11
Friars Way KT16: Chert 5J 37
Friars Wood CR0: Sels 5H 65
Friary, The
GU1: Guil 5B 202 (4M 113)
SL4: O Win 9M 5
Friary Bri.
GU1: Guil 6B 202 (5M 113)
Friary Ct. GU21: Wok 5J 73
FRIARY ISLAND 9M 5
Friary Island TW19: Wray 9M 5
Friary Pas.
GU1: Guil 6B 202 (5M 113)
Friary Rd. SL5: Asc 5L 33
TW19: Wray 1M 19
Friary St.
GU1: Guil 6B 202 (5N 113)
Friary Way RH10: Craw 4B 182
Friday Rd. CR4: Mit 8D 28
FRIDAYS HILL 9F 188
FRIDAY STREET 3N 137
Friday St. RH5: Ockl 6D 158
RH12: Rusp 4L 179
RH12: Warnh 1E 196
Friday St. Rd. RH5: A Com 3M 137
Friend Av. GU12: Alde 3B 110
Friends Cl. RH11: Craw 9B 162
Friendship Way RG12: Brac 2N 31
Friends Rd.
CR0: Croy 4D 200 (9A 46)
CR8: Pur 8M 63
Friends Wlk. TW18: Stain 6H 21
Friesian Cl. GU51: Fleet 1C 88
FRIMLEY 6A 70
Frimley Av. SM6: W'ton 2J 63
Frimley Bus. Pk. GU16: Frim 6A 70
Frimley By-Pass GU16: Frim 6A 70
Frimley Cl. CR0: N Add 4M 65
SW19 .....3K 27
Frimley Cres. CR0: N Add 4M 65
Frimley Gdns. CR4: Mit 2C 44
FRIMLEY GREEN 8D 70
Frimley Grn. Rd.
GU16: Frim, Frim G 5B 70
Frimley Gro. Gdns.
GU16: Frim 5B 70
Frimley Hall Dr.
GU15: Camb 9D 50
Frimley High St. GU16: Frim 6A 70
Frimley Lodge Pk. 9D 70
Frimley Lodge Pk.
GU16: Frim G 9D 70
FRIMLEY RIDGE 3F 70
Frimley Rd. GU12: Ash V 4E 90
GU15: Camb 1M 69
GU16: Camb, Frim 3N 69
KT9: Ches 2K 59
Frimley Station (Rail) 6A 70
Frinton Rd. SW17 .....7E 28
Friston St. SW6 .....5N 13
Friston Wlk. RH11: Craw 1M 181
Fritham Cl. KT3: N Mal 5D 42
FRITH END 6A 148
Frith End Rd. GU35: Slea 5A 148
FRITH HILL 5G 132
Frith Hill Rd. GU7: Godal 4G 133
GU16: Deep, Frim 5E 70
Frith Knowle KT12: Hers 2J 57
Frith Pk. RH19: E Grin 7A 166
Frith Rd.
CR0: Croy 3B 200 (8N 45)
Friths Dr. RH2: Reig 9N 101
Frithwald Rd. KT16: Chert 6H 37
Frobisher RG12: Brac 6A 32
Frobisher Cl. CR8: Ken 4N 83
Frobisher Ct. SM3: Chea 4K 61
Frobisher Cres.
TW19: Stan 1N 21
Frobisher Gdns. GU1: Guil 2C 114
TW19: Stan 1N 21
Frodsham Way GU47: Owls 5K 49
Froggetts La.
RH5: W'wood 9K 157
Frog Gro. La.
GU3: Wood V 1C 112
Frog Hall RG40: W'ham 3E 30
Froghall Dr. RG40: W'ham 2D 30
FROGHOLE 1M 127
Froghole La. TN8: C Hil 1M 127
Frog La. GU4: Sut G 3A 94
RG12: Brac 2M 31
FROGMORE
GU17 .....2H 69
SL4 .....5H 5
Frogmore SW18 .....8M 13
Frogmore Border SL4: W'sor 6H 5
Frogmore Cl. SM3: Chea 9J 43
Frogmore Ct. GU17: B'water 2H 69
UB2: S'hall 1N 9
Frogmore Dr. SL4: W'sor 4H 5
Frogmore Gdns. SM3: Chea 1K 61
Frogmore Gro.
GU17: B'water 2H 69
Frogmore House 5J 5
Frogmore Leisure Cen. 1F 68
Frogmore Pk. Dr.
GU17: B'water 2H 69
Frogmore Rd.
GU17: B'water 1G 69
Frome Cl. GU14: Cove 8J 69
Fromondes Rd. SM3: Chea 2K 61
Fromow Gdns. GU20: Windl 3A 52
Froxfield Down RG12: Brac 4D 32
Fruen Rd. TW14: Felt 1G 23
Fry Cl. RH11: Craw 8N 181
Fryday Gro. M. SW12 .....1G 29
(off Weir Rd.)
Fryern Wood CR3: Cate 2N 103
Frylands Ct. CR0: N Add 7M 65
Fry La. GU19: Bag 5H 51
Frymley Vw. SL4: W'sor 4A 4
Fry's Acre GU12: Ash V 1E 110
Fry's La. GU46: Yate 8D 48
Fryston Av. CR0: Croy 8D 46
CR5: Coul 1F 82
Fuchsia Way GU24: W End 9B 52
Fuel Farm Rd. RH6: Gatw 1C 162
Fugelmere Rd. GU51: Fleet 3D 88
Fugelmere Wlk. GU51: Fleet 3D 88
Fulbourn KT1: K Tham 4M 203
Fulbourne Cl. RH1: Red 1C 122
Fulbrook Av. KT15: N Haw 7J 55
Fulbrook La. GU8: Els 6G 130
Fulford Ho. KT19: Ewe 4C 60
Fulford Rd. CR3: Cate 8A 84
KT19: Ewe 4C 60
Fulfords Hill RH13: Itch 9A 196
Fulfords Rd. RH13: Itch 9B 196
FULHAM 5K 13
FULHAM BROADWAY 3M 13
Fulham B'way. SW6 .....3M 13
Fulham Broadway Shop. Cen.
SW6 .....3M 13
Fulham Broadway Station
(Underground) 3M 13
Fulham Cl. RH11: Craw 7N 181
Fulham Ct. SW6 .....4M 13
Fulham FC 4J 13
Fulham High St. SW6 .....5K 13
Fulham Island SW6 .....3M 13
(off Fulham Rd.)
Fulham Palace 5K 13
Fulham Pal. Rd. SW6 .....1H 13
W6 .....1H 13
Fulham Pk. Gdns. SW6 .....5L 13
Fulham Pk. Rd. SW6 .....5L 13
Fulham Pools
Virgin Active 2K 13
Fulham Rd. SW6 .....3N 13
(Fulham B'way.)
SW6 .....5K 13
(Fulham High St.)
SW10 .....3N 13
Fullbrooks Av. KT4: W Pk 7E 42
Fullbrook School Sports Cen.
.....8J 55
Fullers Av. KT6: Surb 8M 41
Fullers Farm Rd.
KT24: W Hors 2B 116
Fuller's Griffin Brewery &
Visitors Cen. 2E 12
Fullers Hill TN16: Weste 4M 107
Fullers Rd. GU10: Rowl 7C 128
Fullers Va.
GU35: Head, Head D 4E 168
Fullers Way Nth.
KT6: Surb 9M 41
Fullers Way Sth. KT9: Ches 1L 59
Fuller's Wood CR0: Croy 2K 65
Fullers Wood La.
RH1: Sth N 4G 123
Fullerton Cl. KT14: Byf 1A 76
Fullerton Ct. TW11: Tedd 7G 25
Fullerton Dr. KT14: Byf 1N 75
Fullerton Rd. CR0: Croy 6C 46
KT14: Byf 1N 75
SM5: Cars 5C 62
SW18 .....8N 13
Fullerton Way KT14: Byf 1N 75
Fuller Way UB3: Harl 1G 8
Fullmer Way KT15: Wood 6H 55
Fulmar Cl. KT5: Surb 5M 41
RH11: Ifield 4J 181
Fulmar Cres. RG12: Brac 4J 31
Fulmar Dr. RH19: E Grin 7C 166
Fulmead St. SW6 .....4N 13
Fulmer Cl. TW12: Hamp 6M 23
Fulstone Cl. TW4: Houn 7N 9
Fulvens GU5: P'lake 2F 136
FULWELL 5D 24
Fulwell Golf Course 5D 24
Fulwell Pk. Av. TW2: Twick 3B 24
Fulwell Rd. TW11: Tedd 5D 24
Fulwell Station (Rail) 5D 24
Fulwood Gdns. TW1: Twick 9F 10
Fulwood Wlk. SW19 .....2K 27
Funky Footprints Nature Reserve
.....5B 38
Furlong Cl. SM6: W'ton 7F 44
Furlong Rd. RH4: Westc 6C 118
Furlongs, The KT10: Esh 9B 40
Furlong Way RH6: Gatw 2D 162
Furlough, The GU22: Wok 3C 74
Furmage St. SW18 .....1N 27
Furnace Dr. RH10: Craw 5D 182
Furnace Farm Rd.
RH10: Craw 5E 182
RH19: Felb 7E 164
FURNACE GREEN 5E 182
Furnace La. TN8: Cow 5K 167
Furnace Pde. RH10: Craw 5E 182
Furnace Pl. RH10: Craw 5E 182
FURNACE WOOD 6F 164
Furneaux Av. SE27 .....6M 29
Furness SL4: W'sor 5A 4
Furness Pl. SL4: W'sor 5A 4
(off Furness)
Furness Rd. SM4: Mord 5N 43
SW6 .....5N 13
Furness Row SL4: W'sor 5A 4
Furniss Ct. GU6: Cranl 8H 155
Furnival Cl. GU25: V Wat 5N 35
Furrows, The KT12: Wal T 8K 39
Furrows Pl. CR3: Cate 1C 104
Furse Cl. GU15: Camb 2G 70
Furtherfield GU6: Cranl 6N 155
Furtherfield Cl. CR0: Croy 5L 45
Further Vell-Mead
GU52: Chu C 9A 88
Furzebank SL5: S'hill 3A 34
Furze Cl. GU12: Ash V 5E 90
RH1: Red 2D 122
RH6: Horl 8H 143
FURZEDOWN 6F 28
Furzedown Cl. TW20: Egh 7A 20
Furzedown Dr. SW17 .....6F 28
Furzedown Recreation Cen. 6F 28
Furzedown Rd. SM2: Sut 7A 62
SW17 .....6F 28
Furze Fld. KT22: Oxs 9D 58
Furzefield RH11: Craw 2N 181
Furzefield Chase
RH19: D Pk 4A 166
Furzefield Cres. RH2: Reig 5A 122
Furzefield Rd. RH2: Reig 5A 122
RH12: Hors 3A 198
RH19: E Grin 6N 165
Furze Gro. KT20: K'wood 8L 81
Furze Hall KT20: K'wood 8L 81
FURZE HILL 8L 81
Furze Hill CR8: Pur 7J 63
GU10: Run 9B 110
KT20: K'wood 7L 81
RH1: Red 2C 122
Furzehill Cotts. GU24: Pirb 9N 71
Furzehill Cres. RG45: Crowt 3H 49
Furze Hill Rd.
GU35: Head D 5G 168
Furze La. CR8: Pur 7J 63
GU7: Godal 3J 133
RH19: E Grin 6L 165
Furzemoors RG12: Brac 4N 31
Furzen La. RH5: W'wood 6H 177
RH12: Rudg, W'wood 6H 177
Furze Pl. RH1: Red 2D 122
Furze Rd. CR7: T Hea 2N 45
KT15: Addl 3H 55
RH12: Rudg 9E 176
Furze Va. Rd.
GU35: Head D 5G 169
Furzewood TW16: Sunb 9H 23
Fusiliers Way TW4: Houn 6K 9
Fusion RH1: Red 2D 122
Fuzzens Wlk. SL4: W'sor 5B 4
Fydler's Cl. SL4: Wink 7M 17
Fyfield Cl. BR2: Brom 3N 47
GU17: B'water 1J 69
KT17: Eps 8M 201 (1E 80)

G

Gable Ct. RH1: Red 2E 122
(off St Anne's Mt.)
Gable End GU14: Farnb 1N 89
Gables, The GU2: Guil 9L 93
GU26: G'hott 6B 170
KT13: Weybr 2D 56
KT22: Oxs 8C 58
Gables, The RH6: Horl 9E 142
RH10: Copt 7M 163
RH12: Hors 4K 197
SM7: Ban 4L 81
Gables Av. TW15: Ashf 6A 22
Gables Cl. GU12: Ash V 8E 90
GU14: Cove 1M 89
GU22: Wok 7B 74
SL3: Dat 2K 5
Gables Ct. CR8: Pur 8M 63
GU22: Wok 7B 74
Gables Rd. GU52: Chu C 9A 88
Gables Way SM7: Ban 4L 81
Gabriel Cl. TW13: Hanw 5M 23
Gabriel Dr. GU15: Camb 2F 70
Gabriel Rd. RH10: Craw 7G 183
Gabriel's M. BR3: Beck 1G 46
Gadbridge La. GU6: Ewh 6F 156
Gadbrook Rd. RH3: Betch 9B 120
Gadd Cl. RG40: W'ham 1E 30
Gadesden Rd. KT19: Ewe 3B 60
Gaffney Cl. GU11: Alde 6B 90
Gage Cl. RH10: Craw D 9F 164
Gage M.
CR2: S Croy 8A 200 (2M 63)
Gage Ridge RH18: F Row 7G 187
Gaggle Wood
RH13: Mann H 9B 198
Gainsborough RG12: Brac 5A 32
Gainsborough Cl.
GU14: Farnb 3B 90
GU15: Camb 8D 50
KT10: Esh 7E 40
Gainsborough Ct.
GU51: Fleet 4B 88
KT12: Wal T 1H 57
KT19: Ewe 3E 60
W4 .....1A 12
(off Chaseley Dr.)
Gainsborough Dr.
CR2: Sande 9D 64
SL5: Asc 2H 33
Gainsborough Gdns.
TW7: Isle 8D 10
Gainsborough Mans. W14 .....2K 13
(off Queen's Club Gdns.)
Gainsborough Pl.
KT11: Cob 2M 77
Gainsborough Rd.
KT3: N Mal 5C 42
KT19: Eps 6B 60
RH10: Craw 7D 182
TW9: Rich 5M 11
Gainsborough Ter. SM2: Sut 4L 61
(off Belmont Ri.)
Gainsford Pl. RH7: Crow 7M 125
Gaist Av. CR3: Cate 9E 84
Gala Bingo
Aldershot 2M 109
Feltham 3J 23
Hounslow 7A 10
Tooting 6C 28
Woking 4B 74
(within The Big Apple)
Gala Ct. CR7: T Hea 4L 45
Galahad Rd. RH11: Ifield 3K 181
Galata Rd. SW13 .....3F 12
Galba Ct. TW8: Brent 3K 11
Gale Cl. CR4: Mit 2B 44
TW12: Hamp 7M 23
Gale Cres. SM7: Ban 4M 81
Gale Dr. GU18: Ligh 6L 51
Galena Arches W6 .....1G 13
(off Galena Rd.)
Galena Rd. W6 .....1G 13
Galen Cl. KT19: Eps 7N 59
Gales Cl. GU4: Guil 9F 94
GU27: Hasl 3C 188
Gales Dr. RH10: Craw 3D 182
Gales Pl. RH10: Craw 3D 182
Galgate Cl. SW19 .....2J 27
Galileo Ct. RG12: Brac 1C 32
Galleries, The
GU11: Alde 2M 109
(off High St.)
Gallery Ct. SW10 .....2N 13
(off Gunter Gro.)
Galleymead Rd. SL3: Poy 4H 7
Gallica Ct. SM1: Sut 7N 43
Gallop, The CR2: Sels 4E 64
GU46: Yate 8C 48
SL4: W'sor 1F 18
SM2: Sut 5B 62
Gallops, The KT10: Esh 9B 40
Galloway Cl. GU51: Fleet 1D 88
Galloway Path
CR0: Croy 7D 200 (1A 64)
Gallwey Rd. GU11: Alde 1N 109
Gally Hill Rd. GU52: Chu C 8A 88
Gallys Rd. SL4: W'sor 5A 4
Galpins Rd. CR7: T Hea 4J 45
Galsworthy Rd.
KT2: K Tham 8A 26
KT16: Chert 6J 37
Galton Rd. SL5: S'dale 5C 34
Galvani Way CR0: Wad 7K 45
Galveston Rd. SW15 .....8L 13
Galvins Cl. GU2: Guil 9K 93
Galway Rd. GU46: Yate 2B 68
Gambles La. GU23: Rip 2L 95
Gambole Rd. SW17 .....5C 28
Gamlen Rd. SW15 .....7J 13
Gamma Ct. CR0: Croy 1D 200
Gander Grn. Cres.
TW12: Hamp 9A 24

Gander Grn. La.—Glen, The

Gander Grn. La. SM1: Sut 9L 43
SM3: Chea 8K 43
Gangers Hill CR3: Wold 6H 105
RH9: Gods 6H 105
Ganghill GU1: Guil 1C 114
Ganymede Ct. RH11: Craw 6K 181
Gapemouth Rd. GU24: Pirb 9H 71
Gap Rd. SW19 .....6M 27
Garbetts Way GU10: Tong 6C 110
Garbrand Wlk. KT17: Ewe 5E 60
Garden Av. CR4: Mit 8F 28
Garden Cl. GU5: Sha G 7F 134
GU14: Cove 2K 89
KT3: N Mal 3D 42
KT15: Addl 1M 55
KT22: Leat 2J 99
RH19: E Grin 2B 186
SM6: W'ton 2J 63
SM7: Ban 2M 81
SW15 .....1H 27
TW12: Hamp 6N 23
TW15: Ashf 7D 22
Garden Ct. CR0: Croy 8C 46
TW9: Kew 4M 11
TW12: Hamp 6N 23
Gardener Gro. TW13: Hanw 3N 23
Gardeners Cl.
RH12: Warnh 9E 178
Gardeners Ct. RH13: Hors 7K 197
GARDENERS GREEN 6E 30
Gardeners Grn.
RH12: Rusp 3B 180
Gardener's Hill Rd.
GU10: Fren, Lwr Bou, Wrec
.....6G 128
Gardeners Rd.
CR0: Croy 1A 200 (7M 45)
RG42: Wink R 7F 16
Gardener's Wlk. KT23: Book 4B 98
Gardenfields KT20: Tad 6K 81
Garden Ho. La.
RH19: E Grin 2B 186
Garden Houses, The *W6* *2J 13*
(off Bothwell St.)
Gardenia Dr. GU24: W End 9C 52
Garden La. SW2 .....2K 29
Garden Pl. RH12: Hors 4J 197
Garden Rd. KT12: Wal T 5J 39
SE20 .....1F 46
TW9: Rich 6N 11
Garden Royal SW15 .....9J 13
Gardens, The BR3: Beck 1M 47
GU10: Tong 5D 110
GU24: Pirb 9C 72
KT10: Esh 1A 58
KT11: Cob 6D 76
TW14: Felt 8E 8
Garden Wlk. BR3: Beck 1J 47
CR5: Coul 1F 102
RH11: Craw 3A 182
RH12: Hors 4J 197
Garden Wood Rd.
RH19: E Grin 9L 165
Gardiner Ct. CR2: S Croy 3A 64
Gardner Ho. TW13: Hanw 3N 23
Gardner La. RH10: Craw D 1D 184
Gardner Pl. TW14: Felt 9J 9
Gardner Rd.
GU1: Guil 2C 202 (3N 113)
Garendon Gdns. SM4: Mord 6N 43
Garendon Rd. SM4: Mord 6N 43
Gareth Cl. KT4: W Pk 8J 43
Gareth Ct. SW16 .....4H 29
Garfield Pl. SL4: W'sor 5G 4
Garfield Rd. GU15: Camb 1A 70
KT15: Addl 2L 55
SW19 .....6A 28
TW1: Twick 2G 25
Garibaldi Rd. RH1: Red 4D 122
Garland Ct. *RH19: E Grin* *9N 165*
(off Garland Rd.)
Garland Dr. TW3: Houn 5C 10
Garland Ho. KT2: K Tham 2J 203
Garland Rd. RH19: E Grin 8N 165
Garlands Ct. CR0: Croy 6E 200
TN8: Eden *1L 147*
(off Minstrels Cl.)
Garlands Rd. KT22: Leat 8H 79
RH1: Red 4D 122
Garland Way CR3: Cate 9A 84
Garlichill Rd. KT18: Tat C 4G 81
Garner Ct. *TW19: Stan* *9M 7*
(off Douglas Rd.)
Garnet Rd. CR7: T Hea 3N 45
Garrad's Rd. SW16 .....4H 29
Garrard Rd. SM7: Ban 3M 81
Garratt Cl. CR0: Bedd 1J 63
Garratt Ct. SW18 .....1N 27
Garratt La. SW17 .....4A 28
SW18 .....9N 13
Garratts La. SM7: Ban 3L 81
Garratt Ter. SW17 .....5C 28
Garraway Ct. *SW13* *3H 13*
(off Wyatt Dr.)
Garrett Cl. RH10: Craw 5G 183
Garrett M. GU11: Alde 3M 109
Garrick Cl. KT12: Hers 1J 57
TW9: Rich 8K 11
TW18: Stain 8J 21
Garrick Cres.
CR0: Croy 3F 200 (8B 46)
Garrick Gdns. KT8: W Mole 2A 40
Garrick Ho. KT1: K Tham 8J 203
W4 .....2D 12
Garrick Rd. TW9: Rich 5N 11
Garricks Ho. KT1: K Tham 4H 203
Garrick Wlk. RH10: Craw 6C 182
Garrick Way GU16: Frim G 7C 70
Garrison Cl. TW4: Houn 8N 9
Garrison La. KT9: Ches 4K 59
Garrison Sports Cen.
Aldershot 7A 90
Garrones, The RH10: Craw 2H 183
Garsdale Ter. *W14* *1L 13*
(off Aisgill Av.)
Garside Cl. TW12: Hamp 7B 24
Garside Ct. TW11: H Wic 9J 25
Garson Cl. KT10: Esh 2N 57
Garson La. TW19: Wray 1N 19
Garson Rd. KT10: Esh 3N 57
Garson's La. RG42: Warf 2E 16
Garston Gdns. CR8: Ken 2A 84
Garston La. CR8: Ken 1A 84
Garstons, The KT23: Book 3A 98
Garswood RG12: Brac 5B 32
Garth, The GU12: Ash 3D 110
GU14: Farnb 1B 90
KT11: Cob 9M 57
TW12: H Hill 7B 24
Garth Cl. GU9: Farnh 4F 128
KT2: K Tham 6M 25
SM4: Mord 6J 43
Garth Ct. RH4: Dork 7H 119
W4 .....1C 12
Garth Hunt Cotts.
RG42: Brac 7N 15
Garth Rd. KT2: K Tham 6M 25
SM4: Mord 5H 43
W4 .....1C 12
Garth Rd. Ind. Centre, The
SM4: Mord 7J 43
Garthside TW10: Ham 6L 25
Garth Sq. RG42: Brac 8N 15
Gartmoor Gdns. SW19 .....2L 27
Garton Bank SM7: Ban 4M 81
Garton Cl. RH11: Ifield 4K 181
Garton Pl. SW18 .....9N 13 & 1A 28
Gascoigne Rd. CR0: N Add 6M 65
KT13: Weybr 9C 38
Gasden Copse GU8: Wit 5A 152
Gasden Dr. GU8: Wit 4A 152
Gasden La. GU8: Wit 4A 152
Gaskarth Rd. SW12 .....1F 28
Gaskyns Cl. RH12: Rudg 1E 194
Gassiot Rd. SW17 .....5D 28
Gassiot Way SM1: Sut 9B 44
Gasson Wood Rd.
RH11: Craw 5K 181
Gastein Rd. W6 .....2J 13
Gaston Bell Cl. TW9: Rich 6M 11
Gaston Bri. Rd. TW17: Shep 5E 38
Gaston Rd. CR4: Mit 2E 44
Gaston Way TW17: Shep 4E 38
Gatcombe Cres. SL5: Asc 9K 17
Gate Centre, The
TW8: Brent 3G 11
Gateford Dr. RH12: Hors 2M 197
Gatehouse Cl. KT2: K Tham 8B 26
SL4: W'sor 7E 4
Gates, The GU51: Fleet 1D 88
Gates Cl. RH10: Craw 7G 182
Gatesden Cl. KT22: Fetc 1C 98
Gatesden Rd. KT22: Fetc 9C 78
Gates Grn. Rd. BR2: Kes 1B 66
BR4: W Wick 1B 66
Gateside Rd. SW17 .....4D 28
Gate St. GU5: Braml 1C 154
(not continuous)
Gateway KT13: Weybr 9C 38
Gateway, The GU21: Wok 1D 74
Gateway Bus. Pk. CR5: Coul 2H 83
Gateways GU1: Guil 3C 114
KT6: Surb 8K 203
Gateways, The *TW9: Rich* *7K 11*
(off Park La.)
Gateways Ct. SM6: W'ton 2F 62
Gatfield Gro. TW13: Hanw 3A 24
Gatfield Ho. TW13: Hanw 3N 23
Gatley Av. KT19: Ewe 2A 60
Gatley Dr. GU4: B'ham 9B 94
GATTON 6D 102
GATTON BOTTOM 4F 102
Gatton Bottom RH1: Mers 7A 102
RH2: Reig 7A 102
Gatton Cl. RH2: Reig 9A 102
SM2: Sut 5N 61
Gatton Manor Golf Course 8N 157
Gatton Pk. Bus. Cen.
RH1: Mers 7F 102
Gatton Pk. Ct. RH1: Red 8D 102
Gatton Pk. Rd. RH1: Red 1B 122
RH2: Reig 1B 122
Gatton Rd. RH2: Reig 1A 122
SW17 .....5C 28
GATWICK 5K 131
GATWICK AIRPORT
North Terminal 2C 162
South Terminal 3E 162
Gatwick Airport Beehive Area
RH6: Craw 5E 162
Gatwick Airport Station (Rail)
.....3F 162
Gatwick Aviation Mus. 4L 161
Gatwick Bus. Pk.
RH6: Craw 6F 162
RH6: Hookw 9A 142
Gatwick Ga. RH11: Low H 5C 162
Gatwick Ga. Ind. Est.
RH11: Low H 5C 162
(not continuous)
Gatwick Intl. Distribution Cen.
RH10: Craw 6F 162
Gatwick Metro Cen.
RH6: Horl 8F 142
Gatwick Rd. RH6: Craw 5E 162
RH10: Craw 9E 162
SW18 .....1L 27
Gatwick Rd. Rdbt.
RH6: Craw 5E 162
Gatwick Way RH6: Gatw 2D 162
Gauntlett Rd. SM1: Sut 2B 62
Gavell Rd. KT11: Cob 9H 57
Gaveston Cl. KT14: Byf 9A 56
Gaveston Rd. KT22: Leat 7G 78
Gavina Cl. SM4: Mord 4C 44
Gawton Cres. CR5: Coul 9G 83
Gayfere Pl. *SE25* *1B 46*
(off Grange Hill)
Gayfere Rd. KT17: Ewe 2F 60
Gayhouse La. RH1: Out 3A 144
Gayler Cl. RH1: Blet 2C 124
Gaynesford Rd. SM5: Cars 4D 62
Gay St. SW15 .....6J 13
Gayton Cl. KT21: Asht 5L 79
Gayton Ct. RH2: Reig 2M 121
Gayville Rd. SW11 .....1D 28
Gaywood Cl. SW2 .....2K 29
Gaywood Rd. KT21: Asht 5M 79
Gearing Cl. SW17 .....5E 28
Geary Cl. RH6: Smallf 1M 163
Geffers Ride SL5: Asc 2J 33
Gemini Cl. RH11: Craw 5K 181
Gemini Gdns.
RG40: W'ham 1E 30
Gemini Pl. TW15: Ashf 7F 22
Gemmell Cl. CR8: Pur 1K 83
Genesis Bus. Cen.
RH13: Hors 5M 197
Genesis Bus. Pk.
GU21: Wok 2E 74
Genesis Cl. TW19: Stan 2A 22
Geneva Cl. TW17: Shep 1F 38
Geneva Rd. CR7: T Hea 4N 45
KT1: K Tham 8K 203 (3L 41)
Genoa Av. SW15 .....8H 13
Genoa Rd. SE20 .....1F 46
Gentles La. GU30: Pass 8F 168
GU35: Head 6F 168
Genyn Rd.
GU2: Guil 5A 202 (4L 113)
George Ct. *TW15: Ashf* *5A 22*
(off Church Rd.)
George Denyer Cl.
GU27: Hasl 1G 189
George Eliot Cl. GU8: Wit 5C 152
George Gdns. GU11: Alde 5A 110
GU51: Fleet 4C 88
George Groves Rd. SE20 .....1D 46
Georgeham Rd. GU47: Owls 5J 49
George Horley Pl.
RH5: Newd 1A 160
Georgelands GU23: Rip 8K 75
George Lindgren Ho. *SW6* *3L 13*
(off Clem Attlee Ct.)
George Pinion Ct.
RH12: Hors 5H 197
George Rd.
GU1: Guil 3C 202 (3N 113)
GU7: Godal 4H 133
GU8: Mil 9C 132
GU51: Fleet 4C 88
KT2: K Tham 8A 26
KT3: N Mal 3E 42
Georges Pl. KT10: Esh 1C 58
George Sq. SW19 .....2M 43
George's Rd. TN16: Tats 7F 86
George's Sq. *SW6* *2L 13*
(off North End Rd.)
Georges Ter. CR3: Cate 9A 84
George St.
CR0: Croy 3C 200 (8N 45)
GU24: B'wood 8L 71
TW3: Houn 5N 9
TW9: Rich 8K 11
TW18: Stain 5H 21
George Street Stop
(London Tramlink)
.....3C 200 (8N 45)
George Wyver Cl. SW19 .....1K 27
Georgian Cl. GU15: Camb 8C 50
RH10: Craw 4H 183
TW18: Stain 5K 21
Georgian Ct. CR0: Croy 1E 200
SW16 .....5J 29
Georgia Rd. CR7: T Hea 9M 29
KT3: N Mal 3B 42
Georgina Ct. GU51: Fleet 4B 88
Gerald Ct. RH13: Hors 6L 197
Geraldine Rd. W4 .....2N 11
Gerald's Gro. SM7: Ban 1J 81
Geranium Cl. RG45: Crowt 8G 30
Gerard Av. TW4: Houn 1A 24
Gerardes Lodge
GU27: Hasl 9H 171
Gerard Rd. SW13 .....4E 12
Germander Dr. GU24: Bis 2D 72
Gernigan Ho. SW18 .....1B 28
Gerrards Mead SM7: Ban 3L 81
Gervis Ct. TW7: Isle 3C 10
Ghyll Cres. RH13: Hors 8M 197
Giant Arches Rd. SE24 .....1N 29
Gibbet La. GU15: Camb 7E 50
Gibbins La. RG42: Warf 6B 16
Gibbon Rd.
KT2: K Tham 1K 203 (9L 25)
Gibbons Cl. GU47: Sandh 7H 49
RH10: Craw 6G 183
Gibbon Wlk. SW15 .....7F 12
Gibb's Acre GU24: Pirb 1C 92
Gibbs Brook La. RH8: Oxt 5N 125
Gibbs Grn. W14 .....1L 13
(not continuous)
Gibbs Way GU46: Yate 2A 68
Giblets La. RH12: Hors 1M 197
Giblets Way RH12: Hors 1L 197
Gibraltar Cres. KT19: Ewe 6D 60
Gibson Cl. KT9: Ches 2J 59
TW7: Isle 6E 10
Gibson Ct. KT10: Hinc W 8F 40
SL3: Lang 1B 6
Gibson Dr. RG12: Brac 2B 32
Gibson Ho. SM1: Sut 1M 61
Gibson M. TW1: Twick 9J 11
Gibson Pl. RH10: Craw 1C 182
TW19: Stan 9L 7
Gibson Rd. SM1: Sut 2N 61
Gibsons Hill SW16 .....8L 29
(not continuous)
Gidd Hill CR5: Coul 3E 82
Giffard Dr.
GU14: Cove, Farnb 9L 69
Giffards Cl. RH19: E Grin 9B 166
Giffards Mdw. GU9: Farnh 2K 129
Giffard Way GU2: Guil 9K 93
GIGGSHILL 6G 40
Giggs Hill Gdns. KT7: T Dit 7G 40
Giggs Hill Rd. KT7: T Dit 6G 40
Gilbert Cl. *SW19* *9N 27*
(off High Path)
Gilbert Ho. *SW13* *3G 13*
(off Trinity Chu. Rd.)
Gilbert Rd. GU16: Camb 5A 70
SW19 .....8A 28
Gilbert Scott Bldg. SW15 .....9K 13
Gilberts Lodge KT17: Eps 8D 60
Gilbert St. TW3: Houn 6C 10
Gilbert Way CR0: Wad 8K 45
SL3: Lang 1B 6
Gilbey Rd. SW17 .....5C 28
Gilders Rd. KT9: Ches 4M 59
Gilesmead KT18: Eps 8L 201
Giles Travers Cl.
TW20: Thor 2E 36
Gilham La. RH18: F Row 7G 187
Gilhams Av. SM7: Ban 8J 61
Gill Av. GU2: Guil 4H 113
Gillespie Ho. *GU25: V Wat* *3A 36*
(off Holloway Dr.)
Gillett Ct. RH13: Hors 4A 198
GILLETTE CORNER 3G 11
Gillett Rd. CR7: T Hea 3A 46
Gillham's La. GU27: Hasl 4A 188
Gilliam Gro. CR8: Pur 6L 63
Gillian Av. GU12: Alde 4A 110
Gillian Cl. GU12: Alde 4B 110
Gillian Pk. Rd. SM3: Sut 7L 43
Gilliat Dr. GU4: Guil 1F 114
Gilligan Cl. RH12: Hors 6H 197
Gillis Sq. SW15 .....9F 12
Gill Ri. RG42: Warf 7A 16
Gilmais KT23: Book 3C 98
Gilman Cres. SL4: W'sor 6A 4
Gilmore Cres. TW15: Ashf 6B 22
Gilpin Av. SW14 .....7C 12
Gilpin Cl. CR4: Mit 1C 44
Gilpin Cres. TW2: Whitt 1B 24
Gilpin Way UB3: Harl 3E 8
Gilsland Pl. CR7: T Hea 3A 46
Gilsland Rd. CR7: T Hea 3A 46
Gilstead Rd. SW6 .....5N 13
Gingers Cl. GU6: Cranl 8A 156
Ginhams Rd. RH11: Craw 3N 181
Gipsy La. RG12: Brac 1B 32
RG40: W'ham 3B 30
SW15 .....6G 12
Gipsy Rd. SE27 .....5N 29
Gipsy Rd. Gdns. SE27 .....5N 29
Girdlestoneites GU7: Godal 4F 132
Girdwood Rd. SW18 .....1K 27
Girling Way TW14: Felt 6H 9
Gironde Rd. SW6 .....3L 13
Girton Cl. GU47: Owls 6K 49
Girton Gdns. CR0: Croy 9K 47
Gisbourne Cl. SM6: Bedd 9H 45
GIVONS GROVE 4J 99
Givons Gro. KT22: Leat 3H 99
Givons Gro. Rdbt.
KT22: Leat 2H 99
Glade, The BR4: W Wick 9L 47
CR0: Croy 4G 46
CR5: Coul 6L 83
GU9: Heath E 5J 109
GU10: Bucks O 1A 148
GU16: Mytc 3E 90
KT14: W By 9G 54
KT17: Ewe 3F 60
KT20: K'wood 8M 81
KT22: Fetc 9A 78
RH10: Craw 5E 182
RH13: Hors 5N 197
SL5: S'hill 4N 33
SM2: Chea 5K 61
TW18: Stain 7K 21
Glade Cl. KT6: Surb 8K 41
Glade Gdns. CR0: Croy 6H 47
Glade M. GU1: Guil 4B 114
Glades, The KT6: Surb 6L 41
RH19: E Grin 9D 166
Gladeside CR0: Croy 5G 47
Gladeside Cl. KT9: Ches 4K 59
Gladeside Ct. CR6: Warl 7E 84
Glade Spur KT20: K'wood 8N 81
Gladiator Way GU14: Farnb 5M 89
Gladioli Cl. TW12: Hamp 7A 24
Gladsmuir Cl. KT12: Wal T 8K 39
Gladstone Av. TW2: Twick 2D 24
TW14: Felt 9H 9
Gladstone Gdns. TW3: Houn 4C 10
Gladstone Ho. CR4: Mit 1D 44
Gladstone Pl. KT8: E Mol 4E 40
Gladstone Rd. BR6: Farnb 2L 67
CR0: Croy 6A 46
KT1: K Tham 2N 41
KT6: Surb 8K 41
KT21: Asht 5K 79
RH12: Hors 5K 197
SW19 .....8M 27
Gladstone Ter. *SE27* *6N 29*
(off Bentons La.)
Gladwyn Rd. SW15 .....6J 13
Glamis Cl. GU16: Frim 7D 70
Glamorgan Cl. CR4: Mit 2J 45
Glamorgan Rd. KT1: H Wic 8J 25
Glanfield Rd. BR3: Beck 3J 47
GLANTY 5E 20
Glanty, The TW20: Egh 5D 20
Glanville Wlk. RH11: Craw 6M 181
Glanville Way KT19: Eps 8L 59
Glasbrook Av. TW2: Whitt 2N 23
Glasford St. SW17 .....7D 28
Glassonby Wlk.
GU15: Camb 1G 70
Glastonbury Rd. SM4: Mord 6M 43
Glayshers Hill
GU35: Head D 3F 168
Glazbury Rd. W14 .....1K 13
Glazebrook Rd. TW11: Tedd 8F 24
Glaziers La.
GU3: Flex, Norm 9M 91
Gleave Cl. RH19: E Grin 8C 166
Glebe, The GU6: Ewh 4F 156
GU17: Haw 2K 69
KT4: W Pk 7E 42
RH2: Leigh 1F 140
RH6: Horl 8D 142
RH10: Copt 7M 163
RH19: Felb 6K 165
SW16 .....5H 29
Glebe Av. CR4: Mit 1C 44
Glebe Cl. CR2: Sande 7C 64
GU11: Alde 5M 109
GU18: Ligh 6N 51
KT23: Book 4A 98
RH7: Ling 7N 145
RH10: Craw 2C 182
W4 .....1D 12
Glebe Cotts. GU4: W Cla 1K 115
TW13: Hanw *4A 24*
(off Twickenham Rd.)
Glebe Ct. CR4: Mit 2D 44
GU1: Guil 3B 114
GU51: Fleet 4A 88
Glebe Farm Bus. Pk.
BR2: Kes 5F 66
Glebe Gdns. KT3: N Mal 6D 42
KT14: Byf 1M 75
Glebe Hyrst CR2: Sande 8C 64
Glebeland Gdns.
TW17: Shep 5D 38
Glebeland Rd. GU15: Camb 2L 69
Glebelands KT8: W Mole 4B 40
KT10: Clay 5F 58
RH10: Craw D 2D 184
RH14: Loxw 4H 193
Glebelands Mdw. GU6: Alf 8H 175
Glebelands Rd.
RG40: W'ham 1B 30
TW14: Felt 2H 23
Glebe La. GU10: Rush 5A 150
RH5: A Com 3L 137
Glebe Path CR4: Mit 2D 44
Glebe Rd. CR6: Warl 4G 84
GU6: Cranl 7M 155
GU14: Cove 9L 69
GU35: Head 4D 168
KT21: Asht 5K 79
RH1: Mers 2F 102
RH4: Dork 3G 201 (5F 118)
SL4: O Win 8L 5
SM2: Chea 5K 61
SM5: Cars 3D 62
SW13 .....5F 12
TW18: Stain 6K 21
TW20: Egh 6E 20
Glebe Side TW1: Twick 9F 10
Glebe Sq. CR4: Mit 2D 44
Glebe St. W4 .....1D 12
Glebe Ter. W4 .....1D 12
Glebe Way BR4: W Wick 8M 47
CR2: Sande 7C 64
TW13: Hanw 4A 24
Glebewood RG12: Brac 4A 32
Gledhow Gdns. SW5 .....1N 13
Gledhow Wood
KT20: K'wood 8N 81
Gledstanes Rd. W14 .....1K 13
Gleeson Dr. BR6: Chels 2N 67
Gleeson M. KT15: Addl 1L 55
Glegg Pl. SW15 .....7J 13
Glen, The CR0: Croy 9G 47
GU9: Up Hale 6H 109
KT15: Addl 2H 55
RH1: Red 5D 122
SL5: S'hill 3A 34
UB2: S'hall 1N 9

Glen Albyn Rd.—Granard Av.

Glen Albyn Rd. SW19 ... 3J 27
Glenallan Ho. *W14* ... *1L 13*
(off North End Cres.)
Glenalmond Ho. TW15: Ashf ... 4N 21
Glena Mt. SM1: Sut ... 1A 62
Glen Av. TW15: Ashf ... 5B 22
Glenavon Cl. KT10: Clay ... 3G 58
Glenavon Ct. KT4: W Pk ... 8G 43
Glenavon Gdns. GU46: Yate ... 2C 68
Glenbuck Ct. KT6: Surb ... 5L 41
Glenbuck Rd. KT6: Surb ... 5K 41
Glenburnie Rd. SW17 ... 4D 28
Glencairn Rd. SW16 ... 9J 29
Glencar Ct. SE19 ... 7M 29
Glen Cl. GU26: Hind ... 3A 170
KT20: K'wood ... 1K 101
TW17: Shep ... 3B 38
Glencoe Cl. GU16: Frim ... 6E 70
Glencoe Rd. KT13: Weybr ... 9B 38
Glen Ct. GU21: Wok ... 6K 73
GU26: Hind ... 3A 170
KT14: Byf ... 7M 55
KT15: Addl ... 2H 55
TW18: Stain ... *8H 21*
(off Riverside Rd.)
Glendale Cl. GU21: Wok ... 5M 73
RH12: Hors ... 2N 197
Glendale Dr. GU4: B'ham ... 9E 94
SW19 ... 6L 27
Glendale M. BR3: Beck ... 1L 47
Glendale Ri. CR8: Ken ... 2M 83
Glendarvon St. SW15 ... 6J 13
Glendene Av. KT24: E Hor ... 4F 96
Glendon Ho. RH10: Craw ... 4B 182
Glendower Gdns. SW14 ... 6C 12
Glendower Rd. SW14 ... 6C 12
Glendyne Cl. RH19: E Grin ... 1C 186
Glendyne Way
RH19: E Grin ... 1C 186
Gleneagle M. SW16 ... 6H 29
Gleneagle Rd. SW16 ... 6H 29
Gleneagles Cl. TW19: Stan ... 9L 7
Gleneagles Ct. RH10: Craw ... 4B 182
Gleneagles Dr. GU14: Cove ... 2H 89
Gleneagles Ho. *RG12: Brac* ... *5K 31*
(off St Andrews)
Gleneldon M. SW16 ... 5J 29
Gleneldon Rd. SW16 ... 5J 29
Glenfield Cl. RH3: Brock ... 7A 120
Glenfield Cotts.
RH6: Charlw ... 3J 161
Glenfield Ho. RG12: Brac ... 3A 32
Glenfield Rd. RH3: Brock ... 6A 120
SM7: Ban ... 2N 81
SW12 ... 2G 29
TW15: Ashf ... 7C 22
Glen Gdns. CR0: Wad ... 9L 45
Glenhaven Dr. TW19: Stan M ... 8J 7
Glenheadon Cl. KT22: Leat ... 1K 99
Glenheadon Ri. KT22: Leat ... 1K 99
Glenhurst GU20: Windl ... 1L 51
Glenhurst Cl. GU17: Haw ... 2K 69
Glenhurst Ri. SE19 ... 8N 29
Glenhurst Rd. TW8: Brent ... 2J 11
Glen Innes GU47: Coll T ... 6L 49
Glenister Pk. Rd. SW16 ... 8H 29
Glen Lea GU26: Hind ... 8C 170
Glenlea Hollow GU26: Hind ... 9C 170
Glenlee GU22: Wok ... 6M 73
Glenmill TW12: Hamp ... 6N 23
Glenmore Cl. KT15: Addl ... 9K 37
Glenmount Rd. GU16: Mytc ... 3E 90
Glenn Av. CR8: Pur ... 7M 63
Glennie Rd. SE27 ... 4L 29
Glen Rd. GU26: G'hott ... 6B 170
GU26: Hind ... 3B 170
GU51: Fleet ... 5A 88
KT9: Ches ... 1M 59
Glen Rd. End SM6: W'ton ... 5F 62
Glenrosa St. SW6 ... 5N 13
Glenside Cl. CR8: Ken ... 2A 84
Glentanner Way SW17 ... 4B 28
Glentham Gdns. SW13 ... 2G 12
Glentham Rd. SW13 ... 2F 12
Glenthorne Av. CR0: Croy ... 7E 46
Glenthorne Cl. SM3: Sut ... 7M 43
Glenthorne Gdns. SM3: Sut ... 7M 43
Glenthorne Rd.
KT1: K Tham ... 7L 203 (3M 41)
Glenthorpe Av. SW15 ... 7F 12
Glenthorpe Rd. SM4: Mord ... 4J 43
Glenvern Ct. *TW7: Isle* ... *5G 11*
(off White Lodge Cl.)
Glenview Cl. RH10: Craw ... 1D 182
Glenville Gdns. GU26: Hind ... 5D 170
Glenville M. SW18 ... 1N 27
Glenville M. Ind. Est. SW18 ... 1M 27
Glenville Rd.
KT2: K Tham ... 1M 203 (9N 25)
Glen Vue RH19: E Grin ... 9A 166
Glen Wlk. TW7: Isle ... 8D 10
(not continuous)
Glenwood GU9: Up Hale ... 6H 109
RG12: Brac ... 3B 32
RH5: Dork ... 7J 119
Glenwood Ct. GU14: Farnb ... 1M 89
Glenwood Rd. KT17: Ewe ... 3F 60
TW3: Houn ... 6D 10
Glenwood Way CR0: Croy ... 5G 47
Gliddon Rd. W14 ... 1K 13
G Live
Guildford ... 4E 202 (4A 114)
Globe Farm La.
GU17: B'water ... 1G 68
Glorney Mead GU9: B Lea ... 6M 109
Glory Mead RH4: Dork ... 8H 119
Glossop Rd. CR2: Sande ... 5A 64
Gloster Cl. GU12: Ash V ... 8D 90
GU14: Farnb ... 1N 89
Gloster Ct. *GU21: Wok* ... *3B 74*
(off Walton Rd.)
Gloster Rd. GU22: Wok ... 7C 74
KT3: N Mal ... 3D 42
Gloucester *W14* ... *1L 13*
(off Kensington Village)
Gloucester Cl. GU16: Frim G ... 8C 70
KT7: T Dit ... 7G 40
RH19: E Grin ... 1C 186
Gloucester Ct. CR4: Mit ... 4J 45
RH1: Red ... *2D 122*
(off Gloucester Rd.)
TW9: Kew ... 3N 11
Gloucester Cres.
TW18: Stain ... 7M 21
Gloucester Dr. TW18: Stain ... 4E 20
Gloucester Gdns. GU19: Bag ... 4J 51
SM1: Sut ... 8N 43
Gloucester Ho. TW10: Rich ... 8N 11
Gloucester Pl. SL4: W'sor ... 5G 5
Gloucester Rd. CR0: Croy ... 7A 46
GU2: Guil ... 1J 113
GU11: Alde ... 5A 110
GU19: Bag ... 4J 51
KT1: K Tham ... 1N 41
RH1: Red ... 2D 122
RH10: Craw ... 7C 182
TW2: Twick ... 2C 24
TW4: Houn ... 7M 9
TW9: Kew ... 3N 11
TW11: Tedd ... 6E 24
TW12: Hamp ... 8B 24
TW13: Felt ... 2K 23
Gloucestershire Lea
RG42: Warf ... 8D 16
Gloucester Sq. GU21: Wok ... 4A 74
Gloucester Wlk. GU21: Wok ... 4A 74
Glovers Cl. TN16: B Hil ... 3D 86
Glovers Fld. GU27: Hasl ... 2D 188
Glover's Rd. RH2: Reig ... 4N 121
RH6: Charlw ... 3J 161
Glover's Wood ... 3G 161
Gloxinia Wlk. TW12: Hamp ... 7A 24
Glyn Cl. KT17: Ewe ... 5F 60
SE25 ... 1B 46
Glyn Ct. SW16 ... 4L 29
Glyndale Grange SM2: Sut ... 3N 61
Glynde Ho. RH10: Craw ... 1C 182
Glynde Pl. *RH12: Hors* ... *6J 197*
(off South St.)
Glyn Rd. KT4: W Pk ... 8J 43
Glynswood GU10: Wrec ... 7F 128
GU15: Camb ... 3D 70
Goals Soccer Cen.
Heathrow ... 1D 8
Isleworth ... 2F 10
Sutton ... 9J 43
Tolworth ... 8B 42
Wimbledon ... 2F 42
Go Ape
Alice Holt Forest ... 2B 148
Bracknell ... 7B 32
Goater's All. *SW6* ... *3L 13*
(off Dawes Rd.)
GOATERS HILL ... 9G 17
Goaters Rd. SL5: Asc ... 1G 33
Goat Ho. Bri. SE25 ... 2D 46
Goat Rd. CR4: Cars, Mit ... 6D 44
Goatsfield Rd. TN16: Tats ... 7E 86
Goat Wharf TW8: Brent ... 2L 11
GODALMING ... 7H 133
Godalming Av. SM6: W'ton ... 2J 63
Godalming Bus. Cen.
GU7: Godal ... 7J 133
Godalming Leisure Cen. ... 4K 133
Godalming Mus. ... 7G 133
Godalming Rd.
GU8: Hasc, Loxh ... 7A 154
Godalming Station (Rail) ... 7G 132
Goddard Cl. GU2: Guil ... 8K 93
RH10: Craw ... 6F 182
TW17: Shep ... 2A 38
Goddard Rd. BR3: Beck ... 3G 47
Goddard's ... 4L 137
Goddards Cl. GU14: Cove ... 7J 69
Goddards La.
GU15: Camb ... 3N 69
Goddard Way RG42: Brac ... 7B 16
Godfrey Av. TW2: Whitt ... 1D 24
Godfrey Cl. GU47: Coll T ... 7J 49
Godfrey Way TW4: Houn ... 1M 23
Godley Rd. KT14: Byf ... 1A 76
SW18 ... 2B 28
Godolphin Cl. SM2: Chea ... 7L 61
Godolphin Ct.
RH10: Craw ... 5B 182
Godolphin Ho. *SL4: Eton* ... *2G 4*
(off Common La.)
Godolphin Rd. KT13: Weybr ... 3E 56
Godric Cres. CR0: N Add ... 6N 65
Godson Rd. CR0: Wad ... 9L 45
GODSTONE ... 9F 104
Godstone By-Pass
RH9: Gods ... 7F 104
Godstone Farm & Playbarn
... 1F 124
Godstone Golf Course ... 8H 105
Godstone Grn. RH9: Gods ... 9E 104
Godstone Hill RH9: Gods ... 5E 104
GODSTONE INTERCHANGE ... 7F 104
Godstone Mt. CR8: Pur ... 8M 63
Godstone Rd. CR3: Cate ... 2D 104
CR3: Warl, Whyte ... 5C 84
CR8: Pur, Ken ... 8M 63
RH1: Blet ... 2A 124
RH7: Ling ... 6M 145
RH8: Oxt ... 9K 105
SM1: Sut ... 1A 62
TW1: Twick ... 9H 11
Godstone Station (Rail) ... 7H 125
Godstone Vineyards ... 6F 104
Godwin Cl. KT19: Ewe ... 3B 60
RG41: W'ham ... 4A 30
Godwin Way RH13: Hors ... 4M 197
Goepel Ct. RH10: Craw ... 2E 182
Goffs Cl. RH11: Craw ... 4A 182
Goffs La. RH11: Craw ... 3N 181
Goffs Park ... 4N 181
Goffs Pk. Rd. RH11: Craw ... 4A 182
Goffs Rd. TW15: Ashf ... 7E 22
Gogmore Farm Cl.
KT16: Chert ... 6H 37
Gogmore La. KT16: Chert ... 6J 37
Goidel Cl. SM6: Bedd ... 1H 63
Goldcliff Cl. SM4: Mord ... 6M 43
Goldcrest Cl. GU46: Yate ... 9A 48
RH6: Horl ... 7C 142
Goldcrest Rd. RG12: Brac ... 4J 31
Goldcrest Way CR0: N Add ... 5N 65
CR8: Pur ... 6H 63
Gold Cup La. SL5: Asc ... 9H 17
Golden Ct. TW7: Isle ... 5D 10
TW9: Rich ... 8K 11
Golden La. BR4: W Wick ... 9M 47
Golden Mile Ho. *TW8: Brent* ... *1L 11*
(off Clayponds La.)
Golden Orb Wood RG42: Bin ... 9J 15
Goldfinch Cl. GU11: Alde ... 4L 109
RH11: Craw ... 1B 182
RH12: Hors ... 1J 197
Goldfinch Cres. RG12: Brac ... 3J 31
Goldfinch Gdns. GU4: Guil ... 2F 114
Goldfinch Rd. CR2: Sels ... 6H 65
Goldfort Wlk. GU21: Knap ... 3H 73
Gold Hill GU10: Lwr Bou ... 5H 129
Golding Cl. KT9: Ches ... 3J 59
RH10: Craw ... 4G 182
Golding La. RH13: Mann H ... 9C 198
Goldings, The GU21: Wok ... 3J 73
Golding's Hill
RH13: Mann H ... 9C 198
Gold La. GU11: Alde ... 9C 90
GU12: Alde ... 9C 90
Goldney Rd. GU15: Camb ... 2F 70
Goldrings Rd. KT22: Oxs ... 9B 58
Golds Gym
Camberley ... 1A 70
Goldsmith Cl. TN16: B Hil ... 4G 87
Goldsmiths Cl. GU21: Wok ... 5M 73
Goldsmith Way RG45: Crowt ... 3G 48
Goldstone Farm Vw.
KT23: Book ... 5A 98
GOLDSWORTH ... 5N 73
Goldsworth Orchard
GU21: Wok ... 5K 73
GOLDSWORTH PARK ... 4K 73
Goldsworth Pk. Centre, The
GU21: Wok ... 4K 73
Goldsworth Pk. Trad. Est.
GU21: Wok ... 3K 73
Goldsworth Rd. GU21: Wok ... 5M 73
Goldsworth Rd. Ind. Est.
GU21: Wok ... 4N 73
Goldvale Ho. *GU21: Wok* ... *4A 74*
(off Church St. W.)
Gold Valley Lakes ... 9C 90
Goldwell Rd. CR7: T Hea ... 3K 45
Gole Rd. GU24: Pirb ... 8N 71
Golf Cl. CR7: T Hea ... 9L 29
GU22: Pyr ... 1G 75
Golf Club Cotts. SL5: S'dale ... 7F 34
Golf Club Dr. KT2: K Tham ... 8C 26
Golf Club Rd. GU22: Wok ... 7K 73
KT13: Weybr ... 5C 56
Golf Dr. GU15: Camb ... 2D 70
Golf Ho. Rd. RH8: Limp ... 7E 106
Golf Links Av. GU26: Hind ... 3N 169
Golf Rd. CR8: Ken ... 5A 84
Golf Side SM2: Chea ... 7K 61
TW2: Twick ... 4D 24
Golfside Cl. KT3: N Mal ... 1D 42
Gomer Gdns. TW11: Tedd ... 7G 24
Gomer Pl. TW11: Tedd ... 7G 24
Gomer Rd. GU19: Bag ... 5H 51
GOMSHALL ... 8E 116
Gomshall Av. SM6: W'ton ... 2J 63
Gomshall Gdns. CR8: Ken ... 2B 84
Gomshall La. GU5: Shere ... 8B 116
Gomshall Rd.
GU5: Gom, Shere ... 8C 116
SM2: Chea ... 6H 61
Gomshall Station (Rail) ... 8E 116
Gong Hill GU10: Fren ... 8J 129
Gong Hill Dr.
GU10: Fren, Lwr Bou ... 7J 129
Gonston Cl. SW19 ... 3K 27
Gonville Rd. CR7: T Hea ... 4K 45
Gonville St. SW6 ... 6K 13
Gonville Works
RH6: Smallf ... 9M 143
Goodacre Cl. KT13: Weybr ... 2D 56
Goodchild Rd. RG40: W'ham ... 2C 30
Goodden Cres. GU14: Cove ... 2L 89
Goodenough Cl. CR5: Coul ... 7L 83
Goodenough Rd. SW19 ... 8L 27
Goodenough Way CR5: Coul ... 7K 83
Goodhart Ho. SM7: Ban ... 5A 82
Goodhart Way BR4: W Wick ... 6N 47
Goodhew Rd. CR0: Croy ... 5D 46
Gooding Cl. KT3: N Mal ... 3B 42
Goodings Grn.
RG40: W'ham ... 2E 30
GOODLEY STOCK ... 8K 107
Goodley Stock Rd.
TN8: C Hil ... 9K 107
TN16: Weste ... 9K 107
Goodman Cres. CR0: Croy ... 5M 45
SW2 ... 3J 29
Goodman Pl. TW18: Stain ... 5H 21
Goodson Ho. *SM4: Mord* ... *6A 44*
(off Green La.)
Goodways Dr. RG12: Brac ... 1A 32
Goodwin Cl. CR4: Mit ... 2B 44
RH11: Craw ... 6L 181
TN8: Eden ... 1K 147
Goodwin Ct. SW19 ... 8C 28
Goodwin Gdns. CR0: Wad ... 3M 63
Goodwin Rd.
CR0: Wad ... 8A 200 (2M 63)
Goodwins Cl. RH19: E Grin ... 7N 165
Goodwood Cl. GU15: Camb ... 7A 50
RH10: Craw ... 6E 182
SM4: Mord ... 3M 43
Goodwood Ho. *SL4: W'sor* ... *4C 4*
(off Paddock Cl.)
Goodwood Pde. BR3: Beck ... 3H 47
Goodwood Pl. GU14: Farnb ... 2C 90
Goodwood Rd. RH1: Red ... 1D 122
Goodworth Rd. RH1: Red ... 1F 122
Goodwyns Pl. RH4: Dork ... 7H 119
Goodwyns Rd. RH4: Dork ... 8J 119
Goose Cnr. RG42: Warf ... 6D 16
GOOSE GREEN ... 2E 196
Goose Grn. GU5: Gom ... 8D 116
KT11: Down ... 6H 77
Goosegreen Cl.
RH12: Hors ... 3K 197
Goose La. GU22: Wok ... 9L 73
Goosens Cl. SM1: Sut ... 2A 62
Goosepool KT16: Chert ... 6H 37
Goose Rye Rd. GU3: Worp ... 4G 93
Gordon Av. CR2: Sande ... 6N 63
GU15: Camb ... 2N 69
GU52: Chu C ... 7C 88
SW14 ... 7D 12
TW1: Twick ... 8G 11
Gordon Cl. KT16: Chert ... 9G 37
TW18: Stain ... 6K 21
Gordon Ct. GU15: Camb ... 1A 70
RH1: Red ... *5D 122*
(off St John's Ter. Rd.)
Gordon Cres. CR0: Croy ... 7B 46
GU15: Camb ... 2A 70
Gordondale Rd. SW19 ... 3M 27
Gordon Dr. KT16: Chert ... 9G 37
TW17: Shep ... 6E 38
Gordon Rd. BR3: Beck ... 2J 47
CR3: Cate ... 8A 84
GU11: Alde ... 3M 109
GU14: Farnb ... 5B 90
(not continuous)
GU15: Camb ... 2A 70
KT2: K Tham ... 2L 203 (9M 25)
KT5: Surb ... 6M 41
KT10: Clay ... 4E 58
RG45: Crowt ... 4J 49
RH1: Red ... 9E 102
RH12: Hors ... 4K 197
SL4: W'sor ... 5C 4
SM5: Cars ... 3D 62
TW3: Houn ... 7C 10
TW9: Rich ... 5M 11
TW15: Ashf ... 4N 21
TW17: Shep ... 5E 38
TW18: Stain ... 5E 20
UB2: S'hall ... 1M 9
W4 ... 2A 12
Gordons Way RH8: Oxt ... 6N 105
Gordon Wlk. GU46: Yate ... 1D 68
Gore Rd. SW20 ... 1H 43
Goring Rd. TW18: Stain ... 6F 20
Goring's Mead RH13: Hors ... 7K 197
Gorings Sq. TW18: Stain ... 5G 21
Gorling Cl. RH11: Ifield ... 4K 181
GORRICK ... 7C 30
Gorrick Sq. RG41: W'ham ... 5A 30
Gorringe Pk. Av. CR4: Mit ... 8D 28
Gorringes Brook
RH12: Hors ... 2K 197
Gorse Bank GU18: Ligh ... 8L 51
Gorse Cl. GU10: Wrec ... 5F 128
KT20: Tad ... 7G 81
RH10: Copt ... 8M 163
RH11: Craw ... 9N 181
Gorse Cotts. GU10: Fren ... 1H 149
Gorse Ct. GU4: Guil ... 1E 114
Gorse Dr. RH6: Smallf ... 8M 143
Gorse End RH12: Hors ... 3K 197
Gorse Hill GU22: Wok ... 8J 73
Gorse Hill La. GU25: V Wat ... 3N 35
Gorse Hill Rd. GU25: V Wat ... 3N 35
Gorselands GU9: Up Hale ... 5H 109
GU46: Yate ... 2B 68
Gorselands Cl. GU12: Ash V ... 8E 90
GU35: Head D ... 5H 169
KT14: W By ... 7L 55
Gorse La. GU10: Wrec ... 5G 128
GU24: Chob ... 4H 53
Gorse Path GU10: Wrec ... 5F 128
Gorse Pl. RG42: Wink R ... 8F 16
Gorse Ri. SW17 ... 6E 28
Gorse Rd. CR0: Croy ... 1K 65
GU16: Frim ... 4C 70
Gorseway GU52: Fleet ... 6B 88
Gorsewood Rd. GU21: Wok ... 6G 73
Gort Cl. GU11: Alde ... 6C 90
Gosberton Rd. SW12 ... 2D 28
Gosbury Hill KT9: Ches ... 1L 59
Gosden Cl. GU5: Braml ... 3B 134
RH10: Craw ... 4E 182
GOSDEN COMMON ... 3A 134
Gosden Comn. GU5: Braml ... 4A 134
Gosden Cotts. GU5: Braml ... 4B 134
Gosden Hill Rd. GU4: B'ham ... 8E 94
Gosden Rd. GU24: W End ... 9C 52
Gosfield Rd.
KT19: Eps ... 5J 201 (8C 60)
Goslar Way SL4: W'sor ... 5E 4
Gosnell Cl. GU16: Frim ... 3H 71
GOSPEL GREEN ... 5B 190
Gossops Dr. RH11: Craw ... 4L 181
GOSSOPS GREEN ... 4L 181
Gossops Grn. La.
RH11: Craw ... 4M 181
Gossops Pde. *RH11: Craw* ... *4L 181*
(off Gossops Dr.)
Gostling Rd. TW2: Whitt ... 2A 24
Goston Gdns. CR7: T Hea ... 2L 45
Gostrode La. GU8: Chid ... 2D 190
Goswell Hill SL4: W'sor ... 4G 4
Goswell Rd. SL4: W'sor ... 4G 4
Gothic Ct. UB3: Harl ... 2E 8
Gothic Rd. TW2: Twick ... 3D 24
Gotwick Mnr. RH19: Hamm ... 6H 167
Goudhurst Cl. RH10: Worth ... 3J 183
Goudhurst Keep
RH10: Worth ... 3J 183
Gough Ho. KT1: K Tham ... 3J 203
Gough Rd. GU51: Fleet ... 3A 88
Gough's Barn La.
RG42: Warf ... 1M 15
Gough's La. RG12: Brac ... 8B 16
Gough's Mdw. GU47: Sandh ... 8B 48
Gould Ct. GU4: Guil ... 1F 114
Goulding Gdns. CR7: T Hea ... 1N 45
Gould Rd. TW2: Twick ... 2E 24
TW14: Felt ... 1F 22
Government Ho. Rd.
GU11: Alde ... 5M 89
Government Rd. GU11: Alde ... 9B 90
Governor's Rd. GU15: Camb ... 9L 49
Govett Av. TW17: Shep ... 4D 38
Govett Gro. GU20: Windl ... 2A 52
Gowan Av. SW6 ... 4K 13
Gower, The TW20: Thor ... 2D 36
Gower Ho. KT13: Weybr ... 3E 56
Gower Lodge *KT13: Weybr* ... *3E 56*
(off St George's Rd.)
Gower Pk. GU47: Coll T ... 8J 49
Gower Rd. KT13: Weybr ... 3E 56
RH6: Horl ... 8C 142
TW7: Isle ... 2F 10
Gowland Pl. BR3: Beck ... 1J 47
Gowlland Cl. CR0: Croy ... 6D 46
Gownboys GU7: Godal ... 4F 132
Gowrie Pl. CR3: Cate ... 9N 83
Graburn Way KT8: E Mol ... 2D 40
Grace Bennett Cl.
GU14: Farnb ... 7M 69
Grace Bus. Cen. CR4: Mit ... 5D 44
Grace Ct. CR0: Croy ... 4A 200
RH12: Hors ... 4N 197
SM2: Sut ... 5N 61
Gracedale Rd. SW16 ... 6F 28
Gracefield Gdns. SW16 ... 4J 29
Grace Gdns. GU51: Fleet ... 5A 88
Grace M. *SE20* ... *1F 46*
(off Marlow Rd.)
Grace Reynolds Wlk.
GU15: Camb ... 9A 50
Grace Rd. CR0: Croy ... 5N 45
RH11: Craw ... 8M 181
Gracious Pond Rd.
GU24: Chob ... 4K 53
Graemesdyke Av. SW14 ... 6A 12
Graffham Cl. RH11: Craw ... 1N 181
GRAFHAM ... 2E 154
Grafton Cl. KT4: W Pk ... 9D 42
KT14: W By ... 9H 55
TW4: Houn ... 2M 23
Grafton Ct. TW14: Bedf ... 2E 22
Grafton Pk. Rd. KT4: W Pk ... 8D 42
Grafton Rd. CR0: Croy ... 7L 45
KT3: N Mal ... 2D 42
KT4: W Pk ... 9C 42
Grafton Way KT8: W Mole ... 3N 39
Graham Av. CR4: Mit ... 9E 28
Graham Cl. CR0: Croy ... 8K 47
Grahame Ho. RH1: Red ... 1C 122
Graham Gdns. KT6: Surb ... 7L 41
Graham Ho. KT23: Book ... 2N 97
Graham Rd. CR4: Mit ... 9E 28
CR8: Pur ... 9L 63
GU20: Windl ... 3N 51
SW19 ... 8L 27
TW12: H Hill ... 5A 24
Grailands Cl. GU27: Fern ... 9G 188
Grainford Ct. *RG40: W'ham* ... *3B 30*
(off Sturges Rd.)
Grainger Rd. TW7: Isle ... 5F 10
Grampian Cl. SM2: Sut ... 4A 62
UB3: Harl ... 3E 8
Grampian Rd. GU47: Sandh ... 5E 48
Grampian Way SL3: Lang ... 1C 6
Granada St. SW17 ... 6D 28
Granard Av. SW15 ... 8G 13

Granard Rd.—Green Leas

Granard Rd. SW12 1D 28
Granary Cl. RH6: Horl 6E 142
RH12: Hors 7F 196
Granary Way RH12: Hors 7F 196
Granard Av. GU15: Camb 9A 50
KT5: Surb 4A 42
Grand Dr. SW20 1H 43
Granden Rd. SW16 1J 45
Grandfield Ct. W4 2C 12
Grandis Cotts. GU23: Rip 9K 75
Grandison Rd. KT4: W Pk 8H 43
Grand Pde. KT6: Surb 7N 41
RH10: Craw 3B 182
SW14 7B 12
(off Up. Richmond Rd. W.)
Grand Pde. M. SW15 8K 13
Grand Regency Hgts.
SL5: Asc 1J 33
Grandstand Rd.
KT17: Eps D 4E 80
Grand Vw. Av. TN16: B Hil 4E 86
Grange, The CR0: Croy 8J 47
GU2: Guil 9L 93
GU10: Fren 3J 149
GU24: Chob 6H 53
GU25: V Wat 3A 36
(off Holloway Dr.)
KT3: N Mal 4E 42
KT4: W Pk 1C 60
KT12: Wal T 8J 39
RH6: Horl 5F 142
SL4: O Win 8L 5
SW19 7J 27
W4 1A 12
Grange Av. RG45: Crowt 1G 48
SE25 1B 46
TW2: Twick 3E 24
Grangecliffe Gdns. SE25 1B 46
Grange Cl. GU2: Guil 8L 93
GU7: Godal 6K 133
GU15: Camb 7F 50
KT8: W Mole 3B 40
KT22: Leat 7K 79
RH1: Blet 2A 124
RH1: Mers 6F 102
RH10: Craw 1E 182
TN8: Eden 2L 147
TN16: Weste 4L 107
TW5: Hest 2N 9
TW19: Wray 9A 6
Grange Ct. GU10: Tong 6C 110
KT12: Wal T 8H 39
RH1: Mers 6F 102
RH9: S Gods 7H 125
SM2: Sut 4N 61
SM6: W'ton 9F 44
TW17: Shep 3B 38
TW18: Stain 6J 21
TW20: Egh 6B 20
Grange Cres.
RH10: Craw D 2E 184
Grange Dr. GU21: Wok 2A 74
RH1: Mers 6F 102
Grange End RH6: Smallf 8L 143
Grange Est. GU52: Chu C 8A 88
Grange Farm Rd.
GU12: Ash 1E 110
Grangefields Rd.
GU4: J Wel 6N 93
Grange Gdns. SE25 1B 46
SM7: Ban 9N 61
Grange Hill SE25 1B 46
Grange Lodge SW19 7J 27
Grange Mans. KT17: Ewe 4E 60
Grange Mdw. SM7: Ban 9N 61
Grange M. TW13: Felt 5H 23
Grangemount KT22: Leat 7K 79
Grange Pk. GU6: Cranl 7A 156
GU21: Wok 2A 74
Grange Pk. Pl. SW20 8G 26
Grange Pk. Rd. CR7: T Hea 3A 46
Grange Pl. KT12: Wal T 8H 39
TW18: Lale 1L 37
Grange Rd. CR2: S Croy 6N 63
CR3: Cate 3D 104
CR7: T Hea 3A 46
GU2: Guil 7L 93
GU10: Til 2N 149
GU10: Tong 6C 110
GU12: Ash 2F 110
GU14: Farnb 7N 69
GU15: Camb 1C 70
GU21: Wok 1A 74
GU24: Pirb 9N 71
GU52: Chu C 8A 88
KT1: K Tham 5J 203 (2L 41)
KT8: W Mole 3B 40
KT9: Ches 1L 59
KT12: Hers 1M 57
KT15: N Haw 6J 55
KT22: Leat 7K 79
RG12: Brac 9A 16
RH10: Craw D 2D 184
SE19 3A 46
SE25 3A 46
SM2: Sut 4M 61
SW13 4F 12
TW20: Egh 6B 20
W4 1A 12
Grange Va. SM2: Sut 4N 61
Grange Way RH6: Smallf 8L 143
Grangewood Dr.
TW16: Sunb 8G 23
Grangewood Ter. SE25 1A 46
Gransden Cl. GU6: Ewh 5F 156
Grantchester *KT1: K Tham 1N 41*
(off St Peters Rd.)
Grant Cl. TW17: Shep 5C 38
Grantham Cl. GU47: Owls 6K 49
Grantham Ct. KT2: K Tham 6K 25
Grantham Dr. GU14: Cove 9J 69
Grantham Ho.
TW16: Sunb 8F 22
Grantham Rd. W4 3D 12
Grantley Av. GU5: Wone 5D 134
Grantley Cl. GU4: Chil 1A 134
Grantley Ct. GU9: Farnh 5E 128
Grantley Dr. GU52: Fleet 6A 88
Grantley Gdns. GU2: Guil 2K 113
Grantley Pl. KT10: Esh 2C 58
Grantley Rd. GU2: Guil 2K 113
TW4: C'ford 5K 9
Granton Rd. SW16 9G 29
Grant Pl. CR0: Croy 7C 46
Grant Rd. CR0: Croy 7C 46
RG45: Crowt 4H 49
Grants La. RH8: Limp 1E 126
TN8: Eden, Limp 5E 126
Grant Wlk. SL5: S'dale 7B 34
Grant Way TW7: Isle 2G 10
Grantwood Cl. RH1: Red 8E 122
Granville Av. TW3: Houn 8A 10
TW13: Felt 3H 23
Granville Cl.
CR0: Croy 3F 200 (8B 46)
KT13: Weybr 3D 56
KT14: Byf 9A 56
Granville Gdns. SW16 9K 29
Granville Pl. SW6 3N 13
Granville Rd. GU22: Wok 7B 74
KT13: Weybr 4D 56
RH8: Oxt 7B 106
SW18 1L 27
SW19 8M 27
TN16: Weste 4L 107
Granwood Ct. TW7: Isle 4E 10
Grapsome Cl. KT9: Ches 4J 59
Grasholm Way SL3: Lang 1E 6
Grasmere SL4: W'sor 3B 4
Grasmere Av. SW15 5C 26
SW19 2M 43
TW3: Houn 9B 10
Grasmere Cl. GU1: Guil 2D 114
TW14: Felt 2G 22
TW20: Egh 8D 20
Grasmere Ct. *RH10: Craw 5H 183*
(off Grayrigg Rd.)
SM2: Sut 3A 62
SW13 2F 12
(off Verdun Rd.)
Grasmere Gdns.
RH12: Hors 2A 198
Grasmere Rd. CR8: Pur 7M 63
GU9: Up Hale 6F 108
GU14: Cove 2K 89
GU18: Ligh 6M 51
SE25 5E 46
SW16 6J 29
Grasmere Way KT14: Byf 8A 56
Grassfield Cl. CR5: Coul 6F 82
Grasslands RH6: Smallf 8L 143
Grassmere RH6: Horl 7G 142
Grassmount CR8: Pur 6G 63
Grassway SM6: W'ton 1G 62
Gratton Dr. SL4: W'sor 7B 4
Grattons, The RH13: Slinf 5M 195
Grattons Dr. RH10: Craw 9G 162
Gravel Hill CR0: A'ton 3G 64
KT22: Leat 8H 79
Gravel Hill Rd.
GU10: Holt P 8A 128
Gravel Hill Stop
(London Tramlink) 3H 65
Gravelly Hill CR3: Cate 6B 104
Gravelpits Cotts.
GU5: Gom 8D 116
Gravelpits La. GU5: Gom 8D 116
Gravel Rd. GU9: Up Hale 5G 108
GU14: Farnb 5B 90
GU52: Chu C 7C 88
TW2: Twick 2E 24
Gravenel Gdns. *SW17 6C 28*
(off Nutwell St.)
Graveney Rd. RH10: Craw 4G 182
SW17 5C 28
Gravesham Way BR3: Beck 6J 47
Gravetts La. GU3: Guil 8H 93
GRAVETYE 7K 185
Gravetye Cl. RH10: Craw 5E 182
Gray Cl. KT15: Addl 2K 55
RH7: Ling 7A 146
Gray Ct. SL4: W'sor 5D 4
Grayham Cres. KT3: N Mal 3C 42
Grayham Rd. KT3: N Mal 3C 42
Graylands GU21: Wok 3A 74
Graylands Cl. GU21: Wok 3A 74
Graylands Ct. GU1: Guil 4B 114
Grayling KT16: Chert 7L 37
Gray Pl. KT16: Otter 3F 54
RG42: Brac 9K 15
Grayrigg Rd.
RH10: Craw 5H 183
Grays Cl. GU27: Hasl 9J 171
Grayscroft Rd. SW16 8H 29
Grayshot Dr. GU17: B'water 1H 69
GRAYSHOTT 6A 170
Grayshott Laurels
GU35: Lind 4B 168
Grayshott Rd.
GU35: Head D 3G 169
Grays La. KT18: Eps D 7N 79
KT21: Asht 6M 79
TW15: Ashf 5C 22
Grays Rd. GU7: Godal 4J 133
TN16: Weste 8K 87
GRAYSWOOD 7K 171
Grays Wood RH6: Horl 8G 143
Grayswood Comn.
GU27: G'wood 8K 171
Grayswood Dr. GU16: Mytc 4E 90
Grayswood Gdns. SW20 1G 42
Grayswood M.
GU27: G'wood 7K 171
Grayswood Pl. GU27: Hasl 9J 171
Grayswood Point SW15 2F 26
Grayswood Rd.
GU27: Hasl, G'wood 1H 189
Great Austins GU9: Farnh 3J 129
Gt. Austins Ho. GU9: Farnh 3J 129
Great Benty UB7: W Dray 1N 7
GREAT BOOKHAM 4B 98
Great Bookham Common 8N 77
GREAT BURGH 4H 81
Gt. Chertsey Rd.
TW2: Twick 4N 23
TW13: Hanw, Twick 4N 23
W4 4B 12
(not continuous)
Gt. Church La. W6 1J 13
Great Cockcrow Railway 7F 36
Gt. Daux Rdbt.
RH12: Warnh 1H 197
Great Ellshams SM7: Ban 3M 81
GREAT ENTON 6D 152
Greatfield Cl. GU14: Farnb 6N 69
Great Fld. Pl. RH19: E Grin 7D 166
Greatfield Rd. GU14: Farnb 6M 69
Greatford Dr. GU1: Guil 3F 114
Gt. Gatton Cl. CR0: Croy 6H 47
Gt. George St. GU7: Godal 7H 133
Gt. Goodwin Dr. GU1: Guil 1D 114
Greatham Rd. RH10: Craw 6G 182
Greatham Wlk. SW15 2F 26
GREAT HOLLANDS 5L 31
Gt. Hollands Rd. RG12: Brac 5K 31
Gt. Hollands Sq. RG12: Brac 5L 31
Great Ho. Ct. RH19: E Grin 1B 186
Greathurst End KT23: Book 2N 97
Greatlake Ct. *RH6: Horl 7F 142*
(off Tanyard Way)
Great Mead TN8: Eden 9L 127
Great Oaks Pk. GU4: B'ham 7D 94
Great Quarry
GU1: Guil 8D 202 (6N 113)
Great Sth. West Rd.
TW4: Houn 7G 9
TW14: Bedf, Felt 1D 22
Great Tangley GU5: Wone 2D 134
Great Tattenhams
KT18: Tat C 5G 81
Gt. West Rd. TW5: Hest 5L 9
TW7: Brent, Isle 3E 10
TW8: Brent 3E 10
W4 1A 12
(Cedars Rd.)
W4 1E 12
(Dorchester Gro.)
W6 1E 12
Gt. West Trad. Est.
TW8: Brent 2H 11
Greatwood Cl. KT16: Otter 5E 54
Gt. Woodcote Dr. CR8: Pur 6H 63
Gt. Woodcote Pk. CR8: Pur 6H 63
Greaves Pl. SW17 5C 28
Grebe Ct. SM1: Sut 2L 61
Grebe Cres. RH13: Hors 7N 197
Grebe Ter.
KT1: K Tham 5J 203 (2L 41)
Grecian Cres. SE19 7M 29
Green, The CR0: Sels 5J 65
CR3: Wold 1K 105
CR6: Warl 4G 84
GU5: Sha G 6F 134
GU6: Ewh 5F 156
GU8: Chid 5F 172
GU8: Duns 3B 174
GU8: Els 7H 131
GU9: B Lea 7M 109
GU9: Up Hale 6H 109
GU10: Seal 2C 130
GU16: Frim G 8D 70
GU17: B'water 2H 69
GU23: Rip 8L 75
GU46: Yate 9A 48
KT3: N Mal 2C 42
KT10: Clay 3F 58
KT12: Hers 2L 57
KT12: Whit V 6F 56
KT17: Ewe 7F 60
KT20: Tad 6K 81
(Oatlands Rd.)
KT20: Tad 1J 101
(Stokes Riding)
KT22: Fetc 2D 98
RG12: Brac 3N 31
RH3: Buckl 2F 120
RH5: Ockl 5D 158
RH9: Gods 1E 124
RH10: Copt 7M 163
RH11: Craw 2A 182
SL3: Dat 3L 5
SM1: Sut 9N 43
SM4: Mord 3K 43
SM5: Cars 1E 62
SM6: W'ton 8E 44
Green, The SW19 6J 27
TN16: Weste 4M 107
TW2: Twick 2E 24
TW5: Hest 2A 10
TW9: Rich 8K 11
TW13: Felt 3J 23
TW15: Ashf 6M 21
TW17: Shep 3F 38
TW19: Wray 9A 6
TW20: Eng G 5M 19
Green Acre GU11: Alde 3L 109
Greenacre GU21: Knap 3H 73
SL4: W'sor 5B 4
Greenacre Ct. TW20: Eng G 7M 19
Greenacre Pl. SM6: W'ton 8F 44
Green Acres CR0: Croy 9C 46
Greenacres GU10: Run 1A 130
GU35: Bor 5A 168
KT20: Lwr K 6L 101
KT23: Book 2B 98
RH8: Oxt 5A 106
RH10: Craw 4E 182
RH12: Hors 4J 197
Greenacres Cl. BR6: Farnb 1L 67
Greenaways Dr. TW4: Houn 7M 9
Greenaway Ter. *TW19: Stan 2N 21*
(off Victory Cl.)
Green Bank Cotts.
RH5: For G 3M 157
Greenbank Ct. *TW7: Isle 5F 10*
(off Lanadron Cl.)
Greenbank Way
GU15: Camb 4B 70
Greenbush La. GU6: Cranl 9A 156
Green Bus. Centre, The
TW18: Stain 5E 20
Green Cl. SM5: Cars 8D 44
TW13: Hanw 6M 23
Green Ct. TW16: Sunb 7G 23
Greencourt Av. CR0: Croy 8E 46
Greencourt Gdns. CR0: Croy 7E 46
Green Cft. GU9: B Lea 6N 109
RG40: W'ham 9D 14
Greencroft GU1: Guil 3D 114
GU14: Farnb 1N 89
Greencroft Rd. TW5: Hest 4N 9
GREEN CROSS 9M 149
Green Cross La.
GU10: Churt 9M 149
Green Curve SM7: Ban 1L 81
Green Dene KT24: E Hor 4D 116
Green Dragon La.
TW8: Brent 1L 11
Green Dragons Airsports 7L 85
Green Dr. GU23: Rip 1H 95
RG40: W'ham 4D 30
SL3: Lang 1A 6
Greene Fielde End
TW18: Stain 8M 21
Green End GU46: Yate 8C 48
KT9: Ches 1L 59
Greener Ct. *CR0: Croy 5N 45*
(off Goodman Cres.)
Green Farm Rd. GU19: Bag 4K 51
Greenfield GU9: Farnh 4F 128
TN8: Eden 2M 147
Greenfield Av. KT5: Surb 6A 42
Greenfield Ho. SW19 2J 27
TW20: Eng G 7L 19
(off Kings La.)
Greenfield Link CR5: Coul 2J 83
Greenfield Rd. GU9: Farnh 4E 128
RH13: Slinf 5L 195
Greenfields Cl. RH6: Horl 8C 142
RH12: Hors 2N 197
Greenfields Pl. RH5: B Grn 7K 139
Greenfields Rd. RH6: Horl 6D 142
RH12: Hors 3N 197
Greenfields Way
RH12: Hors 2N 197
Greenfield Way RG45: Crowt 9F 30
Green Finch Cl.
RG45: Crowt 1E 48
Greenfinch Cl. GU47: Owls 7J 49
Greenfinch Way
RH12: Hors 1J 197
Greenford Rd. SM1: Sut 1N 61
(not continuous)
Green Gables GU14: Cove 6L 69
Green Gdns. BR6: Farnb 2L 67
Green Glades GU52: Chu C 8A 88
Greenham Ho. TW7: Isle 6D 10
Greenham Wlk. GU21: Wok 5M 73
Greenham Wood RG12: Brac 5A 32
Greenhanger GU10: Churt 1M 169
Greenhaven GU46: Yate 1A 68
Greenhayes Av. SM7: Ban 1M 81
Greenhayes Cl. RH2: Reig 3A 122
Greenhayes Gdns.
SM7: Ban 2M 81
Green Hedges TW1: Twick 8J 11
Green Hedges Av.
RH19: E Grin 8N 165
Green Hedges Cl.
RH19: E Grin 8N 165
Greenheys Pl. GU22: Wok 5B 74
Green Hill BR6: Dow 8H 67
Greenhill SM1: Sut 8A 44
Greenhill Av. CR3: Cate 8E 84
Green Hill Cl. GU15: Camb 9G 51
Greenhill Cl. GU7: Godal 8G 132
GU9: Farnh 4F 128
Greenhill Gdns. GU4: Guil 1E 114
Green Hill La. CR6: Warl 4H 85
Green Hill Rd. GU15: Camb 9G 51
Greenhill Rd. GU9: Farnh 4J 129
Greenhills GU9: Farnh 3K 129
Greenhill Way GU9: Farnh 5F 128
Greenholme GU15: Camb 1H 71
Greenhow RG12: Brac 2M 31
Greenhurst La. RH8: Oxt 1B 126
Greenhurst Rd. SE27 6L 29
Greening Wood
GU26: Hind 4D 170
Greenlake Ter. TW18: Stain 8J 21
Greenlands KT16: Chert 9E 36
KT19: Ewe 2A 60
Greenlands Rd.
GU15: Camb 5N 69
KT13: Weybr 9C 38
TW18: Stain 5J 21
Greenland Way CR0: Bedd 6H 45
Green La. CR3: Cate 9N 83
CR5: Coul 4L 101
CR6: Warl 3H 85
CR7: T Hea 8K 29
CR8: Pur 7G 63
GU1: Guil 3D 114
GU3: Wood V 1D 112
GU4: W Cla 5J 95
GU5: Alb, Sha G 5H 135
GU6: Alf 5H 175
GU7: Godal 2G 133
GU8: Mil 2B 152
GU9: B Lea, Weybo 6L 109
GU9: Farnh 3F 128
GU10: Churt 1L 169
GU10: Dock 4D 148
GU10: Til 5B 130
GU17: B'water 2G 69
GU17: Haw 2K 69
GU19: Bag 9F 32
(Bagshot Rd.)
GU19: Bag 5K 51
(Broomsquires Rd.)
GU22: Wok 8L 73
GU23: Ockh 2C 96
GU24: Chob 6J 53
GU27: Hasl 4F 188
GU46: Yate 9A 48
GU47: Sandh 8H 49
KT3: N Mal 4B 42
KT4: W Pk 7F 42
KT8: W Mole 4B 40
KT9: Ches 5K 59
KT11: Cob 8M 57
KT12: Hers 3J 57
KT14: Byf 8A 56
KT15: Addl 8G 36
KT16: Chert 8G 36
KT20: Lwr K 4L 101
KT21: Asht 4J 79
KT22: Leat 8K 79
(not continuous)
RG40: W'ham 6F 14
RH1: Blet 9B 104
RH1: Out 1J 143
RH1: Red 8E 122
(Jordans Cl.)
RH1: Red 1C 122
(Timperley Gdns.)
RH2: Leigh 3D 140
RH2: Reig 3L 121
RH5: B Grn 1H 159
RH5: Newd 2C 160
RH5: Ockl 7M 157
RH6: Ship B 3K 163
RH7: Ling 8M 145
RH10: Craw 1C 182
RH10: Craw D 6C 164
RH10: Worth 3H 183
(not continuous)
RH12: Hors 5L 179
SL3: Dat 4L 5
SL4: W'sor 5D 4
SL5: Asc 9B 18
SM4: Mord 5M 43
(Central Rd.)
SM4: Mord 6H 43
(Lwr. Morden La.)
SW16 8K 29
TW4: Houn 6J 9
TW13: Hanw 6M 23
TW16: Sunb 8G 22
TW17: Shep 5D 38
TW18: Stain 9G 20
TW20: Egh 5D 20
(The Avenue)
TW20: Egh 6D 20
(Vicarage Cres.)
TW20: Thor 1E 36
Green La. Av. KT12: Hers 2K 57
Green La. Cl. GU15: Camb 8A 50
KT14: Byf 8A 56
KT16: Chert 8G 36
Green La. Cotts.
GU10: Churt 9L 149
Green La. E. GU3: Flex 4K 111
Green La. Gdns.
CR7: T Hea 1N 45
Green Lanes KT19: Ewe 5D 60
Green La. W. GU12: Ash G 4J 111
KT24: W Hors 3B 96
Greenlaw Gdns. KT3: N Mal 6E 42
Greenlawn La. TW8: Brent 1K 11
Green Leaf Av. SM6: Bedd 1H 63
Greenleaf Cl. SW2 1L 29
Greenlea Pk. SW19 8B 28
Green Leas KT1: K Tham 5K 203
TW16: Sunb 7G 23

Greenleas—Gunnersbury Station (Underground & Overground)

Greenleas GU16: Frim ... 4C 70
Green Leas Cl. TW16: Sunb ... 7G 23
Greenleas Cl. GU46: Yate ... 8B 48
Greenleaves Ct. TW15: Ashf ... 7C 22
Green Leys GU52: Chu C ... 9A 88
Greenlink Wlk. TW9: Kew ... 4A 12
Green Man La. TW14: Felt ... 7H 9
(not continuous)
Green Mead KT10: Esh ... 3N 57
Greenmead Cl. SE25 ... 4D 46
Greenmeads GU22: Wok ... 9A 74
Greenoak Ri. TN16: B Hil ... 5E 86
Green Oaks UB2: S'hall ... 1L 9
Greenoak Way SW19 ... 5J 27
Greenock Rd. SW16 ... 9H 29
Greeno Cres. TW17: Shep ... 4B 38
Green Pde. TW3: Houn ... 8B 10
Green Pk. TW18: Stain ... 4G 20
Green Ride RG12: Brac ... 6D 32
Green Rd. GU23: Ockh ... 2D 96
TW20: Thor ... 3C 36
Greenrod Pl. TW8: Brent ... 1L 11
(off Clayponds La.)
Greensand Cl. RH1: Mers ... 6H 103
Green Sand Rd. RH1: Red ... 2E 122
Greenside RG45: Crowt ... 2E 48
Greenside Cl. GU4: Guil ... 1E 114
Greenside Cotts.
GU23: Rip ... 8L 75
Greenside Dr. KT21: Asht ... 5H 79
Greenside Rd. CR0: Croy ... 6L 45
Greenside Wlk.
TN16: B Hil ... 5D 86
Greenslade Av. KT21: Asht ... 6A 80
Greens La. RH5: Newd ... 3N 159
RH13: Mann H ... 9C 198
Green's School La.
GU14: Farnb ... 1M 89
Greenstead Gdns. SW15 ... 8G 12
Greensted Ct. CR3: Whyte ... 6D 84
(off Godstone Rd.)
Greenstede Av.
RH19: E Grin ... 7B 166
Green St. TW16: Sunb ... 9H 23
GREEN STREET GREEN ... 3N 67
Greenvale Rd. GU21: Knap ... 5G 73
Green Vw. KT9: Ches ... 4M 59
RH9: Gods ... 9E 104
Green View, The
RH11: Pease P ... 1N 199
Greenview Av. BR3: Beck ... 5H 47
CR0: Croy ... 5H 47
Greenview Ct. TW15: Ashf ... 5A 22
Greenview Dr. SW20 ... 2H 43
Green Wlk. RG12: Brac ... 2K 31
RH10: Craw ... 1C 182
TW12: Hamp ... 7N 23
UB2: S'hall ... 1A 10
Green Way GU12: Alde ... 1C 110
KT23: Book ... 1B 98
RH1: Red ... 1C 122
TW16: Sunb ... 3H 39
Greenway RH12: Hors ... 5H 197
SM6: W'ton ... 1G 62
SW20 ... 3H 43
TN16: Tats ... 7E 86
Greenway, The KT18: Eps ... 1N 79
RH8: Oxt ... 2D 126
TW4: Houn ... 7N 9
Greenway Cl. KT14: W By ... 9J 55
Greenway Dr. TW18: Stain ... 9M 21
Greenway Gdns. CR0: Croy ... 9J 47
Greenways BR3: Beck ... 2K 47
GU47: Sandh ... 6G 49
GU52: Fleet ... 7A 88
KT10: Hinc W ... 1E 58
KT20: Wal H ... 3G 100
TW20: Egh ... 6A 20
Greenways, The TW1: Twick ... 9G 11
Greenways Dr. SL5: S'dale ... 7B 34
Greenways Wlk.
RH11: Craw ... 8A 182
Greenwell Cl. RH9: Gods ... 8E 104
Greenwich Cl. RH11: Craw ... 7A 182
Greenwood SL5: Asc ... 9G 17
Greenwood, The GU1: Guil ... 2C 114
Greenwood Bus. Cen.
CR0: Croy ... 6C 46
Greenwood Cl. KT7: T Dit ... 7G 41
KT15: Wood ... 7H 55
SM4: Mord ... 3K 43
Greenwood Cotts.
SL5: S'dale ... 5F 34
Greenwood Ct. RH11: Craw ... 8N 181
Greenwood Dr. RH1: Red ... 8E 122
Greenwood Gdns.
CR3: Cate ... 3D 104
RH8: Oxt ... 3C 126
Greenwood La. TW12: H Hill ... 6B 24
Greenwood Pk.
KT2: K Tham ... 8D 26
Greenwood Rd. CR0: Croy ... 6M 45
CR4: Mit ... 2H 45
GU21: Wok ... 7H 73
GU24: B'wood ... 8M 71
KT7: T Dit ... 7G 41
RG45: Crowt ... 1F 48
TW7: Isle ... 6F 10
Green Wrythe Cres.
SM5: Cars ... 7C 44
Green Wrythe La. SM5: Cars ... 5B 44
Gregory Cl. GU21: Wok ... 4M 73
RH10: Craw ... 7G 182
Gregory Dr. SL4: O Win ... 9L 5
Gregsons RH12: Warnh ... 9E 178
Grenaby Av. CR0: Croy ... 6A 46
Grenaby Rd. CR0: Croy ... 6A 46
Grenadier Pl. CR3: Cate ... 9N 83
Grenadier Rd. GU12: Ash V ... 9F 90
Grenadiers Way GU14: Cove ... 2H 89
Grena Gdns. TW9: Rich ... 7M 11
Grena Rd. TW9: Rich ... 7M 11
Grendon Cl. RH6: Horl ... 6D 142
Grenehurst Pk. RH5: Cap ... 6H 159
Grenfell Rd. CR4: Mit ... 7D 28
Grennell Cl. SM1: Sut ... 8B 44
Grennell Rd. SM1: Sut ... 8A 44
Grenside Rd. KT13: Weybr ... 9C 38
Grenville Cl. KT5: Surb ... 7B 42
KT11: Cob ... 9L 57
Grenville Gdns.
GU16: Frim G ... 8C 70
Grenville M. TW12: H Hill ... 6B 24
Grenville Pl. RG12: Brac ... 1A 32
(off The Ring)
Grenville Rd. CR0: N Add ... 5M 65
GU8: S'ford ... 4A 132
Gresham Av. CR6: Warl ... 5H 85
Gresham Cl. RH8: Oxt ... 7B 106
Gresham Ct. CR8: Pur ... 7L 63
GU15: Camb ... 2D 70
TW18: Stain ... 6J 21
Gresham Ho. GU22: Wok ... 9C 74
Gresham Ind. Est.
GU12: Alde ... 2C 110
Gresham Pk. Rd.
GU22: Wok ... 8D 74
Gresham Pl. RH8: Oxt ... 7B 106
Gresham Rd. BR3: Beck ... 1H 47
RH8: Oxt ... 6B 106
SE25 ... 3D 46
TW3: Houn ... 4C 10
TW12: Hamp ... 7A 24
TW18: Stain ... 6H 21
Greshams Way TN8: Eden ... 1J 147
Gresham Wlk. RH10: Craw ... 6C 182
(not continuous)
Gresham Way GU16: Frim G ... 8C 70
SW19 ... 4N 27
Gresham Way Ind. Est.
SW19 ... 4N 27
(off Gresham Way)
Gressenhall Rd. SW18 ... 9L 13
Greswell St. SW6 ... 4J 13
Greta Bank KT24: W Hors ... 4D 96
Greville Av. CR2: Sels ... 6G 64
Greville Cl. GU2: Guil ... 3H 113
GU11: Alde ... 1M 109
KT21: Asht ... 6L 79
TW1: Twick ... 1H 25
Greville Ct. KT21: Asht ... 5L 79
(off Greville Pk. Rd.)
KT23: Book ... 3B 98
Greville Pk. Av. KT21: Asht ... 5L 79
Greville Pk. Rd. KT21: Asht ... 5L 79
Greville Rd. TW10: Rich ... 9M 11
Grey Alders SM7: Ban ... 1H 81
Greybury La. TN8: Marsh G ... 9K 147
Greyfields Cl. CR8: Pur ... 9M 63
Greyford Cl. KT22: Leat ... 1J 99
Greyfriars Dr. GU24: Bis ... 2D 72
SL5: Asc ... 4M 33
Greyfriars Rd. GU23: Rip ... 2J 95
Greyhound Cl. GU12: Ash ... 3D 110
Greyhound La. SW16 ... 7H 29
Greyhound Mans. W6 ... 2K 13
(off Greyhound Rd.)
Greyhound Rd. SM1: Sut ... 2A 62
W6 ... 2J 13
W14 ... 2J 13
Greyhound Slip
RH10: Craw ... 2H 183
Greyhound Ter. SW16 ... 9G 29
Greylees GU7: Godal ... 6H 133
Greys Ct. GU11: Alde ... 2K 109
Greys Pk. Cl. BR2: Kes ... 2F 66
Greystead Pk. GU10: Wrec ... 6D 128
Greystock Rd. RG42: Warf ... 7B 16
Greystoke Ct. RG45: Crowt ... 3F 48
Greystone Cl. CR2: Sels ... 7F 64
Greystones Cl. RH1: Red ... 5B 122
Greystones Dr. RH2: Reig ... 1A 122
Greyswood St. SW16 ... 7F 28
Greythorne Rd. GU21: Wok ... 5K 73
Greywaters Dr. GU5: Braml ... 5C 134
Grice Av. TN16: B Hil ... 9D 66
Grier Cl. RH11: Ifield ... 4K 181
Grierson Ho. SW16 ... 5G 29
Grieve Cl. GU10: Tong ... 5C 110
Griffin Cen. TW14: Felt ... 8J 9
Griffin Centre, The
KT1: K Tham ... 4H 203
Griffin Ct. KT21: Asht ... 6M 79
KT23: Book ... 4B 98
TW8: Brent ... 2L 11
W4 ... 1E 12
Griffin Ho. CR0: Croy ... 6M 45
W6 ... 1J 13
(off Hammersmith Rd.)
Griffin M. SW12 ... 2G 28
Griffin Park ... 2K 11
Griffin Way KT23: Book ... 4A 98
TW16: Sunb ... 1H 39
Griffiths Cl. KT4: W Pk ... 8G 43
Griffiths Rd. SW19 ... 8M 27
Griffits Path RH18: F Row ... 7G 187
Griffon Cl. GU14: Cove ... 2J 89
Griggs Mdw. GU8: Duns ... 2B 174
Grimston Rd. SW6 ... 5L 13
Grimwade Av. CR0: Croy ... 9D 46
Grimwood Rd. TW1: Twick ... 1F 24
Grindall Cl.
CR0: Wad ... 7A 200 (1M 63)
Grindley Gdns. CR0: Croy ... 5C 46
Grindstone Cres.
GU21: Knap ... 5E 72
GRINDSTONE HANDLE CORNER
... 5E 72
Grinstead La. RH19: F Row ... 8L 185
Grisedale Cl. CR8: Pur ... 1B 84
RH11: Craw ... 5A 182
Grisedale Gdns. CR8: Pur ... 1B 84
Grobars Av. GU21: Wok ... 2M 73
Grogan Cl. TW12: Hamp ... 7N 23
Groombridge Cl.
KT12: Hers ... 2J 57
Groombridge Way
RH12: Hors ... 7F 196
Groom Cres. SW18 ... 1B 28
Groomfield Cl. SW17 ... 5E 28
Grooms, The RH10: Craw ... 1H 183
Groom Wlk. GU1: Guil ... 9A 94
Grosse Way SW15 ... 9G 13
Grosvenor Av. SM5: Cars ... 3D 62
SW14 ... 6D 12
TW10: Rich ... 8L 11
Grosvenor Cl. RH6: Horl ... 1E 162
Grosvenor Ct. GU4: B'ham ... 9D 94
GU17: Haw ... 3J 69
RH19: E Grin ... 9N 165
(off Grosvenor Rd.)
SM2: Sut ... 3N 61
SM4: Mord ... 3M 43
TW11: Tedd ... 7G 25
Grosvenor Gdns.
KT2: K Tham ... 7K 25
SM6: W'ton ... 4G 62
SW14 ... 6D 12
Grosvenor Hill SW19 ... 7K 27
Grosvenor Ho. GU1: Guil ... 4B 114
SM1: Sut ... 2N 61
(off West St.)
Grosvenor M. KT18: Eps D ... 6C 80
RH2: Reig ... 6N 121
Grosvenor Pl. GU21: Wok ... 4B 74
(off Stanley Rd.)
KT13: Weybr ... 9E 38
Grosvenor Rd.
BR4: W Wick ... 7L 47
GU7: Godal ... 8H 133
GU11: Alde ... 2M 109
GU24: Chob ... 9G 53
KT18: Eps D ... 6C 80
RH19: E Grin ... 9N 165
SE25 ... 3C 46
SM6: W'ton ... 3F 62
TW1: Twick ... 2G 24
TW3: Houn ... 6N 9
TW8: Brent ... 2K 11
TW10: Rich ... 8L 11
TW18: Stain ... 8J 21
W4 ... 1A 12
Grosvenor Way SW17 ... 4B 28
Groton Rd. SW18 ... 3N 27
Grotto Rd. KT13: Weybr ... 9C 38
TW1: Twick ... 3F 24
Grouse Mdws.
RG12: Brac ... 2J 31
Grouse Rd.
RH11: Colg, Pease P ... 3K 199
RH13: Plum P, Colg ... 9E 198
Grove, The BR4: W Wick ... 9L 47
CR3: Cate ... 8M 83
CR5: Coul ... 2H 83
GU9: Farnh ... 1G 128
GU11: Alde ... 3M 109
GU14: Farnb ... 4B 90
GU16: Frim ... 5B 70
GU21: Wok ... 3B 74
GU26: G'hott ... 6B 170
KT12: Wal T ... 6J 39
KT15: Addl ... 2K 55
KT17: Eps ... 7M 201 (9D 60)
KT17: Ewe ... 6E 60
KT24: Eff ... 6L 97
RH6: Horl ... 9F 142
RH11: Craw ... 3A 182
SL5: Asc ... 9G 17
TN16: B Hil ... 5F 86
TW1: Twick ... 9H 11
TW7: Isle ... 4E 10
TW11: Tedd ... 5G 24
TW20: Egh ... 6C 20
Grove Av.
KT17: Eps ... 6M 201 (9D 60)
SM1: Sut ... 3M 61
TW1: Twick ... 2F 24
Grovebarns TW18: Stain ... 7J 21
Grovebell Ind. Est.
GU10: Wrec ... 4E 128
Grove Cl. GU6: Cranl ... 9A 156
KT1: K Tham ... 7L 203 (3M 41)
KT19: Eps ... 6N 59
RG40: W'ham ... 9D 30
SL4: O Win ... 1L 19
TW13: Hanw ... 5M 23
Grove Cnr. KT23: Book ... 4B 98
Grove Cotts. W4 ... 2D 12
Grove Ct. KT1: K Tham ... 6J 203
KT8: E Mol ... 3D 40
RH1: Red ... 1F 122
(off Gumbrell M.)
RH10: Craw ... 3E 182
TW3: Houn ... 7A 10
TW20: Egh ... 6C 20
Grove Cres.
KT1: K Tham ... 6J 203 (2L 41)
KT12: Wal T ... 6J 39
TW13: Hanw ... 5M 23
Grove Cross Rd. GU16: Frim ... 5B 70
Grove End GU19: Bag ... 3K 51
Grove End La. KT10: Esh ... 7D 40
Grove End Rd. GU9: Farnh ... 4G 128
Grove Farm Pk.
GU16: Mytc ... 4D 90
Grovefields Av. GU16: Frim ... 5B 70
Grove Footpath
KT5: Surb ... 8K 203 (3L 41)
Grove Gdns. TW10: Rich ... 9M 11
TW11: Tedd ... 5G 24
GROVE HEATH ... 1K 95
Grove Heath Ct. GU23: Rip ... 2L 95
Grove Heath Nth. GU23: Rip ... 9K 75
Grove Heath Rd. GU23: Rip ... 1K 95
Grovehill Rd. RH1: Red ... 3D 122
Grove Ho. RH1: Red ... 3D 122
(off Huntingdon Rd.)
Groveland Av. SW16 ... 8K 29
Groveland Rd. BR3: Beck ... 2J 47
Grovelands GU10: Lwr Bou ... 4K 129
KT1: K Tham ... 8H 203
KT8: W Mole ... 3A 40
RH6: Horl ... 9F 142
Grovelands Rd. CR8: Pur ... 8J 63
Groveland Way KT3: N Mal ... 4B 42
Grove La. CR5: Ban, Coul ... 8D 62
KT1: K Tham ... 7K 203 (3L 41)
RG42: Wink R ... 6F 16
Groveley Rd. TW13: Felt ... 6G 23
TW16: Sunb ... 6F 22
Grove Mill Pl. SM5: Cars ... 9E 44
GROVE PARK ... 4B 12
Grove Pk. Bri. W4 ... 3B 12
Grove Pk. Gdns. W4 ... 3A 12
Grove Pk. M. W4 ... 3B 12
Grove Pk. Rd. W4 ... 3A 12
Grove Pk. Ter. W4 ... 3A 12
Grove Pl. KT13: Weybr ... 2D 56
SW12 ... 1F 28
Grove Rd. CR4: Mit ... 2E 44
(not continuous)
CR7: T Hea ... 3L 45
GU1: Guil ... 3E 114
GU6: Cranl ... 9A 156
GU7: Godal ... 8F 132
GU12: Ash V ... 9E 90
GU15: Camb ... 1D 70
GU21: Wok ... 3B 74
GU26: Hind ... 3N 169
GU52: Chu C ... 8C 88
KT6: Surb ... 8G 203 (4K 41)
KT8: E Mol ... 3D 40
KT16: Chert ... 5H 37
KT17: Eps ... 7M 201 (9D 60)
KT21: Asht ... 5M 79
RH1: Red ... 3D 122
RH6: Horl ... 7C 142
RH7: Ling ... 6A 146
RH8: Tand ... 2M 125
SL4: W'sor ... 5F 4
SM1: Sut ... 3M 61
SW13 ... 5E 12
SW19 ... 8A 28
TN16: Tats ... 7E 86
TW2: Twick ... 4D 24
TW3: Houn ... 7A 10
TW7: Isle ... 4E 10
TW8: Brent ... 1J 11
TW10: Rich ... 9M 11
TW17: Shep ... 5D 38
Grovers Farm Cotts.
KT15: Wood ... 7G 55
Grovers Gdns. GU26: Hind ... 3B 170
Grover's Mnr. GU26: Hind ... 3B 170
Grove Shaw KT20: K'wood ... 2K 101
Groveside KT23: Book ... 4A 98
Groveside Cl. KT23: Book ... 5A 98
SM5: Cars ... 8C 44
Grovestile Waye TW14: Bedf ... 1E 22
Grove Ter. TW11: Tedd ... 5G 24
Grove Way KT10: Esh ... 6C 40
Grovewood TW9: Kew ... 4N 11
Grove Wood Hill CR5: Coul ... 1G 83
Grub St. RH8: Limp ... 6E 106
G's Health Club ... 5M 185
Guards Av. CR3: Cate ... 9N 83
Guards Ct. SL5: S'dale ... 6E 34
Guards Polo Club ... 9H 19
Guards Rd. SL4: W'sor ... 5A 4
Guards Wlk. SL4: W'sor ... 5A 4
Guards Way CR3: Cate ... 9N 83
Guerdon Pl. RG12: Brac ... 6B 32
Guernsey Cl. GU4: B'ham ... 7C 94
RH11: Craw ... 7M 181
TW5: Hest ... 3A 10
Guernsey Dr. GU51: Fleet ... 1C 88
Guernsey Farm Dr.
GU21: Wok ... 2N 73
Guernsey Gro. SE24 ... 1N 29
Guildables La. TN8: Eden ... 4G 127
Guildcroft GU1: Guil ... 3C 114
Guildersfield Rd. SW16 ... 8J 29
GUILDFORD ... 6C 202 (3K 113)
Guildford & Godalming By-Pass Rd.
GU2: Guil ... 9D 112
GU3: Comp, Guil ... 9D 112
GU8: Mil, P Har, S'ford ... 1B 152
Guildford Av. TW13: Felt ... 3G 23
Guildford Boat House
... 7C 202 (5N 113)
Guildford Bus. Pk.
GU2: Guil ... 2L 113
Guildford Bus. Pk. Rd.
GU2: Guil ... 2L 113
Guildford Castle ... 6C 202 (5N 113)
Guildford Cathedral ... 3K 113
Guildford Ct. GU2: Guil ... 3K 113
Guildford Crematorium
GU7: Godal ... 3L 133
Guildford Golf Course ... 3E 114
Guildford Ind. Est.
GU2: Guil ... 3K 113
Guildford La. GU5: Alb ... 6G 115
GU22: Wok ... 6N 73
Guildford Lido ... 1D 202 (2N 113)
Guildford Lodge Dr.
KT24: E Hor ... 7G 96
Guildford Mus. ... 6C 202 (5N 113)
GUILDFORD PARK ... 4L 113
Guildford Pk. Av.
GU2: Guil ... 4A 202 (4L 113)
Guildford Pk. Rd.
GU2: Guil ... 5A 202 (4L 113)
Guildford Rd. CR0: Croy ... 5A 46
GU3: Norm ... 1K 111
GU3: Worp ... 2C 92
GU4: Sut G ... 5N 93
GU5: Sha G ... 6F 134
(Northcote La.)
GU5: Sha G ... 1J 155
(Up. House La.)
GU6: Alf ... 3J 175
GU6: Alf, Rudg ... 7K 175
GU6: Cranl ... 3J 155
GU7: Godal ... 4K 133
GU9: Farnh ... 9J 109
GU10: Farnh, Run ... 8L 109
GU12: Alde ... 5B 110
GU12: Ash ... 2G 110
GU16: Deep, Frim G ... 8D 70
GU18: Ligh ... 6L 51
GU19: Bag ... 4J 51
(High St.)
GU19: Bag ... 5K 51
(Regent Ct.)
GU21: Knap ... 8B 52
GU21: Wok ... 7D 54
GU22: Wok ... 9N 73
(Bourne Way)
GU22: Wok ... 6A 74
(Wych Hill La.)
GU24: Bis, W End ... 8B 52
GU24: Chob ... 9G 53
GU24: Pirb ... 1C 92
GU51: Fleet ... 5D 88
KT16: Otter, Chert ... 2E 54
KT22: Fetc ... 3D 98
KT23: Book ... 6L 97
KT24: E Hor, Eff ... 7G 96
RH4: Westc ... 7A 118
RH5: A Ham, Wott ... 9G 116
RH12: Hors ... 5F 196
RH12: Rudg ... 7K 175
RH12: Slinf, Broadb H ... 1L 195
RH13: Rudg, Slinf ... 1H 195
RH14: Loxw ... 3H 193
Guildford Rd. E.
GU14: Farnb ... 4A 90
Guildford Rd. Trad. Est.
GU9: Farnh ... 9J 109
Guildford Rd. W.
GU14: Farnb ... 4A 90
Guildford Station (Rail)
... 5A 202 (4M 113)
Guildford St. KT16: Chert ... 6H 37
TW18: Stain ... 7J 21
Guildford Way SM6: W'ton ... 2J 63
Guildford Guildhall & House Gallery
... 5D 202 (4N 113)
Guildown Av.
GU2: Guil ... 8A 202 (6L 113)
Guildown Rd.
GU2: Guil ... 8A 202 (6L 113)
Guildway, The GU3: Art ... 9M 113
Guileshill La. GU23: Ockh ... 1N 95
Guilford Av.
KT5: Surb ... 8L 203 (4M 41)
Guillemont Flds.
GU14: Cove ... 9J 69
Guillemont Pk. GU17: Min ... 8H 69
Guillemot Path RH11: Ifield ... 4J 181
Guillemot St. RG12: Brac ... 4J 31
Guinea Wlk. RG12: Brac ... 3J 31
Guinevere Rd. RH11: Ifield ... 3K 181
Guinness Ct. CR0: Croy ... 8C 46
GU21: Wok ... 5J 73
RH11: Craw ... 7A 182
Guinness Trust Bldgs. W6 ... 1J 13
(off Fulham Pal. Rd.)
Guion Rd. SW6 ... 5L 13
Gull La. RG12: Brac ... 4J 31
Gumbrell M. RH1: Red ... 1F 122
Gumbrells Cl. GU3: Worp ... 8F 92
Gumley Gdns. TW7: Isle ... 6G 10
Gun Hill GU11: Alde ... 1N 109
Gunnell Cl. CR0: Croy ... 5D 46
SE25 ... 5D 46
(off Backley Gdns.)
GUNNERSBURY ... 1A 12
Gunnersbury Av. W4 ... 1N 11
Gunnersbury Cl. W4 ... 1A 12
Gunnersbury M. W4 ... 1A 12
Gunnersbury Station
(Underground & Overground)
... 1A 12

Gunnersbury Triange Nature Reserve—Harcourt Av.

Gunnersbury Triangle
Nature Reserve ... 1B 12
Gunners Rd. SW18 ... 3B 28
Gunning Cl. RH11: Craw ... 6M 181
Gun Pit Rd. RH7: Ling ... 7N 145
Gunter Gro. SW10 ... 2N 13
Gunter Hall Studios *SW10* ... *2N 13*
(off Gunter Gro.)
Gunters Mead KT10: Esh ... 7C 58
(not continuous)
KT22: Oxs ... 7C 58
Gunterstone Rd. W14 ... 1K 13
Gunton Rd. SW17 ... 7E 28
Gurdon's La. GU8: Worm ... 9B 152
Gurney Cres. CR0: Croy ... 7K 45
Gurney Ho. UB3: Harl ... 1F 8
Gurney Rd. SM5: Cars ... 1E 62
Gurney's Cl. RH1: Red ... 4D 122
Guyatt Gdns. CR4: Mit ... 1E 44
Guy Rd. SM6: Bedd ... 9H 45
Gwalior Rd. SW15 ... 7J 13
Gwendolen Av. SW15 ... 7J 13
Gwendolen Cl. SW15 ... 8J 13
Gwendolen Ho. *TW19: Stan* ... *2N 21*
(off Yeoman Dr.)
Gwendwr Rd. W14 ... 1K 13
Gwydor Rd. BR3: Beck ... 2G 47
Gwyn Cl. SW6 ... 3N 13
Gwynedd Cl. TN16: Tats ... 9F 86
Gwynne Av. CR0: Croy ... 6G 46
Gwynne Cl. SL4: W'sor ... 4B 4
W4 ... 2E 12
Gwynne Ct. *GU2: Guil* ... *8L 93*
(off Grange Rd.)
Gwynne Gdns.
RH19: E Grin ... 8M 165
Gwynne Rd. CR3: Cate ... 1A 104
Gym, The
Hounslow ... 6B 10

H

Habershon Dr. GU16: Frim ... 4H 71
Haccombe Rd. SW19 ... 7A 28
HACKBRIDGE ... 7E 44
Hackbridge Pk. Gdns.
SM5: Cars ... 8D 44
Hackbridge Rd. SM6: W'ton ... 8E 44
Hackbridge Station (Rail) ... 8F 44
Hackenden Cl.
RH19: E Grin ... 7A 166
Hackenden Cotts.
RH19: E Grin ... 7A 166
Hackenden La.
RH19: E Grin ... 8A 166
Hacketts La. GU22: Pyr ... 1H 75
Hackhurst Down
(Local Nature Reserve)
... 6F 116
Hackhurst La. RH5: A Ham ... 8G 116
Haddenhurst Ct. RG42: Bin ... 7H 15
Haddon Cl. KT3: N Mal ... 4E 42
KT13: Weybr ... 9F 38
Haddon Rd. SM1: Sut ... 1N 61
(not continuous)
Hadfield Rd. TW19: Stan ... 9M 7
Hadleigh Cl. SW20 ... 1L 43
Hadleigh Dr. SM2: Sut ... 5M 61
Hadleigh Gdns.
GU16: Frim G ... 8C 70
Hadley Ct. *SL3: Poy* ... *4G 7*
(off Coleridge Cres.)
Hadley Gdns. UB2: S'hall ... 1N 9
W4 ... 1C 12
Hadley Pl. KT13: Weybr ... 4B 56
Hadley Rd. CR4: Mit ... 3H 45
Hadleys GU10: Rowl ... 8D 128
Hadley Wood Ri. CR8: Ken ... 1M 83
Hadmans Cl. RH12: Hors ... 7J 197
Hadrian Cl. TW19: Stan ... 1N 21
Hadrian Ct. SM2: Sut ... 4N 61
Hadrian M. CR4: Mit ... 2F 44
Hadrians GU9: Farnh ... 8K 109
Hadrian Way TW19: Stan ... 1M 21
(not continuous)
Haggard Rd. TW1: Twick ... 1H 25
Haigh Cres. RH1: Red ... 5F 122
Haig La. GU52: Chu C ... 8C 88
Haig Pl. SM4: Mord ... 5M 43
Haig Rd. GU12: Alde ... 3A 110
GU15: Camb ... 9L 49
TN16: B Hil ... 4G 86
Hailes Cl. CR0: Bedd ... 8H 45
SW19 ... 7A 28
Hailey Pl. GU6: Cranl ... 6A 156
Hailsham Av. SW2 ... 3K 29
Hailsham Cl. GU47: Owls ... 6J 49
KT6: Surb ... 6K 41
Hailsham Rd. SW17 ... 7E 28
Haines Ct. KT13: Weybr ... 2E 56
Haines Wlk. SM4: Mord ... 6N 43
Haining Cl. W4 ... 1N 11
Haining Gdns. GU16: Mytc ... 2E 90
Hainthorpe Rd. SE27 ... 4M 29
Halcyon *GU9: Up Hale* ... *5F 108*
(off Lawday Link)
Halcyon Cl. KT22: Oxs ... 2D 78
Haldane Pl. SW18 ... 2N 27
Haldane Rd. SW6 ... 3L 13
Haldon Rd. SW18 ... 9L 13
HALE ... 7J 109
Hale SL4: W'sor ... 4B 4
Halebourne La.
GU24: Chob, W End ... 4D 52
Hale Cl. BR6: Farnb ... 1L 67
Hale End RG12: Brac ... 3D 32
Hale Ends GU22: Wok ... 8L 73
Hale Ho. GU9: Farnh ... 8J 109
Hale Ho. Cl. GU10: Churt ... 9L 149
Hale Ho. La. GU10: Churt ... 9L 149
Hale Path SE27 ... 5M 29
Hale Pit Rd. KT23: Book ... 4C 98
Hale Pl. GU9: Hale ... 7K 109
Hale Reeds GU9: Heath E ... 6J 109
Hale Rd. GU9: Farnh, Hale ... 7J 109
Hales Fld. GU27: Hasl ... 2G 189
Hales Oak KT23: Book ... 4C 98
Halesowen Rd. SM4: Mord ... 6N 43
Hale St. TW18: Stain ... 5G 21
Haleswood KT11: Cob ... 1J 77
Hale Way GU16: Frim ... 6B 70
Halewood RG12: Brac ... 5L 31
Half Acre TW8: Brent ... 2K 11
Halfacres RH10: Craw ... 2C 182
Half Moon Cotts. GU23: Rip ... 8L 75
Half Moon Hill GU27: Hasl ... 2G 189
Half Moon St. GU19: Bag ... 4J 51
Halford Rd. SW6 ... 2M 13
TW10: Rich ... 8L 11
Halfpenny Cl. GU4: Guil ... 9F 114
Halfpenny La. GU4: Guil ... 6E 114
SL5: S'dale ... 6D 34
Halfway Grn. KT12: Wal T ... 9J 39
Halfway La. GU7: Eash ... 7D 132
Haliburton Rd. TW1: Twick ... 8G 11
Halifax Cl. GU14: Cove ... 2L 89
RH10: Craw ... 9J 163
TW11: Tedd ... 7E 24
Halifax Rd. RG12: Brac ... 2A 32
Halimote Rd. GU11: Alde ... 3M 109
Haling Down Pas.
CR2: S Croy ... 5N 63
CR8: Pur ... 6M 63
(not continuous)
Haling Gro. CR2: S Croy ... 4N 63
Haling Pk. Gdns.
CR2: S Croy ... 3M 63
Haling Pk. Rd.
CR2: S Croy ... 8A 200 (2M 63)
Haling Rd. CR2: S Croy ... 3A 64
Hallam Ct. *CR0: Croy* ... *6N 45*
(off Whitehorse Rd.)
Hallam Rd. GU7: Godal ... 5J 133
SW13 ... 6G 13
Halland Cl. RH10: Craw ... 2E 182
Halland Ct. *TN8: Eden* ... *2L 147*
(off Stangrove Rd.)
Hallane Ho. SE27 ... 6N 29
Hallbrooke Gdns. RG42: Bin ... 8K 15
Hall Cl. GU7: Godal ... 4H 133
GU15: Camb ... 9C 50
Hall Ct. SL3: Dat ... 3L 5
TW11: Tedd ... 6F 24
Hall Dene Cl. GU1: Guil ... 2E 114
Hall Dr. GU52: Fleet ... 7C 88
Halley Cl. RH11: Craw ... 8N 181
Halley Dr. SL5: Asc ... 1H 33
Halley's App. GU21: Wok ... 4K 73
Halley's Ct. GU21: Wok ... 5K 73
Halley's Wlk. KT15: Addl ... 4L 55
Hall Farm Cres. GU46: Yate ... 1C 68
Hall Farm Dr. TW2: Whitt ... 1D 24
Hallgrove Bottom GU19: Bag ... 2K 51
Hall Gro. Farm Ind. Est.
GU19: Bag ... 2K 51
Hall Hill RH8: Oxt ... 9N 105
Hall Hurst Cl. RH14: Loxw ... 4H 193
Halliards, The KT12: Wal T ... 5H 39
Halliford Cl. TW17: Shep ... 3E 38
Halliford Rd. TW16: Sunb ... 4F 38
TW17: Shep ... 4F 38
Halliloo Valley Rd.
CR3: Wold ... 7G 85
Hallington Cl. GU21: Wok ... 4L 73
Hall La. GU46: Yate ... 1B 68
UB3: Harl ... 3E 8
Hallmark Cl. GU47: Coll T ... 7K 49
Hallmead Rd. SM1: Sut ... 9N 43
Hallowell Av. CR0: Bedd ... 1J 63
Hallowell Cl. CR4: Mit ... 2E 44
Hallowell Gdns. CR7: T Hea ... 1N 45
Hallowes Cl. GU2: Guil ... 7L 93
Hallowfield Way CR4: Mit ... 2B 44
Hallows Gro. TW16: Sunb ... 6G 23
HALL PLACE ... 1G 175
Hall Pl. GU21: Wok ... 3C 74
Hall Pl. Dr. KT13: Weybr ... 2F 56
Hall Rd. GU5: Braml ... 5B 134
SM6: W'ton ... 5F 62
TW7: Isle ... 8D 10
Halls Dr. RH12: Fay ... 8E 180
Halls Farm Cl. GU21: Knap ... 4G 73
Hallsland RH10: Craw D ... 1F 184
Hallsland Way RH8: Oxt ... 2B 126
Hall Way CR8: Pur ... 9M 63
Halnaker Wlk. RH11: Craw ... 6L 181
Halsford Cft. RH19: E Grin ... 7L 165
Halsford Grn. RH19: E Grin ... 7L 165
Halsford La. RH19: E Grin ... 8L 165
Halsford Pk. Rd.
RH19: E Grin ... 8M 165
Halstead Cl.
CR0: Croy ... 4B 200 (9N 45)
Halters End GU26: G'hott ... 6M 169
Halton Rd. CR8: Ken ... 7B 84
HAM ... 4J 25
Ham, The TW8: Brent ... 3J 11
Hamble Av. GU17: B'water ... 1J 69
Hamble Cl. GU21: Wok ... 4K 73
Hambleden Ct. RG12: Brac ... 3C 32
HAMBLEDON ... 9F 152
Hambledon Gdns. SE25 ... 2C 46
Hambledon Hill KT18: Eps ... 3B 80
Hambledon Pk. GU8: Hamb ... 9E 152
Hambledon Pl. KT23: Book ... 1A 98
Hambledon Rd. CR3: Cate ... 1A 104
GU7: Bus ... 9J 133
GU8: Bus, Hamb ... 7G 153
SW18 ... 1L 27
Hambledon Va. KT18: Eps ... 3B 80
Hamblehyrst BR3: Beck ... 1L 47
Hamble St. SW6 ... 6N 13
Hambleton *SL4: O Win* ... *2M 19*
(off Burfield Rd.)
Hambleton Cl. GU16: Frim ... 3F 70
KT4: W Pk ... 8H 43
Hambleton Ct. RH11: Craw ... 5A 182
Hambleton Hill RH11: Craw ... 5A 182
Hamble Wlk. GU21: Wok ... 5K 73
Hambridge Way SW2 ... 1L 29
Hambrook Rd. SE25 ... 2E 46
Hambro Rd. SW16 ... 7H 29
Ham Cl. TW10: Ham ... 4J 25
(not continuous)
Ham Comn. TW10: Ham ... 4K 25
Ham Common (Nature Reserve)
... 5L 25
Ham Cft. Cl. TW13: Felt ... 4H 23
Hamesmoor Rd. GU16: Mytc ... 1C 90
Hamesmoor Way
GU16: Mytc ... 1D 90
Ham Farm Rd. TW10: Ham ... 5K 25
Hamfield Cl. RH8: Oxt ... 5M 105
Ham Flds. TW10: Ham ... 4H 25
Ham Ga. Av. TW10: Ham ... 4K 25
Hamhaugh Island
TW17: Shep ... 8B 38
Ham House & Gardens ... 2J 25
Hamilton Av. GU22: Pyr ... 2G 75
KT6: Surb ... 8N 41
KT11: Cob ... 9H 57
SM3: Chea ... 8K 43
Hamilton Cl. CR8: Pur ... 8M 63
GU2: Guil ... 7K 93
GU19: Bag ... 4J 51
GU35: Bor ... 5A 168
KT16: Chert ... 7H 37
KT19: Eps ... 8B 60
RH6: Horl ... 9E 142
TW11: Tedd ... 7H 25
TW13: Felt ... 6G 22
Hamilton Ct. CR0: Croy ... 7D 46
KT11: Cob ... 9H 57
KT23: Book ... 3B 98
SW15 ... 6K 13
TW3: Houn ... *7B 10*
(off Hanworth Rd.)
Hamilton Cres. TW3: Houn ... 8B 10
Hamilton Dr. GU2: Guil ... 7K 93
SL5: S'dale ... 6B 34
Hamilton Gdns. GU14: Cove ... 9H 69
Hamilton Gordon Ct.
GU1: Guil ... 1B 202 (2M 113)
Hamilton Ho. W4 ... 2D 12
Hamilton M. *KT13: Weybr* ... *1B 56*
(off Holstein Av.)
SW18 ... 2M 27
SW19 ... 8M 27
Hamilton Pde. TW13: Felt ... 5G 23
Hamilton Pl. GU2: Guil ... 7K 93
GU11: Alde ... 3L 109
KT14: W By ... 9H 55
KT20: K'wood ... 9L 81
TW16: Sunb ... 8J 23
Hamilton Rd. CR7: T Hea ... 2A 46
GU52: Chu C ... 7C 88
RH12: Hors ... 5H 197
SW19 ... 8N 27
TW2: Twick ... 2E 24
TW8: Brent ... 2K 11
TW13: Felt ... 5G 22
Hamilton Rd. M. SW19 ... 8N 27
Hamilton Way SM6: W'ton ... 5H 63
HAM ISLAND ... 7M 5
Ham Lands Nature Reserve ... 3G 25
Ham La. GU8: Els ... 7H 131
SL4: O Win ... 8M 5
TW20: Eng G ... 5L 19
Hamlash La. GU10: Fren ... 1H 149
Hamlet Gdns. W6 ... 1F 12
Hamlet M. SE21 ... 2N 29
Hamlet St. RG42: Warf ... 9C 16
Hamlyn Ho. TW13: Felt ... 2J 23
Hamm Ct. KT13: Weybr ... 8N 37
HAMMER ... 3B 188
HAMMER BOTTOM ... 2A 188
Hammerfield Dr.
RH5: A Ham ... 1G 136
Hammer Hill GU27: Hasl ... 4A 188
Hammer La. GU6: Cranl ... 3M 175
GU10: Churt ... 1K 169
GU26: G'hott ... 1K 169
GU27: Lip ... 2A 188
Hammer Pond Cotts.
GU8: Thur ... 4K 151
Hammerpond Rd.
RH13: Hors, Colg, Mann H, Plum P
... 7M 197
Hammersley Rd.
GU11: Alde ... 6N 89
HAMMERSMITH ... 1H 13
Hammersmith Apollo ... 1H 13
Hammersmith Bri. SW13 ... 2G 13
Hammersmith Bri. Rd. W6 ... 1H 13
Hammersmith B'way. W6 ... 1H 13
Hammersmith Emb. W6 ... 2H 13
Hammersmith Fitness &
Squash Cen. ... *1J 13*
(off Chalk Hill Rd.)
HAMMERSMITH FLYOVER ... 1H 13
Hammersmith Flyover W6 ... 1H 13
Hammersmith Rd. W6 ... 1J 13
W14 ... 1J 13
Hammersmith Station
(Underground) ... 1H 13
Hammersmith Ter. W6 ... 1F 12
Hammer Va. GU27: Lip ... 2A 188
HAMMERWOOD ... 7K 167
Hammerwood Copse
GU27: Hasl ... 3B 188
Hammerwood Park ... 8L 167
Hammerwood Rd.
RH19: Ash W ... 3F 186
Hammer Yd. RH10: Craw ... 4B 182
Hamm Moor La.
KT15: Addl ... 2N 55
Hammond Av. CR4: Mit ... 1F 44
Hammond Cl. GU21: Wok ... 2M 73
TW12: Hamp ... 9A 24
Hammond Ct. RG42: Brac ... 9M 15
Hammond Rd. GU21: Wok ... 2M 73
RH11: Craw ... 9N 181
Hammond's Copse Nature Reserve
... 6D 140
Hammondswood Rd.
GU10: Fren ... 2H 149
Hammond Way GU18: Ligh ... 6M 51
HAM MOOR ... 1N 55
Hamond Cl. CR2: S Croy ... 5M 63
Hampden Av. BR3: Beck ... 1H 47
Hampden Cl. RH10: Craw ... 9J 163
Hampden Cres. RG12: Brac ... 2A 32
Hampden Rd. BR3: Beck ... 1H 47
KT1: K Tham ... 2N 41
Hampers Ct. RH13: Hors ... 6K 197
Hamper's La. RH13: Hors ... 6N 197
Hampshire Cl. GU12: Alde ... 5B 110
Hampshire Ct. KT15: Addl ... 2L 55
Hampshire Hog La. W6 ... 1G 12
Hampshire Ri. RG42: Warf ... 7D 16
Hampshire Rd.
GU15: Camb ... 7D 50
Hampstead La. RH4: Dork ... 6F 118
Hampstead M. BR3: Beck ... 3L 47
Hampstead Rd. RH4: Dork ... 6G 119
Hampstead Wlk.
RH11: Craw ... 7A 182
HAMPTON ... 9B 24
Hampton & Richmond Borough FC
... 9B 24
Hampton Bus. Pk.
TW13: Hanw ... 4M 23
Hampton Cl. GU21: Knap ... 6F 72
GU52: Chu C ... 9B 88
SW20 ... 8H 27
HAMPTON COURT ... 3E 40
HAMPTON COURT ... 2E 40
Hampton Ct. Av. KT8: E Mol ... 5D 40
Hampton Ct. Bri. KT8: E Mol ... 3E 40
Hampton Ct. Cres.
KT8: E Mol ... 2D 40
Hampton Ct. Est. KT7: T Dit ... 3E 40
Hampton Ct. M. *KT8: E Mol* ... *3E 40*
(off Feltham Av.)
Hampton Court Palace ... 3F 40
Hampton Court Palace Golf Course
... 4J 41
Hampton Ct. Pde.
KT8: E Mol ... 3E 40
Hampton Ct. Rd. KT1: H Wic ... 2F 40
KT8: E Mol ... 2F 40
TW12: E Mol, Hamp ... 1C 40
Hampton Court Station (Rail)
... 3E 40
Hampton Ct. Way KT7: T Dit ... 8E 40
KT8: E Mol ... 8E 40
KT10: T Dit ... 8E 40
Hampton Golf Course ... 4A 24
Hampton Gro. KT17: Ewe ... 7E 60
HAMPTON HILL ... 6C 24
Hampton Hill Bus. Pk.
TW12: H Hill ... *6C 24*
(off High St.)
Hampton Hill Playhouse Theatre
... 6C 24
Hampton La. TW13: Hanw ... 5M 23
Hampton Lodge RH6: Horl ... 9E 142
Hampton Open Air Pool ... 8C 24
Hampton Rd. CR0: Croy ... 5N 45
GU9: Up Hale ... 6F 108
KT4: W Pk ... 8F 42
RH1: Red ... 8D 122
TW2: Twick ... 4D 24
TW11: Tedd ... 6D 24
TW12: H Hill ... 6D 24
Hampton Rd. E.
TW13: Hanw ... 5N 23
Hampton Rd. Ind. Pk.
CR0: Croy ... 5N 45
Hampton Rd. W.
TW13: Hanw ... 4M 23
Hampton Sports & Fitness Cen.
... 6A 24
Hampton Station (Rail) ... 9A 24
Hampton Way
RH19: E Grin ... 2B 186
HAMPTON WICK ... 2G 203 (9J 25)
Hampton Wick Station (Rail)
... 2G 203 (9J 25)
Hampton Youth Project (Sports Hall)
... 7N 23
Ham Ridings TW10: Ham ... 6M 25
HAMSEY GREEN ... 3F 84
Hamsey Grn. Gdns.
CR6: Warl ... 3E 84
Hamsey Way CR2: Sande ... 2E 84
Ham St. TW10: Ham ... 2H 25
Ham Vw. CR0: Croy ... 5H 47
Hanah Ct. SW19 ... 8J 27
Hanbury Dr. TN16: B Hil ... 9D 66
Hanbury Path GU21: Wok ... 1F 74
Hanbury Rd. RH11: Ifield ... 4K 181
Hanbury Way GU15: Camb ... 3A 70
Hancocks Mt. SL5: S'hill ... 5A 34
Hancombe Rd. GU47: Sandh ... 6F 48
Handcroft Rd.
CR0: Croy ... 1A 200 (6M 45)
HANDCROSS ... 8N 199
Handel Mans. SW13 ... 3H 13
Handford La. GU46: Yate ... 1B 68
Handinhand La.
KT20: Box H ... 8B 100
Handley Page Rd.
SM6: W'ton ... 4K 63
Handside Cl. KT4: W Pk ... 7J 43
Hanford Cl. SW18 ... 2M 27
Hanford Row SW19 ... 7H 27
Hanger, The GU35: Head ... 2D 168
Hanger Ct. GU21: Knap ... 4H 73
Hangerfield Cl. GU46: Yate ... 1B 68
Hanger Hill KT13: Weybr ... 3C 56
Hangrove Hill BR6: Dow ... 9K 67
Hankins Ct. GU52: Fleet ... 6B 88
Hankley Common Golf Course
... 1B 150
Hanley Cl. SL4: W'sor ... 4A 4
Hannah Cl. BR3: Beck ... 2M 47
Hannah M. SM6: W'ton ... 4G 63
Hannah Peschar Sculpture Garden
... 8A 158
Hannay Ho. SW15 ... 9K 13
Hannay Wlk. SW16 ... 3H 29
Hannell Rd. SW6 ... 3K 13
Hannen Rd. SE27 ... 4M 29
Hannibal Rd. TW19: Stan ... 1M 21
Hannibal Way CR0: Wad ... 2K 63
Hanno Cl. SM6: W'ton ... 4H 63
Hanover Av. TW13: Felt ... 2H 23
Hanover Cl. GU16: Frim ... 5C 70
GU46: Yate ... 8C 48
RH1: Mers ... 6G 102
RH10: Craw ... 5D 182
(not continuous)
SL4: W'sor ... 4C 4
SM3: Chea ... 1K 61
TW9: Kew ... 3N 11
TW15: Ashf ... 5N 21
TW20: Eng G ... 7L 19
Hanover Ct. GU1: Guil ... 1N 113
GU22: Wok ... 6A 74
RH4: Dork ... 2G 201 (5F 118)
RH13: Hors ... 5M 197
SW15 ... 7E 12
Hanover Dr. GU51: Fleet ... 1D 88
Hanover Gdns. GU14: Cove ... 8K 69
RG12: Brac ... 6L 31
Hanover Pk. SL5: Asc ... 9K 17
Hanover Rd. SW19 ... 8A 28
Hanover St.
CR0: Croy ... 4A 200 (9M 45)
Hanover Ter. TW7: Isle ... 4G 11
Hanover Wlk. KT13: Weybr ... 9E 38
Hanover Way SL4: W'sor ... 5C 4
Hansler Ct. *SW19* ... *2K 27*
(off Princes Way)
Hansler Gro. KT8: E Mol ... 3D 40
Hanson Cl. GU4: B'ham ... 9B 94
GU15: Camb ... 8F 50
SW12 ... 1F 28
SW14 ... 6B 12
Hansworth Ho. *RH10: Craw* ... *4B 182*
(off Brighton Rd.)
HANWORTH
RG12 ... 6M 31
TW13 ... 5L 23
Hanworth Air Pk. Leisure Cen.
... 3L 23
Hanworth Cl. RG12: Brac ... 5A 32
Hanworth La. KT16: Chert ... 7H 37
Hanworth Rd. RG12: Brac ... 7M 31
RH1: Red ... 8D 122
TW3: Houn ... 2M 23
TW4: Houn ... 2M 23
TW12: Hamp ... 5N 23
TW13: Felt ... 2J 23
TW16: Sunb ... 8H 23
(not continuous)
Hanworth Ter. TW3: Houn ... 7B 10
Hanworth Trad. Est.
KT16: Chert ... 7H 37
TW13: Hanw ... 4M 23
Harbans Ct. SL3: Poy ... 4G 7
Harberson Rd. SW12 ... 2F 28
Harbledown Rd. CR2: Sande ... 7D 64
SW6 ... 4M 13
Harbord St. SW6 ... 4J 13
Harborough Rd. SW16 ... 5K 29
Harbour Cl. CR4: Mit ... 9E 28
GU14: Farnb ... 6M 69
Harbourfield Rd. SM7: Ban ... 2N 81
Harbridge Av. SW15 ... 1E 26
Harbury Rd. SM5: Cars ... 5C 62
Harcourt TW19: Wray ... 9A 6
Harcourt Av. SM6: W'ton ... 1F 62

Holehill La.—Horatius Way

Holehill La. RH4: Westc ... 4A 118
Hole La. TN8: Eden ... 5H 127
Holford Rd. GU1: Guil ... 3E 114
Holford Way SW15 ... 9F 12
HOLLAND ... 2C 126
Holland Av. SM2: Sut ... 5M 61
SW20 ... 9E 26
Holland Cl. GU9: Farnh ... 3K 129
KT19: Eps ... 7B 60
RH1: Red ... 3D 122
Holland Ct. KT6: Surb ... 6K 41
Holland Cres. RH8: Oxt ... 2C 126
Holland Gdns.
GU51: Fleet ... 5B 88
TW8: Brent ... 2M 11
TW20: Thor ... 1H 37
Holland Ho. SL4: Eton ... 2F 4
(off Common La.)
Holland La. RH8: Oxt ... 2C 126
Holland Pines RG12: Brac ... 6L 31
Holland Rd. RH8: Oxt ... 2C 126
SE25 ... 4D 46
Hollands, The GU22: Wok ... 5A 74
KT4: W Pk ... 7E 42
TW13: Hanw ... 5L 23
Hollands Ct. RH19: E Grin ... 6C 166
Hollands Fld.
RH12: Broadb H ... 4E 196
Hollands Way RH12: Warnh ... 9F 178
RH19: E Grin ... 6C 166
Hollerith Ri. RG12: Brac ... 5N 31
Holles Cl. TW12: Hamp ... 7A 24
Hollie Cl. RH6: Smallf ... 9M 143
Hollies, The GU17: Haw ... 5M 69
KT15: Addl ... 2L 55
(off Bourne Way)
RH8: Oxt ... 2D 126
Hollies Av. KT14: W By ... 9H 55
Hollies Cl. SW16 ... 7L 29
TW1: Twick ... 3F 24
Hollies Ct. KT15: Addl ... 2L 55
Hollies Way SW12 ... 1E 28
Hollin Ct. RH10: Craw ... 9C 162
Hollingbourne Cres.
RH11: Craw ... 9A 182
Hollingsworth Ct. KT6: Surb ... 6K 41
Hollingsworth Rd. CR0: Croy ... 3E 64
Hollington Cres. KT3: N Mal ... 5E 42
Hollingworth Cl.
KT8: W Mole ... 3N 39
Hollingworth Way
TN16: Weste ... 4M 107
Hollis Row RH1: Red ... 5D 122
Hollis Wood Dr.
GU10: Wrec ... 6D 128
Hollman Gdns. SW16 ... 7M 29
Hollow, The GU7: Eash ... 7C 132
GU10: Ews ... 5A 108
RH11: Craw ... 4L 181
Holloway Cl. UB7: Harm ... 1N 7
Holloway Dr. GU25: V Wat ... 3A 36
HOLLOWAY HILL ... 9H 133
Holloway Hill GU7: Godal ... 7G 133
KT16: Chert, Lyne ... 9E 36
Holloway Ho. TW20: Egh ... 6B 20
(off Stoneylands Rd.)
Holloway La.
UB7: Harm, W Dray ... 2M 7
Holloway St. TW3: Houn ... 6B 10
Hollow Cl. GU2: Guil ... 4L 113
Hollow La. GU25: V Wat ... 2M 35
GU35: Head ... 3D 168
RH5: A Com, Wott ... 9L 117
RH7: Dorm ... 1D 166
RH19: E Grin ... 4F 166
Hollows, The TW8: Brent ... 2M 11
Hollow Way GU26: G'hott ... 5A 170
Holly Acre GU46: Yate ... 1C 68
Holly Av. GU16: Frim ... 3F 70
KT12: Wal T ... 7L 39
KT15: N Haw ... 6J 55
Hollybank GU24: W End ... 9C 52
Hollybank Cl. TW12: Hamp ... 6A 24
Holly Bank Rd. GU22: Wok ... 8L 73
Hollybank Rd. KT14: W By ... 1J 75
Hollybrook Pk. GU35: Bor ... 6A 168
Hollybush Bus. Cen.
RH10: Ship B ... 6K 163
Hollybush Cl. RH10: Craw ... 2C 182
Hollybush Ind. Est.
GU11: Alde ... 8C 90
Holly Bush La. GU10: Fren ... 1H 149
TW12: Hamp ... 8N 23
Hollybush La. GU11: Alde ... 8C 90
GU23: Rip ... 6M 75
Hollybush Ride GU20: Windl ... 9K 33
RG40: Finch ... 2B 48
RG45: Crowt ... 3B 48
Hollybush Rd.
KT2: K Tham ... 6L 25
RH10: Craw ... 2C 182
Holly Cl. BR3: Beck ... 3M 47
GU12: Alde ... 2A 110
GU14: Cove ... 1M 89
GU21: Wok ... 6L 73
GU35: Head D ... 4H 169
KT16: L'cross ... 9K 35
KT19: Eps ... 5C 60
RH10: Craw ... 1E 182
RH12: Hors ... 3A 198
SM6: W'ton ... 4F 62
TW13: Hanw ... 6M 23
TW16: Sunb ... 2J 39
TW20: Eng G ... 7L 19
Hollycombe TW20: Eng G ... 5M 19
Holly Ct. KT16: Chert ... 7H 37
(off King St.)
KT22: Leat ... 9G 79
(off Belmont Rd.)
RG45: Crowt ... 3D 48
SM2: Sut ... 4M 61
Holly Cres. BR3: Beck ... 4J 47
SL4: W'sor ... 5A 4
Hollycroft Cl.
CR2: S Croy ... 8F 200 (2B 64)
UB7: Sip ... 2B 8
Hollycroft Gdns. UB7: Sip ... 2B 8
Hollydale Dr. BR2: Brom ... 1H 67
Holly Dr. SL4: O Win ... 9H 5
Holly Farm Rd. UB2: S'hall ... 1M 9
Hollyfield Rd. KT5: Surb ... 6M 41
Hollyfields Cl.
GU15: Camb ... 1N 69
Holly Ga. KT15: Addl ... 1K 55
Holly Grn. KT13: Weybr ... 1E 56
Hollygrove Cl. TW3: Houn ... 7N 9
Holly Hedge Cl. GU16: Frim ... 4C 70
Holly Hedge Rd. GU16: Frim ... 4C 70
Hollyhedge Rd. KT11: Cob ... 1J 77
HOLLY HILL ... 9N 187
Holly Hill Dr. SM7: Ban ... 3M 81
Holly Hill Pk. SM7: Ban ... 4M 81
Hollyhock Dr. GU24: Bis ... 2D 72
Hollyhook Cl. RG45: Crowt ... 1F 48
Holly Ho. RG12: Brac ... 5N 31
TW8: Brent ... 2J 11
Holly La. GU3: Worp ... 7F 92
GU7: Godal ... 7F 132
SM7: Ban ... 3M 81
Holly La. E. SM7: Ban ... 3M 81
Holly La. W. SM7: Ban ... 4M 81
Holly Lea GU4: J Wel ... 6N 93
Holly Lodge GU22: Wok ... 4B 74
(off Heathside Cres.)
KT20: Lwr K ... 4K 101
Hollymead SM5: Cars ... 9D 44
Hollymead Rd. CR5: Chip ... 5E 82
Hollymeoak Rd. CR5: Coul ... 6F 82
Hollymoor La. KT19: Ewe ... 6C 60
Holly Pde. KT11: Cob ... 1J 77
(off High St.)
TW13: Felt ... 4G 23
(off High St.)
Hollyridge GU27: Hasl ... 2F 188
Holly Rd. GU12: Alde ... 2A 110
GU14: Cove ... 1L 89
RH2: Reig ... 5N 121
TW1: Twick ... 2F 24
TW3: Houn ... 7B 10
TW12: H Hill ... 7C 24
W4 ... 1C 12
Holly Spring Cotts.
RG12: Brac ... 8B 16
Holly Spring La. RG12: Brac ... 9A 16
Holly Tree Cl. SW19 ... 2J 27
Hollytree Gdns. GU16: Frim ... 6B 70
Holly Tree Rd. CR3: Cate ... 9B 84
Holly Wlk. SL4: W'sor ... 5B 18
HOLLYWATER ... 8A 168
Hollywater Rd. GU30: Pass ... 9A 168
GU35: Bor, White ... 8A 168
Holly Way CR4: Mit ... 3H 45
GU17: B'water ... 2J 69
Hollywood Bowl
Bracknell ... 1N 31
Crawley ... 2B 182
Tolworth ... 8A 42
Hollywood Rd. SW10 ... 2N 13
Hollywoods CR0: Sels ... 5J 65
Holman Cl. RH11: Craw ... 9N 181
Holman Ct. KT17: Ewe ... 5F 60
Holman Hunt Ho. W6 ... 1K 13
(off Field Rd.)
Holman Rd. KT19: Ewe ... 2B 60
Holmbank Dr. TW17: Shep ... 3F 38
Holmbrook Cl. GU14: Cove ... 1H 89
Holmbrook Gdns.
GU14: Cove ... 1H 89
Holmbury Av. RG45: Crowt ... 9F 30
Holmbury Cl. RH11: Craw ... 5A 182
Holmbury Ct. CR2: S Croy ... 2B 64
SW17 ... 4D 28
SW19 ... 8C 28
Holmbury Dr. RH5: Nth H ... 8J 119
Holmbury Gro. CR0: Sels ... 4J 65
Holmbury Hill Rd.
RH5: Holm M ... 9J 137
Holmbury Keep RH6: Horl ... 7G 142
(off Maize Cft.)
Holmbury La.
RH5: For G, Holm M ... 9L 137
Holmbury Rd. GU6: Ewh ... 9H 137
RH5: Holm M ... 9H 137
HOLMBURY ST MARY ... 6K 137
Holmbush Cl. RH12: Hors ... 2K 197
Holmbush Ct. RH12: Fay ... 8G 181
Holmbush Farm World ... 8G 181
Holmbush Potteries Ind. Est.
RH12: Fay ... 8H 181
Holmbush Rd. SW15 ... 9K 13
Holm Cl. KT15: Wood ... 8G 55
Holm Ct. GU7: Godal ... 4G 132
Holmcroft KT20: Wal H ... 3G 101
RH10: Craw ... 4C 182
Holmdene Cl. BR3: Beck ... 1M 47
Holmead Rd. SW6 ... 3N 13
Holme Chase KT13: Weybr ... 3D 56
Holme Cl. RG45: Crowt ... 9F 30
Holme Ct. TW7: Isle ... 6G 10
Holmefield Pl. KT15: N Haw ... 6K 55
Holme Grange Bus. Pk.
RG40: W'ham ... 6D 30
HOLME GREEN ... 5E 30
Holmes Cl. CR8: Pur ... 9K 63
GU22: Wok ... 8B 74
SL5: S'hill ... 5N 33
Holmes Ct. GU26: G'hott ... 6B 170
(off Boundary Rd.)
Holmesdale KT13: Weybr ... 3E 56
(off Bridgewater Rd.)
Holmesdale Av. RH1: Mers ... 9G 102
SW14 ... 6A 12
Holmesdale Cl. GU1: Guil ... 2D 114
SE25 ... 2C 46
Holmesdale Mnr. RH1: Red ... 1E 122
Holmesdale Natural History Mus.
... 3N 121
Holmesdale Pk. RH1: Nut ... 3K 123
Holmesdale Rd. CR0: Croy ... 4A 46
RH1: Sth N ... 5K 123
RH2: Reig ... 2M 121
RH5: Nth H ... 9H 119
SE25 ... 4A 46
TW9: Kew ... 4M 11
TW11: Tedd ... 8J 25
Holmesdale Ter.
RH5: Nth H ... 9H 119
Holmesdale Vs.
RH5: Mid H ... 2H 139
Holmes Pl. GU26: Hind ... 5D 170
Holmes Rd. SW19 ... 8A 28
TW1: Twick ... 3F 24
Holmeswood SM2: Sut ... 3N 61
HOLMETHORPE ... 9F 102
Holmethorpe Av. RH1: Red ... 9F 102
Holmethorpe Ind. Est.
RH1: Red ... 9F 102
Holmethorpe Lagoons
Nature Reserve ... 9G 102
Holmewood Gdns. SW2 ... 1K 29
Holmewood Rd. SE25 ... 2B 46
SW2 ... 1K 29
Holmgrove Ho. CR8: Pur ... 8L 63
Holming End RH12: Hors ... 3A 198
Holmlea Ct. CR0: Croy ... 6E 200
Holmlea Rd. SL3: Dat ... 4N 5
Holmlea Wlk. SL3: Dat ... 4M 5
Holm Oak Cl. SW15 ... 9L 13
Holmoak Cl. CR8: Pur ... 6K 63
Holmoaks Ho. BR3: Beck ... 1M 47
Holmside Rd. SW12 ... 1E 28
Holmsley Cl. KT3: N Mal ... 5E 42
Holmsley Ho. SW15 ... 1E 26
(off Tangley Gro.)
Holmstead Ct.
CR2: S Croy ... 8E 200 (2A 64)
Holm Ter. RH4: Dork ... 8H 119
Holmwood Av. CR2: Sande ... 9C 64
Holmwood Cl. KT15: Addl ... 2J 55
KT24: E Hor ... 6F 96
SM2: Chea ... 5J 61
HOLMWOOD CORNER ... 6J 139
Holmwood Gdns.
SM6: W'ton ... 3F 62
Holmwood Rd. KT9: Ches ... 2K 59
SM2: Chea ... 5H 61
Holmwood Station (Rail) ... 7J 139
Holmwood Vw. Rd.
RH5: Mid H ... 2H 139
Holne Chase SM4: Mord ... 5L 43
Holroyd Cl. KT10: Clay ... 5F 58
Holroyd Rd. KT10: Clay ... 5F 58
SW15 ... 7H 13
Holsart Cl. KT20: Tad ... 9G 81
Holstein Av. KT13: Weybr ... 1B 56
Holst Mans. SW13 ... 2H 13
Holsworthy Way KT9: Ches ... 2J 59
Holt, The SM4: Mord ... 3M 43
SM6: W'ton ... 1G 62
Holt Cl. GU14: Farnb ... 7A 70
Holt La. RG41: W'ham ... 1A 30
Holton Heath RG12: Brac ... 3D 32
HOLT POUND ... 7C 128
Holt Pound Cotts.
GU10: Holt P ... 7B 128
Holt Pound La.
GU10: Holt P ... 6B 128
Holtwood Rd. KT22: Oxs ... 9C 58
HOLTYE ... 7N 167
Holtye Av. RH19: E Grin ... 7B 166
HOLTYE COMMON ... 6N 167
Holtye Comn. TN8: Cow ... 7N 167
Holtye Golf Course ... 7N 167
Holtye Hill TN8: Cow ... 7N 167
Holtye Pl. RH19: E Grin ... 7C 166
Holtye Rd.
RH19: E Grin, Hamm ... 8B 166
TN8: Cow, Hamm ... 6K 167
Holtye Wlk. RH10: Craw ... 5E 182
Holwood Cl. KT12: Wal T ... 8K 39
Holwood Pk. Av. BR6: Farnb ... 1H 67
Holybourne Av. SW15 ... 1F 26
Holyhead Ct. KT1: K Tham ... 8H 203
Holyoake Av. GU21: Wok ... 4M 73
Holyoake Cres. GU21: Wok ... 4M 73
Holyport Rd. SW6 ... 3J 13
Holyrood RH19: E Grin ... 2C 186
Holyrood Pl. RH11: Craw ... 7N 181
Holywell Cl. GU14: Farnb ... 7M 69
TW19: Stan ... 2N 21
Holywell Way TW19: Stan ... 2N 21
Hombrook Dr. RG42: Brac ... 9K 15
Hombrook Ho. RG42: Brac ... 9K 15
Homebeech Ho. GU22: Wok ... 5A 74
(off Mt. Hermon Rd.)
Home Cl. GU25: V Wat ... 5N 35
KT22: Fetc ... 8D 78
RH10: Craw ... 1G 183
SM5: Cars ... 8D 44
Home Ct.
KT6: Surb ... 8H 203 (4K 41)
Home Farm Cl.
GU14: Farnb ... 8B 70
KT7: T Dit ... 6F 40
KT10: Esh ... 3B 58
KT16: Otter ... 4C 54
KT20: Tad ... 4J 81
RH3: Betch ... 4D 120
TW17: Shep ... 3F 38
Home Farm Cotts.
GU8: P Har ... 6A 132
Home Farm Gdns.
KT12: Wal T ... 8K 39
Home Farm Ho.
RH12: Hors ... 6J 197
(off Springfield Rd.)
Home Farm Rd. GU7: Bus ... 9H 133
Homefield GU8: Thur ... 7G 150
SM4: Mord ... 3M 43
Homefield Av. KT12: Hers ... 1L 57
Homefield Cl. KT15: Wood ... 8G 55
KT22: Leat ... 8J 79
RH6: Horl ... 7F 142
Homefield Gdns. CR4: Mit ... 1A 44
KT20: Tad ... 7H 81
Homefield Pk. SM1: Sut ... 3N 61
Homefield Pl. CR0: Croy ... 8C 46
Homefield Rd. CR3: Coul ... 6M 83
CR5: Coul ... 6M 83
CR6: Warl ... 6F 84
KT12: Wal T ... 6M 39
SW19 ... 7J 27
W4 ... 1E 12
Homegreen Ho. GU27: Hasl ... 2E 188
Homeland Dr. SM2: Sut ... 5N 61
Homelands KT22: Leat ... 8J 79
Homelands Pl. TN16: B Hil ... 4G 86
Homelea Cl. GU14: Farnb ... 6N 69
Homeleigh Ct. SW16 ... 4J 29
Homeleigh Cres.
GU12: Ash V ... 5E 90
Home Mdw. SM7: Ban ... 3M 81
Homemead Rd. CR0: Croy ... 5G 46
Home Pk. KT8: E Mol ... 4J 41
RH8: Oxt ... 9C 106
Home Pk. Cl. GU5: Braml ... 5B 134
Home Pk. Ct. KT1: K Tham ... 8H 203
Homepark Ho. GU9: Farnh ... 1H 129
Home Pk. Pde. KT1: H Wic ... 3G 203
Home Pk. Rd. GU46: Yate ... 9C 48
SW19 ... 5L 27
Home Pk. Ter. KT1: H Wic ... 3G 203
Home Pk. Wlk.
KT1: K Tham ... 8H 203 (3K 41)
Homer Rd. CR0: Croy ... 5G 47
Homersham Rd.
KT1: K Tham ... 1N 41
Homers Rd. SL4: W'sor ... 4A 4
Homesdale Rd. CR3: Cate ... 1A 104
Homestall GU2: Guil ... 3G 113
Homestall Rd.
RH19: Ash W ... 9G 166
Homestead GU6: Cranl ... 6A 156
Homestead Dr. GU3: Norm ... 9A 92
Homestead Gdns.
KT10: Clay ... 2E 58
Homestead Rd. CR3: Cate ... 1A 104
SW6 ... 3L 13
TN8: Eden ... 7K 127
TW18: Stain ... 7K 21
Homestead Way
CR0: N Add ... 7M 65
Homestream Ho.
RH12: Hors ... 7H 197
Homethorne Ho.
RH11: Craw ... 4A 182
Home Vs. GU5: Alb ... 3L 135
Homewater Ho.
KT17: Eps ... 6M 201 (9D 60)
Homewaters Av.
TW16: Sunb ... 9G 23
Homewood GU6: Cranl ... 7B 156
Homewood Cl. TW12: Hamp ... 7N 23
Homewoods SW12 ... 1G 28
Homeworth Ho. GU22: Wok ... 5A 74
(off Ashdown Cl.)
Hone Hill GU47: Sandh ... 7G 48
Hones Yd. Business Pk.
GU9: Farnh ... 1J 129
Honeybrook Rd. SW12 ... 1G 28
Honeycrock Ct. RH1: Salf ... 1E 142
Honeycrock La. RH1: Salf ... 1E 142
Honeydown Cotts.
GU28: Northc ... 8E 190
HONEYHILL ... 7E 30
Honey Hill RG40: W'ham ... 6E 30
Honeyhill Rd. RG42: Brac ... 9M 15
Honey La. RH5: Oak ... 6M 177
RH12: Oak, Rowh ... 6M 177
Honey La. Ho. SW10 ... 2N 13
(off Finborough Rd.)
Honey M. SE27 ... 5N 29
(off Norwood High St.)
Honeypot La. TN8: Eden ... 8F 126
Honeypots Rd. GU22: Wok ... 9N 73
Honeysuckle Bottom
KT24: E Hor ... 3F 116
Honeysuckle Cl.
RG45: Crowt ... 9F 30
RH6: Horl ... 7G 143
Honeysuckle Gdns.
CR0: Croy ... 6G 46
Honeysuckle La.
GU35: Head D ... 4G 168
RH5: Nth H ... 8J 119
RH11: Craw ... 9A 162
Honeysuckle Wlk.
RH12: Hors ... 3N 197
Honeywood La. RH5: Oak ... 4M 177
Honeywood Mus. ... 2D 62
Honeywood Rd.
RH13: Hors ... 4N 197
TW7: Isle ... 7G 11
Honeywood Wlk. SM5: Cars ... 1D 62
Honington M. GU14: Farnb ... 5N 89
Honister Gdns. GU51: Fleet ... 3D 88
Honister Hgts. CR8: Pur ... 1A 84
Honister Wlk. GU15: Camb ... 2H 71
Honnor Gdns. TW7: Isle ... 5D 10
Honnor Rd. TW18: Stain ... 8M 21
Hood Av. SW14 ... 8B 12
Hood Cl.
CR0: Croy ... 1A 200 (7M 45)
Hood Rd. SW20 ... 8E 26
HOOK ... 1K 59
Hooke Rd. KT24: E Hor ... 3G 97
Hookfield
KT19: Eps ... 6G 201 (9B 60)
Hookfield M.
KT19: Eps ... 6G 201 (9B 60)
HOOK HEATH ... 7L 73
Hook Heath Av. GU22: Wok ... 6L 73
Hook Heath Gdns.
GU22: Wok ... 8J 73
Hook Heath Rd. GU22: Wok ... 8H 73
Hook Hill CR2: Sande ... 6B 64
Hook Hill La. GU22: Wok ... 8L 73
Hook Hill Pk. GU22: Wok ... 8L 73
Hook Ho. La. GU8: Duns ... 3M 173
Hookhouse La. GU8: Loxh ... 1N 173
Hookhouse Rd.
GU8: Duns, Loxh ... 1N 173
HOOK JUNC. ... 9L 41
Hook La. GU3: Put ... 8N 111
GU5: Shere ... 1B 136
GU24: W End ... 9N 51
Hookley Cl. GU8: Els ... 8J 131
Hookley La. GU8: Els ... 8J 131
Hook Mill La. GU18: Ligh ... 5A 52
Hook Rise Nth. KT6: Surb ... 9L 41
Hook Rise Sth. KT6: Surb ... 9L 41
Hook Rise Sth. Ind. Pk.
KT6: Surb ... 9M 41
Hook Rd. KT6: Surb ... 8L 41
KT9: Ches ... 2K 59
KT19: Eps, Ewe
... 5K 201 (4B 60)
Hookstile La. GU9: Farnh ... 2H 129
Hookstone La. GU24: W End ... 7C 52
Hook St. GU6: Alf ... 8K 175
HOOKWOOD ... 9B 142
Hookwood Cnr. RH8: Limp ... 6D 106
Hookwood Cotts.
KT18: Head ... 2B 100
HOOKWOOD PARK ... 6D 106
Hookwood Pk. RH8: Limp ... 7D 106
HOOLEY ... 8F 82
Hooley La. RH1: Red ... 4D 122
Hooper Ho. TW15: Ashf ... 4N 21
Hope Av. RG12: Brac ... 6C 32
Hope Cl. SM1: Sut ... 2A 62
TW8: Brent ... 1L 11
Hope Cotts. RG12: Brac ... 2A 32
Hope Ct. RH11: Craw ... 8N 181
Hope Fountain GU15: Camb ... 2E 70
Hope Grant's Rd.
GU11: Alde ... 9M 89
(not continuous)
Hope Ho. CR0: Croy ... 6F 200
Hope La. GU9: Up Hale ... 6G 108
Hopeman Cl. GU47: Coll T ... 7J 49
Hopes Cl. TW5: Hest ... 2A 10
Hope St. GU8: Els ... 7H 131
Hope Way GU11: Alde ... 1L 109
Hopfield GU21: Wok ... 3A 74
Hopfield Av. KT14: Byf ... 8N 55
Hopfields Cl. GU9: Farnh ... 3G 128
Hopgarden, The SL4: Eton ... 1G 4
(off Common La.)
Hopgarden Cl. TN8: Eden ... 9M 127
Hophurst Cl. RH10: Craw D ... 1E 184
Hophurst Dr. RH10: Craw D ... 1E 184
Hophurst Hill
RH10: Craw D ... 8G 164
Hophurst La. RH10: Craw D ... 1E 184
Hopkin Cl. GU2: Guil ... 8L 93
Hopkins Ct. RH11: Craw ... 8N 181
Hop Oast (Horsham)
(Park & Ride) ... 9G 196
Hopper Va. RG12: Brac ... 5M 31
Hoppety, The KT20: Tad ... 9J 81
Hoppingwood Av.
KT3: N Mal ... 2D 42
Hopton Ct. GU2: Guil ... 3H 113
(off Park Barn Dr.)
Hopton Gdns. KT3: N Mal ... 5F 42
Hopton Rd. SW16 ... 6J 29
Hopwood Cl. SW17 ... 4A 28
Horace Rd.
KT1: K Tham ... 6L 203 (2M 41)
Horatio Av. RG42: Warf ... 9C 16
Horatio Ho. W6 ... 1J 13
(off Fulham Pal. Rd.)
Horatio Pl. SW19 ... 9M 27
Horatius Way CR0: Wad ... 2K 63

Hordern Ho.—Hyperion Wlk.

Hordern Ho. RH12: Hors 7G **196**
Horder Rd. SW6 4K **13**
Horewood Rd. RG12: Brac 5N **31**
Horizon Bus. Village
KT13: Weybr 8B **56**
Horizon Ct. *SM2: Chea 4K 61*
(off Up. Mulgrave Rd.)
Horizon Ho.
KT17: Eps 6L **201** (9D **60**)
HORLEY 8F **142**
Horley Leisure Cen. 8C 142
Horley Lodge La. RH1: Salf 3D **142**
Horley Rd. RH1: Red 5D **122**
RH6: Charlw 4L **161**
Horley Row RH6: Horl 7D **142**
Horley Station (Rail) 9F 142
Hormer Cl. GU47: Owls 6J **49**
Hornbeam Cl. GU14: Cove 9H **69**
GU47: Owls 6J **49**
RH13: Hors 7M **197**
Hornbeam Copse
RG42: Warf 9E **16**
Hornbeam Cres.
TW8: Brent 3H **11**
Hornbeam Gdns. KT3: N Mal 5F **42**
Hornbeam Rd. GU1: Guil 9M **93**
RH2: Reig 6N **121**
Hornbeam Ter. SM5: Cars 7C **44**
Hornbeam Wlk.
KT12: Whit V 5G **56**
TW10: Rich 3M **25**
Hornbrook Copse
RH13: Hors 8M **197**
Hornbrook Hill RH13: Hors 8M **197**
Hornby Av. RG12: Brac 6B **32**
Hornchurch Cl. KT2: K Tham 5K **25**
Hornchurch Hill
CR3: Whyte 5C **84**
Hornchurch Sq. GU14: Farnb 5N **89**
Horndean Cl. RH10: Craw 8H **163**
SW15 2F **26**
Horndean Rd. RG12: Brac 5D **32**
HORNE 5C **144**
Hornecourt Hill RH6: Horne 4C **144**
Horne Pk. Golf Course 7D 144
Horner La. CR4: Mit 1B **44**
Horne Rd. TW17: Shep 3B **38**
Hornets, The RH13: Hors 7K **197**
Horne Way SW15 5H **13**
Hornhatch GU4: Guil 9D **114**
Hornhatch Cl. GU4: Guil 9D **114**
Hornhatch La. GU4: Guil 9C **114**
Horn Rd. GU14: Cove 9K **69**
HORNS GREEN 4N **87**
HORNS HILL 8N **107**
Hornshill La. RH12: Rudg 2A **194**
Horseblock Hollow
GU6: Cranl 3B **156**
Horsebrass Dr. GU19: Bag 5J **51**
Horsecroft SM7: Ban 4L **81**
Horsecroft Mdws.
SM7: Ban 3L **81**
Horse Fair
KT1: K Tham 3G **203** (1K **41**)
Horsegate Ride SL5: Asc 5L **33**
(Friary Rd.)
SL5: Asc 4F **32**
(Windsor Ride)
Horse Hill RH6: Sid 6M **141**
HORSELL 3M **73**
Horsell Birch GU21: Wok 2K **73**
HORSELL COMMON 9N **53**
Horsell Comn. Rd.
GU21: Wok 1M **73**
Horsell Ct. KT16: Chert 6K **37**
Horsell Moor GU21: Wok 4N **73**
Horsell Pk. GU21: Wok 3N **73**
Horsell Pk. Cl. GU21: Wok 3N **73**
Horsell Ri. GU21: Wok 2N **73**
Horsell Ri. Cl. GU21: Wok 2N **73**
Horsell Va. GU21: Wok 3A **74**
Horsell Way GU21: Wok 3M **73**
Horse Ride SM5: Cars 6C **62**
SM7: Ban 8D **62**
Horseshoe, The CR5: Coul 9H **63**
GU7: Godal 8F **132**
SM7: Ban 2L **81**
Horseshoe Bend
GU26: G'hott 6M **169**
Horseshoe Cl. GU15: Camb 7D **50**
RH10: Craw 2H **183**
Horseshoe Cres.
GU15: Camb 7D **50**
GU35: Bor 6A **168**
Horse Shoe Grn. SM1: Sut 8N **43**
Horseshoe Lake Watersports Cen.
6C 48
Horseshoe La. GU6: Cranl 6L **155**
GU12: Ash V 6E **90**
Horseshoe La. E.
GU1: Guil 2D **114**
Horseshoe La. W.
GU1: Guil 2D **114**
HORSHAM 6J **197**
Horsham Gates
RH13: Hors 5L **197**
Horsham Golf Course 9H 197
Horsham Indoor Bowls Cen.
6D 196
Horsham La.
GU6: Ewh, W'wood 8G **157**
Horsham Mus. *7J 197*
(off Morth Gdns.)
Horsham Northern By-Pass
RH12: Warnh, Hors 2H **197**
Horsham Rd. GU4: Chil 2A **134**
GU5: Braml 1E **154**
(Rooks Hill)
GU5: Braml 2N **133**
(Trunley Heath Rd.)
GU6: Alf 6J **175**
GU6: Cranl 8F **154**
GU6: Cranl, Rudg 8N **155**
GU47: Owls 6J **49**
RH4: Dork 4J **201** (6G **119**)
RH5: A Ham, Holm M 2G **136**
RH5: B Grn, Holm, Mid H, Nth H
9H **119**
RH5: Cap 2J **179**
RH5: For G, Ockl, W'wood
1L **177**
RH5: W'wood 8G **157**
RH11: Craw 7K **181**
RH11: Pease P 2M **199**
RH12: Rudg 8N **155**
RH12: Rusp 5N **179**
RH17: Plum P, Hand 9K **199**
TW14: Bedf 9D **8**
Horsham Station (Rail) 5K 197
Horsham Trad. Est.
RH13: Hors 4L **197**
Horsley Camping & Caravanning Club Site
KT24: W Hors 2D **96**
Horsley Cl.
KT19: Eps 6J **201** (9C **60**)
Horsley Ct. KT24: E Hor 4F **96**
Horsley Dr. CR0: N Add 4M **65**
KT2: K Tham 6K **25**
Horsley Rd. KT11: Down 9H **77**
Horsley Station (Rail) 3F 96
Horsnape Gdns. RG42: Bin 7G **15**
Horsneile La. RG42: Brac 8N **15**
Hortensia Ho. *SW10 3N 13*
(off Gunter Gro.)
Hortensia Rd. SW10 3N **13**
Horticultural Pl. W4 1C **12**
HORTON
KT19 7B 60
SL3 6C 6
Horton Country Pk. 6M 59
Horton Country Pk. Local Nature Reserve 5M 59
Horton Cres. KT19: Eps 7N **59**
Horton Footpath KT19: Eps 7B **60**
Horton Gdns. KT19: Eps 7B **60**
SL3: Hort 6B **6**
Horton Halls SW17 4B **28**
Horton Hill KT19: Eps 7B **60**
Horton Ho. *W6 1K 13*
(off Field Rd.)
Horton La. KT19: Eps 8N **59**
Horton Pk. Children's Farm 6N 59
Horton Pk. Golf Course 4B 60
Horton Pl. TN16: Weste 4M **107**
Horton Rd. SL3: Coln, Hort 5C **6**
SL3: Dat, Hort 3L **5**
SL3: Poy 6G **6**
TW19: Stan M 7H **7**
Hortons Way TN16: Weste 4M **107**
Horton Trad. Est. SL3: Hort 6E **6**
Horton Way CR0: Croy 4G **47**
Horvath Cl. KT13: Weybr 1E **56**
Hosack Rd. SW17 3E **28**
Hosey Comn. La.
TN16: Weste 7N **107**
Hosey Comn. Rd.
TN8: C Hil, Weste 2L **127**
TN16: Weste 7N **107**
HOSEY HILL 6N 107
Hosey Hill TN16: Weste 5N **107**
Hoskins, The *RH8: Oxt 7A 106*
(off Station Rd. W.)
Hoskins Cl. UB3: Harl 1G **8**
Hoskins Ct. GU15: Camb 3N **69**
Hoskins Pl. RH19: E Grin 6C **166**
Hoskins Rd. RH8: Oxt 7A **106**
(not continuous)
Hoskins Wlk. *RH8: Oxt 7A 106*
(off Station Rd. W.)
Hospital Bri. Rd.
TW2: Twick, Whitt 1B **24**
HOSPITAL BRIDGE RDBT. 3B **24**
Hospital Hill GU11: Alde 1M **109**
Hospital Rd. GU11: Alde 1M **109**
TW3: Houn 6A **10**
Hotham Cl. KT8: W Mole 2A **40**
Hotham Rd. SW15 6H **13**
SW19 8A **28**
Hotham Rd. M. SW19 8A **28**
Houblon Rd. TW10: Rich 8L **11**
Houghton Cl. TW12: Hamp 7M **23**
Houghton Rd. RH10: Craw 6G **182**
Houlder Cres. CR0: Wad 3M **63**
Houlton Ct. GU19: Bag 5J **51**
Hound Ho. Rd. GU5: Shere 1B **136**
Houndown La. GU8: Thur 6E **150**
HOUNSLOW 6B 10
Hounslow and District Indoor Bowls Club 5N 9
Hounslow Av. TW3: Houn 8B **10**
Hounslow Bus. Pk.
TW3: Houn 7A **10**
Hounslow Central Station (Underground) 6B 10
Hounslow Cen. TW3: Houn 6B **10**
Hounslow East Station (Underground) 5C 10
Hounslow Gdns. TW3: Houn 8B **10**
Hounslow Heath Golf Course 8K 9
Hounslow Heath Nature Reserve
9M 9
Hounslow Rd. TW2: Whitt 9B **10**
TW13: Hanw 5L **23**
TW14: Felt 2J **23**
Hounslow Station (Rail) 8B 10
Hounslow Urban Farm 8H 9
HOUNSLOW WEST 6M 9
Hounslow West Station (Underground) 5M 9
Houseman Rd. GU14: Farnb 8L **69**
Housman Way RH19: Felb 6J **165**
Houston Pl. KT10: Esh 7D **40**
Houston Rd. KT6: Surb 5H **41**
Houston Way RG45: Crowt 2C **48**
Houstoun Ct. TW5: Hest 3N **9**
Hove Gdns. SM1: Sut 7N **43**
Howard Av. KT17: Ewe 6F **60**
Howard Cl. GU51: Fleet 4D **88**
KT20: Wal H 3E **100**
KT21: Asht 5M **79**
KT22: Leat 1J **99**
KT24: W Hors 3E **96**
RG12: Brac 4M **31**
TW12: Hamp 8C **24**
TW16: Sunb 7G **22**
Howard Cole Way
GU11: Alde 2K **109**
Howard Ct. *GU21: Knap 6F 72*
(off Tudor Way)
RH2: Reig 2A **122**
Howard Dr. GU14: Cove 1G **89**
Howard Gdns. GU1: Guil 2C **114**
Howard Pl. RH2: Reig 1M **121**
Howard Ridge GU4: B'ham 8C **94**
Howard Rd. CR5: Coul 2G **83**
KT3: N Mal 2D **42**
KT5: Surb 5M **41**
KT23: Book 5B **98**
KT24: E Jun 9H **77**
RG40: W'ham 3B **30**
RH2: Reig 4N **121**
RH4: Dork 2H **201** (5G **118**)
RH5: Nth H 9J **119**
RH11: Craw 7K **181**
RH13: Hors 4N **197**
SE25 4D **46**
TW7: Isle 6F **10**
Howards Cl. GU22: Wok 7C **74**
Howards Crest Cl.
BR3: Beck 1M **47**
Howards Ho. RH2: Reig 2N **121**
Howards La. KT15: Addl 3H **55**
SW15 7G **13**
Howards Rd. GU22: Wok 7B **74**
Howard St. KT7: T Dit 6H **41**
Howberry Chase
GU27: Hasl 2F **188**
Howberry Rd.
CR7: T Hea 9N **29** & 1A **46**
Howden Dr. KT15: Addl 4J **55**
Howden Rd. SE25 1C **46**
Howe, The GU14: Farnb 4F **88**
Howe Dr. CR3: Cate 9A **84**
Howe La. RG42: Bin 2J **15**
Howell Cl. RG42: Warf 7A **16**
Howell Hill SM2: Chea 6H **61**
Howell Hill Cl. KT17: Ewe 7H **61**
Howell Hill Gro. KT17: Ewe 6H **61**
Howell Hill Nature Reserve 7J 61
Howgate Rd. SW14 6C **12**
Howitts Cl. KT10: Esh 3A **58**
Howland Ho. SW16 4J **29**
Howlands Ct. RH10: Craw 3D **182**
How La. CR5: Chip 4E **82**
Howley Rd.
CR0: Croy 4A **200** (9M **45**)
Howorth Ct. RG12: Brac 3D **32**
Howsman Rd. SW13 2F **12**
Howson Ter. TW10: Rich 9L **11**
Hoylake Cl. RH11: Ifield 4J **181**
Hoylake Gdns. CR4: Mit 2G **44**
Hoyland Ho. RH11: Craw 3L **181**
Hoyle Cotts. RH5: B Grn 1K **159**
Hoyle Rd. SW17 6C **28**
Hub, The TW20: Egh 6B **20**
Hubbard Dr. KT9: Ches 3K **59**
Hubbard Rd. SE27 5N **29**
Hubberholme RG12: Brac 2M **31**
Huddleston Cres.
RH1: Mers 6H **103**
Hudson Ct. GU2: Guil 3J **113**
Hudson Ho.
KT19: Eps 6K **201** (9C **60**)
SW10 3N 13
(off Hortensia Rd.)
Hudson Pl. SL3: Lang 1B **6**
Hudson Rd. RH10: Craw 5C **182**
UB3: Harl 2E **8**
Hudsons KT20: Tad 8J **81**
Huggins Pl. SW2 2K **29**
Hugh Dalton Av. SW6 2L **13**
Hugh De Port La.
GU51: Fleet 2A **88**
Hughenden Rd. KT4: W Pk 6F **42**
Hughes Rd. RG40: W'ham 1C **30**
TW15: Ashf 8D **22**
Hughes Wlk. CR0: Croy 6N **45**
Hugh Gaitskell Cl. SW6 2L **13**
Hugh Herland Ho.
KT1: K Tham 6K **203** (2L **41**)
Hugon Rd. SW6 6N **13**
Hullbrook La. GU5: Sha G 7F **134**
Hullmead GU5: Sha G 7G **134**
Hulton Cl. KT22: Leat 1J **99**
Hulverston Cl. SM2: Sut 6N **61**
Humber Cl. GU47: Sandh 7J **49**
Humber Way GU47: Sandh 7J **49**
SL3: Lang 1C **6**
Humbolt Cl. GU2: Guil 3J **113**
Humbolt Rd. W6 2K **13**
Hummer Rd. TW20: Egh 5C **20**
Humphrey Cl. KT22: Fetc 9C **78**
Humphrey Pk.
GU52: Chu C 1A **108**
(not continuous)
Humphries Yd. RG12: Brac 3A **32**
Hungerford Cl. GU47: Sandh 7H **49**
Hungerford Sq. KT13: Weybr 1E **56**
Hungry Hill La.
GU23: Rip, Send 4L **95**
Hunstanton Cl. RH11: Ifield 4J **181**
SL3: Coln 3E **6**
Hunston Rd. SM4: Mord 7N **43**
Hunter Cl. SM6: W'ton 4J **63**
SW12 2E **28**
Hunter Ct. KT19: Eps 6N **59**
Hunter Ho. RH10: Craw 6B **182**
SW5 1M 13
(off Old Brompton Rd.)
TW13: Felt 2H 23
(off Lemon Gro.)
Hunter Rd. CR7: T Hea 2A **46**
GU1: Guil 5F **202** (4A **114**)
GU14: Cove 2L **89**
RH10: Craw 6B **182**
SW20 9H **27**
Hunters Chase RH9: S Gods 6J **125**
Hunters Cl.
KT19: Eps 6H **201** (9B **60**)
Hunters Ct. TW9: Rich 8K **11**
Huntersfield Cl. RH2: Reig 9N **101**
Hunters Ga. RH1: Nut 2K **123**
Hunters Gro. BR6: Farnb 1L **67**
Hunters M. SL4: W'sor 4F **4**
Hunter's Rd. KT9: Ches 9L **41**
Hunters Way CR0: Croy 1B **64**
TN8: Eden 1K **147**
Hunting Cl. KT10: Esh 1A **58**
Huntingdon Cl. CR4: Mit 2J **45**
Huntingdon Gdns.
KT4: W Pk 9H **43**
W4 3B **12**
Huntingdon Ho. Dr.
GU26: Hind 5C **170**
Huntingdon Rd. GU21: Wok 4J **73**
RH1: Red 3D **122**
Huntingfield CR0: Sels 4J **65**
Huntingfield Rd. SW15 7F **12**
Huntingfield Way TW20: Egh 8F **20**
Huntingford Cl. GU26: Hind 2A **170**
Hunting Ga. Dr. KT9: Ches 4L **59**
Hunting Ga. M. SM1: Sut 9N **43**
TW2: Twick 2E **24**
Huntley Cl. TW19: Stan 1N **21**
Huntley Ho. KT12: Whit V 5G **56**
Huntley Way SW20 1F **42**
Huntly Rd. SE25 3B **46**
Hunts Cl. GU2: Guil 2G **112**
Huntsgreen Ct. RG12: Brac 1A **32**
HUNTS HILL 9M 91
Hunts Hill Rd. GU3: Norm 8L **91**
Huntsmans Cl. CR6: Warl 6F **84**
KT22: Fetc 2D **98**
TW13: Felt 5J **23**
Huntsmans Ct. *CR3: Cate 8N 83*
(off Coulsdon Rd.)
Huntsmans Mdw. SL5: Asc 9K **17**
Huntsman's M. GU16: Mytc 2D **90**
Huntsmoor Rd. KT19: Ewe 2C **60**
Huntspill St. SW17 4A **28**
Hurland La. GU35: Head 5E **168**
Hurlands Bus. Cen.
GU9: Farnh 8L **109**
Hurlands Cl. GU9: Farnh 8L **109**
Hurlands La. GU8: Duns 7B **174**
Hurlands Pl. GU9: Farnh 8L **109**
Hurley Cl. KT12: Wal T 8J **39**
SM7: Ban 3L **81**
Hurley Ct. RG12: Brac 3C **32**
SW17 7E 28
(off Mitcham Rd.)
Hurley Gdns. GU4: B'ham 9C **94**
Hurlford GU21: Wok 4K **73**
HURLINGHAM 6N 13
Hurlingham Bus. Pk.
SW6 6M **13**
Hurlingham Club, The 6M 13
Hurlingham Ct. SW6 6L **13**
Hurlingham Gdns. SW6 6L **13**
Hurlingham Pk. 5L 13
Hurlingham Retail Pk.
SW6 6N **13**
Hurlingham Rd. SW6 5L **13**
Hurlingham Sq. SW6 6M **13**
Hurlingham Yacht Club 6K 13
Hurlstone Rd. SE25 4B **46**
Hurn Ct. TW4: Houn 5L **9**
Hurn Ct. Rd. TW4: Houn 5L **9**
Hurnford Cl. CR2: Sande 6B **64**
Huron Cl. BR6: Chels 3N **67**
Huron Rd. SW17 3E **28**
Hurricane Rd. SM6: W'ton 4J **63**
Hurricane Way SL3: Lang 1D **6**
Hurst-An-Clays
RH19: E Grin 1A **186**
Hurst Av. RH12: Hors 5K **197**
Hurstbourne KT10: Clay 3F **58**
Hurstbourne Ho. *SW15 9E 12*
(off Tangley Gro.)
Hurst Cl. GU22: Wok 7M **73**
KT9: Ches 2N **59**
KT18: Head 2B **100**
RG12: Brac 4M **31**
RH11: Craw 5L **181**
Hurst Ct. RH12: Hors 5K **197**
Hurstcourt Rd. SM1: Sut 8N **43**
Hurst Cft.
GU1: Guil 8F **202** (6A **114**)
Hurstdene Av. TW18: Stain 7K **21**
Hurst Dr. KT20: Wal H 4F **100**
Hurst Farm Cl. GU8: Mil 9C **132**
Hurst Farm Rd.
RH19: E Grin 1N **185**
Hurstfield Rd. KT8: W Mole 2A **40**
HURST GREEN 1C 126
Hurst Grn. Cl. RH8: Oxt 1C **126**
Hurst Grn. Rd. RH8: Oxt 1B **126**
Hurst Green Station (Rail) 1B 126
Hurst Gro. KT12: Wal T 7G **39**
Hurst Hill RH12: Hors 7N **179**
Hurst Hill Cotts.
GU5: Braml 6C **134**
Hurstlands RH8: Oxt 1C **126**
Hurst La. KT8: E Mol 3C **40**
KT18: Head 2B **100**
TW20: Egh 1C **36**
Hurstleigh Cl. RH1: Red 1D **122**
Hurstleigh Dr. RH1: Red 1D **122**
Hurst Lodge *KT13: Weybr 3E 56*
(off Gower Rd.)
Hurstmere Cl. GU26: G'hott 6B **170**
HURST PARK 1C 40
Hurst Pk. RH12: Hors 5K **197**
Hurst Pool 2B 40
Hurst Rd.
CR0: Croy 8D **200** (2A **64**)
GU11: Alde 9A **90**
GU14: Farnb 6N **69**
KT8: W Mole, E Mol 4K **39**
KT12: Wal T 4K **39**
KT18: Head 1C **100**
KT19: Eps 7C **60**
KT20: Wal H 1C **100**
RH6: Horl 7C **142**
RH12: Hors 4J **197**
Hurstview Grange
CR2: S Croy 4M **63**
Hurst Vw. Rd. CR2: S Croy 4B **64**
Hurst Way CR2: S Croy 3B **64**
GU22: Pyr 1G **75**
Hurstwood SL5: Asc 5L **33**
Hurtbank Cotts.
RH5: Holm M 5K **137**
HURTMORE 4C 132
HURTMORE BOTTOM 5C 132
Hurtmore Chase GU7: Hurt 4E **132**
Hurtmore Golf Course 4C 132
Hurtmore Rd.
GU7: Hurt, Godal 4C **132**
Hurtwood La.
GU5: Alb, Shere 5N **135**
Hurtwood Rd. KT12: Wal T 6N **39**
Huson Rd. RG42: Warf 7A **16**
Hussar Ct. GU11: Alde 2K **109**
Hussars Cl. TW4: Houn 6M **9**
Hutchingsons Rd.
CR0: N Add 7M **65**
Hutchinson's Bank Nature Reserve
8M 65
Hutchins Way RH6: Horl 6D **142**
Hutsons Cl. RG40: W'ham 9C **14**
Hutton Cl. GU20: Windl 4A **52**
KT12: Hers 2J **57**
Hutton M. SW15 8G **12**
Hutton Rd. GU12: Ash V 7E **90**
Huxley Cl. GU7: Godal 4G **132**
Huxley Rd. GU2: Guil 4G **113**
Huxley's (Bird of Prey & Garden)
8M 197
Hyacinth Cl. TW12: Hamp 7A **24**
Hyacinth Rd. SW15 2F **26**
Hyde Cl. TW15: Ashf 7F **22**
Hyde Dr. RH11: Ifield 4K **181**
Hyde Farm M. SW12 2H **29**
Hyde Heath Ct.
RH10: Craw 1H **183**
Hyde Ho. TW3: Houn 6C **10**
Hydehurst La. RH10: Craw 7C **162**
Hyde La. GU8: Thur 8E **150**
GU10: Churt 9B **150**
GU23: Ockh 7C **76**
Hyde Rd. CR2: Sande 9B **64**
TW10: Rich 8M **11**
HYDESTILE 4G 153
Hydestile Cotts.
GU8: Hamb 5G **152**
Hyde Ter. TW15: Ashf 7F **22**
Hydethorpe Rd. SW12 2G **28**
Hyde Wlk. SM4: Mord 6M **43**
HYDON HEATH 5J 153
Hydon Heath 6J 153
Hydons, The GU8: Hamb 5H **153**
Hydro Ho. KT16: Chert 7L **37**
Hylands Cl. KT18: Eps 2B **80**
RH10: Craw 4E **182**
Hylands M. KT18: Eps 2B **80**
Hylands Rd. KT18: Eps 2B **80**
Hylle Cl. SL4: W'sor 4B **4**
Hylton Pl. RH1: Mers 9G **102**
Hyndman Cl. RH11: Craw 9N **181**
Hyperion Ct. RH11: Craw 5K **181**
Hyperion Ho. SW2 1K **29**
Hyperion Pl. KT19: Ewe 5C **60**
Hyperion Wlk. RH6: Horl 1F **162**

Joseph's Rd.—Killy Hill

Joseph's Rd.
GU1: Guil ... 1C 202 (2N 113)
Joshua Cl. CR2: S Croy ... 4M 63
Jourdelay's SL4: Eton ... 2G 4
(off Jourdelay's Pas.)
Jourdelay's Pas. SL4: Eton ... 2G 4
Jubilee Arch SL4: W'sor ... 4G 4
Jubilee Av. RG41: W'ham ... 1A 30
SL5: Asc ... 9J 17
TW2: Whitt ... 2C 24
Jubilee Cl. GU14: Cove ... 1J 89
KT1: H Wic ... 9J 25
SL5: Asc ... 9J 17
TW19: Stan ... 1L 21
Jubilee Cotts. SL3: Lang ... 1E 6
Jubilee Ct. BR4: W Wick ... 7M 47
RG12: Brac ... 2A 32
SL5: Asc ... 8J 17
TW3: Houn ... 6B 10
(off Bristow Rd.)
TW18: Stain ... 6J 21
Jubilee Cres. KT15: Addl ... 2M 55
Jubilee Dr. GU12: Ash V ... 7E 90
Jubilee Est. RH13: Hors ... 4L 197
Jubilee Hall Rd.
GU14: Farnb ... 1A 90
Jubilee La. GU10: Wrec ... 7F 128
GU26: G'hott ... 6A 170
Jubilee Rd. GU11: Alde ... 5N 109
GU16: Mytc ... 3E 90
RH12: Rudg ... 9E 176
SM3: Chea ... 4J 61
Jubilee Sq. GU21: Wok ... 4B 74
(off Church St. E.)
Jubilee Statue ... 5D 18
Jubilee Ter. RH3: Brock ... 7B 120
RH4: Dork ... 1L 201 (4H 119)
Jubilee Vs. KT10: Esh ... 7D 40
Jubilee Wlk. RH10: Craw ... 3E 182
RH12: Hors ... 6J 197
(off Albion Way)
Jubilee Way CR5: Coul ... 5K 83
KT9: Ches ... 1N 59
SL3: Dat ... 3M 5
SW19 ... 9N 27
TW14: Felt ... 2H 23
Jubilee Way Training Track ... 9A 42
Judge's Ter. RH19: E Grin ... 1A 186
Judge Wlk. KT10: Clay ... 3E 58
Judy's Pas. SL4: Eton ... 1F 4
Jug Hill TN16: B Hil ... 3F 86
Jugshill La. RH5: Oak ... 2B 178
Julian Cl. GU21: Wok ... 5M 73
Julian Hill KT13: Weybr ... 4B 56
Julien Rd. CR5: Coul ... 2H 83
Juliet Gdns. RG42: Warf ... 9D 16
Julius Hill RG42: Warf ... 9D 16
Jumps Rd. GU10: Churt ... 7K 149
Junction Pl. GU27: Hasl ... 2D 188
Junction Rd. CR2: S Croy ... 2A 64
GU18: Ligh ... 6M 51
RH4: Dork ... 2J 201 (5G 119)
TW8: Brent ... 1K 11
TW15: Ashf ... 6D 22
W5 ... 1K 11
June Cl. CR5: Coul ... 1F 82
June La. RH1: Salf ... 1F 142
Junewood Cl. KT15: Wood ... 7H 55
Juniper RG12: Brac ... 7A 32
Juniper Cl. GU1: Guil ... 7L 93
KT9: Ches ... 2M 59
KT19: Eps ... 5C 60
RH2: Reig ... 5A 122
RH8: Oxt ... 2D 126
TN16: B Hil ... 4G 87
Juniper Ct. KT8: W Mole ... 3B 40
TW3: Houn ... 7B 10
(off Grove Rd.)
Juniper Dr. GU24: Bis ... 2D 72
Juniper Gdns. SW16 ... 9G 28
TW16: Sunb ... 7G 23
Juniper Ho. TW9: Kew ... 4A 12
Juniper Pl. GU4: Chil ... 1N 133
Juniper Rd. GU14: Cove ... 9H 69
RH2: Reig ... 5A 122
RH11: Craw ... 9N 161
Juniper Wlk. RH3: Brock ... 5B 120
Jupiter Cl. GU14: Farnb ... 3N 89
Jura Cl. RH11: Craw ... 6N 181
Jurassic Encounter ... 2F 42
Justin Cl. TW8: Brent ... 3K 11
Justin Plaza CR4: Mit ... 3C 44
Jutland Gdns. CR5: Coul ... 7K 83
Jutland Ho. SL4: W'sor ... 5C 4
Jutland Pl. TW20: Egh ... 6E 20
Juxon Cl. RH11: Craw ... 5L 181

K

K2 Leisure Cen. ... 7B 182
Kaine Pl. CR0: Croy ... 6H 47
Kalima Caravan Site
GU24: Chob ... 6L 53
Kamran Ct. GU11: Alde ... 5M 109
(off Boxall's La.)
Karenza Ct. RH13: Hors ... 5L 197
Kashmir Cl. KT15: N Haw ... 5M 55
Kashmir Ct. GU14: Farnb ... 4A 90
Katana GU22: Wok ... 6A 74
(off Brooklyn Rd.)
Katharine Ho. CR0: Croy ... 4C 200
Katharine St.
CR0: Croy ... 4C 200 (9N 45)
Katherine Cl. KT15: Addl ... 3J 55
Katherine Ct. GU15: Camb ... 1B 70
(off Up. Gordon Rd.)
GU21: Knap ... 6F 72
(off Tudor Way)
Katherine M. CR3: Whyte ... 4C 84
Katherine Rd. TN8: Eden ... 3L 147
TW1: Twick ... 2G 24
Kathleen Godfree Ct. SW19 ... 7M 27
Kavanagh Ct. KT18: Eps ... 8L 201
Kavsan Pl. TW5: C'ford ... 3H 9
Kay Av. KT15: Addl ... 9N 37
Kay Cres. GU35: Head D ... 3F 168
Kaye Ct. GU1: Guil ... 9M 93
Kaye Don Way KT13: Weybr ... 6B 56
Kayemoor Rd. SM2: Sut ... 3B 62
Kaynes Pk. SL5: Asc ... 9J 17
Keable Rd. GU10: Wrec ... 4E 128
Kean Ho. TW1: Twick ... 9K 11
(off Arosa Rd.)
Kearton Cl. CR8: Ken ... 4N 83
Kearton Pl. CR3: Cate ... 9D 84
Keate Ho. SL4: Eton ... 2G 4
(off Keates La.)
Keates Grn. RG42: Brac ... 9N 15
Keates La. SL4: Eton ... 2F 4
Keats Av. RH1: Red ... 1E 122
Keats Cl. RH12: Hors ... 1M 197
SW19 ... 7B 28
Keats Gdns. GU51: Fleet ... 4C 88
Keats Pl. RH19: E Grin ... 9N 165
Keats Way CR0: Croy ... 5F 46
GU46: Yate ... 2A 68
RG45: Crowt ... 9G 30
UB7: W Dray ... 1A 8
Keaver Dr. GU16: Frim ... 5D 70
Keble Cl. KT4: W Pk ... 7E 42
RH10: Craw ... 9H 163
Keble Pl. SW13 ... 2G 13
Keble St. SW17 ... 5A 28
Keble Way GU47: Owls ... 5K 49
Kedeston Ct. SM1: Sut ... 7N 43
Keel KT16: Chert ... 7L 37
Keeler Cl. SL4: W'sor ... 6B 4
Keeley Rd.
CR0: Croy ... 3B 200 (8N 45)
Keens Cl. SW16 ... 6H 29
Keens La. GU3: Guil ... 8J 93
Keens Pk. Rd. GU3: Guil ... 8J 93
Keens Rd.
CR0: Croy ... 6C 200 (1N 63)
Keep, The KT2: K Tham ... 7M 25
Keepers Cl. GU4: Guil ... 9F 94
Keepers Coombe
RG12: Brac ... 5B 32
KEEPER'S CORNER ... 4N 163
Keepers Ct. CR2: S Croy ... 8B 200
Keepers Farm Cl. SL4: W'sor ... 5B 4
(not continuous)
Keepers M. TW11: Tedd ... 7J 25
Keepers Wlk. GU25: V Wat ... 4N 35
Keephatch Ho.
RG40: W'ham ... 1E 30
Keephatch Local Nature Reserve
... 1D 30
Keephatch Rd.
RG40: W'ham ... 9D 14
Keevil Dr. SW19 ... 1J 27
Keir, The SW19 ... 6H 27
Keir Hardie Ho.
RH11: Craw ... 8N 181
W6 ... 2J 13
(off Fulham Pal. Rd.)
Keith Lucas Rd. GU14: Cove ... 3L 89
Keith Pk. Cres. TN16: B Hil ... 9D 66
Keldholme RG12: Brac ... 2M 31
Kelling Gdns. CR0: Croy ... 6M 45
Kellino St. SW17 ... 5D 28
Kelly Cl. TW17: Shep ... 1F 38
Kelmscott House ... 1F 12
(off Upper Mall)
Kelmscott Pl. KT21: Asht ... 4J 79
Kelmscott Ri. RH11: Craw ... 9N 181
Kelsall M. TW9: Kew ... 4A 12
Kelsall Pl. SL5: Asc ... 6M 33
Kelsey Cl. KT9: Ches ... 4K 59
RH6: Horl ... 8D 142
Kelsey Ga. BR3: Beck ... 1L 47
Kelsey Gro. GU46: Yate ... 1D 68
Kelsey La. BR3: Beck ... 1K 47
Kelsey Pk. Av. BR3: Beck ... 1L 47
Kelsey Pk. Rd. BR3: Beck ... 1K 47
Kelsey Sq. BR3: Beck ... 1K 47
Kelsey Way BR3: Beck ... 2K 47
Kelso Cl. RH10: Craw ... 2J 183
Kelso Rd. SM5: Cars ... 6A 44
Kelvedon Av. KT12: Hers ... 4F 56
Kelvedon Cl. KT2: K Tham ... 7N 25
Kelvedon Rd. SW6 ... 3L 13
Kelvin Av. KT22: Leat ... 6F 78
TW11: Tedd ... 7E 24
Kelvinbrook KT8: W Mole ... 2B 40
Kelvin Bus. Cen.
RH10: Craw ... 9D 162
Kelvin Cl. KT19: Ewe ... 3N 59
Kelvin Ct. TW7: Isle ... 5E 10
Kelvin Dr. TW1: Twick ... 9H 11
Kelvin Gdns. CR0: Wad ... 6J 45
Kelvin Ga. RG12: Brac ... 1B 32
Kelvin Gro. KT9: Ches ... 9K 41
Kelvington Cl. CR0: Croy ... 6H 47
Kelvin La. RH10: Craw ... 8D 162
Kelvin Way RH10: Craw ... 8D 162
Kelway Ho. W14 ... 1L 13
Kemble Av. KT15: Addl ... 4H 55
Kemble Cl. KT13: Weybr ... 1E 56
Kemble Cotts. KT15: Addl ... 1J 55
Kemble Rd. CR0: Wad ... 9M 45
Kembleside Rd. TN16: B Hil ... 5E 86
Kemerton Rd. BR3: Beck ... 1L 47
CR0: Croy ... 6C 46
Kemishford GU22: Wok ... 1K 93
Kemnal Pk. GU27: Hasl ... 1H 189
Kemp Ct. GU19: Bag ... 5K 51
Kemp Gdns. CR0: Croy ... 5N 45
Kempsford Gdns. SW5 ... 1M 13
Kempshott M. RH12: Hors ... 4H 197
Kempshott Rd.
RH12: Hors ... 4H 197
SW16 ... 8H 29
Kempson Rd. SW6 ... 4M 13
Kempton Av. TW16: Sunb ... 9J 23
Kempton Ct. GU14: Cove ... 3L 89
TW16: Sunb ... 9J 23
Kempton Ga. TW12: Hamp ... 9N 23
Kempton Ho. SL4: W'sor ... 4C 4
(off Paddock Cl.)
Kempton Local Nature Reserve
... 7L 23
Kempton Park Racecourse ... 8K 23
Kempton Park Station (Rail) ... 8J 23
Kemptons, The TW15: Ashf ... 3B 22
Kempton Wlk. CR0: Croy ... 5H 47
Kemsing Cl. CR7: T Hea ... 3N 45
Kemsley Rd. TN16: Tats ... 6F 86
Kendal Cl. GU14: Cove ... 1N 89
RH2: Reig ... 2B 122
TW14: Felt ... 2G 22
Kendale Cl. RH10: Craw ... 7G 183
Kendal Gdns. SM1: Sut ... 8A 44
Kendal Gro. GU15: Camb ... 2H 71
Kendal Ho. SE20 ... 1D 46
(off Derwent Rd.)
Kendall Av. BR3: Beck ... 1H 47
CR2: Sande ... 5A 64
Kendall Av. Sth. CR2: Sande ... 6N 63
Kendall Ct. SW19 ... 7B 28
Kendall Rd. BR3: Beck ... 1H 47
TW7: Isle ... 5G 10
Kendal Pl. SW15 ... 8L 13
Kendor Av. KT19: Eps ... 7B 60
Kendra Hall Rd.
CR2: S Croy ... 4M 63
Kendrey Gdns. TW2: Whitt ... 1E 24
Kendrick Cl. RG40: W'ham ... 3B 30
Kenilford Rd. SW12 ... 1F 28
Kenilworth Av. KT11: Sto D ... 1B 78
RG12: Brac ... 9A 16
SW19 ... 6M 27
Kenilworth Cl. RH11: Craw ... 7N 181
SM7: Ban ... 3N 81
Kenilworth Ct. SW15 ... 6K 13
(off Lwr. Richmond Rd.)
Kenilworth Cres.
GU51: Fleet ... 3D 88
Kenilworth Dr. KT12: Wal T ... 9L 39
Kenilworth Gdns.
TW18: Stain ... 6L 21
Kenilworth Rd. GU14: Cove ... 9H 69
GU51: Fleet ... 4C 88
KT17: Ewe ... 2F 60
TW15: Ashf ... 4M 21
KENLEY ... 1N 83
KENLEY AERODROME ... 6A 84
Kenley Gdns. CR7: T Hea ... 3M 45
Kenley La. CR8: Ken ... 1N 83
Kenley Pl. GU14: Farnb ... 5N 89
Kenley Rd. GU35: Head D ... 4G 169
KT1: K Tham ... 1A 42
SW19 ... 1M 43
TW1: Twick ... 9H 11
Kenley Station (Rail) ... 1N 83
Kenley Wlk. SM3: Chea ... 1J 61
Kenlor Rd. SW17 ... 6B 28
Kenmara Cl. RH10: Craw ... 9E 162
Kenmara Ct. RH10: Craw ... 8E 162
Kenmare Dr. CR4: Mit ... 8D 28
Kenmare Rd. CR7: T Hea ... 5L 45
Kenmore Cl. GU16: Frim ... 6B 70
GU52: Chu C ... 8C 88
TW9: Kew ... 3N 11
Kenmore Rd. CR8: Ken ... 1M 83
Kennard Ct. RH18: F Row ... 6G 187
Kenneally SL4: W'sor ... 5A 4
Kenneally Cl. SL4: W'sor ... 5A 4
(off Kenneally)
Kenneally Pl. SL4: W'sor ... 5A 4
(off Kenneally)
Kenneally Row SL4: W'sor ... 5A 4
(off Kenneally)
Kenneally Wlk. SL4: W'sor ... 5A 4
Kennedy Av. RH19: E Grin ... 7N 165
Kennedy Cl. CR4: Mit ... 9E 28
Kennedy Ct. TW15: Ashf ... 6D 22
Kennedy Rd. RH13: Hors ... 7K 197
Kennel Av. SL5: Asc ... 9K 17
Kennel Cl. KT22: Fetc ... 2C 98
SL5: Asc ... 7K 17
Kennel Grn. SL5: Asc ... 9J 17
Kennel La. GU10: Fren ... 9H 129
GU20: Windl ... 2N 51
KT22: Fetc ... 9B 78
RG42: Brac ... 8N 15
RH6: Hookw ... 9B 142
Kennel Ride SL5: Asc ... 9K 17
Kennels La.
GU14: Cove, Farnb ... 2G 88
(not continuous)
Kennel Wood SL5: Asc ... 9K 17
Kennelwood Cres.
CR0: N Add ... 7N 65
Kennet Cl. GU12: Ash ... 3E 110
GU14: Cove ... 8K 69
RH11: Craw ... 4L 181
Kennet Ho. SW18 ... 7M 13
(off Enterprise Way)
Kenneth Rd. SM7: Ban ... 2B 82
Kenneth Younger Ho. SW6 ... 2L 13
(off Clem Attlee Ct.)
Kennet Rd. TW7: Isle ... 6F 10
Kennet Sq. CR4: Mit ... 9C 28
Kennett Ct. W4 ... 3A 12
Kenny Dr. SM5: Cars ... 5E 62
Kenrick Sq. RH1: Blet ... 2B 124
Kensington Av. CR7: T Hea ... 9L 29
Kensington Dr.
GU15: Camb ... 2F 70
Kensington Gdns.
KT1: K Tham ... 6H 203 (2K 41)
Kensington Hall Gdns. W14 ... 1L 13
Kensington Mans. SW5 ... 1M 13
(off Trebovir Rd., not continuous)
Kensington Rd.
RH11: Craw ... 7N 181
Kensington Ter. CR2: S Croy ... 4A 64
Kensington Village W14 ... 1L 13
Kent & Surrey Golf Course, The
... 1J 147
Kent Cl. BR6: Chels ... 3N 67
CR4: Mit ... 3J 45
TW18: Stain ... 7M 21
Kent Dr. TW11: Tedd ... 6E 24
Kent Folly RG42: Warf ... 7D 16
Kent Ga. Way CR0: A'ton ... 3J 65
KENT HATCH ... 9K 107
Kent Hatch Rd.
RH8: C Hil, Limp ... 7E 106
TN8: C Hil ... 7E 106
Kent Ho. W4 ... 1D 12
(off Devonshire St.)
Kentigern Dr. RG45: Crowt ... 2J 49
Kenton Av. TW16: Sunb ... 1L 39
Kenton Cl. GU16: Frim ... 4D 70
RG12: Brac ... 1B 32
Kenton Ct. TW1: Twick ... 9K 11
Kentone Ct. SE25 ... 3E 46
Kentons La. SL4: W'sor ... 5B 4
Kenton Way GU21: Wok ... 4J 73
Kent Rd. BR4: W Wick ... 7L 47
GU20: Windl ... 2A 52
GU22: Wok ... 3D 74
GU51: Fleet ... 4C 88
KT1: K Tham ... 5H 203 (2K 41)
KT8: E Mol ... 3C 40
TW9: Kew ... 3N 11
Kent's Pas. TW12: Hamp ... 9N 23
Kent Way KT6: Surb ... 9L 41
Kentwode Grn. SW13 ... 3F 12
Kentwood Farm
RG40: W'ham ... 9D 14
Kentwyns Dr. RH13: Hors ... 8L 197
Kentwyns Pl. RH13: Hors ... 8L 197
Kentwyns Ri. RH1: Sth N ... 4K 123
Kenward Ct. RH3: Brock ... 7B 120
Kenway Rd. SW5 ... 1N 13
Kenwith Av. GU51: Fleet ... 4D 88
Kenwood Cl. UB7: Sip ... 2B 8
Kenwood Dr. BR3: Beck ... 2M 47
KT12: Hers ... 3J 57
Kenwood Pk. KT13: Weybr ... 3E 56
Kenwood Ridge CR8: Ken ... 4M 83
Kenworth Gro. GU18: Ligh ... 6L 51
Kenwyn Rd. SW20 ... 9H 27
Kenya Ct. RH6: Horl ... 7D 142
Kenyngton Ct. TW16: Sunb ... 6H 23
Kenyngton Dr. TW16: Sunb ... 6H 23
Kenyon Mans. W14 ... 2K 13
(off Queen's Club Gdns.)
Kenyons KT24: W Hors ... 6C 96
Kenyon St. SW6 ... 4J 13
Keogh Barracks GU12: Ash V ... 4F 90
Keogh Cl. GU12: Ash V ... 3F 90
Keppel Rd. RH4: Dork ... 3H 119
Keppel Spur SL4: O Win ... 1L 19
Kepple Pl. GU19: Bag ... 4J 51
Kepplestone M. BR3: Beck ... 1M 47
Kepple St. SL4: W'sor ... 5G 5
Kernel Ct.
GU1: Guil ... 2A 202 (3M 113)
Kerr Cl. CR2: Sels ... 4H 65
Kerria Way GU24: W End ... 9B 52
Kerrill Av. CR5: Coul ... 6L 83
Kerry Cl. GU51: Fleet ... 9C 68
Kerry Ter. GU21: Wok ... 3D 74
Kersey Dr. CR2: Sels ... 8F 64
Kersfield Ho. SW15 ... 9J 13
Kersfield Rd. SW15 ... 9J 13
Kersland Cotts. GU7: Hurt ... 4C 132
Kerves La. RH13: Hors ... 9K 197
Kerwin Ct. RH13: Slinf ... 6B 196
KESTON ... 2E 66
Keston Av. BR2: Kes ... 2E 66
CR5: Coul ... 6L 83
KT15: N Haw ... 7J 55
Keston Ct. KT5: Surb ... 8L 203
Keston Gdns. BR2: Kes ... 1E 66
KESTON MARK ... 1G 67
KESTON MARK ... 1G 66
Keston Pk. Cl. BR2: Kes ... 1H 67
Keston Rd. CR7: T Hea ... 5L 45
Kestrel Av. TW18: Stain ... 4H 21
Kestrel Cl. GU4: Guil ... 1F 114
GU10: Ews ... 5C 108
GU12: Ash V ... 6E 90
KT2: K Tham ... 5K 25
KT19: Eps ... 8N 59
Kestrel Cl. RH11: Craw ... 1A 182
RH12: Hors ... 3L 197
TN8: Eden ... 9M 127
Kestrel Ct. CR2: S Croy ... 3N 63
SM6: W'ton ... 2G 63
Kestrel Cres. RG12: Brac ... 4J 31
Kestrel Ho. GU9: Farnh ... 3F 128
Kestrel Rd. GU14: Farnb ... 3N 89
Kestrel Wlk. RH10: Turn H ... 4F 184
Kestrel Way CR0: N Add ... 5N 65
GU21: Wok ... 2L 73
Keswick Av. SW15 ... 6D 26
SW19 ... 1M 43
TW17: Shep ... 2F 38
Keswick B'way. SW15 ... 8L 13
(off Up. Richmond Rd.)
Keswick Cl. GU15: Camb ... 2H 71
RH11: Ifield ... 5J 181
SM1: Sut ... 1A 62
Keswick Dr. GU18: Ligh ... 7M 51
Keswick Rd. GU8: Wit ... 4A 152
KT22: Fetc ... 2C 98
KT23: Book ... 3B 98
SW15 ... 8K 13
TW2: Whitt ... 9C 10
TW20: Egh ... 8D 20
Ketcher Grn. RG42: Bin ... 5H 15
Kettering Ct. CR7: T Hea ... 3N 45
Kettering St. SW16 ... 7G 28
Kettlewell Cl. GU21: Wok ... 1N 73
Kettlewell Dr. GU21: Wok ... 1A 74
Kettlewell Hill GU21: Wok ... 1A 74
Ketton Grn. RH1: Mers ... 6H 103
Kevan Dr. GU23: Send ... 2G 95
Kevin Cl. TW4: Houn ... 5L 9
Kevins Dr. GU46: Yate ... 8D 48
Kevins Gro. GU51: Fleet ... 4C 88
KEW ... 4N 11
KEW BRIDGE ... 1M 11
Kew Bri. TW8: Brent ... 2N 11
Kew Bri. Arches TW9: Kew ... 2N 11
Kew Bri. Ct. W4 ... 1N 11
Kew Bri. Distribution Cen.
TW8: Brent ... 1M 11
Kew Bri. Rd. TW8: Brent ... 2M 11
Kew Bridge Station (Rail) ... 1M 11
Kew Bridge Steam Mus. ... 1M 11
Kew Ct.
KT2: K Tham ... 1J 203 (9L 25)
Kew Cres. SM3: Chea ... 9K 43
Kew Foot Rd. TW9: Rich ... 7L 11
Kew Gardens ... 3L 11
Kew Gdns. Rd. TW9: Kew ... 3M 11
Kew Gardens Station
(Underground & Overground)
... 4N 11
KEW GREEN ... 3N 11
Kew Grn. TW9: Kew ... 2M 11
Kew Mdw. Path TW9: Kew ... 5B 12
(Clifford Av.)
TW9: Kew ... 4A 12
(Magnolia Ct.)
Kew Retail Pk. TW9: Kew ... 4A 12
Kew Riverside Pk.
TW9: Kew ... 3A 12
Kew Rd. TW9: Kew, Rich ... 2N 11
Keymer Cl. TN16: B Hil ... 3E 86
Keymer Rd. RH11: Craw ... 4A 182
SW2 ... 3K 29
Keynes Cl. GU52: Chu C ... 9C 88
Keynsham Rd. SM4: Mord ... 7N 43
Keynsham Wlk. SM4: Mord ... 7N 43
Keynsham Way GU47: Owls ... 5J 49
Keys Ct. CR0: Croy ... 5D 200
Keysham Av. TW5: C'ford ... 4H 9
Keywood Dr. TW16: Sunb ... 7H 23
Khama Rd. SW17 ... 5C 28
Khartoum Rd. GU8: Wit ... 4B 152
SW17 ... 5B 28
Kibble Grn. RG12: Brac ... 5A 32
Kidborough Down
KT23: Book ... 5A 98
Kidborough Rd.
RH11: Craw ... 4L 181
KIDBROOKE PARK ... 8F 186
Kidbrooke Ri.
RH18: F Row ... 7G 187
Kidderminster Pl.
CR0: Croy ... 7M 45
Kidderminster Rd.
CR0: Croy ... 7M 45
Kidd's Hill TN7: C Hat, Hart ... 9N 187
Kidmans Cl. RH12: Hors ... 3M 197
Kidspace
Croydon ... 3L 63
Kidworth Cl. RH6: Horl ... 6D 142
Kielder Wlk. GU15: Camb ... 2G 71
Kier Pk. SL5: Asc ... 2N 33
Kilberry Cl. TW7: Isle ... 4D 10
Kilcorral Cl. KT17: Eps ... 1F 80
Kilkie St. SW6 ... 5N 13
Killasser Ct. KT20: Tad ... 1H 101
Killburns Mill Cl.
SM6: W'ton ... 8F 44
Killester Gdns. KT4: W Pk ... 1G 61
Killick Ho. SM1: Sut ... 1N 61
Killick M. SM3: Chea ... 3K 61
Killicks GU6: Cranl ... 6A 156
Killieser Av. SW2 ... 3J 29
Killigrew Ho. TW16: Sunb ... 8F 22
Killinghurst La. GU8: Chid ... 2N 189
GU27: Chid, Hasl ... 2N 189
KILLINGHURST PARK ... 9A 172
Killowen Cl. KT20: Tad ... 9J 81
Killy Hill GU24: Chob ... 4H 53

254 A-Z Surrey

Kilmaine Rd.—Kingswood Ri.

Kilmaine Rd. SW6 3K 13
Kilmarnock Pk. RH2: Reig 2N 121
Kilmartin Av. SW16 2L 45
Kilmartin Gdns. GU16: Frim 5D 70
Kilmington Cl. RG12: Brac 6C 32
Kilmington Rd. SW13 2F 12
Kilmiston Av. TW17: Shep 5D 38
Kilmiston Ho. TW17: Shep 5D 38
Kilmore Dr. GU15: Camb 2F 70
Kilmorey Gdns. TW1: Twick 8H 11
Kilmorey Rd. TW1: Twick 7H 11
Kilmuir Cl. GU47: Coll T 8J 49
Kilmuir Ho. KT17: Eps 6L 201
Kiln Av. GU27: Hasl 9G 171
Kiln Cl. RG40: Finch 9A 30
RH10: Craw D 2E 184
UB3: Harl 2E 8
Kiln Copse GU6: Cranl 6N 155
Kiln Cotts. RH5: Newd 7C 140
Kilnfield Rd. RH12: Rudg 9E 176
Kiln Heath Farm Bus. Cen.
RH6: Ship B 5L 163
Kiln Ho. *RH19: E Grin 8N 165*
(off Fosters Pl.)
Kiln La. GU10: Lwr Bou 5G 129
GU23: Rip 2J 95
GU24: Bis 4E 72
KT17: Eps 7D 60
RG12: Brac 1M 31
RH3: Betch, Brock 4A 120
RH6: Horl 6E 142
SL4: Wink 7M 17
SL5: S'dale 4D 34
Kilnmead RH10: Craw 2B 182
Kilnmead Cl. RH10: Craw 2C 182
Kiln Mdws. GU3: Worp 8F 92
Kiln M. SW17 6B 28
Kiln Pl. GU14: Cove 2M 89
Kiln Ride RG40: Finch 8A 30
Kiln Ride Extension
RG40: Finch 1A 48
Kiln Rd. RH10: Craw D 2E 184
Kilns, The RH1: Mers, Red 9F 102
Kilnside KT10: Clay 4G 58
Kiln Wlk. RH1: Red 8E 122
Kiln Way GU11: Alde 5N 109
GU26: G'hott 4K 169
Kilnwood La. RH11: Fay 6E 180
RH12: Fay 6E 180
Kilometre, The RG45: Crowt 3E 48
Kilross Rd. TW14: Bedf 2E 22
Kilrue La. KT12: Hers 1G 57
Kilrush Ter. GU21: Wok 3C 74
Kilsha Rd. KT12: Wal T 5K 39
Kimbell Gdns. SW6 4K 13
Kimber Cl. SL4: W'sor 6D 4
Kimber Ct. GU4: Guil 1F 114
Kimberley GU52: Chu C 9C 88
RG12: Brac 7A 32
Kimberley Bus. Pk.
BR2: Kes 5E 66
Kimberley Cl. RH6: Horl 8C 142
SL3: Lang 1B 6
Kimberley Pl. CR8: Pur 7L 63
Kimberley Ride KT11: Cob 9B 58
Kimberley Rd. BR3: Beck 1G 47
CR0: Croy 5M 45
RH10: Craw 2F 182
Kimberley Wlk. KT12: Wal T 6J 39
Kimber Pl. TW4: Houn 1N 23
(Conway Rd.)
TW4: Houn 7N 9
(Marryat Cl.)
Kimber Rd. SW18 1M 27
Kimbers La. GU9: Farnh 9J 109
Kimble Rd. SW19 7B 28
Kimmeridge RG12: Brac 5C 32
Kimpton Ho. SW15 1F 26
Kimpton Ind. Est. SM3: Sut 8L 43
Kimpton Link Bus. Cen.
SM3: Sut 8L 43
Kimpton Pk. Way SM1: Sut 8K 43
SM3: Sut 8K 43
Kimpton Rd. SM3: Sut 8L 43
Kimpton Trade & Business Cen.
SM3: Sut 8L 43
Kinburn Dr. TW20: Egh 6A 20
Kincha Lodge KT2: K Tham 1L 203
Kindersley Cl.
RH19: E Grin 7D 166
Kinfauns Rd. SW2 3L 29
King Acre Ct. TW18: Stain 4G 20
King Charles Cres.
KT5: Surb 6M 41
King Charles Ho. *SW6 3N 13*
(off Wandon Rd.)
King Charles Rd. KT5: Surb 4M 41
King Charles Wlk. SW19 2K 27
Kingcup Cl. CR0: Croy 6G 46
Kingcup Dr. GU24: Bis 2D 72
King Edward VII Av.
SL4: W'sor 3H 5
King Edward Cl.
RH13: Hors 9D 196
King Edward Ct. Shop. Cen.
SL4: W'sor 4G 4
King Edward Dr. KT9: Ches 9L 41
King Edward M. SW13 4F 12
King Edward Rd.
RH13: Hors 9D 196
King Edwards Cl. SL5: Asc 9J 17
King Edwards Gro.
TW11: Tedd 7H 25
King Edwards Mans. *SW6 3M 13*
(off Fulham Rd.)
King Edwards Ri. SL5: Asc 8J 17
King Edwards Rd. SL5: Asc 9J 17
KINGFIELD 7C 74
Kingfield Cl. GU22: Wok 7B 74
Kingfield Dr. GU22: Wok 7B 74
Kingfield Gdns. GU22: Wok 7B 74
KINGFIELD GREEN 7B 74
Kingfield Grn. GU22: Wok 7B 74
Kingfield Rd. GU22: Wok 7A 74
Kingfield Stadium 7B 74
Kingfisher Chase RG12: Brac 4J 31
Kingfisher Cl. GU14: Cove 8H 69
GU52: Chu C 8B 88
KT12: Hers 2M 57
KT22: Leat 7J 79
RH10: Craw 8E 162
Kingfisher Ct. CR0: Croy 5C 200
GU21: Wok 4A 74
(off Vale Farm Rd.)
GU21: Wok 1E 74
(Woodlands Ho.)
GU51: Fleet 5A 88
(off Connaught Rd.)
KT8: E Mol 3E 40
RH4: Dork 1J 201
SM1: Sut 2L 61
SW19 3J 27
TW3: Houn 8B 10
TW7: Isle 5D 10
Kingfisher Dr. GU4: Guil 1E 114
GU46: Yate 9A 48
RH1: Red 9E 102
TW10: Ham 5H 25
TW18: Stain 5H 21
Kingfisher Gdns. CR2: Sels 7G 65
Kingfisher La.
RH10: Turn H 4F 184
Kingfisher Leisure Cen.
4K 203 (1L 41)
Kingfisher Ri. RH19: E Grin 1B 186
Kingfisher Rd. GU9: Farnh 3E 128
Kingfisher Wlk. GU12: Ash 2D 110
Kingfisher Way BR3: Beck 4G 46
RH12: Hors 3J 197
King Gdns.
CR0: Wad 8A 200 (2M 63)
King George VI Av. CR4: Mit 3D 44
TN16: B Hil 3F 86
King George Av. KT12: Wal T 7L 39
RH19: E Grin 7M 165
King George Cl.
GU14: Farnb 3B 90
TW16: Sunb 6F 22
King George M. SW17 6D 28
King George's Dr.
KT15: N Haw 6J 55
KING GEORGE'S HILL 5N 137
King George Sq.
TW10: Rich 9M 11
King George's Trad. Est.
KT9: Ches 1N 59
Kingham Cl. SW18 1A 28
Kingham Pl. *GU9: Farnh 1G 129*
(off West St.)
King Henry Rd. GU51: Fleet 2A 88
King Henry's Dr. CR0: N Add 5L 65
King Henry's Drive Stop
(London Tramlink) 5L 65
King Henry's Reach W6 2H 13
King Henry's Rd.
KT1: K Tham 2A 42
King John La. TW19: Wray 8N 5
King John's Cl. TW19: Wray 8N 5
King Johns Pl. TW20: Egh 6A 20
King John St. GU51: Fleet 2A 88
Kinglake Ct. GU21: Wok 5H 73
Kingpost Pde. GU1: B'ham 9D 94
Kings Acre RH1: Sth N 6K 123
Kings Apartments
GU15: Camb 2A 70
Kings Arbour UB2: S'hall 1M 9
King's Arms All. TW8: Brent 2K 11
Kings Av. GU10: Tong 4C 110
GU24: B'wood 6A 72
KT3: N Mal 3D 42
KT14: Byf 8M 55
RH1: Red 5C 122
SM5: Cars 4C 62
SW4 2H 29
SW12 2H 29
TW3: Houn 4B 10
TW16: Sunb 6G 23
Kingsbridge Cotts.
RG40: W'ham 9C 30
Kingsbridge Rd. KT12: Wal T 6J 39
SM4: Mord 5J 43
UB2: S'hall 1N 9
Kingsbrook KT22: Leat 5G 79
Kingsbury Cres. TW18: Stain 5F 20
Kingsbury Dr. SL4: O Win 1K 19
Kings Chase KT8: E Mol 2C 40
Kingsclear Pk. GU15: Camb 2B 70
Kingsclere Cl. SW15 1F 26
Kingscliffe Gdns. SW19 2L 27
Kings Cl. KT7: T Dit 5G 41
KT12: Wal T 7J 39
TW18: Stain 8M 21
King's Club, The 7H 27
Kings Copse RH19: E Grin 1B 186
KINGSCOTE 5H 185
Kingscote Hill RH11: Craw 5N 181
Kingscote Rd. CR0: Croy 6E 46
KT3: N Mal 2C 42
Kingscote Station
Bluebell Railway 5J 185
Kings Ct. GU10: Tong 4C 110
KT12: Wal T 9J 39
KT14: Byf 7M 55
KT20: Tad 9G 81
RH13: Hors 5L 197
Kings Ct. Mans. *SW6 4L 13*
(off Fulham Rd.)
Kings Ct. M. KT8: E Mol 4D 40
Kingscourt Rd. SW16 4H 29
King's Cres. GU15: Camb 7A 50
Kingscroft GU51: Fleet 5B 88
Kingscroft La. RG42: Warf 3D 16
Kingscroft Rd. KT22: Leat 7H 79
SM7: Ban 2B 82
Kings Cross La.
RH1: Sth N 5H 123
Kingsdene KT20: Tad 8G 80
Kingsdown Av. CR2: S Croy 6M 63
Kingsdowne Ho.
GU7: Godal 5J 133
Kingsdowne Rd. KT6: Surb 6L 41
Kingsdown Point SW2 3L 29
Kingsdown Rd. KT17: Eps 9F 60
SM3: Chea 2K 61
Kings Dr. KT5: Surb 6N 41
KT7: T Dit 6H 41
KT12: Whit V 5G 57
TW11: Tedd 6D 24
Kings Farm Av. TW10: Rich 7N 11
Kingsfield GU5: Alb 4N 135
SL4: W'sor 4A 4
Kingsfield Bus. Cen.
RH1: Red 4E 122
Kingsfield Way RH1: Red 4E 122
KINGSFOLD 3H 179
Kingsfold Ct. RH12: K'fold 4H 179
Kings Gdns. KT12: Wal T 7J 39
Kings Ga. *GU7: Godal 5J 133*
(off King's Rd.)
KT15: Addl 1K 55
RH12: Hors 6H 197
Kingsgate RH10: Craw 3C 182
Kingsgate Bus. Cen.
KT2: K Tham 2J 203
Kingsgate Rd.
KT1: K Tham 2J 203 (9L 25)
KT2: K Tham 2J 203 (9L 25)
Kings Glade GU46: Yate 9E 48
Kingsgrove Ind. Est.
GU14: Cove 2M 89
Kingshead La. KT14: Byf 7M 55
Kingshill Av. KT4: W Pk 6F 42
Kings Keep GU47: Sandh 6G 49
GU52: Fleet 7B 88
KT1: K Tham 8J 203 (3L 41)
SW15 8J 13
KINGSLAND 2N 159
Kingsland RH5: Newd 2N 159
Kingsland Ct. RH10: Craw 3E 182
Kings La. GU10: Wrec 5E 128
GU20: Windl 2B 52
SM1: Sut 3B 62
TW20: Eng G 6K 19
Kingslawn Cl. SW15 8G 13
Kingslea KT22: Leat 7G 79
RH13: Hors 5L 197
Kingslee Ct. SM2: Sut 4N 61
Kingsleigh Cl. TW8: Brent 2K 11
Kingsleigh Pl. CR4: Mit 2D 44
Kings Leisure Cen. 9A 166
Kingsley Av. GU15: Camb 2A 70
SM1: Sut 1B 62
SM7: Ban 2M 81
TW3: Houn 5C 10
TW20: Eng G 7L 19
Kingsley Cl. RG45: Crowt 4G 49
RH6: Horl 6D 142
Kingsley Ct. *GU11: Alde 2N 109*
(off Windsor Way)
KT4: W Pk 8E 42
(off The Avenue)
KT12: Wal T 9H 39
(off Ashley Pk. Rd.)
Kingsley Dr. KT4: W Pk 8E 42
Kingsley Gdns. KT16: Otter 3F 54
KINGSLEY GREEN 7F 188
Kingsley Gro. RH2: Reig 6M 121
Kingsley Mans. *W14 2K 13*
(off Greyhound Rd.)
Kingsley Rd. CR0: Croy 7L 45
GU14: Farnb 8L 69
RH6: Horl 6D 142
RH11: Craw 6M 181
SW19 6N 27
TW3: Houn 4B 10
Kingslyn Cres. SE19 1B 46
Kings Mall W6 1H 13
Kings Mead RH1: Sth N 5J 123
RH6: Smallf 8M 143
Kingsmead GU6: Cranl 7N 155
GU14: Farnb 1N 89
GU16: Frim G 7C 70
GU21: Wok 3C 74
KT13: Weybr 3E 56
TN16: B Hil 3F 86
TW10: Rich 9M 11
Kingsmead Av. CR4: Mit 2G 45
KT4: W Pk 8G 42
KT6: Surb 8N 41
TW16: Sunb 1K 39
Kingsmead Cl. KT19: Ewe 4C 60
RH12: Hors 2A 198
TW11: Tedd 7H 25
Kingsmead Lodge
SM2: Sut 3B 62
Kingsmeadow 2N 41
Kingsmeadow Athletics Cen.
2N 41
Kings Mead Pk. KT10: Clay 4E 58
Kingsmead Pk. GU8: Els 9G 130
Kingsmead Pl.
RH12: Broadb H 5C 196
Kingsmead Rd.
RH12: Broadb H 5D 196
SW2 3L 29
Kingsmead Shop. Cen.
GU14: Farnb 1N 89
Kingsmere Cl. SW15 6J 13
Kingsmere Rd. RG42: Brac 9L 15
SW19 3J 27
Kings M. GU16: Frim G 8D 70
RH12: Hors 6H 197
Kingsmill Bus. Pk.
KT1: K Tham 6M 203 (2M 41)
Kings Mill La.
RH1: Red, Sth N 8F 122
Kingsnympton Pk.
KT2: K Tham 8A 26
Kingsoak Ho. GU21: Wok 3C 74
King's Paddock
TW12: Hamp 9C 24
Kings Pde. GU51: Fleet 3B 88
SM5: Cars 9D 44
(off Wrythe La.)
Kings Pk. SL3: Coln 3F 6
Kingspark Bus. Cen.
KT3: N Mal 3B 42
Kings Pas.
KT1: K Tham 4H 203 (1K 41)
KT2: K Tham 1H 203 (9K 25)
Kings Peace, The
GU26: G'hott 6B 170
Kings Pl. RH13: Hors 5L 197
W4 1B 12
King's Ride GU15: Camb 6B 50
SL5: Asc 4G 33
Kings Ride Ga. TW10: Rich 7N 11
Kings Ride Pk. SL5: Asc 4G 33
Kingsridge SW19 3K 27
Kings Rd. CR4: Mit 2E 44
GU1: Guil 3D 202 (3N 113)
GU4: Chil 1A 134
GU6: Cranl 8N 155
GU7: Godal 5J 133
GU11: Alde 3K 109
GU21: Wok 3C 74
GU24: W End 1D 72
GU27: Hasl 2D 188
GU51: Fleet 3B 88
KT2: K Tham 1K 203 (8L 25)
KT6: Surb 7J 41
KT12: Wal T 8J 39
KT15: N Haw 6K 55
RG45: Crowt 3G 49
RH6: Horl 8E 142
RH12: Rudg 9E 176
RH13: Hors 5L 197
SE25 2D 46
SL4: W'sor 5G 5
SL5: S'dale, S'hill 4A 34
SM2: Sut 6M 61
SW6 3N 13
SW10 3N 13
SW14 6C 12
SW19 7M 27
TN16: B Hil 3E 86
TW1: Twick 9H 11
TW10: Rich 9M 11
TW11: Tedd 6D 24
TW13: Felt 2K 23
TW20: Egh 5C 20
King's Rd. Ind. Est.
GU27: Hasl 2D 188
King's Shade Wlk.
KT19: Eps 7K 201 (9C 60)
King Stable St. SL4: Eton 3G 4
Kings Ter. GU10: Fren 1J 149
SL3: Lang 2D 6
TW7: Isle 7G 11
Kingston Av. KT22: Leat 8H 79
KT24: E Hor 4F 96
SM3: Chea 9K 43
TW14: Felt 9F 8
Kingston Bri.
KT1: K Tham 3G 203 (1K 41)
Kingston Bus. Cen.
KT9: Ches 9L 41
Kingston By-Pass
KT3: N Mal 4D 42
KT6: Surb 9K 41
SW15 5D 26
SW20 1F 42
Kingston By-Pass Rd.
KT6: Surb 8E 40
KT10: Hinc W, Surb 8E 40
Kingston Cl. TW11: Tedd 7H 25
Kingston Crematorium
KT1: K Tham 2N 41
Kingston Cres. TW15: Ashf 6L 21
Kingston Gdns. CR0: Bedd 9J 45
Kingston Hall Rd.
KT1: K Tham 5H 203 (2K 41)
Kingston Hill KT2: K Tham 9N 25
Kingston Hill Pl.
KT2: K Tham 5B 26
Kingston Ho. KT1: K Tham 7H 203
Kingston Ho. Est. KT6: Surb 5H 41
Kingston Ho. Gdns.
KT22: Leat 8H 79
Kingstonian FC 2N 41
Kingston La. KT24: W Hors 5B 96
TW11: Tedd 6G 25
Kingston Lodge
KT3: N Mal 3D 42
Kingston Ri. KT15: N Haw 6J 55
Kingston Rd. GU15: Camb 7D 50
KT1: K Tham 2A 42
KT3: N Mal 2A 42
KT4: W Pk 8A 42
KT5: Surb 8A 42
KT17: Ewe 5E 60
KT19: Ewe 8A 42
KT22: Leat 5G 79
SW15 3F 26
SW19 3F 26
(Norstead Pk.)
SW19 1K 43
(Rothesay Av.)
SW20 1J 43
TW11: Tedd 6H 25
TW15: Ashf 7N 21
TW18: Stain 5H 21
Kingstons Ind. Est.
GU12: Ash 2C 110
Kingston Sq. *KT22: Leat 6G 79*
(off Buffers La.)
Kingston Station (Rail)
2J 203 (9L 25)
Kingston University
Kingston Hill Campus 6C 26
Knights Park Campus
6K 203 (2L 41)
Penrhyn Road Campus
7J 203 (3L 41)
Roehampton Vale Cen. 4E 26
KINGSTON UPON THAMES
4J 203 (1K 41)
Kingston upon Thames
(Park & Ride) 5J 59
Kingston upon Thames
Art Gallery & Museum
3K 203 (1L 41)
KINGSTON VALE 5D 26
Kingston Va. SW15 5C 26
King St. KT16: Chert 7J 37
RH19: E Grin 9A 166
TW1: Twick 2G 24
TW9: Rich 8K 11
W6 1F 12
King St. Cloisters *W6 1G 13*
(off King St.)
King St. Pde.
TW1: Twick 2G 24
(off King St.)
Kings Wlk. CR2: Sande 1E 84
GU15: Camb 9L 49
Kings Warren KT22: Oxs 7C 58
King's Way CR0: Wad 2K 63
Kingsway BR4: W Wick 1B 66
GU11: Alde 3K 109
GU17: B'water 1J 69
GU21: Wok 5N 73
KT3: N Mal 3H 43
SW14 6A 12
TW19: Stan 2M 21
Kingsway, The KT17: Ewe 7D 60
Kingsway Av. CR2: Sels 5F 64
GU21: Wok 5N 73
Kingsway Bus. Pk.
TW12: Hamp 9N 23
Kingsway Rd. SM3: Chea 4K 61
Kingsway Ter. KT13: Weybr 5B 56
Kingswey Bus. Pk.
GU21: Wok 1E 74
Kingswick Cl. SL5: S'hill 3B 34
Kingswick Dr. SL5: S'hill 3A 34
KINGSWOOD 2K 101
Kingswood SL5: Asc 3G 33
Kingswood Av. BR2: Brom 2N 47
CR2: Sande 2E 84
CR7: T Hea 4L 45
TW3: Houn 4N 9
TW12: Hamp 7B 24
Kingswood Cl. GU1: Guil 2E 114
GU15: Camb 7E 50
KT3: N Mal 5E 42
KT6: Surb 6L 41
KT13: Weybr 4C 56
RH11: Craw 9A 182
TW15: Ashf 6E 22
TW20: Eng G 5N 19
Kingswood Ct. GU21: Wok 3A 74
GU51: Fleet 4B 88
KT20: K'wood 2K 101
Kingswood Creek
TW19: Wray 8N 5
Kingswood Dr. SM2: Sut 5N 61
SM5: Cars 7D 44
Kingswood Flds. Bus. Pk.
KT20: K'wood 3M 101
Kingswood Firs
GU26: G'hott 7N 169
Kingswood Golf Course 2M 101
Kingswood Grange
KT20: Lwr K 6M 101
Kingswood Ho.
KT20: K'wood 7L 81
Kingswood La. CR6: Warl 2F 84
GU26: G'hott 7A 170
Kingswood Pk.
KT20: K'wood 8K 81
Kingswood Pl. CR3: Cate 1C 104
TN8: Eden 9L 127
Kingswood Ri.
TW20: Eng G 6N 19

Kingswood Rd.—Laneway

Kingswood Rd. BR2: Brom . . . 3N 47
KT20: Tad . . . 8G 81
SW2 . . . 1J 29
SW19 . . . 8L 27
Kingswood Station (Rail) . . . 8L 81
Kingswood Way
CR2: Sande, Sels . . . 9F 64
(not continuous)
SM6: W'ton . . . 2J 63
Kingsworth Cl. BR3: Beck . . . 4H 47
Kingsworthy Cl.
KT1: K Tham . . . 5M 203 (2M 41)
Kings Yd. GU2: Guil . . . 9J 93
SL5: Asc . . . 3J 33
SW15 . . . 6H 13
(off Lwr. Richmond Rd.)
Kingwood Rd. SW6 . . . 4K 13
Kinloss Rd. SM5: Cars . . . 6A 44
Kinnaird Av. W4 . . . 3B 12
Kinnersley Mnr. RH2: Sid . . . 2A 142
Kinnersley Wlk. RH2: Reig . . . 8M 121
Kinnibrugh Dr. RH7: Dorm . . . 1C 166
Kinnoul Rd. W6 . . . 2K 13
Kinross Av. KT4: W Pk . . . 8F 42
SL5: Asc . . . 4K 33
Kinross Cl. TW16: Sunb . . . 6G 23
Kinross Ct. SL5: Asc . . . 4K 33
Kinross Dr. TW16: Sunb . . . 6G 22
Kinsella Gdns. SW19 . . . 6G 26
Kintyre Cl. SW16 . . . 1K 45
Kintyre Ct. SW2 . . . 1J 29
Kipings KT20: Tad . . . 8J 81
Kipling Cl. GU46: Yate . . . 2B 68
RH10: Craw . . . 1G 182
Kipling Ct. RH13: Hors . . . 4N 197
SL4: W'sor . . . 5E 4
Kipling Dr. SW19 . . . 7B 28
Kipling Hall RG45: Crowt . . . 2G 48
Kipling Way RH19: E Grin . . . 9M 165
Kirby Cl. KT19: Ewe . . . 2E 60
Kirby Rd. GU21: Wok . . . 4M 73
Kirby Way KT12: Wal T . . . 5K 39
Kirdford Cl. RH11: Craw . . . 1M 181
Kirkby Ct. GU16: Frim . . . 5C 70
Kirkefields GU2: Guil . . . 9K 93
Kirkgate, The
KT17: Eps . . . 6L 201 (9D 60)
Kirkham Cl. GU47: Owls . . . 5J 49
Kirk Knoll GU35: Head . . . 4E 168
Kirkland Av. GU21: Wok . . . 3H 73
Kirkleas Rd. KT6: Surb . . . 7L 41
Kirklees Rd. CR7: T Hea . . . 4L 45
Kirkley Rd. SW19 . . . 9M 27
Kirkly Cl. CR2: Sande . . . 5B 64
Kirk Ri. SM1: Sut . . . 9N 43
Kirkstall RH4: Dork . . . 4J 201
Kirkstall Gdns. SW2 . . . 2J 29
Kirkstall Rd. SW2 . . . 2H 29
Kirksted Rd. SM4: Mord . . . 7N 43
Kirkstone Cl. GU15: Camb . . . 2H 71
Kirrane Cl. KT3: N Mal . . . 4E 42
Kirriemuir Gdns.
GU12: Ash . . . 1H 111
Kirsty Cl. RH5: Dork . . . 7J 119
Kirton Lodge SW18 . . . 9N 13
Kitchener Rd. CR7: T Hea . . . 2A 46
GU11: Alde . . . 7B 90
(not continuous)
Kites Cl. RH11: Craw . . . 3A 182
Kithurst Cl. RH11: Craw . . . 5B 182
Kitsbridge Ho. *RH10: Copt . . . 8L 163*
(off Brookhill Rd.)
Kitsmead RH10: Copt . . . 8L 163
Kitsmead La.
KT16: L'cross, V Wat . . . 7M 35
Kitson Rd. SW13 . . . 4F 12
Kittiwake Chase RG12: Brac . . . 4J 31
Kittiwake Cl. CR2: Sels . . . 6H 65
RH11: Ifield . . . 5J 181
Kittiwake Pl. SM1: Sut . . . 2L 61
Kitts La. GU10: Churt . . . 9K 149
Klondyke Vs.
GU27: G'wood . . . 8L 171
KNAPHILL . . . 4G 72
Knapp Rd. TW15: Ashf . . . 5A 22
Knapton M. SW17 . . . 7E 28
Knaresborough Dr. SW18 . . . 2N 27
Kneller Gdns. TW7: Isle . . . 9D 10
Kneller Rd. KT3: N Mal . . . 6D 42
TW2: Whitt . . . 9C 10
Knepp Cl. RH10: Craw . . . 3G 182
Knepp Ho. *RH13: Hors . . . 7K 197*
(off Kennedy Rd.)
Knevett Ter. TW3: Houn . . . 7A 10
Knighton Cl. CR2: S Croy . . . 5M 63
RH10: Craw . . . 8H 163
Knighton Pl. KT11: Cob . . . 3M 77
Knighton Rd. RH1: Red . . . 5E 122
Knightons La. GU8: Duns . . . 5B 174
Knightsbridge Ct. *SL3: Lang . . . 1C 6*
(off High St.)
Knightsbridge Cres.
TW18: Stain . . . 7K 21
Knightsbridge Gro.
GU15: Camb . . . 8C 50
Knightsbridge Ho.
GU1: Guil . . . 4B 114
(off St Lukes Sq.)
Knightsbridge Rd.
GU15: Camb . . . 8C 50
Knights Cl. KT8: W Mole . . . 4N 39
SL4: W'sor . . . 4A 4
TW20: Egh . . . 7F 20
Knights Ct.
KT1: K Tham . . . 5J 203 (2L 41)
Knights Hill SE27 . . . 6M 29
Knight's Hill Sq. SE27 . . . 5M 29
Knight's Ho. *W14 . . . 1L 13*
(off Baron's Ct. Rd.)
Knights Mead KT16: Chert . . . 6K 37
RH7: Ling . . . 5N 145
Knight's Pk.
KT1: K Tham . . . 5K 203 (2L 41)
Knights Pl. RH1: Red . . . 2E 122
SL4: W'sor . . . 5F 4
TW2: Twick . . . 2E 24
Knights Rd. GU9: Heath E . . . 5K 109
Knights Way GU15: Camb . . . 2G 70
Knightswood GU21: Wok . . . 5J 73
RG12: Brac . . . 7N 31
Knightwood Cl. GU14: Farnb . . . 3C 90
RH2: Reig . . . 5M 121
Knightwood Cres.
KT3: N Mal . . . 5D 42
Knipp Hill KT11: Cob . . . 9N 57
Knivet Rd. SW6 . . . 2M 13
Knobfield RH5: A Ham . . . 3G 136
Knob Hill RH12: Warnh . . . 9F 178
Knockholt Cl. SM2: Sut . . . 6N 61
Knockholt Main Rd.
TN14: Knoc . . . 6N 87
Knockhundred La.
GU26: Lip . . . 9N 169
Knole Cl. CR0: Croy . . . 5F 46
RH10: Craw . . . 2H 183
Knole Gro. RH19: E Grin . . . 7M 165
Knole Wood SL5: S'dale . . . 7B 34
Knoll, The BR3: Beck . . . 1L 47
KT11: Cob . . . 9A 58
KT16: Chert . . . 7H 37
KT22: Leat . . . 8J 79
Knoll Cl. GU51: Fleet . . . 3B 88
Knoll Ct. GU51: Fleet . . . 2B 88
Knoll Farm Rd. RH5: Cap . . . 7G 159
Knollmead KT5: Surb . . . 7B 42
Knoll Pk. Rd. KT16: Chert . . . 7H 37
Knoll Quarry GU7: Godal . . . 5H 133
Knoll Rd. GU7: Godal . . . 5G 133
GU15: Camb . . . 9B 50
GU51: Fleet . . . 3B 88
RH4: Dork . . . 7G 119
SW18 . . . 8N 13
KNOLL RDBT. . . . 8J 79
Knoll Rdbt. KT22: Leat . . . 8J 79
Knolls, The KT17: Eps D . . . 3H 81
Knolls Cl. KT4: W Pk . . . 9G 42
Knoll Wlk. GU15: Camb . . . 9B 50
Knoll Wood GU7: Godal . . . 5G 133
Knollys Cl. SW16 . . . 4L 29
Knollys Rd. GU11: Alde . . . 1L 109
SW16 . . . 4K 29
Knook, The GU47: Coll T . . . 8J 49
Knotley Way BR4: W Wick . . . 8L 47
Knowle, The GU35: Head . . . 3G 168
KT20: Tad . . . 8H 81
Knowle Cl. RH10: Copt . . . 7N 163
Knowledge Ct. SW16 . . . 2K 45
Knowle Dr. RH10: Copt . . . 7M 163
Knowle Gdns. KT14: W By . . . 9H 55
KNOWLE GREEN . . . 6K 21
Knowle Grn. TW18: Stain . . . 6J 21
Knowle Gro. GU25: V Wat . . . 6M 35
Knowle Gro. Cl.
GU25: V Wat . . . 6M 35
KNOWLE HILL . . . 6M 35
Knowle Hill GU25: V Wat . . . 6L 35
Knowle La.
GU6: Cranl, Rudg . . . 8M 155
RH12: Rudg . . . 4M 175
Knowle Lodge CR3: Cate . . . 1D 104
Knowle Pk. KT11: Cob . . . 3M 77
Knowle Pk. Av. TW18: Stain . . . 7K 21
Knowle Rd. TW2: Twick . . . 2E 24
Knowles Av. RG45: Crowt . . . 2E 48
Knowles Ho. *SW18 . . . 9N 13*
(off Neville Gill Cl.)
Knowl Hill GU22: Wok . . . 6D 74
Knox Grn. RG42: Bin . . . 6H 15
Knox Rd. GU2: Guil . . . 7K 93
Kohat Ct. GU11: Alde . . . 2L 109
Kohat Rd. SW19 . . . 6N 27
Kohima Cl. GU11: Alde . . . 1N 109
Koonowla Cl. TN16: B Hil . . . 2F 86
Kooringa CR6: Warl . . . 6E 84
Korda Cl. TW17: Shep . . . 2A 38
Korea Cotts. KT11: Cob . . . 3L 77
Kotan Dr. TW18: Stain . . . 5E 20
Kramer M. SW5 . . . 1M 13
Kreisel Wlk. TW9: Kew . . . 2M 11
Kristina Ct. *SM2: Sut . . . 3M 61*
(off Overton Rd.)
Krooner Rd. GU15: Camb . . . 3N 69
Kuala Gdns. SW16 . . . 9K 29
Kurdish Mus. . . . 1F 12
Kwesi M. SE27 . . . 6L 29
Kyle Cl. RG12: Brac . . . 2N 31
Kynaston Av. CR7: T Hea . . . 4N 45
Kynaston Ct. CR3: Cate . . . 3B 104
Kynaston Cres. CR7: T Hea . . . 4N 45
Kynaston Rd. CR7: T Hea . . . 4N 45
Kynersley Cl. SM5: Cars . . . 9D 44
Kyngeshene Gdns.
GU1: Guil . . . 4D 114

L

Laburnum Av. SM1: Sut . . . 9C 44
Laburnum Cl. GU1: Guil . . . 9M 93
GU11: Alde . . . 3M 109
Laburnum Ct. (Caravan Pk.)
RH6: Smallf . . . 1N 163
Laburnum Cres.
TW16: Sunb . . . 9J 23
Laburnum Gdns. CR0: Croy . . . 6G 46
GU52: Chu C . . . 8C 88
Laburnum Gro. KT3: N Mal . . . 1C 42
SL3: Lang . . . 2D 6
TW3: Houn . . . 7N 9
Laburnum Ho. BR2: Brom . . . 1N 47
Laburnum Pas.
GU11: Alde . . . 2M 109
Laburnum Pl. TW20: Eng G . . . 7L 19
Laburnum Rd. CR4: Mit . . . 1E 44
GU9: Weybo . . . 5K 109
GU11: Alde . . . 3M 109
GU22: Wok . . . 7N 73
KT16: Chert . . . 7J 37
KT18: Eps . . . 7L 201 (9D 60)
SW19 . . . 8A 28
UB3: Harl . . . 1H 9
Laburnums, The
GU17: B'water . . . 1G 68
Laburnum Way TW19: Stan . . . 2A 22
Lacey Av. CR5: Coul . . . 7L 83
Lacey Cl. TW20: Egh . . . 8F 20
Lacey Dr. CR5: Coul . . . 7M 83
TW12: Hamp . . . 9N 23
Lacey Grn. CR5: Coul . . . 7L 83
Lackford Rd. CR5: Chip . . . 5D 82
Lackland Ct. *GU51: Fleet . . . 2A 88*
(off King John St.)
Lacock Cl. SW19 . . . 7A 28
Lacrosse Way SW16 . . . 9H 29
Lacy Rd. SW15 . . . 7J 13
Ladas Rd. SE27 . . . 5N 29
Ladbroke Cotts. *RH1: Red . . . 2E 122*
(off Ladbroke Rd.)
Ladbroke Ct. RH1: Red . . . 1E 122
Ladbroke Gro. RH1: Red . . . 2E 122
Ladbroke Hurst RH7: Dorm . . . 1C 166
Ladbroke Rd.
KT18: Eps . . . 8K 201 (1C 80)
RH1: Red . . . 2E 122
RH6: Horl . . . 6F 142
Ladbrook Rd. SE25 . . . 3A 46
Ladderstile Ride
KT2: K Tham . . . 6A 26
Ladybank RG12: Brac . . . 7N 31
Lady Booth Rd.
KT1: K Tham . . . 4J 203 (1L 41)
Ladycroft Gdns. BR6: Farnb . . . 2L 67
Ladycroft Way BR6: Farnb . . . 2L 67
Ladycross GU8: Mil . . . 2B 152
Ladyegate Cl. RH5: Dork . . . 4K 119
Ladyegate Rd. RH5: Dork . . . 5J 119
Lady Elizabeth Ho. SW14 . . . 6B 12
Lady Forsdyke Way
KT19: Eps . . . 5N 59
Ladygate Dr. GU26: G'hott . . . 6M 169
Ladygrove CR0: Sels . . . 5H 65
Ladygrove Dr. GU4: B'ham . . . 7C 94
Lady Harewood Way
KT19: Eps . . . 5N 59
Lady Hay KT4: W Pk . . . 8E 42
Lady Jane Ct.
KT2: K Tham . . . 3M 203
Lady Margaret Rd.
RH11: Craw . . . 2M 181
SL5: S'dale . . . 7C 34
Lady Margaret Wlk.
RH11: Craw . . . 2M 181
Ladymead
GU1: Guil . . . 1B 202 (2M 113)
Ladymead Cl. RH10: Craw . . . 6G 183
Ladymead Retail Cen.
GU1: Guil . . . 1B 202 (2M 113)
Ladythorpe Cl.
KT15: Addl . . . 1K 55
Ladywood Av. GU14: Cove . . . 1H 89
Ladywood Rd. KT6: Surb . . . 8N 41
Laffan's Rd. GU11: Alde . . . 7H 89
LA Fitness
Croydon . . . 4L 63
Epsom . . . 1C 60
Ewell . . . 8H 61
Gatwick . . . 8L 163
Goldsworth . . . 4N 73
Guildford . . . 2G 114
Isleworth . . . 6H 11
(off Swan St.)
Purley . . . 6N 63
Lafone Av. TW13: Felt . . . 3K 23
Lagham Pk. RH9: S Gods . . . 6H 125
Lagham Rd. RH9: S Gods . . . 7H 125
Laglands Cl. RH2: Reig . . . 1A 122
Laings Av. CR4: Mit . . . 1D 44
Lainlock Pl. TW3: Houn . . . 4B 10
Lainson St. SW18 . . . 1M 27
Lairdale Cl. SE21 . . . 2N 29
Laird Ct. GU19: Bag . . . 6J 51
Laitwood Rd. SW12 . . . 2F 28
Lake Cl. KT14: Byf . . . 8M 55
SW19 . . . 6L 27
Lake End Way
RG45: Crowt . . . 3F 48
Lake Gdns. SM6: W'ton . . . 9F 44
TW10: Ham . . . 3H 25
Lakehall Gdns. CR7: T Hea . . . 4M 45
Lakehall Rd. CR7: T Hea . . . 4M 45
Lakehurst Rd. KT19: Ewe . . . 2D 60
Lakeland Dr. GU16: Frim . . . 5C 70
Lake La. GU10: Dock . . . 4D 148
RH6: Horl . . . 6G 142
Laker Ct. RH10: Craw . . . 3E 182
Lake Rd. CR0: Croy . . . 8J 47
GU16: Deep . . . 8E 70
GU25: V Wat . . . 4L 35
SW19 . . . 6L 27
Laker Pl. SW15 . . . 9K 13
LAKER'S GREEN . . . 5H 175
Lakers Lea RH14: Loxw . . . 7H 193
Lakers Ri. SM7: Ban . . . 3C 82
Lakes Cl. GU4: Guil . . . 9D 114
Lakeside BR3: Beck . . . 2L 47
GU21: Wok . . . 6H 73
KT2: K Tham . . . 8A 26
KT13: Weybr . . . 8F 38
KT19: Ewe . . . 3D 60
RG42: Brac . . . 8A 16
RH1: Red . . . 1E 122
RH12: Hors . . . 3J 197
SM6: W'ton . . . 1F 62
Lakeside, The GU17: B'water . . . 2J 69
Lakeside Bus. Pk.
GU47: Sandh . . . 8F 48
Lakeside Cl. GU12: Ash V . . . 9D 90
GU21: Wok . . . 6H 73
SE25 . . . 1D 46
Lakeside Ct. GU51: Fleet . . . 2C 88
Lakeside Dr. GU24: Chob . . . 9H 53
KT10: Esh . . . 3C 58
Lakeside Fishery . . . 3F 190
Lakeside Gdns. GU14: Cove . . . 7J 69
Lakeside Grange
KT13: Weybr . . . 9D 38
Lakeside Ind. Est. SL3: Coln . . . 2J 7
Lakeside (Local Nature Reserve)
. . . 9D 90
Lakeside Pk. KT16: Chert . . . 7L 37
Lakeside Rd. GU11: Alde . . . 8C 90
GU12: Ash V . . . 8C 90
GU14: Farnb . . . 6M 89
SL0: R Pk . . . 3H 7
SL3: Coln, R Pk . . . 3H 7
Lakes La. GU8: Wit . . . 5C 152
Lakes Rd. BR2: Kes . . . 2E 66
Lakestreet Grn. RH8: Limp . . . 7F 106
Lake Vw. RH5: Nth H . . . 8J 119
RH19: D Pk . . . 5B 166
Lakeview Pk. Caravan Site
SL4: Wink . . . 2J 17
Lake Vw. Rd. RH19: Felb . . . 7E 164
Lakeview Rd. SE27 . . . 6L 29
Lakewood KT10: Esh . . . 7N 57
LALEHAM . . . 2L 37
Laleham Abbey TW18: Lale . . . 3L 37
Laleham Camping Site
TW18: Lale . . . 4L 37
Laleham Cl. TW18: Stain . . . 9K 21
Laleham Ct. GU21: Wok . . . 3A 74
SM1: Sut . . . 2A 62
Laleham Golf Course . . . 3K 37
Laleham Park . . . 3L 37
LALEHAM REACH . . . 2J 37
Laleham Reach KT16: Chert . . . 2J 37
Laleham Rd. TW17: Shep . . . 3N 37
TW18: Stain . . . 6H 21
Lalor St. SW6 . . . 5K 13
Lamberhurst Rd. SE27 . . . 5L 29
Lamberhurst Wlk.
RH10: Craw . . . 4E 182
Lambert Av. TW9: Rich . . . 6N 11
Lambert Cl. TN16: B Hil . . . 3F 86
Lambert Cotts. RH1: Blet . . . 2B 124
Lambert Ct. KT13: Weybr . . . 4A 56
Lambert Cres.
GU17: B'water . . . 2H 69
Lambert Lodge *TW8: Brent . . . 1K 11*
(off Layton Rd.)
Lambert Rd. SM7: Ban . . . 1M 81
Lambert's Pl.
CR0: Croy . . . 1E 200 (7A 46)
Lamberts Rd. KT5: Surb . . . 4L 41
Lambeth Cl. RH11: Craw . . . 7N 181
Lambeth Crematorium
SW17 . . . 5A 28
Lambeth Rd. CR0: Croy . . . 6L 45
Lambeth Wlk. RH11: Craw . . . 7N 181
Lambly Hill GU25: V Wat . . . 2A 36
Lamborne Cl. GU47: Sandh . . . 6F 48
Lambourn Cl. CR2: S Croy . . . 5M 63
RH19: E Grin . . . 7A 166
Lambourne Av. SW19 . . . 5L 27
Lambourne Cl. RH10: Craw . . . 5D 182
Lambourne Cres.
GU21: Wok . . . 9F 54
Lambourne Dr. GU19: Bag . . . 5H 51
KT11: Cob . . . 2L 77
Lambourne Way
GU10: Tong . . . 5C 110
Lambourn Gro. KT1: K Tham . . . 1A 42
RG12: Brac . . . 1C 32
Lambrook Ter. SW6 . . . 4K 13
Lambs Bus. Pk.
RH9: S Gods . . . 7E 124
Lambs Cres. RH12: Hors . . . 3M 197
Lambs Farm Cl.
RH12: Hors . . . 3N 197
Lambs Farm Rd.
RH12: Hors . . . 3M 197
LAMBS GREEN . . . 3E 180
Lambs Grn. RH12: Rusp . . . 4E 180
Lambton Ho. SL4: W'sor . . . 6D 4
Lambton Rd. SW20 . . . 9H 27
Lambyn Cft. RH6: Horl . . . 7G 143
LAMDA . . . *1J 13*
(off Talgarth Rd.)
Lammas Av. CR4: Mit . . . 1E 44
SL4: W'sor . . . 5F 4
Lammas Cl. GU7: Godal . . . 5K 133
TW18: Stain . . . 4G 20
Lammas Ct. *GU7: Godal . . . 6H 133*
(off Old Station Way)
SL4: W'sor . . . 5F 4
TW19: Stain . . . 3F 20
Lammas Dr. TW18: Stain . . . 5F 20
Lammas Hill KT10: Esh . . . 1B 58
Lammas La.
KT10: Esh, Hers . . . 1N 57
Lammas Mead RG42: Bin . . . 8K 15
Lammas Rd. GU7: Godal . . . 6K 133
TW10: Ham . . . 5J 25
Lammermoor Rd. SW12 . . . 1F 28
Lampard La. GU10: Churt . . . 8J 149
Lampeter Cl. GU22: Wok . . . 5A 74
Lampeter Sq. W6 . . . 2K 13
Lamports Ct. *GU9: Farnh . . . 2H 129*
(off Arthur Rd.)
Lampson Ct. RH10: Copt . . . 7N 163
LAMPTON . . . 4B 10
Lampton Av. TW3: Houn . . . 4B 10
Lampton Ct. TW3: Houn . . . 4B 10
Lampton Ho. Cl. SW19 . . . 5J 27
Lampton Pk. Rd. TW3: Houn . . . 5B 10
Lampton Rd. TW3: Houn . . . 5A 10
Lampton Sports Cen. . . . 5A 10
Lanadron Cl. TW7: Isle . . . 5F 10
Lanark Cl. GU16: Frim . . . 4C 70
RH13: Hors . . . 6L 197
Lancashire Hill RG42: Warf . . . 7D 16
Lancaster Av. CR4: Mit . . . 4J 45
GU1: Guil . . . 5B 114
GU9: Farnh . . . 3H 129
SE27 . . . 3M 29
SW19 . . . 6J 27
Lancaster Cl. GU12: Ash V . . . 8D 90
GU21: Wok . . . 3C 74
KT2: K Tham . . . 6K 25
RH10: Craw . . . 9H 163
TW15: Ashf . . . 5N 21
TW19: Stan . . . 9N 7
TW20: Eng G . . . 6N 19
Lancaster Cotts. TW10: Rich . . . 9L 11
Lancaster Ct. KT12: Wal T . . . 6H 39
KT19: Ewe . . . 6C 60
SE27 . . . 3M 29
SM2: Sut . . . 4M 61
(off Mulgrave Rd.)
SM7: Ban . . . 1L 81
SW6 . . . 3L 13
TW19: Stan . . . 2N 21
Lancaster Dr. GU15: Camb . . . 9B 50
RH19: E Grin . . . 7C 166
Lancaster Gdns.
KT2: K Tham . . . 6K 25
RH7: Blin H . . . 3H 145
SW19 . . . 6K 27
Lancaster Ho. RG12: Brac . . . 4N 31
RH1: Red . . . 6C 122
TW7: Isle . . . 3F 10
Lancaster M. SW18 . . . 8N 13
TW10: Rich . . . 9L 11
Lancaster Pk. TW10: Rich . . . 8L 11
Lancaster Pl. SW19 . . . 6J 27
TW1: Twick . . . 9G 11
TW4: Houn . . . 5K 9
Lancaster Rd. SE25 . . . 1C 46
SW19 . . . 6J 27
Lancaster Way GU14: Farnb . . . 7A 70
KT4: W Pk . . . 6G 43
Lancastrian Rd. SM6: W'ton . . . 4J 63
Lancelot Cl. RH11: Ifield . . . 3K 181
Lancer Ct. GU11: Alde . . . 2K 109
Lanchester Dr. RG45: Crowt . . . 9H 31
Lancing Cl. RH11: Craw . . . 1M 181
Lancing Ct. RH12: Hors . . . 4N 197
Lancing Ho. CR0: Croy . . . 6D 200
Lancing Rd. CR0: Croy . . . 6K 45
TW13: Felt . . . 3G 22
Landau Ct. CR2: S Croy . . . 8B 200
Landen Ct. RG40: W'ham . . . 4A 30
Landen Ho. RG40: W'ham . . . 1B 30
Landen Pk. RH6: Horl . . . 6C 142
Landford Rd. SW15 . . . 6H 13
Landgrove Rd. SW19 . . . 6M 27
Landmark Arts Cen. . . . 6H 25
Landmark Ho. *W6 . . . 1H 13*
(off Hammersmith Bri. Rd.)
Landon Way TW15: Ashf . . . 7C 22
Landridge Rd. SW6 . . . 5L 13
Landscape Rd. CR6: Warl . . . 6E 84
Landseer Cl. GU47: Coll T . . . 9K 49
SW19 . . . 9A 28
Landseer Rd. KT3: N Mal . . . 6C 42
SM1: Sut . . . 3M 61
Lands End La. GU35: Lind . . . 4A 168
Lane, The GU8: Thur . . . 6G 150
GU25: V Wat . . . 2A 36
KT16: Chert . . . 2J 37
RH14: Ifo . . . 4E 192
Lane Cl. KT15: Addl . . . 2K 55
Lane End GU8: Hamb . . . 1E 172
KT18: Eps . . . 1A 80
RH7: Dorm . . . 1C 166
SW15 . . . 9J 13
Lane End Dr. GU21: Knap . . . 4F 72
Lane Gdns. KT10: Clay . . . 4F 58
Lanehurst Gdns.
RH10: Craw . . . 1G 182
Lanercost Cl. SW2 . . . 3L 29
Lanercost Rd. RH11: Craw . . . 4A 182
SW2 . . . 3L 29
Lanesborough Way SW17 . . . 4B 28
Laneway SW15 . . . 8G 12

Lanfrey Pl.—Leech La.

Lanfrey Pl. W14 . . . . .1L 13
Langaller La. KT22: Fetc 9B 78
Langborough Rd.
RG40: W'ham 3B 30
Langbourne Way KT10: Clay . . .3G 58
Lang Cl. KT22: Fetc 1B 98
Langcroft Cl. SM5: Cars 9D 44
Langdale Av. CR4: Mit 2D 44
Langdale Cl. GU14: Cove 1K 89
GU21: Wok 3M 73
SW14 . . . . .7A 12
Langdale Ct. *GU12: Ash V 8D 90*
(off Lakeside Cl.)
Langdale Dr. SL5: Asc 1J 33
Langdale Pde. CR4: Mit 2D 44
Langdale Rd. CR7: T Hea 3L 45
RH11: Ifield 5J 181
Langdon Cl. GU15: Camb 2G 70
Langdon Pk. TW11: Tedd 8J 25
Langdon Pl. SW14 . . . . .6B 12
Langdon Rd. SM4: Mord 4A 44
Langdon Wlk. SM4: Mord 4A 44
Langford Rd. SW6 . . . . .5N 13
Langham Cl. GU7: Godal 6J 133
Langham Ct. GU9: Farnh 4H 129
SW20 . . . . .1H 43
Langham Dene CR8: Ken 2M 83
Langham Gdns. TW10: Ham . . .5J 25
Langham Ho. Cl.
TW10: Ham 5K 25
Langham Mans. *SW5 . . . . .1N 13*
(off Earl's Ct. Sq.)
Langham Pk. GU7: Godal 6J 133
Langham Pl. TW20: Egh 6B 20
W4 . . . . .2D 12
Langham Rd. SW20 . . . . .9H 27
TW11: Tedd 6H 25
Langholm Cl. SW12 . . . . .1H 29
Langhorn Dr. TW2: Twick 1E 24
Lang Ho. TW19: Stan 2N 21
LANGHURST
RH12, Lambs Green 9F 160
RH12, Lipscomb's Corner
. . . . .5L 179
TN8 . . . . .5G 127
Langhurst Cl. RH12: Hors 5K 179
Langhurst La. RH12: Rusp 1F 180
Langhurstwood Rd.
RH12: Hors 8J 179
Langland Gdns. CR0: Croy 8J 47
Langlands Ri.
KT19: Eps 6H 201 (9B 60)
LANGLEY 1C 6
Langley Av. KT4: W Pk 7J 43
KT6: Surb 7K 41
LANGLEY BOTTOM 6C 80
Langley Broom SL3: Lang 1B 6
Langley Cl.
GU1: Guil 1B 202 (2M 113)
GU52: Chu C 9A 88
KT18: Eps D 6C 80
Langley Ct. RH2: Reig 2N 121
Langley Cres. UB3: Harl 3G 9
Langley Dr. GU11: Alde 4M 109
GU15: Camb 9C 50
RH11: Craw 1A 182
LANGLEY GREEN 9A 162
Langley Gro. KT3: N Mal 1D 42
Langley La. KT18: Head 3A 100
RH11: Ifield 1M 181
Langley Oaks Av.
CR2: Sande 6D 64
Langley Pde. RH11: Craw 9A 162
Langley Pk. Golf Course 5N 47
Langley Pk. Rd. SM1: Sut 2A 62
SM2: Sut 2A 62
Langley Pk. Sports Cen. 5M 47
Langley Pl. RH11: Craw 9A 162
Langley Rd. BR3: Beck 3H 47
CR2: Sels 5G 64
KT6: Surb 6L 41
SW19 . . . . .9L 27
TW7: Isle 5F 10
TW18: Stain 7H 21
LANGLEY RDBT. 1C 6
LANGLEY VALE 6D 80
Langley Va. Rd.
KT18: Eps D 7B 80
Langley Wlk. GU14: Farnb 5N 89
GU22: Wok 6A 74
RH11: Craw 9N 161
Langley Way BR4: W Wick 7N 47
Langmans La. GU21: Wok 5L 73
Langmans Way GU21: Wok 3H 73
Langmead St. SE27 . . . . .5M 29
Langport Ct. KT12: Wal T 7K 39
Langridge Dr. RH19: E Grin . . .1A 186
Langridge Ho. RH12: Hors . . .6G 197
Langridge M. TW12: Hamp 7N 23
Langroyd Rd. SW17 . . . . .3D 28
LANGSHOTT 7G 143
Langshott RH6: Horl 6F 142
Langshott Cl. KT15: Wood 7G 55
Langshott La. RH6: Horl 8G 142
(not continuous)
Langside Av. SW15 . . . . .7F 12
Langsmead RH7: Blin H 3H 145
Langstone Cl. RH10: Craw . . .6G 183
Langthorne Ho. UB3: Harl 1F 8
Langthorne St. SW6 . . . . .3J 13
Langton Av. KT17: Ewe 7E 60
Langton Cl. GU21: Wok 4J 73
KT15: Addl 9K 37
Langton Dr. GU35: Head 2F 168
Langton Pl. SW18 . . . . .2M 27
Langton Rd. KT8: W Mole 3C 40
Langton Way CR0: Croy 9B 46
TW20: Egh 7E 20
Langtry Ct. TW7: Isle 5F 10
Langtry Ho. *KT2: K Tham 2M 203*
(off London Rd.)
Langtry Pl. SW6 . . . . .2M 13
Langwood Chase
TW11: Tedd 7J 25
Langwood Cl. KT21: Asht 4N 79
Lanigan Dr. TW3: Houn 8B 10
Lankester Sq. RH8: Oxt 6N 105
Lankton Cl. BR3: Beck 1M 47
Lannoy Point *SW6 . . . . .3K 13*
(off Pellant Rd.)
Lansbury Av. TW14: Felt 9J 9
Lansbury Est. GU21: Knap 5G 73
Lansbury Rd. RH11: Craw 7N 181
Lansdell Ho. SW2 . . . . .1L 29
Lansdell Rd. CR4: Mit 1E 44
Lansdown GU1: Guil 3C 114
Lansdown Cl. GU21: Wok 6J 73
KT12: Wal T 7K 39
RH12: Hors 2A 198
Lansdowne Cl. KT6: Surb 8A 42
SW20 . . . . .9J 27
TW1: Twick 2F 24
Lansdowne Ct. CR8: Pur 6M 63
KT4: W Pk 8F 42
Lansdowne Hill SE27 . . . . .4M 29
Lansdowne Ho. KT18: Eps 8H 201
Lansdowne Rd.
CR0: Croy 2C 200 (8A 46)
CR8: Pur 8L 63
GU11: Alde 3M 109
GU16: Frim 6E 70
KT19: Ewe 4B 60
SW20 . . . . .8H 27
TW3: Houn 6C 10
TW18: Stain 8K 21
Lansdowne Wood Cl. SE27 . . . .4M 29
Lantern Cl. BR6: Farnb 1K 67
SW15 . . . . .7F 12
Lanyon Cl. RH12: Hors 2N 197
Lanyon M. RH12: Hors 2N 197
Lapwing Cl. CR2: Sels 6H 65
RH13: Hors 5M 197
Lapwing Ct. KT6: Surb 9N 41
Lapwing Gro. GU4: Guil 1F 114
Lara Cl. KT9: Ches 4L 59
Larbert Rd. SW16 . . . . .8G 29
Larby Pl. KT17: Ewe 6D 60
Larch Av. GU1: Guil 1M 113
SL5: S'dale 4B 34
Larch Cl. CR6: Warl 6H 85
GU15: Camb 6C 50
KT20: K'wood 8A 82
RH1: Red 5A 122
SW12 . . . . .3F 28
Larch Cres. KT19: Ewe 3A 60
Larch Dr. W4 . . . . .1N 11
Larch End RH12: Hors 5H 197
Larches, The GU21: Wok 3A 74
RG42: Warf 8E 16
RH12: Hors 2B 198
RH19: E Grin 6D 166
Larches Av. SW14 . . . . .7C 12
Larches Ho. RH19: E Grin 6D 166
Larches Way GU17: B'water 1G 68
RH10: Craw D 1E 184
Larchfield Ct. KT13: Weybr 9G 38
Larchfield Rd. GU52: Fleet 6B 88
Larch Rd. GU35: Head D 3G 168
Larch Tree Way CR0: Croy 9K 47
Larchvale Ct. SM2: Sut 4N 61
Larch Way GU14: Cove 2H 89
Larchwood RG12: Brac 4D 32
Larchwood Cl. SM7: Ban 2K 81
Larchwood Dr. TW20: Eng G 7L 19
Larchwood Glade
GU15: Camb 8E 50
Larchwood Rd. GU21: Wok 7G 73
Larcombe Cl. CR0: Croy 1C 64
Larcombe Ct. *SM2: Sut 4N 61*
(off Worcester Rd.)
Larges Bri. Dr. RG12: Brac 2A 32
Larges La. RG12: Brac 1A 32
Largewood Av. KT6: Surb 8N 41
Lark Av. TW18: Stain 4H 21
Larkfield GU6: Ewh 6F 156
KT11: Cob 9H 57
Larkfield Cl. GU9: Farnh 9E 108
Larkfield Ct. RH6: Smallf 8L 143
Larkfield Rd. GU9: Farnh 1E 128
TW9: Rich 7L 11
Larkhall Cl. KT12: Hers 3K 57
Larkham Cl. TW13: Felt 4F 22
Larkin Cl. CR5: Coul 4K 83
Larkins Rd. RH6: Gatw 3B 162
Lark Ri. KT24: E Hor 9F 96
RH10: Turn H 4F 184
RH11: Craw 1A 182
Larksfield RH6: Horl 7F 142
TW20: Eng G 8L 19
Larkspur Cl. GU11: Alde 5M 109
Larkspur Way KT19: Ewe 2B 60
RH5: Nth H 8K 119
Larks Way GU21: Knap 3F 72
Larkswood Cl. GU47: Sandh 6F 48
Larkswood Dr. RG45: Crowt 2G 49
Lark Way SM5: Cars 6C 44
Larnach Rd. W6 . . . . .2J 13
Larpent Av. SW15 . . . . .8H 13
Lascar Cl. TW3: Houn 6N 9
Lascombe La. GU3: Put 8L 111
Laserquest
Horsham 6J 197
(within Superbowl)
Sutton 2N 61
(within Superbowl)
Woking 4B 74
(within The Big Apple)
Wokingham 3A 30
(within Superbowl)
Lashmere GU6: Cranl 7J 155
RH10: Copt 7A 164
Laski Ct. RH11: Craw 8N 181
Las Palmas Est.
TW17: Shep 6D 38
Lasswade Ct. KT16: Chert 6G 37
Lasswade Rd. KT16: Chert 6G 37
Lastingham Ct. TW18: Stain 7J 21
Latchmere Cl. TW10: Ham 6L 25
Latchmere La. KT2: K Tham . . .7M 25
TW10: Ham 7M 25
Latchmere Pl. TW15: Ashf 3N 21
Latchmere Rd. KT2: K Tham . . .8L 25
Latchwood La.
GU10: Lwr Bou 6J 129
Lateward Rd. TW8: Brent 2K 11
Latham Av. GU16: Frim 4C 70
Latham Cl. TN16: B Hil 3E 86
TW1: Twick 1G 24
Latham Ct. *SW5 . . . . .1M 13*
(off W. Cromwell Rd.)
Latham Rd. TW1: Twick 1F 24
Latham's Way CR0: Wad 7K 45
Lathkill Ct. BR3: Beck 1J 47
Latimer RG12: Brac 7N 31
Latimer Cl. GU22: Wok 3D 74
KT4: W Pk 1G 61
RH11: Craw 9B 162
Latimer Ct. RH1: Red 5D 122
Latimer Ho. GU51: Fleet 2A 88
Latimer Rd.
CR0: Croy 4A 200 (9M 45)
GU7: Godal 7H 133
RG41: W'ham 3A 30
SW19 . . . . .7N 27
TW11: Tedd 6F 24
Latitude *KT16: Chert 7L 37*
(off Bridge Wharf)
Latitude Apartments
CR0: Croy 4E 200
Lattimer Pl. W4 . . . . .3D 12
Latton Cl. KT10: Esh 1B 58
KT12: Wal T 6M 39
Latymer Cl. KT13: Weybr 1D 56
Laubin Cl. TW1: Twick 7H 11
Laud Dr. RH10: Craw 4H 183
Lauder Cl. GU16: Frim 4C 70
Lauderdale GU14: Cove 3J 89
Lauderdale Dr. TW10: Ham 4K 25
Lauderdale Ho. *TW18: Stain 6H 21*
(off Gresham Rd.)
Laud St. CR0: Croy . . .5B 200 (9N 45)
Laud Way RG40: W'ham 2D 30
Laughton Rd. RH12: Hors 3M 197
Laundry Cotts. RH11: Craw . . .7L 181
Laundry La. GU47: Coll T 9K 49
Laundry Rd.
GU1: Guil 4B 202 (4M 113)
W6 . . . . .2K 13
Laundry Way RH5: Cap 5J 159
Lauradale RG12: Brac 3M 31
Laurel Av. TW1: Twick 2F 24
TW20: Eng G 6L 19
Laurel Bank *GU24: Chob 7H 53*
(off Bagshot Rd.)
Laurel Bank Gdns. SW6 . . . . . . .5L 13
Laurel Cl. GU14: Cove 2H 89
GU15: Camb 2B 70
RH10: Craw 6E 182
SL3: Poy 3G 6
SW17 . . . . .6C 28
Laurel Ct. CR2: S Croy 7F 200
RG12: Brac 3D 32
(off Wayland Cl.)
Laurel Cres. CR0: Croy 9K 47
GU21: Wok 9E 54
Laurel Dene RH19: E Grin 9B 166
Laureldene GU3: Flex 3M 111
Laurel Dr. RH8: Oxt 9B 106
Laurel Gdns. GU11: Alde 5M 109
KT15: N Haw 6K 55
TW4: Houn 7M 9
TW15: Ashf 6D 22
Laurel Gro. GU10: Wrec 6E 128
Laurel Ho. BR2: Brom 1N 47
Laurel Mnr. SM2: Sut 4A 62
Laurel Rd. SW13 . . . . .5F 12
SW20 . . . . .9G 26
TW12: H Hill 6D 24
Laurels, The GU9: Weybo 5L 109
GU51: Fleet 4B 88
KT11: Cob 2M 77
KT13: Weybr 9E 38
KT22: Fetc 2D 98
RH10: Craw 9E 162
SM7: Ban 4L 81
Laurel Wlk. RH13: Hors 7M 197
Laurence Rd. TW3: Houn 6C 10
Laurier Rd. CR0: Croy 6C 46
Lauriston Cl. GU21: Knap 4G 72
Lauriston Rd. SW19 . . . . .7J 27
Lauser Rd. TW19: Stan 1L 21
Laustan Cl. GU1: Guil 3E 114
Lavant Cl. RH11: Craw 4L 181
Lavender Av. CR4: Mit 9C 28
KT4: W Pk 9H 43
Lavender Cl. CR3: Cate 3N 103
CR5: Coul 6G 82
KT22: Leat 9J 79
RH1: Red 8F 122
SM5: Cars 1F 62
Lavender Ct. KT8: W Mole 2B 40
KT22: Leat 9J 79
SM2: Sut 4A 62
TW14: Felt 9J 9
Lavender Ga. KT22: Oxs 1B 78
Lavender Gro. CR4: Mit 9C 28
Lavender Ho. TW9: Kew 4A 12
Lavender La.
GU10: Rowl 7E 128
Lavender Pk. Golf Course 2G 32
Lavender Pk. Rd.
KT14: W By 8J 55
Lavender Rd. CR0: Croy 5K 45
GU22: Wok 3D 74
KT19: Ewe 2A 60
SM1: Sut 1B 62
SM5: Cars 1E 62
Lavender Va. SM6: W'ton 3H 63
Lavender Wlk. CR4: Mit 2E 44
Lavender Way CR0: Croy 5G 47
Lavengro Rd. SE27 . . . . .3N 29
Lavenham Rd. SW18 . . . . .3L 27
Laverstoke Gdns. SW15 . . . . . . .1E 26
Laverton Pl. SW5 . . . . .1N 13
Lavington Cl. RH11: Craw 2L 181
Lavington Rd. CR0: Bedd 9K 45
Lawbrook La.
GU5: P'lake, Shere 6D 136
Lawday Link GU9: Up Hale 5F 108
Lawday Pl. GU9: Up Hale 5F 108
Lawday Pl. La.
GU9: Up Hale 5F 108
Lawdons Gdns.
CR0: Wad 7A 200 (1M 63)
Lawford Cres. GU46: Yate 9C 48
Lawford Gdns. CR8: Ken 3N 83
Lawford Rd. W4 . . . . .3B 12
Lawford's Hill Cl.
GU3: Worp 2F 92
Lawford's Hill Rd.
GU3: Worp 2F 92
Lawley Ho. TW1: Twick 9K 11
Lawn, The SL3: Dat 4M 5
UB2: S'hall 1A 10
Lawn Cl. KT3: N Mal 1D 42
SL3: Dat 3M 5
Lawn Cres. TW9: Kew 5N 11
Lawn Rd.
GU2: Guil 8B 202 (6M 113)
Lawns, The GU8: Mil 1C 152
GU14: Cove 2K 89
SE19 . . . . .1A 46
SL3: Poy 4G 7
SL5: Asc 2H 33
SM2: Chea 4K 61
SW19 . . . . .6L 27
Lawns Cotts. RH12: Rudg 6B 176
Lawnsmead GU5: Wone 4D 134
Lawnsmead Cotts.
GU5: Wone 4D 134
Lawns Rd. RH12: Rudg 6B 176
Lawnwood Cotts.
GU7: Godal 6K 133
(off Catteshall La.)
Lawrence Av. KT3: N Mal 5C 42
Lawrence Cl. GU4: B'ham 7D 94
RG40: W'ham 2C 30
RH10: Craw 5H 183
Lawrence Ct. SL4: W'sor 5F 4
Lawrence Cres.
GU20: Windl 3A 52
Lawrence Est. TW4: Houn 7K 9
Lawrence Gro. RG42: Bin 9J 15
Lawrence La. RH3: Buckl 1G 120
Lawrence Lodge
GU15: Camb 8B 50
Lawrence M. SW15 . . . . .7H 13
Lawrence Pde. *TW7: Isle 6H 11*
(off Lower Sq.)
Lawrence Rd. BR4: W Wick 1C 66
GU52: Fleet 5A 88
SE25 . . . . .3C 46
TW4: Houn 7K 9
TW10: Ham 5J 25
TW12: Hamp 8N 23
Lawrence Way GU15: Camb 2L 69
Lawrence Weaver Cl.
SM4: Mord 5M 43
Lawrie Ho. *SW19 . . . . .6N 27*
(off Durnsford Rd.)
Laws Cl. RH11: Ifield 4K 181
SE25 . . . . .3A 46
Lawson Cl. SW19 . . . . .4J 27
Lawson Ct. KT6: Surb 6K 41
Lawson Hunt Ind. Pk.
RH12: Broadb H 4D 196
Lawson Wlk. SM5: Cars 5E 62
Lawson Way SL5: S'dale 5E 34
Laws Ter. GU11: Alde 1A 110
Laxton Ct. CR7: T Hea 3N 45
Laxton Gdns. RH1: Mers 6H 103
Layard Rd. CR7: T Hea 1A 46
Layburn Cres. SL3: Lang 2D 6
Layhams Rd. BR2: Kes 9N 47
BR4: W Wick . . . .9N 47 & 1A 66
CR6: Warl 8B 66
Layton Ct. KT13: Weybr 1C 56
TW8: Brent 1K 11
Layton Cres. CR0: Wad 2L 63
Layton Pl. TW9: Kew 4N 11
Layton Rd. TW3: Houn 7B 10
TW8: Brent 1K 11
Layton's La. TW16: Sunb 1G 38
Lazare Ct. *TW18: Stain 6H 21*
(off Gresham Rd.)
Lazell Gdns. RH3: Betch 9B 120
Lazenbys Est.
RH5: W'wood 9L 157
Lea, The TW20: Egh 8E 20
Leach Gro. KT22: Leat 9J 79
Lea Cl. GU9: B Lea 6M 109
GU12: Ash 3E 110
RH11: Craw 4L 181
TW2: Whitt 1N 23
Lea Coach Rd.
GU8: Thur, Wit 5L 151
Lea Ct. GU9: Weybo 5L 109
Lea Cft. RG45: Crowt 1G 49
Leacroft RH19: E Grin 8N 165
SL5: S'dale 4D 34
TW18: Stain 6J 21
Leacroft Av. SW12 . . . . .1D 28
Leacroft Cl. CR8: Ken 3N 83
TW18: Stain 5K 21
Leaden Hill CR5: Coul 2H 83
Leaf Cl. KT7: T Dit 4E 40
Leafey La. GU26: G'hott 3K 169
Leaf Gro. SE27 . . . . .6L 29
Leafield Cl. GU21: Wok 5M 73
SW16 . . . . .7M 29
Leafield Copse RG12: Brac 3D 32
Leafield Rd. SM1: Sut 8M 43
SW20 . . . . .2L 43
Leafy Gro. BR2: Kes 2E 66
Leafy Way CR0: Croy 8C 46
Leamington Av. BR6: Orp 1N 67
SM4: Mord 3K 43
Leamington Cl. TW3: Houn 8C 10
Leamore St. W6 . . . . .1H 13
Leander Ct. KT6: Surb 6K 41
Leander Rd. CR7: T Hea 3K 45
SW2 . . . . .1K 29
Leapale La.
GU1: Guil 5C 202 (4N 113)
Leapale Rd.
GU1: Guil 5C 202 (4N 113)
Lea Rd. BR3: Beck 1K 47
GU15: Camb 4N 69
UB2: S'hall 1M 9
Leas Cl. KT9: Ches 4M 59
Leaside GU28: Northc 8D 190
KT23: Book 1A 98
Leas La. CR6: Warl 5G 84
Leas Rd. CR6: Warl 5G 84
GU1: Guil 4B 202 (4M 113)
Leather Cl. CR4: Mit 1E 44
TN8: Eden 3L 147
LEATHERHEAD 9H 79
Leatherhead Bus. Pk.
KT22: Leat 6F 78
LEATHERHEAD COMMON 6G 79
Leatherhead Fitness &
Wellbeing Cen. *9H 79*
(off The Crescent)
Leatherhead Golf Course 3G 79
Leatherhead Leisure Cen. 1G 99
Leatherhead Museum of
Local History 9H 79
Leatherhead Rd. KT9: Ches 1H 79
KT21: Asht 8K 79
KT22: Leat 8K 79
KT22: Oxs 1D 78
KT23: Book 4B 98
Leatherhead Station (Rail) . . .8G 79
Leatherhead Theatre 9H 79
Leatherhead Trade Pk.
KT22: Leat 8G 78
Leather La. GU5: Gom 8D 116
Leaveland Cl. BR3: Beck 3K 47
Leavesden Rd. KT13: Weybr . . .2C 56
LEAVES GREEN 7F 66
Leaves Grn. RG12: Brac 5B 32
Leaves Grn. Cres. BR2: Kes 7E 66
Leaves Grn. Rd. BR2: Kes 7F 66
Lea Way GU12: Alde 1D 110
Leaway GU9: B Lea 7M 109
Leazes Av. CR3: Cate 1L 103
Leazes La. CR3: Cate 1L 103
Lebanon Av. TW13: Hanw 6L 23
Lebanon Ct. TW1: Twick 1H 25
Lebanon Dr. KT11: Cob 9A 58
Lebanon Gdns. SW18 . . . . .9M 13
TN16: B Hil 4F 86
Lebanon Pk. TW1: Twick 1H 25
Lebanon Rd. CR0: Croy 7B 46
SW18 . . . . .8M 13
Lebanon Road Stop
(London Tramlink) 8B 46
Le Chateau CR0: Croy 5E 200
Lechford Rd. RH6: Horl 9E 142
Leckford Rd. SW18 . . . . .3A 28
Leckhampton Pl. SW2 . . . . .1L 29
Leconfield Av. SW13 . . . . .6E 12
Ledbury Pl.
CR0: Croy 7C 200 (1N 63)
Ledbury Rd.
CR0: Croy 8C 200 (1A 64)
RH2: Reig 3M 121
Ledger Cl. GU1: Guil 1D 114
Ledger Dr. KT15: Addl 2H 55
Ledgers La. CR6: Warl 4L 85
Ledgers Rd. CR6: Warl 3K 85
Lee Acre RH4: Dork 7J 119
Leechcroft Rd. SM6: W'ton 9E 44
Leech La. KT18: Head 4A 100

Leechpool La.—Link 10

Leechpool La. RH13: Hors . . . 4N 197
Lee Ct. GU11: Alde . . . 4A 110
Leegate Cl. GU21: Wok . . . 3L 73
Lee Grn. La. KT18: Head . . . 2A 100
Leehurst GU8: Mil . . . 1B 152
Lee M. BR3: Beck . . . 2H 47
Lee Rd. GU11: Alde . . . 2K 109
SW19 . . . 9N 27
Lees, The CR0: Croy . . . 8J 47
Leeside RH12: Rusp . . . 3B 180
Leeson Gdns. SL4: E Wic . . . 1B 4
Leeson Ho. TW1: Twick . . . 1H 25
Lee St. RH6: Horl . . . 8C 142
Leeward Gdns. SW19 . . . 6K 27
Leeways, The SM3: Chea . . . 3K 61
Leewood Way KT24: Eff . . . 5K 97
Le Freth Dr. GU51: Fleet . . . 2A 88
Lefroy Pk. GU51: Fleet . . . 4A 88
Legge Cres. GU11: Alde . . . 3K 109
Leggyfield Ct. RH12: Hors . . . 3H 197
Legion Ct. SM4: Mord . . . 5M 43
Legoland . . . 8A 4
Leg O'Mutton Local Nature Reserve
. . . 3E 12
Legrace Av. TW4: Houn . . . 5L 9
Legsheath La.
RH19: F Row . . . 8M 185
Leicester RG12: Brac . . . 6C 32
Leicester Av. CR4: Mit . . . 3J 45
Leicester Cl. KT4: W Pk . . . 1H 61
Leicester Ct. RH10: Craw . . . 3H 183
TW1: Twick . . . 9K 11
(off Clevedon Rd.)
Leicester Rd. CR0: Croy . . . 6B 46
LEIGH . . . 1F 140
Leigh, The KT2: K Tham . . . 8D 26
Leigham Av. SW16 . . . 4J 29
Leigham Cl. SW16 . . . 4K 29
Leigham Ct. SM6: W'ton . . . 3G 63
Leigham Ct. Rd. SW16 . . . 3J 29
Leigham Dr. TW7: Isle . . . 3E 10
Leigham Hall Pde. SW16 . . . 4J 29
(off Streatham High Rd.)
Leigham Va. SW2 . . . 4K 29
SW16 . . . 4K 29
Leigh Cl. KT3: N Mal . . . 3B 42
KT15: Addl . . . 4H 55
Leigh Cl. Ind. Est.
KT3: N Mal . . . 3C 42
Leigh Cnr. KT11: Cob . . . 2K 77
Leigh Ct. KT11: Cob . . . 1L 77
Leigh Ct. Cl. KT11: Cob . . . 1K 77
Leigh Cres. CR0: N Add . . . 4L 65
Leigh Hill Rd. KT11: Cob . . . 2K 77
Leighlands RH10: Craw . . . 1G 183
Leigh La. GU9: Farnh . . . 3K 129
Leigh Orchard Cl. SW16 . . . 4K 29
Leigh Pk. SL3: Dat . . . 3L 5
Leigh Pl. KT11: Cob . . . 2K 77
TW13: Felt . . . 2K 23
Leigh Pl. Cotts. RH2: Leigh . . . 9F 120
Leigh Pl. La. RH9: Gods . . . 1G 125
Leigh Pl. Rd. RH2: Leigh . . . 9F 120
Leigh Rd. KT11: Cob . . . 1J 77
RH3: Betch . . . 9B 120
TW3: Houn . . . 7D 10
Leigh Sq. SL4: W'sor . . . 5A 4
Leighton Gdns. CR0: Croy . . . 7M 45
CR2: Sande . . . 9E 64
Leighton Mans. W14 . . . 2K 13
(off Greyhound Rd.)
Leighton St.
CR0: Croy . . . 1A 200 (7M 45)
Leighton Way
KT18: Eps . . . 8K 201 (1C 80)
Leinster Av. SW14 . . . 6B 12
Leipzig Rd. GU52: Chu C . . . 1C 108
Leisure La. KT14: W By . . . 8K 55
Leisure Pursuits . . . 3G 186
Leisure West TW13: Felt . . . 3J 23
Leith Cl. RG45: Crowt . . . 9F 30
Leithcote Gdns. SW16 . . . 5K 29
Leithcote Path SW16 . . . 4K 29
Leith Dr. GU11: Alde . . . 1L 109
Leith Gro. RH5: B Grn . . . 7K 139
Leith Hill La.
RH5: A Com, Holm M . . . 4M 137
Leith Hill Place (East) . . . 9B 138
Leith Hill Place (West) . . . 1N 157
Leith Hill Rd.
RH5: Holm M . . . 9A 138
Leith Hill Tower . . . 8B 138
Leith Lea RH5: B Grn . . . 7K 139
Leith Rd. KT17: Eps . . . 8D 60
RH5: B Grn . . . 8J 139
Leith Towers SM2: Sut . . . 4N 61
Leith Va. Cotts. RH5: Ockl . . . 7A 158
Leith Vw. RH5: Nth H . . . 9J 119
Leith Vw. Cotts.
RH12: K'fold . . . 3H 179
Leith Vw. Rd. RH12: Hors . . . 3N 197
Lela Av. TW4: Houn . . . 5K 9
Le Marchant Rd.
GU15: Camb . . . 3D 70
GU16: Frim . . . 3D 70
Le May Cl. RH6: Horl . . . 7E 142
Lemington Gro. RG12: Brac . . . 5N 31
Lemmington Way
RH12: Hors . . . 1M 197
Lemon Gro. TW13: Felt . . . 2H 23
Lemon's Farm Rd.
RH5: A Com . . . 5N 137
Lemuel St. SW18 . . . 9N 13
Lendore Rd. GU16: Frim . . . 6B 70
Lendy Pl. TW16: Sunb . . . 3H 39
Lenelby Rd. KT6: Surb . . . 7N 41
Leney Cl. RG40: W'ham . . . 9C 14
Len Freeman Pl. SW6 . . . 2L 13
Lenham Rd. CR7: T Hea . . . 1A 46
SM1: Sut . . . 1N 61
Lennard Rd.
CR0: Croy . . . 1B 200 (7N 45)
Lennel Gdns. GU52: Chu C . . . 7D 88
Lennox Ct. RH1: Red . . . 2E 122
(off St Anne's Ri.)
Lennox Gdns.
CR0: Wad . . . 7A 200 (1M 63)
Lennox Ho. TW1: Twick . . . 9K 11
(off Clevedon Rd.)
Lenten Cl. GU5: P'lake . . . 2E 136
Lenton Ri. TW9: Rich . . . 6L 11
Leo Ct. TW8: Brent . . . 3K 11
Leominster Rd. SM4: Mord . . . 5A 44
Leominster Wlk. SM4: Mord . . . 5A 44
Leonard Av. SM4: Mord . . . 4A 44
Leonard Cl. GU16: Frim . . . 6B 70
Leonard Rd. SW16 . . . 9G 28
Leonardslee Ct.
RH10: Craw . . . 5F 182
Leonard Way RH13: Hors . . . 6M 197
Leopold Av. GU14: Farnb . . . 9N 69
SW19 . . . 6L 27
Leopold Ct. KT10: Esh . . . 3C 58
(off Princess Sq.)
Leopold Rd. RH11: Craw . . . 3A 182
SW19 . . . 5L 27
Leopold Ter. SW19 . . . 6L 27
Le Personne Homes
CR3: Cate . . . 9A 84
(off Banstead Rd.)
Le Personne Rd. CR3: Cate . . . 9A 84
Leppington RG12: Brac . . . 7N 31
Leret Way KT22: Leat . . . 8H 79
Lerry Cl. W14 . . . 2L 13
Lesbourne Rd. RH2: Reig . . . 4N 121
Leslie Dunne Ho. SL4: W'sor . . . 5B 4
Leslie Gdns. SM2: Sut . . . 3M 61
Leslie Gro.
CR0: Croy . . . 1F 200 (7B 46)
Leslie Gro. Pl.
CR0: Croy . . . 1F 200 (7B 46)
Leslie Pk. Rd.
CR0: Croy . . . 1F 200 (7B 46)
Leslie Rd. GU24: Chob . . . 6H 53
RH4: Dork . . . 3K 119
Lessingham Av. SW17 . . . 5D 28
Lessness Rd. SM4: Mord . . . 5A 44
Lestock Cl. SE25 . . . 2D 46
(off Manor Rd.)
Lestock Way GU51: Fleet . . . 4D 88
Letchworth Av. TW14: Felt . . . 1G 22
Letchworth Ct. RH11: Craw . . . 6K 181
Letchworth St. SW17 . . . 5D 28
Letcombe Sq. RG12: Brac . . . 3C 32
Letterstone Rd. SW6 . . . 3L 13
Lettice St. SW6 . . . 4L 13
Levana Cl. SW19 . . . 2K 27
Levehurst Ho. SE27 . . . 6N 29
Leveret Cl. CR0: N Add . . . 7N 65
Leveret La. RH11: Craw . . . 1N 181
Leverette Cl. GU12: Alde . . . 1B 110
Leverkusen Rd. RG12: Brac . . . 2N 31
Levern Dr. GU9: Up Hale . . . 6H 109
Leverson St. SW16 . . . 7G 28
Levett Rd. KT22: Leat . . . 7H 79
Levylsdene GU1: Guil . . . 3E 114
Levylsdene Ct. GU1: Guil . . . 3F 114
Lewen Cl.
CR0: Croy . . . 1E 200 (7A 46)
Lewes Cl. RH10: Craw . . . 3G 183
Lewes Ct. CR4: Mit . . . 2D 44
(off Chatsworth Pl.)
Lewesdon Cl. SW19 . . . 2J 27
Lewes Rd.
RH18: F Row, W Cros . . . 9F 186
RH19: Ash W, E Grin, F Row
. . . 1B 186
Lewin Rd. SW14 . . . 6C 12
SW16 . . . 7H 29
Lewins Rd. KT18: Eps . . . 1A 80
Lewin Ter. TW14: Bedf . . . 1E 22
Lewis Cl. KT15: Addl . . . 1L 55
Lewis Ct. KT22: Leat . . . 8G 78
(off Highbury Dr.)
Lewis Elton Gallery . . . 3K 113
Lewisham Cl. RH11: Craw . . . 7A 182
Lewisham Way GU47: Owls . . . 6J 49
Lewis Ho. RG12: Brac . . . 5N 31
Lewis Rd. CR4: Mit . . . 1B 44
SM1: Sut . . . 1N 61
TW10: Rich . . . 8K 11
Lewiston Cl. KT4: W Pk . . . 6G 43
Leworth Pl. SL4: W'sor . . . 4G 4
Lexden Rd. CR4: Mit . . . 3H 45
Lexington Ct. CR8: Pur . . . 6N 63
Lexington Pl.
KT1: H Wic . . . 1G 203 (8K 25)
Lexton Gdns. SW12 . . . 2H 29
Leyborne Pk. TW9: Kew . . . 4N 11
Leybourne Av. KT14: Byf . . . 9A 56
Leybourne Cl. KT14: Byf . . . 9A 56
RH11: Craw . . . 8A 182
Leybourne Pl. RH19: Felb . . . 6J 165
Leyburn Gdns. CR0: Croy . . . 8B 46
Leycester Cl. GU20: Windl . . . 1M 51
Leyfield KT4: W Pk . . . 7D 42
Leylands SW18 . . . 9L 13
Leylands La. TW19: Stan M . . . 7H 7
(not continuous)
Ley Rd. GU14: Farnb . . . 6M 69
Leys, The KT12: Hers . . . 1N 57
Leyside RG45: Crowt . . . 2F 48
Leys Rd. KT22: Oxs . . . 8D 58
Leyton Rd. SW19 . . . 8A 28
Liberty Av. SW19 . . . 9B 28
Liberty Cl. KT4: W Pk . . . 7H 43
Liberty Ct. CR8: Pur . . . 8L 63
Liberty Hall Rd.
KT15: Addl . . . 2J 55
Liberty Ho. KT16: Chert . . . 7H 37
(off Guildford St.)
Liberty La. KT15: Addl . . . 2J 55
Liberty Point CR0: Croy . . . 6D 46
(off Blackhorse La.)
Liberty Ri. KT15: Addl . . . 3J 55
Libra Cres. RG40: W'ham . . . 1F 30
Library Way TW2: Whitt . . . 1C 24
Lichfield Ct. KT6: Surb . . . 8J 203
TW9: Rich . . . 8L 11
Lichfield Gdns. TW9: Rich . . . 7L 11
Lichfield La. TW2: Whitt . . . 2C 24
Lichfield Rd. TW4: Houn . . . 6K 9
TW9: Kew . . . 4M 11
Lichfields RG12: Brac . . . 1C 32
Lichfield Ter. TW9: Rich . . . 8L 11
(off Sheen Rd.)
Lichfield Way CR2: Sels . . . 6G 65
Lickey Ho. W14 . . . 2L 13
(off North End Rd.)
Lickfolds Rd. GU10: Rowl . . . 9D 128
Liddell SL4: W'sor . . . 6A 4
Liddell Pl. SL4: W'sor . . . 6A 4
Liddell Sq. SL4: W'sor . . . 5A 4
Liddell Way SL4: W'sor . . . 6A 4
SL5: Asc . . . 4K 33
Liddington Hall Dr.
GU3: Guil . . . 9H 93
Liddington New Rd.
GU3: Guil . . . 9H 93
Lidiard Rd. SW18 . . . 3A 28
Lido Rd. GU1: Guil . . . 1D 202 (2N 113)
Lidsey Cl. RH10: Craw . . . 5G 183
Lidstone Cl. GU21: Wok . . . 4L 73
Liffords Pl. SW13 . . . 5E 12
Lifford St. SW15 . . . 7J 13
Lightbox Museum, The . . . 3A 74
Lighterage Ct. TW8: Brent . . . 2L 11
Lightermans Wlk. SW18 . . . 7M 13
LIGHTWATER . . . 6M 51
Lightwater By-Pass
GU18: Ligh . . . 5L 51
Lightwater Country Pk. . . . 7J 51
Lightwater Leisure Cen. . . . 6K 51
Lightwater Mdw.
GU18: Ligh . . . 7M 51
Lightwater Rd. GU18: Ligh . . . 7M 51
Lightwood RG12: Brac . . . 5B 32
Lilac Av. GU22: Wok . . . 7N 73
Lilac Cl. GU1: Guil . . . 8M 93
Lilac Ct. TW11: Tedd . . . 5F 24
Lilac Gdns. CR0: Croy . . . 9K 47
Lilian Rd. SW16 . . . 9G 28
Lille Barracks GU11: Alde . . . 6B 90
Lilleshall Rd. SM4: Mord . . . 5B 44
Lilley Ct. RG45: Crowt . . . 3G 49
Lilley Dr. KT20: K'wood . . . 9N 81
Lilley Mead RH1: Mers . . . 9G 102
Lillian Rd. SW13 . . . 2F 12
Lillie Bri. Dpt. W14 . . . 1L 13
Lillie Mans. SW6 . . . 2K 13
(off Lillie Rd.)
Lillie Rd. SW6 . . . 2K 13
TN16: B Hil . . . 5F 86
Lillie Road Fitness Cen. . . . 3J 13
Lillie Yd. SW6 . . . 2M 13
Lilliot's La. KT22: Leat . . . 6G 79
Lillywhite Cl. GU12: Alde . . . 5B 110
Lily Cl. W14 . . . 1J 13
Lily Ct. RG41: W'ham . . . 2A 30
Lilyfields Chase GU6: Ewh . . . 6F 156
Lily Hill Dr. RG12: Brac . . . 1C 32
Lily Hill Rd. RG12: Brac . . . 1C 32
Lilyville Rd. SW6 . . . 4L 13
Lime Av. GU15: Camb . . . 9E 50
RH12: Hors . . . 4N 197
SL4: W'sor . . . 4J 5
(Adelaide Rd.)
SL4: W'sor . . . 4C 18
(Holly Wlk.)
SL5: Asc . . . 5F 32
Limebush Cl. KT15: N Haw . . . 5L 55
Lime Cl. GU4: W Cla . . . 6K 95
RH2: Reig . . . 6N 121
RH10: Copt . . . 7M 163
RH11: Craw . . . 9A 162
SM5: Cars . . . 8D 44
Lime Ct. CR4: Mit . . . 1B 44
Lime Cres. GU12: Ash . . . 2F 110
TW16: Sunb . . . 1K 39
Limecroft GU46: Yate . . . 1B 68
Limecroft Cl. KT19: Ewe . . . 4C 60
Limecroft Rd. GU21: Knap . . . 4E 72
Lime Dr. GU51: Fleet . . . 1C 88
Lime Gro. CR6: Warl . . . 5H 85
GU1: Guil . . . 8L 93
GU4: W Cla . . . 6J 95
GU22: Wok . . . 8A 74
KT3: N Mal . . . 2C 42
KT15: Addl . . . 1J 55
TW1: Twick . . . 9F 10
Lime Ho. TW9: Kew . . . 4A 12
Lime Lodge TW16: Sunb . . . 8G 22
(off Forest Dr.)
Lime Mdw. Av. CR2: Sande . . . 9D 64
Lime Quarry M. GU1: Guil . . . 2F 114
Limerick Cl. RG42: Brac . . . 9M 15
SW12 . . . 1G 28
Lime Rd. TW9: Rich . . . 7M 11
Limes, The GU21: Wok . . . 3C 74
(off Maybury Rd.)
GU21: Wok . . . 2N 73
(Ridgeway)
KT8: W Mole . . . 3B 40
KT19: Eps . . . 6A 60
KT22: Leat . . . 1H 99
RG42: Warf . . . 6D 16
RH12: Hors . . . 4J 197
(off Trafalgar Rd.)
RH19: Felb . . . 5K 165
SL4: W'sor . . . 4A 4
SW18 . . . 9M 13
TN8: Eden . . . 2L 147
Limes Av. CR0: Wad . . . 9L 45
RH6: Horl . . . 9F 142
SM5: Cars . . . 7D 44
SW13 . . . 5E 12
Limes Cl. KT22: Leat . . . 8J 79
TW15: Ashf . . . 6B 22
Limes Fld. Rd. SW14 . . . 6D 12
Limes Gdns. SW18 . . . 9M 13
Limes M. TW20: Egh . . . 6B 20
Limes Pl. CR0: Croy . . . 6A 46
Limes Rd. BR3: Beck . . . 1L 47
CR0: Croy . . . 6A 46
GU14: Cove . . . 9H 69
KT13: Weybr . . . 1B 56
TW20: Egh . . . 6B 20
Limes Row BR6: Farnb . . . 2K 67
Lime St. GU11: Alde . . . 2L 109
Lime Tree Av. KT7: T Dit . . . 7D 40
KT10: Esh . . . 7D 40
Lime Tree Cl. KT23: Book . . . 2A 98
Limetree Cl. SW2 . . . 2K 29
Lime Tree Copse
RG42: Warf . . . 8E 16
Lime Tree Ct. CR2: S Croy . . . 3N 63
KT21: Asht . . . 5L 79
Lime Tree Gro. CR0: Croy . . . 9J 47
Lime Tree Pl. CR4: Mit . . . 9F 28
Lime Tree Rd. TW5: Hest . . . 4B 10
Lime Tree Wlk.
BR4: W Wick . . . 1B 66
GU14: Farnb . . . 5C 90
GU21: Wok . . . 3N 73
GU25: V Wat . . . 3A 36
Limetree Wlk. SW17 . . . 6E 28
Lime Wlk. GU5: Shere . . . 8A 116
KT8: E Mol . . . 3F 40
RG12: Brac . . . 3A 32
Limeway Ter. RH4: Dork . . . 3G 118
Limewood Cl. BR3: Beck . . . 4M 47
GU21: Wok . . . 7G 73
Limewood Ho. KT19: Eps . . . 5C 60
Lime Works Rd.
RH1: Mers . . . 4G 102
LIMPSFIELD . . . 7D 106
Limpsfield Av. CR7: T Hea . . . 4K 45
SW19 . . . 3J 27
LIMPSFIELD CHART . . . 8G 107
Limpsfield Chart Golf Course
. . . 7E 106
Limpsfield Rd. CR2: Sande . . . 8D 64
CR6: Warl . . . 3F 84
Linacre Ct. W6 . . . 1J 13
Linacre Dr. GU6: Cranl . . . 7D 176
RH12: Cranl, Rudg . . . 7D 176
Lince La. RH4: Westc . . . 5D 118
Linchfield Rd. SL3: Dat . . . 4M 5
LINCHMERE . . . 6A 188
Linchmere Pl. RH11: Craw . . . 2M 181
Linchmere Ridge
GU27: Hasl . . . 5B 188
Linchmere Rd.
GU27: Linch, Hasl . . . 5A 188
Lincoln Av. SW19 . . . 4J 27
TW2: Twick . . . 3C 24
Lincoln Cl. GU12: Ash V . . . 8D 90
GU15: Camb . . . 2F 70
RH6: Horl . . . 9E 142
RH10: Craw . . . 6C 182
SE25 . . . 5D 46
Lincoln Ct. CR2: S Croy . . . 8C 200
KT13: Weybr . . . 3E 56
(off Old Av.)
Lincoln Dr. GU22: Pyr . . . 2G 75
Lincoln Gro. KT13: Weybr . . . 9C 38
Lincoln Ho. TW8: Brent . . . 1L 11
(off Ealing Rd.)
Lincoln M. SE21 . . . 3N 29
Lincoln Rd. CR4: Mit . . . 4J 45
GU2: Guil . . . 1J 113
KT3: N Mal . . . 2B 42
KT4: W Pk . . . 7G 42
RH4: Dork . . . 3J 119
SE25 . . . 2E 46
TW13: Hanw . . . 4N 23
Lincolnshire Gdns.
RG42: Warf . . . 8C 16
Lincolns Mead RH7: Ling . . . 8M 145
Lincoln Wlk. KT19: Ewe . . . 6C 60
Lincoln Way TW16: Sunb . . . 9F 22
Lincombe Ct. KT15: Addl . . . 2K 55
Lindale Cl. GU25: V Wat . . . 3J 35
Lindbergh Rd. SM6: W'ton . . . 4J 63
Linden RG12: Brac . . . 4D 32
SL3: Lang . . . 1D 6
Linden Av. CR5: Coul . . . 3F 82
CR7: T Hea . . . 3M 45
RH19: E Grin . . . 8M 165
TW3: Houn . . . 8B 10
Linden Cl. KT7: T Dit . . . 6F 40
KT15: N Haw . . . 7J 55
KT20: Tad . . . 7J 81
RH10: Craw . . . 6E 182
RH12: Hors . . . 4L 197
Linden Ct. GU15: Camb . . . 8D 50
KT22: Leat . . . 8H 79
TW20: Eng G . . . 7L 19
Linden Cres.
KT1: K Tham . . . 4M 203 (1M 41)
Linden Dr. CR3: Cate . . . 2N 103
Linden Gdns. KT22: Leat . . . 8J 79
W4 . . . 1D 12
Linden Gro. CR6: Warl . . . 5H 85
KT3: N Mal . . . 2D 42
KT12: Wal T . . . 8G 39
TW11: Tedd . . . 6F 24
Lindenhill Rd. RG42: Brac . . . 9L 15
Linden Ho. TW12: Hamp . . . 7A 24
Linden Lea RH4: Dork . . . 7J 119
(off Stubs Hill)
Linden Leas BR4: W Wick . . . 8N 47
Linden Pit Path KT22: Leat . . . 7J 79
(Kingfisher Cl.)
KT22: Leat . . . 8H 79
(Linden Rd.)
Linden Pl. CR4: Mit . . . 3C 44
KT17: Eps . . . 5M 201 (8D 60)
KT24: E Hor . . . 4F 96
TW18: Stain . . . 5J 21
Linden Rd.
GU1: Guil . . . 2C 202 (3N 113)
GU35: Head D . . . 4G 169
KT13: Weybr . . . 5D 56
KT22: Leat . . . 8H 79
TW12: Hamp . . . 8A 24
Lindens, The CR0: N Add . . . 3M 65
GU9: Farnh . . . 2J 129
GU16: Mytc . . . 2D 90
GU35: Lind . . . 3B 168
RH10: Copt . . . 7M 163
W4 . . . 4B 12
Lindens Cl. KT24: Eff . . . 6M 97
Linden Way CR8: Pur . . . 6G 63
GU22: Wok . . . 8B 74
GU23: Rip . . . 3H 95
TW17: Shep . . . 4D 38
Lindfield Gdns. GU1: Guil . . . 2B 114
Lindfield Rd. CR0: Croy . . . 5C 46
LINDFORD . . . 4A 168
Lindford Chase GU35: Lind . . . 4A 168
Lindford Rd.
GU35: Bor, Lind . . . 3A 168
Lindford Wey GU35: Lind . . . 4A 168
Lindgren Wlk. RH11: Craw . . . 8N 181
Lindisfarne Ho.
RH11: Craw . . . 5N 181
(off St Aidan Cl.)
Lindisfarne Rd. SW20 . . . 8F 26
Lindley Ct. KT1: H Wic . . . 9J 25
Lindley Pl. TW9: Kew . . . 4N 11
Lindley Rd. KT12: Wal T . . . 9L 39
RH9: Gods . . . 8F 104
Lindores Rd. SM5: Cars . . . 6A 44
Lind Rd. SM1: Sut . . . 2A 62
Lindrop St. SW6 . . . 5N 13
Lindsay Cl. KT9: Ches . . . 4L 59
KT19: Eps . . . 7G 201 (9B 60)
TW19: Stan . . . 8M 7
Lindsay Ct. CR0: Croy . . . 6D 200
Lindsay Dr. TW17: Shep . . . 5E 38
Lindsay Rd. KT4: W Pk . . . 8G 43
KT15: N Haw . . . 6J 55
TW12: H Hill . . . 5B 24
Lindsey Cl. CR4: Mit . . . 3J 45
Lindsey Gdns. TW14: Bedf . . . 1E 22
Lindum Cl. GU11: Alde . . . 3M 109
Lindum Dene GU11: Alde . . . 3M 109
Lindum Rd. TW11: Tedd . . . 8J 25
Lindvale GU21: Wok . . . 2A 74
Lindway SE27 . . . 6M 29
Linersh Dr. GU5: Braml . . . 5C 134
Linersh Wood GU5: Braml . . . 5C 134
Linersh Wood Cl.
GU5: Braml . . . 6C 134
Lines Cl. RH18: F Row . . . 7L 187
Lines Rd. GU11: Alde . . . 6B 90
Linfield Cl. KT12: Hers . . . 2J 57
Ling Cres. GU35: Head D . . . 3G 169
Ling Dr. GU18: Ligh . . . 8K 51
LINGFIELD . . . 7N 145
Lingfield Av.
KT1: K Tham . . . 8K 203 (3L 41)
LINGFIELD COMMON . . . 6M 145
Lingfield Comn. Rd.
RH7: Ling . . . 6M 145
Lingfield Dr. RH10: Craw . . . 2J 183
Lingfield Gdns. CR5: Coul . . . 6M 83
Lingfield Pk. Golf Course . . . 9B 146
Lingfield Pk. Racecourse . . . 9A 146
Lingfield Rd. KT4: W Pk . . . 9H 43
RH19: E Grin . . . 6N 165
SW19 . . . 6J 27
TN8: Eden . . . 3H 147
Lingfield Station (Rail) . . . 7A 146
Lingmala Gro. GU52: Chu C . . . 8C 88
Lings Coppice SE21 . . . 3N 29
Lingwell Rd. SW17 . . . 4C 28
Lingwood RG12: Brac . . . 5A 32
Lingwood Gdns. TW7: Isle . . . 3E 10
Link, The GU46: Yate . . . 4B 68
RH11: Craw . . . 3B 182
(not continuous)
TW11: Tedd . . . 7F 24
Link 10 RH10: Craw . . . 9D 162

Link Av.—Longdown

Link Av. GU22: Pyr . . . 2F 74
Linkfield KT8: W Mole . . . 2B 40
Linkfield Cnr. RH1: Red . . . 2C 122
Linkfield Gdns. RH1: Red . . . 3C 122
Linkfield La. RH1: Red . . . 2C 122
Linkfield Lodge RH1: Red . . . 2C 122
Linkfield Rd. TW7: Isle . . . 5F 10
Linkfield St. RH1: Red . . . 3C 122
Link La. SM6: W'ton . . . 3H 63
Link Rd. KT15: Addl . . . 1N 55
SL3: Dat . . . 4M 5
SM6: W'ton . . . 7E 44
TW14: Felt . . . 1G 23
Links, The KT12: Wal T . . . 8H 39
SL5: Asc . . . 1J 33
Links Av. SM4: Mord . . . 3M 43
Links Brow KT22: Fetc . . . 2E 98
Links Bus. Cen. GU22: Wok . . . 6E 74
Links Cl. GU6: Ewh . . . 4F 156
KT21: Asht . . . 4J 79
Linkscroft Av. TW15: Ashf . . . 7C 22
Links Gdns. SW16 . . . 8L 29
Links Grn. Way KT11: Cob . . . 1A 78
LINKSIDE . . . 2N 169
Linkside KT3: N Mal . . . 1D 42
Linkside E. GU26: Hind . . . 2A 170
Linkside Nth. GU26: Hind . . . 2N 169
Linkside Sth. GU26: Hind . . . 3A 170
Linkside W. GU26: Hind . . . 2N 169
Links Pl. KT21: Asht . . . 4K 79
Links Rd. BR4: W Wick . . . 7M 47
GU5: Braml . . . 4A 134
KT17: Eps . . . 9F 60
KT21: Asht . . . 5J 79
SW17 . . . 7E 28
TW15: Ashf . . . 6N 21
Links Vw. Av. RH3: Brock . . . 3N 119
Linksview Ct. TW12: H Hill . . . 5D 24
Links Vw. Rd. CR0: Croy . . . 9K 47
TW12: H Hill . . . 6C 24
Links Way BR3: Beck . . . 5K 47
GU14: Cove . . . 2H 89
KT23: Book . . . 6M 97
Link Way TW18: Stain . . . 7K 21
Linkway GU2: Guil . . . 2J 113
GU15: Camb . . . 2A 70
GU22: Wok . . . 4E 74
GU52: Fleet . . . 7A 88
RG45: Crowt . . . 2E 48
SW20 . . . 2G 43
TW10: Ham . . . 3H 25
Linkway, The SM2: Sut . . . 5A 62
Linkway Pde. GU52: Fleet . . . 7A 88
Linley Ct. SM1: Sut . . . 1A 62
Linnell Cl. RH11: Craw . . . 9N 181
Linnell Rd. RH1: Red . . . 4E 122
Linnet Cl. CR2: Sels . . . 6G 65
RG12: Brac . . . 3J 31
Linnet Gro. GU4: Guil . . . 1F 114
Linnet M. SW12 . . . 1E 28
Linnett Cl. RH10: Turn H . . . 4F 184
Linsford Bus. Pk.
GU16: Mytc . . . 2C 90
Linsford La. GU16: Mytc . . . 2D 90
Linslade Cl. TW4: Houn . . . 8M 9
Linstead Rd. GU14: Cove . . . 6K 69
Linstead Way SW18 . . . 1K 27
Linsted La. GU35: Head . . . 2C 168
Lintaine Cl. W6 . . . 2K 13
Linters Ct. RH1: Red . . . 1D 122
Linton Cl. CR4: Mit . . . 6D 44
Linton Glade CR0: Sels . . . 5H 65
Linton Gro. SE27 . . . 6M 29
Lintons La. KT17: Eps . . . 8D 60
Lintott Ct. TW19: Stan . . . 9M 7
Lintott Gdns. RH13: Hors . . . 5L 197
Linver Rd. SW6 . . . 5M 13
Lion & Lamb Way
GU9: Farnh . . . 1G 128
Lion & Lamb Yd.
GU9: Farnh . . . 1G 129
Lion Av. TW1: Twick . . . 2F 24
Lion Cl. GU27: Hasl . . . 1D 188
TW17: Shep . . . 2N 37
Lionel Rd. Nth. TW8: Brent . . . 1L 11
Lionel Rd. Sth. TW8: Brent . . . 1M 11
Liongate Ent. Pk. CR4: Mit . . . 3B 44
Lion Ga. Gdns. TW9: Rich . . . 6M 11
Lion Ga. M. SW18 . . . 1M 27
Liongate M. KT8: E Mol . . . 2F 40
Lion Grn. GU27: Hasl . . . 2D 188
Lion Grn. Rd. CR5: Coul . . . 3H 83
Lion Head Ct. CR0: Croy . . . 6C 200
Lion La. GU27: Hasl . . . 9D 170
RH1: Red . . . 2D 122
RH10: Turn H . . . 5D 184
Lion Mead GU27: Hasl . . . 2D 188
Lion Pk. Av. KT9: Ches . . . 1N 59
Lion Retail Pk.
GU22: Wok . . . 3D 74
Lion Rd. CR0: Croy . . . 4N 45
GU14: Farnb . . . 3N 89
TW1: Twick . . . 2F 24
Lion's La. GU6: Cranl . . . 3K 175
Lion Way GU52: Chu C . . . 8C 88
TW8: Brent . . . 3K 11
Lion Wharf Rd. TW7: Isle . . . 6H 11
Lipcombe Cotts. GU5: Alb . . . 3L 135
Liphook Rd. GU27: Hasl . . . 2C 188
GU27: Hasl, Linch, Lip . . . 4A 188
GU30: Pass . . . 6D 168
GU35: Head . . . 6D 168
GU35: Lind . . . 4A 168
GU35: White . . . 9A 168
LIPSCOMB'S CORNER . . . 2M 179
Lipsham Cl. SM7: Ban . . . 9B 62
Lisbon Av. TW2: Twick . . . 3C 24
Liscombe RG12: Brac . . . 6N 31
Liscombe Ho. RG12: Brac . . . 6N 31
Liskeard Dr. GU14: Farnb . . . 8M 69
Liskeard Lodge
CR3: Cate . . . 4D 104
Lisle Cl. SW17 . . . 5F 28
Lismore *SW19* . . . *6L 27*
(off Woodside)
Lismore Cl. TW7: Isle . . . 5G 10
Lismore Cres. RH11: Craw . . . 6N 181
Lismore Rd. CR2: S Croy . . . 3B 64
Lismoyne Cl. GU51: Fleet . . . 3A 88
Lissant Cl. KT6: Surb . . . 6K 41
Lissoms Rd. CR5: Chip . . . 5E 82
Lister Av. RH19: E Grin . . . 3A 186
Lister Cl. CR4: Mit . . . 9C 28
Listergate Ct. SW15 . . . 7H 13
Lister Ho. UB3: Harl . . . 1F 8
Lister Pl. GU15: Camb . . . 1M 69
Litchfield Av. SM4: Mord . . . 6L 43
Litchfield Gdns. KT11: Cob . . . 1J 77
Litchfield Rd. SM1: Sut . . . 1A 62
Litchfield Way GU2: Guil . . . 5J 113
Lithgow's Rd. TW6: Lon A . . . 7F 8
Little Acre BR3: Beck . . . 2K 47
Little All. TN8: Marsh G . . . 6K 147
Little Angels Playworld . . . 8E 48
Lit. Austins Rd. GU9: Farnh . . . 3J 129
Little Benty UB7: W Dray . . . 1M 7
Lit. Birch Cl. KT15: N Haw . . . 5M 55
LITTLE BIRKETTS . . . 1L 157
Lit. Boltons, The SW5 . . . 1N 13
SW10 . . . 1N 13
LITTLE BOOKHAM . . . 2N 97
LITTLE BOOKHAM COMMON
. . . 9M 77
Lit. Bookham St.
KT23: Book . . . 1N 97
Little Borough RH3: Brock . . . 4N 119
Littlebrook Cl. CR0: Croy . . . 5G 47
Lit. Browns La. TN8: Eden . . . 8H 127
Little Buntings SL4: W'sor . . . 6C 4
Little Chesters KT20: Wal H . . . 3F 100
Little Collins RH1: Out . . . 4M 143
Littlecombe Cl. SW15 . . . 9J 13
Little Comn. La. RH1: Blet . . . 1M 123
Little Comptons
RH13: Hors . . . 6M 197
Little Copse GU46: Yate . . . 8C 48
GU52: Fleet . . . 6A 88
Littlecote Cl. SW19 . . . 1K 27
Little Crabtree RH11: Craw . . . 2A 182
Lit. Cranmore La.
KT24: W Hors . . . 6C 96
Little Cft. GU46: Yate . . . 1C 68
Littlecroft Rd. TW20: Egh . . . 6B 20
Littledale Cl. RG12: Brac . . . 2C 32
Little Dimocks SW12 . . . 3F 28
Lit. East Fld. CR5: Coul . . . 8H 83
Little Elms UB3: Harl . . . 3E 8
Lit. Ferry Rd. TW1: Twick . . . 2H 25
Littlefield Cl. GU3: Worp . . . 8G 92
GU12: Ash . . . 3E 110
KT1: K Tham . . . 4K 203 (1L 41)
LITTLEFIELD COMMON . . . 7E 92
Littlefield Gdns. GU12: Ash . . . 3E 110
Littlefield Ho. KT1: K Tham . . . 4J 203
Littlefield Way GU3: Worp . . . 8F 92
Littleford La. GU4: B'eath . . . 2G 135
GU5: Sha G . . . 2G 135
Little Fryth RG40: Finch . . . 1B 48
Little Grebe RH12: Hors . . . 3J 197
Little Green TW9: Rich . . . 7K 11
Lit. Green La. GU9: Farnh . . . 4F 128
KT16: Chert . . . 9G 36
Little Gro. *RH4: Dork* . . . *7J 119*
(off Stubs Hill)
Little Halliards KT12: Wal T . . . 5H 39
Lit. Hammer La.
GU26: Hasl . . . 9A 170
Little Hatch RH12: Hors . . . 3M 197
LITTLE HAVEN . . . 3L 197
Littlehaven La.
RH12: Hors . . . 3M 197
Littlehaven Station (Rail) . . . 3M 197
Littleheath La.
KT11: Cob, Sto D . . . 1A 78
Lit. Heath Rd. GU24: Chob . . . 5H 53
Littleheath Rd. CR2: Sels . . . 4E 64
Little Hide GU1: Guil . . . 1D 114
Lit. Holland Bungs.
CR3: Cate . . . 1A 104
Little Holland House . . . 4D 62
Little Kiln GU7: Godal . . . 3H 133
Lit. King St. RH19: E Grin . . . 9A 166
LITTLE LONDON . . . 1A 136
Little London GU5: Alb . . . 1N 135
GU8: Wit . . . 5B 152
Lit. London Hill
RH12: Warnh . . . 8G 179
Little Lullenden RH7: Ling . . . 6N 145
Lit. Manor Gdns.
GU6: Cranl . . . 8N 155
Little Mead GU6: Cranl . . . 8K 155
Littlemead GU21: Wok . . . 3J 73
KT10: Esh . . . 1D 58
Lit. Mead Ind. Est.
GU6: Cranl . . . 7K 155
Little Moor GU47: Sandh . . . 6H 49
Lit. Moreton Cl. KT14: W By . . . 8K 55
Little Oaks *RH19: E Grin* . . . *7N 165*
(off Springfield)
Lit. Oaks Cl. TW17: Shep . . . 3A 38
Little Orchard GU21: Wok . . . 1C 74
KT15: Wood . . . 7J 55
Lit. Orchard Pl. KT10: Esh . . . 9C 40
Little Orchards KT18: Eps . . . 8L 201
Lit. Orchard Way GU4: Chil . . . 1A 134
Little Paddock GU15: Camb . . . 7E 50
Lit. Paddock Cl.
RH11: Craw . . . 1M 181
Lit. Park Dr. TW13: Felt . . . 3M 23
Lit. Park Enterprises
RH11: Ifield . . . 7K 161
LITTLE PARROCK . . . 7M 187
Little Platt GU2: Guil . . . 2G 112
Lit. Queen's Rd. TW11: Tedd . . . 7F 24
Little Riding GU22: Wok . . . 3D 74
Little Ringdale RG12: Brac . . . 3C 32
Lit. Roke Av. CR8: Ken . . . 1M 83
Lit. Roke Rd. CR8: Ken . . . 1N 83
Littlers Cl. SW19 . . . 9B 28
Little St Leonard's SW14 . . . 6B 12
LITTLE SANDHURST . . . 6F 48
Lit. Stanford Cl. RH7: Ling . . . 8N 145
Little St. GU2: Guil . . . 8L 93
Lit. Sutton La. SL3: Lang . . . 1E 6
(Hurricane Way)
SL3: Lang . . . 2D 6
(Kings Ter.)
Little Thatch GU7: Godal . . . 5J 133
Lit. Thurbans Cl.
GU9: Farnh . . . 5F 128
LITTLETON
GU3 . . . 8K 113
TW17 . . . 2B 38
LITTLETON COMMON . . . 8D 22
Littleton Ho. *RH2: Reig* . . . *2M 121*
(off Somers Cl.)
Littleton La. GU3: Art . . . 8K 113
RH2: Reig . . . 5J 121
TW17: Shep . . . 6M 37
Littleton Rd. TW15: Ashf . . . 8D 22
Littleton St. SW18 . . . 3A 28
Lit. Tumners Ct.
GU7: Godal . . . 4H 133
Little Vigo GU46: Yate . . . 2A 68
Lit. Warren Cl. GU4: Guil . . . 5D 114
Lit. Wellington St.
GU11: Alde . . . 2M 109
LITTLEWICK . . . 3H 73
LITTLEWICK COMMON . . . 2H 73
Littlewick Rd.
GU21: Knap, Wok . . . 3H 73
Littlewold Dr. CR6: Warl . . . 6G 84
Littlewood GU6: Cranl . . . 7A 156
LITTLE WOODCOTE . . . 7F 62
Lit. Woodcote Est.
SM5: W'ton . . . 7F 62
Lit. Woodcote La. CR8: Pur . . . 8F 62
SM5: Cars . . . 8F 62
Little Woodlands SL4: W'sor . . . 6C 4
Lit. Wood St.
KT1: K Tham . . . 3H 203 (1K 41)
Littleworth Av. KT10: Esh . . . 2D 58
Littleworth Comn. Rd.
KT10: Esh . . . 9D 40
Littleworth La. KT10: Esh . . . 1D 58
Littleworth Pl. KT10: Esh . . . 1D 58
Littleworth Rd. GU10: Seal . . . 2C 130
KT10: Esh . . . 2D 58
Liverpool Rd. CR7: T Hea . . . 2N 45
KT2: K Tham . . . 8N 25
Livesey Cl.
KT1: K Tham . . . 5L 203 (2M 41)
Livingstone Cl. GU6: Cranl . . . 9A 156
Livingstone Ct. *TW19: Stan* . . . *2N 21*
(off Explorer Av.)
Livingstone Mans. *W14* . . . *2K 13*
(off Queen's Club Gdns.)
Livingstone Rd. CR3: Cate . . . 9A 84
CR7: T Hea . . . 1N 45
RH10: Craw . . . 5C 182
RH13: Hors . . . 7K 197
TW3: Houn . . . 7C 10
LivingWell Health Club
Bracknell . . . 6A 32
London Heathrow Hilton
. . . 9D 8
Wokingham . . . 2G 30
Llanaway Cl. GU7: Godal . . . 5J 133
Llanaway Ho. *GU7: Godal* . . . *5J 133*
(off Meadrow)
Llanaway Rd. GU7: Godal . . . 5J 133
Llangar Gro. RG45: Crowt . . . 2F 48
Llanthony Rd. SM4: Mord . . . 4B 44
Llanvair Cl. SL5: Asc . . . 5L 33
Llanvair Dr. SL5: Asc . . . 5K 33
Lloyd Av. CR5: Coul . . . 1E 82
SW16 . . . 9J 29
Lloyd Ho. *CR0: Croy* . . . *7A 46*
(off Tavistock Rd.)
Lloyd Pk. Av. CR0: Croy . . . 1C 64
Lloyd Park Stop
(London Tramlink) . . . 1C 64
Lloyd Rd. KT4: W Pk . . . 9H 43
Lloyds Ct. RH10: Craw . . . 9C 162
Lloyds Lanes Raynes Pk. . . . 2J 43
Lloyds Way BR3: Beck . . . 4H 47
Lobelia Rd. GU24: Bis . . . 2D 72
Locarno Cl. SW16 . . . 6G 29
Lochaline St. W6 . . . 2H 13
Lochinvar St. SW12 . . . 1F 28
Lochinver RG12: Brac . . . 6N 31
Lock Cl. KT15: Wood . . . 8G 55
Locke King Cl. KT13: Weybr . . . 4B 56
Locke King Rd. KT13: Weybr . . . 4B 56
Lockesley Sq. KT6: Surb . . . 5K 41
Lockestone KT13: Weybr . . . 3A 56
Lockestone Cl. KT13: Weybr . . . 3A 56
Lockets Cl. SL4: W'sor . . . 4A 4
Locke Way GU21: Wok . . . 4B 74
Lockfield Dr. GU21: Wok . . . 3H 73
Lockhart Rd. KT11: Cob . . . 9K 57
Lockhurst Hatch La.
GU5: Alb . . . 5N 135
Lockie Pl. SE25 . . . 2D 46
Lockites *GU7: Godal* . . . *4F 132*
(off Queen's Dr.)
Lock La. GU22: Pyr . . . 3K 75
LOCKNER HOLT . . . 9H 115
Lock Path SL4: Dorn, E Wic . . . 2A 4
Lock Rd. GU1: Guil . . . 9N 93
GU11: Alde . . . 8B 90
TW10: Ham . . . 5J 25
Locks La. CR4: Mit . . . 9E 28
Locksley Dr. GU21: Wok . . . 4J 73
Locksmeade Rd.
TW10: Ham . . . 5J 25
Locks Mdw. RH7: Dorm . . . 1C 166
Locks Ride SL5: Asc . . . 8F 16
Lockswood GU24: B'wood . . . 7E 72
Lockton Chase SL5: Asc . . . 2B 33
Lockton Ho. *RG40: W'ham* . . . *2B 30*
(off Palmer School Rd.)
Lockwood Cl. GU14: Cove . . . 6K 69
RH12: Hors . . . 3N 197
Lockwood Ct. RG41: W'ham . . . 3A 30
RH10: Craw . . . 1D 182
Lockwood Path GU21: Wok . . . 9F 54
Lockwood Way KT9: Ches . . . 2N 59
Lockyer Ho. SW15 . . . 6J 13
Locomotive Dr. TW14: Felt . . . 2H 23
Loddon Cl. GU15: Camb . . . 9E 50
Loddon Rd. GU14: Cove . . . 8J 69
Loddon Way GU12: Ash . . . 3E 110
Loder Cl. GU21: Wok . . . 9F 54
Lodge, The RH7: Newchap . . . 1H 165
SM7: Ban . . . 4A 82
Lodge Av. CR0: Wad . . . 9L 45
SW14 . . . 6D 12
Lodgebottom Rd.
KT18: Head . . . 5N 99
RH5: Mick . . . 5N 99
Lodge Cl. GU11: Alde . . . 4A 110
KT11: Sto D . . . 3N 77
KT17: Ewe . . . 6H 61
KT22: Fetc . . . 9D 78
RH5: Nth H . . . 9J 119
RH11: Craw . . . 3A 182
RH19: E Grin . . . 9M 165
SL5: Asc . . . 1N 33
SM6: W'ton . . . 7E 44
TW7: Isle . . . 4H 11
TW20: Eng G . . . 6N 19
Lodge Gdns. BR3: Beck . . . 4J 47
Lodge Gro. GU46: Yate . . . 9E 48
Lodge Hill CR8: Pur . . . 2L 83
Lodge Hill Cl.
GU10: Lwr Bou . . . 5J 129
Lodge Hill Rd.
GU10: Lwr Bou . . . 5J 129
Lodge La. CR0: N Add . . . 3K 65
RH1: Salf . . . 3C 142
RH5: Holm . . . 4L 139
TN16: Weste . . . 5L 107
Lodge Pl. SM1: Sut . . . 2N 61
Lodge Rd. CR0: Croy . . . 5M 45
KT22: Fetc . . . 9C 78
SM6: W'ton . . . 2F 62
Lodge Wlk. CR6: Warl . . . 3K 85
RH6: Horl . . . *8D 142*
(off Thornton Pl.)
Lodge Way SL4: W'sor . . . 6B 4
TW15: Ashf . . . 3N 21
TW17: Shep . . . 1D 38
Lodkin Hill GU8: Hasc . . . 4N 153
Lodsworth GU14: Cove . . . 2J 89
Lofthouse Pl. KT9: Ches . . . 3J 59
Lofts, The GU8: Worm . . . 1C 172
Logan Cl. TW4: Houn . . . 6N 9
Logmore La.
RH4: Dork, Westc . . . 7B 118
Lois Dr. TW17: Shep . . . 4C 38
Lollesworth La.
KT24: W Hors . . . 4D 96
Loman Rd. GU16: Mytc . . . 1E 90
Lomas Cl. CR0: N Add . . . 4M 65
Lombard Bus. Pk.
CR0: Croy . . . 6K 45
SW19 . . . 1N 43
Lombard Rd. SW19 . . . 1N 43
LOMBARD RDBT. . . . 6K 45
Lombard St. GU8: S'ford . . . 5K 131
Lombardy Cl. GU21: Wok . . . 4J 73
Lomond Gdns. CR2: Sels . . . 4H 65
Loncin Mead Av.
KT15: N Haw . . . 5L 55
LONDON BIGGIN HILL AIRPORT
. . . 8F 66
London Broncos RLFC . . . 1E 24
London Bus Museum, The . . . 4A 56
London Flds. Ho.
RH11: Craw . . . 8A 182
LONDON GATWICK AIRPORT
North Terminal . . . 2C 162
South Terminal . . . 3E 162
LONDON HEATHROW AIRPORT
Terminals 1, 2, 3 . . . 6B 8
Terminal 4 . . . 8C 8
Terminal 5 . . . 6L 7
London La. GU5: Shere . . . 7B 116
KT24: E Hor . . . 9G 97
London Rd. CR0: Croy . . . 6M 45
CR3: Cate . . . 1A 104
CR4: Mit . . . 6E 44
(Mill Grn. Rd.)
CR4: Mit . . . 4C 44
(Brookfields Av.)
CR7: T Hea . . . 1A 200 (4L 45)
GU1: Guil . . . 4E 202 (4A 114)
GU4: B'ham . . . 8D 94
(not continuous)
GU15: Camb . . . 2J 69
GU17: B'water, Min . . . 4A 68
GU19: Bag . . . 6F 50
GU20: Windl . . . 2K 51
GU23: Send . . . 4G 94
GU25: V Wat . . . 2K 35
GU26: Hind . . . 5D 170
KT2: K Tham . . . 3L 203 (1M 41)
KT17: Ewe . . . 5E 60
RG12: Bin . . . 1G 31
RG12: Brac . . . 1B 32
RG40: W'ham . . . 2C 30
RG42: Bin . . . 1G 31
RH1: Red . . . 2D 122
RH2: Reig . . . 3M 121
RH4: Dork . . . 1L 201 (4H 119)
RH5: Dork . . . 3H 119
RH10: Craw, Low H . . . 2B 182
RH11: Craw . . . 1B 182
RH12: Hors . . . 6J 197
RH18: F Row . . . 5G 186
RH19: E Grin . . . 6K 165
SL3: Dat . . . 3L 5
(not continuous)
SL3: Lang . . . 1A 6
SL5: Asc . . . 2E 32
SL5: Asc, S'hill . . . 2M 33
SL5: S'dale . . . 7B 34
SM3: Chea . . . 4F 60
SM4: Mord . . . 4M 43
SM6: W'ton . . . 1F 62
SW16 . . . 9K 29
SW17 . . . 8D 28
TN16: Weste . . . 1L 107
TW1: Twick . . . 1G 24
TW3: Houn, Isle . . . 6C 10
TW7: Brent, Isle . . . 5F 10
TW7: Isle, Twick . . . 8G 10
TW8: Brent . . . 5F 10
TW14: Bedf . . . 3A 22
TW15: Ashf . . . 4K 21
TW18: Stain . . . 5J 21
TW20: Eng G . . . 9L 19
London Rd. Nth.
RH1: Mers . . . 4F 102
LONDON ROAD RDBT. . . . 9G 10
London Rd. Sth.
RH1: Mers, Red . . . 8E 102
London Road Station (Rail)
. . . 3F 202 (3A 114)
London Scottish & Richmond
Rugby Football Ground . . . 6K 11
London Scottish Golf Course
. . . 4G 27
London Sq.
GU1: Guil . . . 3F 202 (3B 114)
London Stile W4 . . . 1N 11
London St. KT16: Chert . . . 6J 37
London Wetland Cen. . . . 4G 13
London Wetland Cen. Vis. Cen.
. . . 4G 12
Loneacre GU20: Windl . . . 3B 52
Lone Oak RH6: Smallf . . . 1M 163
LONESOME . . . 9G 28
Lonesome Caravan Site
SW16 . . . 9F 28
Lonesome La.
RH2: Reig, Sid . . . 7N 121
Lonesome Way SW16 . . . 9F 28
Long Acre RH10: Craw D . . . 1D 184
Longacre GU12: Ash . . . 2E 110
Longacre Pl. SM5: Cars . . . 3E 62
Long Acres Caravan & Camping Pk.
RH7: Ling . . . 1J 165
Long Beech Dr. GU14: Cove . . . 2H 89
Longbourn SL4: W'sor . . . 6D 4
Longbourne Grn.
GU7: Godal . . . 3H 133
Longbourne Way
KT16: Chert . . . 5H 37
Longboyds KT11: Cob . . . 2J 77
Longbridge GU9: Farnh . . . 1H 129
Longbridge Ga. *RH6: Gatw* . . . *2C 162*
(off Arrivals Rd.)
Longbridge Rd. RH6: Horl . . . 1D 162
Longbridge Rdbt.
RH6: Horl . . . 9C 142
Longbridge Wlk. RH6: Horl . . . 1D 162
Longbridge Way
RH6: Gatw . . . 1D 162
Longchamps Cl. RH6: Horl . . . 8G 143
Long Cl. RH10: Craw . . . 3H 183
Long Comn. GU5: Sha G . . . 8E 134
Long Copse Cl. KT23: Book . . . 1B 98
Longcroft Av. SM7: Ban . . . 1A 82
LONGCROSS . . . 9K 35
Long Cross Hill
GU35: Head . . . 4D 168
Longcross Rd. KT16: L'cross . . . 9J 35
Longcross Station (Rail) . . . 7J 35
Longden Av. KT15: Addl . . . 4H 55
Longdene Rd. GU27: Hasl . . . 2F 188
LONG DITTON . . . 7J 41
Longdon Wood BR2: Kes . . . 1G 66
Longdown GU52: Fleet . . . 7A 88

Longdown Chase Cotts.—Lymbourne Cl.

Longdown Chase Cotts.
GU26: Hind ... 6E 170
Longdown Cl.
GU10: Lwr Bou ... 5H 129
Longdown La. Nth.
KT17: Eps ... 1F 80
Longdown La. Sth.
KT17: Eps, Eps D ... 1F 80
Longdown Lodge
GU47: Sandh ... 7G 48
Longdown Rd. GU4: Guil ... 6D 114
GU10: Lwr Bou ... 6G 128
GU47: Sandh ... 6F 48
KT17: Eps ... 1F 80
Long Dyke GU1: Guil ... 1D 114
Longfellow Cl.
RH12: Hors ... 1L 197
Longfellow Rd. KT4: W Pk ... 8F 42
Longfield Av. SM6: W'ton ... 7E 44
Longfield Cl. GU14: Farnb ... 6M 69
Longfield Cres. KT20: Tad ... 7H 81
Longfield Dr. CR4: Mit ... 9C 28
SW14 ... 8A 12
Longfield Rd. GU12: Ash ... 2E 110
RH4: Dork ... 6F 118
RH12: Hors ... 8G 196
Longfield St. SW18 ... 1M 27
LONGFORD ... 4K 7
Longford Av. TW14: Felt ... 9F 8
TW19: Stan ... 2N 21
Longford Cir. UB7: L'ford ... 4K 7
Longford Cl. GU15: Camb ... 2B 70
TW12: H Hill ... 5A 24
TW13: Hanw ... 4M 23
Longford Ct. KT19: Ewe ... 1B 60
TW12: H Hill ... 7B 24
Longford Gdns. SM1: Sut ... 9A 44
Longford Ho. TW12: H Hill ... 5A 24
Longford Ind. Est.
TW12: Hamp ... 7B 24
LONGFORDMOOR ... 4J 7
Longford Rd. TW2: Whitt ... 2A 24
Longford Wlk. SW2 ... 1L 29
Longford Way TW19: Stan ... 2N 21
Long Gdn. M. *GU9: Farnh ... 1G 129*
(off Castle St.)
Long Gdn. Pl. GU9: Farnh ... 9G 109
Long Gdn. Wlk.
GU9: Farnh ... 1G 129
Long Gdn. Wlk. E.
GU9: Farnh ... 9G 109
Long Gdn. Wlk. W.
GU9: Farnh ... 9G 108
Long Gdn. Way GU9: Farnh ... 1G 128
Long Gore GU7: Godal ... 2H 133
Long Gro. Rd. KT19: Eps ... 7B 60
Long Heath Dr. KT23: Book ... 2M 97
Longheath Gdns. CR0: Croy ... 4F 46
Long Hedges TW3: Houn ... 5A 10
Long Hill CR3: Wold ... 8G 85
GU10: Seal ... 2C 130
Long Hill Rd. RG12: Brac ... 1E 32
SL5: Asc ... 1E 32
Longhope Dr. GU10: Wrec ... 5F 128
Long Houses GU24: Pirb ... 2A 92
Longhurst Av. RH12: Hors ... 6E 196
Longhurst Rd. CR0: Croy ... 5E 46
KT24: E Hor ... 7F 96
RH11: Craw ... 8M 181
Longitude Apartments
CR0: Croy ... 3E 200
Longland Pl. KT19: Eps ... 8L 59
Longlands Av. CR5: Coul ... 1E 82
Longlands Ct. CR4: Mit ... 9E 28
Longlands Way GU15: Camb ... 1H 71
Long La. CR0: Croy ... 5F 46
RG40: W'ham ... 7E 14
TW19: Stan ... 3A 22
Longleat Sq. GU14: Farnb ... 2C 90
Longleat Way TW14: Bedf ... 1E 22
Longley Rd. CR0: Croy ... 6M 45
GU9: Farnh ... 2J 129
SW17 ... 7C 28
Long Lodge Dr. KT12: Wal T ... 9K 39
Longmead GU1: Guil ... 3E 114
GU52: Fleet ... 7B 88
SL4: W'sor ... 4B 4
Longmead Bus. Pk.
KT19: Eps ... 7C 60
Longmead Cl. CR3: Cate ... 9B 84
Longmead Ho. SE27 ... 6N 29
Longmeadow GU16: Frim ... 3D 70
KT23: Book ... 3N 97
Long Meadow Cl.
BR4: W Wick ... 6M 47
Long Meadow Vs.
RH6: Charlw ... 5K 161
Longmead Rd. KT7: T Dit ... 6E 40
KT19: Eps, Ewe ... 7C 60
SW17 ... 6D 28
Longmere Gdns. KT20: Tad ... 6H 81
Longmere Rd. RH10: Craw ... 1B 182
Long Mickle GU47: Sandh ... 6F 48
Longmoor Point *SW15 ... 2G 26*
(off Norley Va.)
Longmoors RG42: Brac ... 9K 15
Longmore Rd. KT12: Hers ... 1M 57
Long Orchards
KT20: K'wood ... 7K 81
Longpoles Rd. GU6: Cranl ... 8A 156
Long Reach GU23: Ockh ... 1B 96
KT24: W Hors ... 1B 96
Longridge Gro. GU22: Pyr ... 1H 75
Longridge Rd. SW5 ... 1M 13
Longridge Vw. CR5: Chip ... 7D 82
Long Road, The
GU10: Rowl ... 8E 128
Longroyd *KT24: E Hor ... 4F 96*
(off Cobham Way)
Longs Cl. GU22: Pyr ... 3J 75
Longs Ct. TW9: Rich ... 7M 11
Longsdon Way CR3: Cate ... 2D 104
Longshaw KT22: Leat ... 7G 79
Longshot Ind. Est.
RG12: Brac ... 1K 31
Longshot La. RG12: Brac ... 2K 31
(Butler Dr.)
RG12: Brac ... 1K 31
(Longshot Ind. Est.)
Longside Cl. TW20: Egh ... 9E 20
Longstaff Cres. SW18 ... 9M 13
Longstaff Rd. SW18 ... 9M 13
Longstone Rd. SW17 ... 6F 28
Long's Way RG40: W'ham ... 1D 30
Longthornton Rd. SW16 ... 1G 45
Long Wlk. GU4: E Cla ... 8N 95
KT3: N Mal ... 2B 42
KT14: W By ... 1L 75
KT18: Tat C ... 6H 81
SL4: W'sor ... 7G 5
SW13 ... 5D 12
TN8: C Hil ... 9K 107
Long Walk, The SL4: W'sor ... 3G 19
Longwall RH19: E Grin ... 6K 165
Longwater Ho.
KT1: K Tham ... 6H 203
Longwater Rd. RG12: Brac ... 5A 32
Longwood Av. SL3: Lang ... 1D 6
Longwood Bus. Pk.
TW16: Sunb ... 4G 38
Longwood Dr. SW15 ... 9F 12
Longwood Rd. CR8: Ken ... 3A 84
Longwood Vw. RH10: Craw ... 6E 182
Longyard Ho. RH6: Horl ... 6F 142
Lonsdale Ct. KT6: Surb ... 6K 41
Lonsdale Gdns. CR7: T Hea ... 3K 45
Lonsdale M. TW9: Kew ... 4N 11
Lonsdale Pl. RH4: Dork ... 1L 201
Lonsdale Rd. KT13: Weybr ... 4B 56
RH4: Dork ... 1L 201 (4H 119)
SE25 ... 3E 46
SW13 ... 4E 12
Look Out Discovery Centre, The
... 7B 32
Loop Rd. GU22: Wok ... 7B 74
KT18: Eps ... 3B 80
Loppets Rd. RH10: Craw ... 5D 182
Lorac Ct. SM2: Sut ... 4M 61
Loraine Gdns. KT21: Asht ... 4L 79
Loraine Ho. SM6: W'ton ... 1F 62
Loraine Rd. W4 ... 2A 12
Lord Chancellor Wlk.
KT2: K Tham ... 9B 26
Lord Darby M. TN14: Cud ... 2M 87
Lordell Pl. SW19 ... 7H 27
Lord Knyvett Cl. TW19: Stan ... 9M 7
Lord Knyvetts Ct. TW19: Stan ... 9M 7
Lord Napier Pl. W6 ... 1F 12
Lord Raglan Ho. SL4: W'sor ... 6F 4
Lord Roberts M. SW6 ... 3N 13
Lord Rosebery Lodge
KT18: Eps ... 1B 80
Lordsbury Fld. SM6: W'ton ... 6G 62
Lords Cl. SE21 ... 3N 29
TW13: Hanw ... 3M 23
Lordsgrove Cl. KT20: Tad ... 7G 81
LORDSHILL COMMON ... 7E 134
Lords Hill Cotts.
GU5: Sha G ... 7E 134
Lordshill Rd. GU5: Sha G ... 6E 134
Lords Wood Ho. CR5: Coul ... 9H 83
Loretto Cl. GU6: Cranl ... 7A 156
Lorian Dr. RH2: Reig ... 2A 122
Loriners RH10: Craw ... 6B 182
Loriners Cl. KT11: Cob ... 1H 77
Loring Rd. SL4: W'sor ... 4C 4
TW7: Isle ... 5F 10
Lorne, The KT23: Book ... 4A 98
Lorne Av. CR0: Croy ... 6G 47
Lorne Gdns. CR0: Croy ... 6G 47
GU21: Knap ... 6G 72
Lorne Rd. TW10: Rich ... 8M 11
Lorraine Rd. GU15: Camb ... 7D 50
Lory Ridge GU19: Bag ... 3J 51
Loseberry Rd. KT10: Clay ... 2D 58
Loseley Pk. ... 9H 113
Loseley Rd. GU7: Godal ... 3H 133
Losfield Rd. SL4: W'sor ... 4B 4
Lothian Rd. GU24: B'wood ... 8L 71
Lothian Wood KT20: Tad ... 9G 80
Lots Rd. SW10 ... 3N 13
Lotus Cl. SE21 ... 4N 29
Lotus Pk. TW18: Stain ... 5F 20
Lotus Rd. TN16: B Hil ... 5H 87
Loubet St. SW17 ... 7D 28
Loudwater Cl.
TW16: Sunb ... 3H 39
Loudwater Rd.
TW16: Sunb ... 3H 39
Loughborough RG12: Brac ... 5C 32
Louisa Ct. TW2: Twick ... 3E 24
Louise Margaret Rd.
GU11: Alde ... 1A 110
Louis Flds. GU3: Worp ... 8F 92
Louisville Rd. SW17 ... 4E 28
Lovatt Ct. SW12 ... 2F 28
Lovat Wlk. TW5: Hest ... 3M 9
Loveday Ho. GU6: Cranl ... 5L 155
Lovedean Ct. RG12: Brac ... 5C 32
Lovegrove Cl. CR2: Sande ... 6A 64
Lovejoy La. SL4: W'sor ... 5A 4
Lovekyn Cl.
KT2: K Tham ... 3L 203 (1L 41)
Lovelace Cl. KT24: E Jun ... 1H 97
Lovelace Dr. GU22: Pyr ... 3G 75
Lovelace Gdns. KT6: Surb ... 6K 41
KT12: Hers ... 2K 57
Lovelace Rd. KT6: Surb ... 6J 41
RG12: Brac ... 3K 31
SE21 ... 3N 29
Lovelace Vs. *KT7: T Dit ... 6H 41*
(off Portsmouth Rd.)
Lovelands La. GU24: Chob ... 9F 52
KT20: Lwr K ... 5N 101
Love La. CR4: Mit ... 2C 44
(not continuous)
GU12: Ash ... 2F 110
KT6: Surb ... 8J 41
KT20: Wal H ... 5E 100
RH5: Ockl ... 6D 158
RH9: Gods ... 1F 124
SE25 ... 2E 46
SM1: Sut ... 3L 61
SM3: Chea, Sut ... 3K 61
SM4: Mord ... 6M 43
Loveletts RH11: Craw ... 4M 181
Lovel La. SL4: Wink ... 5L 17
Lovell Path RH11: Ifield ... 4K 181
Lovell Rd. TW10: Ham ... 4J 25
Lovells Cl. GU18: Ligh ... 6M 51
Lovelock Cl. CR8: Ken ... 4N 83
Lovel Rd. SL4: Wink ... 5K 17
Lovers La. GU10: Fren ... 3H 149
RH13: Hors ... 9J 197
Lovett Dr. SM5: Cars ... 6A 44
Lovett Rd. TW18: Stain ... 5D 20
Lovett's Pl. SW18 ... 7N 13
Lovibonds Av. BR6: Farnb ... 1K 67
Lowbury RG12: Brac ... 3C 32
Lowburys RH4: Dork ... 8H 119
Lowdell's Cl. RH19: E Grin ... 6M 165
Lowdells Dr. RH19: E Grin ... 6M 165
Lowdells La. RH19: E Grin ... 6L 165
Lowe Cl. GU11: Alde ... 1L 109
RH11: Craw ... 9N 181
Lwr. Addiscombe Rd.
CR0: Croy ... 1F 200 (7B 46)
Lwr. Ash Est. TW17: Shep ... 5G 39
LOWER ASHTEAD ... 6K 79
Lwr. Barn Cl. RH12: Hors ... 3M 197
Lwr. Barn Rd. CR8: Pur ... 8N 63
LOWER BOURNE ... 4J 129
Lwr. Breache Rd.
GU6: Ewh ... 6H 157
Lwr. Bridge Rd. RH1: Red ... 3D 122
Lwr. Broadmoor Rd.
RG45: Crowt ... 3H 49
Lwr. Charles St.
GU15: Camb ... 9A 50
Lwr. Church La.
GU9: Farnh ... 1G 129
Lwr. Church Rd.
GU47: Sandh ... 6D 48
Lwr. Church St.
CR0: Croy ... 3A 200 (8M 45)
Lwr. Common Sth. SW15 ... 6G 13
Lwr. Coombe St.
CR0: Croy ... 6B 200 (1N 63)
Lower Ct. Rd. KT19: Eps ... 7B 60
Lower Dene RH19: E Grin ... 9C 166
Lwr. Downs Rd. SW20 ... 9J 27
Lwr. Drayton Pl.
CR0: Croy ... 3A 200 (8M 45)
Lower Dunnymans SM7: Ban ... 1L 81
LOWER EASHING ... 7C 132
Lower Eashing GU7: Eash ... 7B 132
Lwr. Edgeborough Rd.
GU1: Guil ... 4B 114
Lwr. Farm Rd. KT24: Eff ... 2J 97
Lwr. Farnham Rd.
GU11: Alde ... 5N 109
GU12: Alde ... 5N 109
LOWER FELTHAM ... 4H 23
Lwr. George St. TW9: Rich ... 8K 11
LOWER GREEN ... 8B 40
Lower Grn. Gdns. KT4: W Pk ... 7F 42
Lower Grn. Rd. KT10: Esh ... 8B 40
Lower Grn. W. CR4: Mit ... 2C 44
Lower Gro. Rd. TW10: Rich ... 9M 11
Lwr. Guildford Rd.
GU21: Knap ... 4G 72
LOWER HALLIFORD ... 6E 38
Lwr. Ham La. GU8: Els ... 7J 131
Lwr. Hampton Rd.
TW16: Sunb ... 2K 39
Lwr. Ham Rd.
KT2: K Tham ... 1J 203 (6K 25)
Lower Hanger GU27: Hasl ... 2A 188
Lwr. Hill Rd. KT19: Eps ... 8A 60
Lwr. Hook Bus. Pk.
BR6: Dow ... 4H 67
Lowerhouse La.
RH5: For G, W'wood ... 7K 157
Lower Ho. Rd. GU8: Bow G ... 9K 151
Lwr. King's Rd.
KT2: K Tham ... 1J 203 (9L 25)
LOWER KINGSWOOD ... 5L 101
Lower Lodge Shooting Grounds
... 6G 194
Lower Mall W6 ... 1G 12
Lwr. Manor Rd.
GU7: Godal ... 5H 133
GU8: Mil ... 1B 152
Lwr. Marsh La.
KT1: K Tham ... 7L 203 (3M 41)
Lower Mead RH1: Red ... 1D 122
Lower Mere RH19: E Grin ... 1B 186
Lower Mill KT17: Ewe ... 4E 60
Lwr. Mill Fld. GU19: Bag ... 5H 51
Lower Moor GU46: Yate ... 1C 68
Lwr. Morden La. SM4: Mord ... 5H 43
Lwr. Mortlake Rd.
TW9: Rich ... 7L 11
Lwr. Moushill La. GU8: Mil ... 1A 152
Lwr. Nelson St.
GU11: Alde ... 2M 109
Lwr. Newport Rd.
GU12: Alde ... 4B 110
Lower Northfield SM7: Ban ... 1L 81
Lower Nursery SL5: S'dale ... 4D 34
Lwr. Park Rd. CR5: Chip ... 5C 82
Lower Peryers KT24: E Hor ... 6F 96
Lwr. Pillory Down CR5: Coul ... 9F 62
SM6: W'ton ... 9F 62
Lwr. Pyrford Rd. GU22: Pyr ... 3K 75
Lwr. Richmond Rd. SW14 ... 6A 12
SW15 ... 6G 13
TW9: Rich ... 6N 11
Lower Rd. CR8: Ken ... 9M 63
GU27: G'wood ... 7K 171
KT22: Fetc ... 1D 98
KT23: Book ... 5L 97
KT24: Eff ... 5L 97
RH1: Red ... 5B 122
RH18: F Row ... 6H 187
SM1: Sut ... 1A 62
Lower Sandfields
GU23: Send ... 2F 94
Lwr. Sand Hills KT6: Surb ... 6J 41
Lwr. Sandhurst Rd.
GU47: Sandh ... 5A 48
RG40: Finch ... 5A 48
Lwr. Sawley Wood SM7: Ban ... 1L 81
Lower Shott KT23: Book ... 4A 98
LOWER SOUTH PARK ... 9D 124
Lwr. South Pk.
RH9: S Gods ... 9D 124
Lwr. South St. GU7: Godal ... 7G 133
Lwr. South Vw. GU9: Farnh ... 9H 109
Lower Sq. RH18: F Row ... 6H 187
TW7: Isle ... 6H 11
Lower Square, The
SM1: Sut ... 2N 61
(off St Nicholas Way)
Lower St. GU5: Shere ... 8B 116
GU27: Hasl ... 2F 188
Lwr. Sunbury Rd.
TW12: Hamp ... 1N 39
Lwr. Tanbridge Way
RH12: Hors ... 6H 197
Lwr. Teddington Rd.
KT1: H Wic ... 1G 203 (9K 25)
Lower Ter. *SE27 ... 6M 29*
(off Woodcote Pl.)
Lwr. Village Rd. SL5: S'hill ... 4M 33
Lwr. Weybourne La.
GU9: B Lea, Weybo ... 6L 109
Lwr. Wokingham Rd.
RG40: Finch ... 9C 30
RG45: Crowt ... 9C 30
Lwr. Wood Rd. KT10: Clay ... 3H 59
Lowestoft Wlk. RH10: Craw ... 5F 182
Loweswater Wlk.
GU15: Camb ... 2H 71
Lowfield Cl. GU18: Ligh ... 7L 51
LOWFIELD HEATH ... 5C 162
Lowfield Heath Rd.
RH6: Charlw, Gatw ... 4L 161
Lowfield Heath Rdbt.
RH10: Low H ... 6C 162
(off London Rd.)
Lowfield Rd. RH13: Slinf ... 5L 195
Lowfield Way RH11: Low H ... 5C 162
Lowicks Rd. GU10: Rush ... 4N 149
Lowlands Dr. TW19: Stan ... 8M 7
Lowlands Rd. GU17: B'water ... 2H 69
Low La. GU9: B Lea ... 6N 109
Lownde M. SW16 ... 3J 29
Lowndes Bldgs.
GU9: Farnh ... 9G 109
Lowndes M. SW16 ... 3J 29
Lowry Cl. GU47: Coll T ... 9J 49
Lowry Cres. CR4: Mit ... 1C 44
Lowther Rd.
KT2: K Tham ... 1M 203 (9M 25)
SW13 ... 4E 12
Lowthorpe GU21: Wok ... 5K 73
Loxford Cl. CR3: Cate ... 3C 104
Loxford Ct. GU6: Cranl ... 8H 155
Loxford Ho.
KT17: Eps ... 5M 201 (8D 60)
Loxford Rd. CR3: Cate ... 3C 104
Loxford Way CR3: Cate ... 3C 104
LOXHILL ... 9A 154
Loxley Cl. KT14: Byf ... 1N 75
Loxley Rd. SW18 ... 2B 28
TW12: Hamp ... 5N 23
Loxmeadow Cl. RH14: Ifo ... 5F 192
LOXWOOD ... 4H 193
Loxwood KT13: Weybr ... 9F 38
Loxwood Cl. TW14: Bedf ... 2E 22
Loxwood Farm Pl.
RH14: Loxw ... 5H 193
Loxwood Rd. GU6: Alf ... 1H 193
RH12: Rudg ... 4N 193
RH14: Loxw ... 5J 193
RH14: Plais ... 6B 192
Loxwood Wlk. RH11: Craw ... 1L 181
(not continuous)
Lucan Dr. TW18: Stain ... 8M 21
Lucas Cl. GU46: Yate ... 1C 68
RH10: Craw ... 6F 182
RH19: E Grin ... 9C 166
Lucas Dr. GU46: Yate ... 1C 68
Lucas Fld. GU27: Hasl ... 2C 188
LUCAS GREEN ... 2A 72
Lucas Grn. Rd.
GU24: W End ... 2A 72
Lucas Ho. *SW10 ... 3N 13*
(off Coleridge Gdns.)
Lucas Pl. RG12: Brac ... 2J 31
Lucas Rd. RH12: Warnh ... 9E 178
Lucerne Cl. GU22: Wok ... 6A 74
Lucerne Dr. RH10: Craw ... 6H 183
Lucerne Rd. CR7: T Hea ... 4M 45
Lucie Av. TW15: Ashf ... 7C 22
Lucien Rd. SW17 ... 5E 28
SW19 ... 3N 27
Lucilina Dr. TN8: Eden ... 3L 147
Lucinda Wlk. GU19: Bag ... 5H 51
Luckley Path RG40: W'ham ... 2B 30
Luckley Rd. RG40: W'ham ... 5A 30
RG41: W'ham ... 5A 30
Luckley Wood RG41: W'ham ... 5A 30
Luddington Av. GU25: V Wat ... 1B 36
Ludford Cl.
CR0: Wad ... 6A 200 (9M 45)
Ludgrove RG40: W'ham ... 5C 30
Ludlow RG12: Brac ... 6N 31
Ludlow Cl. GU16: Frim ... 7E 70
Ludlow Rd.
GU2: Guil ... 5A 202 (4L 113)
TW13: Felt ... 5H 23
Ludovick Wlk. SW15 ... 7D 12
Ludshott Gro.
GU35: Head D ... 4G 169
Ludshott Mnr.
GU30: Brams ... 8H 169
Luff Cl. SL4: W'sor ... 6B 4
Luffs Mdw. GU28: Northc ... 9D 190
Luke Rd. GU11: Alde ... 4K 109
Luke Rd. E. GU11: Alde ... 4K 109
Lullarook Cl. TN16: B Hil ... 3E 86
LULLENDEN ... 5H 167
Lulworth Av. TW5: Hest ... 4B 10
Lulworth Cl. GU14: Farnb ... 7M 69
RH11: Craw ... 6M 181
Lulworth Cres. CR4: Mit ... 1C 44
Lulworth Pl. KT19: Eps ... 8L 59
Lumiere Ct. SW17 ... 3E 28
Lumley Ct. RH6: Horl ... 7E 142
Lumley Gdns. SM3: Chea ... 2K 61
Lumley Rd. RH6: Horl ... 7E 142
SM3: Chea ... 2K 61
Lunar Cl. TN16: B Hil ... 3F 86
Luna Rd. CR7: T Hea ... 2N 45
Lundy Cl. RH11: Craw ... 6A 182
Lundy Dr. UB3: Harl ... 1F 8
Lunghurst Rd. CR3: Wold ... 7J 85
Lupin Cl. CR0: Croy ... 7G 46
GU19: Bag ... 6G 51
SW2 ... 3M 29
UB7: W Dray ... 1M 7
Lupin Ride RG45: Crowt ... 8G 30
Lurgan Av. W6 ... 2J 13
Lushington Dr. KT11: Cob ... 1J 77
Lushington Ho.
KT12: Wal T ... 5K 39
Lusted Hall La.
TN16: B Hil, Tats ... 7D 86
Lusteds Cl. RH4: Dork ... 8J 119
Lutea Ho. *SM2: Sut ... 4A 62*
(off Walnut M.)
Luther M. TW11: Tedd ... 6F 24
Luther Rd. TW11: Tedd ... 6F 24
Lutterworth Cl. RG42: Brac ... 8A 16
Luttrell Av. SW15 ... 8G 13
Lutyens Cl. KT24: Eff ... 5L 97
RH11: Craw ... 5K 181
Luxford Cl. RH12: Hors ... 3M 197
Luxford's La. RH19: E Grin ... 4D 186
LUXTED ... 1J 87
Luxted Rd. BR6: Dow ... 8J 67
Lyall Pl. GU9: Up Hale ... 5G 108
Lych Ga. Cl. GU47: Sandh ... 7E 48
Lych Way GU21: Wok ... 3N 73
Lyconby Gdns. CR0: Croy ... 6H 47
Lydbury RG12: Brac ... 2D 32
Lydden Gro. SW18 ... 1N 27
Lydden Rd. SW18 ... 1N 27
Lydele Cl. GU21: Wok ... 2B 74
Lydens La.
TN8: Eden, Hev ... 6N 147
Lydford Cl. GU14: Farnb ... 7M 69
GU16: Frim ... 7E 70
Lydger Cl. GU22: Wok ... 7D 74
Lydhurst Av. SW2 ... 3K 29
Lydia Ct. KT1: K Tham ... 6J 203
Lydia Pk. GU6: Cranl ... 1E 174
Lydney RG12: Brac ... 6N 31
Lydney Cl. SW19 ... 3K 27
Lydon Ho. RH11: Craw ... 9B 162
Lye, The KT20: Tad ... 9H 81
Lye Copse Av. GU14: Farnb ... 6N 69
Lyefield La. RH5: For G ... 4K 157
Lyell Rd. SL4: W'sor ... 6A 4
Lyfield KT22: Oxs ... 1B 78
Lyford Rd. SW18 ... 1B 28
Lygon Ho. *SW6 ... 4K 13*
(off Fulham Pal. Rd.)
Lyham Cl. SW2 ... 1J 29
Lyham Rd. SW2 ... 1J 29
Lyle Cl. CR4: Mit ... 6E 44
Lyle Ct. SM4: Mord ... 5B 44
Lymbourne Cl. SM2: Sut ... 6M 61

Lymden Gdns.—Manor Cl.

Lymden Gdns. RH2: Reig 4N 121
Lyme Regis Rd. SM7: Ban 4L 81
Lymescote Gdns. SM1: Sut 8M 43
Lyminge Gdns. SW18 2C 28
Lymington Av. GU46: Yate 1A 68
Lymington Cl. SW16 1H 45
Lymington Ct. SM1: Sut 9N 43
Lymington Gdns.
KT19: Ewe 2E 60
Lynchborough Rd.
GU30: Pass 9C 168
Lynchen Cl. TW5: C'ford 4J 9
Lynchford La. GU14: Farnb 5C 90
Lynchford Rd. GU12: Ash V 5D 90
GU14: Farnb 5N 89
Lynchmere Pl. GU2: Guil 9K 93
Lynch Rd. GU9: Farnh 1J 129
Lyncroft Gdns. KT17: Ewe 5E 60
TW3: Houn 8C 10
Lyndale KT7: T Dit 6E 40
Lyndale Ct. KT14: W By 9J 55
RH1: Red 9E 102
Lyndale Dr. GU51: Fleet 4E 88
Lyndale Rd. RH1: Red 9D 102
Lynde Ho. KT12: Wal T 5K 39
Lynden Hyrst CR0: Croy 8C 46
Lyndford Ter. GU52: Fleet 6A 88
Lyndhurst Av. GU11: Alde 6A 110
GU17: B'water 9H 49
KT5: Surb 7A 42
SW16 1H 45
TW2: Whitt 2N 23
TW16: Sunb 2H 39
Lyndhurst Cl. BR6: Farnb 1K 67
CR0: Croy 9C 46
GU21: Wok 2N 73
RG12: Brac 2E 32
RH11: Craw 4B 182
Lyndhurst Ct. *SM2: Sut* 4M 61
(off Grange Rd.)
Lyndhurst Dr. KT3: N Mal 6D 42
Lyndhurst Farm Cl.
RH19: Felb 6G 165
Lyndhurst Rd. CR5: Coul 3E 82
CR7: T Hea 3L 45
RH2: Reig 6M 121
SL5: Asc 3L 33
Lyndhurst Vs. RH1: Red 9D 102
Lyndhurst Way KT16: Chert 9G 36
SM2: Sut 5M 61
Lyndon Av. SM6: W'ton 9E 44
Lyndons, The GU30: Pass 9C 168
Lyndon Yd. SW17 5A 28
Lyndsey Cl. GU14: Cove 1G 88
Lyndum Pl. GU35: Lind 4A 168
Lyndwood Dr. SL4: O Win 9K 5
Lyndwood Pde. *SL4: O Win* 9K 5
(off St Luke's Rd.)
LYNE 7C 36
Lyne Cl. GU25: V Wat 5B 36
Lyne Crossing Rd.
KT16: Lyne 5C 36
Lyne Gdns. TN16: B Hil 5G 87
Lynegrove Av. TW15: Ashf 6D 22
Lyneham Rd. RG45: Crowt 2G 48
Lyne La. GU25: V Wat 5C 36
KT16: Lyne 5C 36
TW20: Thor 5C 36
Lyne Rd. GU25: V Wat 5N 35
Lynford Ct. CR2: S Croy 7F 200
Lyngarth Cl. KT23: Fetc 3D 98
Lynhurst KT13: Weybr 3C 56
Lynmead Cl. TN8: Eden 8K 127
Lynmouth Av. SM4: Mord 5J 43
Lynmouth Gdns. TW5: Hest 3L 9
Lynn Cl. TW15: Ashf 6E 22
Lynn Ct. CR3: Whyte 5C 84
Lynne Cl. BR6: Chels 3N 67
CR2: Sels 7F 64
Lynne Ct. CR2: S Croy 7F 200
Lynne Wlk. KT10: Esh 2C 58
Lynn Rd. SW12 1F 28
Lynn Wlk. RH2: Reig 6N 121
Lynn Way GU14: Cove 7L 69
Lynscott Way CR2: S Croy 5M 63
Lynstead Ct. BR3: Beck 1H 47
Lynton Cl. GU9: Farnh 4F 128
KT9: Ches 1L 59
RH19: E Grin 8B 166
TW7: Isle 7F 10
Lynton Ct. KT17: Ewe 7E 60
Lynton Ho. *GU22: Wok* 5A 74
(off Station App.)
Lynton Pk. Av.
RH19: E Grin 8B 166
Lynton Rd. CR0: Croy 5L 45
KT3: N Mal 4C 42
LYNWICK 9B 176
Lynwick St. RH12: Rudg 1C 194
Lynwood GU2: Guil 4L 113
SL5: S'dale 5B 34
Lynwood Av. CR5: Coul 2F 82
KT17: Eps 1E 80
TW20: Egh 7A 20
Lynwood Chase
RG12: Brac 8A 16
Lynwood Cl. GU21: Wok 9F 54
GU35: Lind 4B 168
Lynwood Ct. KT1: K Tham 1A 42
KT17: Eps 9E 60
RH12: Hors 5J 197
Lynwood Cres. SL5: S'dale 5B 34
Lynwood Dr. GU16: Mytc 2E 90
KT4: W Pk 8F 42
Lynwood Gdns. CR0: Wad 1K 63
Lynwood Rd. KT7: T Dit 8F 40
KT17: Eps 1E 80
RH1: Red 1E 122
SW17 4D 28
(not continuous)
Lynx Ct. GU14: Farnb 3A 90
Lynx Hill KT24: E Hor 6G 96
Lyon Cl. RH10: Craw 7G 183
Lyon Ct. RH13: Hors 6L 197
Lyon Oaks RG42: Warf 7N 15
Lyon Rd. KT12: Wal T 8M 39
RG45: Crowt 1H 49
SW19 9A 28
Lyons Cl. RH13: Slinf 5L 195
Lyons Ct.
RH4: Dork 2K 201 (5H 119)
Lyonsdene KT20: Lwr K 5L 101
Lyons Dr. GU2: Guil 7K 93
Lyons Farm Est.
RH13: Slinf 6A 196
Lyons Rd. RH13: Slinf 5L 195
Lyon Way GU16: Frim 5A 70
Lyon Way Ind. Est.
GU16: Frim 5A 70
Lyric Cl. RH10: Craw 5H 183
Lyric Rd. SW13 4E 12
Lyric Sq. *W6* 1H 13
(off King St.)
Lyric Theatre
Hammersmith 1H 13
Lysander Dr. RG12: Brac 3A 32
Lysander Gdns. KT6: Surb 5M 41
Lysander Rd. CR0: Wad 3K 63
Lysia Ct. *SW6* 3J 13
(off Lysia St.)
Lysias Rd. SW12 1F 28
Lysia St. SW6 3J 13
Lysons Av. GU12: Ash V 5D 90
Lyson's Rd. GU11: Alde 3M 109
Lysons Wlk. SW15 7F 12
Lyster M. KT11: Cob 9K 57
Lytchett Minster Cl.
RG12: Brac 4D 32
Lytchgate Cl. CR2: S Croy 4B 64
Lytcott Dr. KT8: W Mole 2N 39
Lytham RG12: Brac 5K 31
Lytham Ct. SL5: S'hill 4N 33
LYTHE HILL 2L 189
Lythe Hill Pk. GU27: Hasl 3J 189
Lytton Dr. RH10: Craw 2H 183
Lytton Gdns. SM6: Bedd 1H 63
Lytton Gro. SW15 8J 13
Lytton Pk. KT11: Cob 8N 57
Lytton Rd. GU22: Wok 3D 74
Lyveden Rd. SW17 7D 28
Lywood Cl. KT20: Tad 9H 81

M

Mabbots KT20: Tad 8J 81
Mabel St. GU21: Wok 5N 73
Maberley Rd. BR3: Beck 2G 47
Mablethorpe Rd. SW6 3K 13
Macadam Av. RG45: Crowt 9H 31
McAlmont Ridge
GU7: Godal 4G 132
McArdle Way SL3: Coln 3F 6
Macaulay Av. KT10: Hinc W 8F 40
Macaulay Cl. RG12: Brac 1J 31
Macaulay Rd. CR3: Cate 9B 84
Macbeth Ct. RG42: Warf 9C 16
Macbeth St. W6 1G 13
McCarthy Rd. TW13: Hanw 6L 23
McClaren Technology Cen.
GU21: Wok 7C 54
Macclesfield Rd. SE25 4F 46
Macdonald Rd.
GU9: Up Hale 5G 109
GU18: Ligh 8K 51
McDonalds Almshouses
GU9: Farnh 2F 128
(off West St.)
McDonough Cl. KT9: Ches 1L 59
McDougall Ct. TW9: Rich 5N 11
Macdowall Rd. GU2: Guil 7L 93
Mace Ho. TW7: Isle 4H 11
Mace La. TN14: Cud 9M 67
Macfarlane La. TW7: Isle 2F 10
McIndoe Rd. RH19: E Grin 7N 165
McIntosh Cl. SM6: W'ton 4J 63
McIver Cl. RH19: Felb 6J 165
McKay Cl. GU11: Alde 1A 110
McKay Rd. SW20 8G 27
McKay Trad. Est. SL3: Poy 5G 7
Mackenzie Rd. BR3: Beck 1F 46
McKenzie Way KT19: Eps 5N 59
McKernan Ct. GU47: Sandh 7E 48
Mackie Rd. SW2 1L 29
Mackies Hill GU5: P'lake 4E 136
Mackrells RH1: Red 6A 122
Maclaren Dr. RG42: Warf 9D 16
Maclaren M. SW15 7H 13
Macleod Rd. RH13: Hors 7L 197
(not continuous)
Macmahon Cl. GU24: Chob 6H 53
Macmillan Ho. *SM7: Ban* 1L 81
(off Basing Rd.)
Macmillan Way SW17 5F 28
Macnaghten Woods
GU15: Camb 9C 50
McNaughton Cl. GU14: Cove 2H 89
Macphail Cl. RG40: W'ham 9D 14
McRae La. CR4: Mit 6D 44
Macrae Rd. GU46: Yate 9A 48
Madan Cl. TN16: Weste 3N 107
Madan Rd. TN16: Weste 3M 107
Madans Wlk.
KT18: Eps 8K 201 (2C 80)
(not continuous)
Maddison Cl. TW11: Tedd 7F 24
Maddox Dr. RH10: Worth 4H 183
Maddox La. KT23: Book 9M 77
Maddox Pk. KT23: Book 1M 97
Madehurst Ct. RH11: Craw 6L 181
Madeira Av. RH12: Hors 6J 197
Madeira Cl. KT14: W By 9J 55
Madeira Cres. KT14: W By 9H 55
Madeira Rd. CR4: Mit 3D 44
KT14: W By 9H 55
SW16 6J 29
Madeira Wlk. RH2: Reig 2B 122
SL4: W'sor 4G 5
Madeley Rd. GU52: Chu C 7C 88
Madgehole La. GU5: Sha G 7J 135
Madingley RG12: Brac 7N 31
Madison Cl. SM2: Sut 4B 62
Madox Brown End
GU47: Coll T 8K 49
Madrid Rd. GU2: Guil 4L 113
SW13 4F 12
Maesmaur Rd. TN16: Tats 8F 86
Mafeking Av. TW8: Brent 2L 11
Mafeking Rd. TW19: Wray 3D 20
Magazine Pl. KT22: Leat 9H 79
Magazine Rd. CR3: Cate 9M 83
GU14: Farnb 5J 89
Magdala Rd. CR2: S Croy 4A 64
TW7: Isle 6G 11
Magdalen Cl. KT14: Byf 1N 75
Magdalen Cres. KT14: Byf 1N 75
Magdalene Cl. RH10: Craw 9G 162
Magdalene Rd. GU47: Owls 5L 49
TW17: Shep 3A 38
Magdalen Rd. SW18 2A 28
Magellan Ter. RH10: Craw 8E 162
Magistrates' Court
Aldershot 2L 109
Crawley 3C 182
Croydon 4E 200 (9A 46)
East Berkshire, Bracknell
1A 32
Feltham 2J 23
Guildford 4B 202 (4M 113)
Hammersmith 1J 13
Horsham 5K 197
Redhill 3B 122
Richmond-upon-Thames
7K 11
Staines Upon Thames 6J 21
Wimbledon 7M 27
Magna Carta La.
TW19: Wray 2N 19
Magna Carta Memorial 3N 19
Magna Ct. TW18: Stain 6G 20
Magna Rd. TW20: Eng G 7L 19
Magna Sq. *SW14* 6B 12
(off Moore Cl.)
Magnolia Cl. GU47: Owls 6J 49
KT2: K Tham 7A 26
RG42: Warf 9E 16
Magnolia Ct. RH6: Horl 8E 142
SM2: Sut 4M 61
(off Grange Rd.)
SM6: W'ton 2F 62
TW9: Kew 4A 12
TW13: Felt 2H 23
(off Plum Cl.)
Magnolia Dr. SM7: Ban 3L 81
TN16: B Hil 3F 86
Magnolia Pl. GU1: Guil 9M 93
Magnolia Rd. W4 2A 12
Magnolia St. UB7: W Dray 1M 7
Magnolia Vs. TW18: Stain 8K 21
Magnolia Way GU52: Fleet 6B 88
KT19: Ewe 2B 60
RH5: Nth H 8K 119
Magnolia Wharf W4 2A 12
Magpie Cl. CR5: Coul 5G 83
GU10: Ews 4C 108
Magpie Grn. *TN8: Eden* 9M 127
(off Woodland Dr.)
Magpie Wlk. RH10: Craw 1D 182
Maguire Dr. GU16: Frim 3G 71
TW10: Ham 5J 25
Mahonia Cl. GU24: W End 9C 52
Maibeth Gdns. BR3: Beck 3H 47
Maida Rd. GU11: Alde 9N 89
MAIDENBOWER 5G 183
Maidenbower Bus. Pk.
RH10: Worth 5J 183
Maidenbower Community Sports Cen.
5F 182
Maidenbower Dr.
RH10: Craw 5G 182
Maidenbower La.
RH10: Craw 4G 182
(Blackett Rd.)
RH10: Craw 5F 182
(Marion Rd.)
Maidenbower Pl.
RH10: Craw 5G 183
Maidenbower Sq.
RH10: Craw 5G 183
Maidenhead Rd.
RG40: W'ham 6C 14
RG42: Warf 3N 15
SL4: W'sor 3A 4
Maiden La. RH11: Craw 1A 182
MAIDEN'S GREEN 3F 16
Maiden's Grn. SL4: Wink 3F 16
Maidenshaw Rd.
KT19: Eps 5J 201 (8C 60)
Maids of Honour Row
TW9: Rich 8K 11
Main Dr. RG42: Warf 8D 16
(Forest Way)
RG42: Warf 8F 16
(The Plateau)
Mainprize Rd. RG12: Brac 9C 16
Main Rd. BR2: Kes 9E 66
GU10: Bucks O 2A 148
SL4: W'sor 3A 4
TN8: C Hil, Eden 6K 127
TN16: B Hil, Weste 9E 66
Mainstone Cl. GU16: Deep 7G 71
Mainstone Cres.
GU24: B'wood 8A 72
Mainstone Rd. GU24: Bis 3C 72
Main St. KT15: Addl 9N 37
TW13: Hanw 6L 23
Mainwaring Ct. CR4: Mit 1E 44
Maisie Webster Cl.
TW19: Stan 1M 21
Maisonettes, The SM1: Sut 2L 61
Maitland Cl. KT12: Wal T 8M 39
KT14: W By 9J 55
TW4: Houn 6N 9
Maitland Rd. GU14: Farnb 5N 89
Maitlands Cl. GU10: Tong 6C 110
Maize Cft. RH6: Horl 7G 142
Maize La. RG42: Warf 7B 16
Majestic Way CR4: Mit 1D 44
Majors Farm Rd. SL3: Dat 3N 5
Major's Hill RH10: Worth 4N 183
Makepiece Rd. RG42: Brac 8N 15
Malacca Farm GU4: W Cla 5K 95
Malan Cl. TN16: B Hil 4G 87
Malbrook Rd. SW15 7G 13
Malcolm Dr. KT6: Surb 7L 41
Malcolm Gdns.
RH6: Hookw 1B 162
Malcolm Rd. CR5: Coul 2H 83
SE25 5D 46
SW19 7K 27
Malden Av. SE25 3E 46
Malden Centre, The 3E 42
Malden Ct. KT3: N Mal 2G 42
Malden Golf Course 1D 42
MALDEN GREEN 7F 42
Malden Grn. Av. KT4: W Pk 7E 42
Malden Grn. M. KT4: W Pk 7F 42
Malden Hill KT3: N Mal 2E 42
Malden Hill Gdns.
KT3: N Mal 2E 42
MALDEN JUNC. 4E 42
Malden Manor Station (Rail)
6D 42
Malden Pk. KT3: N Mal 5E 42
Malden Rd. KT3: N Mal 4D 42
KT4: W Pk 5E 42
SM3: Chea 1J 61
MALDEN RUSHETT 7J 59
Malden Way KT3: N Mal 6C 42
Maldon Ct. SM6: W'ton 2G 62
Maldon District Society of
Model Engineers, The 7G 41
Maldon Rd. SM6: W'ton 2F 62
Malet Cl. TW20: Egh 7F 20
Maley Av. SE27 3M 29
Malham Cl. RH10: Craw 6G 183
Malham Fell RG12: Brac 3M 31
Mall, The
CR0: Croy 2B 200 (8N 45)
KT6: Surb 4K 41
KT12: Hers 2L 57
(off Hersham Grn. Shop. Cen.)
SW14 8B 12
TW8: Brent 2K 11
Mallard Cl. GU12: Ash 1D 110
GU27: Hasl 2C 188
RH1: Red 9E 102
RH6: Horl 6E 142
RH12: Hors 3J 197
TW2: Whitt 1A 24
Mallard Ct. *GU11: Alde* 5M 109
(off Boxall's La.)
RH4: Dork 1J 201
Mallard Pl. GU14: Cove 6M 69
RH19: E Grin 1B 186
TW1: Twick 4G 24
Mallard Rd. CR2: Sels 6G 65
Mallards, The GU16: Frim 4D 70
TW18: Lale 1K 37
Mallards Reach
KT13: Weybr 8E 38
Mallards Way GU18: Ligh 7L 51
Mallard Wlk. BR3: Beck 4G 47
Mallard Way GU46: Yate 9A 48
SM6: W'ton 5G 63
TN8: Eden 9L 127
Malling Cl. CR0: Croy 5F 46
Malling Gdns. SM4: Mord 5A 44
Mallinson Rd. CR0: Bedd 9H 45
Mallow Cl. CR0: Croy 7G 46
GU35: Lind 4B 168
KT20: Tad 7G 81
RH12: Hors 2L 197
Mallow Cres. GU4: B'ham 9D 94
Mallowdale Rd. RG12: Brac 6C 32
Mall Rd. W6 1G 13
Mall Vs. *W6* 1G 13
(off Mall Rd.)
Malmains Cl. BR3: Beck 3N 47
Malmains Way BR3: Beck 3M 47
Malmesbury Rd. SM4: Mord 6A 44
Malmstone Av. RH1: Mers 6G 103
Malory Cl. BR3: Beck 1H 47
Malta Rd. GU16: Deep 6J 71
Maltby Rd. KT9: Ches 3N 59
Malt Hill RG42: Warf 4C 16
TW20: Egh 6A 20
Malt House, The GU10: Til 8A 130
Malt Ho. Cl. SL4: O Win 1L 19
Malthouse Ct. GU24: W End 8C 52
TW8: Brent 2L 11
(off High St.)
Malthouse Dr. TW13: Hanw 6L 23
W4 2E 12
Malthouse La. GU3: Worp 2F 92
GU8: Hamb 9F 152
GU24: Pirb 1E 92
GU24: W End 9C 52
TW20: Egh 6C 20
Malthouse Mead GU8: Wit 5C 152
Malthouse Pas. *SW13* 5E 12
(off Clevelands Gdns.)
Malthouse Rd. RH10: Craw 5B 182
Malthouses, The
GU6: Cranl 7N 155
Maltings, The KT14: Byf 9A 56
RH8: Oxt 9B 106
TW18: Stain 5G 20
W4 1N 11
(off Spring Gro.)
Maltings Cl. SW13 5E 12
Maltings Lodge *W4* 2D 12
(off Corney Reach Way)
Maltings Pl. SW6 4N 13
Malting Way TW7: Isle 6F 10
Malus Cl. KT15: Addl 4H 55
Malus Dr. KT15: Addl 4H 55
Malva Cl. SW18 8N 13
Malvern Cl. CR4: Mit 2G 44
KT6: Surb 7L 41
KT16: Otter 3E 54
SE20 1D 46
Malvern Ct.
KT18: Eps 8K 201 (1C 80)
SL3: Lang 2C 6
SM2: Sut 4M 61
Malvern Dr. TW13: Hanw 6L 23
Malvern Rd. CR7: T Hea 3L 45
GU14: Cove 7J 69
GU17: Min 5E 68
KT6: Surb 8L 41
RH11: Craw 4A 182
TW12: Hamp 8A 24
UB3: Harl 3F 8
Malwood Rd. SW12 1F 28
Malyons, The TW17: Shep 5E 38
Manatee Pl. SM6: Bedd 9H 45
Manawey Bus. Units
GU12: Alde 3C 110
Manbre Rd. W6 2H 13
Manchester Rd. CR7: T Hea 2N 45
Mandalay *GU9: Up Hale* 5F 108
(off Lawday Pl. La.)
Mandel Ho. SW18 7M 13
Mandeville Cl. GU2: Guil 9K 93
SW20 8K 27
Mandeville Ct. TW20: Egh 5C 20
Mandeville Dr. KT6: Surb 7K 41
Mandeville Rd. TW7: Isle 5G 10
TW17: Shep 4B 38
Mandora Rd. GU11: Alde 9N 89
Mandrake Rd. SW17 4D 28
Manfield Pk. GU6: Cranl 5K 155
Manfield Rd. GU12: Ash 2E 110
Manfred Rd. SW15 8L 13
Mangles Ct.
GU1: Guil 4B 202 (4M 113)
Mangles Rd. GU1: Guil 1N 113
Manitoba Gdns. BR6: Chels 3N 67
Manley Bri. Rd.
GU10: Rowl, Wrec 6D 128
Mannamead KT18: Eps D 6D 80
Mannamead Cl.
KT18: Eps D 6D 80
Mann Cl.
CR0: Croy 4B 200 (9N 45)
RH11: Craw 9N 181
Manning Cl.
RH19: E Grin 8N 165
Manning Gdns. CR0: Croy 6E 46
Manning Pl. TW10: Rich 9M 11
Mannings Cl. RH10: Craw 9H 163
MANNINGS HEATH 9B 198
Mannings Heath Golf Course
9D 198
Mannings Hill
GU6: Cranl 4M 155
Manningtree Cl. SW19 2K 27
Mann's Cl. TW7: Isle 8F 10
Manny Shinwell Ho. *SW6* 2L 13
(off Clem Attlee Ct.)
Manoel Rd. TW2: Twick 3C 24
Manor, The GU8: Mil 1C 152
Manor Av. CR3: Cate 2B 104
TW4: Houn 6L 9
Manor Chase KT13: Weybr 2C 56
MANOR CIRCUS 6N 11
Manor Cl. CR6: Warl 4H 85
GU10: Tong 5D 110
GU22: Pyr 4H 75
GU27: Hasl 2C 188
KT4: W Pk 7D 42
KT24: E Hor 6F 96
RG42: Brac 8M 15
RH6: Horl 8D 142
RH9: S Gods 7J 125

Manor Ct.—Marsham Ho.

Manor Ct. BR4: W Wick 7L 47
GU52: Chu C 9B 88
KT2: K Tham 9N 25
KT8: W Mole 3A 40
KT13: Weybr 1C 56
RH10: Craw 9D 162
RH12: Hors 3N 197
SM5: Cars 9E 44
SW6 . . . . 4N 13
SW16 . . . . 4J 29
TW2: Twick 3C 24
TW18: Stain 6F 20
Manor Cres. GU2: Guil 1L 113
GU24: B'wood 7A 72
GU27: Hasl 2C 188
KT5: Surb 5N 41
KT14: Byf 9A 56
KT19: Eps 8N 59
Manorcrofts Rd. TW20: Egh 7C 20
Manordene Cl. KT7: T Dit 7G 40
Manor Dr. KT5: Surb 5M 41
KT10: Hinc W 8F 40
KT15: N Haw 6J 55
KT19: Ewe 3D 60
RH6: Horl 8D 142
TW13: Hanw 6L 23
TW16: Sunb 1H 39
Manor Drive, The
KT4: W Pk 7D 42
Manor Dr. Nth. KT3: N Mal . . . 6C 42
KT4: W Pk 6C 42
Manor Farm GU3: Wan 6N 111
TW20: Egh 6C 20
Mnr. Farm Av. TW17: Shep . . . 5C 38
Mnr. Farm Bus. Cen.
GU10: Tong 7D 110
Mnr. Farm Cl. GU3: Norm 1M 111
GU12: Ash 3D 110
KT4: W Pk 7D 42
SL4: W'sor 6C 4
Mnr. Farm Cotts.
GU3: Wan 6N 111
SL4: O Win 8K 5
Mnr. Farm Ct. TW20: Egh 6C 20
Manor Farm Craft Cen. 8F 110
MANOR FARM ESTATE 1M 19
Mnr. Farm Ho.
SL4: W'sor 6C 4
Mnr. Farm La. TW20: Egh 6C 20
Mnr. Farm M.
GU10: Dock 6E 148
Mnr. Farm Rd. SW16 . . . . 1L 45
Manor Flds. GU8: Mil 9B 132
GU10: Seal 7F 110
RH13: Hors 4N 197
SW15 . . . . 9J 13
Manorfields RH11: Craw 7J 181
Manor Gdns. CR2: S Croy 3C 64
GU2: Guil 1L 113
GU7: Godal 4H 133
GU10: Lwr Bou 6J 129
KT24: Eff 6L 97
SW20 . . . . 1L 43
TW9: Rich 7M 11
TW12: Hamp 8B 24
TW16: Sunb 9H 23
W4 . . . . 1D 12
Manor Ga. RH10: Craw 9D 162
Manorgate Rd.
KT2: K Tham 9N 25
Manor Grn. GU8: Mil 1B 152
Manor Grn. Rd. KT19: Eps 9A 60
Manor Gro. BR3: Beck 1L 47
TW9: Rich 7N 11
Manor Hill SM7: Ban 2D 82
Manor Ho. SL4: Eton 2G 4
(off Common La.)
Manor House, The
GU15: Camb 9B 50
KT20: K'wood 1A 102
Manor Ho. Ct.
KT18: Eps 7H 201 (9B 60)
TW17: Shep 6C 38
Manor Ho. Dr. KT12: Hers 2G 57
SL5: Asc 8L 17
Manor Ho. Flats
GU10: Tong 6C 110
Manor Ho. Gdns.
TN8: Eden 2L 147
Manor Ho. La. KT23: Book 4M 97
SL3: Dat 4L 5
Manor Ho. Way TW7: Isle 6H 11
Manor La. GU5: Sha G 8G 134
KT20: Lwr K 7M 101
RH13: Hors 8A 198
SM1: Sut 2A 62
TW13: Felt 3H 23
TW16: Sunb 1H 39
UB3: Harl 2E 8
Manor Lea GU27: Hasl 2C 188
Manor Lea Cl. GU8: Mil 9B 132
Manor Lea Rd. GU8: Mil 9B 132
Manor Leaze TW20: Egh 6D 20
Manor Lodge GU2: Guil 1L 113
Manor Pk. TW9: Rich 7M 11
TW13: Felt 3H 23
TW18: Stain 4F 20
Manor Pk. Cl. BR4: W Wick . . . 7L 47
Manor Pk. Dr. GU46: Yate 1C 68
Manor Pk. Est.
GU12: Alde 3A 110
Manor Pk. Rd. BR4: W Wick . . . 7L 47
SM1: Sut 2A 62
Manor Pk. Village
GU2: Guil 4H 113
Manor Pl. CR4: Mit 2G 45
KT12: Wal T 6G 39
(not continuous)
KT23: Book 4A 98
SM1: Sut 1N 61
TW14: Felt 2H 23
TW18: Stain 6K 21
Manor Rd. BR3: Beck 1L 47
BR4: W Wick 8L 47
CR4: Mit 3G 44
GU2: Guil 1L 113
GU9: Farnh 8K 109
GU10: Tong 5D 110
GU11: Alde 4L 109
GU12: Ash 5D 110
GU14: Farnb 1B 90
GU21: Wok 3M 73
GU23: Rip 1H 95
KT8: E Mol 3D 40
KT12: Wal T 6G 39
RH1: Mers 7G 102
RH2: Reig 1L 121
RH12: Hors 3N 197
RH19: E Grin 8M 165
SE25 . . . . 3D 46
SL4: W'sor 5B 4
SM2: Chea 4L 61
SM6: W'ton 1F 62
SW20 . . . . 1L 43
TN8: Eden 2K 147
TN16: Tats 7G 86
TW2: Twick 3C 24
TW9: Rich 7N 11
TW11: Tedd 6G 25
(not continuous)
TW15: Ashf 6A 22
Manor Rd. Nth. KT7: T Dit 9F 40
KT10: Hinc W, T Dit 9F 40
SM6: W'ton 1F 62
Manor Rd. Sth.
KT10: Hinc W 1E 58
Manor Royal RH10: Craw 9C 162
Mnr. Royal Ind. Est.
RH10: Craw 9C 162
Manor Ter. GU7: Godal 5J 133
Manor Va. TW8: Brent 1J 11
Manor Wlk. GU12: Alde 3N 109
KT13: Weybr 2C 56
RH6: Horl 8D 142
(off Manor Dr.)
Manor Way BR3: Beck 1K 47
CR2: S Croy 3B 64
CR4: Mit 2G 44
CR8: Pur 8J 63
GU2: Guil 6H 113
GU19: Bag 5J 51
GU22: Wok 8D 74
KT4: W Pk 7D 42
KT22: Oxs 2C 78
SM7: Ban 3D 82
TW20: Egh 7B 20
Manor Way, The SM6: W'ton . . 1F 62
Mnr. Wood Rd. CR8: Pur 9J 63
Mansard Beeches SW17 . . . . . 6E 28
Manse Cl. UB3: Harl 2E 8
Mansel Cl. GU2: Guil 7L 93
Mansell Cl. SL4: W'sor 4B 4
Mansell Way CR3: Cate 9A 84
Mansel Rd. SW19 . . . . 7K 27
Mansfield Cl. SL5: Asc 9H 17
Mansfield Cres. RG12: Brac . . . 5N 31
Mansfield Dr. RH1: Mers 6H 103
Mansfield Pl. CR2: S Croy 3A 64
SL5: Asc 1H 33
Mansfield Rd. CR2: S Croy . . . 3A 64
KT9: Ches 2J 59
Manship Rd. CR4: Mit 8E 28
Mansions, The SW5 . . . . 1N 13
Manston Av. UB2: S'hall 1A 10
Manston Cl. SE20 . . . . 1F 46
Manston Dr. RG12: Brac 5A 32
Manston Gro. KT2: K Tham 6K 25
Manston Rd. GU4: B'ham 8C 94
Mantilla Rd. SW17 . . . . 5E 28
Mantle Cl. SL4: W'sor 6A 4
Mantle Ct. SW18 . . . . 9N 13
(off Mapleton Rd.)
Mantlet Cl. SW16 . . . . 8G 29
Manville Ct. GU4: Chil 2A 134
Manville Gdns. SW17 . . . . 4F 28
Manville Rd. SW17 . . . . 3E 28
Manygate La. TW17: Shep 6D 38
Manygate Pk. Caravan Site
TW17: Shep 5E 38
(off Mitre Cl.)
Manygates SW12 . . . . 3F 28
Maori Rd. GU1: Guil 3B 114
Maple Av. GU14: Cove 9J 69
Maple Cl. CR3: Whyte 4C 84
CR4: Mit 9F 28
GU12: Ash V 6D 90
GU17: B'water 1H 69
GU47: Sandh 6E 48
KT19: Eps 5C 60
RH11: Craw 9A 162
RH12: Hors 3N 197
TW12: Hamp 7N 23
Maple Ct. CR0: Croy 6C 200
(Keens Rd.)
CR0: Croy 6B 200
(The Waldrons)
GU21: Wok 3M 73
KT3: N Mal 2C 42
KT22: Leat 7F 78
RG12: Brac 3D 32
Maple Ct. SL4: W'sor 6F 4
TW15: Ashf 8E 22
TW20: Eng G 7L 19
Mapledale Av. CR0: Croy 8D 46
Mapledrakes Cl. GU6: Ewh 5F 156
Mapledrakes Rd. GU6: Ewh . . . 5F 156
Maple Dr. GU18: Ligh 7K 51
KT23: Book 3B 98
RG45: Crowt 9H 31
RH1: Red 9D 122
RH19: E Grin 9C 166
Maple Gdns. GU46: Yate 1C 68
KT17: Eps 6L 201
TW19: Stan 3N 21
Maple Grn. RH11: Craw 4A 182
Maple Gro. GU1: Guil 1N 113
GU22: Wok 8A 74
KT23: Book 5A 98
TW8: Brent 3H 11
Maple Gro. Bus. Cen.
TW4: Houn 7K 9
Maplehatch Cl. GU7: Godal . . . 9H 133
Maple Ho. KT1: K Tham 8J 203
RH1: Red 3D 122
(off Chapel Rd.)
TW9: Kew 4A 12
Maplehurst BR2: Brom 1N 47
KT22: Fetc 1D 98
Maplehurst Cl.
KT1: K Tham 8J 203 (3L 41)
Maple Ind. Est. TW13: Felt 4H 23
Maple Leaf Cl. GU14: Cove . . . 2L 89
TN16: B Hil 3F 86
Mapleleaf Cl. CR2: Sels 7G 64
Maple Lodge GU27: Hasl 4J 189
Maple M. SW16 . . . . 6K 29
Maple Pl. SM7: Ban 1J 81
Maple Rd. CR3: Whyte 4C 84
GU23: Rip 2J 95
KT6: Surb 8J 203 (5K 41)
KT21: Asht 6K 79
RH1: Red 7D 122
SE20 . . . . 1E 46
Maplers Dr. GU51: Fleet 2A 88
Maples, The KT10: Clay 4G 59
KT16: Otter 3D 54
SM7: Ban 1N 81
Maplestead Rd. SW2 . . . . 1K 29
Maplethorpe Rd. CR7: T Hea . . . 3L 45
Mapleton Cres. SW18 . . . . 9N 13
Mapleton Rd. SW18 . . . . 9M 13
(not continuous)
TN16: Weste 8N 107
Maple Wlk. GU12: Alde 4B 110
SM2: Sut 6N 61
Maple Way CR5: Coul 8F 82
GU35: Head D 3G 169
TW13: Felt 4H 23
Maplewood Ct. TW15: Ashf 5N 21
Marbaix Gdns. TW7: Isle 4D 10
Marbeck Cl. SL4: W'sor 4A 4
Marble Hill Cl. TW1: Twick . . . 1H 25
Marble Hill Gdns.
TW1: Twick 1H 25
Marble Hill House 1J 25
(off High St.)
Marbles Way KT20: Tad 6J 81
Marbull Way RG42: Warf 7N 15
Marcellina Way BR6: Orp 1N 67
Marchant's Hill (Activity Cen.)
. . . . 2B 170
Marchbank Rd. W14 . . . . 2L 13
March Ct. SW15 . . . . 7G 12
Marcheria Cl. RG12: Brac 5N 31
Marches, The RH12: K'fold 4H 179
Marches Rd.
RH12: Warnh, K'fold 5D 178
Marchmont Gdns.
TW10: Rich 8M 11
Marchmont Pl. RG12: Brac 2A 32
Marchmont Rd. SM6: W'ton 4G 62
TW10: Rich 8M 11
March Rd. KT13: Weybr 2B 56
TW1: Twick 1G 24
Marchside Cl. TW5: Hest 4L 9
Marcus Ct. GU22: Wok 5B 74
Marcuse Rd. CR3: Cate 1A 104
Marcus St. SW18 . . . . 9N 13
Marcus Ter. SW18 . . . . 9N 13
Mardale GU15: Camb 2G 71
Mardell Rd. CR0: Croy 4G 46
Marden Cres. CR0: Croy 5K 45
MARDEN PARK 1H 105
Marden Rd. CR0: Croy 5K 45
Mardens, The RH11: Craw 2N 181
Mare La. GU8: Hasc 6L 153
RG42: Bin 1K 15
Mareschal Rd.
GU2: Guil 7A 202 (5M 113)
Maresfield CR0: Croy 9B 46
Maresfield Ho. GU4: Guil 2F 114
(off Merrow St.)
Mareshall Av. RG42: Warf 7N 15
Mare St. GU8: Hasc 6N 153
Mareth Cl. GU11: Alde 2N 109
Marfleet Cl. SM5: Cars 8C 44
Margaret Cl. TW18: Stain 7M 21
Margaret Herbison Ho. SW6 . . . 2L 13
(off Clem Attlee Ct.)
Margaret Ho. W6 . . . . 1H 13
(off Queen Caroline St.)
Margaret Ingram Cl. SW6 . . . . 2L 13
Margaret Lockwood Cl.
KT1: K Tham . . . 7M 203 (3M 41)
Margaret Rd.
GU1: Guil 4B 202 (4M 113)
Margaret Rutherford Pl.
SW12 . . . . 2G 28
Margaret Way CR5: Coul 6M 83
MARGERY 7M 101
Margery Gro. KT20: Lwr K 7K 101
Margery La. KT20: Lwr K 7L 101
Margery Wood La.
KT20: Lwr K, Reig 7L 101
Margin Dr. SW19 . . . . 6J 27
Margravine Gdns. W6 . . . . 1J 13
Margravine Rd. W6 . . . . 1J 13
Marham Gdns.
SM4: Mord 5A 44
SW18 . . . . 2C 28
Maria Ct. SE25 . . . . 1B 46
Marian Ct. SM1: Sut 2N 61
Marian Rd. SW16 . . . . 9G 29
Maria Theresa Cl.
KT3: N Mal 4C 42
Mariette Way SM6: W'ton 5J 63
Marigold Cl. RG45: Crowt 9E 30
Marigold Ct. GU1: Guil 9A 94
Marigold Dr. GU24: Bis 2D 72
Marigold Way CR0: Croy 7G 46
Marina Av. KT3: N Mal 4G 42
Marina Cl. KT16: Chert 7L 37
Marina Pl.
KT1: H Wic 3G 203 (9K 25)
Marina Way TW11: Tedd 8K 25
Marinefield Rd. SW6 . . . . 5N 13
Mariner Bus. Cen.
CR0: Wad 2L 63
Mariner Gdns. TW10: Ham 4J 25
Mariners Dr. GU3: Norm 9M 91
GU14: Farnb 8A 70
Marion Av. TW17: Shep 4C 38
Marion M. SE21 . . . . 4N 29
Marion Rd. CR7: T Hea 4N 45
RH10: Craw 5F 182
Marius Mans. SW17 . . . . 3E 28
Marius Rd. SW17 . . . . 3E 28
Marjoram Cl. GU2: Guil 8K 93
GU14: Cove 1G 89
Marjoram Ct. RH6: Horl 6G 142
(off Newman Rd.)
Marjorie Fosters Way
GU24: B'wood 6A 72
Marke Cl. BR2: Kes 1G 66
Markedge La. CR5: Coul 2D 102
RH1: Mers 2D 102
Markenfield Rd.
GU1: Guil 3C 202 (3N 113)
Markenhorn GU7: Godal 4G 132
Market, The SM1: Sut 7A 44
Market Centre, The
UB2: S'hall 1J 9
Market Dr. W4 . . . . 3D 12
Marketfield Rd. RH1: Red 3D 122
Marketfield Way
RH1: Red 3D 122
Market House, The
RH19: E Grin 9B 166
(off Cantelupe Rd.)
Market Pde. KT17: Ewe 5E 60
(off High St.)
SE25 . . . . 3D 46
TW13: Hanw 4M 23
Market Pl.
KT1: K Tham . . . 3H 203 (1K 41)
RG12: Brac 1N 31
RG40: W'ham 2B 30
SL3: Coln 3E 6
TW8: Brent 3J 11
Market Rd. TW9: Rich 6N 11
Market Sq. GU21: Wok 4A 74
KT1: K Tham 4H 203
(off Market Pl.)
RH12: Hors 7J 197
TN16: Weste 4M 107
TW18: Stain 6G 21
Market St.
GU1: Guil 5C 202 (4N 113)
RG12: Brac 1N 31
SL4: W'sor 4G 5
Market Ter. TW8: Brent 2L 11
(off Albany Rd.)
Market Way TN16: Weste 4M 107
Markfield CR0: Sels 6J 65
(not continuous)
Markfield Rd. CR3: Cate 4E 104
Markham Ct. GU15: Camb 9B 50
Markham Ho. GU14: Farnb 5N 89
(off Kenley Pl.)
Markham M. RG40: W'ham 2A 30
Markham Rd. RH5: Cap 5J 159
Markhole Cl.
TW12: Hamp 8N 23
Mark Oak La. KT22: Fetc 9A 78
Marksbury Av. TW9: Rich 6N 11
Marks Rd. CR6: Warl 5H 85
Mark St. RH2: Reig 2N 121
Markville Gdns. CR3: Cate 3D 104
Mark Way
GU7: Hurt, Godal 3E 132
Markway TW16: Sunb 1K 39
Markwick La. GU8: Loxh 6L 153
Marlborough SW19 . . . . 2J 27
(off Inner Pk. Rd.)
Marlborough Bus. Cen.
KT16: Chert 8H 37
Marlborough Cl. GU51: Fleet . . . 5E 88
KT12: Hers 9L 39
RH11: Craw 7A 182
RH12: Hors 3K 197
SW19 . . . . 7C 28
Marlborough Ct.
CR2: S Croy 7F 200
RG40: W'ham 1C 30
RH4: Dork 3K 201 (5H 119)
SM6: W'ton 4G 62
TN16: Weste 4L 107
(off Croydon Rd.)
Marlborough Cres. UB3: Harl . . . 3E 8
Marlborough Dr.
KT13: Weybr 9D 38
Marlborough Gdns.
KT6: Surb 6K 41
Marlborough Hill
RH4: Dork 3K 201 (5H 119)
Marlborough M. SM7: Ban 2M 81
MARLBOROUGH PARK 6C 90
Marlborough Pl.
RH12: Hors 5H 197
(off Rushams Rd.)
Marlborough Ri.
GU15: Camb 9C 50
Marlborough Rd.
CR2: S Croy 4N 63
GU21: Wok 3C 74
RH4: Dork 2K 201 (5H 119)
SL3: Lang 1A 6
SM1: Sut 9M 43
SW19 . . . . 7C 28
TW7: Isle 4H 11
TW10: Rich 9M 11
TW12: Hamp 7A 24
TW13: Felt 3L 23
TW15: Ashf 6M 21
W4 . . . . 1B 12
Marlborough Vw.
GU14: Cove 9H 69
Marld, The KT21: Asht 5M 79
Marles La. RH14: T Have 7D 194
Marley Av. GU27: Hasl 5C 188
Marley Cl. KT15: Addl 3H 55
Marley Combe Rd.
GU27: Hasl 3D 188
MARLEY COMMON 5D 188
Marley Hanger GU27: Hasl 5E 188
Marley Hgts.
GU27: K Grn 8D 188
Marley La.
GU27: Hasl, K Grn 3C 188
Marley Ri. RH4: Dork 8G 119
Marl Fld. Cl. KT4: W Pk 7F 42
Marl Hurst TN8: Eden 8K 127
Marlin Cl. TW16: Sunb 7F 22
Marling Ct. TW12: Hamp 7N 23
Marlingdene Cl.
TW12: Hamp 7A 24
MARLING PARK 8N 23
Marlings Cl. CR3: Whyte 4B 84
Marlins Cl. SM1: Sut 2A 62
Marlis Cl. GU19: Bag 5J 51
Marlow Cl. SE20 . . . . 2E 46
Marlow Ct. RH10: Craw 2B 182
Marlow Cres. TW1: Twick 9F 10
Marlow Dr. SM3: Chea 8J 43
Marlowe Ho. KT1: K Tham 8H 203
Marlowe Sq. CR4: Mit 3G 44
Marlowe Way CR0: Bedd 8J 45
Marlow Ho. KT5: Surb 8K 203
TW11: Tedd 5G 25
Marlow Rd. SE20 . . . . 2E 46
Marlpit Av. CR5: Coul 4J 83
Marlpit Cl. RH19: E Grin 7A 166
TN8: Eden 8L 127
MARLPIT HILL 8K 127
Marlpit La. CR5: Coul 3H 83
Marl Rd. SW18 . . . . 7N 13
Marlyns Cl. GU4: B'ham 9C 94
Marlyns Dr. GU4: B'ham 8C 94
Marmot Rd. TW4: Houn 6L 9
Marncrest Cl. KT12: Hers 2J 57
Marnell Way TW4: Houn 6L 9
Marneys Cl. KT18: Eps 2N 79
Marnfield Cres. SW2 . . . . 2L 29
Marnham Pl. KT15: Addl 1L 55
Marqueen Towers SW16 . . . . . 8K 29
Marquis Ct. KT1: K Tham 8H 203
KT19: Eps 6J 201 (9C 60)
TW19: Stan 2N 21
Marrick Cl. SW15 . . . . 7F 12
Marriott Cl. TW14: Felt 9E 8
Marriott Lodge Cl.
KT15: Addl 1L 55
Marrowbrook Cl.
GU14: Cove 2M 89
Marrowbrook La.
GU14: Cove 3L 89
Marrowells KT13: Weybr 9G 38
Marrow Meade GU51: Fleet . . . 2A 88
Marryat Cl. TW4: Houn 7N 9
Marryat Pl. SW19 . . . . 5K 27
Marryat Rd. SW19 . . . . 6J 27
Marryat Sq. SW6 . . . . 4K 13
Marsden Way BR6: Orp 1N 67
Marshall Cl. CR2: Sande 9D 64
GU14: Cove 7L 69
GU16: Frim 4H 71
TW4: Houn 8N 9
Marshall Pde. GU22: Pyr 2H 75
Marshall Pl. KT15: N Haw 5L 55
Marshall Rd. GU7: Godal 6H 133
GU47: Coll T 8J 49
RH10: Craw 5G 183
Marshalls Cl.
KT19: Eps 6H 201 (9B 60)
Marshall's Rd. SM1: Sut 1N 61
Marsham Ho. RG42: Brac 8N 15

Orchard Way—Parbury Ri.

Orchard Way RH4: Dork 6H 119
RH8: Oxt 2C 126
RH19: E Grin 9A 166
SM1: Sut 1B 62
TW15: Ashf 3A 22
Orchid Cl. KT9: Ches 4J 59
Orchid Ct. TW20: Egh 5D 20
Orchid Dr. GU24: Bis 2D 72
Orchid Gdns. TW3: Houn 7N 9
Orchid Mead SM7: Ban 1N 81
Orde Cl. RH10: Craw 9H 163
Ordnance Cl. TW13: Felt 3H 23
Ordnance Rd. GU11: Alde 2N 109
Ordnance Rdbt. GU11: Alde 2N 109
Oregano Way GU2: Guil 7K 93
Oregon Cl. KT3: N Mal 3B 42
Orestan La. KT24: Eff 5J 97
Orewell Gdns. RH2: Reig 5N 121
Orford Ct. SE27 3M 29
Orford Gdns. TW1: Twick 3F 24
ORGAN CROSSROADS 4F 60
Oriel, The RH6: Horl 9E 142
Oriel Cl. CR4: Mit 3H 45
RH10: Craw 9G 162
Oriel Ct. CR0: Croy 1D 200 (7A 46)
Oriel Dr. SW13 2H 13
Oriel Hill GU15: Camb 2B 70
Oriental Cl. GU22: Wok 4B 74
Oriental Rd. GU22: Wok 4B 74
SL5: S'hill 3A 34
Orion RG12: Brac 7M 31
Orion Centre, The CR0: Bedd 3J 45
Orion Ct. RH11: Craw 5J 181
Orion M. SM4: Mord 3M 43
Orlando Gdns. KT19: Ewe 6C 60
Orleans Cl. KT10: Esh 8D 40
Orleans Ct. KT12: Wal T 8K 39
TW1: Twick 1H 25
Orleans House Gallery 2H 25
Orleans Pk. School Sports Cen. 1H 25
Orleans Rd. TW1: Twick 1H 25
Orltons La. RH12: Rusp 8E 160
Ormathwaites Cnr.
RG42: Warf 8C 16
Ormeley Rd. SW12 2F 28
Orme Rd. KT1: K Tham 1A 42
SM1: Sut 3N 61
Ormerod Gdns. CR4: Mit 1E 44
Ormesby Wlk. RH10: Craw 5F 182
Ormond Av. TW10: Rich 8K 11
TW12: Hamp 9B 24
Ormond Cres. TW12: Hamp 9B 24
Ormond Dr. TW12: Hamp 8B 24
Ormonde Av. KT19: Ewe 6C 60
Ormonde Ct. SW15 7H 13
Ormonde Pl. KT13: Weybr 3E 56
Ormonde Rd. GU7: Godal 5H 133
GU21: Wok 3M 73
RG41: W'ham 3A 30
SW14 6B 12
Ormond Rd. TW10: Rich 8K 11
Ormsby SM2: Sut 4N 61
Ormside Way RH1: Red 8F 102
Orpen Ho. *SW5* 1M 13
(off Trebovir Rd.)
Orpheus Centre, The 8D 104
Orpin Rd. RH1: Mers 8F 102
Orpwood Cl. TW12: Hamp 7N 23
Orwell Cl. GU14: Cove 8K 69
SL4: W'sor 6G 4
Orwell Ct. *SW17* 4B 28
(off Grosvenor Way)
Osborne Av. TW19: Stan 2N 21
Osborne Cl. BR3: Beck 3H 47
GU16: Frim 6D 70
TW13: Hanw 6L 23
Osborne Ct. GU14: Farnb 5A 90
GU51: Fleet 5A 88
RH11: Craw 7N 181
SL4: W'sor 5F 4
Osborne Dr. GU18: Ligh 7L 51
GU52: Fleet 6C 88
Osborne Gdns. CR7: T Hea 1N 45
Osborne La. RG42: Warf 6A 16
Osborne M. SL4: W'sor 5F 4
Osborne Pl. SM1: Sut 2B 62
Osborne Rd. CR7: T Hea 1N 45
GU14: Farnb 4A 90
KT2: K Tham 8L 203
KT12: Wal T 7H 39
RG40: W'ham 2B 30
RH1: Red 9E 102
SL4: W'sor 5F 4
TW3: Houn 6N 9
TW20: Egh 7B 20
Osborne Ter. *SW17* 6D 28
(off Church La.)
Osborne Way KT9: Ches 2M 59
KT19: Eps 8L 59
Osborn Rd. GU9: Farnh 8J 109
Osbourne Ho. TW2: Twick 3C 24
Oscar Cl. CR8: Pur 6L 63
Osier Ct. *TW8: Brent* 2L 11
(off Ealing Rd.)
Osier M. W4 2D 12
Osier Pl. TW20: Egh 7E 20
Osiers Ct. KT1: K Tham 2H 203
Osiers Rd. SW18 7M 13
Osiers Twr. *SW18* 7M 13
(off Enterprise Way)
Osier Way CR4: Mit 4D 44
SM7: Ban 1K 81
Osman's Cl. RG42: Wink R 8F 16
Osmond Gdns. SM6: W'ton 2G 62
Osmunda Bank RH19: D Pk 4A 166
Osmund Cl. RH10: Worth 3J 183
Osnaburgh Hill
GU15: Camb 1N 69
Osney Cl. RH11: Craw 4A 182
Osney Wlk. SM5: Cars 5B 44
Osprey Av. RG12: Brac 3J 31
Osprey Cl. KT22: Fetc 9C 78
SM1: Sut 2L 61
Osprey Ct. CR0: Croy 5C 200
Osprey Dr. KT18: Tat C 4G 81
Osprey Gdns. CR2: Sels 6H 65
GU11: Alde 5M 109
Ostade Rd. SW2 1K 29
OSTERLEY 3D 10
Osterley Av. TW7: Isle 3D 10
Osterley Cl. RG40: W'ham 3E 30
Osterley Ct. TW7: Isle 4D 10
Osterley Cres. TW7: Isle 4E 10
Osterley Gdns. CR7: T Hea 1N 45
Osterley La. TW7: Isle 1C 10
UB2: S'hall 1A 10
Osterley Lodge *TW7: Isle* 3E 10
(off Church Rd.)
Osterley Pk. 2C 10
Osterley Pk. House 2C 10
Osterley Rd. TW7: Isle 3E 10
Osterley Sports & Athletics Cen. 3E 10
Osterley Station
(Underground) 3D 10
Ostlers Dr. TW15: Ashf 6D 22
Oswald Cl. KT22: Fetc 9C 78
RG42: Warf 8C 16
Oswald Rd. KT22: Fetc 9C 78
Osward CR0: Sels 5J 65
(not continuous)
Osward Rd. SW17 3D 28
Otford Cl. RH11: Craw 9A 182
Othello Gro. RG42: Warf 9C 16
Otho Ct. TW8: Brent 3K 11
Otterbourne Pl.
RH19: E Grin 9L 165
Otterbourne Rd.
CR0: Croy 2B 200 (8N 45)
Otterburn Gdns. TW7: Isle 3G 10
Otterburn St. SW17 7D 28
Otter Cl. GU12: Alde 1B 110
KT16: Otter 3D 54
RG45: Crowt 9F 30
Otterden Cl. BR6: Orp 1N 67
Otter Dr. SM5: Cars 7D 44
Ottermead La. KT16: Otter 3E 54
Otter Mdw. KT22: Leat 6F 78
OTTERSHAW 3E 54
Ottershaw Pk. KT16: Otter 4C 54
(not continuous)
Ottway's Av. KT21: Asht 6K 79
Ottways La. KT21: Asht 7K 79
Otway Cl. RH11: Craw 5L 181
Oulton Wlk. RH10: Craw 5F 182
Ouseley Lodge SL4: O Win 1M 19
Ouseley Rd. SL4: O Win 1M 19
SW12 2D 28
TW19: Wray 1M 19
Outdowns KT24: Eff 8J 97
Outfield Cres. RG40: W'ham 3A 30
Outram Pl. KT13: Weybr 2D 56
Outram Rd. CR0: Croy 8C 46
OUTWOOD 3N 143
OUTWOOD COMMON 3N 143
Outwood Ho. *SW2* 1K 29
(off Deepdene Gdns.)
Outwood La.
CR5: Chip, K'wood 7C 82
KT20: K'wood 9N 81
RH1: Blet, Sth N 2A 124
RH1: Out 3A 144
Outwood Windmill 3A 144
Ouzel Chase RG12: Brac 4J 31
Oval, The GU2: Guil 4K 113
GU3: Wood V 2E 112
GU7: Godal 4J 133
SM7: Ban 1M 81
Oval Ho. CR0: Croy 1F 200
Oval Rd. CR0: Croy 2E 200 (8A 46)
Overbrook GU7: Godal 6K 133
KT24: W Hors 7C 96
Overbury Av. BR3: Beck 2L 47
Overbury Cres. CR0: N Add 6M 65
Overdale KT21: Asht 2L 79
RH1: Blet 2N 123
RH5: Dork 4J 119
Overdale Av. KT3: N Mal 1B 42
Overdale Ri. GU16: Frim 3C 70
Overdene Dr. RH11: Craw 3M 181
Overford Cl. GU6: Cranl 8M 155
Overford Dr. GU6: Cranl 8N 155
Overhill CR6: Warl 6F 84
Overhill Rd. CR8: Pur 5L 63
Overhill Way BR3: Beck 4N 47
Overlord Cl. GU15: Camb 7A 50
Overlord Ct. KT22: Fetc 8D 78
Overstand Cl. BR3: Beck 4K 47
Overstone Gdns. CR0: Croy 6J 47
Overthorpe Cl. GU21: Knap 4H 73
Overton Cl. GU11: Alde 6A 110
TW7: Isle 4F 10
Overton Ct. GU10: Tong 6D 110
RH19: E Grin 9A 166
SM2: Sut 4M 61
Overton Ho. *SW15* 1E 26
(off Tangley Gro.)
Overton Rd. SM2: Sut 3M 61
Overton Shaw RH19: E Grin 6A 166
Overton's Yd.
CR0: Croy 4B 200 (9N 45)
Oveton Way KT23: Book 4A 98
Ovington Ct. GU21: Wok 3J 73
Owen Cl. CR0: Croy 5A 46
SL3: Lang 1B 6
TW16: Sunb 9F 22
Owen Ho. TW1: Twick 1H 25
TW14: Felt 1H 23
Owen Mans. *W14* 2K 13
(off Queen's Club Gdns.)
Owen Pl. KT22: Leat 9H 79
Owen Rd. GU7: Godal 5J 133
GU20: Windl 2A 52
Owers Cl. RH13: Hors 6L 197
Owlbeech Ct. RH13: Hors 4A 198
Owlbeech Pl. RH13: Hors 4A 198
Owlbeech Way RH13: Hors 4A 198
Owl Cl. CR2: Sels 6G 65
Owletts RH10: Craw 2H 183
Owlscastle Cl.
RH12: Hors 3K 197
OWLSMOOR 6K 49
Owlsmoor Rd.
GU47: Coll T, Owls 7J 49
Ownstead Gdns.
CR2: Sande 7C 64
Ownsted Hill CR0: N Add 6M 65
Oxberry Av. SW6 5K 13
Oxdowne Cl. KT11: Sto D 1B 78
Oxenden Ct. GU10: Tong 4C 110
Oxenden Rd. GU10: Tong 4C 110
Oxenhope RG12: Brac 3M 31
Oxfield *TN8: Eden* 9M 127
(off Woodpecker Cl.)
Oxford Av. SW20 1K 43
TW5: Hest 1A 10
UB3: Harl 1G 8
Oxford Cl. CR4: Mit 2G 44
TW15: Ashf 8D 22
Oxford Ct.
KT18: Eps 8L 201 (1D 80)
TW13: Hanw 5L 23
W4 1A 12
Oxford Cres. KT3: N Mal 5C 42
Oxford Gdns. W4 1N 11
Oxford Rd.
GU1: Guil 6D 202 (5N 113)
GU14: Farnb 4A 90
GU47: Owls 5K 49
RG41: W'ham 2A 30
RH1: Red 2C 122
RH10: Craw 7C 182
RH13: Hors 6K 197
SL4: W'sor 4F 4
SM5: Cars 3C 62
SM6: W'ton 2G 62
SW15 7K 13
TW11: Tedd 6D 24
Oxford Rd. E. SL4: W'sor 4F 4
Oxford Rd. Nth. W4 1M 11
Oxford Rd. Sth. W4 1N 11
Oxfordshire Pl. RG42: Warf 8D 16
Oxford Ter.
GU1: Guil 6D 202 (5N 113)
Oxford Way TW13: Hanw 5L 23
Ox La. KT17: Ewe 5F 60
Oxleigh Cl. KT3: N Mal 4D 42
Oxlip Cl. CR0: Croy 7G 46
OXSHOTT 9D 58
Oxshott Lodge KT22: Oxs 1D 78
Oxshott Ri. KT11: Cob 9L 57
Oxshott Rd. KT22: Leat 3E 78
Oxshott Station (Rail) 9C 58
Oxshott Village Sports Club 1C 78
Oxshott Way KT11: Cob 2M 77
OXTED 7A 106
Oxted Cl. CR4: Mit 2B 44
Oxted Ct. *RH1: Red* 1F 122
(off Reynolds Av.)
Oxted Grn. GU8: Mil 3B 152
Oxted Rd. RH9: Gods 8F 104
Oxted Station (Rail) 7A 106
Oxtoby Way SW16 9H 29
Oyster La. KT14: Byf 6M 55

P

Pachesham Dr. KT22: Leat 3F 78
PACHESHAM PARK 3F 78
Pachesham Pk. KT22: Leat 3G 78
Pachesham Pk. Golf Course 5E 78
Pacific Cl. TW14: Felt 2G 23
Packer Cl. RH19: E Grin 6C 166
Packham Ct. KT4: W Pk 9H 43
Packway GU9: Farnh 4K 129
Padbrook RH8: Limp 7C 106
(not continuous)
Padbrook Cl. RH8: Limp 7C 106
Padbury Cl. TW14: Bedf 2E 22
Padbury Oaks UB7: L'ford 4K 7
Paddock, The GU1: Guil 2F 114
GU6: Cranl 7M 155
GU6: Ewh 6F 156
GU7: Godal 8H 133
GU10: Wrec 7E 128
GU18: Ligh 7M 51
GU26: G'hott 5M 169
GU27: Hasl 9E 170
GU35: Head 4D 168
RG45: Crowt 1F 48
RH4: Westc 6B 118
RH10: Craw 2H 183
Paddock, The SL3: Dat 4L 5
SL4: Wink 1J 17
(Lakeview Pk. Caravan Site)
SL4: Wink 2M 17
(Squirrel La.)
TN16: Weste 4L 107
Paddock Cl. BR6: Farnb 1K 67
GU8: Hamb 9F 152
GU15: Camb 9E 50
KT4: W Pk 7D 42
RH5: B Grn 7K 139
RH7: Ling 8M 145
RH8: Oxt 9B 106
SL4: W'sor 4C 4
TN8: Eden 9L 127
Paddock Gdns.
RH19: E Grin 2A 186
Paddock Ga. SL4: Wink 3M 17
Paddock Gro. RH5: B Grn 7K 139
Paddock Ho. *GU4: Guil* 2F 114
(off Merrow St.)
Paddockhurst Rd.
RH10: Turn H 9K 183
RH11: Craw 4M 181
RH17: Turn H 9K 183
Paddock Mobile Home Pk.
BR2: Kes 5G 67
Paddocks, The CR0: A'ton 3K 65
GU3: Flex 3N 111
GU25: V Wat 5A 36
KT13: Weybr 9F 38
KT15: N Haw 6K 55
KT23: Book 4B 98
Paddocks Cl. KT11: Cob 1K 77
KT21: Asht 5L 79
Paddocks Mead GU21: Wok 3H 73
Paddocks Rd. GU4: B'ham 8C 94
Paddocks Way KT16: Chert 7K 37
KT21: Asht 5L 79
Paddock Wlk. CR6: Warl 6E 84
Paddock Way GU21: Wok 1D 74
GU27: G'wood 7L 171
RH8: Oxt 9B 106
SW15 1H 27
Padley Cl. KT9: Ches 2M 59
Padstow Wlk. RH11: Craw 5K 181
TW14: Felt 2G 22
Padwick Rd. RH13: Hors 6N 197
Pageant Wlk.
CR0: Croy 4F 200 (9B 46)
Page Cl. TW12: Hamp 7M 23
Page Ct. RH10: Craw 4D 182
RH13: Hors 7K 197
Page Cres. CR0: Wad 2M 63
Page Cft. KT15: Addl 8K 37
Pagehurst Rd. CR0: Croy 6E 46
Pageites GU7: Godal 4E 132
Page Rd. TW14: Bedf 9E 8
Page's Cft. RG40: W'ham 3C 30
Pages Yd. W4 2E 12
Paget Av. SM1: Sut 9B 44
Paget Cl. GU15: Camb 8F 50
RH13: Hors 8L 197
TW12: H Hill 5D 24
Paget La. TW7: Isle 6D 10
Paget Pl. KT2: K Tham 7B 26
KT7: T Dit 7F 40
PAGEWOOD 3J 161
Pagewood Cl. RH10: Craw 5H 183
Pagoda Av. TW9: Rich 6M 11
Pagoda Gro. SE27 3N 29
Paice Grn. RG40: W'ham 1C 30
Painesfield Dr. KT16: Chert 7J 37
Pain's Cl. CR4: Mit 1F 44
PAINS HILL
KT11 1G 76
RH8 9E 106
PAINSHILL 9G 56
Pains Hill RH8: Limp 1E 126
Pains Hill Ho. KT11: Cob 1G 77
Painshill Pk. 1G 76
Paisley Rd. SM5: Cars 7B 44
Paisley Ter. SM5: Cars 6B 44
Pakenham Cl. SW12 2E 28
Pakenham Dr. GU11: Alde 1M 109
Pakenham Rd. RG12: Brac 6B 32
Palace Ct. *GU21: Wok* 3C 74
(off Maybury Rd.)
Palace Dr. KT13: Weybr 9C 38
Palace Grn. CR0: Sels 4J 65
Palace Mans. KT1: K Tham 8H 203
Palace M. SW6 3L 13
Palace Rd.
KT1: K Tham 8H 203 (3K 41)
KT8: E Mol 2C 40
SW2 2K 29
TN16: Weste 8J 87
Palace Vw. CR0: Croy 1J 65
Palace Way GU22: Wok 7D 74
KT13: Weybr 9C 38
Palace Wharf *W6* 3H 13
(off Rainville Rd.)
Palemead Cl. SW6 4J 13
Palestine Gro. SW19 9B 28
Palewell Comn. Dr. SW14 8C 12
Palewell Pk. SW14 8C 12
Palgrave Ct. TW11: H Wic 8J 25
Palgrave Ho. TW2: Whitt 1C 24
Palladino Ho. *SW17* 6C 28
(off Laurel Cl.)
Palladio Ct. *SW18* 9N 13
(off Mapleton Cres.)
Pallant Way BR6: Farnb 1J 67
Pallingham Dr.
RH10: Craw 6G 182
Palliser Ct. *W14* 1K 13
(off Palliser Rd.)
Palliser Rd. W14 1K 13
Pallister Ter. SW15 4E 26
Palmer Av. SM3: Chea 1H 61
Palmer Cl. BR4: W Wick 9N 47
RG40: W'ham 8F 30
RH1: Red 4E 122
RH6: Horl 6D 142
TW5: Hest 4A 10
Palmer Ct. RG40: W'ham 2B 30
Palmer Cres.
KT1: K Tham 5J 203 (2L 41)
KT16: Otter 3F 54
Palmer Rd. RH10: Craw 6G 182
Palmer School Rd.
RG40: W'ham 2B 30
PALMERS CROSS 4F 154
Palmersfield Rd. SM7: Ban 1M 81
Palmers Gro. KT8: W Mole 3A 40
Palmers Lodge GU2: Guil 4K 113
Palmers Pas. *SW14* 6B 12
(off Little St Leonard's)
Palmers Rd. SW14 6B 12
SW16 1K 45
Palmerston Cl. GU14: Cove 2J 89
GU21: Wok 1C 74
RH1: Red 6E 122
Palmerston Ct. KT6: Surb 6K 41
Palmerstone Ct.
GU25: V Wat 4A 36
(off Ridge Way)
Palmerston Gro. SW19 8M 27
Palmerston Ho. *SM7: Ban* 2L 81
(off Basing Rd.)
Palmerston Mans. *W14* 2K 13
(off Queen's Club Gdns.)
Palmerston Rd. BR6: Farnb 1L 67
CR0: Croy 4A 46
SM1: Sut 2A 62
SM5: Cars 1D 62
SW14 7B 12
SW19 8M 27
TW2: Twick 9E 10
TW3: Houn 4C 10
Palmers Wharf
KT1: K Tham 4G 203
Palm Gro. GU1: Guil 7M 93
Pampisford Rd.
CR2: S Croy 5M 63
CR8: Pur 7L 63
Pams Way KT19: Ewe 2C 60
Pankhurst Cl. TW7: Isle 6F 10
Pankhurst Ct. RH11: Craw 8N 181
Pankhurst Dr. RG12: Brac 4B 32
Pankhurst Rd. KT12: Wal T 6K 39
Panmuir Rd. SW20 9G 27
Pannell Cl. RH19: E Grin 1N 185
Pannells GU10: Lwr Bou 6J 129
Pannells Ash RH14: Ifo 5E 192
Pannells Cl. KT16: Chert 7H 37
Pannells Ct.
GU1: Guil 5D 202 (4N 113)
TW5: Hest 2A 10
Pan's Gdns. GU15: Camb 2D 70
Pantile Rd. KT13: Weybr 1E 56
Pantiles Cl. GU21: Wok 5L 73
Panton Cl.
CR0: Croy 1A 200 (7M 45)
Papercourt La. GU23: Rip 9H 75
Papercourt Sailing Club 9H 75
Paper M.
RH4: Dork 1L 201 (4H 119)
Papermill Cl. SM5: Cars 1E 62
Papworth Way SW2 1L 29
Parade, The CR0: Croy 5J 45
GU2: Guil 7L 93
(off Burden Way)
GU12: Ash V 9E 90
GU16: Frim 6B 70
GU25: V Wat 5N 35
GU46: Yate 9D 48
KT2: K Tham 3K 203
KT4: W Pk 1E 60
KT10: Clay 3E 58
KT17: Eps 7K 201 (9C 60)
KT18: Eps 1N 79
(off Spa Dr.)
KT20: Tad 6K 81
KT22: Leat 7G 79
(off Kingston Rd.)
RH1: Red 4E 122
RH10: Craw 2C 182
RH12: Hors 5G 197
(off Cootes Av.)
RH19: E Grin 7L 165
SL4: W'sor 4A 4
SM1: Sut 9L 43
SM5: Cars 2D 62
(off Beynon Rd.)
TN16: Tats 8E 86
(off Ship Hill)
TW12: H Hill 6D 24
TW16: Sunb 8G 23
TW18: Stain 6F 20
(off Meadow Gdns.)
Parade Ct. KT24: E Hor 4F 96
Parade M. SE27 3M 29
Paradise Rd. TW9: Rich 8K 11
Paragon *TW8: Brent* 1J 11
(off Boston Pk. Rd.)
Paragon Cotts. GU4: E Cla 9M 95
Paragon Gro. KT5: Surb 5M 41
Paragon Pl. KT5: Surb 5M 41
Parbury Ri. KT9: Ches 3L 59

Parchmore Rd.—Pawsons Rd.

Parchmore Rd. CR7: T Hea 1M 45
Parchmore Way CR7: T Hea . . .1M 45
Pares Cl. GU21: Wok 3N 73
Parfitts Cl. GU9: Farnh 1F 128
Parfour Dr. CR8: Ken 3N 83
Parfrey St. W6 . . . . .2H 13
Parham Rd. RH11: Craw 2L 181
Parish Cl. GU9: Up Hale 6F 108
GU12: Ash 3F 110
Parish Ct. KT6: Surb 4L 41
Parish Ho. RH11: Craw 4B 182
Parish Rd. GU14: Farnb 5A 90
Parison Cl. TW9: Rich 6N 11
Park, The KT23: Book 1A 98
RH4: Dork 7G 118
SM5: Cars 2D 62
Park & Ride
Artington (Guildford) . . .8M 113
Hop Oast (Horsham) 9G 196
Kingston upon Thames . . .5J 59
Merrow (Guildford) 2G 115
Spectrum (Guildford) . . .1B 114
Windsor Home Park 2H 5
Windsor Legoland 8B 4
Park Av. BR4: W Wick 8M 47
CR3: Cate 2B 104
CR4: Mit 8F 28
GU8: P Har 6N 131
GU15: Camb 2A 70
RG40: W'ham 3A 30
RH1: Salf 2D 142
SM5: Cars 3E 62
SW14 . . . . .7C 12
TN8: Eden 1K 147
TW3: Houn 9B 10
TW17: Shep 2F 38
TW18: Stain 7H 21
TW19: Wray 8N 5
TW20: Egh 7E 20
Park Av. E. KT17: Ewe 3F 60
Park Av. M. CR4: Mit 8F 28
Park Av. W. KT17: Ewe 3F 60
PARK BARN 2H 113
Park Barn Dr. GU2: Guil 1H 113
Park Barn E. GU2: Guil 2J 113
Park Barn Pde. GU2: Guil 3H 113
(off Southway)
Park Chase
GU1: Guil 3E 202 (3A 114)
GU7: Godal 9H 133
Park Cl. GU27: G'wood 8K 171
KT2: K Tham 1M 203 (9N 25)
KT10: Esh 3A 58
KT12: Wal T 8G 38
KT14: Byf 9M 55
KT15: N Haw 6K 55
KT22: Fetc 2D 98
RH3: Brock 8A 120
RH8: Oxt 6B 106
SL4: W'sor 5G 5
SM5: Cars 3D 62
TW3: Houn 8C 10
TW12: Hamp 9C 24
W4 . . . . .2C 12
Park Copse RH5: Dork 5K 119
Park Corner SL4: W'sor 6B 4
Park Cnr. Dr. KT24: E Hor 6F 96
Park Cotts. RH5: For G 2L 157
Park Ct. CR2: S Croy 8B 200
GU9: Farnh 9J 109
GU22: Wok 5B 74
KT1: H Wic 9J 25
KT3: N Mal 3C 42
KT14: W By 9J 55
SE21 . . . . .4N 29
SM6: W'ton 2J 63
Park Crematorium, The
GU12: Alde 6B 110
Park Cres. RH18: F Row 7J 187
SL5: S'dale 5C 34
TW2: Twick 2D 24
Parkdale Cres. KT4: W Pk 9C 42
Park Dr. GU5: Braml 5B 134
GU6: Cranl 6A 156
GU22: Wok 5B 74
KT13: Weybr 2C 56
KT21: Asht 5N 79
SL5: S'dale 5C 34
SW14 . . . . .8C 12
Parker Cl. RH10: Craw 4H 183
SM5: Cars 3D 62
Parke Rd. SW13 . . . . .4F 12
TW16: Sunb 3H 39
Parker Rd.
CR0: Croy 6C 200 (1N 63)
Parker's Cl. KT21: Asht 6L 79
Parkers Ct. GU19: Bag 4J 51
Parker's Hill KT21: Asht 6L 79
Parker's La. KT21: Asht 6L 79
RG42: Wink R 4F 16
Park Farm Cl. RH12: Hors 1K 197
Park Farm Ind. Est.
GU16: Camb 5A 70
Park Farm Rd. KT2: K Tham 8L 25
RH12: Hors 1K 197
Parkfield GU7: Bus 9H 133
RH12: Hors 5J 197
TW7: Isle 4E 10
Parkfield Av. SW14 . . . . .7D 12
TW13: Felt 4H 23
Parkfield Cl. RH11: Craw 4L 181
Parkfield Cres. TW13: Felt 4H 23
Parkfield Ho. RG45: Crowt 3H 49
(off Cambridge Rd.)
Parkfield Pde. TW13: Felt 4H 23
Parkfield Rd. SW4 . . . . .1H 29
TW13: Felt 4H 23
Parkfields CR0: Croy 7J 47
GU46: Yate 1C 68
KT22: Oxs 7D 58
SW15 . . . . .7H 13
Parkfields Av. SW20 . . . . .9G 26
Parkfields Cl. SM5: Cars 1E 62
Parkfields Rd.
KT2: K Tham 6M 25
Park Gdns. KT2: K Tham 6M 25
PARKGATE 7C 140
Parkgate Cl. KT2: K Tham 7A 26
Park Gate Cotts.
GU6: Cranl 7K 155
Park Gate Ct. GU22: Wok 5A 74
TW12: H Hill 7C 24
Parkgate Gdns. SW14 . . . . .8C 12
Parkgate Rd. RH2: Reig 4N 121
RH5: Newd 9A 140
SM6: W'ton 2E 62
Park Grn. KT23: Book 2A 98
Park Hall Rd. RH2: Reig 1M 121
SE21 . . . . .4N 29
Park Hall Trad. Est. SE21 . . . . .4N 29
Parkham Ho. RH1: Red 1F 122
(off Reynolds Av.)
Park Hgts. GU22: Wok 5A 74
(off Constitution Hill)
KT18: Eps 8J 201 (1C 80)
Park Hill GU52: Chu C 8A 88
SM5: Cars 3C 62
TW10: Rich 9M 11
Parkhill KT10: Esh 1C 58
Park Hill Cl. SM5: Cars 2C 62
Parkhill Cl. GU17: B'water 2J 69
Park Hill Ct. SW17 . . . . .4D 28
Park Hill M.
CR2: S Croy 8E 200 (2A 64)
Park Hill Ri. CR0: Croy 8B 46
Park Hill Rd. BR2: Brom 1N 47
CR0: Croy
. . . . . .3F 200 & 6F 200 (8B 46)
KT17: Ewe 7E 60
SM6: W'ton 4F 62
Parkhill Rd. GU17: B'water 2J 69
Park Horsley KT24: E Hor 7H 97
Park Ho. Dr. RH2: Reig 5L 121
Park Ho. Gdns. TW1: Twick 8J 11
Parkhurst KT19: Eps 6B 60
Parkhurst Flds.
GU10: Churt 9L 149
Parkhurst Gro. RH6: Horl 7C 142
Parkhurst Rd. GU2: Guil 2K 113
RH6: Horl 7C 142
SM1: Sut 1B 62
Parkland Av. SL3: Lang 1N 5
Parkland Dr. RG12: Brac 9C 16
Parkland Gdns. SW19 . . . . .2J 27
Parkland Gro. GU9: Weybo . . .4L 109
TW15: Ashf 4B 22
Parkland Rd. TW15: Ashf 5B 22
PARKLANDS 1A 136
Parklands GU2: Guil 8K 93
KT5: Surb 4M 41
KT15: Addl 2L 55
KT23: Book 1A 98
RH1: Red 1E 122
RH5: Nth H 9H 119
RH8: Oxt 9A 106
Parklands Cl. GU9: Farnh 4K 129
SW14 . . . . .8B 12
Parklands Cotts.
GU5: Shere 1A 136
Parklands Ct. KT19: Eps 8L 59
TW5: Hest 5L 9
Parklands Dr. GU6: Cranl 7B 156
Parklands Gro. TW7: Isle 4F 10
Parklands Pde. TW5: Hest 5L 9
(off Parklands Ct.)
Parklands Pl. GU1: Guil 3D 114
Parklands Rd. SW16 . . . . .6F 28
Parklands Way KT4: W Pk 8D 42
Park La. CR0: Croy . . .3D 200 (9A 46)
CR5: Coul 8H 83
GU4: Guil 9F 94
GU8: Brook 2J 171
GU10: Churt 9G 149
GU15: Camb 1A 70
KT21: Asht 5M 79
RG42: Bin 8K 15
RH2: Reig 4K 121
RH5: B Grn, Ockl 4F 158
RH19: Ash W, E Grin 3F 186
SL3: Hort 6C 6
SL4: Wink 2M 17
SM3: Chea 3K 61
SM5: Cars 1E 62
SM6: W'ton 2E 62
TW5: C'ford 3H 9
TW9: Rich 7K 11
TW11: Tedd 7F 24
Park La. E. RH2: Reig 6L 121
Park La. Mans. CR0: Croy 5D 200
PARK LANGLEY 3M 47
Parklangley Club, The 3M 47
Parklawn Av. KT18: Eps 9A 60
RH6: Horl 6D 142
Park Lawn Rd. KT13: Weybr . . .1D 56
Parkleigh Rd. SW19 . . . . .1N 43
Park Ley Rd. CR3: Wold 7G 85
Parkleys TW10: Ham 5K 25
Parkleys Pde. TW10: Ham 5K 25
Park Mnr. SM2: Sut 4A 62
(off Christchurch Pk.)
Parkmead GU6: Cranl 6A 156
SW15 . . . . .9G 12
Parkmead Cl. CR0: Croy 5G 46
Park M. RH8: Oxt 6B 106
SE24 . . . . .1N 29
TW19: Stan 1A 22
Parkpale La.
RH3: Betch, Brock 8N 119
Park Pl. GU17: Haw 3L 69
GU22: Wok 5B 74
(off Hill Vw. Rd.)
GU52: Chu C 8A 88
RH12: Hors 7J 197
TW12: H Hill 7C 24
Park Ride SL4: W'sor 1A 18
Park Ri. KT22: Leat 8H 79
RH12: Hors 4H 197
Park Ri. Cl. KT22: Leat 8H 79
Park Rd. CR3: Cate 1B 104
CR6: Warl 1A 86
CR8: Ken 2M 83
GU1: Guil 3C 202 (3N 113)
GU5: Alb 9N 115
GU7: Godal 9H 133
GU9: Farnh 8J 109
GU11: Alde 4N 109
GU14: Farnb 4C 90
GU15: Camb 9B 50
GU22: Wok 4B 74
(not continuous)
GU27: Hasl 2G 188
GU47: Sandh 8H 49
KT1: H Wic 9J 25
KT2: K Tham . . .1M 203 (6M 25)
KT3: N Mal 3C 42
KT5: Surb 5M 41
KT8: E Mol 3C 40
KT10: Esh 1B 58
KT21: Asht 5L 79
RG12: Brac 1B 32
RG40: W'ham 2A 30
RH1: Red 1D 122
(not continuous)
RH6: Smallf 1N 163
RH7: Crow 9A 126
RH8: Oxt 6B 106
RH12: Fay 8E 180
RH13: Slinf 5L 195
RH17: Hand 9N 199
RH18: F Row 7J 187
RH19: D Pk 4A 166
RH19: E Grin 9N 165
SE25 . . . . .3B 46
SM3: Chea 3K 61
SM6: W'ton 2F 62
(Clifton Rd.)
SM6: W'ton 8F 44
(Elmwood Cl.)
SM7: Ban 2N 81
SW19 . . . . .7B 28
TW1: Twick 9J 11
TW3: Houn 8B 10
TW7: Isle 4H 11
TW10: Rich 9M 11
TW11: Tedd 7F 24
TW12: H Hill 5B 24
TW13: Hanw 5L 23
TW15: Ashf 6C 22
TW16: Sunb 8J 23
TW17: Shep 7B 38
TW19: Stan, Stan M 9K 7
TW20: Egh 5C 20
W4 . . . . .3B 12
Park Rd. Ho.
KT2: K Tham 1M 203 (8N 25)
Park Rd. Nth. W4 . . . . .1C 12
Park Rd. Rdbt. GU14: Farnb 5C 90
Park Row GU9: Farnh 9G 109
SW2 . . . . .1L 29
Parkshot TW9: Rich 7K 11
Parkside GU9: Up Hale 6H 109
KT15: N Haw 7K 55
RH10: Craw 3C 182
RH19: E Grin 9M 165
SM3: Chea 3K 61
SW19 . . . . .4J 27
TW12: H Hill 6D 24
Parkside Av. SW19 . . . . .6J 27
Parkside Cl. KT24: E Hor 3G 96
Parkside Cotts. GU4: W Cla . . .1J 115
Parkside Ct. KT13: Weybr 1B 56
RH1: Red 8D 102
Parkside Cres. KT5: Surb 5B 42
Parkside Gdns. CR5: Coul 4F 82
SW19 . . . . .5J 27
Parkside M. CR6: Warl 3K 85
RH12: Hors 6K 197
Parkside Pl. KT24: E Hor 3G 96
TW18: Stain 7J 21
Parkside Rd. SL5: S'dale 4D 34
TW3: Houn 8B 10
Parkside Ter. BR6: Farnb 1K 67
(off Willow Wlk.)
Park Sq. KT10: Esh 1B 58
SL4: Wink 2M 17
Parkstead Rd. SW15 . . . . .8F 12
Parkstone Dr. GU15: Camb 2A 70
PARK STREET 5K 195
Park St. CR0: Croy . . .3C 200 (8N 45)
GU1: Guil 6B 202 (5M 113)
GU15: Camb 9A 50
GU19: Bag 4J 51
RH12: Hors 6K 197
RH13: Slinf 5K 195
SL3: Coln 4F 6
Park St. SL4: W'sor 4G 5
SW6 . . . . .4N 13
TW11: Tedd 7E 24
Park St. La. RH13: Slinf 5G 195
Park Ter. KT4: W Pk 7F 42
SM5: Cars 9C 44
Park Ter. Courtyard
RH13: Hors 7K 197
(off Park Ter. E.)
Park Ter. E. RH13: Hors 7K 197
Park Ter. W. RH12: Hors 7K 197
Parkthorne Rd. SW12 . . . . .1H 29
Park Vw. CR3: Cate 3D 104
GU19: Bag 4H 51
KT3: N Mal 2E 42
KT12: Hers 2K 57
KT15: Addl 2L 55
(off Bourne Way)
KT23: Book 3A 98
RH6: Horl 8E 142
RH11: Craw 4A 182
Park Vw. Cl. TN8: Eden 1K 147
Parkview Cl. SM5: Cars 4D 62
Park Vw. Ct. GU22: Wok 6B 74
Parkview Ct. SW6 . . . . .5K 13
SW18 . . . . .9M 13
Parkview Cres. KT4: W Pk 6H 43
Park Vw. Dr. CR4: Mit 1B 44
Park Vw. Gdns.
RH19: E Grin 7N 165
Park Vw. Ho. GU11: Alde 2M 109
(off High St.)
Park Vw. Rd. CR3: Wold 9H 85
KT22: Leat 7F 78
RH1: Salf 1E 142
Parkview Rd. CR0: Croy 7D 46
Parkview Va. GU4: Guil 9E 94
Parkview Way KT19: Eps 6C 60
Park Vs. GU17: Haw 4L 69
Parkville Rd. SW6 . . . . .3L 13
Park Wlk. KT21: Asht 6M 79
Park Way KT8: W Mole 2B 40
KT23: Book 1A 98
RH6: Horl 8E 142
RH10: Craw 1G 182
RH12: Hors 6J 197
TW14: Felt 1J 23
Parkway CR0: N Add 5L 65
GU1: Guil 1D 202 (2N 113)
GU15: Camb 3A 70
KT13: Weybr 1E 56
RG45: Crowt 2F 48
RH4: Dork 1J 201 (4G 119)
SW20 . . . . .3J 43
Parkway, The TW4: C'ford 5J 9
TW5: C'ford 1H 9
UB2: S'hall 1H 9
Parkway Trad. Est. TW5: Hest . . .2K 9
Parkwood Av. KT10: Esh 7C 40
Parkwood Cl. KT22: Fetc 1C 98
SM7: Ban 2J 81
Park Wood Golf Course 9G 86
Parkwood Gro. TW16: Sunb 2H 39
Parkwood Rd. RH1: Nut 2J 123
SM7: Ban 2J 81
SW19 . . . . .6L 27
TN16: Tats 8G 87
TW7: Isle 4F 10
Parkwood Vw. SM7: Ban 3H 81
Park Works Rd. RH1: Nut 2K 123
Parley Dr. GU21: Wok 4M 73
Parliamentary Rd.
GU24: B'wood 8L 71
Parliament M. SW14 . . . . .5B 12
Parnell Cl. RH10: Craw 5H 183
Parnell Gdns. KT13: Weybr 7B 56
Parnham Av. GU18: Ligh 7A 52
Parr Av. KT17: Ewe 5G 61
Parr Cl. KT22: Leat 7F 78
Parr Ct. GU21: Knap 6F 72
(off Tudor Way)
TW13: Hanw 5K 23
Parrington Ho. SW4 . . . . .1H 29
Parris Cft. RH4: Dork 8J 119
Parritt Rd. RH1: Red 1F 122
Parrock La. TN7: Up Hart 8M 187
Parrs Cl. CR2: Sande 5A 64
Parrs Pl. TW12: Hamp 8A 24
Parry Cl. KT17: Ewe 4G 60
RH13: Hors 4B 198
Parry Dr. KT13: Weybr 6B 56
Parry Rd. SE25 . . . . .2B 46
Parsley Gdns. CR0: Croy 7G 46
Parsonage Bus. Pk.
RH12: Hors 4L 197
Parsonage Cl. CR6: Warl 3J 85
RH4: Westc 7C 118
Parsonage Farm Ind. Est.
RH12: Hors 3L 197
Parsonage La. RH4: Westc 6C 118
SL4: W'sor 4D 4
Parsonage Rd. GU6: Cranl . . .7M 155
RH12: Hors 4K 197
TW20: Eng G 6N 19
Parsonage Sq. RH4: Dork 2H 201
Parsonage Way GU16: Frim 5C 70
RH12: Hors 4L 197
Parsons Cl. GU11: Alde 2A 110
GU27: Hasl 9G 171
GU52: Chu C 8A 88
RH6: Horl 7C 142
SM1: Sut 9N 43
Parsons Cotts. GU12: Ash 1G 111
Parsons Fld. GU47: Sandh 7G 49
Parsonsfield Cl. SM7: Ban 2J 81
Parsonsfield Rd. SM7: Ban 3J 81
Parsons Ga. M. SW6 . . . . .5M 13
PARSONS GREEN 5L 13
Parsons Grn. GU1: Guil 1N 113
GU27: Hasl 9G 171
SW6 . . . . .4M 13
Parsons Grn. Ct. GU1: Guil 9N 93
Parson's Grn. La. SW6 . . . . . . .4M 13
Parsons Green Station
(Underground) 4M 13
Parsons La. GU26: Hind 3A 170
Parsons Mead
CR0: Croy 1A 200 (7M 45)
KT8: E Mol 2C 40
Parson's Ride RG12: Brac 6D 32
Parsons Rd. SL3: Lang 1B 6
Parsons Wlk. RH12: Hors 8F 196
Parthenia Dr. TW7: Isle 6G 11
Parthenia Rd. SW6 . . . . .4M 13
Parthia Cl. KT20: Tad 6G 81
Parthings La. RH13: Hors 9E 196
Partridge Av. GU46: Yate 9A 48
Partridge Cl. GU10: Ews 4C 108
GU16: Frim 5C 70
RG12: Brac 3K 31
Partridge Knoll CR8: Pur 8M 63
Partridge La. RH5: Newd 7C 140
RH12: Newd, Rusp 8C 160
Partridge Mead SM7: Ban 2H 81
Partridge Pl. RH10: Turn H . . .3F 184
Partridge Rd. TW12: Hamp 7N 23
Partridge Way GU4: Guil 1F 114
Parvis Rd. KT14: W By, Byf 9K 55
Paschal Rd. GU15: Camb 7D 50
Passage, The TW9: Rich 8L 11
PASSFIELD 8D 168
Passfield Ent. Cen.
GU30: Pass 9C 168
Passfield Mill Bus. Pk.
GU30: Pass 8C 168
Passfield Rd. GU30: Pass 9D 168
Passfields W14 . . . . .1L 13
(off Star Rd.)
Passingham Ho. TW5: Hest 2A 10
Pastens Rd. RH8: Limp 9E 106
Paston Cl. SM6: W'ton 9G 44
Pasture, The RH10: Craw 3G 182
Pasturewood Rd.
RH5: A Com, Holm M 6K 137
Patching Cl. RH11: Craw 2L 181
Patchings RH13: Hors 5M 197
Paterson Rd. TW15: Ashf 6M 21
Pates Mnr. Dr. TW14: Bedf 1E 22
Path, The SW19 . . . . .9N 27
Pathfield GU8: Chid 5E 172
Pathfield Cl. GU8: Chid 5E 172
RH12: Rudg 1E 194
Pathfield Rd. RH12: Rudg 1E 194
SW16 . . . . .7H 29
Pathfields GU5: Shere 9B 116
GU27: Hasl 1G 189
Pathfields Cl. GU27: Hasl 1G 189
Pathfinders, The
GU14: Cove 2H 89
Path Link RH10: Craw 2C 182
Pathway, The GU23: Send 3H 95
RG42: Bin 6H 15
Patmore La. KT12: Hers 3G 56
Patricia Gdns. SM2: Sut 7M 61
Patrick Gdns. RG42: Warf 8C 16
Patrington Cl. RH11: Craw . . .6M 181
Patten All. TW10: Rich 8K 11
Patten Ash Dr. RG40: W'ham . . .1D 30
Patten Av. GU46: Yate 1B 68
Patten Rd. SW18 . . . . .1C 28
Patterdale Cl. RH11: Craw 5N 181
Patterson Cl. GU16: Frim 3G 71
Paul Cl. GU11: Alde 4K 109
Paul Ct. TW20: Egh 7F 20
Paulet Cl. GU51: Fleet 2A 88
Paul Gdns. CR0: Croy 8C 46
Pauline Cres. TW2: Whitt 2C 24
Paul Robeson Theatre, The
Hounslow 6B 10
Pauls Mead RH7: Ling 6A 146
Paul's Pl. KT21: Asht 6A 80
Paul Vanson Ct. KT12: Hers 3L 57
Paved Ct. TW9: Rich 8K 11
Pavement, The
RH10: Craw 3C 182
TW7: Isle 6G 11
(off South St.)
Pavement Sq. CR0: Croy 7D 46
Pavilion, The
KT20: K'wood 1A 102
RH2: Reig 1C 122
Pavilion Ct. GU6: Cranl 7L 155
(off East Vw. La.)
Pavilion Gdns. TW18: Stain 8K 21
Pavilion La. GU11: Alde 1K 109
Pavilion Rd. GU11: Alde 3K 109
Pavilions, The KT14: Byf 7M 55
RH10: Worth 2J 183
RH11: Pease P 2N 199
SL4: W'sor 4E 4
Pavilions End, The
GU15: Camb 3B 70
Pavilions in the Park, The . . .5J 197
Pavilion Sports & Fitness Club, The
. . . . .2C 40
Pavilion Sq. SW17 . . . . .4D 28
Pavilion Way RH19: E Grin . . .1A 186
Paviours GU9: Farnh 9G 109
Pawley Cl. GU10: Tong 5D 110
Pawsons Rd. CR0: Croy 5N 45

Pax Cl.—Pickets St.

Pax Cl. RH11: Craw . . . 5K 181
Paxton Cl. KT12: Wal T . . . 6K 39
TW9: Kew . . . 5M 11
Paxton Ct. *CR4: Mit . . . 1D 44*
(off Armfield Cres.)
Paxton Gdns. GU21: Wok . . . 8F 54
Paxton Rd. W4 . . . 2D 12
Payley Dr. RG40: W'ham . . . 9D 14
Payne Cl. RH10: Craw . . . 1H 183
Paynesfield Av. SW14 . . . 6C 12
Paynesfield Rd. TN16: Tats . . . 8E 86
(not continuous)
PAYNES GREEN . . . 1D 178
Paynes Wlk. W6 . . . 2K 13
Paynetts Ct. KT13: Weybr . . . 2E 56
Peabody Cl. CR0: Croy . . . 7F 46
Peabody Est. SE24 . . . 1M 29
SW6 . . . 2M 13
(off Lillie Rd.)
W6 . . . 1H 13
Peabody Hill SE21 . . . 2M 29
Peabody Rd. GU14: Farnb . . . 4B 90
Peace Cl. SE25 . . . 3B 46
Peacemaker Cl.
RH11: Craw . . . 5K 181
Peaches Cl. SM2: Chea . . . 4K 61
Peach Rd. TW13: Felt . . . 2H 23
Peach St. RG40: W'ham . . . 2B 30
Peach Tree Cl. GU14: Farnb . . . 7M 69
Peacock Av. TW14: Bedf . . . 2E 22
Peacock Cl. KT19: Eps . . . 8M 59
Peacock Cotts. RG12: Brac . . . 3H 31
Peacock Gdns. CR2: Sels . . . 6H 65
Peacock La. RG12: Brac . . . 4G 31
RG40: W'ham . . . 4G 31
Peacocks Shop. Centre, The
GU21: Wok . . . 4A 74
Peacock Wlk.
RH4: Dork . . . 4J 201 (6G 119)
RH11: Craw . . . 6M 181
PEAKED HILL . . . 1A 110
Peakfield GU10: Fren . . . 3H 149
Peak Fitness
Woking . . . 4B 74
(off Chertsey Rd.)
Peak Rd. GU2: Guil . . . 9K 93
Peaks Hill CR8: Pur . . . 6H 63
Peaks Hill Ri. CR8: Pur . . . 6J 63
Peall Rd. CR0: Croy . . . 5K 45
Peall Rd. Ind. Est.
CR0: Croy . . . 5K 45
Pearce Cl. CR4: Mit . . . 1E 44
Pearing Cl. KT4: W Pk . . . 8J 43
Pearl Ct. GU21: Wok . . . 3H 73
Pearmain Cl. TW17: Shep . . . 4C 38
Pears Av. TW17: Shep . . . 2F 38
Pearscroft Ct. SW6 . . . 4N 13
Pearscroft Rd. SW6 . . . 4N 13
Pearson Cl. CR8: Pur . . . 7M 63
Pearson Rd. RH10: Craw . . . 2G 182
Pearson Way CR4: Mit . . . 9E 28
Pears Rd. TW3: Houn . . . 6C 10
Pear Tree Av. GU51: Fleet . . . 3A 88
Peartree Av. SW17 . . . 4A 28
Pear Tree Cl. CR4: Mit . . . 1C 44
GU35: Lind . . . 5A 168
KT9: Ches . . . 2N 59
KT15: Addl . . . 2J 55
KT19: Eps . . . 5C 60
Peartree Cl. CR2: Sande . . . 1E 84
Pear Tree Ct. GU15: Camb . . . 7F 50
Pear Tree Grn. GU8: Duns . . . 2N 173
Pear Tree Hill RH1: Salf . . . 3E 142
Pear Tree La. GU10: Rowl . . . 8E 128
Pear Tree Rd. GU35: Lind . . . 5A 168
KT15: Addl . . . 2J 55
TW15: Ashf . . . 6D 22
Peary Cl. RH12: Hors . . . 2K 197
Peascod Pl. *SL4: W'sor . . . 4G 4*
(off Peascod St.)
Peascod St. SL4: W'sor . . . 4F 4
PEASE POTTAGE . . . 2N 199
Pease Pottage Golf Course
. . . 2M 199
Pease Pottage Hill
RH11: Craw . . . 8A 182
PEASE POTTAGE SERVICE AREA
. . . 9A 182
PEASLAKE . . . 5E 136
Peaslake La. GU5: P'lake . . . 5E 136
Peaslake Rd. GU6: Ewh . . . 2E 156
PEASMARSH . . . 2M 133
Peat Comn. GU8: Els . . . 9G 131
Peat Cotts. GU8: Els . . . 9G 131
Peatmoor Cl. GU51: Fleet . . . 3A 88
Peatmore Av. GU22: Pyr . . . 3J 75
Peatmore Cl. GU22: Pyr . . . 3J 75
Peatmore Dr. GU24: B'wood . . . 8N 71
Pebble Cl. KT20: Wal H . . . 7D 100
Pebblehill Rd. RH3: Betch . . . 7D 100
Pebble La. KT18: Eps D . . . 9N 79
KT22: Leat . . . 2M 99
Pebworth Ct. RH1: Red . . . 1E 122
Peddlars Gro. GU46: Yate . . . 9D 48
Peeble Hill KT24: W Hors . . . 2D 116
Peek Cres. SW19 . . . 6J 27
Peeks Brook La.
RH6: Ship B, Horl . . . 4J 163
Peel Av. GU16: Frim . . . 7E 70
Peel Centre, The
RG12: Brac . . . 1M 31
Peel Cl. SL4: W'sor . . . 6E 4
Peel Ct. GU14: Farnb . . . 5A 90
Peel Rd. BR6: Farnb . . . 2L 67
Pegasus Av. GU12: Alde . . . 1C 110
Pegasus Cl. GU27: Hasl . . . 3B 188
Pegasus Ct. CR3: Cate . . . 1C 104
GU12: Alde . . . 3C 110
GU51: Fleet . . . 3A 88
KT1: K Tham . . . 6H 203 (2K 41)
KT22: Leat . . . 8J 79
(off Epsom Rd.)
RH11: Craw . . . 5K 181
SM7: Ban . . . 2M 81
TW8: Brent . . . 1M 11
TW20: Egh . . . 6D 20
Pegasus Pl. SW6 . . . 4M 13
Pegasus Rd. CR0: Wad . . . 3L 63
GU14: Cove . . . 7L 69
Pegasus Way RH19: E Grin . . . 7D 166
Peggotty Pl. GU47: Owls . . . 5K 49
Pegg Rd. TW5: Hest . . . 3L 9
Pegler Ct. *RH11: Craw . . . 3B 182*
(off Pegler Way)
Pegler Way RH11: Craw . . . 3B 182
Pegwell Cl. RH11: Craw . . . 5L 181
Peket Cl. TW18: Stain . . . 9G 21
Pelabon Ho. *TW1: Twick . . . 9K 11*
(off Clevedon Rd.)
Peldon Ct. TW9: Rich . . . 7M 11
Peldon Pas. TW10: Rich . . . 7M 11
Pelham Ct. RH11: Craw . . . 7N 181
RH12: Hors . . . 6H 197
TW18: Stain . . . 6K 21
(off Kingston Rd.)
Pelham Dr. RH11: Craw . . . 7M 181
Pelham Ho. CR3: Cate . . . 2C 104
W14 . . . 1L 13
(off Mornington Av.)
Pelham Pl. GU10: Wrec . . . 7F 128
RH11: Craw . . . 7N 181
Pelham Rd. BR3: Beck . . . 1F 46
SW19 . . . 8M 27
Pelham's Cl. KT10: Esh . . . 1A 58
Pelham's Wlk. KT10: Esh . . . 9A 40
Pelham Way KT23: Book . . . 4B 98
Pellant Rd. SW6 . . . 3K 13
Pelling Hill SL4: O Win . . . 1L 19
Pelman Ho. KT19: Eps . . . 6A 60
Pelman Way KT19: Eps . . . 6A 60
Pelton Av. SM2: Sut . . . 6N 61
Pemberley Chase KT19: Ewe . . . 2A 60
Pemberley Cl. KT19: Ewe . . . 2A 60
Pemberley Ho. *KT19: Ewe . . . 2A 60*
(off Pemberley Chase)
Pemberley Lodge SL4: W'sor . . . 6D 4
Pemberton Cl. TW19: Stan . . . 2N 21
Pemberton Pl. KT10: Esh . . . 9C 40
Pemberton Rd. KT8: E Mol . . . 3C 40
Pembley Grn. RH10: Copt . . . 7A 164
Pembridge Av. TW2: Whitt . . . 2N 23
Pembridge Pl. SW15 . . . 8M 13
Pembroke RG12: Brac . . . 6L 31
W14 . . . 1L 13
(off Kensington Village)
Pembroke Av. KT5: Surb . . . 4A 42
KT12: Hers . . . 1L 57
Pembroke B'way.
GU15: Camb . . . 1A 70
Pembroke Cl. SL5: S'hill . . . 4A 34
SM7: Ban . . . 4N 81
Pembroke Gdns. GU22: Wok . . . 5C 74
Pembroke M. SL5: S'hill . . . 4A 34
Pembroke Pde. GU46: Yate . . . 8D 48
Pembroke Pl. TW7: Isle . . . 5E 10
Pembroke Rd. CR4: Mit . . . 1E 44
GU22: Wok . . . 5C 74
RH10: Craw . . . 9G 163
SE25 . . . 3B 46
Pembroke Vs. TW9: Rich . . . 7K 11
Pembury Av. KT4: W Pk . . . 7F 42
Pembury Cl. CR5: Coul . . . 1E 82
Pembury Ct. UB3: Harl . . . 2E 8
Pembury Pl. GU12: Alde . . . 3A 110
Pembury Rd. SE25 . . . 3D 46
Pemdevon Rd. CR0: Croy . . . 6L 45
Pemerich Cl. UB3: Harl . . . 1G 8
Penart Ct. SM2: Sut . . . 4A 62
Penates KT10: Esh . . . 1D 58
Penbury Rd. UB2: S'hall . . . 1N 9
Pendarves Rd. SW20 . . . 9H 27
Pendarvis Ct. GU26: G'hott . . . 6A 170
Pendell Av. UB3: Harl . . . 3G 8
Pendell Rd. RH1: Blet . . . 9M 103
Pendennis Cl. KT14: W By . . . 1J 75
Pendennis Rd. SW16 . . . 5J 29
Pendenza KT11: Cob . . . 3M 77
Penderel Rd. TW3: Houn . . . 8A 10
Pendine Pl. RG12: Brac . . . 4N 31
Pendlebury RG12: Brac . . . 6M 31
Pendlebury Ct. KT5: Surb . . . 8K 203
Pendle Rd. SW16 . . . 7F 28
Pendleton Cl. RH1: Red . . . 4D 122
Pendleton Rd. RH1: Red . . . 6A 122
RH2: Reig . . . 6A 122
Pendragon Way
GU15: Camb . . . 2H 71
Pendry's La. RG42: Warf . . . 1M 15
Penfold Cl. CR0: Wad . . . 9L 45
Penfold Cft. GU9: Farnh . . . 8L 109
Penfold Mnr. GU27: Hasl . . . 2H 189
Penfold Rd. RH10: Craw . . . 7F 182
Penfurzen La. RG42: Warf . . . 1B 16
Penge Rd. SE20 . . . 2D 46
SE25 . . . 2D 46
Pengilly Ho. GU1: Guil . . . 3E 114
Pengilly Rd. GU9: Farnh . . . 1G 128
Penhurst GU21: Wok . . . 1B 74
Penhurst Mans. *SW6 . . . 4L 13*
(off Rostrevor Rd.)
Peninsular Cl. GU15: Camb . . . 8F 50
TW14: Felt . . . 9E 8
Peninsular Pl. RG45: Crowt . . . 3H 49
Penistone Rd. SW16 . . . 8J 29
Penlee Cl. TN8: Eden . . . 1L 147
Pennards, The TW16: Sunb . . . 2K 39
Penn Cl. RH11: Craw . . . 9B 162
Penn Ct. RH11: Craw . . . 3L 181
Pennefather's Rd.
GU11: Alde . . . 1L 109
Penner Cl. SW19 . . . 3K 27
Penners Gdns. KT6: Surb . . . 6L 41
Pennethorne GU15: Camb . . . 7F 50
Penn Ho. *SL4: Eton . . . 1G 4*
(off Common La.)
Pennine Cl. RH11: Craw . . . 3N 181
Pennine Way GU14: Cove . . . 7J 69
UB3: Harl . . . 3E 8
Pennings Av. GU2: Guil . . . 1J 113
Pennington Dr. KT13: Weybr . . . 9F 38
Pennington Lodge
KT5: Surb . . . 8K 203
Penn Rd. SL3: Dat . . . 4N 5
Penns Wood GU14: Farnb . . . 4B 90
Pennycroft CR0: Sels . . . 5H 65
Penny Dr. GU3: Wood V . . . 2E 112
Pennyfield KT11: Cob . . . 9H 57
Penny Hill Caravan Pk.
GU17: Min . . . 4B 68
PENNYHILL PARK . . . 5F 50
Penny La. TW17: Shep . . . 6F 38
Pennymead Dr. KT24: E Hor . . . 5G 96
Pennymead Pl. KT10: Esh . . . 3N 57
Pennymead Ri. KT24: E Hor . . . 5G 96
Penny M. SW12 . . . 1F 28
PENNY POT . . . 8F 52
Pennypot La. GU24: Chob . . . 9E 52
Penny Royal SM6: W'ton . . . 3H 63
Penrhyn Cl. CR3: Cate . . . 7A 84
GU12: Alde . . . 3N 109
Penrhyn Cres. SW14 . . . 7B 12
Penrhyn Gdns.
KT1: K Tham . . . 7H 203 (3K 41)
Penrhyn Rd.
KT1: K Tham . . . 7J 203 (3L 41)
Penrith Cl. RH2: Reig . . . 2C 122
SW15 . . . 8K 13
Penrith Pl. SE27 . . . 3M 29
Penrith Rd. CR7: T Hea . . . 1N 45
KT3: N Mal . . . 3C 42
Penrith St. SW16 . . . 7G 28
Penrose Ct. TW20: Eng G . . . 7M 19
(not continuous)
Penrose Dr. KT19: Eps . . . 7N 59
Penrose Gdns. GU12: Ash V . . . 7E 90
Penrose Rd. KT22: Fetc . . . 9C 78
Penryn Dr. GU35: Head D . . . 4H 169
Penryn Ho. *RH1: Red . . . 1E 122*
(off London Rd.)
Pensfold La. RH12: Rudg . . . 3F 194
Pensford Av. TW9: Kew . . . 5N 11
Pensford Cl. RG45: Crowt . . . 9G 30
Penshurst Cl. RH10: Craw . . . 2H 183
Penshurst Ri. GU16: Frim . . . 6D 70
Penshurst Rd. CR7: T Hea . . . 4M 45
Penshurst Way SM2: Sut . . . 4M 61
Penstock M. GU7: Godal . . . 6K 133
Pentelow Gdns. TW14: Felt . . . 9H 9
Pentire Cl. GU21: Wok . . . 1A 74
Pentland Av. TW17: Shep . . . 4B 38
Pentland Gdns. SW18 . . . 9N 13
Pentland Pl. GU14: Cove . . . 7K 69
Pentlands Cl. CR4: Mit . . . 2F 44
Pentland St. SW18 . . . 9N 13
Pentlow St. SW15 . . . 6H 13
Pentney Rd. SW12 . . . 2G 28
SW19 . . . 9K 27
Penton Av. TW18: Stain . . . 8H 21
Penton Ct. TW18: Stain . . . 7H 21
Penton Hall TW18: Stain . . . 9J 21
Penton Hall Dr. TW18: Stain . . . 9J 21
Penton Hook Marina . . . 1H 37
Penton Hook Rd.
TW18: Stain . . . 8J 21
Penton Hook Yacht Club . . . 2J 37
Penton Pk. KT16: Chert . . . 2K 37
Penton Rd. TW18: Stain . . . 8H 21
Pentreath Av. GU2: Guil . . . 4J 113
Penwerris Av. TW7: Isle . . . 3C 10
Penwerris Ct. TW5: Hest . . . 3C 10
Penwith Dr. GU27: Hasl . . . 4B 188
Penwith Rd. SW18 . . . 3M 27
Penwith Wlk. GU22: Wok . . . 6N 73
Penwood End GU22: Wok . . . 8L 73
Penwood Gdns. RG12: Brac . . . 5J 31
Penwood Ho. SW15 . . . 9E 12
Penwortham Rd.
CR2: Sande . . . 6N 63
SW16 . . . 7F 28
Pen-y-Bos Track
GU27: Hasl . . . 5K 189
Penywern Rd. SW5 . . . 1M 13
Peperham Ho. GU27: Hasl . . . 1G 189
Peperham Rd. GU27: Hasl . . . 9G 171
PEPER HAROW . . . 6N 131
Peper Harow La.
GU8: S'ford . . . 5N 131
Peper Harow Pk.
GU8: P Har . . . 6N 131
Peperharow Rd.
GU7: Godal . . . 5E 132
Peppard Rd. RH10: Craw . . . 5H 183
Pepperbox La. GU5: Braml . . . 5F 154
Pepper Cl. CR3: Cate . . . 3B 104
Peppercorn Cl. CR7: T Hea . . . 1A 46
Peppermint Cl. CR0: Croy . . . 6J 45
Peppers Yd. RH12: Hors . . . 5K 197
Pepys Cl. KT21: Asht . . . 4N 79
SL3: Lang . . . 2D 6
Pepys Rd. SW20 . . . 9H 27
Percheron Cl. TW7: Isle . . . 6F 10
Percheron Dr. GU21: Knap . . . 6F 72
Percival Cl. KT22: Oxs . . . 7B 58
Percival Rd. SW14 . . . 7B 12
TW13: Felt . . . 3G 22
Percival Way KT19: Ewe . . . 1C 60
Percy Av. TW15: Ashf . . . 6B 22
Percy Bilton Ct. *TW5: Hest . . . 4B 10*
(off Skinners La.)
Percy Bryant Rd.
TW16: Sunb . . . 8F 22
Percy Gdns. KT4: W Pk . . . 7C 42
TW7: Isle . . . 6H 11
Percy Laurie Ho. *SW15 . . . 7J 13*
(off Nursery Cl.)
Percy Pl. SL3: Dat . . . 4L 5
Percy Rd. CR4: Mit . . . 6E 44
GU2: Guil . . . 1L 113
RH12: Hors . . . 5H 197
SE20 . . . 1G 46
SE25 . . . 4D 46
TW2: Whitt . . . 2B 24
TW7: Isle . . . 7G 11
TW12: Hamp . . . 8A 24
Percy Way TW2: Whitt . . . 2C 24
Peregrine Cl. GU6: Cranl . . . 6N 155
RG12: Brac . . . 4N 31
Peregrine Ct. SW16 . . . 5K 29
Peregrine Gdns. CR0: Croy . . . 8H 47
Peregrine Rd. TW16: Sunb . . . 1G 38
Peregrine Way SW19 . . . 8H 27
Perendale Dr. TW17: Shep . . . 9D 22
Perham Rd. W14 . . . 1K 13
Perifield SE21 . . . 2N 29
Perimeter Rd. RH6: Gatw . . . 3F 162
Perimeter Rd. E.
RH6: Gatw . . . 5E 162
Perimeter Rd. Nth.
RH6: Gatw . . . 2B 162
Perimeter Rd. Sth.
RH6: Gatw . . . 5A 162
Periwinkle Cl. GU35: Lind . . . 4B 168
Perkin Cl. TW3: Houn . . . 7A 10
Perkins Ct. TW15: Ashf . . . 6A 22
Perkstead Ct. *RH11: Craw . . . 6M 181*
(off Kingsley Rd.)
Perleybrooke La.
GU21: Wok . . . 4K 73
Perowne St. GU11: Alde . . . 2L 109
Perran Rd. SW2 . . . 2M 29
Perran Wlk. TW8: Brent . . . 1L 11
Perrin Cl. TW15: Ashf . . . 6A 22
Perrin Ct. GU21: Wok . . . 2D 74
TW15: Ashf . . . 5B 22
Perring Av. GU14: Cove . . . 6K 69
Perring Rd. GU14: Farnb . . . 4M 89
Perrior Rd. GU7: Godal . . . 4H 133
Perry Av. RH19: E Grin . . . 7A 166
Perry Cl. GU7: Godal . . . 6K 133
Perry Ct. KT1: K Tham . . . 3K 203
Perrycroft SL4: W'sor . . . 6B 4
Perryfield Ho. *RH11: Craw . . . 4B 182*
(off Perryfield Rd.)
Perryfield Rd. RH11: Craw . . . 4A 182
Perryfield Way TW10: Ham . . . 4H 25
Perry Hill GU3: Worp . . . 5H 93
(not continuous)
Perryhill Dr. GU47: Sandh . . . 6E 48
Perry How KT4: W Pk . . . 7E 42
Perrylands RH6: Charlw . . . 3L 161
Perrylands La.
RH6: Horl, Smallf . . . 9K 143
Perrymead St. SW6 . . . 4M 13
Perryn Ct. TW1: Twick . . . 9G 10
Perry Oaks RG12: Brac . . . 1C 32
Perry Way GU9: Up Hale . . . 5G 109
GU18: Ligh . . . 8K 51
GU35: Head . . . 5E 168
RG12: Brac . . . 1C 32
Perrywood Bus. Pk.
RH1: Salf . . . 2F 142
Perseverance Cotts.
GU23: Rip . . . 8L 75
Perseverance Pl. TW9: Rich . . . 7L 11
Persfield Cl. KT17: Ewe . . . 6E 60
Persfield M. KT17: Ewe . . . 6E 60
Pershore Gro. SM5: Cars . . . 5B 44
Perth Cl. RH11: Craw . . . 9B 162
SW20 . . . 1E 42
Perth Rd. BR3: Beck . . . 1M 47
Perth Way RH12: Hors . . . 4M 197
Petavel Rd. TW11: Tedd . . . 7E 24
Peter Av. RH8: Oxt . . . 7N 105
Peterborough M. SW6 . . . 5M 13
Peterborough Rd.
GU2: Guil . . . 1J 113
RH10: Craw . . . 7C 182
SM5: Cars . . . 5C 44
SW6 . . . 5M 13
Peterborough Vs. SW6 . . . 4N 13
Peterhead M. SL3: Lang . . . 1C 6
Peterhouse Cl. GU47: Owls . . . 5L 49
Peterhouse Pde.
RH10: Craw . . . 9G 162
Peter Kennedy Ct. CR0: Croy . . . 5J 47
Peterlee Wlk. RH11: Craw . . . 7K 181
Petersfield Av. TW18: Stain . . . 6L 21
Petersfield Cres. CR5: Coul . . . 2J 83
Petersfield Ri. SW15 . . . 2G 26
Petersfield Rd. TW18: Stain . . . 6L 21
PETERSHAM . . . 2L 25
Petersham Av. KT14: Byf . . . 8N 55
Petersham Cl. KT14: Byf . . . 8N 55
SM1: Sut . . . 2M 61
TW10: Ham . . . 3K 25
Petersham Rd.
TW10: Rich, Ham . . . 9K 11
Petersham Ter. *CR0: Bedd . . . 9J 45*
(off Richmond Grn.)
Petersmead Cl. KT20: Tad . . . 1H 101
Peterstow Cl. SW19 . . . 3K 27
Peters Wood RH5: Cap . . . 5J 159
Peterwood Pk. CR0: Wad . . . 8K 45
Peterwood Way CR0: Wad . . . 8K 45
Petley Rd. W6 . . . 2J 13
Petridge Rd. RH1: Red . . . 8D 122
PETRIDGE WOOD COMMON
. . . 8D 122
Petters Rd. KT21: Asht . . . 3M 79
Pettiward Cl. SW15 . . . 7H 13
Petts La. TW17: Shep . . . 3B 38
Petworth Cl. CR5: Coul . . . 6G 82
GU16: Frim . . . 6D 70
Petworth Ct. *GU15: Camb . . . 2D 70*
(off Portsmouth Rd.)
GU27: Hasl . . . 2H 189
RH11: Craw . . . 6L 181
SL4: W'sor . . . 4D 4
Petworth Dr. RH12: Hors . . . 1M 197
Petworth Gdns. SW20 . . . 2G 42
Petworth Rd. GU8: Chid . . . 2C 190
(not continuous)
GU8: Hasl . . . 3A 190
GU8: Mil, Wit, Worm . . . 3B 152
GU8: Worm . . . 8C 152
GU27: Hasl . . . 2H 189
Pevensey Cl. RH10: Craw . . . 4G 182
TW7: Isle . . . 3C 10
Pevensey Ct. SW16 . . . 4L 29
Pevensey Rd. SW17 . . . 5B 28
TW13: Felt . . . 2M 23
Pevensey Way GU16: Frim . . . 6D 70
Peverel Rd. RH11: Ifield . . . 4K 181
Peveril Dr. TW11: Tedd . . . 6D 24
Pewley Bank
GU1: Guil . . . 6F 202 (5A 114)
Pewley Down (Local Nature Reserve)
. . . 6B 114
Pewley Hill
GU1: Guil . . . 6D 202 (5N 113)
Pewley Point
GU1: Guil . . . 7F 202 (5A 114)
Pewley Way
GU1: Guil . . . 6F 202 (5A 114)
Pewsey Va. RG12: Brac . . . 4D 32
Peyton's Cotts. RH1: Nut . . . 1K 123
Pharaoh Cl. CR4: Mit . . . 6D 44
Pharaoh's Island
TW17: Shep . . . 8A 38
Pheasant Cl. CR8: Pur . . . 9M 63
GU8: Mil . . . 2C 152
Pheasantry Welcome Centre, The
. . . 9F 24
Pheasant Vw. RG12: Brac . . . 3J 31
Phelps Way UB3: Harl . . . 1G 9
Philanthropic Rd.
RH1: Red . . . 4E 122
Philbeach Gdns. SW5 . . . 1M 13
Philip Gdns. CR0: Croy . . . 8J 47
Philip Rd. TW18: Stain . . . 7M 21
Philips Cl. SM5: Cars . . . 7E 44
Phillip Copse RG12: Brac . . . 6B 32
Phillippines Cl. TN8: Eden . . . 3M 147
Phillips Cl. GU7: Godal . . . 9G 132
GU10: Tong . . . 4C 110
GU35: Head . . . 4E 168
RH10: Craw . . . 8F 182
Phillips Cres. GU35: Head . . . 4E 168
Phillips Hatch GU5: Wone . . . 3E 134
Phillip's Quad.
GU22: Wok . . . 5A 74
Philpot La. GU24: Chob . . . 9L 53
Philpot Sq. SW6 . . . 6N 13
Phipps Bri. Rd. CR4: Mit . . . 1A 44
SW19 . . . 1A 44
Phipps Bridge Stop
(London Tramlink) . . . 2B 44
Phoenix Bus. Pk.
RG12: Brac . . . 1H 31
Phoenix Cen. . . . 4J 63
Phoenix Cl. BR4: W Wick . . . 8N 47
KT19: Eps . . . 8N 59
Phoenix Ct. CR2: S Croy . . . 2C 64
GU1: Guil . . . 6C 202 (5N 113)
GU11: Alde . . . 3M 109
KT3: N Mal . . . 2E 42
KT17: Eps . . . 6L 201
TW3: Houn . . . 6A 10
TW4: Houn . . . 8L 9
TW8: Brent . . . 1L 11
TW13: Felt . . . 5F 22
Phoenix Dr. BR2: Kes . . . 1F 66
Phoenix Ho. SM1: Sut . . . 1N 61
Phoenix La. RH19: Ash W . . . 3G 186
Phoenix Trad. Pk.
TW8: Brent . . . 1K 11
Phoenix Way TW5: Hest . . . 2L 9
Phyllis Av. KT3: N Mal . . . 4G 42
Phyllis Ho. CR0: Wad . . . 7A 200
Piccards, The GU2: Guil . . . 7M 113
Pickering RG12: Brac . . . 3M 31
Pickering Gdns. CR0: Croy . . . 5C 46
Pickering Pl. GU2: Guil . . . 1K 113
Picket Post Cl. RG12: Brac . . . 2D 32
Pickets St. SW12 . . . 1F 28

Picketts Hill—Poppy Cl.

Picketts Hill
GU35: Head, Slea 9A **148**
RH6: Gatw 4H **163**
Picketts La. RH1: Salf 2G **142**
Pickford Ho. *GU11: Alde 2N 109*
(off Pickford St.)
Pickford St. GU11: Alde 2N **109**
Pickhurst Ri. BR4: W Wick 6M **47**
Pickhurst Rd. GU8: Chid 6F **172**
Pickins Piece SL3: Hort 5C **6**
Pickwick Cl. TW4: Houn 8M **9**
Pickwick Gdns.
GU15: Camb 2F **70**
Picquets Way SM7: Ban 3K **81**
Picton Cl. GU15: Camb 8G **50**
Picton Mt. CR6: Warl 6D **84**
Picton Pl. KT6: Surb 7N **41**
Picts Hill RH13: Hors 9G **197**
Picture Ho. SW16 . . . . .3J **29**
Pieris Ho. *TW13: Felt 3H 23*
(off High St.)
Pierrefonde's Av.
GU14: Farnb 9M **69**
Pier Rd. TW14: Felt 8J **9**
Pierson Rd. SL4: W'sor 4A **4**
Pier Ter. SW18 . . . . .7N **13**
Pigbush La. RH14: Loxw 1H **193**
Pigeon Gro. RG12: Brac 3J **31**
Pigeon Ho. La. CR5: Coul 3A **102**
Pigeonhouse La. SL4: Wink 4H **17**
Pigeon La. TW12: Hamp 5A **24**
Pigeon Pass RH10: Turn H 4F **184**
Piggy Wood Local Nature Reserve
. . . . .7A 16
Pigott Ct. RG40: W'ham 2C **30**
Pigott Rd. RG40: W'ham 9C **14**
Pig Pound Wlk.
RH17: Hand 6N **199**
Pike Cl. GU11: Alde 2A **110**
Pikes Hill
KT17: Eps 6M **201** (9D **60**)
Pikes La. RH7: Crow 2A **146**
Pilgrim Cl. SM4: Mord 6N **43**
Pilgrim Ct. GU8: Mil 2C **152**
Pilgrim Hill SE27 . . . . .5N **29**
Pilgrim M. RH2: Reig 3M **121**
Pilgrims Cl. GU5: Shere 8B **116**
GU9: Farnh 3F **128**
RH5: Westh 9G **99**
Pilgrims La. CR3: Cate 4K **103**
RH8: T'sey 3D **106**
TN16: Weste 1G **106**
Pilgrims Pl. RH2: Reig 1M **121**
Pilgrims Vw.
GU12: Ash G 4G **111**
Pilgrims Way CR2: S Croy 3C **64**
GU4: Guil 7N **113**
GU5: Alb 6H **115**
GU5: Shere 8B **116**
GU24: Bis 3D **72**
GU35: Head 4D **168**
RH2: Reig 1L **121**
RH5: Westh 9H **99**
TN16: Weste, Brast 1H **107**
Pilgrims Way Cotts.
RH3: Betch 2B **120**
Pilsdon Cl. SW19 . . . . .2J **27**
Pilton Estate, The
CR0: Croy 2A **200** (8M **45**)
Pimms Cl. GU4: B'ham 8C **94**
Pinckards GU8: Chid 4D **172**
Pincott La. KT24: W Hors 7C **96**
Pincott Rd. SW19 . . . . .8A **28**
Pine Av. BR4: W Wick 7L **47**
GU15: Camb 2B **70**
Pine Bank GU26: Hind 5C **170**
Pine Cl. CR8: Ken 4A **84**
GU12: Ash V 7E **90**
GU15: Camb 8K **49**
GU21: Wok 3M **73**
KT15: N Haw 7K **55**
KT19: Eps 5B **60**
RH11: Craw 9A **162**
Pine Coombe CR0: Croy 1G **65**
Pinecote Dr. SL5: S'dale 6C **34**
Pine Ct. GU11: Alde 2M **109**
GU16: Mytc 2E **90**
KT13: Weybr 2D **56**
KT15: Addl 1K 55
(off Church Rd.)
RG12: Brac 3C **32**
Pine Cres. SM5: Cars 7B **62**
Pinecrest Gdns. BR6: Farnb 1K **67**
Pine Cft. *KT13: Weybr 3E 56*
(off St George's Rd.)
Pine Dean KT23: Book 3B **98**
Pine Dr. GU17: Haw 3K **69**
Pinefields *KT15: Addl 1K 55*
(off Church Rd.)
Pinefields Cl.
RG45: Crowt 2G **48**
Pine Gdns. KT5: Surb 5N **41**
RH6: Horl 9E **142**
Pine Glade BR6: Farnb 1H **67**
Pine Gro. GU10: Lwr Bou 5K **129**
GU20: Windl 3A **52**
GU52: Chu C 8C **88**
KT13: Weybr 2C **56**
RH19: E Grin 7L **165**
SW19 . . . . .6L **27**
TN8: Eden 1K **147**
Pine Gro. M. KT13: Weybr 2D **56**
Pine Hill KT18: Eps 2C **80**
Pinehill Ri. GU47: Sandh 7H **49**
Pinehill Rd. RG45: Crowt 3G **49**
Pinehurst *GU22: Wok 5B 74*
(off Park Dr.)
RH12: Hors 4J **197**
SL5: S'hill 4A **34**
TW20: Eng G 8M **19**
Pinehurst Av. GU14: Farnb 3N **89**
Pinehurst Cl. KT20: K'wood 9M **81**
Pinehurst Cotts.
GU14: Farnb 3N **89**
Pinehurst Gdns. KT14: W By . . .8L **55**
Pinehurst Pas. GU14: Farnb . . .3N **89**
Pinehurst Rd. GU14: Farnb . . .3M **89**
Pinehurst Rdbt.
GU14: Farnb 2N **89**
Pinel Cl. GU25: V Wat 3A **36**
Pine Lodge *KT11: Cob 2K 77*
(off Leigh Cnr.)
Pinemount Rd. GU15: Camb . . .2B **70**
Pine Pk. GU3: Worp 7D **92**
Pine Pl. SM7: Ban 1J **81**
Piner Cotts. SL4: W'sor 6B **4**
Pine Ridge SM5: Cars 4E **62**
Pineridge Cl. KT13: Weybr 1F **56**
Pine Ridge Dr.
GU10: Lwr Bou 6G **129**
Pine Ridge Golf Course 4H 71
Pine Ridge Mobile Home Pk.
RG40: W'ham 9D **30**
Pine Rd. GU22: Wok 7M **73**
Pines, The CR5: Coul 5F **82**
CR8: Pur 9N **63**
GU15: Camb 8D **50**
GU21: Wok 1B **74**
KT9: Ches 9L **41**
RH4: Dork 6H **119**
RH10: Worth 3H **183**
RH12: Hors 3B **198**
SE19 . . . . .7M **29**
TW16: Sunb 2H **39**
Pine Shaw RH10: Craw 2H **183**
Pines Ridge RH12: Hors 6F **196**
Pines Rd. GU51: Fleet 3A **88**
Pines Trad. Estate, The
GU3: Guil 1H **113**
Pinetops RH12: Hors 3B **198**
Pine Tree Cl. TW5: C'ford 4J **9**
Pine Tree Hill GU22: Pyr 3F **74**
Pine Trees Bus. Pk.
TW18: Stain 6G **20**
Pinetrees Cl. RH10: Copt 7M **163**
Pine Vw. GU35: Head D 3H **169**
Pine Vw. Cl. GU4: Guil 9H **115**
GU9: B Lea 7M **109**
GU27: Hasl 9G **170**
Pine Wlk. CR3: Cate 9B **84**
KT5: Surb 5N **41**
KT11: Cob 1L **77**
KT23: Book 3B **98**
KT24: E Hor 6G **97**
SM5: Cars 6B **62**
SM7: Ban 4D **82**
Pine Wlk. E. SM5: Cars 7B **62**
Pine Wlk. W. SM5: Cars 6B **62**
Pine Way TW20: Eng G 7L **19**
Pine Way Cl. RH19: E Grin 2A **186**
PINEWOOD 1G 48
Pine Wood TW16: Sunb 9H **23**
Pinewood Av. KT15: N Haw 5L **55**
RG45: Crowt 1H **49**
Pinewood Caravan Pk.
RG40: W'ham 8H **31**
Pinewood Cl. CR0: Croy 9H **47**
GU21: Wok 2C **74**
GU47: Sandh 7E **48**
RH12: Broadb H 5D **196**
Pinewood Ct. GU51: Fleet 3B **88**
KT15: Addl 1M **55**
Pinewood Cres. GU14: Cove 9H **69**
Pinewood Dr. BR6: Orp 2N **67**
KT15: N Haw 6L **55**
TW18: Stain 6J **21**
Pinewood Gdns. GU19: Bag 4G **50**
Pinewood Gro. KT15: N Haw 6K **55**
Pinewood Hill GU51: Fleet 3B **88**
Pinewood Leisure Cen. 8G 31
Pinewood M. TW19: Stan 9M **7**
Pinewood Pk. GU14: Cove 7H **69**
KT15: N Haw 7K **55**
Pinewood Pl. KT19: Ewe 1C **60**
Pinewood Rd. GU12: Ash 1H **111**
GU25: V Wat 3K **35**
TW13: Felt 4J **23**
Pinfold Rd. SW16 . . . . .5J **29**
Pinglestone Cl. UB7: Harm 3N **7**
Pinkcoat Cl. TW13: Felt 4J **23**
Pinkerton Pl. SW16 . . . . .5H **29**
Pinkham Mans. W4 . . . . .1N **11**
Pinkhurst La. RH13: Slinf 6A **196**
PINKS HILL 1F 112
Pinners Cl. SM5: Cars 8C **44**
Pinova Cl. RH11: Ifield 9M **161**
Pioneer Pl. CR0: Sels 5K **65**
Pioneers Ind. Pk. CR0: Bedd 7J **45**
Piper Building, The SW6 . . . . . .6N **13**
Piper Rd.
KT1: K Tham 5M **203** (2N **41**)
Pipers Cl. KT11: Cob 2L **77**
Pipers Cft. GU52: Chu C 9B **88**
Pipers End GU25: V Wat 2N **35**
RH13: Slinf 5M **195**
Piper's Gdns. CR0: Croy 6H **47**
Pipers La. GU28: Northc 8D **190**
Pipers Patch GU14: Farnb 1N **89**
Pipers Rd. CR5: Coul 3H **83**
Pipewell Rd. SM5: Cars 5C **44**
Pipit Grn. RG12: Brac 4H **31**
PIPPBROOK 1L 201 (4H 119)
Pippbrook Gdns.
RH4: Dork 1L **201** (4H **119**)
Pippin Cl. CR0: Croy 7J **47**
TW13: Hanw 4N **23**
Pippin Link RH11: Ifield 9M **161**
Pippins Ct. TW15: Ashf 7C **22**
Pipson La. GU46: Yate 1C **68**
Pipsons Cl. GU46: Yate 9C **48**
Piquet Rd. SE20 . . . . .1F **46**
PIRBRIGHT 1C 92
PIRBRIGHT CAMP 8M 71
Pirbright Cres. CR0: N Add 3M **65**
Pirbright Golf Course 8A 72
Pirbright Grn. GU24: Pirb 1C **92**
Pirbright Rd. GU3: Norm 1J **111**
GU14: Farnb 2A **90**
SW18 . . . . .2L **27**
Pirbright Ter. GU24: Pirb 1C **92**
Piries Pl. *RH12: Hors 6J 197*
(off Carfax)
Pisley La. RH5: Ockl 6N **157**
Pitcairn Rd. CR4: Mit 8D **28**
Pitchfont La.
RH8: Limp, T'sey 3B **106**
PITCH HILL 1D 156
Pitch Hill GU6: Ewh 9C **136**
PITCH PLACE
GU2 . . . . .7K 93
GU8 . . . . .7E 150
Pitch Pl. RG42: Bin 6J **15**
Pit Farm Rd. GU1: Guil 3C **114**
Pit Farm Tennis Club 3C 114
Pitfold Av. GU27: Hasl 2B **188**
Pitfold Cl. GU27: Hasl 2C **188**
Pitlake CR0: Croy 2A **200** (8M **45**)
PITLAND STREET 6K 137
Pitland St. RH5: Holm M 6K **137**
Pit La. TN8: Eden 8L **127**
Pitlochry Ho. *SE27 . . . . .3M 29*
(off Elmcourt Rd.)
Pitson Cl. KT15: Addl 1M **55**
Pitt Cres. SW19 . . . . .5N **27**
Pitt La. GU10: Fren 4F **148**
Pitt Pl. KT17: Eps 8M **201** (1D **80**)
Pitt Rivers Cl. GU1: Guil 4D **114**
Pitt Rd. BR6: Farnb 1L **67**
CR0: Croy 4N **45**
CR7: T Hea 4N **45**
KT17: Eps 8M **201** (1D **80**)
Pitts Cl. RG42: Bin 7J **15**
Pitts Rd. GU11: Alde 9N **89**
Pittville Gdns. SE25 . . . . .2D **46**
Pitt Way GU14: Cove 9L **69**
Pitwood Grn. KT20: Tad 7H **81**
Pitwood Pk. Ind. Est.
KT20: Tad 7G **81**
PIXHAM 3K 119
Pixham End RH4: Dork 2J **119**
Pixham La. RH4: Dork 2J **119**
Pixholme Gro. RH4: Dork 3J **119**
PIXTON HILL 5K 187
Pixton Way CR0: Sels 5H **65**
Place Ct. GU11: Alde 5A **110**
Place Farm Rd. RH1: Blet 8A **104**
Placehouse La. CR5: Coul 6K **83**
Plain Ride SL4: W'sor 2N **17**
PLAISTOW 6A 192
Plaistow Rd. GU8: Chid 4C **190**
GU8: Duns 1M **191**
RH14: Kird 8D **192**
RH14: Plais, Loxw 5D **192**
Plaistow St. RH7: Ling 7N **145**
Plane Ho. BR2: Brom 1N **47**
Planes, The KT16: Chert 6L **37**
Plane Tree Cres. TW13: Felt 4J **23**
Plantagenet Cl. KT4: W Pk 1C **60**
Plantagenet Pk. RG42: Warf 9D **16**
Plantain Cres. RH11: Craw . . .7M **181**
Plantation La.
CR3: Warl, Wold 6H **85**
CR6: Warl 6H **85**
Plantation Row
GU15: Camb 1N **69**
Plas Newydd RH19: D Pk 4B **166**
Plat, The RH12: Hors 5G **197**
TN8: Eden 2M **147**
Plateau, The RG42: Warf 8E **16**
Platt, The RH7: Dorm 1C **166**
SW15 . . . . .6J **13**
Platt Mdw. GU4: Guil 9F **94**
Platt's Eyot TW12: Hamp 1A **40**
Plaws Hill GU5: P'lake 5E **136**
Playden Ct. RH11: Craw 6L **181**
Playfair Mans. *W14 . . . . .2K 13*
(off Queen's Club Gdns.)
Playfair St. W6 . . . . .1H **13**
Playground Cl. BR3: Beck 1G **47**
Playing Fld. Cl.
GU27: Hasl 9G **171**
Plaza, The RG40: W'ham 3B **30**
Pleasance, The SW15 . . . . .7G **12**
Pleasance Rd. SW15 . . . . .8G **12**
Pleasant Gro. CR0: Croy 9J **47**
Pleasant Pl. KT12: Hers 3K **57**
Pleasant Vw. Pl.
BR6: Farnb 2K **67**
Pleasure Pit Rd.
KT21: Asht 5A **80**
Plesman Way SM6: W'ton 5J **63**
Plevna Rd. TW12: Hamp 9B **24**
Plough Cl. RH11: Ifield 1L **181**
Plough Ind. Est. KT22: Leat 7G **79**
Ploughlands RG42: Brac 9L **15**
Plough La. CR8: Pur 5J **63**
GU6: Ewh 6G **156**
KT11: Cob 4H **77**
RG40: W'ham 1E **30**
RH12: Hors 3L **197**
SM6: Bedd, W'ton 1J **63**
SW17 . . . . .6N **27**
SW19 . . . . .6N **27**
TW11: Tedd 6G **24**
Plough La. Cl. SM6: Bedd 2J **63**
Ploughmans End
TW7: Isle 8D **10**
Plough Rd. GU46: Yate 8D **48**
KT19: Ewe 5C **60**
RH6: Smallf 8M **143**
RH7: Dorm 9C **146**
Plough Wlk. *TN8: Eden 9L 127*
(off Fircroft Way)
Plover Cl. RH11: Craw 1A **182**
TN8: Eden 9M **127**
TW18: Stain 4H **21**
Plovers Ri. GU24: B'wood 7B **72**
Plovers Rd. RH13: Hors 5M **197**
Plum Cl. TW13: Felt 2H **23**
Plum Gth. TW8: Brent 1K **11**
Plummer La. CR4: Mit 1D **44**
Plummer Rd. SW4 . . . . .1H **29**
Plumpton Way SM5: Cars 9C **44**
Plumtree Cl. SM6: W'ton 4H **63**
Plymen Ho. KT8: W Mole 4A **40**
Plymouth Ct. KT5: Surb 8K **203**
Pocket Cl. RG12: Bin 1J **31**
Pockford Rd. GU8: Chid 5F **172**
Pocklington Ct. SW15 . . . . .2F **26**
Pococks La. SL4: Eton 1H **5**
Podmore Rd. SW18 . . . . .7N **13**
Poels Ct. RH19: E Grin 8A **166**
Poets Ct. SE25 . . . . .3D **46**
Point, The *GU21: Wok 3B 74*
(off Chertsey Rd.)
Point Bingo
Bracknell 1N 31
(within The Point Leisure Cen.)
Pointers, The KT21: Asht 7L **79**
Pointers Cotts. TW10: Ham 3J **25**
POINTERS GREEN 5H 77
Pointers Hill RH4: Westc 7C **118**
Pointers Rd. KT11: Cob 3D **76**
Point Leisure Centre, The 1N 31
Point Pleasant SW18 . . . . .7M **13**
Point Wharf TW8: Brent 3L **11**
Point Wharf La. TW8: Brent 3K **11**
Polar Pk. UB7: Harm 3A **8**
Polden Cl. GU14: Cove 7K **69**
POLECAT 8D 170
Polecat Hill GU26: Hind 8D **170**
GU27: Hasl 8D **170**
Polecat Valley GU26: Hind . . .8D **170**
Polehamptons, The
TW12: Hamp 8C **24**
Polesden Gdns. SW20 . . . . .1G **42**
POLESDEN LACEY 8B 98
Polesden Lacey 8B 98
Polesden La. GU23: Rip 9H **75**
Polesden Rd. KT23: Book 7B **98**
Polesden Vw. KT23: Book 5B **98**
Poles La. RH11: Low H 6A **162**
Polesteeple Hill TN16: B Hil 4F **86**
Police Sta. Rd. KT12: Hers 3K **57**
Polka Theatre for Children 7N 27
Polkerris Way GU52: Chu C 9C **88**
Pollard Cl. SL4: O Win 8L **5**
Pollard Gro. GU15: Camb 2G **71**
Pollard Ho. KT4: W Pk 1H **61**
Pollard Rd. GU22: Wok 3D **74**
SM4: Mord 4B **44**
Pollardrow Av. RG42: Brac 9L **15**
Pollards RH11: Craw 4M **181**
Pollards Cres. SW16 . . . . .2J **45**
Pollards Dr. RH13: Hors 5L **197**
Pollards Hill E. SW16 . . . . .2K **45**
Pollards Hill Nth. SW16 . . . . . . .2J **45**
Pollards Hill Sth. SW16 . . . . . . .2J **45**
Pollards Hill W. SW16 . . . . .2K **45**
Pollards Oak Cres.
RH8: Oxt 1C **126**
Pollards Oak Rd. RH8: Oxt . . .1C **126**
Pollards Wood Hill
RH8: Oxt 8D **106**
Pollards Wood Rd.
RH8: Oxt 9D **106**
SW16 . . . . .2J **45**
Pollocks Path GU26: Hind 7B **170**
Polmear Cl. GU52: Chu C 9C **88**
Polo Centre, The SL5: S'hill 2F **34**
Polsted La. GU3: Comp 1E **132**
Poltimore Rd. GU2: Guil 5K **113**
Polworth Rd. SW16 . . . . .6J **29**
Polyanthus Way
RG45: Crowt 8G **31**
Polygon Bus. Cen. SL3: Poy 5H **7**
Pomeroy Cl. TW1: Twick 7H **11**
Pond Cl. KT12: Hers 3G **57**
(not continuous)
RH14: Loxw 4H **193**
Pond Copse La.
RH14: Loxw 3H **193**
Pond Cott. La. BR4: W Wick 7K **47**
Pond Cft. GU46: Yate 9D **48**
Pond Farm Cl.
KT20: Wal H 2G **100**
Pondfield Ho. SE27 . . . . .6N **29**
Pondfield Rd. CR8: Ken 3M **83**
GU7: Godal 4J **133**
RH12: Rudg 9F **176**
Pond Head La.
RH5: For G, Ockl 6L **157**
Pond Hill Gdns. SM3: Chea 3K **61**
Pond Ho. KT16: Chert 6K **37**
Pond La. GU5: P'lake 4D **136**
GU10: Churt 6H **149**
Pond Mdw. GU2: Guil 3H **113**
Pondmoor Rd. RG12: Brac 4N **31**
Pond Piece KT22: Oxs 9B **58**
Pond Pl. KT21: Asht 4L **79**
Pond Rd. GU14: Farnb 3N **89**
GU22: Wok 7K **73**
GU35: Head D 5F **168**
TW20: Egh 7E **20**
Ponds, The KT13: Weybr 3E **56**
Pondside Av. KT4: W Pk 7H **43**
Pondside Cl. UB3: Harl 2E **8**
Ponds La. GU5: Alb 2N **135**
PONDTAIL
GU51 . . . . .5D 88
TN8 . . . . .5M 167
Pondtail Cl. GU51: Fleet 5D **88**
RH12: Hors 2K **197**
Pondtail Copse RH12: Hors . . .2K **197**
Pondtail Dr. RH12: Hors 1K **197**
Pondtail Gdns. GU51: Fleet 5D **88**
Pondtail Pk. RH12: Hors 2K **197**
Pondtail Rd. GU51: Fleet 5D **88**
RH12: Hors 3J **197**
Pond Vw. Cl. GU51: Fleet 3C **88**
Pond Way RH19: E Grin 9D **166**
TW11: Tedd 7J **25**
Pond Wood Rd.
RH10: Craw 1E **182**
Ponsonby Rd. SW15 . . . . .1G **26**
Pontes Av. TW3: Houn 7N **9**
Pony Chase KT11: Cob 9N **57**
Pook Hill GU8: Chid, Hasl 5B **172**
Pool Cl. KT8: W Mole 4N **39**
Poole Ct. TW4: Houn 5M **9**
Poole Ct. Rd. TW4: Houn 5M **9**
POOL END 4B 38
Pool End Cl. TW17: Shep 4B **38**
Poole Rd. GU21: Wok 5A **74**
KT19: Ewe 3C **60**
Pooles Cotts. TW10: Ham 3K **25**
Pooley Av. TW20: Egh 6D **20**
Pooley Dr. SW14 . . . . .6B **12**
POOLEY GREEN 6E 20
Pooley Grn. Cl. TW20: Egh 6E **20**
Pooley Grn. Rd. TW20: Egh 6D **20**
Pool in the Park 6B 74
Poolmans Rd. SL4: W'sor 6A **4**
Pool Rd. GU11: Alde 5A **110**
KT8: W Mole 4N **39**
Pools on the Park 7K 11
POOTINGS 5N 127
Pootings Rd. TN8: C Hil 3M **127**
Pope Cl. SW19 . . . . .7B **28**
TW14: Felt 2G **22**
Popejoy Dr. GU19: Bag 5H **51**
Popes Av. TW2: Twick 3E **24**
Popes Cl. SL3: Coln 3D **6**
Popes Ct. TW2: Twick 3E **24**
Popes Gro. CR0: Croy 9J **47**
TW1: Twick 3F **24**
TW2: Twick 3F **24**
Popes La. RH8: Oxt 3A **126**
Popes Mead GU27: Hasl 1G **189**
POPESWOOD 8J 15
Popeswood Rd. RG42: Bin 8J **15**
Popeswood Rdbt. RG42: Bin . . .9J **15**
Popham Cl. RG12: Brac 4D **32**
TW13: Hanw 4N **23**
Popham Gdns. TW9: Rich 6N **11**
Popinjays Row *SM3: Chea 2J 61*
(off Netley Cl.)
Poplar Av. CR4: Mit 9D **28**
GU20: Windl 1L **51**
KT22: Leat 9H **79**
Poplar Cl. GU14: Cove 9H **69**
GU16: Mytc 2E **90**
KT17: Eps D 2G **81**
RG12: Brac 2B **32**
RH11: Craw 9A **162**
SL3: Poy 4G **7**
Poplar Cotts. GU3: Guil 9H **93**
Poplar Ct. SW19 . . . . .6M **27**
TW1: Twick 9J **11**
Poplar Cres. KT19: Ewe 3B **60**
Poplar Dr. SM7: Ban 1J **81**
Poplar Farm Cl. KT19: Ewe 3B **60**
Poplar Gdns. KT3: N Mal 1C **42**
Poplar Gro. GU22: Wok 6A **74**
KT3: N Mal 1C **42**
Poplar Ho. KT19: Eps 5C **60**
SL3: Lang 1B **6**
Poplar La. RH18: F Row 8G **187**
Poplar Rd. GU4: Chil 1A **134**
KT10: Surb 9H **41**
KT22: Leat 9H **79**
SM3: Sut 7L **43**
SW19 . . . . .1M **43**
TW15: Ashf 6D **22**
Poplar Rd. Sth. SW19 . . . . .2M **43**
Poplars, The RH13: Hors 5L **197**
SL5: Asc 4L **33**
Poplar Vs. *GU16: Frim G 8D 70*
(off Beech Rd.)
Poplar Wlk.
CR0: Croy 1B **200** (8N **45**)
CR3: Cate 1B **104**
GU9: Heath E 5J **109**
Poplar Way TW13: Felt 4H **23**
Poppy Cl. SM6: W'ton 7E **44**

Poppyhills Rd.—Puddenhole Cotts.

Poppyhills Rd. GU15: Camb . . .7D 50
Poppy La. CR0: Croy 6F 46
Poppy Pl. RG40: W'ham 2A 30
Porchester SL5: Asc 3L 33
Porchester Rd.
KT1: K Tham 1A 42
Porchfield Cl. SM2: Sut 6N 61
Porridge Pot All.
GU1: Guil 7B 202 (5N 113)
Portal Cl. SE27 . . . . .4L 29
Porters Lodge, The SW10 . . . . .3N 13
(off Coleridge Gdns.)
Portesbery Hill Dr.
GU15: Camb 9C 50
Portesbery Rd. GU15: Camb . . .9B 50
Portia Gro. RG42: Warf 9C 16
Portinscale Rd. SW15 . . . . .8K 13
Portland Av. KT3: N Mal 6E 42
Portland Bus. Cen. SL3: Dat 4L 5
Portland Cl. KT4: W Pk 6G 42
Portland Cotts. CR0: Bedd 6H 45
Portland Cres. TW13: Felt 5E 22
Portland Dr. GU52: Chu C 9A 88
RH1: Mers 7H 103
Portland Ho. RH1: Mers 7H 103
SW15 . . . . .8J 13
Portland Pl. KT17: Eps 8D 60
SE25 . . . . .3D 46
(off Sth. Norwood Hill)
Portland Rd. CR4: Mit 1C 44
KT1: K Tham . . .6K 203 (2L 41)
RH4: Dork 1J 201 (4G 119)
RH19: E Grin 1A 186
SE25 . . . . .3D 46
TW15: Ashf 4N 21
Portland Ter. GU1: Guil 5F 202
TW9: Rich 7K 11
Portley La. CR3: Cate 8B 84
Portley Wood Rd.
CR3: Whyte 7C 84
Portman Av. SW14 . . . . .6C 12
Portman Cl. RG42: Brac 9M 15
Portman Rd.
KT1: K Tham . . .4M 203 (1M 41)
Portmore Pk. Rd.
KT13: Weybr 1B 56
Portmore Pl. KT13: Weybr 9E 38
(off Oatlands Dr.)
Portmore Quays
KT13: Weybr 1A 56
Portmore Way KT13: Weybr 9B 38
Portnall Dr. GU25: V Wat 3J 35
Portnall Ri. GU25: V Wat 4J 35
Portnall Rd. GU25: V Wat 4J 35
Portnalls Cl. CR5: Coul 3F 82
Portnalls Ri. CR5: Coul 3G 82
Portnalls Rd. CR5: Coul 5F 82
Porton Ct. KT6: Surb 5J 41
Portsmouth Av. KT7: T Dit 6G 40
Portsmouth Rd.
GU2: Guil 8B 202 (7M 113)
GU3: Art 7M 113
GU7: Godal 1D 152
GU8: Godal, Mil 1D 152
GU8: Mil, Thur 9G 151
GU15: Camb 9E 50
GU16: Frim 5B 70
GU23: Rip, Wis 8M 75
GU23: Send, Rip 3H 95
GU26: Brams, Lip, Hind
. . . . .9M 169
(not continuous)
KT1: K Tham . . .8G 203 (6G 41)
KT6: Surb 8G 203 (6G 41)
KT7: T Dit 8G 203 (6G 41)
KT10: Esh 3A 58
(Hawkshill Cl.)
KT10: Esh 1C 58
(Sandown Rd.)
KT10: Esh 9G 56
(Seven Hills Rd. Sth.)
KT11: Cob 9G 56
SW15 . . . . .1G 27
Portswood Pl. SW15 . . . . .9E 12
Portugal Gdns. TW2: Twick 3C 24
Portugal Rd. GU21: Wok 3B 74
Port Way GU24: Bis 3D 72
Portway KT17: Ewe 5F 60
Portway Cres. KT17: Ewe 5F 60
POSK 1F 12
(off King St.)
Post Boys Row KT11: Cob 1H 77
Postford Farm Cotts.
GU5: Alb 1J 135
Postford Mill Cotts.
GU4: Guil 7H 115
Post Horn Cl. RH18: F Row . . .8K 187
Post Horn La. RH18: F Row . . .8J 187
Post Ho. La. KT23: Book 3A 98
Post La. TW2: Twick 2D 24
Postmill Cl. CR0: Croy 9F 46
Post Office All. W4 . . . . .2A 12
(off Thames Rd.)
Post Office Row RH8: Limp . . .9G 107
Potbury Cl. SL4: Wink 7M 17
POT COMMON 8G 131
Potkiln Ho. GU51: Fleet 1A 88
Potley Hill Rd. GU46: Yate 9E 48
Potter Cl. CR4: Mit 1F 44
Potteries, The GU14: Cove 8J 69
KT16: Otter 3G 54
Potteries La. GU16: Mytc 2D 90
Potterne Cl. SW19 . . . . .1J 27
Potters Cl. CR0: Croy 7H 47
GU8: Mil 9C 132
Potters Ct. SM1: Sut 3L 61
(off Rosebery Rd.)
Potters Cres. GU12: Ash 1F 110
Potter's Cft. RH13: Hors 6L 197
Pottersfield RH10: Craw 2B 182
Potters Ga. GU9: Farnh 1F 128
Potters Gro. KT3: N Mal 3B 42
Potter's Hill GU8: Ent G 5F 152
Potters Ind. Pk.
GU52: Chu C 8D 88
Potters La. GU23: Send 1D 94
SW16 . . . . .7H 29
Potters Pl. RH12: Hors 6J 197
Potters Way RH2: Reig 7A 122
Pottery Cl. SE25 . . . . .2D 46
Pottery Ct. GU10: Wrec 5E 128
Pottery Ho. RH19: E Grin 8N 165
(off Fosters Pl.)
Pottery La. GU10: Wrec 5E 128
Pottery Rd. TW8: Brent 2L 11
Poulcott TW19: Wray 9A 6
Poulett Gdns. TW1: Twick 2G 24
Poulters Wood BR2: Kes 2F 66
Poulton Av. SM1: Sut 9B 44
Pound Cl. GU7: Godal 7H 133
GU35: Head 4E 168
KT6: Surb 7J 41
KT19: Eps 7C 60
RH14: Loxw 3H 193
Pound Ct. GU3: Wood V 2E 112
KT21: Asht 5M 79
Pound Cres. KT22: Fetc 8D 78
Pound Farm Cl. KT10: Esh 7D 40
Pound Farm La.
GU12: Ash, Ash G 2H 111
Pound Fld.
GU1: Guil 2C 202 (2N 113)
Poundfield Ct. GU22: Wok 8E 74
Poundfield Gdns.
GU22: Wok 7E 74
(not continuous)
Poundfield La. RH14: Plais . . .4D 192
POUND HILL 3G 183
Pound Hill GU3: Wood V 2E 112
Pound Hill Pde.
RH10: Craw 2G 183
Pound Hill Pl. RH10: Craw 3G 183
Pound La. GU3: Wood V 2E 112
GU7: Godal 7H 133
(not continuous)
GU20: Windl 3N 51
KT19: Eps 5G 201 (8B 60)
RG10: Hurst 4A 14
Pound La. Caravan Site
GU3: Wood V 2E 112
Pound Pl. GU4: Chil 9B 114
RG42: Bin 6H 15
Pound Pl. Cl. GU4: Chil 9B 114
Pound Rd. GU12: Alde 3A 110
KT16: Chert 6K 37
SM7: Ban 4L 81
Pound St. SM5: Cars 2D 62
POVEY CROSS 1B 162
Povey Cross Rd. RH6: Horl . . .1B 162
Powderham Ct. GU21: Knap 5G 72
Powder Mill La. TW2: Whitt . . .1N 23
Powell Cl. GU2: Guil 5J 113
KT9: Ches 2K 59
RH6: Horl 7C 142
Powell Ct. CR2: S Croy 7A 200
Powell Gdns. RH1: Red 1F 122
Powells Cl. RH4: Dork 8J 119
Powell's Wlk. W4 . . . . .2D 12
Power Cl.
GU1: Guil 1B 202 (2M 113)
Powerleague
Croydon 3K 63
Power Rd. W4 . . . . .1N 11
Powers Ct. TW1: Twick 1K 25
Pownall Gdns. TW3: Houn 7B 10
Pownall Rd. TW3: Houn 7B 10
POYLE 5G 7
Poyle Gdns. RG12: Brac 9B 16
Poyle Ho. GU4: Guil 2F 114
(off Merrow St.)
Poyle Ind. Est. SL3: Poy 6H 7
Poyle New Cotts. SL3: Poy 5H 7
Poyle Pk. SL3: Poy 6G 6
Poyle Rd.
GU1: Guil 7E 202 (5A 114)
GU10: Tong 6D 110
SL3: Poy 6G 6
Poyle Technical Cen.
SL3: Poy 5G 7
Poyle Ter.
GU1: Guil 6D 202 (5N 113)
Poyle Trad. Est. SL3: Poy 6G 7
Poynders Ct. SW4 . . . . .1G 29
Poynders Gdns. SW4 . . . . .1G 29
Poynders Rd. SW4 . . . . .1G 29
Poynes Rd. RH6: Horl 6C 142
Poynings Rd. RH11: Ifield 4J 181
Prado Path TW1: Twick 2F 24
(off Laurel Av.)
Prairie Cl. KT15: Addl 9K 37
Prairie Rd. KT15: Addl 9K 37
Pratts La. KT12: Hers 1L 57
Pratts Pas.
KT1: K Tham 4J 203 (1L 41)
Prebend Gdns. W4 . . . . .1E 12
Prebend Mans. W4 . . . . .1E 12
(off Chiswick High Rd.)
Precinct, The GU6: Cranl 6N 155
TW20: Egh 6C 20
Precincts, The SM4: Mord 5M 43
Premier Ho. RH10: Craw 8B 162
Premier Pde. RH6: Horl 8F 142
(off High St.)
Premier Pl. SW15 . . . . .7K 13
Prentice Cl. GU14: Farnb 6N 69
Prentice Ct. SW19 . . . . .6L 27
Prentis Rd. SW16 . . . . .5H 29
Presburg Rd. KT3: N Mal 4D 42
Presbury Ct. GU21: Wok 5K 73
Prescott RG12: Brac 6L 31
Prescott Cl. SW16 . . . . .8J 29
Prescott Rd. SL3: Poy 5G 6
Presentation M. SW2 . . . . .3K 29
Preshaw Cres. CR4: Mit 2C 44
Prestbury Cres. SM7: Ban 3D 82
Preston Cl. TW2: Twick 4E 24
Preston Ct. KT12: Wal T 7K 39
Preston Dr. KT19: Ewe 3D 60
Preston Gro. KT21: Asht 4J 79
Preston La. KT20: Tad 8G 81
Preston Pl. TW10: Rich 8L 11
Preston Rd. SE19 . . . . .7M 29
SW20 . . . . .8E 26
TW17: Shep 4B 38
Prestwick Cl. RH11: Ifield 4J 181
UB2: S'hall 1M 9
Prestwick La. GU8: Chid 7L 171
GU27: G'wood, Chid 7L 171
Prestwood Cl. RH11: Craw . . .9N 161
Prestwood Gdns. CR0: Croy . . .6N 45
Prestwood La. RH11: Ifield . . .9H 161
RH12: Rusp 9F 160
Pretoria Rd. KT16: Chert 7H 37
SW16 . . . . .7F 28
Pretty La. CR5: Coul 8G 82
Prewetts Mill RH12: Hors 7H 197
PREY HEATH 1M 93
Prey Heath Cl. GU22: Wok 2M 93
Prey Heath Rd. GU22: Wok 2L 93
Preymead Ind. Est.
GU9: B Lea 5N 109
Price Cl. SW17 . . . . .4D 28
Price Gdns. RG42: Warf 7N 15
Price Rd.
CR0: Wad 8A 200 (2M 63)
Prices La. RH2: Reig 6M 121
Price Way TW12: Hamp 7M 23
Priddy Pl. RH1: Mers 9G 102
Priddy's Yd.
CR0: Croy 3B 200 (8N 45)
Prideaux Gdns. RH5: Ockl 6D 158
Prides Crossing SL5: Asc 8L 17
Pridham Rd. CR7: T Hea 3A 46
Priest Av. RG40: W'ham 3E 30
Priestcroft Cl. RH11: Craw 3M 181
Priest Hill RH8: Limp 7D 106
SL4: O Win 4M 19
TW20: Eng G, O Win 4M 19
Priestlands Cl. RH6: Horl 7D 142
Priest La. GU24: W End 9N 51
Priestley Rd. CR4: Mit 1E 44
GU2: Guil 3G 112
Priestley Way RH10: Craw 8E 162
Priestly Gdns. GU22: Wok 7C 74
Priests Bri. SW14 . . . . .6D 12
SW15 . . . . .6D 12
PRIESTWOOD 9M 15
Priestwood Av. RG42: Brac 9L 15
Priestwood Ct. Rd.
RG42: Brac 9M 15
Priestwood Sq. RG42: Brac 9L 15
Primeplace M. CR7: T Hea 1N 45
Primrose Av. RH6: Horl 1F 162
Primrose Cl. RH11: Craw 6N 181
SM6: W'ton 6F 44
Primrose Copse
RH12: Hors 1K 197
Primrose Ct. GU12: Ash 2E 110
SW12 . . . . .1H 29
Primrose Dr. GU24: Bis 2D 72
Primrose Gdns. GU14: Cove 2K 89
Primrose Ho. KT18: Eps 7H 201
Primrose La. CR0: Croy 7F 46
RH18: F Row 8J 187
Primrose Pl. GU7: Godal 9E 132
TW7: Isle 5F 10
Primrose Ridge GU7: Godal . . .9E 132
Primrose Rd. KT12: Hers 2K 57
Primrose Wlk. GU46: Yate 9A 48
GU51: Fleet 3A 88
KT17: Ewe 4E 60
RG12: Brac 4A 32
Primrose Way GU5: Braml 6N 133
GU47: Sandh 6G 49
Primula Rd. GU35: Bor 6A 168
Prince Albert Ct.
TW16: Sunb 8G 22
Prince Albert Dr. SL5: Asc 3H 33
Prince Albert Sq. RH1: Red . . .8D 122
Prince Albert's Wlk.
SL4: W'sor 4K 5
Prince Andrew Way
SL5: Asc 1H 33
Prince Charles Cres.
GU14: Farnb 6N 69
Prince Charles Way
SM6: W'ton 9F 44
Prince Consort Cotts.
SL4: W'sor 5G 4
Prince Consort Dr. SL5: Asc . . .3H 33
Prince Consort's Dr.
SL4: W'sor 9C 4
Prince Dr. GU47: Sandh 6F 48
Prince George's Av. SW20 . . . . .1H 43
Prince George's Rd. SW19 . . . .9B 28
Prince of Wales Ct.
GU11: Alde 2L 109
(off Queen Elizabeth Dr.)
Prince of Wales Rd.
RH1: Out 2L 143
SM1: Sut 8B 44
Prince of Wales Ter. W4 . . . . . .1D 12
Prince of Wales Wlk.
GU15: Camb 9A 50
Prince Regent Pl.
GU14: Farnb 4A 90
Prince Regent Rd.
TW3: Houn 6B 10
Prince Rd. SE25 . . . . .4B 46
Princes Av. CR2: Sande 2E 84
GU7: Godal 4F 132
GU11: Alde 8N 89
KT6: Surb 7N 41
SM5: Cars 4D 62
Princes Cl. CR2: Sande 2E 84
SL4: E Wic 1C 4
TW11: Tedd 5D 24
Princes Club 3C 22
Princes Ct. GU1: Guil 2C 202
KT13: Weybr 2C 56
(off Princes Rd.)
Prince's Dr. KT22: Oxs 8E 58
Princes Hall
Aldershot 2M 109
Princes Mead (Shop. Cen.)
GU14: Farnb 1N 89
Princes M. TW3: Houn 7A 10
W6 . . . . .1G 13
(off Down Pl.)
Princes Rd. KT2: K Tham 8N 25
KT13: Weybr 2C 56
RH1: Red 5D 122
SW14 . . . . .6C 12
SW19 . . . . .7M 27
TW9: Kew 4M 11
TW10: Rich 8M 11
TW11: Tedd 5D 24
TW13: Felt 3G 22
TW15: Ashf 6A 22
TW20: Egh 7B 20
Princess Anne Rd.
RH12: Rudg 1E 194
Princess Av. SL4: W'sor 6E 4
Princess Ct. KT1: K Tham 6L 203
Princess Gdns. GU22: Wok 3D 74
Princess Ho. RH1: Red 2E 122
Princess Margaret Rd.
RH12: Rudg 1E 194
Princess Mary Cl. GU2: Guil . . .8K 93
Princess Marys Rd.
KT15: Addl 1L 55
Princess M.
KT1: K Tham . . .6L 203 (2M 41)
Princess Pde. BR6: Farnb 1J 67
Princess Pk. KT15: Addl 1J 55
Princess Pct. RH6: Horl 8E 142
(off High St.)
Princess Rd. CR0: Croy 5N 45
GU22: Wok 3D 74
RH11: Craw 3A 182
Princess Sq. KT10: Esh 3C 58
RG12: Brac 1N 31
Princes St. SM1: Sut 1B 62
TW9: Rich 7L 11
Princess Way GU15: Camb 9A 50
RH1: Red 2E 122
Princes Way BR4: W Wick 1B 66
CR0: Wad 2K 63
GU11: Alde 2M 109
GU19: Bag 6J 51
SW19 . . . . .1J 27
Princeton Ct. SW15 . . . . .6J 13
Princeton M.
KT2: K Tham 2M 203 (9N 25)
Prince William Ct.
TW15: Ashf 6A 22
(off Clarendon Rd.)
Pringle Gdns. CR8: Pur 6K 63
SW16 . . . . .5G 28
(not continuous)
Printing Ho. Ct. GU11: Alde . . .2N 109
(off Sebastopol Rd.)
Prior Av. SM2: Sut 4C 62
Prior Cft. Cl. GU15: Camb 2E 70
Prior End GU15: Camb 1E 70
Prioress Rd. SE27 . . . . .4M 29
Prior Rd. GU15: Camb 1E 70
Priors, The KT21: Asht 6K 79
Priors Cl. GU14: Farnb 6M 69
Priors Ct. GU12: Ash 3D 110
GU21: Wok 5K 73
Prior's Cft. GU22: Wok 7C 74
Priorsfield Rd.
GU3: Comp 9C 112
GU7: Hurt 9C 112
Priors Hatch La.
GU7: Hurt 2C 132
Priors Keep GU52: Fleet 5C 88
Prior's La. GU17: B'water 1F 68
Priors Mead KT23: Book 3C 98
Priors Rd. SL4: W'sor 6A 4
Priors Wlk. RH10: Craw 3C 182
Priors Wood GU27: Hasl 2D 188
KT10: Hinc W 8F 40
RG45: Crowt 3C 48
Priorswood GU3: Comp 1C 132
Priory, The CR0: Wad 1L 63
KT22: Leat 9H 79
RH9: Gods 9E 104
Priory Av. SM3: Chea 1J 61
Priory Cl. BR3: Beck 2H 47
GU21: Wok 9F 54
KT12: Wal T 9H 39
RH4: Dork 7G 119
RH6: Horl 7D 142
SL5: S'dale 6D 34
SW19 . . . . .9N 27
TW12: Hamp 9N 23
TW16: Sunb 8H 23
Priory Ct. GU2: Guil 7M 113
GU15: Camb 1L 69
KT1: K Tham 5J 203
KT17: Ewe 5E 60
RH4: Dork 7H 119
SM3: Chea 1K 61
TW3: Houn 6B 10
TW20: Egh 7E 20
Priory Cres. SE19 . . . . .8N 29
SM3: Chea 1J 61
Priory Dr. RH2: Reig 5M 121
Priory Gdns. SE25 . . . . .3C 46
SW13 . . . . .6E 12
TW12: Hamp 8N 23
TW15: Ashf 6E 22
Priory Grn. TW18: Stain 6K 21
Priory La. GU10: Fren, Til 2K 149
KT8: W Mole 3B 40
RG42: Brac 8A 16
SW15 . . . . .9D 12
Priory Lodge W4 . . . . .1N 11
(off Kew Bri. Ct.)
Priory M. TW18: Stain 6K 21
Priory Pl. KT12: Wal T 9H 39
Priory Retail Pk. SW19 . . . . . . .8B 28
Priory Rd. CR0: Croy 6L 45
KT9: Ches 9L 41
RH2: Reig 5M 121
RH18: F Row 9D 186
SL5: Asc 9F 16
SL5: S'dale 6D 34
SM3: Chea 1J 61
SW19 . . . . .8B 28
TW3: Houn 8C 10
TW9: Kew 2N 11
TW12: Hamp 8N 23
Priory St. GU14: Farnb 1B 90
Priory Ter. TW16: Sunb 8H 23
Priory Wlk. RG12: Brac 3D 32
Priory Way SL3: Dat 3L 5
UB7: Harm 2N 7
Privet M. CR8: Pur 8G 63
Privet Rd. GU35: Lind 4B 168
Probyn Rd. SW2 . . . . .3M 29
Proctor Cl. CR4: Mit 9E 28
RH10: Craw 5G 183
Proctor Gdns. KT23: Book 3B 98
Proctors Cl. TW14: Felt 2H 23
Proctors Rd. RG40: W'ham 2E 30
Proffits Cotts. KT20: Tad 9J 81
Profumo Rd. KT12: Hers 2L 57
Progress Bus. Pk. CR0: Wad . . .8K 45
Progress Way CR0: Wad 8K 45
Prologis Pk. CR0: Bedd 6H 45
Promenade, The W4 . . . . .5D 12
Promenade App. Rd. W4 . . . . . .3D 12
Promenade de Verdun
CR8: Pur 7H 63
Propeller Cres. CR0: Wad 2L 63
Prospect Av. GU14: Farnb 8N 69
Prospect Cl. TW3: Houn 4N 9
Prospect Cotts. GU12: Ash V . . .9E 90
(off South Rd.)
SW18 . . . . .7M 13
Prospect Cres. TW2: Whitt 9C 10
Prospect Hill GU35: Head 1D 168
Prospect Ho. KT19: Eps 5A 60
SW19 . . . . .9B 28
(off Chapter Way)
Prospect La. TW20: Eng G 6K 19
Prospect Pl. CR2: S Croy 3N 63
KT17: Eps 6L 201 (8D 60)
RH11: Craw 3A 182
SL4: W'sor 6G 4
(off Osborne Rd.)
SW20 . . . . .8G 27
TW18: Stain 6H 21
W4 . . . . .1C 12
Prospect Quay SW18 . . . . .7M 13
(off Lightermans Wlk.)
Prospect Rd. GU10: Rowl 8D 128
GU12: Ash V 8E 90
GU14: Cove, Farnb 1M 89
KT6: Surb 5J 41
Prossers KT20: Tad 8J 81
Prothero Rd. SW6 . . . . .3K 13
Providence La. UB3: Harl 3E 8
Providence Pl. GU22: Pyr 1J 75
KT17: Eps 5M 201 (8D 60)
Providence Ter.
RH10: Turn H 5D 184
Prudence La. BR6: Farnb 1J 67
Prune Hill
TW20: Egh, Eng G 8N 19
Prunus Cl. GU24: W End 9B 52
Pryors Wood RH12: K'fold 3J 179
Ptarmigan Hgts. RG12: Brac 3J 31
Puccinia Ct. TW19: Stan 2N 21
(off Yeoman Dr.)
Puckridge Hill Rd.
GU11: Alde 7K 89
Pucks Hill GU21: Knap 4G 73
Puckshott Way GU27: Hasl 9H 171
Puddenhole Cotts.
RH3: Betch 2N 119

Pudding La.—Radnor Way

Pudding La. RH6: Charlw 2K 161
Puffin Cl. BR3: Beck 4G 46
Puffin Hill RH10: Turn H 4F 184
Puffin Rd. RH11: Ifield 4J 181
Pulborough Rd. SW18 . . . . .1L 27
Pulborough Way TW4: Houn 7K 9
Pullman Ct. SW2 . . . . .2J 29
Pullman Gdns. SW15 . . . . .9H 13
Pullman La. GU7: Godal 9F 132
Pullman Pl. *RH1: Mers 6G 102*
(off Station Rd.)
Pullmans Pl. TW18: Stain 6J 21
Pulteney Cl. TW7: Isle 6G 10
Pulton Pl. SW6 . . . . .3M 13
Pump All. TW8: Brent 3K 11
Pumping Sta. Rd. W4 . . . . .3D 12
Pump La. SL5: Asc 9B 18
Pump Pail Nth.
CR0: Croy 5B 200 (9N 45)
Pump Pail Sth.
CR0: Croy 5B 200 (9N 45)
Punch Bowl La. GU8: Thur 3E 170
Punchbowl La. RH5: Dork 4K 119
Punch Copse Rd.
RH10: Craw 2D 182
Puniper Cl. TW13: Felt 4J 23
Punnetts Ct. RH11: Craw 6L 181
Purbeck Av. KT3: N Mal 5E 42
Purbeck Cl. RH1: Mers 6G 103
(not continuous)
Purbeck Ct. GU2: Guil 3H 113
Purbeck Dr. GU21: Wok 1B 74
Purberry Gro. KT17: Ewe 6E 60
Purberry Shot KT17: Ewe 6E 60
Purbrook Ct. RG12: Brac 5C 32
Purcell Cl. CR8: Ken 1N 83
Purcell Cres. SW6 . . . . .3J 13
Purcell Mans. *W14 . . . . .2K 13*
(off Queen's Club Gdns.)
Purcell Rd. RG45: Crowt 9G 30
RH11: Craw 6L 181
Purcell's Cl. KT21: Asht 5M 79
Purdy Ct. KT4: W Pk 8F 42
PURLEY 7L 63
Purley Bury Av. CR8: Pur 7N 63
Purley Bury Cl. CR8: Pur 7N 63
Purley Cl. RH10: Craw 6H 183
PURLEY CROSS 7L 63
Purley Downs Golf Course 7A 64
Purley Downs Rd.
CR2: Sande 6N 63
CR8: Pur 6N 63
Purley Hill CR8: Pur 8M 63
Purley Knoll CR8: Pur 7K 63
Purley Leisure Cen. 7L 63
Purley Oaks Rd. CR2: Sande 5A 64
Purley Oaks Station (Rail) 5A 64
Purley Pde. CR8: Pur 7L 63
Purley Pk. Rd. CR8: Pur 6M 63
Purley Ri. CR8: Pur 8K 63
Purley Rd. CR2: S Croy 4A 64
CR8: Pur 7L 63
Purley Station (Rail) 7L 63
Purley Va. CR8: Pur 9M 63
Purley Vw. Ter. *CR2: S Croy . . .4A 64*
(off Sanderstead Rd.)
Purley Way CR0: Croy, Wad 6K 45
CR8: Pur 6L 63
GU16: Frim 6C 70
Purley Way Centre, The
CR0: Wad 8L 45
Purley Way Cres. CR0: Croy . . .6K 45
Purmerend Cl. GU14: Cove 9H 69
Purser Ho. SW2 . . . . .1L 29
Pursers Cross Rd. SW6 . . . . . .4L 13
Pursers La. GU5: P'lake 2E 136
Pursers Lea GU5: P'lake 4E 136
Purslane RG40: W'ham 3C 30
Purton Rd. RH12: Hors 4H 197
Purvis Ho. CR0: Croy 6A 46
PUTNEY 7J 13
Putney Arts Theatre 7J 13
Putney Bri. SW15 . . . . .6K 13
Putney Bri. App. SW6 . . . . .6K 13
Putney Bri. Rd. SW15 . . . . .7K 13
SW18 . . . . .7K 13
Putney Bridge Station
(Underground) 6L 13
Putney Comn. SW15 . . . . .6H 13
Putney Exchange (Shop. Centre)
SW15 . . . . .7J 13
PUTNEY HEATH 9H 13
Putney Heath SW15 . . . . .9G 13
Putney Heath La. SW15 . . . . . . .9J 13
Putney High St. SW15 . . . . .7J 13
Putney Hill SW15 . . . . .1J 27
(not continuous)
Putney Leisure Cen. 7H 13
Putney Pk. Av. SW15 . . . . .7F 12
Putney Pk. La. SW15 . . . . .7G 12
(not continuous)
Putney Pier (Riverbus) 6K 13
Putney Station (Rail) 7K 13
PUTNEY VALE 4F 26
Putney Va. Crematorium
SW19 . . . . .3G 26
Putney Wharf SW15 . . . . .6K 13
PUTTENHAM 8N 111
Puttenham Golf Course 8A 112
Puttenham Heath Rd.
GU3: Comp, Put 8A 112
Puttenham Hill GU3: Put 7N 111
Puttenham La. GU8: S'ford . . .2N 131
Puttenham Rd. GU10: Seal 8F 110
Puttocks Cl. GU27: Hasl 3B 188
Pye Cl. CR3: Cate 1A 104
Pyecombe Ct. RH11: Craw 6L 181
Pyegrove Chase RG12: Brac . . .6C 32
PYESTOCK 4F 88
Pyestock Cres. GU14: Cove 1H 89
Pyke Cl. RG40: W'ham 2C 30
Pylbrook Rd. SM1: Sut 9M 43
Pyle Cl. KT15: Addl 1L 55
PYLE HILL 2N 93
Pyle Hill GU22: Wok 2N 93
Pylon Way CR0: Bedd 7J 45
Pymers Mead SE21 . . . . .2N 29
Pyne Rd. KT6: Surb 7N 41
Pyramid Ct. KT1: K Tham 4M 203
Pyramid Ho. TW4: Houn 5M 9
Pyrcroft La. KT13: Weybr 2C 56
Pyrcroft Rd. KT16: Chert 6G 36
PYRFORD 3J 75
Pyrford Comn. Rd.
GU22: Pyr 3F 74
Pyrford Ct. GU22: Pyr 4G 75
Pyrford Golf Course 4K 75
PYRFORD GREEN 4K 75
Pyrford Heath GU22: Pyr 3H 75
Pyrford Lock GU23: Wis 3L 75
Pyrford Rd. GU22: Pyr 9J 55
KT14: W By 9J 55
PYRFORD VILLAGE 5J 75
Pyrford Wood Est.
GU22: Pyr 3H 75
Pyrford Woods GU22: Pyr 2G 75
Pyrford Woods Cl.
GU22: Pyr 2H 75
Pyrian Cl. GU22: Wok 3F 74
Pyrland Rd. TW10: Rich 9M 11
Pyrmont Gro. SE27 . . . . .4M 29
Pyrmont Rd. W4 . . . . .2N 11
Pytchley Cres. SE19 . . . . .7N 29

Q

QUABROOK 9L 187
Quadrangle, The GU2: Guil 4K 113
GU16: Frim 6A 70
RH6: Horl 8E 142
SW6 . . . . .3K 13
Quadrant, The *GU1: Guil 5B 202*
(off Bridge St.)
GU12: Ash V 9E 90
KT17: Eps 6L 201 (9D 60)
SM2: Sut 3A 62
SW20 . . . . .9K 27
TW9: Rich 7K 11
Quadrant Ct. RG12: Brac 2C 32
Quadrant Courtyard, The
KT13: Weybr 1B 56
(off Quadrant Way)
Quadrant Rd. CR7: T Hea 3M 45
TW9: Rich 7K 11
Quadrant Way KT13: Weybr 1B 56
Quadrella Gdns. SL5: Asc 8J 17
Quadrum Pk. GU3: P'marsh . . .1L 133
Quail Cl. RH12: Hors 1K 197
Quail Cnr. RG12: Brac 3K 31
Quail Gdns. CR2: Sels 6H 65
Quain Mans. *W14 . . . . .2K 13*
(off Queen's Club Gdns.)
Quakers La. TW7: Isle 3G 10
Quakers Way GU3: Worp 8F 92
Qualitas RG12: Brac 7L 31
Quality St. RH1: Mers 6F 102
Quantock Cl. RH11: Craw 3N 181
SL3: Lang 1C 6
UB3: Harl 3E 8
Quantock Dr. KT4: W Pk 8H 43
Quarrendon St. SW6 . . . . .5M 13
Quarr Rd. SM5: Cars 5B 44
Quarry, The RH3: Betch 1C 120
Quarry Bank GU18: Ligh 7L 51
Quarry Cl. KT22: Leat 8K 79
RH8: Oxt 8A 106
RH12: Hors 2M 197
Quarry Cotts. RH2: Reig 9N 101
Quarry Gdns. KT22: Leat 8K 79
Quarry Hill GU7: Godal 8E 132
Quarry Hill Pk. RH2: Reig 9A 102
Quarry La. GU46: Yate 1D 68
Quarry Pk. Rd. SM1: Sut 3L 61
Quarry Path RH8: Oxt 9A 106
Quarry Ri. RH19: E Grin 7C 166
SM1: Sut 3L 61
Quarry Rd. GU7: Hurt 4D 132
RH8: Oxt 8A 106
RH9: Gods 6F 104
Quarryside Bus. Pk.
RH1: Red 9F 102
Quarry St.
GU1: Guil 6C 202 (5N 113)
Quarterbrass Farm Rd.
RH12: Hors 1K 197
Quartermaine Av.
GU22: Wok 9B 74
Quartermile Rd.
GU7: Godal 9H 133
Quarters Rd. GU14: Farnb 3N 89
Quayside Wlk.
KT1: K Tham 4H 203
Quebec Av. TN16: Weste 4M 107
Quebec Cl. RH6: Smallf 8L 143
Quebec Cotts.
TN16: Weste 5M 107
Quebec Gdns. GU17: Haw 2J 69
Quebec House 4M 107
Quebec Sq. TN16: Weste 4M 107
Queen Adelaide's Ride
SL4: Wink 9A 4
Queen Alexandra's Ct.
SW19 . . . . .6L 27
Queen Alexandra's Way
KT19: Eps 7N 59
Queen Anne Dr. KT10: Clay 4E 58
Queen Anne's Cl.
SL4: W'sor 4E 18
TW2: Twick 4D 24
Queen Anne's Gdns.
CR4: Mit 2D 44
KT22: Leat 8H 79
Queen Anne's Ga.
GU9: Heath E 5J 109
Queen Anne's Ride
SL4: W'sor 6D 18
Queen Anne's Rd.
SL4: W'sor 7F 4
Queen Anne's Ter.
KT22: Leat 8H 79
Queen Ann's Ct. *SL4: W'sor 4G 4*
(off Peascod St.)
Queen Caroline St. W6 . . . . . . .1H 13
Queen Catherine Ho. *SW6 . . . .3N 13*
(off Wandon Rd.)
Queen Charlotte St.
SL4: W'sor 4G 5
(off Market St.)
Queendale Ct. GU21: Wok 3J 73
Queen Eleanor's Rd.
GU2: Guil 4J 113
Queen Elizabeth Cl.
GU12: Ash 2E 110
Queen Elizabeth Dr.
GU11: Alde 2L 109
Queen Elizabeth Gdns.
SM4: Mord 3M 43
Queen Elizabeth Ho. SW12 . . . .1E 28
QUEEN ELIZABETH PARK 8K 93
Queen Elizabeth Rd.
GU15: Camb 6B 50
KT2: K Tham 3L 203 (1M 41)
RH12: Rudg 1E 194
Queen Elizabeth's Dr.
CR0: N Add 5N 65
Queen Elizabeth's Gdns.
CR0: N Add 6N 65
Queen Elizabeth's Wlk.
SL4: W'sor 5H 5
SM6: Bedd 1H 63
Queen Elizabeth Wlk. SW13 . . .4F 12
Queen Elizabeth Way
GU22: Wok 6B 74
SL4: W'sor 4E 4
Queenhill Rd. CR2: Sels 6E 64
Queenhythe Cres.
GU4: J Wel 6N 93
Queenhythe Rd. GU4: J Wel . . .6N 93
Queen Mary Av.
GU15: Camb 1M 69
SM4: Mord 4J 43
Queen Mary Cl. GU22: Wok . . .3E 74
GU51: Fleet 2A 88
KT6: Surb 9N 41
Queen Mary Ct. TW19: Stan . . .2N 21
Queen Mary Rd. SE19 . . . . .7M 29
TW17: Shep 1D 38
Queen Mary's Av.
SM5: Cars 4D 62
Queen Mary's Dr.
KT15: N Haw 6H 55
Queen Mary's Ho. SW15 . . . . . .9F 12
Queens Acre SL4: W'sor 7G 4
SM3: Chea 4J 61
Queens Acre Ho. SL4: W'sor 6G 4
Queens Av. GU11: Alde 1M 109
KT14: Byf 8M 55
TW13: Hanw 5K 23
Queensberry Ho. TW9: Rich 8J 11
Queensberry Pl. *TW9: Rich 8K 11*
(off Friars La.)
Queensbridge Pk. TW7: Isle . . .8E 10
Queensbury Pl.
GU17: Haw 3H 69
Queens Cl. GU24: Bis 3D 72
KT10: Esh 1B 58
KT20: Wal H 2F 100
SL4: O Win 8K 5
SL5: Asc 9J 17
SM6: W'ton 2F 62
Queen's Club Gdns. W14 . . . . . .2K 13
Queen's Club, The (Tennis Courts)
. . . . .1K 13
Queens Club Ter. *W14 . . . . . . .2L 13*
(off Normand Rd.)
Queens Ct. CR2: S Croy 8C 200
CR7: T Hea 4L 45
GU1: Guil 3D 202
GU9: Up Hale 5G 109
GU14: Farnb 5A 90
GU22: Wok 5B 74
KT13: Weybr 2E 56
KT19: Ewe 6D 60
RH1: Red 2E 122
(off St Anne's Mt.)
RH6: Horl 8E 142
SM2: Sut 7M 61
TN8: Eden 2M 147
TW10: Rich 9M 11
TW18: Stain 7M 21
Queens Ct. Ride KT11: Cob 9H 57
Queen's Cres.
RH4: Dork 4J 201 (6G 119)
TW10: Rich 8M 11
Queens Dr. GU2: Guil 9K 93
GU7: Godal 4E 132
KT5: Surb 6N 41
KT7: T Dit 5G 41
KT22: Oxs 7C 58
Queensfield Ct. SM3: Chea 1H 61
Queen's Gdns. TW5: Hest 4M 9
Queens Gate *GU7: Godal 7H 133*
(off Queen St.)
Queen's Ga. RH6: Gatw 3E 162
Queensgate KT11: Cob 8L 57
Queens Gate Cotts.
SL4: W'sor 7G 4
Queens Gate Gdns. SW15 . . . . .7G 13
Queens Ga. Rd.
GU14: Farnb 3N 89
Queens Hill Ri. SL5: Asc 2N 33
Queens Ho. TW11: Tedd 7F 24
Queens Keep GU15: Camb 1B 70
TW1: Twick 9J 11
Queensland Av. SW19 . . . . .9N 27
Queens La. GU9: Up Hale 5G 109
Queen's Mead GU8: Chid 5E 172
Queensmead GU14: Farnb 1N 89
KT22: Oxs 7C 58
SL3: Dat 3L 5
Queensmead Av. KT17: Ewe . . .6G 61
Queensmere Cl. SW19 . . . . .3J 27
Queensmere Ct. SW13 . . . . .3E 12
Queensmere Rd. SW19 . . . . . . .3J 27
Queensmill Rd. SW6 . . . . .3J 13
Queens Pde. *RH13: Hors 7K 197*
(off Queen St.)
Queen's Pde. Path
GU11: Alde 7N 89
Queen's Pk. Gdns.
TW13: Felt 4G 23
Queen's Pk. Rd. CR3: Cate . . .1B 104
Queens Pine RG12: Brac 5C 32
Queens Pl. SL5: Asc 2L 33
SM4: Mord 3M 43
Queen's Prom.
KT1: K Tham, Surb
. . . . .8G 203 (3K 41)
Queens Reach
KT1: K Tham 4G 203 (1K 41)
KT8: E Mol 3E 40
Queens Ride RG45: Crowt 9F 30
SW13 . . . . .6F 12
SW15 . . . . .6F 12
Queens Ri. TW10: Rich 9M 11
Queens Rd. BR3: Beck 1H 47
CR0: Croy 5M 45
CR4: Mit 2B 44
GU1: Guil 3D 202 (3N 113)
GU9: Up Hale 6H 109
GU11: Alde 3L 109
GU14: Farnb 5A 90
GU15: Camb 2N 69
GU21: Knap 5F 72
GU24: Bis, B'wood 7B 72
GU52: Fleet 6B 88
KT2: K Tham 8N 25
KT3: N Mal 3E 42
KT7: T Dit 4F 40
KT12: Hers 1G 57
KT13: Weybr 1D 56
RH6: Horl 8E 142
RH19: E Grin 1A 186
SL3: Dat 3L 5
SL4: E Wic 1C 4
SL4: W'sor 5F 4
SL5: S'hill 4A 34
SM2: Sut 6M 61
SM4: Mord 3M 43
SM6: W'ton 2F 62
SW14 . . . . .6C 12
SW19 . . . . .7L 27
TW1: Twick 2G 24
TW3: Houn 6B 10
TW10: Rich 1M 25
TW11: Tedd 7F 24
TW12: H Hill 5B 24
TW13: Felt 2J 23
TW20: Egh 6B 20
Queen's Rdbt. GU11: Alde 6N 89
Queen's Royal Surrey Regiment
Museum, The *1J 115*
(off Clandon Pk.)
Queen's Sq. RH10: Craw 3B 182
Queens St. TW15: Ashf 5A 22
Queens Ter. *KT7: T Dit 5G 41*
(off Queens Dr.)
SL4: W'sor 6G 5
TW7: Isle 7G 11
Queen St.
CR0: Croy 6B 200 (1N 63)
GU5: Gom 8D 116
GU7: Godal 7H 133
GU12: Alde 2B 110
KT16: Chert 7J 37
RH13: Hors 7K 197
Queensville Rd. SW12 . . . . . . .1H 29
Queens Wlk. RH19: E Grin 9A 166
TW15: Ashf 5M 21
Queens Way GU24: B'wood 6A 72
TW13: Hanw 5K 23
Queensway BR4: W Wick 1A 66
CR0: Wad 3K 63
GU6: Cranl 8A 156
GU16: Frim G 7E 70
RG42: Brac 9L 15
RH1: Red 2D 122
RH10: Craw 3C 182
RH13: Hors 7J 197
Queensway RH19: E Grin 9A 166
TW16: Sunb 1J 39
Queensway Nth. KT12: Hers . . .1K 57
Queensway Sth. KT12: Hers . . .2K 57
Queens Wharf W6 . . . . .1H 13
Queenswood Av. CR7: T Hea . . .4L 45
SM6: Bedd 1H 63
TW3: Houn 5N 9
TW12: Hamp 7B 24
Queenswood Rd.
GU21: Wok 6G 73
QUEEN VICTORIA 1J 61
Queen Victoria Ct.
GU14: Farnb 9N 69
Queen Victoria Ho.
RG40: W'ham 2C 30
Queen Victoria Rd.
GU24: B'wood 6A 72
Queen Victoria's Wlk.
GU15: Camb 9L 49
Queen Victoria Wlk.
SL4: W'sor 4H 5
Queenwood Golf Course 3B 54
Quell La. GU27: Hasl 9L 189
Quelmans Head Ride
SL4: W'sor 3A 18
Quelm La. RG42: Brac, Warf . . .8N 15
Quennell Cl. KT21: Asht 6M 79
Quennells Hill GU10: Wrec 5D 128
Quentins Dr. TN16: B Hil 3K 87
Quentins Wlk. *TN16: B Hil 3K 87*
(off St Anns Way)
Quentin Way GU25: V Wat 3L 35
Querrin St. SW6 . . . . .5N 13
Questen M. RH10: Craw 1H 183
Quetta Pk. GU52: Chu C 2C 108
Quiberon Ct. TW16: Sunb 2H 39
Quick Rd. W4 . . . . .1D 12
Quicks Rd. SW19 . . . . .8N 27
Quiet Cl. KT15: Addl 1J 55
Quiet Cnr. GU7: Godal 5H 133
Quiet Nook BR2: Hay 1F 66
Quill La. SW15 . . . . .7J 13
Quillot, The KT12: Hers 2G 56
Quince Cl. SL5: S'hill 3N 33
Quince Dr. GU24: Bis 2E 72
Quincy Rd. TW20: Egh 6C 20
Quinney's GU14: Farnb 4A 90
Quintain Ho. KT1: K Tham 2H 203
Quinta M. RH11: Pease P 1N 199
Quintet, The KT12: Wal T 7H 39
Quintilis RG12: Brac 7L 31
Quintin Av. SW20 . . . . .9L 27
Quinton Cl. BR3: Beck 2M 47
SM6: W'ton 1F 62
TW5: C'ford 3J 9
Quinton Rd. KT7: T Dit 7G 41
Quinton St. SW18 . . . . .3A 28
Quintrell Cl. GU21: Wok 4L 73

R

Rabbit La. KT12: Hers 4H 57
Rabies Heath Rd.
RH1: Blet 2B 124
Raby Rd. KT3: N Mal 3C 42
Raccoon Way TW4: Houn 5K 9
Racecourse Rd. RH6: Gatw . . .2D 162
RH7: Dorm, Ling 8A 146
Racecourse Way
RH6: Gatw 2D 162
(off Nth. Terminal App.)
RAC Golf Course 4B 80
Rachael's Lake Vw.
RG42: Warf 8C 16
Rackfield GU27: Hasl 1B 188
Rackham Cl. RH11: Craw 5B 182
Rackham M. SW16 . . . . .7G 29
Rack's Ct.
GU1: Guil 7D 202 (5N 113)
Rackstraw Rd.
GU47: Coll T, Owls 6H 49
Racquets Ct. Hill
GU7: Godal 5F 132
Racton Rd. SW6 . . . . .2M 13
Radbourne Rd. SW12 . . . . .1G 29
Radcliffe Cl. GU16: Frim 7D 70
Radcliffe Gdns. SM5: Cars 5C 62
Radcliffe M. TW12: H Hill 6C 24
Radcliffe Rd. CR0: Croy 8C 46
Radcliffe Sq. SW15 . . . . .9J 13
Radcliffe Way RG42: Brac 9K 15
Radford Cl. GU9: Hale 7K 109
Radford Rd. RH10: Craw 6F 162
Radipole Rd. SW6 . . . . .4L 13
Radius Pk. TW14: Felt 7G 9
Rad La. GU5: P'lake 2E 136
RH5: A Ham 1F 136
Radley Cl. TW14: Felt 2G 23
Radnor Cl. CR4: Mit 3J 45
Radnor Ct. RH1: Red 3C 122
Radnor Gdns. TW1: Twick 3F 24
Radnor Ho. SW16 . . . . .1K 45
Radnor La. RH5: Holm M 9H 137
(Three Mile Rd.)
RH5: Holm M 4H 137
(Woodhouse La.)
Radnor Rd. GU5: P'lake 5E 136
KT13: Weybr 9B 38
RG12: Brac 2D 32
TW1: Twick 2F 24
Radnor Ter. SM2: Sut 4M 61
Radnor Wlk. CR0: Croy 5H 47
Radnor Way SL3: Lang 1A 6

276 A-Z Surrey

Radolphs—Reedham Station (Rail)

Radolphs KT20: Tad 9J **81**
Radstock Way RH1: Mers 6H **103**
Radstone Ct. GU22: Wok 5B **74**
Raeburn Av. KT5: Surb 7A **42**
Raeburn Cl.
KT1: H Wic 1G **203** (8K **25**)
Raeburn Ct. GU21: Wok 6K **73**
Raeburn Gro. GU21: Wok 5K **73**
Raeburn Way GU47: Coll T 9J **49**
RAE Rd. GU14: Farnb 3M **89**
RAFBOROUGH 2K **89**
Rafborough Footpath
GU14: Cove, Farnb 2M **89**
(not continuous)
Rafdene Copse GU22: Wok 6M **73**
RAF Gate Rd. GU14: Farnb 4N **89**
Rag Hill Cl. TN16: Tats 8G **86**
Rag Hill Rd. TN16: Tats 8F **86**
Raglan Cl. GU12: Alde 3A **110**
GU16: Frim 6E **70**
RH2: Reig 1B **122**
TW4: Houn 8N **9**
Raglan Ct.
CR2: S Croy 8A **200** (2M **63**)
Raglan Pct. CR3: Cate 9B **84**
Raglan Rd.
GU21: Knap, Wok 5H **73**
RH2: Reig 9N **101**
Raikes Hollow RH5: A Ham . . .2J **137**
Raikes La. RH5: A Ham 2J **137**
Railey Rd. RH10: Craw 2C **182**
Railpit La. CR6: Warl 2A **86**
Railshead Rd. TW1: Isle 7H **11**
TW7: Isle 7H **11**
Rails La. GU24: Pirb 3N **91**
Railton Cl. KT13: Weybr 4B **56**
Railton Rd. GU2: Guil 8L **93**
Railway App. RH19: E Grin . . .9A **166**
SM6: W'ton 2F **62**
TW1: Twick 1G **24**
Railway Cotts. GU19: Bag 3J **51**
SW19 . . . . .5N **27**
Railway Pas. TW11: Tedd 7G **24**
Railway Rd. TW11: Tedd 5E **24**
Railway Side SW13 . . . . .6D **12**
Railway Ter. *CR5: Coul 2H **83***
(off Station App.)
TN16: Weste 3M **107**
TW13: Felt 2H **23**
TW18: Stain 6F **20**
Railway Vw. SL3: Hort 6B **6**
Railway Wharf
KT1: K Tham 2H **203**
Rainbow Cl. RH6: Horl 6F **142**
Rainbow Ct. GU21: Wok 3H **73**
Rainbow Ind. Est. SW20 . . . . . .1G **43**
Rainbow Leisure Cen.
Epsom 5L 201 (8D 60)
Rainforest Wlk. *RG12: Brac 4N **31***
(off Pondmoor Rd.)
Rainville Rd. W6 . . . . .2H **13**
Rake La. GU8: Mil 3C **152**
Rakers Ridge RH12: Hors 3K **197**
Raleigh Av. SM6: Bedd 1H **63**
Raleigh Ct. RH10: Craw 7E **162**
SM6: W'ton 3F **62**
TW18: Stain 5J **21**
Raleigh Dr. KT5: Surb 7B **42**
KT10: Clay 2D **58**
RH6: Smallf 8L **143**
Raleigh Gdns. CR4: Mit 2D **44**
(not continuous)
Raleigh Rd. TW9: Rich 6M **11**
TW13: Felt 4G **22**
UB2: S'hall 1M **9**
Raleigh Wlk. RH10: Craw 5C **182**
Raleigh Way GU16: Frim 3D **70**
TW13: Hanw 6K **23**
Ralliwood Rd. KT21: Asht 6N **79**
Ralph Perring Ct. BR3: Beck . . .3K **47**
Ralph's Ride RG12: Brac 2C **32**
(Littledale Cl.)
RG12: Brac 4C **32**
(Mendip Rd.)
Ralston Ct. *SL4: W'sor 4G **4***
(off Russell St.)
Rama Cl. SW16 . . . . .8J **29**
Rambler Cl. SW16 . . . . .5G **28**
Ramblers Way RH11: Craw . . .9N **181**
Rame Cl. SW17 . . . . .6E **28**
Ramillies Cl. GU11: Alde 6C **90**
RAMILLIES PARK 7B **90**
Ramin Ct. GU1: Guil 9M **93**
Ramones Ter. *CR4: Mit 3J **45***
(off Yorkshire Rd.)
Ramornie Cl. KT12: Hers 1N **57**
Ram Pas.
KT1: K Tham 4H **203** (1K **41**)
Rampling Ct. RH10: Craw 4D **182**
Ramsay Cl. GU15: Camb 7F **50**
Ramsay Ct. RH11: Craw 8N **181**
Ramsay Rd. GU20: Windl 2B **52**
Ramsbury Cl. RG12: Brac 5K **31**
Ramsdale Rd. SW17 . . . . .6E **28**
Ramsden Rd. GU7: Godal 8G **133**
SW12 . . . . .1E **28**
Ramsey Cl. RH6: Horl 8D **142**
RH12: Hors 3K **197**
Ramsey Ct. CR0: Croy 3A **200**
Ramsey Pl. CR3: Cate 9N **83**
Ramsey Rd. CR7: T Hea 5K **45**
Ramslade Cotts. RG12: Brac . . .2A **32**
Rams La. GU8: Duns 7C **174**
RAMSNEST COMMON 1D **190**
Ramster Cotts. GU8: Chid 1C **190**
Ram St. SW18 . . . . .8N **13**
Ramuswood Av. BR6: Chels 2N **67**
Ranald Ct. SL5: Asc 7K **17**
Rances La. RG40: W'ham 2D **30**
Randal Cres. RH2: Reig 5M **121**
Randall Cl. SL3: Lang 1B **6**
Randall Ct. *SL4: O Win 9K **5***
(off Lyndwood Dr.)
Randall Mead RG42: Bin 7G **15**
Randall Scholfield Ct.
RH10: Craw 2E **182**
Randalls Cres. KT22: Leat 7G **78**
Randalls Pk. Av. KT22: Leat . . .7G **78**
Randalls Pk. Crematorium
(Leatherhead)
KT22: Leat 7E **78**
Randalls Pk. Dr. KT22: Leat 8G **78**
Randalls Rd. KT22: Leat 6E **78**
Randalls Way KT22: Leat 8G **78**
Randell Cl. GU17: Haw 5K **69**
Randell Ho. GU17: Haw 5K **69**
Randle Rd. TW10: Ham 5J **25**
Randolph Cl. GU21: Knap 4H **73**
KT2: K Tham 6B **26**
KT11: Sto D 2A **78**
Randolph Dr. GU14: Cove 2H **89**
Randolph Ho. KT18: Eps 8G **201**
Randolph Rd.
KT17: Eps 8M **201** (1E **80**)
Randolph's La.
TN16: Weste 4K **107**
Ranelagh SL4: Wink 3M **17**
Ranelagh Av. SW6 . . . . .6L **13**
SW13 . . . . .5F **12**
Ranelagh Cres. SL5: Asc 9G **17**
Ranelagh Dr. RG12: Brac 2A **32**
TW1: Twick 7H **11**
Ranelagh Gdns. SW6 . . . . .6K **13**
(not continuous)
W4 . . . . .3B **12**
Ranelagh Gdns. Mans. *SW6 . . . .6K **13***
(off Ranelagh Gdns.)
Ranelagh Pl. KT3: N Mal 4D **42**
Ranelagh Rd. RH1: Red 3C **122**
Ranfurly Rd. SM1: Sut 8M **43**
Range, The GU5: Braml 7C **134**
Range Ride GU15: Camb 8L **49**
Range Rd. GU14: Farnb 5J **89**
RG40: Finch 9A **30**
Ranger Wlk. KT15: Addl 2K **55**
Range Vw. GU47: Coll T 7K **49**
Range Way TW17: Shep 6B **38**
Rankine Cl. GU9: B Lea 6M **109**
Ranmere St. SW12 . . . . .2F **28**
Ranmore Av. CR0: Croy 9C **46**
Ranmore Cl. RH1: Red 9E **102**
RH11: Craw 9A **182**
RANMORE COMMON
RH5, Dogkennel Green
. . . . .3J 117
RH5, Dorking 3D 118
Ranmore Comn. Rd.
RH5: Ran C, Westh 3M **117**
Ranmore Pk. RH4: Dork 3G **118**
Ranmore Pl. KT13: Weybr 2D **56**
RH5: Ran C 3K **117**
Ranmore Rd.
RH4: Dork 1H **201** (3C **118**)
SM2: Chea 5J **61**
Rannoch Rd. W6 . . . . .2H **13**
Ransome Cl. RH11: Craw 6K **181**
Ranyard Cl. KT9: Ches 9M **41**
Rapallo Cl. GU14: Farnb 1A **90**
Rapeland Hill RH12: Hors 7M **179**
Raphael Cl.
KT1: K Tham 8H **203** (3K **41**)
Raphael Dr. KT7: T Dit 6F **40**
Rapley Cl. GU15: Camb 7D **50**
Rapley Grn. RG12: Brac 5A **32**
Rapley's Fld. GU24: Pirb 1B **92**
Rapsley La. GU21: Knap 5E **72**
Rashleigh Ct. GU52: Chu C 9C **88**
Rastell Av. SW2 . . . . .3H **29**
Ratcliffe Rd. GU14: Cove 6L **69**
Rathbone Ho. RH11: Craw 8N **181**
Rathbone Sq.
CR0: Croy 6B **200** (1N **63**)
Rathgar Cl. RH1: Red 8E **122**
Rathlin Rd. RH11: Craw 6N **181**
Rathmell Dr. SW4 . . . . .1H **29**
Ravelin Cl. GU51: Fleet 1A **88**
Raven Cl. GU46: Yate 9A **48**
RH10: Turn H 4F **184**
RH12: Hors 2L **197**
Ravendale Rd. TW16: Sunb 1G **39**
Ravendene Ct. RH11: Craw 4B **182**
Ravenfield TW20: Eng G 7M **19**
Ravenfield Rd. SW17 . . . . .4D **28**
Raven La. RH11: Craw 1A **182**
Ravenna Rd. SW15 . . . . .8J **13**
Raven's Ait
Kingston upon Thames
. . . . .8G 203 (4K 41)
Ravensbourne Av.
TW19: Stan 2N **21**
Ravensbourne Rd.
TW1: Twick 9J **11**
Ravensbourne Ter.
TW19: Stan 2N **21**
Ravensbury Av. SM4: Mord 4A **44**
Ravensbury Ct. *CR4: Mit 3B **44***
(off Ravensbury Gro.)
Ravensbury Gro. CR4: Mit 3B **44**
Ravensbury La. CR4: Mit 3B **44**
Ravensbury Path CR4: Mit 3B **44**
Ravensbury Rd. SW18 . . . . .3N **27**
Ravensbury Ter. SW18 . . . . . . .3N **27**
Ravenscar Rd. KT6: Surb 8M **41**
Ravens Cl. GU21: Knap 3F **72**
KT6: Surb 5K **41**
RH1: Red 2D **122**
Ravens Ct. KT1: K Tham 8H **203**
Ravenscourt TW16: Sunb 9G **23**
Ravenscourt Av. W6 . . . . .1F **12**
Ravenscourt Pl. W6 . . . . .1G **12**
Ravenscourt Rd. W6 . . . . .1G **12**
Ravenscroft Cl. GU12: Ash . . .1G **111**
Ravenscroft Ct. RH12: Hors . . .5J **197**
Ravenscroft Rd. BR3: Beck 1F **46**
KT13: Weybr 7D **56**
Ravensdale Cotts.
GU26: Hind 9A **170**
Ravensdale Gdns.
TW4: Houn 6M **9**
Ravensdale M. TW18: Stain . . .7K **21**
Ravensdale Rd. SL5: Asc 4L **33**
TW4: Houn 6M **9**
Ravensfield Gdns.
KT19: Ewe 2D **60**
Ravenshead Cl. CR2: Sels 7F **64**
Ravenside KT1: K Tham 8G **203**
Ravenslea Rd. SW12 . . . . .1D **28**
Ravensmede Way W4 . . . . .1E **12**
Ravenstone Rd.
GU15: Camb 1H **71**
Ravenstone St. SW12 . . . . .2E **28**
Ravenswold CR8: Ken 2N **83**
Ravenswood Av.
BR4: W Wick 7M **47**
KT6: Surb 8M **41**
RG45: Crowt 2D **48**
Ravenswood Cl. KT11: Cob 2L **77**
Ravenswood Ct. GU22: Wok . . .5B **74**
KT2: K Tham 7A **26**
Ravenswood Cres.
BR4: W Wick 7M **47**
Ravenswood Dr.
GU15: Camb 1E **70**
Ravenswood Gdns.
TW7: Isle 4E **10**
Ravenswood Rd.
CR0: Wad 5A **200** (9M **45**)
SW12 . . . . .1F **28**
Ravensworth Ct. *SW6 . . . . .3M **13***
(off Fulham Rd.)
Rawchester Cl. SW18 . . . . .2L **27**
Rawdon Ri. GU15: Camb 1F **70**
Rawlings Cl. BR3: Beck 4M **47**
Rawlins Cl. CR2: Sels 4J **65**
Rawlinson Rd. GU11: Alde 8A **90**
GU15: Camb 9L **49**
RH10: Craw 5H **183**
Rawnsley Av. CR4: Mit 4B **44**
Raworth Cl. RH10: Craw 5F **182**
Rawsthorne Ct. TW4: Houn 7N **9**
Raybell Ct. TW7: Isle 5F **10**
Ray Cl. KT9: Ches 3J **59**
RH7: Ling 6M **145**
(not continuous)
Ray La. RH7: Blin H, Ling 4J **145**
Rayleigh Av. TW11: Tedd 7E **24**
Rayleigh Ct.
KT1: K Tham . . .3M **203** (1N **41**)
Rayleigh Ri. CR2: S Croy 3B **64**
Rayleigh Rd. SW19 . . . . .9L **27**
Raymead Av. CR7: T Hea 4L **45**
Raymead Cl. KT22: Fetc 9E **78**
Raymead Pas. *CR7: T Hea 4L **45***
(off Raymead Av.)
Raymead Way KT22: Fetc 9E **78**
Raymer Wlk. RH6: Horl 7G **142**
Raymond Cl. SL3: Poy 4G **7**
Raymond Cres. GU2: Guil 4J **113**
Raymond Rd. BR3: Beck 3H **47**
SW19 . . . . .7K **27**
Raymond Way KT10: Clay 3G **59**
Raynald Ho. SW16 . . . . .4J **29**
Rayne Ho. SW12 . . . . .1E **28**
Rayners Cl. SL3: Coln 3E **6**
Rayners Rd. SW15 . . . . .8K **13**
Raynes Cl. GU21: Knap 6E **72**
RAYNES PARK 3H **43**
Raynes Pk. Bri. SW20 . . . . .1H **43**
Raynes Park School Sports Cen.
. . . . .2G 42
Raynes Park Station (Rail) . . .1H **43**
Raynham Cl. GU4: B'ham 8D **94**
Ray Rd. KT8: W Mole 4B **40**
Ray's Av. SL4: W'sor 3C **4**
Rays Rd. BR4: W Wick 6M **47**
Raywood Cl. UB3: Harl 3D **8**
Read Cl. KT7: T Dit 6G **40**
Readens, The SM7: Ban 3C **82**
Reading Arch Rd.
RH1: Red 3D **122**
Reading Rd. GU14: Farnb 4A **90**
GU17: B'water 8A **48**
GU46: Yate 8A **48**
RG41: Win, W'ham 1A **30**
SM1: Sut 2A **62**
Reading Rd. Nth.
GU51: Fleet 4A **88**
Reading Rd. Sth.
GU51: Fleet 5A **88**
GU52: Chu C, Fleet 5A **88**
Read Rd. KT21: Asht 4K **79**
Reads Rest La. KT20: Tad 6L **81**
Reapers Cl. RH12: Hors 3K **197**
Reapers Way TW7: Isle 8D **10**
Reckitt Rd. W4 . . . . .1D **12**
Recognition Ho. SL4: W'sor 5D **4**
Recovery St. SW17 . . . . .6C **28**
Recreation Cl. GU14: Cove 5L **69**
Recreation Rd.
GU1: Guil 2B **202** (3N **113**)
GU10: Rowl 8D **128**
Recreation Way CR4: Mit 2H **45**
Rectory Cl. GU4: Guil 1F **114**
GU6: Ewh 5F **156**
GU7: Bus 9J **133**
GU47: Sandh 7E **48**
KT6: Surb 7J **41**
KT14: Byf 9M **55**
KT21: Asht 6M **79**
RG12: Brac 3A **32**
RG40: W'ham 2B **30**
RH5: Ockl 7C **158**
SL4: W'sor 4D **4**
SW20 . . . . .2H **43**
TW17: Shep 2B **38**
Rectory Ct. SM6: W'ton 1G **63**
TW13: Felt 5K **23**
Rectory Flats RH11: Ifield 1L **181**
Rectory Gdn. GU6: Cranl 7M **155**
Rectory Grn. BR3: Beck 1J **47**
Rectory Gro. CR0: Croy 3A **200**
TW12: Hamp 5N **23**
Rectory La. GU5: Shere 8B **116**
GU20: Windl 3N **51**
GU30: Brams 9K **169**
KT6: Surb 7H **41**
KT14: Byf 9N **55**
KT21: Asht 6M **79**
KT23: Book 4N **97**
RG12: Brac 4N **31**
RH3: Buckl 9E **100**
RH6: Charlw 3J **161**
RH11: Ifield 1L **181**
SM6: W'ton 1G **63**
SM7: Ban 1D **82**
SW17 . . . . .7E **28**
TN16: Weste 1G **106**
Rectory Orchard SW19 . . . . . . .5K **27**
Rectory Pk. CR2: Sande 9B **64**
Rectory Rd. BR2: Kes 4F **66**
BR3: Beck 1K **47**
CR5: Coul 3N **101**
GU14: Farnb 1A **90**
RG40: W'ham 2B **30**
SM1: Sut 9M **43**
SW13 . . . . .5F **12**
TW4: C'ford 5K **9**
Rectory Row RG12: Brac 3N **31**
Red Admiral St.
RH12: Hors 2L **197**
Redan Gdns. GU12: Alde 2A **110**
REDAN HILL 2B **110**
Redan Hill Est. GU12: Alde . . .2A **110**
Redan Rd. GU12: Alde 2A **110**
Redbarn Cl. CR8: Pur 7M **63**
Redcliffe Cl. *SW5 . . . . .1N **13***
(off Old Brompton Rd.)
Redcliffe Gdns. SW10 . . . . .1N **13**
W4 . . . . .3A **12**
Redcliffe M. SW10 . . . . .1N **13**
Redcliffe Sq. SW10 . . . . .1N **13**
Redcliffe St. SW10 . . . . .2N **13**
Redclose Av. SM4: Mord 4M **43**
Redcote Pl. RH4: Dork 3K **119**
Red Cotts. GU27: G'wood 7J **171**
Redcourt CR0: Croy . . .5F **200** (9B **46**)
GU22: Pyr 2F **74**
Redcrest Gdns. GU15: Camb . . .1D **70**
Redcroft Wlk. GU6: Cranl 8N **155**
Red Deer Cl. RH13: Hors 5A **198**
Reddington Cl. CR2: Sande 5A **64**
Reddington Dr. SL3: Lang 1B **6**
Redding Way GU21: Knap 6E **72**
Redditch RG12: Brac 6B **32**
Redditch Cl. RH11: Craw 7K **181**
Reddown Rd. CR5: Coul 5H **83**
Rede Ct. GU14: Farnb 4A **90**
*KT13: Weybr 9C **38***
(off Old Palace Rd.)
Redehall Rd.
RH6: Burs, Smallf 8M **143**
Redenham Ho. *SW15 . . . . .1F **26***
(off Ellisfield Dr.)
Redesdale Gdns. TW7: Isle 3G **10**
Redfern Av. TW4: Houn 1A **24**
Redfields La. GU52: Chu C . . .1A **108**
Redfields Pk. GU52: Chu C . . .1A **108**
Redford Av. CR5: Coul 2F **82**
CR7: T Hea 3K **45**
RH12: Hors 4H **197**
SM6: W'ton 3J **63**
Redford Cl. TW13: Felt 3G **22**
Redford Rd. SL4: W'sor 4A **4**
Redgarth Ct. RH19: E Grin 7L **165**
Redgate Ter. SW15 . . . . .9J **13**
Redgrave Cl. CR0: Croy 5C **46**
Redgrave Ct. GU12: Ash 2D **110**
Redgrave Dr. RH10: Craw 4H **183**
Redgrave Rd. SW15 . . . . .6J **13**
Redhall Ct. CR3: Cate 1A **104**
Redhearn Flds.
GU10: Churt 8K **149**
Redhearn Grn. GU10: Churt . . .8K **149**
RED HILL 1L **109**
REDHILL 2D **122**
Redhill Aerodrome and Heliport
. . . . .8H 123
Redhill & Reigate Golf Course
. . . . .6B 122
Redhill Comn. RH1: Red 4C **122**
Redhill Ct. SW2 . . . . .3L **29**
Redhill Distribution Cen.
RH1: Salf 2E **142**
Redhill Golf Course 7E 122
Redhill Ho. RH1: Red 1D **122**
Redhill Rd. KT11: Cob 8C **56**
Redhill Station (Rail) 2E **122**
Red Ho. La. GU8: Els 8G **131**
KT12: Wal T 8H **39**
Redhouse Rd. CR0: Croy 5H **45**
TN16: Tats 7E **86**
Redkiln Cl. RH13: Hors 5M **197**
Redkiln Cl. Ind. Est.
RH13: Hors 4M **197**
Redkiln Way RH13: Hors 4M **197**
Redknap Ho. TW10: Ham 4J **25**
Redlake La. RG40: W'ham 6E **30**
Redland Gdns. KT8: W Mole . . .3N **39**
REDLANDS
GU10 . . . . .5A **108**
RH5 . . . . .5G **138**
Redlands CR5: Coul 3J **83**
TW11: Tedd 7G **25**
Redlands, The BR3: Beck 1L **47**
Redlands Cotts.
RH5: Mid H 2H **139**
Redlands La.
GU10: Cron, Ews 5A **108**
RH5: Mid H 2G **139**
Redlands Way SW2 . . . . .1K **29**
Red La. GU35: Head D 2G **168**
KT10: Clay 3G **58**
RH5: Holm 1L **139**
RH8: Oxt 3D **126**
Redleaf Cl. KT22: Fetc 2D **98**
Redleaves Av. TW15: Ashf 7C **22**
Redlees Cl. TW7: Isle 7G **10**
Redlin Ct. RH1: Red 1D **122**
Red Lion Bus. Pk.
KT6: Surb 9M **41**
Red Lion Ct. *TW3: Houn 6B **10***
(off Alexandra Rd.)
Red Lion La. GU9: Farnh 2G **129**
GU24: Chob 5H **53**
Red Lion Rd. GU24: Chob 5H **53**
KT6: Surb 8M **41**
Red Lion Sq. SW18 . . . . .8M **13**
Red Lion St. TW9: Rich 8K **11**
Red Lion Wlk. *TW3: Houn 6B **10***
(off High St.)
Red Lodge BR4: W Wick 7M **47**
Red Lodge Rd.
BR4: W Wick 7M **47**
Redmayne Cl. GU15: Camb 2G **71**
Red Oak Cl. CR0: Croy 8K **47**
Red Oaks GU10: Rowl 8C **128**
Red River Ct. RH12: Hors 3H **197**
Red Rd. GU15: Ligh 9H **51**
GU18: Ligh 8M **51**
KT20: Betch, Box H 1A **120**
Red Rose RG42: Bin 6H **15**
RED ROVER 7F **12**
Redruth Gdns. KT10: Clay 4F **58**
Redruth Ho. SM2: Sut 4N **61**
Redsan Cl. CR2: S Croy 4A **64**
Redshank Ct. *RH11: Ifield 4J **181***
(off Stoneycroft Wlk.)
Redstart Cl. CR0: N Add 6N **65**
Redstone Hill RH1: Red 3E **122**
Redstone Hollow RH1: Red . . .4E **122**
Redstone Mnr. RH1: Red 3E **122**
Redstone Pk. RH1: Red 3E **122**
Redstone Rd. RH1: Red 4E **122**
Redtiles Gdns. CR8: Ken 2M **83**
Redvers Buller Rd.
GU11: Alde 6A **90**
Redvers Ct. *CR6: Warl 5G **84***
(off Redvers Rd.)
Redvers Rd. CR6: Warl 5G **84**
RG12: Brac 4N **31**
Redway Dr. TW2: Whitt 1C **24**
Redwing Av. GU7: Godal 2G **133**
Redwing Cl. CR2: Sels 7G **64**
RH13: Hors 5M **197**
Redwing Gdns. KT14: W By 8K **55**
Redwing Pl. RG12: Brac 4J **31**
Redwing Ri. GU4: Guil 1F **114**
Redwing Rd. SM6: W'ton 4J **63**
Redwood TW20: Thor 1G **37**
Redwood Cl. CR8: Ken 1N **83**
RH10: Craw 1C **182**
Redwood Ct. KT6: Surb 6K **41**
KT17: Ewe 7E **60**
*KT22: Leat 7F **78***
(off Park Vw. Rd.)
Redwood Dr. GU15: Camb 2H **71**
KT19: Eps 6B **60**
SL5: S'dale 5E **34**
Redwood Est. TW5: C'ford 2J **9**
Redwood Gro. GU4: Guil 9E **114**
Redwood Ho. TN16: Weste . . .1K **107**
Redwood Mnr. GU27: Hasl 1G **188**
Redwood M. *TW15: Ashf 8E **22***
(off Staines Rd. W.)
Redwood Mt. RH2: Reig 9M **101**
Redwoods KT15: Addl 3J **55**
SW15 . . . . .2F **26**
Redwoods, The SL4: W'sor 6G **4**
Redwoods Way GU52: Chu C . . .8C **88**
Redwood Wlk. KT6: Surb 7K **41**
Reed Cl. GU11: Alde 8B **90**
Reed Dr. RH1: Red 6E **122**
Reedham Dr. CR8: Pur 9K **63**
Reedham Pk. Av. CR8: Pur 3L **83**
Reedham Station (Rail) 9K 63

Reed Ho.—Riverdale Dr.

Reed Ho. SW19 . . . . . 5N 27
Reedings RH11: Ifield 5J 181
Reed Pl. KT14: W By 9G 54
TW17: Shep 7A 38
REEDS, THE 8L 129
Reedsfield Cl. TW15: Ashf 4C 22
Reedsfield Rd. TW15: Ashf 5C 22
Reed's Hill RG12: Brac 4N 31
Reeds Mdw. RH1: Mers 8G 102
Reeds Road, The
GU10: Fren, Til 1J 149
Rees Gdns. CR0: Croy 5C 46
Reeve Ct. *GU2: Guil 8K 93*
(off Tarragon Rd.)
Reeve Rd. RH2: Reig 7A 122
Reeves Cnr.
CR0: Croy 3A 200 (8M 45)
Reeves Corner Stop
(London Tramlink)
. . . . . 3A 200 (8M 45)
Reeves Ho. *RH10: Craw 3F 182*
(off Trafalgar Gdns.)
Reeves Rd. GU12: Alde 3A 110
Regal Ct. CR4: Mit 2D 44
GU1: Guil 2D 202
SW6 . . . . . 3M 13
(off Dawes Rd.)
Regal Cres. SM6: W'ton 9F 44
Regal Dr. RH19: E Grin 1B 186
Regalfield Cl. GU2: Guil 8J 93
Regal Pl. SW6 . . . . . 3N 13
Regan Cl. GU2: Guil 7L 93
Regatta Ho. TW11: Tedd 5G 25
Regatta Point TW8: Brent 2M 11
Regency Cl. TW12: Hamp 6N 23
Regency Ct. *KT15: Addl 9M 37*
(off Albert Rd.)
SM1: Sut 1A 62
TW11: Tedd 7H 25
Regency Dr. KT14: W By 9H 55
Regency Gdns. KT12: Wal T 7K 39
KT13: Weybr 3D 56
Regency Lodge *KT13: Weybr 9F 38*
(off Oatlands Chase)
Regency M. TW7: Isle 8E 10
Regency Wlk. CR0: Croy 5J 47
TW10: Rich 8L 11
(off Grosvenor Av.)
Regent Cl. GU51: Fleet 5B 88
KT15: N Haw 5M 55
RH1: Mers 7G 102
TW4: C'ford 4J 9
Regent Ct. GU2: Guil 1L 113
GU19: Bag 5K 51
SL4: W'sor 4G 5
Regent Cres. RH1: Red 1D 122
Regent Ho. KT17: Eps 7D 60
RH1: Red 2D 122
Regent Pde. SM2: Sut 3A 62
Regent Pk. KT22: Leat 5G 78
Regent Pl. CR0: Croy 7C 46
SW19 . . . . . 6A 28
Regent Rd. KT5: Surb 4M 41
Regents Cl. CR2: S Croy 3B 64
CR3: Whyte 5B 84
RH11: Craw 7A 182
Regents Ct. KT2: K Tham 2J 203
KT13: Weybr 3C 56
Regents Dr. BR2: Kes 2F 66
Regents M. RH6: Horl 8E 142
Regents Pl. GU47: Sandh 7H 49
KT12: Wal T 9K 39
Regent St. GU51: Fleet 5B 88
W4 . . . . . 1N 11
Regents Wlk. SL5: Asc 5N 33
Regent Way GU16: Frim 5D 70
Regiment Cl. GU14: Cove 2H 89
Regina Rd. SE25 . . . . . 2D 46
UB2: S'hall 1M 9
Regis Ct. CR4: Mit 9C 28
Regnolruf Ct. KT12: Wal T 6H 39
Reid Av. CR3: Cate 8A 84
Reid Cl. CR5: Coul 3F 82
Reidonhill Cotts.
GU21: Knap 5E 72
REIGATE 3M 121
Reigate Av. SM1: Sut 7M 43
Reigate Bus. M. RH2: Reig 2L 121
Reigate Cl. RH10: Craw 9H 163
REIGATE HEATH 3J 121
Reigate Heath Golf Course
. . . . . 3H 121
Reigate Heath (Local Nature Reserve)
. . . . . 3J 121
Reigate Hill RH2: Reig 8A 102
Reigate Hill Cl. RH2: Reig 9M 101
Reigate Hill Golf Course 6E 102
REIGATE HILL INTERCHANGE
. . . . . **7N 101**
Reigate Priory Mus. 4M 121
Reigate Rd. KT17: Eps D 7F 60
KT17: Eps, Ewe 6E 60
KT18: Tat C 4J 81
KT20: Tad 4J 81
KT22: Leat 1J 99
RH1: Red 3N 121
RH2: Reig 3N 121
(Chart La.)
RH2: Reig 2D 120
(Station Rd.)
RH2: Sid 1N 141
RH3: Betch, Buckl 4J 119
RH4: Dork 1L 201 (4J 119)
RH6: Hookw, Horl 1N 141
Reigate Station (Rail) 2M 121
Reigate Way SM6: W'ton 2J 63
Reindorp Cl. GU2: Guil 4K 113
Relko Ct. KT19: Eps 7C 60
Relko Gdns. SM1: Sut 2B 62
Rembrandt Ct. KT19: Ewe 3E 60
Rembrandt Way KT12: Wal T 8J 39
Renaissance *KT15: Addl 1L 55*
(off High St.)
Renaissance Ct. SM1: Sut 7A 44
TW3: Houn 6C 10
(off Prince Regent Rd.)
Renaissance Ho.
KT17: Eps 6M 201
Rendel Ho. SM7: Ban 5A 82
Rendle Cl. CR0: Croy 4C 46
Renfree Way TW17: Shep 6B 38
Renfrew Ct. TW4: Houn 5M 9
Renfrew Rd. KT2: K Tham 8A 26
TW4: Houn 5L 9
Renmans, The KT21: Asht 3M 79
Renmuir St. SW17 . . . . . 7D 28
Rennels Way TW7: Isle 5E 10
Rennie Cl. TW15: Ashf 4M 21
Rennie Ter. RH1: Red 4E 122
Renown Cl.
CR0: Croy 1A 200 (7M 45)
Renton Cl. SW2 . . . . . 1K 29
Replingham Rd. SW18 . . . . . 2L 27
Reporton Rd. SW6 . . . . . 3K 13
Repton Av. UB3: Harl 1E 8
Repton Cl. SM5: Cars 2C 62
Reris Grange Cl. GU8: Mil 9C 132
Reservoir Cl. CR7: T Hea 2A 46
Restavon Caravan Site
TN16: B Hil 3K 87
Restmor Way SM6: W'ton 8E 44
Restormel Cl. TW3: Houn 8A 10
Restwell Av. GU6: Cranl 4K 155
Results Health Club 4C 32
Retreat, The CR7: T Hea 3A 46
GU6: Cranl 6L 155
GU51: Chu C 7A 88
KT4: W Pk 8G 43
KT5: Surb 5M 41
SW14 . . . . . 6D 12
TW20: Eng G 6N 19
Retreat Rd. TW9: Rich 8K 11
Reubens Ct. *W4 . . . . . 1A 12*
(off Chaseley Dr.)
Revell Cl. KT22: Fetc 9B 78
Revell Dr. KT22: Fetc 9B 78
Revell Rd. KT1: K Tham 1A 42
SM1: Sut 3L 61
Revelstoke Av. GU14: Farnb 8N 69
Revelstoke Rd. SW18 . . . . . 3L 27
Revere Way KT19: Ewe 5D 60
Revesby Cl. GU24: W End 9A 52
Revesby Rd. SM5: Cars 5B 44
Rewell St. SW6 . . . . . 3N 13
Rewley Rd. SM5: Cars 5B 44
Rex Av. TW15: Ashf 7B 22
Rex Ct. GU27: Hasl 2D 188
Rebon Pl. KT12: Wal T 8J 39
Reynard Bus. Pk.
TW8: Brent 1J 11
Reynard Cl. RH12: Hors 3A 198
Reynolds Av. KT9: Ches 4L 59
RH1: Red 1F 122
Reynolds Cl. SM5: Cars 7D 44
SW19 . . . . . 9B 28
Reynolds Grn. GU47: Coll T 9J 49
Reynolds Pl. RH11: Craw 2A 182
TW10: Rich 9M 11
Reynolds Rd. GU14: Farnb 5G 89
KT3: N Mal 6C 42
RH11: Craw 2A 182
Reynolds St. GU51: Fleet 1A 88
Reynolds Way CR0: Croy 1B 64
Rheingold Way SM6: W'ton 5J 63
Rhine Banks GU14: Cove 9J 69
Rhoda McGaw Theatre *4A 74*
(off Victoria Way)
Rhodes Cl. TW20: Egh 6D 20
Rhodes Ct. *TW20: Egh 6E 20*
(off Rhodes Cl.)
Rhodes Moorhouse Ct.
SM4: Mord 5M 43
Rhodes Way RH10: Craw 6D 182
Rhododendron Cl. SL5: Asc 8J 17
Rhododendron Ride
TW20: Eng G 7J 19
Rhododendron Rd.
GU16: Frim 5E 70
Rhododendron Wlk.
SL5: Asc 8J 17
Rhodrons Av. KT9: Ches 2L 59
RHS Garden Wisley 5N 75
Rhyll Gdns. GU11: Alde 3L 109
Rialto Rd. CR4: Mit 1E 44
Ribble Pl. GU14: Cove 8K 69
Ribblesdale RH4: Dork 7H 119
Ribblesdale Rd. SW16 . . . . . 7F 28
Ricardo Ct. GU5: Braml 6B 134
Ricardo Rd. SL4: O Win 9L 5
Ricards Rd. SW19 . . . . . 6L 27
Ricebridge La. RH2: Reig 6G 120
Rices Cnr. GU4: Chil 2C 134
Rices Hill RH19: E Grin 9B 166
Richard Burbidge Mans.
SW13 . . . . . 2H 13
(off Brasenose Dr.)
Richard Challoner Sports Cen.
. . . . . 6C 42
Richard Meyjes Rd.
GU2: Guil 4H 113
Richards Cl. GU12: Ash V 8E 90
UB3: Harl 2E 8
Richards Fld. KT19: Ewe 5C 60
Richard Sharples Ct.
SM2: Sut 4A 62
Richardson Ct. RH11: Craw 8N 181
Richards Rd. KT11: Sto D 1B 78
Richbell Cl. KT21: Asht 5K 79
Richborough Ct.
RH11: Craw 3A 182
Richens Cl. TW3: Houn 5D 10
Richings Pk. Golf Course 1F 6
Richland Av. CR5: Coul 1E 82
Richlands Av. KT17: Ewe 1F 60
Rich La. SW5 . . . . . 1N 13
RICHMOND 8K 11
Richmond,
The American International
University in London
Richmond Hill Campus . . . 9L 11
Richmond & London Scottish RUFC
. . . . . 6K 11
Richmond Athletic Ground 6K 11
Richmond Av. SW20 . . . . . 9K 27
TW14: Felt 9F 8
Richmond Bri. TW1: Twick 9K 11
RICHMOND CIRCUS 7L 11
Richmond Cl. GU14: Cove 2J 89
GU16: Frim 5D 70
GU52: Fleet 7A 88
KT18: Eps 8L 201 (1D 80)
KT22: Fetc 2C 98
TN16: B Hil 6D 86
Richmond Ct. CR4: Mit 2B 44
GU51: Fleet 5A 88
RH10: Craw 4C 182
Richmond Cres. KT19: Eps 8L 59
TW18: Stain 6H 21
Richmond Cricket Ground 6L 11
Richmond Dr. TW17: Shep 5E 38
Richmond Golf Course 3L 25
Richmond Grn. CR0: Bedd 9J 45
Richmond Gro. KT5: Surb 5M 41
Richmond Hill TW10: Rich 9L 11
Richmond Hill Ct.
TW10: Rich 9L 11
Richmond Ho. CR3: Cate 2C 104
GU47: Coll T 8K 49
Richmond Mans. *SW5 . . . . . 1N 13*
(off Old Brompton Rd.)
TW1: Twick 9K 11
Richmond M. TW11: Tedd 6F 24
Richmond Pde. *TW1: Twick 9J 11*
(off Richmond Rd.)
Richmond Pk. Golf Course 1D 26
Richmond Pk.
(National Nature Reserve)
. . . . . 2M 25
Richmond Pk. Rd.
KT2: K Tham . . . 1J 203 (8L 25)
SW14 . . . . . 8B 12
Richmond Rd. CR0: Bedd 9J 45
CR5: Coul 2F 82
CR7: T Hea 2M 45
GU7: Godal 5G 133
GU47: Coll T 7K 49
KT2: K Tham . . . 1J 203 (6K 25)
RH12: Hors 4J 197
SW20 . . . . . 9G 26
TW1: Twick 1H 25
TW7: Isle 6G 11
TW18: Stain 6H 21
Richmond Sq.
RH19: E Grin 8M 165
Richmond Station
(Rail, Underground &
Overground) 7L 11
Richmond Theatre 7K 11
Richmond Way KT22: Fetc 1B 98
(not continuous)
RH19: E Grin 1B 186
Richmondwood SL5: S'dale 7E 34
Rickard Cl. SW2 . . . . . 2L 29
Rickards Cl. KT6: Surb 8L 41
Ricketts Hill Rd.
TN16: Tats 5F 86
Rickett St. SW6 . . . . . 2M 13
Rickfield RH11: Craw 4M 181
Rickford GU3: Worp 4G 92
Rickford Hill GU3: Worp 4G 93
Rickman Cl. RG12: Brac 5A 32
Rickman Ct. KT15: Addl 9K 37
Rickman Cres. KT15: Addl 9K 37
Rickman Hill CR5: Coul 5F 82
Rickman Hill Rd.
CR5: Chip, Coul 5F 82
RICKMANS GREEN 7H 163
Rickman's La.
RH14: Plais, Kird 6B 192
Ricksons La. KT24: W Hors 5C 96
Rickwood RH6: Horl 7F 142
Rickwood Pk.
RH5: B Grn 1K 159
Rickyard GU2: Guil 3G 113
Riddings, The CR3: Cate 3C 104
RIDDLESDOWN 9N 63
Riddlesdown Av. CR8: Pur 7N 63
Riddlesdown Rd.
CR8: Ken, Pur 6N 63
Riddlesdown Station (Rail) 9N 63
Ride, The RH14: Ifo 5D 192
TW8: Brent 1H 11
Ride La. GU5: Alb 4M 135
Riders Way RH9: Gods 9F 104
Rideway Cl. GU15: Camb 2N 69
Ridge, The CR3: Wold 4K 105
CR5: Coul 1J 83
CR6: Warl 3N 105
CR8: Pur 6G 63
GU22: Wok 4D 74
KT5: Surb 4N 41
KT18: Eps 5B 80
KT22: Fetc 2D 98
RH12: Rudg 9F 176
SL5: S'dale 6D 34
TW2: Whitt 1D 24
RIDGEBRIDGE HILL 1H 155
Ridge Cl. GU22: Wok 8L 73
RH3: Brock 7A 120
Ridge Ct. CR6: Warl 5D 84
SL4: W'sor 6F 4
Ridgegate Cl. RH2: Reig 1B 122
RIDGE GREEN 6J 123
Ridge Grn. RH1: Sth N 6J 123
Ridge Grn. Cl.
RH1: Sth N 6J 123
Ridgehurst Dr. RH12: Hors 7F 196
Ridgelands KT22: Fetc 2D 98
Ridge Langley CR2: Sande 6D 64
Ridgemead Rd.
TW20: Eng G 4K 19
Ridgemoor Cl. GU26: Hind 4C 170
Ridgemount GU2: Guil 4L 113
KT13: Weybr 8F 38
Ridgemount Av. CR0: Croy 7G 47
CR5: Coul 4F 82
Ridgemount Est.
GU16: Deep 7G 70
Ridgemount Rd.
SL5: S'dale 8D 34
Ridgemount Way RH1: Red 5B 122
Ridge Pk. CR8: Pur 6H 63
Ridge Rd. CR4: Mit 8F 28
SM3: Sut 7K 43
Ridges, The GU3: Art 8M 113
RG40: Crowt, Finch 3A 48
Ridgeside RH10: Craw 3D 182
(not continuous)
Ridges Yd.
CR0: Croy 4A 200 (9M 45)
Ridge Way GU25: V Wat 4A 36
TN8: Eden 8L 127
TW13: Hanw 4M 23
Ridge Way, The
CR2: Sande 5B 64
Ridgeway GU21: Wok 2N 73
KT19: Eps 5G 201 (8B 60)
RH19: E Grin 2A 186
Ridgeway, The CR0: Wad 9K 45
GU1: Guil 4C 114
GU6: Cranl 7A 156
GU18: Ligh 6M 51
GU24: B'wood 7C 72
KT12: Wal T 7G 38
KT22: Fetc 1D 98
KT22: Oxs 1C 78
RG12: Brac 2A 32
RH6: Horl 1E 162
RH12: Hors 4H 197
Ridgeway Cl. GU6: Cranl 7B 156
GU18: Ligh 7L 51
GU21: Wok 2N 73
KT22: Fetc 2E 98
KT22: Oxs 1C 78
RH4: Dork 7G 118
Ridgeway Ct. RH1: Red 4D 122
Ridgeway Cres. BR6: Orp 1N 67
Ridgeway Dr. RH4: Dork 8G 119
Ridgeway Gdns.
GU21: Wok 2N 73
Ridgeway Ho. *RH6: Horl 1E 162*
(off The Crescent)
Ridgeway Pde. GU52: Chu C 8B 88
Ridgeway Rd. RH1: Red 3D 122
RH4: Dork 7G 118
TW7: Isle 3E 10
Ridgeway Rd. Nth.
TW7: Isle 2E 10
Ridgewood Dr. GU16: Frim 3H 71
Ridgley Rd. GU8: Chid 5D 172
Ridgmount Rd. SW18 . . . . . 8N 13
RIDGWAY 2J 75
Ridgway GU22: Pyr 2J 75
SW19 . . . . . 8H 27
TW10: Rich 9L 11
Ridgway, The SM2: Sut 4B 62
Ridgway Ct. SW19 . . . . . 7J 27
Ridgway Gdns. SW19 . . . . . 8J 27
Ridgway Hill Rd.
GU9: Farnh 3H 129
Ridgway Pde. *GU9: Farnh 4H 129*
(off Ridgway Rd.)
Ridgway Pl. SW19 . . . . . 7K 27
Ridgway Rd. GU9: Farnh 4H 129
GU22: Pyr 2H 75
Riding, The GU21: Wok 1D 74
Riding Ct. Farm SL3: Dat 2L 5
Riding Ct. Rd.
SL3: Dat, Lang 3M 5
Riding Hill CR2: Sande 9D 64
Ridings, The GU6: Cranl 6N 155
GU16: Frim 3F 70
GU23: Rip 1J 95
KT5: Surb 4N 41
KT11: Cob 8A 58
KT15: Addl 3G 55
KT17: Ewe 5E 60
KT18: Eps 2D 80
KT20: Tad 7L 81
KT21: Asht 4K 79
Ridings, The KT24: E Hor 3F 96
RH2: Reig 1B 122
RH10: Craw 2H 183
TN16: B Hil 4G 86
TW16: Sunb 9H 23
Ridings La. GU23: Ockh 1C 96
Ridlands Gro. RH8: Limp 8G 106
Ridlands La. RH8: Limp 8F 106
Ridlands Ri. RH8: Limp 8G 106
Ridley Cl. GU52: Fleet 6A 88
Ridley Ct. RH10: Craw 9H 163
SW16 . . . . . 7J 29
Ridley Rd. CR6: Warl 5F 84
SW19 . . . . . 8N 27
Ridleys Cnr. Rdbt.
RH10: Craw 1H 183
Ridsdale Rd. GU21: Wok 4L 73
Riesco Dr. CR0: Croy 3F 64
Rifle Butts All. KT18: Eps 1E 80
Rifle Way GU14: Cove 2H 89
Rigault Rd. SW6 . . . . . 5K 13
Rigby Cl. CR0: Wad 9L 45
Riggindale Rd. SW16 . . . . . 6H 29
Riley Cl. KT19: Eps 7A 60
Rillside RH10: Craw 6E 182
Rill Wlk. RH19: E Grin 9D 166
Rimbault Cl. GU11: Alde 6B 90
Rimmer Cl. RH11: Craw 9N 181
Rinaldo Rd. SW12 . . . . . 1F 28
Rindle Cl. GU14: Cove 1H 89
Ring, The RG12: Brac 1N 31
Ringford Rd. SW18 . . . . . 8L 13
Ringley Av. RH6: Horl 8E 142
Ringley Oak RH12: Hors 4M 197
Ringley Pk. Av. RH2: Reig 4B 122
Ringley Pk. Rd. RH2: Reig 3A 122
Ringley Rd. RH12: Hors 4L 197
Ringmead RG12: Brac 4K 31
Ringmer Av. SW6 . . . . . 4K 13
Ringmore Dr. GU4: Guil 9E 94
Ringmore Rd. KT12: Wal T 9K 39
Ring Rd. Nth. RH6: Gatw 2F 162
Ring Rd. Sth. RH6: Gatw 3G 162
Ringside TN8: Eden 1L 147
Ringstead Rd. SM1: Sut 1B 62
Ringway UB2: S'hall 1L 9
Ringwood RG12: Brac 6L 31
Ringwood Av. CR0: Croy 6J 45
RH1: Red 9D 102
Ringwood Cl. RH10: Craw 5C 182
SL5: Asc 3M 33
Ringwood Gdns. SW15 . . . . . 2F 26
Ringwood Lodge RH1: Red 9E 102
Ringwood Rd. GU14: Farnb 7A 70
GU17: B'water 9H 49
Ringwood Way TW12: H Hill 5A 24
RIPLEY 8L 75
Ripley Av. TW20: Egh 7A 20
Ripley By-Pass GU23: Rip 1L 95
Ripley Cl. CR0: N Add 3M 65
Ripley Ct. CR4: Mit 1B 44
Ripley Gdns. SM1: Sut 1A 62
(not continuous)
SW14 . . . . . 6C 12
Ripley La. GU23: Rip 1N 95
KT24: W Hors 3B 96
Ripley Rd. GU4: E Cla 7M 95
GU23: Send 4L 95
TW12: Hamp 8A 24
RIPLEY SPRINGS 7A 20
Ripley Way KT19: Eps 7N 59
Ripon Cl. GU2: Guil 1J 113
GU15: Camb 3H 71
Ripon Gdns. KT9: Ches 2K 59
Ripon Rd. GU17: Min 5E 68
Ripplesmere RG12: Brac 3B 32
Ripplesmore Cl.
GU47: Sandh 7G 48
Ripston Rd. TW15: Ashf 6E 22
Risborough Dr. KT4: W Pk 6F 42
Rise, The CR2: Sels 5F 64
KT17: Ewe 6E 60
KT20: Tad 7H 81
KT24: E Hor 4F 96
RG42: Warf 9E 16
RG45: Crowt 2E 48
RH10: Craw 3G 183
RH19: E Grin 1A 186
Rise Rd. SL5: S'dale 4B 34
Ritchie Cl. RH10: Craw 7G 182
Ritchie Rd. CR0: Croy 5E 46
Ritherdon Rd. SW17 . . . . . 3E 28
Ritz Bingo
Wokingham 2B 30
RIVER ASH ESTATE 6G 38
River Av. KT7: T Dit 6G 41
River Bank KT7: T Dit 4F 40
KT8: E Mol 2E 40
TW12: Hamp 2A 40
Riverbank RH4: Westc 5B 118
TW18: Stain 7H 21
Riverbank, The SL4: W'sor 3E 4
Riverbank Way TW8: Brent 2J 11
River Bourne Health Club 6J 37
River Cl. GU1: Guil 1M 113
River Ct. GU21: Wok 1E 74
KT6: Surb 8H 203
TW17: Shep 6D 38
Rivercourt Rd. W6 . . . . . 1G 12
River Crane Way
TW13: Hanw 3N 23
(off Watermill Way)
Riverdale GU10: Wrec 4D 128
Riverdale Dr. GU22: Wok 8B 74
SW18 . . . . . 2N 27

Riverdale Gdns.—Rose Hill Pk. W.

Riverdale Gdns. TW1: Twick ...9J 11
Riverdale Rd. TW1: Twick ...9J 11
TW13: Hanw ...5M 23
Riverdene Ind. Est.
KT12: Hers ...2L 57
Riverfield Rd. TW18: Stain ...7H 21
River Gdns. SM5: Cars ...8E 44
TW14: Felt ...8J 9
River Gdns. Bus. Cen.
TW14: Felt ...8J 9
River Gro. Pk. BR3: Beck ...1J 47
Riverhead Dr. SM2: Sut ...6N 61
River Hill KT11: Cob ...2J 77
Riverhill KT4: W Pk ...8C 42
Riverhill M. KT4: W Pk ...9C 42
Riverhill Mobile Home Pl.
KT4: W Pk ...8C 42
Riverholme Dr. KT19: Ewe ...5C 60
Riverhouse Barn ...6G 39
River Island Cl. KT22: Fetc ...8D 78
River La. GU9: Farnh ...4D 128
KT11: Cob ...3M 77
KT22: Fetc, Leat ...8D 78
TW10: Ham ...1K 25
River Mead RH11: Ifield ...9M 161
RH12: Hors ...7H 197
Rivermead
KT1: K Tham ...8H 203 (4K 41)
KT8: E Mol ...2C 40
KT14: Byf ...9A 56
Rivermead Cl. KT15: Addl ...4L 55
TW11: Tedd ...6H 25
Rivermead Ct. SW6 ...6L 13
Rivermead Ho. TW16: Sunb ...2K 39
(off Thames St.)
Rivermead Rd. GU15: Camb ...4N 69
River Meads Av. TW2: Twick ...4A 24
Rivermede GU35: Bor ...5A 168
River Mole Bus. Pk.
KT10: Esh ...8A 40
River Mole Local Nature Reserve
...6D 78
River Mt. KT12: Wal T ...6G 38
Rivermount Gdns.
GU2: Guil ...8B 202 (6M 113)
Rivernook Cl. KT12: Wal T ...4K 39
River Pk. Av. TW18: Stain ...5F 20
River Reach TW11: Tedd ...6J 25
River Rd. GU46: Yate ...7A 48
SL4: W'sor ...3A 4
TW18: Stain ...9H 21
River Row GU9: Farnh ...4E 128
River Row Cotts.
GU9: Farnh ...3E 128
Rivers Cl. GU14: Farnb ...4C 90
Riversdale Rd. KT7: T Dit ...4G 40
Riversdell Cl. KT16: Chert ...6H 37
Rivers Ho. TW7: Isle ...7H 11
(off Richmond Rd.)
TW8: Brent ...1N 11
(off Aitman Dr.)
Riverside GU1: Guil ...1N 113
KT16: Chert ...1J 37
RH4: Dork ...3K 119
RH6: Horl ...1E 162
RH12: Hors ...6G 196
RH18: F Row ...6G 187
TN8: Eden ...2L 147
TW1: Twick ...2H 25
TW9: Rich ...8K 11
TW10: Rich ...8K 11
TW16: Sunb ...1L 39
TW17: Shep ...6F 38
TW18: Stain ...9H 21
TW19: Wray ...1M 19
TW20: Egh ...4C 20
W6 ...2H 13
Riverside, The KT8: E Mol ...2D 40
Riverside Arts Cen. ...2K 39
Riverside Av. GU18: Ligh ...7N 51
KT8: E Mol ...4D 40
Riverside Bus. Cen.
GU1: Guil ...3A 202 (3M 113)
SW18 ...2N 27
Riverside Bus. Pk.
GU9: Farnh ...9J 109
SW19 ...9A 28
Riverside Cl. GU14: Cove ...9L 69
GU24: B'wood ...7C 72
KT1: K Tham ...7H 203 (3K 41)
SM6: W'ton ...9F 44
TW18: Stain ...9H 21
Riverside Ct. GU9: Farnh ...9H 109
KT22: Fetc ...9G 79
RH4: Dork ...3K 119
TN8: Eden ...2M 147
TW7: Isle ...5F 10
(off Woodlands Rd.)
TW14: Felt ...9F 8
Riverside Dr. CR4: Mit ...4C 44
GU5: Braml ...4C 134
KT10: Esh ...1A 58
TW10: Ham ...4H 25
TW18: Stain ...6G 21
W4 ...3C 12
Riverside Gdns. GU22: Wok ...8D 74
W6 ...1G 13
Riverside Ind. Pk.
GU9: Farnh ...9J 109
Riverside M. CR0: Bedd ...9J 45
Riverside Pk. GU9: Farnh ...9J 109
KT13: Weybr ...2N 55
SL3: Poy ...5G 6
Riverside Pk. (Local Nature Reserve)
...1E 202 (9A 94)
Riverside Pk. (Watchmoor Pk.)
GU15: Camb ...3M 69
Riverside Pl. TW19: Stan ...9M 7
Riverside Rd. KT12: Hers ...1L 57
SW17 ...5N 27
TW18: Stain ...8H 21
TW19: Stan ...8M 7
Riverside Studios ...1H 13
Riverside Vs. KT6: Surb ...5J 41
Riverside Wlk.
BR4: W Wick ...7L 47
GU7: Godal ...6G 133
KT1: K Tham ...3G 203 (2K 41)
SL4: W'sor ...3G 5
SW6 ...6K 13
TW7: Isle ...6E 10
W4 ...2E 12
(off Chiswick Wharf)
Riverside Walk
Local Nature Reserve ...4M 35
Riverside Way GU15: Camb ...3M 69
Riverside Yd. SW17 ...5A 28
Riverstone Ct.
KT2: K Tham ...2L 203 (9M 25)
River St. SL4: W'sor ...3G 4
River Ter. W6 ...1H 13
River Thames Vis. Cen. ...9K 11
River Vw. KT15: Addl ...2L 55
Riverview
GU1: Guil ...2A 202 (3M 113)
River Vw. Gdns. TW1: Twick ...3F 24
Riverview Gdns. KT11: Cob ...9H 57
SW13 ...2G 13
Riverview Gro. W4 ...2A 12
Riverview Rd. KT19: Ewe ...1B 60
W4 ...3A 12
River Wlk. KT12: Wal T ...5H 39
RH12: Hors ...7F 196
W6 ...3H 13
River Way BR3: Beck ...7K 47
KT19: Ewe ...2C 60
TW2: Twick ...3B 24
Riverway TW18: Stain ...9K 21
Riverway Est.
GU3: P'marsh ...3M 133
Riverwood Ct. GU1: Guil ...1M 113
Rivett Drake Cl. GU2: Guil ...8L 93
Rivey Cl. KT14: W By ...1H 75
Road Ho. Est. GU22: Wok ...8C 74
Roakes Av. KT15: Addl ...8J 37
Roan Gdns. CR4: Mit ...9D 28
Roasthill La. SL4: Dorn ...2A 4
Robert Cl. KT12: Hers ...2J 57
Robert Gentry Ho. W14 ...1K 13
(off Gledstanes Rd.)
Robert Owen Ho. SW6 ...4J 13
Robertsbridge Rd.
SM5: Cars ...7A 44
Roberts Cl. CR7: T Hea ...2A 46
SM3: Chea ...4J 61
TW19: Stan ...9L 7
Roberts Ct. KT9: Ches ...2K 59
Robertson Ct. GU21: Wok ...5H 73
Robertson Gro. SW17 ...6C 28
Robertson Way GU12: Ash ...3D 110
Roberts Rd. GU12: Alde ...3A 110
GU15: Camb ...9M 49
Robert St.
CR0: Croy ...4C 200 (9N 45)
Roberts Way GU6: Cranl ...6N 155
TW20: Eng G ...8M 19
Robert Way GU16: Mytc ...2D 90
RH12: Hors ...1M 197
Robin Cl. GU12: Ash V ...7D 90
KT15: Addl ...2M 55
RH11: Craw ...1A 182
RH19: E Grin ...8B 166
TW12: Hamp ...6M 23
Robin Ct. SM6: W'ton ...2G 63
Robin Gdns. RH1: Red ...1E 122
Robin Gro. TW8: Brent ...2J 11
Robin Hill GU7: Godal ...4G 133
Robin Hill Dr. GU15: Camb ...3E 70
ROBIN HOOD ...4D 26
Robin Hood Cl.
GU14: Farnb ...7M 69
GU21: Wok ...5J 73
Robinhood Cl. CR4: Mit ...2G 45
Robin Hood Cres.
GU21: Knap ...4H 73
Robin Hood La. GU4: Sut G ...2B 94
RH12: Warnh ...3E 196
SM1: Sut ...2M 61
SW15 ...4D 26
Robinhood La. CR4: Mit ...2G 45
Robin Hood Rd.
GU21: Knap, Wok ...4G 73
(not continuous)
SW19 ...6F 26
Robin Hood Rdbt.
RH12: Warnh ...3H 197
Robin Hood Way SW15 ...4D 26
SW20 ...4D 26
Robin Hood Works
GU21: Knap ...4H 73
Robinites GU7: Godal ...4E 132
Robin La. GU47: Sandh ...7G 49
Robin Row RH10: Turn H ...4F 184
Robins, The RG12: Brac ...3J 31
Robin's Bow GU15: Camb ...2N 69
Robins Ct. BR3: Beck ...1N 47
CR2: S Croy ...7F 200
RH6: Horl ...8D 142
Robins Dale GU21: Knap ...4F 72
Robins Gro. Cres.
GU46: Yate ...9A 48
Robinson Cl. GU22: Wok ...7E 74
Robinson Ct. CR7: T Hea ...5M 45
TW9: Rich ...7M 11
Robinson Ho. RH11: Craw ...4B 182
Robinson Rd. SW17 ...7C 28
Robinsway KT12: Hers ...1K 57
Robinswood Ct.
RH12: Hors ...4M 197
Robin Way GU2: Guil ...8L 93
GU8: Worm ...9C 152
TW18: Stain ...4H 21
Robin Willis Way SL4: O Win ...9K 5
Robinwood Pl. SW15 ...5C 26
Robson Rd. SE27 ...4N 29
Roby Dr. RG12: Brac ...6B 32
Robyns Way TN8: Eden ...3M 147
Roche Rd. SW16 ...9K 29
Rochester Av. TW13: Felt ...3G 23
Rochester Cl. SW16 ...8J 29
Rochester Gdns. CR0: Croy ...9B 46
CR3: Cate ...9B 84
Rochester Gro. GU51: Fleet ...5A 88
Rochester Pde. TW13: Felt ...3H 23
Rochester Rd. SM5: Cars ...1D 62
TW18: Stain ...6F 20
Rochester Wlk. RH2: Reig ...8N 121
Roche Wlk. SM5: Cars ...5B 44
Rochford Way CR0: Croy ...5J 45
Rock Av. SW14 ...6C 12
Rock Cl. CR4: Mit ...1B 44
Rockdale Dr. GU26: G'hott ...6B 170
Rockdale Ho. GU26: G'hott ...6B 170
Rockdene Cl. RH19: E Grin ...9C 166
Rockery, The GU14: Cove ...2J 89
Rockfield Cl. RH8: Oxt ...9B 106
Rockfield Rd. RH8: Oxt ...7B 106
Rockfield Way GU47: Coll T ...7J 49
Rock Gdns. GU11: Alde ...3L 109
Rockhampton Cl. SE27 ...5L 29
Rockhampton Rd.
CR2: S Croy ...3B 64
SE27 ...5L 29
Rock Hill GU8: Hamb ...8G 152
Rock Ho. La. GU10: Farnh ...9L 109
Rockingham Cl. SW15 ...7E 12
Rockland Rd. SW15 ...7K 13
Rocklands Dr. CR2: S Croy ...3A 64
Rock La. GU10: Wrec ...6F 128
Rocks, The RH19: Ash W ...3E 186
Rockshaw Rd. RH1: Mers ...5G 103
Rocks La. SW13 ...4F 12
ROCKWOOD PARK ...4M 185
Rocky La. RH1: Red ...6D 102
RH2: Reig ...6D 102
Rocque Ho. SW6 ...3L 13
(off Estcourt Rd.)
Rodale Mans. SW18 ...9N 13
Rodborough Common
(Nature Reserve) ...2N 151
Rodborough Hill Cotts.
GU8: Mil ...3N 151
Rodd Est. TW17: Shep ...4D 38
Roden Gdns. CR0: Croy ...5B 46
Rodenhurst Rd. SW4 ...1G 29
Rodgate La. GU27: Hasl ...3A 190
Rodgers Ho. SW4 ...1H 29
(off Clapham Pk. Est.)
Roding Cl. GU6: Cranl ...8H 155
Rodmel Ct. GU14: Farnb ...4C 90
Rodmill La. SW2 ...1J 29
Rodney Cl.
CR0: Croy ...1A 200 (7M 45)
KT3: N Mal ...4D 42
KT12: Wal T ...7K 39
Rodney Gdns. BR4: W Wick ...1C 66
Rodney Grn. KT12: Wal T ...8K 39
Rodney Pl. SW19 ...9A 28
Rodney Rd. CR4: Mit ...2C 44
KT3: N Mal ...4D 42
KT12: Wal T ...8K 39
TW2: Whitt ...9A 10
Rodney Way GU1: Guil ...2C 114
SL3: Poy ...4G 7
Rodona Rd. KT13: Weybr ...7E 56
Rodsall La. GU3: Put ...3K 131
Rodway Rd. SW15 ...1F 26
Rodwell Ct. KT12: Wal T ...9J 39
KT15: Addl ...1L 55
Roebuck Cl. KT21: Asht ...7L 79
RH2: Reig ...3M 121
RH13: Hors ...4A 198
TW13: Felt ...5J 23
Roebuck Est. RG42: Bin ...8H 15
Roebuck Rd. KT9: Ches ...2N 59
Roedean Cres. SW15 ...9D 12
Roedeer Copse GU27: Hasl ...2C 188
ROEHAMPTON ...1F 26
Roehampton Cl. SW15 ...7F 12
Roehampton Ga. SW15 ...9D 12
Roehampton Golf Course ...7E 12
Roehampton High St. SW15 ...1F 26
ROEHAMPTON LANE ...2G 27
Roehampton La. SW15 ...7F 12
Roehampton Sport & Fitness Cen.
...1F 26
Roehampton University ...9E 12
Roehampton Va. SW15 ...4E 26
Roe Way SM6: W'ton ...3J 63
Roffe's La. CR3: Cate ...2A 104
ROFFEY ...4N 197
Roffey Cl. CR8: Pur ...3M 83
RH6: Horl ...8D 142
ROFFEY PARK ...2E 198
Roffey Pk. RH12: Colg ...2D 198
Roffey's Cl. RH10: Copt ...6L 163
Roffey Social and Sports Club
...3N 197
(off Leith Vw. Rd.)
Roffords GU21: Wok ...4L 73
Roffye Ct. RH12: Hors ...4N 197
Rogers Cl. CR3: Cate ...9E 84
CR5: Coul ...5M 83
Roger Simmons Ct.
KT23: Book ...2N 97
Rogers La. CR6: Warl ...5J 85
Rogers Mead RH9: Gods ...1E 124
Rogers Rd. SW17 ...5B 28
ROGER'S TOWN ...6N 167
Rokeby Cl. RG12: Brac ...9B 16
Rokeby Ct. GU21: Wok ...4J 73
Rokeby Ho. SW12 ...1F 28
(off Lochinvar St.)
Rokeby Pl. SW20 ...8G 27
Roke Cl. CR8: Ken ...1N 83
GU8: Wit ...5B 152
Roke La. GU8: Wit ...6N 151
Roke Lodge Rd. CR8: Ken ...9N 63
Roke Rd. CR8: Ken ...2N 83
Roker Pk. Golf Course ...7G 92
Rokers La. GU8: S'ford ...4A 132
Rokewood Dr. RH11: Ifield ...9M 161
Roland Way KT4: W Pk ...8E 42
Rolinsden Way BR2: Kes ...2F 66
Rollesby Rd. KT9: Ches ...3N 59
Rolleston Rd. CR2: S Croy ...4A 64
Rollit Cres. TW3: Houn ...8A 10
Rolls Royce Cl. SM6: W'ton ...4J 63
Rolston Ho. GU27: Hasl ...2D 188
Romana Ct. TW18: Stain ...5J 21
Romanby Ct. RH1: Red ...4D 122
Roman Cl. TW14: Felt ...8K 9
Roman Ct. TN8: Eden ...2L 147
Roman Farm Rd. GU2: Guil ...2G 113
Romanfield Rd. SW2 ...1K 29
Romanhurst Gdns.
BR2: Brom ...3N 47
Roman Ind. Est. CR0: Croy ...6B 46
Roman Ride RG45: Crowt ...2C 48
Roman Rd. RH4: Dork ...7G 119
TN8: Marsh G ...5M 147
Romans Bus. Pk.
GU9: Farnh ...9J 109
Romans Cl. GU1: Guil ...4D 114
Romans Way GU22: Pyr ...2J 75
Roman Temple
Virginia Water ...2H 35
Roman Way
CR0: Croy ...2A 200 (8M 45)
GU9: Farnh ...8K 109
RG42: Warf ...9D 16
SM5: Cars ...5D 62
Romany, The GU14: Farnb ...4F 88
Romany Gdns. SM3: Sut ...6M 43
Romany Rd. GU21: Knap ...2F 72
Roma Read Cl. SW15 ...1G 26
Romayne Cl. GU14: Cove ...9M 69
Romberg Rd. SW17 ...4E 28
Romeo Hill RG42: Warf ...9D 16
Romeyn Rd. SW16 ...4K 29
Romily Ct. SW6 ...5L 13
Romley Ct. GU9: Farnh ...2J 129
Romney Cl. KT9: Ches ...1L 59
TW15: Ashf ...6D 22
Romney Ho. RG12: Brac ...3C 32
Romney Lock SL4: W'sor ...2H 5
Romney Lock Rd. SL4: W'sor ...3G 5
Romney Rd. KT3: N Mal ...5C 42
Romney Wlk. SL4: W'sor ...3G 5
Romola Rd. SE24 ...2M 29
Romsey Cl. BR6: Farnb ...1K 67
GU11: Alde ...6A 110
GU17: B'water ...9H 49
Romulus Ct. TW8: Brent ...3K 11
Rona Cl. RH11: Craw ...6N 181
Ronald Cl. BR3: Beck ...3J 47
Ronald Ross Rd. GU2: Guil ...4H 113
Ronelean Rd. KT6: Surb ...8M 41
Ronneby Cl. KT13: Weybr ...9F 38
Ronson Way KT22: Leat ...8G 78
Roof of the World Caravan Pk.
KT20: Box H ...9A 100
Rookeries Cl. TW13: Felt ...4J 23
Rookery, The RH4: Westc ...7A 118
Rookery Cl. KT22: Fetc ...2E 98
Rookery Dr. RH4: Westc ...7A 118
Rookery Hill KT21: Asht ...5N 79
RH1: Out ...4L 143
RH6: Out ...4L 143
Rookery La.
RH6: Out, Smallf ...6L 143
Rookery Mead CR5: Coul ...9H 83
Rookery Rd. BR6: Dow ...6H 67
TW18: Stain ...6K 21
Rookery Vs. BR6: Dow ...6H 67
Rookery Way KT20: Lwr K ...5L 101
Rook La. CR3: Cate ...3K 103
Rookley Cl. SM2: Sut ...5N 61
Rooks Hill GU5: Braml ...9E 134
Rooksmead Rd. TW16: Sunb ...1G 39
ROOKS NEST ...8H 105
Rookstone Rd. SW17 ...6D 28
Rookswood RG42: Brac ...8N 15
Rook Way RH12: Hors ...2M 197
Rookwood Av. GU47: Owls ...5K 49
KT3: N Mal ...3F 42
SM6: Bedd ...1H 63
Rookwood Cl. RH1: Mers ...7F 102
Rookwood Ct.
GU2: Guil ...8A 202 (6M 113)
Rookwood Golf Course ...4G 197
Rookwood Pk. RH12: Hors ...5F 196
Rookwood Pl. RH1: Mers ...6F 102
(off London Rd. Sth.)
Roosthole Hill RH13: Colg ...8C 198
Roothill La. RH3: Betch ...1N 139
Ropeland Way RH12: Hors ...1L 197
Ropers Wlk. SW2 ...1L 29
Roper Way CR4: Mit ...1E 44
Rope Wlk. TW16: Sunb ...2K 39
Rorkes Drift GU16: Mytc ...1D 90
Rosa Av. TW15: Ashf ...5B 22
Rosalind Franklin Cl.
GU2: Guil ...4H 113
Rosaline Rd. SW6 ...3K 13
Rosaline Ter. SW6 ...3K 13
(off Rosaline Rd.)
Rosamund Cl.
CR2: S Croy ...7E 200 (1A 64)
Rosamund Rd. RH10: Craw ...5F 182
Rosamun St. UB2: S'hall ...1M 9
Rosary Cl. TW3: Houn ...5M 9
Rosary Gdns. GU46: Yate ...9C 48
TW15: Ashf ...5C 22
Rosaville Rd. SW6 ...3L 13
Roseacre RH8: Oxt ...3C 126
Roseacre Cl. SM1: Sut ...8A 44
TW17: Shep ...4B 38
Roseacre Gdns. GU4: Guil ...9H 115
Rose Av. CR4: Mit ...9D 28
SM4: Mord ...4A 44
Rosebank
KT18: Eps ...8H 201 (1B 80)
SW6 ...3H 13
Rosebank Cl. TW11: Tedd ...7G 25
Rose Bank Cotts.
GU22: Wok ...9A 74
Rosebay RG40: W'ham ...9D 14
Roseberry Gdns. BR6: Orp ...1N 67
Rosebery Av. CR7: T Hea ...1N 45
KT3: N Mal ...1E 42
KT17: Eps ...8M 201 (1D 80)
Rosebery Cl. SM4: Mord ...5J 43
Rosebery Cres. GU22: Wok ...7B 74
Rosebery Gdns. SM1: Sut ...1N 61
Rosebery Rd. KT1: K Tham ...1A 42
KT18: Eps D ...6C 80
SM1: Sut ...3L 61
TW3: Houn ...8C 10
Roseberys, The KT18: Eps ...1D 80
Rosebery Sq. KT1: K Tham ...1A 42
Rosebine Av. TW2: Twick ...1D 24
Rosebriar Cl. GU22: Pyr ...3J 75
Rosebriars CR3: Cate ...7B 84
KT10: Esh ...2C 58
(not continuous)
Rosebury Dr. GU24: Bis ...2D 72
Rosebury Rd. SW6 ...5N 13
Rose Bushes KT17: Eps D ...3G 81
Rose Cotts. BR2: Kes ...7E 66
GU8: Worm ...8D 152
GU52: Chu C ...1A 108
RH12: Fay ...9H 181
RH18: F Row ...6G 187
Rose Ct. RG40: W'ham ...2B 30
Rosecourt Rd. CR0: Croy ...5K 45
Rosecroft Cl. TN16: B Hil ...5H 87
Rosecroft Gdns.
TW2: Twick ...2D 24
Rosedale CR3: Cate ...1B 104
GU12: Alde ...2A 110
KT21: Asht ...5J 79
RG42: Bin ...6H 15
Rosedale Cl. RH11: Craw ...5M 181
Rosedale Gdns. RG12: Brac ...4M 31
Rosedale Pl. CR0: Croy ...6G 47
Rosedale Rd. KT17: Ewe ...2F 60
TW9: Rich ...6L 11
Rosedene Av. CR0: Croy ...6J 45
SM4: Mord ...4M 43
SW16 ...4K 29
Rosedene Gdns. GU51: Fleet ...3A 88
Rosedene La. GU47: Coll T ...9J 49
Rosedew Rd. W6 ...2J 13
Rose End KT4: W Pk ...7J 43
Rosefield Cl. SM5: Cars ...2C 62
Rosefield Gdns.
KT16: Otter ...3F 54
Rosefield Rd. TW18: Stain ...5J 21
Rose Gdns. GU14: Cove ...2K 89
RG40: W'ham ...2B 30
TW13: Felt ...3H 23
TW19: Stan ...1M 21
Roseheath Rd. TW4: Houn ...8N 9
ROSE HILL ...3K 201 (5G 119)
ROSEHILL ...6A 44
Rose Hill RG42: Bin ...6H 15
RH4: Dork ...2J 201 (5G 119)
SM1: Sut ...8N 43
Rosehill KT10: Clay ...3G 58
RH2: Reig ...2B 122
TW12: Hamp ...9A 24
Rose Hill App. RH4: Dork ...2J 201
Rose Hill Arch M.
RH4: Dork ...2K 201
Rosehill Av. GU21: Wok ...3M 73
SM1: Sut ...7A 44
Rosehill Ct. SM4: Mord ...6A 44
(off St Helier Av.)
Rosehill Ct. Pde.
SM4: Mord ...6A 44
(off St Helier Av.)
Rosehill Farm Mdw.
SM7: Ban ...2N 81
Rosehill Gdns. SM1: Sut ...8N 43
Rose Hill Pk. W. SM1: Sut ...7A 44

Rosehill Rd.—Russell Pl.

Rosehill Rd. SW18 .9N 13
TN16: B Hil .4E 86
ROSE HILL RDBT. .6N 43
Rose Ho. CR8: Ken .3C 84
Rose La. GU23: Rip .8L 75
Roseleigh Cl. TW1: Twick .9K 11
Rosemary Av. GU12: Ash V .5E 90
KT8: W Mole .2A 40
TW4: Houn .5L 9
Rosemary Cl. CR0: Croy .5J 45
GU14: Cove .9J 69
RH8: Oxt .2C 126
Rosemary Ct. GU27: Hasl .1G 188
RH6: Horl .7C 142
Rosemary Cres. GU2: Guil .8J 93
Rosemary Gdns.
GU17: B'water .1H 69
KT9: Ches .1L 59
SW14 .6B 12
Rosemary Ga. KT10: Esh .2C 58
Rosemary Hall Cl.
GU12: Ash .3C 110
Rosemary La. GU6: Alf .9E 174
GU10: Rowl .7D 128
GU17: B'water .1G 69
RH6: Charlw .3K 161
RH6: Horl .9F 142
SW14 .6B 12
TW20: Thor .2D 36
Rosemary Rd. SW17 .4A 28
Rosemead KT16: Chert .6K 37
Rosemead Av. CR4: Mit .2G 45
TW13: Felt .3G 22
Rosemead Cl. KT6: Surb .7N 41
RH1: Red .5B 122
Rosemead Gdns.
RH10: Craw .4C 182
(off Richmond Ct.)
Rose Mdw. GU24: W End .9D 52
Rosemont Rd. KT3: N Mal .2B 42
TW10: Rich .9L 11
Rosemount SM6: W'ton .3G 62
(off Clarendon Rd.)
Rosemount Av. KT14: W By .9J 55
Rosemount Point
KT14: W By .9J 55
(off Rosemount Av.)
Rosendale Rd. SE21 .1N 29
SE24 .1N 29
Roseneath Ct. CR3: Cate .3D 104
Roseneath Dr. GU8: Chid .5E 172
Roseneath Pl. SW16 .5K 29
(off Curtis Fld. Rd.)
Rose Pk. KT15: Wood .5G 54
Rosery, The CR0: Croy .5G 46
TW20: Thor .1G 36
Roses Cotts. RH4: Dork .2J 201
Roses La. SL4: W'sor .5A 4
Rose St. RG40: W'ham .2B 30
Rose Theatre Kingston
.4H 203 (1K 41)
Rosethorn Cl. SW12 .1H 29
Rosetree Pl. TW12: Hamp .8A 24
Rosetrees GU1: Guil .4C 114
Rose Vw. KT15: Addl .2L 55
Roseville Av. TW3: Houn .8A 10
Roseville Rd. UB3: Harl .1H 9
Rosevine Rd. SW20 .9H 27
Rose Wlk. BR4: W Wick .8M 47
CR8: Pur .7H 63
GU51: Fleet .3A 88
KT5: Surb .4A 42
RH11: Craw .5N 181
Rosewarne Cl. GU21: Wok .5K 73
Rosewood GU22: Wok .6C 74
KT7: T Dit .8G 40
SM2: Sut .6A 62
Rosewood Ct. KT2: K Tham .8N 25
Rosewood Dr. TW17: Shep .4A 38
Rosewood Gro. SM1: Sut .8A 44
Rosewood Rd. GU35: Lind .4B 168
Rosewood Way
GU24: W End .9B 52
Roshni Ho. SW17 .7C 28
Roskell Rd. SW15 .6J 13
Roslan Ct. RH6: Horl .9F 142
Roslyn Cl. CR4: Mit .1B 44
Roslyn Ct. GU21: Wok .5K 73
Ross Cl. RH10: Craw .6D 182
Ross Ct. RH6: Horl .8F 142
SW15 .1J 27
Rossdale SM1: Sut .2C 62
Rossdale Rd. SW15 .7H 13
Rossett Cl. RG12: Brac .3N 31
Rossetti Gdns. CR5: Coul .5K 83
Rossignol Gdns. SM5: Cars .8E 44
Rossindel Rd. TW3: Houn .8A 10
Rossiter Cl. SE19 .8N 29
Rossiter Lodge GU1: Guil .4C 114
Rossiter Rd. SW12 .2F 28
Rosslare Cl. TN16: Weste .3M 107
Rosslea GU20: Windl .1L 51
Rosslyn Av. SW13 .6D 12
TW14: Felt .9H 9
Rosslyn Cl. TW16: Sunb .7F 22
Rosslyn Pk. KT13: Weybr .1E 56
Rosslyn Rd. TW1: Twick .9J 11
Rossmore Cl. RH10: Craw .8H 163
Rossmore Gdns.
GU11: Alde .3K 109
Ross Pde. SM6: W'ton .3F 62
Ross Rd. KT11: Cob .9K 57
SE25 .2A 46
SM6: W'ton .2G 62
TW2: Whitt .2B 24
Ross Wlk. SE27 .5N 29
Rosswood Gdns.
SM6: W'ton .3G 62
Rostella Rd. SW17 .5B 28
Rostrevor Gdns. UB2: S'hall .1M 9
Rostrevor Mans. SW6 .4L 13
(off Rostrevor Rd.)
Rostrevor M. SW6 .4L 13
Rostrevor Rd. SW6 .4L 13
SW19 .6M 27
Rothbury Gdns. TW7: Isle .3G 11
Rothbury Wlk. GU15: Camb .2G 71
Rother Cl. GU47: Sandh .7H 49
Rother Cres. RH11: Craw .4L 181
Rotherfield Rd. SM5: Cars .1E 62
Rotherhill Av. SW16 .7H 29
Rother Rd. GU14: Cove .8K 69
Rothervale RH6: Horl .5E 142
Rotherwick Ct. GU14: Farnb .5A 90
Rotherwood Cl. SW20 .9K 27
Rotherwood Rd. SW15 .6J 13
Rothesay Av. SW20 .1K 43
TW10: Rich .7A 12
Rothesay Rd. SE25 .3A 46
Rothes Rd.
RH4: Dork .1K 201 (4H 119)
Rothsay Ct. KT13: Weybr .3E 56
Rothschild St. SE27 .5M 29
Rothwell Gdns. KT15: Addl .3H 55
Rothwell Ho. RG45: Crowt .3H 49
TW5: Hest .2A 10
Rotunda Centre, The
.3K 203 (1L 41)
Rotunda Est. GU11: Alde .2N 109
Rougemont Av. SM4: Mord .5M 43
Rough, The GU22: Wok .4F 74
ROUGHETS, THE .7C 104
Roughets La. RH1: Blet .7B 104
Rough Fld. RH19: E Grin .6N 165
Roughgrove Copse
RG42: Bin .7G 15
Roughlands GU22: Pyr .2G 75
Rough Rew RH4: Dork .8H 119
Rough Rd. GU22: Wok .9F 72
Rough Way RH12: Hors .3M 197
Rounce La. GU24: W End .9A 52
Roundabout Rd.
RH10: Copt .6A 164
Roundacre SW19 .3J 27
Roundals La. GU8: Hamb .1H 173
Roundburrow Cl. CR6: Warl .4D 84
Round Cl. GU46: Yate .1E 68
Round Gro. CR0: Croy .6G 47
ROUND HILL .1K 109
Roundhill GU22: Wok .6D 74
Roundhill Dr. GU22: Wok .5D 74
Roundhill Way GU2: Guil .3J 113
KT11: Cob .7B 58
ROUNDHURST .7M 189
Round Oak Rd. KT13: Weybr .1A 56
ROUNDSHAW .4J 63
Roundshaw Downs
Local Nature Reserve .5K 63
Roundshead Dr. RG42: Warf .9B 16
ROUNDS HILL .9L 15
Rounds Hill RG42: Brac .9K 15
Roundthorn Way GU21: Wok .3J 73
Roundway GU15: Camb .9G 50
TN16: B Hil .3E 86
TW20: Egh .6E 20
Roundway, The KT10: Clay .3F 58
Roundway Cl. GU15: Camb .9G 50
Roundway Ct. RH10: Craw .1B 182
Roundwood Vw. SM7: Ban .2J 81
Roundwood Way SM7: Ban .2J 81
Rounton Rd. GU52: Chu C .7B 88
Roupell Ho. KT2: K Tham .1M 203
Roupell Rd. SW2 .2K 29
Rouse Cl. KT13: Weybr .1G 56
Routh Ct. TW14: Bedf .2E 22
Routh Rd. SW18 .1C 28
Row, The TN8: Eden .8K 127
Rowallan Rd. SW6 .3K 13
Rowan RG12: Brac .4D 32
Rowan Av. TW20: Egh .6E 20
Rowan Chase GU10: Wrec .6F 128
Rowan Cl. GU1: Guil .9L 93
GU15: Camb .7D 50
GU51: Fleet .4D 88
KT3: N Mal .1D 42
RH2: Reig .5A 122
RH10: Craw .3D 182
RH12: Hors .3A 198
SM7: Ban .2J 81
SW16 .9G 29
TW15: Ashf .5M 21
Rowan Ct. SW11 .1D 28
Rowan Cres. SW16 .9G 29
Rowan Dale GU52: Chu C .8A 88
Rowan Dr. RG45: Crowt .9H 31
Rowan Gdns. CR0: Croy .9C 46
Rowan Grn. KT13: Weybr .1E 56
Rowan Gro. CR5: Coul .8F 82
Rowan Mead KT20: Tad .6G 81
Rowan Rd. GU35: Lind .5A 168
SW16 .1G 45
TW8: Brent .3H 11
UB7: W Dray .1M 7
Rowans, The GU22: Wok .5A 74
GU26: Hind .7B 170
TW16: Sunb .6G 23
Rowans Cl. GU14: Cove .5K 69
Rowanside Cl.
GU35: Head D .5H 169
Rowan Wlk. RH10: Craw D .1F 184
Rowan Way RH12: Hors .3A 198
Rowbarns Way KT24: E Hor .8G 97
Rowberry Cl. SW6 .3H 13
Rowbury GU7: Godal .3K 133
Rowcliffe Springs
GU8: Hasc .6A 154
Rowcroft Cl. GU12: Ash V .7E 90
Rowden Rd. KT19: Ewe .1A 60
Rowdown Cres. CR0: N Add .5N 65
Rowe La. GU24: Pirb .2D 92
Rowena Ho. RH11: Craw .9B 162
(off Dobson Rd.)
ROWFANT .2A 184
Rowfant Bus. Cen.
RH10: Rowf .3A 184
Rowfant Cl. RH10: Worth .3J 183
Rowfant Rd. SW17 .2E 28
Rowfield TN8: Eden .9M 127
ROWHILL .3H 55
Rowhill KT15: Addl .3H 55
Rowhill Av. GU11: Alde .3L 109
Rowhill Cl. GU14: Cove .1H 89
Rowhill Copse Local Nature Reserve
.4K 109
Rowhill Cres. GU11: Alde .4L 109
Rowhills GU9: Heath E .4J 109
Rowhills Cl. GU9: Weybo .5L 109
ROWHOOK .8M 177
Rowhook Hill RH12: Rowh .8M 177
Rowhook Rd.
RH12: Rowh, Broadb H .9N 177
(not continuous)
Rowhurst Av. KT15: Addl .3K 55
KT22: Leat .4F 78
Rowland Cl. RH10: Copt .5B 164
SL4: W'sor .6A 4
Rowland Hill Almshouses
TW15: Ashf .6B 22
(off Feltham Hill Rd.)
Rowland Pl. CR8: Pur .3L 83
Rowland Rd. GU6: Cranl .7M 155
Rowlands Rd. RH12: Hors .2N 197
Rowland Way SW19 .9N 27
TW15: Ashf .8E 22
Row La. GU5: Alb .8N 135
ROWLEDGE .8D 128
ROWLEY .4K 155
Rowley Cl. GU22: Pyr .3K 75
RG12: Brac .2C 32
Rowley Ct. CR3: Cate .9A 84
Rowlls Rd.
KT1: K Tham .5M 203 (2M 41)
Rowly Dr. GU6: Cranl .5J 155
Rowly Edge GU6: Cranl .4J 155
Rowntree Rd. TW2: Twick .2E 24
Rowplatt Cl. RH19: Felb .6H 165
Rowplatt La. RH19: Felb .7H 165
ROW TOWN .3J 55
Row Town KT15: Addl .4H 55
Roxbee Cox Rd. GU14: Farnb .3E 88
Roxborough Av. TW7: Isle .3F 10
Roxburgh Cl. GU15: Camb .2G 71
Roxburgh Rd. SE27 .6M 29
Roxby Pl. SW6 .2M 13
Roxeth Ct. TW15: Ashf .6B 22
Roxford Cl. TW17: Shep .4F 38
Roxton Gdns. CR0: A'ton .2K 65
Royal Ascot Golf Course .9M 17
Royal Ashdown Forest Golf Course
.8J 187
Royal Av. KT4: W Pk .8D 42
Royal Botanic Gdns.
Kew .4L 11
Royal Cir. SE27 .4L 29
Royal Cl. BR6: Farnb .1K 67
KT4: W Pk .8D 42
SW19 .4J 27
Royal County of Berkshire
Health & Racquet Club, The
.7B 32
Royal Dr. KT18: Tat C .5G 80
Royal Duchess M. SW12 .1F 28
Royal Earlswood Mus. .2D 122
Royal Earlswood Pk.
RH1: Red .6E 122
Royale Cl. GU11: Alde .4A 110
Royal Free Ct. SL4: W'sor .4G 4
(off Bachelors Acre)
Royal Holloway
(University of London) .7N 19
Royal Holloway University
Sports Cen. .8A 20
Royal Horticultural Society Cotts.
GU23: Wis .3N 75
Royal Household Golf Course
.4H 5
Royal Huts Av. GU26: Hind .5D 170
Royal Logistic Corps Museum, The
.6H 71
Royal Mausoleum
Windsor .6H 5
Royal M. GU7: Godal .7H 133
KT8: E Mol .2E 40
SL4: W'sor .4G 5
Royal Mid-Surrey Golf Course
.6K 11
Royal Military Academy Sandhurst
.8M 49
Royal Oak Cl. GU46: Yate .9D 48
Royal Oak Dr. RG45: Crowt .8G 30
Royal Oak Ho.
RH10: Craw D .2E 184
Royal Oak M. TW11: Tedd .6G 25
Royal Oak Rd. GU21: Wok .5M 73
Royal Orchard Cl. SW18 .1K 27
Royal Pde. GU26: Hind .5D 170
SW6 .3K 13
TW9: Kew .4N 11
(off Station App.)
Royal Quarter
KT2: K Tham .2H 203 (9L 25)
Royal Rd. TW11: Tedd .6D 24
Royals, The GU1: Guil .5D 202
Royal Victoria Gdns.
SL5: Asc .4L 33
Royal Wlk. SM6: W'ton .8F 44
Royal Wimbledon Golf Course
.6G 27
Royal Windsor Racecourse .2C 4
Royce Rd. RH10: Craw .7E 162
Roycroft Cl. SW2 .2L 29
Roydon Ct. KT12: Hers .1H 57
TW20: Egh .7F 20
Roy Gro. TW12: Hamp .7B 24
Roymount Ct. TW2: Twick .4E 24
Roy Richmond Way
KT19: Eps .6D 60
Royston Av. KT14: Byf .8N 55
SM1: Sut .9B 44
SM6: Bedd .1H 63
Royston Centre, The
GU12: Ash V .5D 90
Royston Cl. KT12: Wal T .7H 39
RH10: Craw .8E 162
TW5: C'ford .4J 9
Royston Ct. KT10: Hinc W .8F 40
SE24 .1N 29
TW9: Kew .4M 11
Royston Pk. KT14: Byf .8N 55
Royston Rd. KT14: Byf .8N 55
TW10: Rich .8L 11
Roystons, The KT5: Surb .4A 42
Rozeldene GU26: Hind .6C 170
Rozel Ter. CR0: Croy .4B 200
RQ33 SW18 .7M 13
Rubeck Cl. RH1: Red .1F 122
Rubus Cl. GU24: W End .9B 52
Ruckmans La. RH5: Oak .3A 178
Rudd Hall Ri.
GU15: Camb .3B 70
Ruddlesway SL4: W'sor .4A 4
Ruden Way KT17: Eps D .3G 80
Rudge Ho. RH19: E Grin .9B 166
(off Cantelupe Rd.)
Rudge Ri. KT15: Addl .2H 55
RUDGWICK .9E 176
Rudgwick Keep RH6: Horl .7G 142
(off Langshott La.)
Rudgwick Rd. RH11: Ifield .2L 181
Rudloe Rd. SW12 .1G 28
Rudsworth Cl. SL3: Coln .4F 6
Ruffetts, The CR2: Sels .4E 64
Ruffetts Cl. CR2: Sels .4E 64
Ruffetts Way KT20: Tad .5K 81
Rufford Cl. GU52: Fleet .7B 88
Rufford Ga. RG12: Brac .2C 32
Rufus Bus. Cen. SW18 .3N 27
Rufwood RH10: Craw D .1D 184
Rugby Cl. GU47: Owls .6K 49
Rugby La. SM2: Chea .5J 61
Rugby Rd. TW1: Twick .8E 10
Ruggles-Brise Rd.
TW15: Ashf .6M 21
Rugosa Rd. GU24: W End .9B 52
Ruislip St. SW17 .5D 28
Rumbold Rd. SW6 .3N 13
Rumsey Cl. TW12: Hamp .7N 23
RUN COMMON .1G 155
Run Comn. Rd.
GU5: Braml, Sha G .2G 154
Runcorn Cl. RH11: Craw .7K 181
Runes Cl. CR4: Mit .3B 44
RUNFOLD .8A 110
Runfold Rdbt. GU10: B Lea .6B 110
Runfold St George
GU10: B Lea .7N 109
Runnemede Rd. TW20: Egh .5B 20
Running Horse Yd.
TW8: Brent .2L 11
RUNNYMEDE .3N 19
Runnymede .3N 19
Runnymede SW19 .9A 28
Runnymede Cl. TW2: Whitt .9B 10
Runnymede Ct.
GU14: Farnb .7M 69
SM6: W'ton .3F 62
SW15 .2F 26
TW20: Egh .5C 20
Runnymede Cres. SW16 .9H 29
Runnymede Gdns.
TW2: Whitt .9B 10
Runnymede Ho. KT16: Chert .6J 37
(off London St.)
Runnymede Rd. TW2: Whitt .9B 10
Runnymede Rdbt.
TW20: Egh .5D 20
Runshooke Ct.
RH11: Craw .6M 181
Runtley Wood La.
GU4: Sut G .3B 94
Runway Pk. RH11: Low H .5C 162
Runway's End Outdoor Cen. .8L 89
Runwick La. GU10: Farnh .3A 128
Rupert Ct. KT8: W Mole .3A 40
(off St Peter's Rd.)
Rupert Ho. SW5 .1M 13
(off Nevern Sq.)
Rupert Rd.
GU2: Guil .5A 202 (4M 113)
Rural Cl. GU9: Farnh .5E 128
Rural Life Cen. (Old Kiln Mus.)
.8L 129
Rural Way RH1: Red .3E 122
SW16 .8F 28
Ruscoe Dr. GU22: Wok .4C 74
Ruscombe Gdns. SL3: Dat .3K 5
Ruscombe Way TW14: Felt .1G 22
Rush, The SW20 .9L 27
(off Watery La.)
Rusham Ct. TW20: Egh .7C 20
Rusham Pk. Av. TW20: Egh .7B 20
Rusham Rd. SW12 .1D 28
TW20: Egh .7B 20
Rushams Rd. RH12: Hors .6H 197
Rushbridge Cl. CR0: Croy .5N 45
Rushbury Ct. TW12: Hamp .9A 24
Rush Comn. M. SW2 .1K 29
Rush Cft. GU7: Godal .3K 133
Rushdene Wlk. TN16: B Hil .4F 86
Rushden Way GU9: Heath E .5J 109
Rushen Wlk. SM5: Cars .7B 44
Rushes, The TW18: Stain .6G 20
(off Wapshott Rd.)
RUSHETT .5K 127
Rushett Cl. KT7: T Dit .7H 41
RUSHETT COMMON .1E 154
Rushett Dr. RH4: Dork .8H 119
Rushett La. KT9: Ches .7J 59
KT18: Eps .7J 59
Rushett Rd. KT7: T Dit .6H 41
RUSHETTS FARM .7A 122
Rushetts Pl. RH11: Craw .9A 162
Rushetts Rd. RH2: Reig .7A 122
RH11: Craw .9N 161
Rushey Cl. KT3: N Mal .3C 42
Rushfords RH7: Ling .6A 146
Rushley Cl. BR2: Kes .1F 66
Rushmead TW10: Ham .4H 25
Rushmead Cl. CR0: Croy .1C 64
Rushmere Ct. KT4: W Pk .8F 42
Rushmere Pl. SW19 .6J 27
TW20: Eng G .6A 20
Rushmon Gdns.
KT12: Wal T .9J 39
Rushmon Pl. SM3: Chea .3K 61
Rushmon Vs. KT3: N Mal .3E 42
RUSHMOOR .4A 150
Rushmoor Arena
(Army Show Ground) .9K 89
Rushmoor Cl. GU2: Guil .9J 93
GU52: Fleet .6B 88
Rushmoor Ct.
GU14: Farnb .5A 90
Rushmoor Gym .5A 110
Rushmoor Rd. GU11: Alde .8J 89
Rushmoor Stadium .6M 69
Rushmore Ho. SW15 .1F 26
Rusholme Rd. SW15 .9J 13
Rushton Av. RH9: S Gods .7F 124
Rushworth Rd. RH2: Reig .2M 121
Rushy Mdw. La.
SM5: Cars .8C 44
Ruskin Av. TW9: Kew .3N 11
TW14: Felt .9G 9
Ruskin Cl. RH10: Craw .9G 163
Ruskin Ct. RG45: Crowt .3E 48
Ruskin Dr. KT4: W Pk .8G 43
Ruskin Ho. CR2: S Croy .8D 200
Ruskin Mans. W14 .2K 13
(off Queen's Club Gdns.)
Ruskin Pde. CR2: S Croy .8D 200
Ruskin Rd.
CR0: Croy .2A 200 (8M 45)
SM5: Cars .2D 62
TW7: Isle .6F 10
TW18: Stain .7H 21
Ruskin Way SW19 .9B 28
Rusmon Ct. KT16: Chert .6H 37
RUSPER .2C 180
Rusper Ct. Cotts.
RH12: Rusp .3D 180
Rusper Golf Course .6A 160
Rusper Rd. RH5: Cap .6J 159
RH5: Newd .2A 160
RH11: Ifield .2H 181
RH12: Hors, Rusp .4M 197
RH12: Ifield .2F 180
RH12: Newd, Rusp .9C 160
Rusper Rd. Rdbt.
RH12: Hors .1M 197
Ruspers Keep RH11: Ifield .2L 181
Russell Cl. BR3: Beck .2M 47
GU21: Wok .2M 73
KT20: Wal H .3F 100
RG12: Brac .7B 32
W4 .2E 12
Russell Ct. CR8: Pur .6L 63
GU1: Guil .9M 93
GU11: Alde .2M 109
(off Frederick St.)
GU17: B'water .1J 69
GU26: Hind .5D 170
KT22: Leat .9H 79
SM6: W'ton .2G 63
(off Ross Rd.)
SW16 .6K 29
Russell Dr. TW19: Stan .9M 7
Russell Gdns. TW10: Ham .3J 25
UB7: Sip .1B 8
Russell Grn. Cl. CR8: Pur .6L 63
Russell Hill CR8: Pur .6K 63
Russell Hill Pl. CR8: Pur .7L 63
Russell Hill Rd. CR8: Pur .7L 63
Russell Kerr Cl. W4 .3B 12
Russell Pl. SM2: Sut .4N 61

280 A-Z Surrey

Taylor Rd.—Thursley Common National Nature Reserve

Taylor Rd. CR4: Mit ... 8C 28
GU11: Alde ... 6B 90
KT21: Asht ... 4K 79
SM6: W'ton ... 2F 62
Taylor's Bushes Ride
SL4: W'sor ... 3N 17
Taylors Cl. GU35: Lind ... 4A 168
Taylors Ct. TW13: Felt ... 3H 23
Taylors Cres. GU6: Cranl ... 7A 156
Taylors La. GU35: Lind ... 4A 168
Taylor Wlk. RH11: Craw ... 3A 182
Taymans Track RH17: Hand ... 8L 199
Taynton Dr. RH1: Mers ... 8H 103
Teal Cl. CR2: Sels ... 7G 64
RH12: Hors ... 3J 197
Teal Ct. RH4: Dork ... 1J 201
SM6: W'ton ... 2G 63
Teale Cl. GU7: Godal ... 5J 133
Tealing Dr. KT19: Ewe ... 1C 60
Teal Pl. SM1: Sut ... 2L 61
Teamsport Karting
Camberley ... 5A 70
Crawley ... 8F 162
Teasel Cl. CR0: Croy ... 7G 46
RH11: Craw ... 6N 181
Tea Tree Cl. TW15: Ashf ... 6D 22
Teazlewood Pk. KT22: Leat ... 4G 78
Tebbit Cl. RG12: Brac ... 1B 32
Teck Cl. TW7: Isle ... 5G 11
Tedder Cl. KT9: Ches ... 2J 59
Tedder Rd. CR2: Sels ... 4F 64
TEDDINGTON ... 6G 24
Teddington Bus. Pk.
TW11: Tedd ... 7F 24
(off Station Rd.)
Teddington Cl. KT19: Eps ... 6C 60
Teddington Lock ... 5H 25
Teddington Pk. TW11: Tedd ... 6F 24
Teddington Pk. Rd.
TW11: Tedd ... 5F 24
Teddington Pool & Fitness Cen.
... 6G 24
Teddington Sports Cen. ... 7K 25
Teddington Station (Rail) ... 7G 24
Teddy Bear Collection ... *7N 27*
(within Polka Theatre for Children)
Tedham La. RH9: S Gods ... 3E 144
Tees Cl. GU14: Cove ... 8K 69
Teesdale RH11: Craw ... 6A 182
Teesdale Av. TW7: Isle ... 4G 11
Teesdale Gdns. SE25 ... 1B 46
TW7: Isle ... 4G 11
Tees Ho. Ga. GU14: Farnb ... 3N 89
Teevan Cl. CR0: Croy ... 6D 46
Teevan Rd. CR0: Croy ... 7D 46
Tegan Cl. SM2: Sut ... 4M 61
Tegg's La. GU22: Pyr ... 3H 75
Tekels Av. GU15: Camb ... 1B 70
Tekels Pk. GU15: Camb ... 1C 70
Tekels Way GU15: Camb ... 3C 70
Tekram Cl. TN8: Eden ... 2L 147
Telconia Cl. GU35: Head D ... 5H 169
Telegraph Hill GU6: Cranl ... 7D 154
GU8: Cranl, Hasc ... 7D 154
Telegraph La. KT10: Clay ... 1F 58
Telegraph Pas. *SW2 ... 1J 29*
(off New Pk. Rd.)
Telegraph Rd. SW15 ... 1G 27
Telegraph Track SM5: Cars ... 7E 62
Telephone Pl. SW6 ... 2L 13
Telferscot Rd. SW12 ... 2H 29
Telford Av. RG45: Crowt ... 9H 31
SW2 ... 2H 29
Telford Ct. GU1: Guil ... 3B 114
Telford Dr. KT12: Wal T ... 6K 39
Telford Pl. RH10: Craw ... 4C 182
Telford Rd. TW2: Whitt ... 1A 24
Telham Ct. RH11: Craw ... 6L 181
Tellisford KT10: Esh ... 1B 58
Temeraire Pl. TW8: Brent ... 1M 11
Temperley Rd. SW12 ... 1E 28
Tempest M. RG12: Brac ... 3B 32
Tempest Rd. TW20: Egh ... 7E 20
Templar Av. GU9: Farnh ... 3G 129
Templar Cl. GU47: Sandh ... 7F 48
Templar Ct. *TN8: Eden ... 9L 127*
(off Farmstead Dr.)
Templar Pl. TW12: Hamp ... 8A 24
Temple Av. CR0: Croy ... 8J 47
Temple Bar Rd. GU21: Wok ... 6J 73
Temple Cl.
KT19: Eps ... 5J 201 (8C 60)
RH10: Craw ... 4H 183
Templecombe M.
GU22: Wok ... 3D 74
Templecombe Way
SM4: Mord ... 4K 43
Temple Copse Local Nature Reserve
... 8K 15
Temple Ct. KT13: Weybr ... 1C 56
KT19: Eps ... 8C 60
Templecroft TW15: Ashf ... 7E 22
Templedene Av. TW18: Stain ... 8K 21
Templefield Cl. KT15: Addl ... 3K 55
Temple Gdns. TW18: Stain ... 9H 21
Temple La. RH5: Cap ... 4L 159
Templeman Cl. CR8: Pur ... 3M 83
Temple Mkt. KT13: Weybr ... 1C 56
Templemere KT13: Weybr ... 9E 38
Temple Pk. Rdbt. RG42: Bin ... 7L 15
Templer Av. GU14: Farnb ... 3L 89
Temple Rd.
CR0: Croy ... 6D 200 (1A 64)
KT19: Eps ... 5K 201 (8C 60)
SL4: W'sor ... 5F 4
Temple Rd. TN16: B Hil ... 4F 86
TW3: Houn ... 7B 10
TW9: Rich ... 5M 11
Temple's Cl. GU10: Farnh ... 2A 130
Temple Sheen SW14 ... 7B 12
Temple Sheen Rd. SW14 ... 7A 12
Templeton Cl. SE19 ... 1A 46
Templeton Pl. SW5 ... 1M 13
Temple Way RG42: Bin ... 9K 15
SM1: Sut ... 9B 44
Temple Wood Dr.
RH1: Red ... 9D 102
Tenacre GU21: Wok ... 5K 73
Ten Acre La. TW20: Thor ... 1E 36
Ten Acres KT22: Fetc ... 2D 98
Ten Acres Cl. KT22: Fetc ... 2D 98
Ten Acre Wlk.
GU10: Rowl, Wrec ... 7E 128
Tenbury Ct. SW2 ... 2H 29
Tenby Dr. SL5: S'hill ... 4A 34
Tenby Rd. GU16: Frim ... 6E 70
Tenchley's La. RH8: Limp ... 9E 106
Tenham Av. SW2 ... 2H 29
Tenniel Cl. GU2: Guil ... 1L 113
Tennis Ct. La. KT8: E Mol ... 2F 40
Tennison Cl. CR5: Coul ... 7M 83
Tennison Rd. SE25 ... 3C 46
Tennistogether Cen. ... 4D 110
Tennyson Av. KT3: N Mal ... 4G 43
TW1: Twick ... 2F 24
Tennyson Cl. RH10: Craw ... 1F 182
RH12: Hors ... 2L 197
TW14: Felt ... 9G 9
Tennyson Ct. GU26: Hind ... 5D 170
SW6 ... 4N 13
(off Imperial Rd.)
Tennyson Mans. *W14 ... 2L 13*
(off Queen's Club Gdns.)
Tennyson Ri. RH19: E Grin ... 9M 165
Tennyson Rd. KT15: Addl ... 1N 55
SW19 ... 7A 28
TW3: Houn ... 5C 10
TW15: Ashf ... 6N 21
Tennyson's La. GU27: Hasl ... 3H 189
Tennyson's Ridge
GU27: Hasl ... 3H 189
Tenpin
Croydon ... 8K 45
Feltham ... 3J 23
Kingston upon Thames
... 3K 203
(within The Rotunda Cen.)
Tensing Ct. TW19: Stan ... 2N 21
Tentelow La. UB2: S'hall ... 1A 10
Tenterden Gdns. CR0: Croy ... 6D 46
Tenterden Rd. CR0: Croy ... 6D 46
Tenth Av. KT20: Lwr K ... 4K 101
Teresa Va. RG42: Warf ... 7C 16
Terminal 4 Rdbt. TW6: Lon A ... 9D 8
Terminal 5 Rdbt. TW6: Lon A ... 5K 7
Ternhill RG12: Brac ... 4J 31
Tern Rd. RH11: Ifield ... 4J 181
Terrace, The GU14: Farnb ... 2C 90
GU15: Camb ... 1L 69
GU22: Wok ... 7C 74
(not continuous)
KT15: Addl ... 2N 55
RG40: W'ham ... 2A 30
RH5: Dork ... 6J 119
SL5: S'hill ... 4A 34
SW13 ... 5D 12
Terrace Gdns. SW13 ... 5E 12
Terrace Hill CR0: Croy ... 5A 200
Terrace La. TW10: Rich ... 9L 11
Terrace Rd. KT12: Wal T ... 6H 39
Terrace Rd. Nth. RG42: Bin ... 6H 15
Terrace Rd. Sth. RG42: Bin ... 7H 15
Terra Cotta Ct. GU10: Wrec ... 5E 128
Terracotta Rd.
RH9: S Gods ... 7F 124
Terrano Ho. TW9: Kew ... 3A 12
Terrapin Rd. SW17 ... 4F 28
Terrent Ct. SL4: W'sor ... 4D 4
Terry Rd. RH11: Craw ... 8N 181
Tersha St. TW9: Rich ... 7M 11
Testard Rd.
GU2: Guil ... 6A 202 (5M 113)
Tester's Cl. RH8: Oxt ... 9D 106
Testwood Rd. SL4: W'sor ... 4A 4
Tetcott Rd. SW10 ... 3N 13
Teviot Cl. GU2: Guil ... 9K 93
Tewkesbury Cl. KT14: Byf ... 7M 55
Tewkesbury Rd.
SM5: Cars ... 7B 44
Textile Est. GU46: Yate ... 8C 48
Teynham Ct. BR3: Beck ... 2L 47
Thackeray Cl. SW19 ... 8J 27
TW7: Isle ... 5G 11
Thackeray Lodge
TW14: Bedf ... 9E 8
Thames Av. KT4: W Pk ... 7H 43
KT16: Chert ... 2J 37
SL4: W'sor ... 3G 4
Thames Bank SW14 ... 5B 12
Thames Cl. GU14: Cove ... 8K 69
KT16: Chert ... 6K 37
TW12: Hamp ... 1B 40
Thames Cotts. KT7: T Dit ... 5H 41
Thames Ct. KT8: W Mole ... 1B 40
Thames Cres. W4 ... 3D 12
THAMES DITTON ... 5G 40
Thames Ditton & Esher Golf Course
... 8D 40
Thames Ditton Station (Rail)
... 6F 40
Thames Edge Ct.
TW18: Stain ... 5G 21
(off Clarence St.)
Thames Eyot TW1: Twick ... 2G 24
Thamesfield Ct.
TW17: Shep ... 6D 38
Thamesfield M. TW17: Shep ... 6D 38
Thamesgate TW18: Stain ... 1K 37
Thamesgate Cl. TW10: Ham ... 5H 25
Thames Haven KT6: Surb ... 4K 41
Thames Ho. KT1: K Tham ... 7H 203
Thameside KT8: W Mole ... 2B 40
KT16: Chert ... 3L 37
TW11: Tedd ... 8K 25
TW18: Lale, Stain ... 6H 21
(not continuous)
Thameside Cen. TW8: Brent ... 2M 11
Thameside Pl.
KT1: H Wic ... 1G 203 (9K 25)
Thames Lock KT12: Wal T ... 2K 39
KT13: Weybr ... 9B 38
Thames Mead SL4: W'sor ... 4B 4
Thamesmead KT12: Wal T ... 5H 39
Thames Mdw. KT8: W Mole ... 1A 40
TW17: Shep ... 7E 38
Thames Pl. SW15 ... 6J 13
Thamespoint TW11: Tedd ... 8K 25
Thames Reach KT1: H Wic ... 9K 25
W6 ... 2H 13
(off Rainville Rd.)
Thames Rd. W4 ... 2N 11
Thames Side
KT1: K Tham ... 2H 203 (9K 25)
KT7: T Dit ... 5H 41
SL4: W'sor ... 3G 5
Thames St.
KT1: K Tham ... 3H 203 (1K 41)
KT12: Wal T ... 6G 39
KT13: Weybr ... 8C 38
SL4: W'sor ... 4G 4
TW12: Hamp ... 9B 24
TW16: Sunb ... 3H 39
TW18: Stain ... 6H 21
Thamesvale Cl. TW3: Houn ... 6A 10
Thames Valley Athletics Cen.
... 1H 5
Thamesview Ho's.
KT12: Wal T ... 5H 39
Thames Village W4 ... 4B 12
Thames Wlk. *KT12: Wal T ... 6H 39*
(off Mnr. Rd.)
Thames Wharf Studios *W6 ... 2H 13*
(off Rainville Rd.)
Thanescroft Gdns.
CR0: Croy ... 9B 46
Thanet Dr. BR2: Kes ... 1F 66
Thanet Ho. CR0: Croy ... 6C 200
Thanet Pl.
CR0: Croy ... 6C 200 (1N 63)
Tharp Rd. SM6: W'ton ... 2H 63
Thatcher Cl. RH10: Craw ... 6B 182
Thatchers Cl. RH6: Horl ... 6F 142
RH12: Hors ... 4L 197
Thatchers La. GU3: Worp ... 5G 93
Thatchers Way TW7: Isle ... 8D 10
Thaxted Pl. SW20 ... 8J 27
Thaxton Rd. W14 ... 2L 13
Thayers Farm Rd.
BR3: Beck ... 1H 47
The ....
Names prefixed with 'The'
for example 'The Acorns'
are indexed under the main
name such as 'Acorns, The'
Theal Cl. GU47: Coll T ... 7J 49
Theatre Ct.
KT18: Eps ... 7J 201 (9C 60)
Theatre Rd. GU14: Farnb ... 5N 89
Theatre Royal
Windsor ... 3G 5
Thegn Wlk. GU51: Fleet ... 1A 88
Thelma Gro. TW11: Tedd ... 7G 24
Thelton Av.
RH12: Broadb H ... 5D 196
Theobald Rd.
CR0: Croy ... 2A 200 (8M 45)
Theobalds Way GU16: Frim ... 3G 71
Thepps Cl. RH1: Sth N ... 6K 123
Therapia La. CR0: Bedd ... 6H 45
CR0: Croy ... 5J 45
Therapia Lane Stop
(London Tramlink) ... 6J 45
Theresa Rd. W6 ... 1F 12
Theresa's Wlk. CR2: Sande ... 5A 64
Thetford Rd. KT3: N Mal ... 5C 42
TW15: Ashf ... 5N 21
Thetford Wlk. RH11: Craw ... 7K 181
Thetis Ter. TW9: Kew ... 2N 11
Theydon Cl. RH10: Craw ... 5E 182
Theydon Ct. GU6: Cranl ... 8J 155
Thibet Rd. GU47: Sandh ... 7H 49
Thicket Cres. SM1: Sut ... 1A 62
Thicket Rd. SM1: Sut ... 1A 62
Thickthorne La. TW18: Stain ... 8L 21
Third Av. KT20: Lwr K ... 3K 101
Third Cl. KT8: W Mole ... 3C 40
Third Cross Rd. TW2: Twick ... 3D 24
Thirlmere Cl. GU14: Cove ... 1K 89
TW20: Egh ... 8D 20
Thirlmere Cres.
GU52: Chu C ... 8A 88
Thirlmere Ho. TW7: Isle ... 8F 10
Thirlmere Rd. RH11: Ifield ... 5J 181
SW16 ... 5H 29
Thirlmere Wlk. GU15: Camb ... 2H 71
Thirsk Ct. GU12: Alde ... 2B 110
Thirsk Rd. CR4: Mit ... 8E 28
SE25 ... 3A 46
Thirteenth Av. KT20: Lwr K ... 4L 101
Thistlecroft Rd. KT12: Hers ... 1K 57
Thistledene KT7: T Dit ... 5E 40
KT14: W By ... 9H 55
Thistle Down GU26: Hind ... 5C 170
Thistledown Cl.
GU10: Wrec ... 5E 128
Thistledown Va. RH14: Ifo ... 4F 192
Thistles, The KT22: Leat ... 9J 79
Thistle Way RH6: Smallf ... 8N 143
Thistlewood Cres.
CR0: N Add ... 8N 65
Thistleworth Cl. TW7: Isle ... 3D 10
Thistleworth Marina
TW7: Isle ... 7H 11
(off Railshead Rd.)
Thistley Cl. CR5: Coul ... 9H 83
Thistley La. GU6: Cranl ... 6N 155
Thomas Av. CR3: Cate ... 8N 83
Thomas Dr. RG42: Warf ... 8C 16
Thomas Ho. SM2: Sut ... 4N 61
Thomas Moore Ho.
RH2: Reig ... 3A 122
(off Reigate Rd.)
Thomas More Gdns.
KT10: Esh ... 9A 40
Thomas Rd. GU11: Alde ... 6B 90
Thomas Turner Path
CR0: Croy ... 3C 200
Thomas Wall Cl. SM1: Sut ... 2N 61
Thompson Av. TW9: Rich ... 6N 11
Thompson Cl. SL3: Lang ... 1B 6
SM3: Sut ... 7M 43
Thompson Rd. TW3: Houn ... 7B 10
Thompson's Cl. GU24: Pirb ... 1A 92
Thompson's La. GU24: Chob ... 5G 53
Thomson Ct. RH11: Craw ... 8N 181
Thomson Cres. CR0: Croy ... 7L 45
Thorburn Chase
GU47: Coll T ... 9K 49
Thorburn Way SW19 ... 9B 28
Thorkhill Gdns. KT7: T Dit ... 7G 41
Thorkhill Rd. KT7: T Dit ... 7G 41
Thorley Cl. KT14: W By ... 1J 75
Thorley Gdns. GU22: Pyr ... 2J 75
Thornash Cl. GU21: Wok ... 2M 73
Thornash Rd. GU21: Wok ... 2M 73
Thornash Way GU21: Wok ... 2M 73
Thorn Bank GU2: Guil ... 5K 113
Thornbank Cl. TW19: Stan M ... 8J 7
Thornberry Way GU1: Guil ... 8B 94
Thornbury Av. TW7: Isle ... 3D 10
Thornbury Cl. RG45: Crowt ... 2G 48
Thornbury Ct. CR2: S Croy ... 8E 200
CR3: Whyte ... 7C 84
TW7: Isle ... 3E 10
Thornbury Rd. SW2 ... 1J 29
TW7: Isle ... 3D 10
Thorncliffe Rd. SW2 ... 1J 29
UB2: S'hall ... 1N 9
Thorn Cl. GU10: Wrec ... 7E 128
THORNCOMBE STREET ... 1N 153
Thorncombe St.
GU5: Braml ... 8N 133
Thorncroft TW20: Eng G ... 8M 19
Thorncroft Cl. CR5: Coul ... 6L 83
Thorncroft Dr. KT22: Leat ... 1H 99
Thorncroft Rd. SM1: Sut ... 2N 61
Thorndean St. SW18 ... 3A 28
Thorndon Gdns. KT19: Ewe ... 2D 60
Thorndown La. GU20: Windl ... 4A 52
Thorndyke Cl. RH10: Craw ... 4H 183
Thorne Cl. KT10: Clay ... 4G 59
RG45: Crowt ... 9F 30
TW15: Ashf ... 8D 22
Thorneloe Gdns.
CR0: Wad ... 8A 200 (2L 63)
Thorne Pas. SW13 ... 5D 12
Thornes Cl. BR3: Beck ... 2M 47
Thorne St. SW13 ... 6D 12
Thorneycroft Cl.
KT12: Wal T ... 5K 39
Thorney Hedge Rd. W4 ... 1A 12
Thornfield Grn. GU17: Haw ... 3L 69
Thornfield Rd. SM7: Ban ... 4M 81
Thornhill RG12: Brac ... 3C 32
RH11: Craw ... 5N 181
Thornhill Av. KT6: Surb ... 8L 41
Thornhill Ho. *W4 ... 1D 12*
(off Wood St.)
Thornhill M. SW15 ... 7L 13
Thornhill Rd. CR0: Croy ... 6N 45
GU11: Alde ... 9B 90
KT6: Surb ... 8L 41
Thornhill Way TW17: Shep ... 4B 38
Thornlaw Rd. SE27 ... 5L 29
Thornleas Pl. KT24: E Hor ... 4F 96
Thorn Rd. GU10: Wrec ... 6F 128
Thornsett Pl. SE20 ... 1E 46
Thornsett Rd. SE20 ... 1E 46
SW18 ... 2N 27
Thornsett Ter. *SE20 ... 1E 46*
(off Croydon Rd.)
Thornton Av. CR0: Croy ... 5K 45
SW2 ... 2H 29
W4 ... 1D 12
Thornton Cl. GU2: Guil ... 9K 93
RH6: Horl ... 8C 142
Thornton Cres. CR5: Coul ... 6L 83
Thornton Dene BR3: Beck ... 1K 47
Thornton Gdns. SW12 ... 2H 29
THORNTON HEATH ... 3N 45
Thornton Heath Leisure Cen.
... 3N 45
THORNTON HEATH POND ... 4L 45
Thornton Heath Station (Rail)
... 3N 45
Thornton Hill SW19 ... 8K 27
Thornton M. RG45: Crowt ... 3H 49
Thornton Pl. RH6: Horl ... 8C 142
Thornton Rd. CR0: Croy ... 6K 45
CR7: T Hea ... 6K 45
SM5: Cars ... 7B 44
SW12 ... 1H 29
SW14 ... 7C 12
SW19 ... 7J 27
Thornton Rd. E. SW19 ... 7J 27
Thornton Rd. Ind. Est.
CR0: Croy ... 5K 45
Thornton Row CR7: T Hea ... 4L 45
Thornton Side RH1: Mers ... 9F 102
Thornton Wlk. RH6: Horl ... 8C 142
Thornville Gro. CR4: Mit ... 1B 44
Thornycroft Ho. *W4 ... 1D 12*
(off Fraser St.)
Thornyhurst Rd. GU16: Mytc ... 1E 90
Thorold Cl. CR2: Sels ... 6G 65
Thorold Rd. GU9: Farnh ... 9H 109
Thoroughfare, The
KT20: Wal H ... 2F 100
Thorp Cl. RG42: Bin ... 6H 15
THORPE ... 2E 36
Thorpe By-Pass TW20: Thor ... 1D 36
Thorpe Cl. CR0: N Add ... 7M 65
RG41: W'ham ... 5A 30
THORPE GREEN ... 3C 36
Thorpe Hay Meadow Nature Reserve
... 8F 20
Thorpe Ind. Pk. TW20: Thor ... 9E 20
THORPE LEA ... 7E 20
Thorpe Lea Rd.
TW20: Egh, Thor ... 7D 20
Thorpe Park ... 3G 37
Thorpe Rd.
KT2: K Tham ... 1K 203 (8L 25)
KT16: Chert ... 4F 36
TW18: Stain ... 7F 20
Thorpe's Cl. GU2: Guil ... 9K 93
Thorpeside Cl. TW18: Stain ... 1G 37
Thorsden Cl. GU22: Wok ... 6A 74
Thorsden Ct. GU22: Wok ... 5A 74
Thrale Rd. SW16 ... 5G 28
Three Acres RH12: Hors ... 7G 197
Three Arch Bus. Pk.
RH1: Red ... 7E 122
Three Arches Pk. RH1: Red ... 7D 122
Three Arch Rd. RH1: Red ... 7D 122
THREE BRIDGES ... 2E 182
Three Bridges Path
KT1: K Tham ... 6K 203
(off Bellvue Rd.)
Three Bridges Rd.
RH10: Craw ... 3D 182
Three Bridges Station (Rail)
... 3F 182
Three Gates GU1: Guil ... 2E 114
Three Gates La.
GU27: Hasl ... 1H 189
Three Mile Rd.
RH5: Holm M ... 9H 137
Three Pears Rd. GU1: Guil ... 3G 114
Threestile Rd.
RH12: Warnh ... 8F 178
Three Stiles Rd.
GU9: Farnh ... 9E 108
Threshers Cnr. GU51: Fleet ... 1D 88
Threshfield RG12: Brac ... 4M 31
Threshold Way GU24: Chob ... 6A 54
Thrift La. TN14: Cud ... 4N 87
Thrift Va. GU4: Guil ... 9F 94
Thrigby Rd. KT9: Ches ... 3M 59
Throgmorton Rd. GU46: Yate ... 1A 68
Thrower Pl. RH5: Dork ... 7J 119
Throwley Rd. SM1: Sut ... 2N 61
Throwley Way SM1: Sut ... 1N 61
Thrupp Cl. CR4: Mit ... 1F 44
Thrupp Ho. *GU4: Guil ... 2F 114*
(off Merrow St.)
Thrupp's Av. KT12: Hers ... 2L 57
Thrupp's La. KT12: Hers ... 2L 57
Thundery Hill GU10: Seal ... 8D 110
Thundry Meadows Nature Reserve
... 7F 130
Thurbans Rd. GU9: Farnh ... 4F 128
Thurbarns Hill RH5: B Grn ... 1L 159
Thurlby Rd. SE27 ... 5L 29
Thurleigh Ct. SW12 ... 1E 28
Thurleigh Rd. SW12 ... 1D 28
Thurleston Av. SM4: Mord ... 4K 43
Thurlestone Cl. TW17: Shep ... 5D 38
Thurlestone Pde.
TW17: Shep ... 5D 38
(off High St.)
Thurlestone Rd. SE27 ... 4L 29
Thurlow Hill SE21 ... 2N 29
Thurlow Ho. SW16 ... 4J 29
Thurlow Pk. Rd. SE21 ... 3M 29
Thurlow Wlk. GU6: Cranl ... 9N 155
Thurlton Ct. GU21: Wok ... 3A 74
Thurnby Ct. TW2: Twick ... 4E 24
Thurne Way RH12: Rudg ... 1E 194
Thurnham Way KT20: Tad ... 7J 81
Thursby Rd. GU21: Wok ... 5K 73
THURSLEY ... 7G 150
Thursley Common
National Nature Reserve
... 4H 151

A-Z Surrey 291

Thursley Cres.—Trenton Cl.

Thursley Cres. CR0: N Add 4M 65
Thursley Gdns. SW19 . . . . .3J 27
Thursley Ho. SW2 . . . . .1K 29
(off Holmewood Gdns.)
Thursley Rd. GU8: Els 4F 150
GU8: Thur 7A 150
GU10: Churt 7A 150
Thurso St. SW17 . . . . .5B 28
Thurstan Rd. SW20 . . . . .8G 26
Thyer Cl. BR6: Farnb 1L 67
Thyme Ct. GU4: B'ham 9D 94
GU14: Cove 9H 69
Tibbet's Cl. SW19 . . . . .2J 27
TIBBET'S CORNER 1J 27
Tibbet's Ride SW15 . . . . .1J 27
Ticehurst Cl. RH10: Worth 3J 183
Tichborne Cl. GU16: Frim 3D 70
GU17: B'water 1J 69
Tichborne Pl. GU12: Alde 4B 110
Tichmarsh KT19: Eps 6B 60
TICKLEBACK ROW 3N 15
Tickleback Row
RG42: Warf 3N 15
TICKNERS HEATH 6F 174
Tide Cl. CR4: Mit 9E 28
Tidenham Gdns. CR0: Croy 9B 46
Tides End Ct. GU15: Camb 2D 70
Tideswell Rd. CR0: Croy 9K 47
SW15 . . . . .7H 13
Tideway Cl. TW10: Ham 5H 25
Tidwells Lea RG42: Warf 9C 16
Tierney Ct. CR0: Croy 8B 46
Tierney Rd. SW2 . . . . .2J 29
Tiffany Hgts. SW18 . . . . .1M 27
Tiffin Girls Community Sports Cen.
. . . . .7L 25
Tiffin Sports Cen. . . .3L 203 (1M 41)
Tilburstow Hill Rd.
RH9: Gods, S Gods 1F 124
(not continuous)
Tildesley Rd. SW15 . . . . .9H 13
Tile Barn Cl. GU14: Farnb 9M 69
Tile Farm Rd. BR6: Orp 1M 67
Tilehouse Rd. GU4: Guil 7A 114
Tilehurst La. RG42: Bin 6H 15
RH5: Dork 6L 119
Tilehurst Rd. SM3: Chea 2K 61
SW18 . . . . .2B 28
Tilers Cl. RH1: Mers 9G 103
Tiler's Wlk. RH2: Reig 7A 122
Tiler's Way RH2: Reig 7A 122
TILFORD 8A 130
Tilford Av. CR0: N Add 5M 65
TILFORD COMMON 1A 150
Tilford Gdns. SW19 . . . . .2J 27
Tilford Ho. SW2 . . . . .1K 29
(off Holmewood Gdns.)
Tilford Rd. GU9: Farnh 2J 129
GU10: Churt, Rush, Til . . .8A 130
GU26: Hind 1A 170
Tilford St. GU10: Til 8A 130
Tilford Woods Caravan Pk.
GU10: Til 1B 150
TILGATE 6C 182
Tilgate Comn. RH1: Blet 2N 123
Tilgate Dr. RH10: Craw 4E 182
(Hylands Cl.)
RH10: Craw 7B 182
(The Avenue, not continuous)
Tilgate Forest Bus. Cen.
RH11: Craw 8B 182
Tilgate Forest Golf Course . . .7E 182
TILGATE FOREST ROW 3N 199
Tilgate Forest Row
RH11: Pease P 3N 199
Tilgate Forest Theatre 8C 182
Tilgate Mans.
RH10: Craw 8D 182
Tilgate Nature Pk. 8C 182
Tilgate Pde. RH10: Craw 6C 182
Tilgate Park (Country Pk.)
. . . . .8C 182
Tilgate Pl. RH10: Craw 6C 182
Tilgate Way RH10: Craw 6C 182
Tilia Cl. SM1: Sut 2L 61
Tillers Cl. TW18: Stain 7G 20
Tilletts La. RH12: Warnh 9E 178
Tilley La.
KT18: Eps D, Head 9B 80
Tilley Rd. TW13: Felt 2H 23
Tillingbourne Rd.
GU4: Chil 9A 114
Tillingdown Hill
CR3: Cate, Wold 9E 84
Tillingdown La.
CR3: Cate, Wold 2E 104
(not continuous)
Tillotson Cl. RH10: Craw 4H 183
Tillys La. TW18: Stain 5H 21
Tilney Cl. KT22: Leat 7G 78
Tilson Gdns. SW2 . . . . .1J 29
Tilson Ho. SW2 . . . . .1J 29
Tilstone Av. SL4: E Wic 1B 4
Tilstone Cl. SL4: E Wic 1B 4
Tilt Cl. KT11: Cob 3M 77
Tilthams Cnr. Rd.
GU5: Braml 3L 133
GU7: Godal 3L 133
Tilthams Grn. GU7: Godal 3L 133
Tilt Mdw. KT11: Cob 3M 77
Tilton St. SW6 . . . . .2K 13
Tilt Rd. KT11: Cob, Sto D 2K 77
Tilt Vw. KT11: Cob 2K 77
Tiltwood Dr. RH10: Craw D 9F 164
Timber Bank GU16: Frim G 8E 70
Timber Cl. GU9: Farnh 1G 128
(off The Hart)
GU22: Pyr 1H 75
KT23: Book 4C 98
Timber Ct. RH12: Hors 5J 197
Timbercroft KT19: Ewe 1D 60
Timberham Farm Rd.
RH6: Gatw 2B 162
Timberham Way
RH6: Gatw 2C 162
Timberhill KT21: Asht 6L 79
Timber Hill Cl. KT16: Otter 4E 54
Timber Hill Rd. CR3: Cate 2D 104
Timberlands RH11: Craw 8N 181
Timber La. CR3: Cate 2D 104
Timberley Pl. RG45: Crowt 3D 48
Timberling Gdns.
CR2: Sande 5A 64
Timbermill Ct. GU27: Hasl 2D 188
Timbers, The
RH13: Mann H 9B 198
RH19: E Grin 8M 165
SM3: Chea 3K 61
Timberslip Dr. SM6: W'ton 5H 63
Timbertop Rd. TN16: B Hil 5E 86
Timbralls SL4: Eton 1G 4
(off Slough Rd.)
Times Sq. SM1: Sut 2N 61
Timline Grn. RG12: Brac 1D 32
Timothy Pl. KT8: W Mole 4N 39
Timpani Hill CR6: Warl 5E 84
Timperley Ct. RH1: Red 1C 122
(off Timperley Gdns.)
SW19 . . . . .2K 27
Timperley Gdns. RH1: Red . . .1C 122
Timsbury Wlk. SW15 . . . . .2F 26
Timsway TW18: Stain 6H 21
Tindal Cl. GU46: Yate 9C 48
Tindale Cl. CR2: Sande 7A 64
Tinderbox All. SW14 . . . . .6C 12
Tinefields KT20: Tad 6K 81
Tinkers Copse Local Nature Reserve
. . . . .7L 15
Tinkers La. SL4: W'sor 5A 4
SL5: S'dale 5E 34
Tinmans Row KT11: Down 5K 77
Tinsey Cl. TW20: Egh 6D 20
Tinsley Cl. RH10: Craw 9E 162
SE25 . . . . .2E 46
TINSLEY GREEN 6F 162
Tinsley Grn. RH10: Craw 6F 162
Tinsley La. RH10: Craw 8E 162
Tinsley La. Nth.
RH10: Craw 7F 162
Tinsley La. Sth.
RH10: Craw 1E 182
(off Hazelwick Av.)
Tintagel Cl.
KT17: Eps 8M 201 (1E 80)
Tintagel Ct. RH13: Hors 7K 197
Tintagel Dr. GU16: Frim 5D 70
Tintagel Farm Cl.
RG40: Finch 8A 30
Tintagel Rd. RG40: Finch 8A 30
Tintagel Way GU22: Wok 3C 74
Tintells La. KT24: W Hors 6C 96
Tintern Cl. SW15 . . . . .8K 13
SW19 . . . . .7A 28
Tintern Rd. RH11: Craw 5M 181
SM5: Cars 7B 44
Tippits Mead RG42: Brac 9J 15
Tipton Dr. CR0: Croy 1B 64
Tiree Path RH11: Craw 6N 181
Tirlemont Rd. CR2: S Croy 4N 63
Tirrell Rd. CR0: Croy 5N 45
Tisbury Rd. SW16 . . . . .1J 45
TISMAN'S COMMON 2A 194
Tismans Comn.
RH12: Rudg 2A 194
Titan Ct. TW8: Brent 1M 11
Titchfield Rd. SM5: Cars 7B 44
Titchfield Wlk. SM5: Cars 6B 44
Titchwell Rd. SW18 . . . . .2B 28
Tite Hill TW20: Egh, Eng G 6M 19
Tithe, The RH11: Ifield 9M 161
Tithe Barn Cl.
KT2: K Tham 2L 203 (9M 25)
Tithebarns La. GU23: Send 4J 95
Tithe Cl. GU25: V Wat 5N 35
KT12: Wal T 5J 39
Tithe Ct. RG40: W'ham 1B 30
Tithe La. TW19: Wray 9C 6
Tithe Mdws. GU25: V Wat 5M 35
Tithe Orchard RH19: Felb 6H 165
Tithepit Shaw La. CR6: Warl . . .4E 84
Tithing Rd. GU51: Fleet 1A 88
Titlarks Hill SL5: S'dale 8E 34
Titmus Dr. RH10: Craw 6D 182
Titness Pk. SL5: S'hill 2D 34
TITSEY 3D 106
Titsey Hill RH8: T'sey 1C 106
Titsey Place & Gardens 2D 106
Titsey Rd.
RH8: Limp, T'sey 3D 106
Tiverton Cl. CR0: Croy 6C 46
Tiverton Rd. TW3: Houn 5C 10
Tiverton Way GU16: Frim 5D 70
KT9: Ches 2K 59
Tivoli Rd. SE27 . . . . .6N 29
TW4: Houn 7M 9
Toad La. GU17: Haw 2K 69
TW4: Houn 7N 9
Toat Hill RH13: Slinf 8N 195
Tobermory Cl. SL3: Lang 1A 6
Tobin Cl. KT19: Eps 7A 60
Toby Way KT5: Surb 8A 42
Tocker Gdns. RG42: Warf 7N 15
Tockington Ct. GU46: Yate 9C 48
Todds Cl. RH6: Horl 6C 142
Toftwood Cl. RH10: Craw 4G 183
Token Yd. SW15 . . . . .7K 13
Toland Sq. SW15 . . . . .8F 12
Tolgate Ct. RH1: Red 8D 122
Toll Bar Ct. SM2: Sut 5N 61
Tolldene Cl. GU21: Knap 4H 73
Tollers La. CR5: Coul 5K 83
Tolley Cl. GU12: Ash 1F 110
Toll Gdns. RG12: Brac 2D 32
Tollgate GU1: Guil 3F 114
Tollgate Av. RH1: Red 8D 122
Tollgate Ct.
CR2: S Croy 8E 200 (2A 64)
Tollgate Hill RH11: Craw 9A 182
Tollgate Hill Rdbt.
RH11: Craw 9N 181
Tollgate Pl. RH19: E Grin 1B 186
(off Lewes Rd.)
Tollgate Rd. RH4: Dork 8H 119
Tollhouse La. SM6: W'ton 5G 63
Tolpuddle Way GU46: Yate 1E 68
Tolson Rd. TW7: Isle 6G 10
Tolvaddon Cl. GU21: Wok 4K 73
Tolverne Rd. SW20 . . . . .9H 27
TOLWORTH 8A 42
Tolworth B'way. KT6: Surb 7A 42
Tolworth Cl. KT6: Surb 7A 42
TOLWORTH JUNC. (TOBY JUG)
. . . . .8A 42
Tolworth Pk. Rd. KT6: Surb . . .8M 41
Tolworth Recreation Cen. 9M 41
Tolworth Ri. Nth. KT5: Surb . . .7A 42
Tolworth Ri. Sth. KT5: Surb . . .8A 42
Tolworth Rd. KT6: Surb 8L 41
Tolworth Station (Rail) 8A 42
Tolworth Twr. KT6: Surb 8A 42
Tomlin Cl. KT19: Eps 7C 60
Tomlin Ct. KT19: Eps 7C 60
RH10: Craw 3D 182
Tomlins All. TW1: Twick 2G 24
Tomlins Av. GU16: Frim 4D 70
Tomlinscote Sports Cen. 4D 70
Tomlinscote Way
GU16: Frim 4E 70
Tomlinson Cl. W4 . . . . .1A 12
Tomlinson Dr. RG40: Finch 9A 30
TOMPSET'S BANK 9H 187
Tompset's Bank
RH18: F Row 9H 187
Tomtit Cres. RH10: Turn H 4F 184
Tomtits La. RH18: F Row 8G 187
Tom Williams Ho. SW6 . . . . . . .2L 13
(off Clem Attlee Ct.)
Tonbridge Cl. SM7: Ban 1D 82
Tonbridge Rd. KT8: W Mole 3N 39
Tonfield Rd. SM3: Sut 7L 43
Tonge Cl. BR3: Beck 4K 47
TONGHAM 6D 110
Tongham Mdws.
GU10: Tong 5C 110
Tongham Rd. GU10: B Lea 7B 110
GU10: Run 8A 110
(not continuous)
GU12: Alde 4B 110
Tonsley Hill SW18 . . . . .8N 13
Tonsley Pl. SW18 . . . . .8N 13
Tonsley Rd. SW18 . . . . .8N 13
Tonsley St. SW18 . . . . .8N 13
Tonstall Rd. CR4: Mit 1E 44
KT19: Eps 6C 60
Tony Law Ho. SE20 . . . . .1E 46
Toogood Pl. RG42: Warf 6B 16
TOOTING 6C 28
TOOTING BEC 4D 28
Tooting Bec Gdns. SW16 . . . . . .5H 29
(not continuous)
Tooting Bec Lido 5G 29
Tooting Bec Rd. SW16 . . . . .4E 28
SW17 . . . . .4E 28
Tooting Bec Station
(Underground) 4E 28
Tooting B'way. SW17 . . . . .6C 28
Tooting Broadway Station
(Underground) 6C 28
TOOTING GRAVENEY 7D 28
Tooting Gro. SW17 . . . . .6C 28
Tooting High St. SW17 . . . . . . .7C 28
Tooting Leisure Cen. 5B 28
Tooting Mkt. SW17 . . . . .5D 28
Tooting Station (Rail) 7D 28
Topcliffe Dr. BR6: Farnb 1M 67
Top Common RG42: Warf 8B 16
TopGolf
Surrey 4L 55
Topiary, The GU14: Cove 2K 89
KT21: Asht 7L 79
Topiary Sq. TW9: Rich 6M 11
Toplady Pl. GU9: Up Hale 5H 109
Top Pk. BR3: Beck 4N 47
Topsham Rd. SW17 . . . . .4D 28
Torin Ct. TW20: Eng G 6M 19
Torland Dr. KT22: Oxs 9D 58
Tor La. KT13: Weybr 7D 56
Tormead Cl. SM1: Sut 3M 61
Tormead Rd. GU1: Guil 3B 114
Tornado Chase RG12: Brac 3A 32
Toronto Dr. RH6: Smallf 8L 143
Torrens Cl. GU2: Guil 9K 93
Torre Wlk. SM5: Cars 7C 44
Torridge Rd. CR7: T Hea 4M 45
SL3: Lang 2D 6
Torridon Cl. GU21: Wok 4L 73
Torrington Cl. GU35: Lind 4B 168
KT10: Clay 3E 58
Torrington Rd. KT10: Clay 3E 58
Torrington Sq. CR0: Croy 6A 46
Torrington Way
SM4: Mord 5M 43
Tor Rd. GU9: Farnh 1E 128
Torwood La. CR3: Whyte 7C 84
Torwood Rd. SW15 . . . . .8F 12
Totale Ri. RG42: Warf 7N 15
Totford La. GU10: Seal 9J 111
TOT HILL 4B 100
Tot Hill La. KT18: Head 4B 100
Totland Cl. GU14: Farnb 8M 69
Tottenham Rd. GU7: Godal 5H 133
Tottenham Wlk. GU47: Owls 6J 49
Totterdown St. SW17 . . . . .5D 28
Totton Rd. CR7: T Hea 2L 45
Toulouse Cl. GU15: Camb 8F 50
Tourist Info. Cen.
Aldershot 2M 109
Bracknell 7B 32
Crawley 4C 182
East Grinstead 1A 186
Edenbridge 2L 147
Guildford 5D 202 (4N 113)
Heathrow Central 6C 8
Horsham 7J 197
Kingston upon Thames
. . . . .4H 203 (1K 41)
Windsor 4G 4
Tournai Cl. GU11: Alde 6C 90
Tournay Rd. SW6 . . . . .3L 13
Tovil Cl. SE20 . . . . .1E 46
Tower App. Rd. RH6: Gatw . . .4C 162
Tower Cl. GU21: Wok 4N 73
GU26: Hind 5C 170
RH6: Horl 8D 142
RH13: Hors 8G 196
RH19: E Grin 8A 166
Tower Ct. RH13: Hors 7J 197
RH19: E Grin 8A 166
(off Moat Rd.)
TW20: Egh 6C 20
Tower Gdns. KT10: Clay 4G 59
Towergate Bus. Cen.
GU8: Worm 2C 172
Tower Gro. KT13: Weybr 8F 38
TOWER HILL
RH4 . . . . .7H 119
RH13 . . . . .8G 196
Tower Hill GU14: Cove 2M 89
RH4: Dork 7H 119
RH13: Hors 9F 196
Towerhill GU5: Gom 9D 116
Towerhill La. GU5: Gom 8D 116
Towerhill Ri. GU5: Gom 9D 116
Tower Hill Rd. RH4: Dork 7H 119
Tower Ho. KT14: Byf 8N 55
(off High Rd.)
Tower La. RH2: Reig 6C 102
Tower Pl. CR6: Warl 2K 85
Tower Ride SL4: W'sor 4B 18
Tower Ri. TW9: Rich 6L 11
Tower Rd. GU26: Hind 5C 170
KT20: Tad 1H 101
RH12: Fay, Colg 9E 180
TW1: Twick 4F 24
Towers, The CR8: Ken 2N 83
Towers Dr. RG45: Crowt 3G 48
Towers Pl. TW9: Rich 8L 11
Towers Wlk. KT13: Weybr 3C 56
Tower Vw. CR0: Croy 6H 47
Tower Yd. TW10: Rich 8M 11
Towfield Ct. TW13: Hanw 3N 23
Towfield Rd. TW13: Hanw 3N 23
Town Barn Rd. RH11: Craw . . .3A 182
Town End CR3: Cate 9B 84
Town End Cl. CR3: Cate 9B 84
GU7: Godal 7H 133
Town End Pde.
KT1: K Tham 5H 203
Town End St. GU7: Godal 7H 133
Town Farm Way TW19: Stan . . .1M 21
Townfield Ct.
RH4: Dork 4J 201 (6G 119)
Townfield Rd.
RH4: Dork 4J 201 (6G 119)
Town Fld. Way TW7: Isle 5G 11
Towngate KT11: Cob 2M 77
Town Hall Av. W4 . . . . .1C 12
Town Hill RH7: Ling 7N 145
Town La. TW19: Stan 9M 7
(not continuous)
Town Mead RH1: Blet 2A 124
RH11: Craw 2B 182
Townmead Bus. Cen.
SW6 . . . . .6N 13
Town Mdw. TW8: Brent 2K 11
Town Mdw. Rd. TW8: Brent 3K 11
Townmead Rd. SW6 . . . . .6N 13
TW9: Kew 5A 12
Town Quay TW18: Lale 2K 37
(off Blacksmiths La.)
Townsend Cl. RG12: Brac 4C 32
Townsend La. GU22: Wok 8D 74
Townsend M. SW18 . . . . .3A 28
Townsend Rd. TW15: Ashf 6N 21
Townsend Way RH10: Craw . . .5H 183
Townshend Rd. TW9: Rich 7M 11
Townshend Ter. TW9: Rich 7M 11
Townshott Cl. KT23: Book 3A 98
Townside Pl. GU15: Camb 9B 50
Townslow La. GU23: Wis 3L 75
Town Sq. GU15: Camb 9A 50
GU21: Wok 4A 74
RG12: Brac 1A 32
TW7: Isle 6H 11
(off Swan St.)
Town Tree Rd. TW15: Ashf 6B 22
Town Wharf TW7: Isle 6H 11
Towpath KT12: Wal T 4H 39
TW17: Shep 7A 38
Towpath Way CR0: Croy 5C 46
Towton Rd. SE27 . . . . .3N 29
Toynbee Rd. SW20 . . . . .9K 27
Tozer Wlk. SL4: W'sor 6A 4
Tracery, The SM7: Ban 2N 81
Tracious Cl. GU21: Wok 3L 73
Tracious La. GU21: Wok 3L 73
Tracy Av. SL3: Lang 1B 6
Trade City KT13: Weybr 6N 55
Trade City Bus. Pk.
TW16: Sunb 9F 22
Traditions Golf Course 2K 75
Trafalgar Av. KT4: W Pk 7J 43
Trafalgar Ct. GU9: Farnh 2G 129
KT11: Cob 9H 57
Trafalgar Dr. KT12: Wal T 9J 39
Trafalgar Gdns.
RH10: Craw 2F 182
Trafalgar Rd. RH12: Hors 4J 197
SW19 . . . . .8N 27
TW2: Twick 3D 24
Trafalgar Vs. GU14: Cove 1H 89
(off Brownsover Rd.)
Trafalgar Way CR0: Wad 8L 45
GU15: Camb 2L 69
Trafford Rd. CR7: T Hea 4K 45
GU16: Frim 6B 70
Traherne Lodge TW11: Tedd 6F 24
Tramlink, The SW19 . . . . .1A 44
Tramsheds, The CR0: Bedd 6H 45
Tramway Cl. SE20 . . . . .1F 46
Tramway Path CR4: Mit 3C 44
(not continuous)
Tranmere Ct. SM2: Sut 4A 62
Tranmere Rd. SW18 . . . . .3A 28
TW2: Whitt 1B 24
Tranquil Dale RH3: Buckl 1E 120
Transport Av. TW8: Brent 1G 11
Trap La. RH5: Ockl 8N 157
Traps La. KT3: N Mal 9D 26
Traq Motor Racing 6G 34
Trasher Mead RH4: Dork 7J 119
Travellers Way TW4: C'ford 5K 9
Travis La. GU47: Sandh 8H 49
Treadcroft Dr. RH12: Hors 3L 197
Treadwell Rd. KT18: Eps 3D 80
Treasury Cl. SM6: W'ton 2H 63
Treaty Cen. TW3: Houn 6B 10
Trebor Av. GU9: Farnh 2J 129
Trebovir Rd. SW5 . . . . .1M 13
Tredenham Cl. GU14: Farnb 5A 90
Tredwell Cl. SW2 . . . . .3K 29
Tredwell Rd. SE27 . . . . .5M 29
Treebourne Rd. TN16: B Hil 4E 86
Treebys Av. GU4: J Wel 6N 93
Tree Cl. TW10: Ham 2K 25
Treelands RH5: Nth H 8J 119
Treemount Ct.
KT17: Eps 6M 201 (9D 60)
Treen Av. SW13 . . . . .6E 12
Treeside Dr. GU9: Weybo 5K 109
Treetops CR3: Warl 5D 84
RH9: S Gods 6H 125
Tree Tops Av. GU15: Camb 7E 50
Tree Tops Caravan Pk.
GU5: Alb 6N 135
Treeview RH11: Craw 8A 182
Treeview Ct. RH2: Reig 3B 122
(off Wray Comn. Rd.)
Tree Way RH2: Reig 9N 101
Trefoil Cl. RG40: W'ham 1D 30
RH12: Hors 3L 197
Trefoil Cres. RH11: Craw 7M 181
Trefusis Ct. TW5: C'ford 4J 9
Tregaron Gdns. KT3: N Mal 3D 42
Tregarthen Pl. KT22: Leat 8J 79
Tregarth Pl. GU21: Wok 4J 73
Treglos Ct. KT13: Weybr 7F 38
Tregolls Dr. GU14: Farnb 2A 90
Tregunter Rd. SW10 . . . . .2N 13
Trehaven Pde. RH2: Reig 6N 121
Treherne Ct. SW17 . . . . .5E 28
Trehern Rd. SW14 . . . . .6C 12
Trelawn Cl. KT16: Otter 4E 54
Trelawne Dr. GU6: Cranl 8N 155
Trelawney Av. SL3: Lang 1B 6
Trelawney Gro. KT13: Weybr 3B 56
Trellis Ho. SW19 . . . . .8A 28
Tremaine Rd. SE20 . . . . .1E 46
Trematon Pl. TW11: Tedd 8J 25
Tremayne Wlk. GU15: Camb 2G 70
Trenance GU21: Wok 4K 73
Trenchard Cl. KT12: Hers 2K 57
Trenchard Ct. SM4: Mord 5M 43
Trenear Cl. RH13: Hors 6L 197
Trenham Dr. CR6: Warl 3F 84
Trenholme Ct. CR3: Cate 1D 104
Trent Cl. GU14: Cove 8K 69
RH11: Craw 5L 181
Trent Ct. CR2: S Croy 8B 200
Trentham Cres. GU22: Wok 8C 74
Trentham Rd. RH1: Red 5D 122
Trentham St. SW18 . . . . .2M 27
Trent Ho.
KT2: K Tham 1H 203 (9K 25)
Trenton Cl. GU16: Frim 4E 70

292 A-Z Surrey

Wedgwood Pl.—West Humble Chapel (remains of)

Wedgwood Pl. KT11: Cob 9H 57
Wedgwoods TN16: Tats 8E 86
Wedgwood Way SE19 . . . . .8N 29
Weighton M. SE20 . . . . .1E 46
Weighton Rd. SE20 . . . . .1E 46
Weihurst Ct. SM1: Sut 2C 62
Weihurst Gdns. SM1: Sut 2B 62
Weimar St. SW15 . . . . .6K 13
Weint, The SL3: Coln 3E 6
Weir Av. GU14: Cove 2M 89
Weirbrook RH10: Craw 6E 182
Weir Cl. GU14: Cove 2M 89
Weir Ct. KT13: Weybr 8C 38
Weir Pl. TW18: Stain 9G 21
Weir Rd. KT12: Wal T 5H 39
KT16: Chert 6K 37
SW12 . . . . .1G 28
SW19 . . . . .4N 27
WEIR WOOD 7D 186
Weir Wood Reservoir 7B 186
Weir Wood Reservoir
Nature Reserve 8M 185
Weir Wood Sailing Club 6D 186
Weiss Rd. SW15 . . . . .6J 13
Welbeck RG12: Brac 4K 31
Welbeck Cl. GU14: Cove 2L 89
KT3: N Mal 4E 42
KT17: Ewe 4F 60
Welbeck Rd. SM1: Sut 8B 44
SM5: Cars 8B 44
Welbeck Wlk. SM5: Cars 7B 44
Welcomes Cotts.
CR3: Wold 1K 105
Welcomes Rd. CR8: Ken 4A 84
Welcomes Ter. CR3: Whyte 3C 84
Weldin M. *SW18* *8M 13*
(off Lebanon Rd.)
Weldon Cl. GU52: Chu C 8C 88
Weldon Dr. KT8: W Mole 3N 39
Weldon Way RH1: Mers 7H 103
Welford Pl. SW19 . . . . .5K 27
Welham Rd. SW16 . . . . .6E 28
SW17 . . . . .6E 28
Welhouse Rd. SM5: Cars 7C 44
Welland Cl. SL3: Lang 2D 6
Welland Rd. TW6: Lon A 5K 7
Wellbrook Rd. BR6: Farnb 1J 67
Wellburn Cl. GU47: Sandh 8G 49
Well Cl. GU15: Camb 2N 69
GU21: Wok 4M 73
SW16 . . . . .5K 29
Weller Cl. RH10: Worth 4H 183
Weller Dr. GU15: Camb 3A 70
Weller Pl. BR6: Dow 7J 67
Wellers Cl. TN16: Weste 5L 107
Wellers Ct. GU5: Shere 8B 116
Weller's La. RG42: Warf 3A 16
Wellesford Cl. SM7: Ban 4L 81
Wellesley Cl. GU12: Ash V 6D 90
GU19: Bag 4G 51
Wellesley Ct. RG45: Crowt 3E 48
SM3: Sut 7K 43
Wellesley Ct. Rd.
CR0: Croy 3D 200 (8A 46)
Wellesley Cres. TW2: Twick 3E 24
Wellesley Dr. RG45: Crowt 2D 48
Wellesley Gdn.
GU9: Up Hale 5H 109
Wellesley Ga. GU12: Alde 3N 109
Wellesley Gro.
CR0: Croy 3D 200 (8A 46)
Wellesley Ho. *SL4: W'sor* *4E 4*
(off Vansittart Rd.)
Wellesley Mans. *W14* *1L 13*
(off Edith Vs.)
Wellesley Pde. TW2: Twick 4E 24
Wellesley Pas.
CR0: Croy 2C 200 (8N 45)
Wellesley Rd.
CR0: Croy 1C 200 (7N 45)
GU10: Rush 4N 149
GU11: Alde 1J 109
(not continuous)
GU12: Ash V 6D 90
SM2: Sut 3A 62
(not continuous)
TW2: Twick 4D 24
W4 . . . . .1N 11
Wellesley Road Stop
(London Tramlink)
. . . . .2D 200 (8A 46)
Welley Av. TW19: Wray 7A 6
Welley Rd. SL3: Hort 9A 6
TW19: Wray 9A 6
Well Farm Hgts.
CR3: Whyte 6D 84
Well Farm Rd. CR6: Warl 6D 84
Wellfield RH19: E Grin 2E 186
Wellfield Gdns. SM5: Cars 5C 62
Wellfield Rd. SW16 . . . . .5J 29
Wellfield Wlk. SW16 . . . . .5K 29
Well House SM7: Ban 2N 81
Wellhouse La. RH3: Betch 7B 120
Wellhouse Rd. BR3: Beck 3K 47
Wellingham Way
RH12: Fay 7H 181
Wellington Av. GU11: Alde 2K 109
GU25: V Wat 4L 35
GU51: Fleet 3C 88
KT4: W Pk 9H 43
TW3: Houn 8A 10
Wellington Bus. Pk.
RG45: Crowt 3D 48
Wellington Centre, The
GU11: Alde 2M 109
Wellington Cl. GU47: Sandh . . .7H 49
KT12: Wal T 7G 39
RH10: Craw 9J 163
Wellington Cotts.
KT24: E Hor 7F 96
Wellington Ct.
KT19: Eps 5K 201 (8C 60)
SW6 . . . .*4N 13*
(off Maltings Pl.)
TW12: H Hill 6D 24
TW15: Ashf 6N 21
TW19: Stan 1N 21
Wellington Cres.
KT3: N Mal 2B 42
Wellington Dr. CR8: Pur 6K 63
RG12: Brac 4B 32
Wellington Gdns.
GU11: Alde 3L 109
TW2: Twick 5D 24
Wellington Ga.
RH19: E Grin 7C 166
Wellington Health & Fitness Club
. . . . .3E 48
Wellingtonia Av.
GU15: Camb 1H 71
RG45: Crowt 4B 48
Wellingtonia Ho. KT15: Addl . . .2J 55
Wellingtonia Pl.
RH2: Reig 2M 121
Wellingtonia Rdbt.
RG45: Crowt 3D 48
Wellingtonias RG42: Warf 8E 16
Wellingtonia Way
TN8: Eden 1L 147
Wellington La.
GU9: Heath E 5J 109
Wellington Lodge
SL4: Wink 3M 17
Wellington Mans. *W14* *2L 13*
(off Queen's Club Gdns.)
Wellington M. SW16 . . . . .4H 29
Wellington Pl. GU12: Ash V . . .9D 90
KT11: Cob 8A 58
Wellington Rd. CR0: Croy 6M 45
CR3: Cate 9N 83
GU47: Sandh 7G 48
RG40: W'ham 2A 30
RG45: Crowt 3H 49
RH12: Hors 6K 197
SW19 . . . . .3M 27
TW2: Twick 6D 24
TW6: Lon A *6L 7*
(off Whittle Rd.)
TW12: H Hill 6D 24
TW14: Felt 8F 8
TW15: Ashf 6N 21
Wellington Rd. Nth.
TW4: Houn 6N 9
Wellington Rd. Sth.
TW4: Houn 7N 9
Wellington Rdbt.
GU11: Alde 2K 109
Wellington Statue 1K 109
Wellington St. GU11: Alde . . .2M 109
Wellington Ter. GU21: Knap . . .5H 73
GU47: Sandh 7H 49
Wellington Town Rd.
RH19: E Grin 8N 165
Wellington Way
KT13: Weybr 6A 56
RH6: Horl 6D 142
Well La. GU8: Worm 1A 172
GU21: Wok 4M 73
GU27: Hasl 2H 189
SW14 . . . . .8B 12
Wellow Wlk. SM5: Cars 7B 44
Well Path GU21: Wok 4M 73
WELLS, THE 1N 79
Wells Cl. CR2: S Croy 2B 64
KT23: Book 2C 98
RH12: Hors 6F 196
SL4: W'sor 4D 4
Wells Cotts. GU9: Farnh 4F 128
Wells Ct. BR2: Brom 1N 47
Wells Ho. KT18: Eps 1N 79
Wellside Gdns. SW14 . . . . .7B 12
Wells La. GU3: Norm 9N 91
SL5: Asc 2M 33
TW3: Houn 6B 10
Wells Lea RH19: E Grin 7N 165
Wells Mdw. RH19: E Grin 7N 165
Wells Pl. RH1: Mers 8F 102
SW18 . . . . .1A 28
TN16: Weste 5L 107
Wells Pl. Ind. Est.
RH1: Mers 7F 102
Wells Rd. GU4: Guil 9E 94
KT18: Eps 1N 79
RH10: Craw 7C 182
Wellswood SL5: Asc 2M 33
Well Way KT18: Eps 2N 79
Wellwood Cl. CR5: Coul 1J 83
RH13: Hors 4A 198
Wellwynds Rd. GU6: Cranl . . .8N 155
Weltje Rd. W6 . . . . .1F 12
Welwyn Av. TW14: Felt 9G 8
Welwyn Cl. RH11: Craw 7K 181
Wembley Rd. TW12: Hamp 9A 24
Wembury Pk.
RH7: Newchap 1H 165
Wend, The CR5: Coul 1H 83
Wendela Cl. GU22: Wok 5B 74
Wenderholme CR2: S Croy 8E 200
Wendley Dr. KT15: N Haw 6H 55
Wendling Rd. SM1: Sut 7B 44
Wendover Dr. GU16: Frim 3G 70
KT3: N Mal 5E 42
Wendover Pl. TW18: Stain 6F 20
Wendover Rd.
TW18: Stain 6E 20
Wendron Cl. GU21: Wok 5K 73
Wendy Cres. GU2: Guil 1K 113
Wenlock Cl. RH11: Craw 5M 181
Wenlock Edge RH4: Dork 7J 119
Wensleydale RH11: Craw 6A 182
Wensleydale Dr.
GU15: Camb 1H 71
Wensleydale Gdns.
TW12: Hamp 8B 24
Wensleydale Pas.
TW12: Hamp 9A 24
Wensleydale Rd.
TW12: Hamp 7A 24
Wensley Dr. GU51: Fleet 2B 88
WENTWORTH 4J 35
Wentworth Av. SL5: Asc 1G 33
Wentworth Cl. BR6: Farnb 2N 67
GU9: Weybo 6L 109
GU12: Ash V 6E 90
GU23: Rip 8K 75
GU46: Yate 1C 68
KT6: Surb 8K 41
RG45: Crowt 1E 48
SM4: Mord 6M 43
TW15: Ashf 5C 22
Wentworth Ct. *SW18* *9N 13*
(off Garratt La.)
TW2: Twick 4E 24
W6 . . . .*2K 13*
(off Paynes Wlk.)
Wentworth Cres.
GU12: Ash V 7E 90
(not continuous)
Wentworth Dene
KT13: Weybr 2C 56
Wentworth Dr. GU25: V Wat . . .3J 35
RH10: Craw 2H 183
Wentworth Golf Course
East Course 5L 35
Edinburgh Course 7J 35
West Course 4J 35
Wentworth Ho. KT15: Addl 1K 55
Wentworth Pl. *GU15: Camb* . . .*2M 69*
(off Vale Rd.)
Wentworth Rd. CR0: Croy 6L 45
UB2: S'hall 1L 9
Wentworth Tennis & Health Club, The
. . . . .4K 35
Wentworth Way CR2: Sande . . .1D 84
SL5: Asc 1G 33
Werndee Rd. SE25 . . . . .3D 46
Werter Rd. SW15 . . . . .7K 13
Wesco Ct. GU21: Wok 3C 74
Wescott Rd. RG40: W'ham 2C 30
Wesley Av. TW3: Houn 5M 9
Wesley Cl. RH2: Reig 4L 121
RH6: Horl 6E 142
RH11: Craw 6K 181
Wesley Dr. TW20: Egh 7C 20
Wesley Pl. KT18: Tat C 5J 81
SL4: Wink 3M 17
Wesley Rd. KT22: Leat 1J 99
Wessels KT20: Tad 8J 81
Wessex Av. SW19 . . . . .2M 43
Wessex Cl. KT1: K Tham 9A 26
KT7: T Dit 8F 40
Wessex Ct. TW19: Stan 9N 7
Wessex Pl. GU9: Farnh 2H 129
Wessex Rd. GU14: Farnb 4K 89
West Acres KT10: Esh 4N 57
West Av. GU9: Heath E 6J 109
KT12: Whit V 6F 56
RH1: Red 9E 122
RH10: Craw 1E 182
SM6: W'ton 2J 63
West Bank
RH4: Dork 4G 201 (6F 118)
Westbank Rd. TW12: H Hill 7C 24
WEST BARNES 4G 42
W. Barnes La. KT3: N Mal 2G 42
SW20 . . . . .2G 43
WEST BEDFONT 9A 8
WESTBOROUGH 2J 113
Westbourne Av. SM3: Chea 8K 43
Westbourne Ho. TW5: Hest 2A 10
Westbourne Pl. GU9: Farnh . . .4G 129
Westbourne Rd. CR0: Croy 5C 46
GU47: Coll T 8K 49
TW13: Felt 4G 22
TW18: Stain 8K 21
WEST BROMPTON 2N 13
West Brompton Station
(Underground & Overground)
. . . . .2M 13
WESTBROOK 6F 132
Westbrook RH18: F Row 6G 187
Westbrook Av.
TW12: Hamp 8N 23
Westbrook Gdns.
RG12: Brac 9A 16
Westbrook Hill GU8: Els 7F 130
Westbrook Rd.
CR7: T Hea . . . . . .9N 29 & 1A 46
GU7: Godal 6F 132
TW5: Hest 3N 9
TW18: Stain 6H 21
Westbury *SL4: Eton* *2F 4*
(off Eton Wick Rd.)
Westbury Av. GU51: Fleet 5E 88
KT10: Clay 3F 58
Westbury Cl. CR3: Whyte 5C 84
GU51: Fleet 5D 88
RG45: Crowt 1G 48
TW17: Shep 5C 38
Westbury Gdns.
GU9: Farnh 8K 109
GU51: Fleet 5E 88
Westbury Pl. TW8: Brent 2K 11
Westbury Rd. BR3: Beck 2H 47
CR0: Croy 5A 46
KT3: N Mal 3C 42
SE20 . . . . .1G 46
TW13: Felt 2L 23
Westbury Ter.
TN16: Weste 5L 107
Westbury Way GU12: Alde 2B 110
WEST BYFLEET 9J 55
West Byfleet Golf Courses 9H 55
West Byfleet Station (Rail) 8J 55
Westcar La. KT12: Hers 3J 57
WEST CLANDON 7J 95
West Cl. GU9: Heath E 5J 109
GU27: Fern 9F 188
TW12: Hamp 7M 23
TW15: Ashf 5N 21
Westcombe Av. CR0: Croy 6J 45
Westcombe Cl. RG12: Brac 6C 32
West Comn. Rd.
BR2: Hay, Kes 1D 66
Westcoombe Av. SW20 . . . . . . .9E 26
Westcote Rd. KT19: Eps 7A 60
SW16 . . . . .6G 29
WESTCOTT 6C 118
Westcott Cl. CR0: N Add 5L 65
RH11: Craw 9A 182
WESTCOTT COMMON 7B 118
Westcott Keep *RH6: Horl* *7G 142*
(off Langshott La.)
Westcott Rd.
RH4: Dork 3G 201 (6D 118)
Westcotts Grn. RG42: Warf 7B 16
Westcott St. RH4: Westc 6B 118
Westcott Way SM2: Chea 6H 61
West Ct. GU4: B'ham 8D 94
TW7: Isle 3C 10
West Cres. SL4: W'sor 4C 4
Westcroft Gdns. SM4: Mord 2L 43
Westcroft Leisure Cen. 1E 62
Westcroft Rd. SM5: Cars 1E 62
SM6: W'ton 1E 62
W. Cromwell Rd. SW5 . . . . .1L 13
W14 . . . . .1L 13
W. Cross Cen. TW8: Brent 2G 11
W. Cross Way TW8: Brent 2H 11
West Croydon Station
(Rail, Overground &
London Tramlink)
. . . . .1B 200 (7N 45)
Westdean Cl. SW18 . . . . .9N 13
West Dene SM3: Chea 3K 61
Westdene KT12: Hers 1J 57
Westdene Mdws.
GU6: Cranl 7J 155
Westdene Way KT13: Weybr 9F 38
West Down KT23: Book 5B 98
West Dr. GU25: V Wat 6H 35
(not continuous)
KT15: N Haw 6K 55
KT20: Tad 5J 81
SL5: S'dale, V Wat 4G 34
SM2: Chea 5J 61
SM5: Cars 6B 62
SW16 . . . . .5G 28
WEST DULWICH 3N 29
WEST END
GU24 . . . . .8C 52
KT10 . . . . .3N 57
RG42 . . . . .6N 15
West End Cen. *2L 109*
(off Queen's Rd.)
West End Common
(Local Nature Reserve)
. . . . .4M 57
Westende RG40: W'ham 2C 30
West End Gdns. KT10: Esh 2N 57
West End Gro. GU9: Farnh 1F 128
West End La. GU10: Fren 1D 148
GU27: Hasl 9A 172
KT10: Esh 4N 57
RG42: Warf 6N 15
UB3: Harl 3D 8
Westerdale Dr. GU16: Frim 3F 70
Westerfolds Cl. GU22: Wok 4E 74
Westergate Ho.
KT1: K Tham 8H 203
WESTERHAM 4M 107
Westerham Cl. KT15: Addl 3L 55
SM2: Sut 6M 61
WESTERHAM HILL 7J 87
Westerham Hill
TN16: Weste 8K 87
Westerham Rd. BR2: Kes 3F 87
RH8: Limp, Oxt 7B 106
TN16: Weste 6G 107
Westerham Trade Cen.
TN16: Weste 3M 107
Westerley Ware *TW9: Kew* *2N 11*
(off Kew Grn.)
Westermain KT15: N Haw 6L 55
Western Av. KT16: Chert 2J 37
TW20: Thor 2D 36
Western Centre, The
RG12: Brac 1L 31
Western Cl. KT16: Chert 2J 37
Western Dr. TW17: Shep 5E 38
WESTERN INDUSTRIAL AREA
. . . . .1L 31
Western Intl. Mkt. UB2: S'hall . . .1J 9
Western La. SW12 . . . . .1E 28
Western Pde. RH2: Reig 6N 121
Western Perimeter Rd.
TW6: Lon A, L'ford 5K 7
Western Pl. RH4: Dork 3J 201
Western Rd. CR4: Mit 9B 28
GU11: Alde 3K 109
RG12: Brac 9K 15
SM1: Sut 2M 61
SW19 . . . . .9B 28
Western Ter. W6 . . . . .1F 12
WEST EWELL 5C 60
W. Farm Av. KT21: Asht 5J 79
W. Farm Cl. KT21: Asht 6J 79
W. Farm Dr. KT21: Asht 6K 79
WESTFIELD 8A 74
Westfield KT21: Asht 5M 79
RH2: Reig 9N 101
RH5: A Ham 3G 136
Westfield Av. CR2: Sande 9A 64
GU22: Wok 8A 74
Westfield Cl. GU22: Wok 8B 74
SM1: Sut 1L 61
SW10 . . . . .3N 13
Westfield Comn. GU22: Wok . . .9A 74
Westfield Ct. GU51: Fleet 4B 88
KT6: Surb 8H 203
Westfield Dr. KT23: Book 9A 78
Westfield Gdns.
RH4: Dork 2H 201 (5G 118)
Westfield Gro. GU22: Wok 7A 74
Westfield Ho. SW18 . . . . .2N 27
Westfield La. GU10: Wrec 5D 128
Westfield Pde.
KT15: N Haw 6M 55
Westfield Rd. BR3: Beck 1J 47
CR0: Croy 2A 200 (8M 45)
CR4: Mit 1C 44
GU1: Guil 8A 94
GU15: Camb 4N 69
GU22: Wok 9N 73
KT6: Surb 4K 41
KT12: Wal T 6M 39
RH11: Craw 3N 181
SM1: Sut 1L 61
Westfields GU8: Wit 5C 152
SW13 . . . . .6E 12
Westfields Av. SW13 . . . . .6D 12
Westfield Sq. GU22: Wok 9A 74
Westfield Way GU22: Wok 9A 74
W. Flexford La.
GU3: Flex, Wan 3N 111
West Fryerne GU46: Yate 7C 48
West Gdns. KT17: Ewe 6D 60
SW17 . . . . .7C 28
Westgate GU11: Alde 2L 109
Westgate Cl. KT18: Eps 2C 80
Westgate Est. TW14: Bedf 2C 22
Westgate Ho. *KT18: Eps* *2C 80*
(off Chalk La.)
TW7: Isle 5D 10
Westgate Rd. BR3: Beck 1M 47
SE25 . . . . .3E 46
Westgate Ter. SW10 . . . . .2N 13
Westglade GU14: Cove 1J 89
WEST GREEN 2A 182
West Grn. GU46: Yate 8A 48
West Green Dr.
RH11: Craw 2A 182
West Green Pk. 2A 182
West Gro. KT12: Hers 2J 57
West Hall KT14: W By 9L 55
Westhall Pk. CR6: Warl 6F 84
West Hall Rd. TW9: Kew 4A 12
Westhall Rd. CR6: Warl 5D 84
Westhatch La. RG42: Warf 5N 15
Westhay Gdns. SW14 . . . . .8A 12
WEST HEATH
GU14 . . . . .9L 69
RH8 . . . . .8C 106
West Heath GU24: Pirb 1A 92
W. Heath Rd. GU14: Cove 1L 89
WEST HILL 9L 13
West Hill BR6: Dow 8H 67
CR2: Sande 6B 64
GU8: Els 8G 131
KT19: Eps 6G 201 (9A 60)
RH8: Oxt 8N 105
RH19: D Pk 4A 166
RH19: E Grin 1N 185
SW15 . . . . .1J 27
SW18 . . . . .1J 27
West Hill Av.
KT19: Eps 5G 201 (9A 60)
West Hill Bank RH8: Oxt 8N 105
West Hill Cl. GU8: Els 8G 131
GU24: B'wood 7E 72
West Hill Ct. KT19: Eps 6H 201
West Hill Golf Course 7E 72
West Hill Pl. RH8: Oxt 7A 106
West Hill Rd. GU22: Wok 6N 73
SW18 . . . . .9L 13
W. Hoathly Rd.
RH19: E Grin 4N 185
(not continuous)
Westhorpe Rd. SW15 . . . . .6H 13
WEST HORSLEY 7C 96
West House GU6: Cranl 5L 155
West Ho. Cl. SW19 . . . . .2K 27
WESTHUMBLE 9H 99
West Humble Chapel (remains of)
. . . . .9F 98

Whites Rd. GU14: Farnb . . . 4C 90
White Star Cl. GU7: Godal . . . 4J 133
Whitestile Rd. TW8: Brent . . . 1J 11
Whitestone Way CR0: Wad . . . 8L 45
White Swan M. W4 . . . 1D 12
Whitethorn Av. CR5: Coul . . . 2E 82
Whitethorn Cl. GU12: Ash . . . 3F 110
Whitethorn Cotts.
GU6: Cranl . . . 5K 155
Whitethorn Gdns. CR0: Croy . . . 8E 46
Whitethorns *GU9: Heath E* . . . *4J 109*
(off Lwr. Weybourne La.)
Whitewalls *RH11: Craw* . . . *3L 181*
(off Rusper Rd.)
Whitewater Rd. GU51: Fleet . . . 1A 88
Whiteway KT23: Book . . . 4B 98
Whiteways Ct. TW18: Stain . . . 8K 21
WHITEWOOD . . . 5D 144
Whitewood Cotts.
TN16: Tats . . . 7E 86
Whitewood La. RH6: Horne . . . 5D 144
RH9: S Gods . . . 5D 144
Whitfield Cl. GU2: Guil . . . 9K 93
GU27: Hasl . . . 8G 171
Whitfield Rd. GU27: Hasl . . . 9G 171
Whitford Gdns. CR4: Mit . . . 2D 44
Whitgift Av.
CR2: S Croy . . . 8A 200 (2M 63)
Whitgift Cen.
CR0: Croy . . . 2C 200 (8N 45)
Whitgift Ct. CR2: S Croy . . . 8C 200
Whitgift Sq.
CR0: Croy . . . 3C 200 (8N 45)
Whitgift St.
CR0: Croy . . . 5B 200 (9N 45)
Whitgift Wlk. RH10: Craw . . . 6B 182
Whitland Rd. SM5: Cars . . . 7B 44
Whitlet Cl. GU9: Farnh . . . 2G 128
Whitley Cl. TW19: Stan . . . 9N 7
Whitley Ct. *GU11: Alde* . . . *2M 109*
(off Grosvenor Rd.)
Whitley Rd. GU46: Yate . . . 2C 68
Whitlock Dr. SW19 . . . 1K 27
Whitmead Cl. CR2: S Croy . . . 3B 64
Whitmead La. GU10: Til . . . 6C 130
Whitmoor & Rickford Commons
Local Nature Reserve . . . 5K 93
WHITMOOR COMMON . . . 4K 93
Whitmoor La. GU4: Sut G . . . 4N 93
Whitmoor Rd. GU19: Bag . . . 4K 51
Whitmoor Va. Rd.
GU26: G'hott, Hind . . . 2L 169
Whitmore Cl. GU47: Owls . . . 7J 49
Whitmore Grn.
GU9: Heath E . . . 6K 109
Whitmore La.
SL5: S'dale, S'hill . . . 4D 34
Whitmore Rd. BR3: Beck . . . 2J 47
Whitmores Cl. KT18: Eps . . . 2B 80
Whitmore Va. GU26: G'hott . . . 2K 169
Whitmore Va. Rd.
GU26: G'hott . . . 5M 169
Whitmore Way RH6: Horl . . . 7B 142
Whitnell Way SW15 . . . 8H 13
(not continuous)
Whitstable Cl. BR3: Beck . . . 1J 47
Whitstable Pl.
CR0: Croy . . . 7C 200 (1N 63)
Whitstone La. BR3: Beck . . . 4L 47
Whittaker Av. TW9: Rich . . . 8K 11
Whittaker Ct. KT21: Asht . . . 4K 79
Whittaker Pl. *TW9: Rich* . . . *8K 11*
(off Whittaker Av.)
Whittaker Rd. SM3: Sut . . . 9L 43
Whittingham Ct. W4 . . . 3D 12
Whittingstall Rd. SW6 . . . 4L 13
Whittington College
RH19: Felb . . . 6J 165
Whittington Rd.
RH10: Craw . . . 6B 182
Whittlebury Cl. SM5: Cars . . . 4D 62
Whittle Cl. GU12: Ash V . . . 8D 90
GU47: Sandh . . . 6F 48
Whittle Cres. GU14: Cove . . . 7L 69
Whittle Rd. TW5: Hest . . . 3K 9
TW6: Lon A . . . 6K 7
Whittle Way RH10: Craw . . . 6E 162
WHITTON . . . 1C 24
Whitton Dene
TW3: Houn, Isle . . . 8C 10
TW7: Isle . . . 9D 10
Whitton Ho. *RG41: W'ham* . . . *3A 30*
(off Ashville Way)
Whitton Mnr. Rd. TW7: Isle . . . 9C 10
Whitton Rd. RG12: Brac . . . 2D 32
TW1: Twick . . . 9F 10
TW2: Twick . . . 9E 10
TW3: Houn . . . 7B 10
WHITTON ROAD RDBT. . . . 9F 10
Whitton Sports & Fitness Cen.
. . . 3B 24
Whitton Station (Rail) . . . 1C 24
Whitton Waye TW3: Houn . . . 9A 10
Whitwell Hatch GU27: Hasl . . . 3H 189
Whitworth Rd. RH11: Craw . . . 8B 162
SE25 . . . 2B 46
Whopshott Av. GU21: Wok . . . 3M 73
Whopshott Cl. GU21: Wok . . . 3M 73
Whopshott Dr. GU21: Wok . . . 3M 73
Whynstones Rd. SL5: Asc . . . 5L 33
Whyteacre CR3: Warl . . . 7E 84
Whyte Av. GU12: Alde . . . 4B 110
Whytebeam Vw. CR3: Whyte . . . 5C 84
Whytecliffe Rd. Nth.
CR8: Pur . . . 7M 63
Whytecliffe Rd. Sth.
CR8: Pur . . . 7L 63
Whytecroft TW5: Hest . . . 3L 9
WHYTELEAFE . . . 5C 84
Whyteleafe Bus. Village
CR3: Whyte . . . 4C 84
Whyteleafe Hill CR3: Whyte . . . 7B 84
Whyteleafe Rd. CR3: Cate . . . 7B 84
Whyteleafe South Station (Rail)
. . . 6D 84
Whyteleafe Station (Rail) . . . 4C 84
Whyte M. SM3: Chea . . . 4K 61
Wicket, The CR0: A'ton . . . 2K 65
Wicket Hill GU10: Wrec . . . 5F 128
Wickets, The TW15: Ashf . . . 5N 21
Wickham Av. CR0: Croy . . . 8H 47
SM3: Chea . . . 2H 61
Wickham Chase
BR4: W Wick . . . 7N 47
Wickham Cl. GU52: Chu C . . . 7A 88
KT3: N Mal . . . 5E 42
RH6: Horl . . . 7D 142
Wickham Ct. KT5: Surb . . . 8L 203
Wickham Ct. Rd.
BR4: W Wick . . . 8M 47
Wickham Cres.
BR4: W Wick . . . 8M 47
Wickham La. TW20: Egh . . . 8C 20
Wickham Pl. GU52: Chu C . . . 7A 88
Wickham Rd. BR3: Beck . . . 1L 47
CR0: Croy . . . 8G 46
GU15: Camb . . . 7C 50
GU52: Chu C . . . 7A 88
Wickham Theatre Cen. . . . 8N 47
Wickham Va. RG12: Brac . . . 5K 31
Wickham Way BR3: Beck . . . 3M 47
WICK HILL
RG40 . . . 1A 48
RG42 . . . 8B 16
Wick Hill La. RG40: Finch . . . 1A 48
Wick Ho. KT1: H Wic . . . 1G 203
Wickhurst Gdns.
RH12: Broadb H . . . 5E 196
Wickhurst La.
RH12: Broadb H . . . 5E 196
Wickland Ct. RH10: Craw . . . 6B 182
Wick La. TW20: Eng G . . . 7J 19
Wick Rd. TW11: Tedd . . . 8H 25
TW20: Eng G . . . 9K 19
Wick's Grn. RG42: Bin . . . 5H 15
Wicks La. RG10: Shur R . . . 1D 14
Wicksteed Ho. TW8: Brent . . . 1M 11
Wide Way CR4: Mit . . . 2H 45
Widewing Cl. TW11: Tedd . . . 8H 25
Widgeon Rd. TW6: Lon A . . . 5K 7
Widgeon Way RH12: Hors . . . 3J 197
Widmer Ct. TW3: Houn . . . 5M 9
Wiggett Gro. RG42: Bin . . . 7H 15
Wiggie La. RH1: Red . . . 1E 122
Wiggington Ho. *SL4: Eton* . . . *3G 4*
(off High St.)
Wiggins La. TW10: Ham . . . 3J 25
Wiggins Yd. GU7: Godal . . . 7H 133
Wight Ho. KT1: K Tham . . . 6H 203
Wighton M. TW7: Isle . . . 5E 10
Wigley Rd. TW13: Felt . . . 3L 23
Wigmore La. RH5: B Grn . . . 9J 139
Wigmore Rd. SM5: Cars . . . 8B 44
Wigmore Wlk. SM5: Cars . . . 8B 44
Wilberforce Cl.
RH11: Craw . . . 9A 182
Wilberforce Ct. BR2: Kes . . . 4F 66
KT18: Eps . . . 8K 201
Wilberforce Way RG12: Brac . . . 4B 32
SE25 . . . 3C 46
SW19 . . . 7J 27
Wilbury Av. SM2: Chea . . . 6L 61
Wilbury Rd. GU21: Wok . . . 4N 73
Wilcot Cl. GU24: Bis . . . 3D 72
Wilcot Gdns. GU24: Bis . . . 3D 72
Wilcox Gdns. TW17: Shep . . . 2N 37
Wilcox Rd. SM1: Sut . . . 1N 61
TW11: Tedd . . . 5D 24
Wildacre Cl. RH14: Ifo . . . 5F 192
Wildacres KT14: W By . . . 7L 55
Wildbank Ct. GU22: Wok . . . 5B 74
Wildcat Rd. *TW6: Lon A* . . . *6K 7*
(off Wayfarer Rd.)
Wildcroft Dr. RH5: Nth H . . . 8K 119
Wildcroft Mnr. SW15 . . . 1H 27
Wildcroft Rd. SW15 . . . 1H 27
Wildcroft Wood GU8: Wit . . . 4A 152
Wilde Pl. SW18 . . . 1B 28
Wilderness, The
KT8: W Mole, E Mol . . . 4C 40
TW12: H Hill . . . 5B 24
Wilderness Ct. GU2: Guil . . . 5J 113
Wilderness Island Nature Reserve
. . . 8E 44
Wilderness Ri. RH19: D Pk . . . 5C 166
Wilderness Rd. GU2: Guil . . . 5J 113
GU16: Frim . . . 4C 70
RH8: Oxt . . . 8N 105
Wilders Cl. GU16: Frim . . . 3C 70
GU21: Wok . . . 5M 73
RG42: Brac . . . 8M 15
Wilderwick Rd.
RH7: E Grin . . . 3C 166
RH19: E Grin . . . 6D 166
Wilde Theatre . . . 6A 32
Wildfield Cl. GU3: Wood V . . . 2E 112
Wildgoose Dr. RH12: Hors . . . 5F 196
WILDRIDINGS . . . 3M 31
Wildridings Rd. RG12: Brac . . . 3M 31
Wildridings Sq. RG12: Brac . . . 3M 31
Wild Wood RH12: Hors . . . 5F 196
Wildwood Cl. GU6: Cranl . . . 9A 156
GU8: Chid . . . 5E 172
GU22: Pyr . . . 2H 75
KT24: E Hor . . . 3G 96
Wildwood Ct. CR8: Ken . . . 2A 84
Wildwood Gdns. GU46: Yate . . . 2B 68
Wildwood Golf Course . . . 6K 175
Wildwood La.
GU6: Alf, Cranl . . . 4J 175
Wilford Rd. CR0: Croy . . . 5N 45
Wilfred Owen Cl. SW19 . . . 7A 28
Wilfred St. GU21: Wok . . . 5N 73
Wilhelmina Av. CR5: Coul . . . 6G 83
Wilkes Rd. TW8: Brent . . . 2L 11
Wilkins Cl. CR4: Mit . . . 9C 28
UB3: Harl . . . 1G 9
Wilkinson Ct. RH11: Craw . . . 8N 181
SW17 . . . 5B 28
Wilkinson Gdns. SE25 . . . 1B 46
Wilkinson Way
GU9: Weybo . . . 7L 109
Wilks Gdns. CR0: Croy . . . 7H 47
Willard Way RH19: E Grin . . . 7K 165
Willats Cl. KT16: Chert . . . 5H 37
Willbury Rd. GU9: Farnh . . . 8K 109
Willcocks Cl. KT9: Ches . . . 9L 41
Willems Av. GU11: Alde . . . 2L 109
Willems Rdbt. GU11: Alde . . . 2L 109
Willerton Lodge
KT13: Weybr . . . 3E 56
Willets Heath GU10: Fren . . . 1H 149
Willett Pl. CR7: T Hea . . . 4L 45
Willett Rd. CR7: T Hea . . . 4L 45
Willetts Way RH14: Loxw . . . 5H 193
Willey Broom La.
CR3: Cate . . . 3L 103
Willey Farm La. CR3: Cate . . . 4N 103
WILLEY GREEN . . . 9A 92
Willey La. CR3: Cate . . . 3A 104
William Banfield Ho. *SW6* . . . *5L 13*
(off Munster Rd.)
William Ct. *GU14: Farnb* . . . *4A 90*
(off Cambridge Rd. W.)
SE25 . . . *2C 46*
(off Chalfont Rd.)
SW16 . . . *8K 29*
(off Streatham High Rd.)
William Dyce M. SW16 . . . 5H 29
William Ellis Cl. SL4: O Win . . . 8K 5
William Evans Rd.
KT19: Eps . . . 7N 59
William Evelyn Ct.
RH5: Wott . . . 8N 117
William Farm La. SW15 . . . 6G 13
William Farthing Cl.
GU11: Alde . . . 2M 109
William Gdns. RH6: Smallf . . . 8L 143
SW15 . . . 8G 13
William Harvey Ho. *SW19* . . . *2K 27*
(off Whitlock Dr.)
William Hitchcock Ho.
GU14: Farnb . . . 7N 69
William Hunt Mans. SW13 . . . 2H 13
William Morris Ho. W6 . . . 2J 13
William Morris Way
RH11: Craw . . . 9N 181
SW6 . . . 6N 13
William Rd. CR3: Cate . . . 9A 84
GU1: Guil . . . 3B 202 (3M 113)
SM1: Sut . . . 2A 62
SW19 . . . 8K 27
William Russell Ct.
GU21: Wok . . . 5H 73
Williams Cl. KT15: Addl . . . 2K 55
SW6 . . . 3K 13
Williams Dr. TW3: Houn . . . 7A 10
William Sellars Cl.
CR3: Cate . . . 8B 84
Williams Gro. KT6: Surb . . . 5J 41
William Sim Wood
RG42: Wink R . . . 7F 16
Williams La. SM4: Mord . . . 4A 44
SW14 . . . 6B 12
Williamson Cl.
GU27: G'wood . . . 8K 171
Williams Pl. GU6: Ewh . . . 5F 156
Williams Rd. UB2: S'hall . . . 1M 9
Williams Ter. CR0: Wad . . . 3L 63
William St. SL4: W'sor . . . 4G 4
SM5: Cars . . . 9C 44
William's Wlk. GU2: Guil . . . 8L 93
Williams Way GU51: Fleet . . . 4D 88
RH10: Craw . . . 3F 182
Willian Pl. GU26: Hind . . . 3C 170
Willingham Way
KT1: K Tham . . . 2N 41
WILLINGHURST ESTATE . . . 9L 135
Willinghurst Estate Fisheries
. . . 1K 155
Willington Cl. GU15: Camb . . . 9N 49
Willis Av. SM2: Sut . . . 3C 62
Willis Cl. KT18: Eps . . . 1A 80
Willis Ct. BR4: W Wick . . . 8N 47
CR7: T Hea . . . 5L 45
Willis Rd. CR0: Croy . . . 6N 45
Will Miles Ct. SW19 . . . 8A 28
Willmore End SW19 . . . 9N 27
Willoughby Av. CR0: Bedd . . . 1K 63
Willoughby Rd.
KT2: K Tham . . . 1M 203 (9M 25)
RG12: Brac . . . 2L 31
TW1: Twick . . . 8J 11
(not continuous)
Willoughbys, The SW14 . . . 6D 12
Willow Av. SW13 . . . 5E 12
Willow Bank GU22: Wok . . . 9A 74
SW6 . . . 6K 13
TW10: Ham . . . 4H 25
Willowbank CR5: Coul . . . 1J 83
KT7: T Dit . . . 7G 40
Willowbank Gdns.
KT20: Tad . . . 9G 81
Willowbank Pl. CR8: Pur . . . 5M 63
Willow Brean RH6: Horl . . . 7C 142
Willowbrook SL4: Eton . . . 1G 5
TW12: H Hill . . . 6B 24
Willowbrook Rd.
TW19: Stan . . . 3N 21
Willow Cl. GU6: Cranl . . . 9A 156
GU16: Mytc . . . 1C 90
KT15: Wood . . . 7H 55
KT16: Chert . . . 8G 36
RH5: B Grn . . . 7J 139
RH10: Craw . . . 1C 182
RH19: E Grin . . . 7N 165
SL3: Coln . . . 3E 6
SM7: Ban . . . 1K 81
TW8: Brent . . . 2J 11
Willow Cnr. RH6: Charlw . . . 3L 161
Willow Cotts. TW9: Kew . . . 2N 11
TW13: Hanw . . . 4M 23
Willow Ct. GU12: Ash V . . . 6E 90
GU16: Frim . . . 5B 70
RG41: W'ham . . . 2A 30
RH6: Horl . . . 5F 142
SM6: W'ton . . . *4F 62*
(off Willow Rd.)
TW16: Sunb . . . *8F 22*
(off Staines Rd. W.)
W4 . . . *3D 12*
(off Corney Reach Way)
Willow Cres. GU14: Farnb . . . 7N 69
Willowdene Cl. TW2: Whitt . . . 1C 24
Willow Dr. GU3: Flex . . . 3N 111
GU23: Rip . . . 2J 95
RG12: Brac . . . 9A 16
Willow End KT6: Surb . . . 7L 41
Willowfield RH11: Craw . . . 4A 182
Willow Flds. GU12: Ash G . . . 3F 110
Willowford GU46: Yate . . . 9C 48
Willow Gdns. TW3: Houn . . . 4A 10
Willow Glade RH2: Reig . . . 6A 122
Willow Grn. GU24: W End . . . 9C 52
RH5: Nth H . . . 9H 119
Willowhayne Ct.
KT12: Wal T . . . *6J 39*
(off Willowhayne Dr.)
Willowhayne Dr.
KT12: Wal T . . . 6J 39
Willowhayne Gdns.
KT4: W Pk . . . 9H 43
Willowherb Cl.
RG40: W'ham . . . 1D 30
Willow Ho. CR6: Warl . . . 2L 85
Willow La. CR4: Mit . . . 4D 44
GU1: Guil . . . 2C 114
GU17: Haw . . . 2J 69
Willow La. Bus. Pk.
CR4: Mit . . . 5D 44
Willow La. Ind. Est.
CR4: Mit . . . 5D 44
Willow Lodge SW6 . . . 4J 13
TW16: Sunb . . . *8G 23*
(off Forest Dr.)
Willow Mead GU8: Wit . . . 5B 152
RH4: Dork . . . 1J 201 (4G 119)
RH19: E Grin . . . 1B 186
Willowmead TW18: Stain . . . 9K 21
Willowmead Cl.
GU21: Wok . . . 3K 73
Willowmere KT10: Esh . . . 1C 58
Willow M. GU8: Wit . . . 5C 152
Willow Mt. CR0: Croy . . . 9B 46
Willow Pk. GU12: Ash . . . 2D 110
Willow Pl. SL4: Eton . . . 2F 4
Willow Ridge
RH10: Turn H . . . 6D 184
Willow Rd. GU7: Godal . . . 3J 133
KT3: N Mal . . . 3B 42
RH1: Red . . . 6A 122
RH12: Hors . . . 3A 198
SL3: Poy . . . 5G 7
SM6: W'ton . . . 4F 62
Willows, The *GU2: Guil* . . . *7K 93*
(off Weydown La.)
GU4: Guil . . . 1E 114
GU8: Chid . . . 5D 172
GU10: Run . . . 8A 110
GU18: Ligh . . . 7N 51
KT10: Clay . . . 3E 58
KT13: Weybr . . . 9B 38
KT14: Byf . . . 9N 55
RG12: Brac . . . 3D 32
RH1: Red . . . 4D 122
RH12: Hors . . . 3K 197
SL4: W'sor . . . 3A 4
Willows Av. SM4: Mord . . . 4N 43
Willows End GU47: Sandh . . . 7G 48
Willows Lodge SL4: W'sor . . . 3A 4
Willows Pk. GU3: Norm . . . 9A 92
Willows Path KT18: Eps . . . 1A 80
SL4: W'sor . . . 4A 4
Willows Riverside Pk.
SL4: W'sor . . . 3A 4
Willow Tree Cl. SW18 . . . 2N 27
Willowtree Way CR7: T Hea . . . 9L 29
Willow Va. KT22: Fetc . . . 1B 98
(not continuous)
Willow Vw. SW19 . . . 9B 28
Willow Wlk. BR6: Farnb . . . 1K 67
GU5: Shere . . . 8B 116
KT16: Chert . . . 6J 37
KT20: Box H . . . 8A 100
KT23: Book . . . 3C 98
RH1: Red . . . 5F 122
SM3: Sut . . . 9L 43
TW20: Eng G . . . 6M 19
Willow Way GU1: Guil . . . 8L 93
GU9: Hale . . . 6J 109
GU12: Alde . . . 4C 110
GU22: Wok . . . 8A 74
GU47: Sandh . . . 6E 48
KT14: W By . . . 7L 55
KT19: Ewe . . . 3C 60
RH9: Gods . . . 1E 124
TW2: Twick . . . 3B 24
TW16: Sunb . . . 3H 39
Willow Wood Cres. SE25 . . . 5B 46
Wills Cres. TW3: Houn . . . 9B 10
Willson Rd. TW20: Eng G . . . 6L 19
Wilmar Gdns. BR4: W Wick . . . 7L 47
Wilmer Cl. KT2: K Tham . . . 6M 25
Wilmer Cres. KT2: K Tham . . . 6M 25
Wilmerhatch La. KT18: Eps . . . 5A 80
Wilmington Av. W4 . . . 3C 12
Wilmington Cl.
RH11: Craw . . . 8N 181
Wilmington Ct. SW16 . . . 8J 29
Wilmot Cl. RG42: Bin . . . 7H 15
Wilmot Cotts. SM7: Ban . . . 2N 81
Wilmot Ct. *GU14: Farnb* . . . *1N 89*
(off Victoria Rd.)
Wilmot Rd. CR8: Pur . . . 8L 63
SM5: Cars . . . 2D 62
Wilmots Cl. RH2: Reig . . . 2A 122
Wilmot's La. RH1: Horne . . . 4A 144
RH6: Horne . . . 4A 144
Wilmot Way GU15: Camb . . . 3D 70
SM7: Ban . . . 1M 81
Wilna Rd. SW18 . . . 1A 28
Wilson Av. CR4: Mit . . . 8C 28
Wilson Cl.
CR2: S Croy . . . 8D 200 (2A 64)
RH10: Craw . . . 6H 183
Wilson Dr. KT16: Otter . . . 2D 54
Wilson Rd. GU12: Alde . . . 3B 110
GU14: Cove . . . 2L 89
KT9: Ches . . . 3M 59
Wilsons KT20: Tad . . . 8J 81
Wilsons Rd. GU35: Head D . . . 4G 169
W6 . . . 1J 13
Wilson Way GU21: Wok . . . 3N 73
Wilstrode Av. RG42: Bin . . . 8L 15
Wilton Av. W4 . . . 1D 12
Wilton Cl. UB7: Harm . . . 2M 7
Wilton Ct. GU14: Farnb . . . 2B 90
Wilton Cres. SL4: W'sor . . . 7A 4
SW19 . . . 8L 27
Wilton Gdns. KT8: W Mole . . . 2A 40
KT12: Wal T . . . 7L 39
Wilton Gro. KT3: N Mal . . . 5E 42
SW19 . . . 9L 27
Wilton Ho. CR2: S Croy . . . 8B 200
RH11: Craw . . . 3A 182
Wilton Pde. TW13: Felt . . . 3H 23
Wilton Pl. KT15: N Haw . . . 5M 55
Wilton Rd. GU15: Camb . . . 3N 69
RH1: Red . . . 4D 122
SW19 . . . 8C 28
TW4: Houn . . . 6L 9
Wiltshire Av. RG45: Crowt . . . 1G 48
Wiltshire Ct.
CR2: S Croy . . . 8C 200 (2N 63)
Wiltshire Dr. RG40: W'ham . . . 1C 30
Wiltshire Gdns. TW2: Twick . . . 2C 24
Wiltshire Gro. RG42: Warf . . . 7D 16
Wiltshire Pl. RG40: W'ham . . . 1C 30
Wiltshire Rd. CR7: T Hea . . . 2L 45
RG40: W'ham . . . 9B 14
Wilverley Cres. KT3: N Mal . . . 5D 42
Wilwood Rd. RG42: Brac . . . 9K 15
Wimbart Rd. SW2 . . . 1K 29
WIMBLEDON . . . 7K 27
Wimbledon All England
Lawn Tennis & Croquet Club
. . . 5K 27
Wimbledon Bri. SW19 . . . 7L 27
Wimbledon Chase Station (Rail)
. . . 1K 43
Wimbledon Cl.
GU15: Camb . . . 6D 50
SW20 . . . 8J 27
Wimbledon Common . . . 5F 26
Wimbledon Common Golf Course
. . . 6G 27
Wimbledon Hill Rd. SW19 . . . 7K 27
Wimbledon Lawn Tennis Mus.
. . . 4K 27
Wimbledon Leisure Cen. . . . 7N 27
Wimbledon Museum of
Local History . . . 7K 27
WIMBLEDON PARK . . . 4M 27
Wimbledon Pk. Athletics Track
. . . 3L 27
Wimbledon Pk. Ct. SW19 . . . 2L 27
Wimbledon Pk. Golf Course
. . . 4L 27
Wimbledon Pk. Rd. SW18 . . . 3K 27
SW19 . . . 3K 27
Wimbledon Pk. Side SW19 . . . 4J 27
Wimbledon Park Station
(Underground) . . . 4M 27
Wimbledon Pk. Watersports Cen.
. . . 3L 27

Wimbledon Pk. Women's Fitness Suite—Woodbridge Ct.

Wimbledon Pk.
Women's Fitness Suite . . .4L 27
Wimbledon Rd.
GU15: Camb 6D 50
SW17 . . . . .5A 28
Wimbledon Stadium Bus. Cen.
SW17 . . . . .4N 27
Wimbledon Stadium (Greyhound)
. . . . .5A 28
Wimbledon Station
(Rail, Underground &
London Tramlink) 7L 27
Wimbledon Theatre 8M 27
Wimbledon Windmill Mus. . . .3G 27
WIMBLE HILL 1A 128
Wimblehurst Ct.
RH12: Hors 4J 197
Wimblehurst Rd.
RH12: Hors 4J 197
Wimborne Av. RH1: Red 8D 122
Wimborne Cl. KT4: W Pk 7H 43
KT17: Eps 7M 201 (9D 60)
Wimborne Ct. SW12 . . . . .4G 28
Wimborne Ho. GU14: Farnb . . .3B 90
SW12 . . . . .4G 28
Wimborne Way BR3: Beck 2G 47
Wimbourne Ho.
RH11: Craw 3A 182
Wimland Hill RH12: Fay 7C 180
Wimland Rd.
RH12: Fay, Hors, Rusp . . .4A 180
Wimlands La. RH12: Fay 7C 180
Wimpole Cl.
KT1: K Tham . . .4M 203 (1M 41)
Wimshurst Cl. CR0: Wad 7J 45
Wincanton Cl.
RH10: Craw 2H 183
Wincanton Rd. SW18 . . . . .1L 27
Winch Cl. RG42: Bin 6H 15
Winchcombe Cl. GU51: Fleet . . .5B 88
Winchcombe Rd. SM5: Cars . . .6B 44
Winchelsea Cl. SW15 . . . . .8J 13
Winchelsey Ri. CR2: S Croy . . .3C 64
Winchendon Rd. SW6 . . . . .4L 13
TW11: Tedd 5D 24
Winches, The RH13: Colg . . .2H 199
Winchester Av. TW5: Hest 2N 9
Winchester Cl. KT2: K Tham . . .8A 26
KT10: Esh 1A 58
SL3: Poy 4G 7
Winchester Ho. *KT19: Eps 8N 59*
(off Phoenix Cl.)
Winchester M. KT4: W Pk 8J 43
Winchester Rd.
GU10: Rush 3N 149
GU12: Ash 1E 110
KT12: Wal T 7H 39
RH10: Craw 7C 182
TW1: Twick 9H 11
TW13: Hanw 4N 23
UB3: Harl 3F 8
Winchester St. GU14: Farnb . . .5A 90
Winchester Wlk. *SW15 . . . . . . .8L 13*
(off Up. Richmond Rd.)
Winchester Way
GU17: B'water 9H 49
Winchet Wlk. CR0: Croy 5F 46
Winchfield Ho. SW15 . . . . .9E 12
Winchgrove Rd. RG42: Brac . . .8M 15
Winchilsea Cres.
KT8: W Mole 1C 40
Winchstone Cl. TW17: Shep . . .3A 38
Windborough Rd. SM5: Cars . . .4E 62
Windermere Av. SW19 . . . . . . .2N 43
Windermere Cl. GU14: Cove . . .2K 89
TW14: Felt 2G 22
TW19: Stan 2N 21
TW20: Egh 8D 20
Windermere Ct. CR8: Ken 2M 83
GU12: Ash V 9D 90
(off Lakeside Cl.)
GU21: Wok 5K 73
(off St John's Rd.)
SM5: Cars 9E 44
SW13 . . . . .2E 12
Windermere Ga. RG12: Brac . . .2N 31
Windermere Ho. TW7: Isle 8F 10
Windermere Rd. CR0: Croy 7C 46
CR5: Coul 2J 83
GU18: Ligh 6M 51
SW15 . . . . .5D 26
SW16 . . . . .9G 29
Windermere Wlk.
GU15: Camb 1H 71
Windermere Way
GU9: Up Hale 6F 108
RH2: Reig 2C 122
Windfield KT22: Leat 8H 79
Windgates GU4: Guil 9E 94
Windham Av. CR0: N Add 6N 65
Windham Rd. TW9: Rich 6M 11
Windings, The CR2: Sande 7C 64
Winding Wood Dr.
GU15: Camb 2F 70
Windlebrook Grn.
RG42: Brac 9M 15
Windle Cl. GU20: Windl 3A 52
Windlemere Golf Course 7B 52
WINDLESHAM 3A 52
Windlesham Ct.
GU20: Windl 9N 33
Windlesham Ct. Dr.
GU20: Windl 1N 51
Windlesham Golf Course 3K 51
Windlesham Gro. SW19 . . . . . . .2J 27
Windlesham M.
TW12: H Hill 7C 24
Windlesham Rd.
GU24: Chob 4D 52
GU24: W End 7B 52
RG42: Brac 9L 15
Windmill Av. KT17: Ewe 7E 60
Windmill Bri. Ho. *CR0: Croy . . .7B 46*
(off Freemasons Rd.)
Windmill Bus. Village
TW16: Sunb 9F 22
Windmill Cl. CR3: Cate 8N 83
KT6: Surb 7J 41
KT17: Eps 8E 60
RH6: Horl 8F 142
RH13: Hors 4N 197
SL4: W'sor 5E 4
TW16: Sunb 8F 22
Windmill Ct. RH4: Dork 8H 119
RH10: Craw 1B 182
Windmill Dr. BR2: Kes 1E 66
GU35: Head D 3G 168
KT22: Leat 1J 99
RH2: Reig 1B 122
Windmill End KT17: Eps 8E 60
Windmill Fld. GU20: Windl 3N 51
Windmill Grn. *TW17: Shep 6F 38*
(off Walton La.)
Windmill Gro. CR0: Croy 5N 45
Windmill Hill GU12: Alde 3A 110
Windmill La. KT6: Surb 5H 41
KT17: Eps 8E 60
RH19: E Grin 7N 165
(Goodwins Cl.)
RH19: E Grin 2E 186
(Wellfield)
TW7: Isle 1E 10
Windmill M. W4 . . . . .1D 12
Windmill Pas. W4 . . . . .1D 12
Windmill Plain GU6: Cranl 9C 136
Windmill Ri. KT2: K Tham 8A 26
Windmill Rd. CR0: Croy 6N 45
CR4: Mit 4G 44
GU12: Alde 3A 110
RG42: Brac 9L 15
SW19 . . . . .3G 27
TW8: Brent 1J 11
TW12: H Hill 6B 24
TW16: Sunb 9F 22
W4 . . . . .1D 12
W5 . . . . .1J 11
Windmill Rd. W.
TW16: Sunb 1F 38
Windmill Shott TW20: Egh 7B 20
Windmill Ter. TW17: Shep 6F 38
Windmill Way RH2: Reig 1B 122
Windrum Cl. RH12: Hors 8F 196
Windrush KT3: N Mal 3A 42
Windrush Cl. GU5: Braml 5B 134
RH11: Craw 5L 181
W4 . . . . .4B 12
Windrushes CR3: Cate 3D 104
Windrush Hgts.
GU47: Sandh 7F 48
Windsock Way TW6: Lon A 5K 7
WINDSOR 4G 5
Windsor & Royal Borough Mus.
. . . . .4G 5
Windsor Av. KT3: N Mal 4B 42
KT8: W Mole 2A 40
SM3: Chea 9K 43
SW19 . . . . .9A 28
Windsor Boys' School Sports Cen.
. . . . .4E 4
Windsor Bus. Cen.
SL4: W'sor 3F 4
Windsor Castle 3H 5
Windsor Cl. GU2: Guil 5J 113
GU14: Farnb 1N 89
RH11: Craw 7A 182
SE27 . . . . .5N 29
TW6: Lon A 6L 7
(off Whittle Rd.)
TW8: Brent 2H 11
Windsor Ct. CR3: Whyte 5C 84
GU11: Alde 2L 109
(off Queen Elizabeth Dr.)
GU24: Chob 5H 53
GU51: Fleet 4B 88
KT1: K Tham 8H 203
KT18: Eps 7K 201
RG12: Brac 3A 32
RH13: Hors 5M 197
TW16: Sunb 8H 23
Windsor Ct. Rd.
GU24: Chob 5H 53
Windsor Cres.
GU9: Up Hale 6G 108
Windsor Dr. TW15: Ashf 5M 21
Windsor & Eton Central Station
(Rail) 4G 4
Windsor & Eton Riverside Station
(Rail) 3G 5
Windsor Fitness Club, The 4E 4
Windsor Forest Ct. SL5: Asc 9H 17
Windsor Gdns. CR0: Bedd 9J 45
GU12: Ash 2D 110
Windsor Great Pk. 4E 18
Windsor Gro. SE27 . . . . .5N 29
Windsor Home Park
(Park & Ride) 2H 5
Windsor Legoland
(Park & Ride) 8B 4
Windsor Leisure Cen. 3E 4
Windsor Pk. Rd. UB3: Harl 3G 8
Windsor Pl. KT16: Chert 5J 37
RH10: Craw 8D 162
RH19: E Grin 1C 186
Windsor Ride
GU15: Camb 7M 49
RG12: Brac 5D 32
(Abury La.)
RG12: Brac 5A 50
(King's Ride)
SL5: Asc 4F 32
Windsor Rd. CR7: T Hea 1M 45
GU14: Farnb 4B 90
GU24: Chob 1F 52
GU35: Lind 4A 168
KT2: K Tham 8L 25
KT4: W Pk 8F 42
SL3: Dat 3K 5
SL4: O Win 2M 19
SL4: Wink 8L 17
SL4: W'sor 4A 4
SL5: Asc 2J 33
TW4: C'ford 5J 9
TW9: Kew 5M 11
TW11: Tedd 6D 24
TW16: Sunb 7H 23
TW19: Wray 9A 6
TW20: Egh 3A 20
Windsor St. KT16: Chert 5J 37
Windsor Wlk. GU35: Lind 4A 168
KT12: Wal T 7L 39
KT13: Weybr 2C 56
Windsor Way GU11: Alde 2N 109
GU16: Frim 6D 70
GU22: Wok 3E 74
Winds Ridge GU23: Send 3E 94
Windways GU8: Duns 2B 174
Windycroft Cl. CR8: Pur 9H 63
Windy Gap 3M 169
Windyridge RH11: Craw 4M 181
Windy Ridge Cl. SW19 . . . . .6J 27
Windy Wood GU7: Godal 8F 132
Winern Glebe KT14: Byf 9M 55
Winery La.
KT1: K Tham 5L 203 (2M 41)
Winey Cl. KT9: Ches 4J 59
Winfield Gro. RH5: Newd 1N 159
Winfield Way RH11: Craw 7A 182
Winfrith Rd. SW18 . . . . .1A 28
Wingate Ct. GU11: Alde 2L 109
Wingate Cres. CR0: Croy 5J 45
Wingfield Cl. KT15: N Haw 6K 55
Wingfield Ct. SM7: Ban 2M 81
Wingfield Gdns.
GU16: Frim 3H 71
Wingfield Rd. KT2: K Tham 7M 25
Wingford Rd. SW2 . . . . .1J 29
Wingrave Rd. W6 . . . . .2H 13
Wings Cl. GU9: Up Hale 6G 109
SM1: Sut 1M 61
Wings Rd. GU9: Up Hale 6G 109
TW6: Lon A 6K 7
(off Whittle Rd.)
Winifred Rd. CR5: Coul 3E 82
SW19 . . . . .9M 27
TW12: H Hill 5A 24
WINKFIELD 4H 17
Winkfield Cl. RG41: W'ham 5A 30
Winkfield La. SL4: Wink 3F 16
Winkfield Mnr. SL5: Asc 8H 17
Winkfield Rd.
SL4: W'sor, Wink 2N 17
SL5: Asc 7L 17
WINKFIELD ROW 7F 16
Winkfield Row
RG42: Wink R 5E 16
WINKFIELD STREET 3G 16
Winkfield St. SL4: Wink 3F 16
Winkworth Arboretum 3M 153
Winkworth Pl. SM7: Ban 1L 81
Winkworth Rd. SM7: Ban 1M 81
Winnards GU21: Wok 5K 73
Winner Way RH6: Gatw 4B 162
Winnington Way GU21: Wok . . .5L 73
Winnipeg Dr. BR6: Chels 3N 67
Winscombe RG12: Brac 4K 31
Winslow Rd. W6 . . . . .2H 13
Winslow Way KT12: Wal T 9K 39
TW13: Hanw 4L 23
Winstanley Cl. KT11: Cob 1J 77
Winstanley Wlk. *KT11: Cob 1J 77*
(off Winstanley Cl.)
Winston Churchill School
Sports Cen. 5H 73
Winston Cl. GU16: Frim G 8D 70
Winston Dr. KT11: Sto D 3M 77
TN16: B Hil 4F 86
Winston Wlk.
GU10: Lwr Bou 5H 129
Winston Way GU22: Wok 7D 74
Winta Dr. GU51: Fleet 1A 88
Winterborne Av. BR6: Orp 1M 67
Winterbourne RH12: Hors 1M 197
Winterbourne Ct.
RG12: Brac 1A 32
Winterbourne Gro.
KT13: Weybr 3D 56
Winterbourne M. RH8: Oxt 8M 105
Winterbourne Rd.
CR7: T Hea 3L 45
Winterbourne Wlk.
GU16: Frim 6D 70
Winter Box Wlk.
TW10: Rich 8M 11
Winterbrook Rd. SE24 . . . . .1N 29
Winter Cl. GU12: Ash V 5E 90
Winterdown Gdns.
KT10: Esh 3N 57
Winterdown Rd. KT10: Esh 3N 57
Winterfold RH10: Craw 6E 182
Winterfold Cl. SW19 . . . . .3K 27
Winterfold Cotts. GU5: Alb . . .7N 135
WINTERFOLD HEATH 1N 155
Winterfold Heath Rd.
GU6: Cranl 9M 135
Winter Gdns. RH11: Craw 4A 182
TW11: Tedd 5G 25
Winterhill Way GU4: B'ham 8D 94
Wintersells Ind. Est.
KT14: Byf 6N 55
Wintersells Rd. KT14: Byf 6M 55
Winters Rd. KT7: T Dit 6H 41
Winterton Ct. KT1: H Wic 1G 203
RH13: Hors 6K 197
SE20 . . . . .1D 46
TN16: Weste 5M 107
(off Market Sq.)
Winthorpe Rd. SW15 . . . . .7K 13
Winton Cres. GU46: Yate 1C 68
Winton Rd. BR6: Farnb 1K 67
GU9: Farnh 9J 109
GU11: Alde 3M 109
Winton Way SW16 . . . . .6L 29
Winwood SL4: W'sor 4B 4
Wire Cut GU10: Fren 1J 149
Wireless Rd. TN16: B Hil 2F 86
Wire Mill La.
RH7: Newchap 2H 165
Wirra Rd. *TW6: Lon A 5K 7*
(off Wayfarer Rd.)
Wisbeach Rd. CR0: Croy 4A 46
Wisborough Ct.
RH11: Craw 6L 181
Wisborough Rd. CR2: Sande . . .5C 64
Wisdom Ct. *TW7: Isle 6G 11*
(off South St.)
Wise La. UB7: W Dray 1M 7
Wiseton Rd. SW17 . . . . .2C 28
Wishanger La. GU10: Churt . . .8F 148
Wishbone Way GU21: Wok 3J 73
Wishford Ct. KT21: Asht 5M 79
Wishmoor Cl. GU15: Camb 7C 50
Wishmoor Rd. GU15: Camb 7C 50
WISLEY 3N 75
WISLEY COMMON 3B 76
Wisley Common, Ockham &
Chatley Heath Nature Reserve
. . . . .5E 76
Wisley Ct. CR2: Sande 6A 64
RH1: Red 2D 122
(off Clarendon Rd.)
Wisley Gdns. GU14: Cove 2J 89
Wisley Golf Course 4M 75
WISLEY INTERCHANGE 3D 76
Wisley La. GU23: Wis 3L 75
Wispers La. GU27: Hasl 8G 170
Wistaria La. GU46: Yate 1B 68
Wiston Ct. RH11: Craw 6L 181
RH12: Hors 3K 197
(off Woodstock Cl.)
Witham Ct. SW17 . . . . .4D 28
Witham Rd. SE20 . . . . .2F 46
TW7: Isle 4D 10
Witherby Cl. CR0: Croy 2B 64
Wither Dale RH6: Horl 7C 142
Withers Cl. KT9: Ches 3J 59
Witherslack Cl.
GU35: Head D 5G 169
Withey Brook RH6: Hookw 1B 162
Withey Cl. SL4: W'sor 4B 4
Witheygate Av. TW18: Stain 7K 21
Withey Mdws. RH6: Hookw . . .1B 162
Withies, The GU21: Knap 4H 73
KT22: Leat 7H 79
Withies La. GU3: Comp 1F 132
Withybed Cnr. KT20: Wal H . . .1G 101
Withy Cl. GU18: Ligh 6N 51
Withycombe Rd. SW19 . . . . .1J 27
Withypitts RH10: Turn H 6D 184
Withypitts E. RH10: Turn H . . .6D 184
WITLEY 6C 152
Witley Common 4N 151
Witley Cres. CR0: N Add 3M 65
Witley Ho. SW2 . . . . .1J 29
WITLEY PARK 7L 151
Witley Point *SW15 . . . . .2G 26*
(off Wanborough Dr.)
Witley Station (Rail) 1C 172
Wittenham Rd. RG12: Brac 9D 16
Wittering Cl. KT2: K Tham 6K 25
Wittmead Rd. GU16: Mytc 1D 90
Witts Ho. KT1: K Tham 5L 203
Wivenhoe Ct. TW3: Houn 7N 9
Wix Hill KT24: W Hors 8C 96
Wix Hill Cl. KT24: W Hors 9C 96
Woburn Av. CR8: Pur 7L 63
GU14: Farnb 1B 90
Woburn Cl. GU16: Frim 5E 70
SW19 . . . . .7A 28
Woburn Ct.
CR0: Croy 1C 200 (7N 45)
Woburn Hill KT15: Addl 8L 37
WOBURN PARK 8L 37
Woburn Rd.
CR0: Croy 1C 200 (7N 45)
RH11: Craw 5M 181
SM5: Cars 7C 44
Wodeland Av.
GU2: Guil 7A 202 (5L 113)
Woffington Cl. KT1: H Wic 9J 25
WOKING 4B 74
Woking Bus. Pk.
GU21: Wok 2D 74
Woking Cl. SW15 . . . . .7E 12
Woking Crematorium
GU21: Wok 6H 73
Woking FC 7B 74
Woking Golf Course 7K 73
WOKINGHAM 2B 30
Wokingham Bowling Club 1A 30
Wokingham Rd.
GU47: Sandh 3D 48
RG42: Brac 9K 15
RG45: Crowt 3D 48
Wokingham Station (Rail) 2A 30
Wokingham Theatre 9A 14
WOKINGHAM WITHOUT 8E 30
Woking Leisure Cen. 6B 74
Woking Rd.
GU1: Guil 1D 202 (8N 93)
(not continuous)
GU4: J Wel 6M 93
Woking Station (Rail) 4B 74
Wold, The CR3: Wold 9K 85
Wold Cl. RH11: Craw 5L 181
Woldhurstlea Cl.
RH11: Craw 5M 181
WOLDINGHAM 1K 105
WOLDINGHAM GARDEN VILLAGE
. . . . .7H 85
Woldingham Golf Course 7G 85
Woldingham Rd. CR3: Wold 7E 84
Woldingham Station (Rail) 9G 85
Wolds Dr. BR6: Farnb 1J 67
Wolesley Ct. *GU21: Knap 5F 72*
(off Tudor Way)
Wolfe Cotts. TN16: Weste 5M 107
Wolfendale Cl. RH1: Mers 8G 103
Wolfe Rd. GU12: Alde 3A 110
Wolfington Rd. SE27 . . . . .5M 29
Wolf La. SL4: W'sor 6A 4
Wolf's Hill RH8: Oxt 9C 106
Wolf's Rd. RH8: Limp 8D 106
Wolf's Row RH8: Limp 7D 106
Wolfs Wood RH8: Oxt 1C 126
Wolseley Av. SW19 . . . . .3M 27
Wolseley Gdns. W4 . . . . .2A 12
Wolseley Rd. CR4: Mit 6E 44
GU7: Godal 5H 133
GU11: Alde 3M 109
Wolsey Av. KT7: T Dit 4F 40
Wolsey Cl. KT2: K Tham 9A 26
KT4: W Pk 1F 60
SW20 . . . . .8G 26
TW3: Houn 7C 10
Wolsey Cres. CR0: N Add 5M 65
SM4: Mord 6K 43
Wolsey Dr. KT2: K Tham 6L 25
KT12: Wal T 7L 39
Wolsey Gro. KT10: Esh 1B 58
Wolsey Pl. Shop. Cen.
GU21: Wok 4A 74
Wolsey Rd. KT8: E Mol 3D 40
KT10: Esh 1B 58
TW12: H Hill 7B 24
TW15: Ashf 5N 21
TW16: Sunb 8G 23
Wolsey Wlk. GU21: Wok 4A 74
Wolsey Way KT9: Ches 2N 59
Wolstonbury Cl.
RH11: Craw 5A 182
Wolvens La. RH4: Dork 9A 118
RH5: A Com, Cold 2B 138
Wolverton Av. KT2: K Tham 9N 25
Wolverton Cl. RH6: Horl 1D 162
Wolverton Gdns. RH6: Horl . . .9D 142
Wolves Hill RH5: Cap 6J 159
Wondesford Dale RG42: Bin 5H 15
WONERSH 4D 134
WONERSH COMMON 2D 134
Wonersh Comn. Rd.
GU5: Wone 2D 134
Wonersh Pk. GU5: Wone 5D 134
Wonersh Way SM2: Chea 5J 61
Wonford Cl. KT2: K Tham 9D 26
KT20: Wal H 4F 100
Wonham La. RH3: Betch 4D 120
Wonham Pl. RH9: S Gods 4J 125
Wonham Way
GU5: Gom, P'lake 8E 116
Wontford Rd. CR8: Pur 2L 83
Wontner Rd. SW17 . . . . .3D 28
Woodall Cl. KT9: Ches 4J 59
Woodbarn, The *GU9: Farnh . . .2H 129*
(off Alfred Rd.)
Woodberry Cl. GU8: Chid 4D 172
TW16: Sunb 7H 23
Woodbine Cl. GU47: Sandh 8H 49
TW2: Twick 3D 24
Woodbine La. KT4: W Pk 9G 43
Woodbines Av.
KT1: K Tham 6H 203 (2K 41)
Woodborough Rd. SW15 . . . . . .7G 12
Woodbourne GU9: Weybo 5K 109
Woodbourne Av. SW16 . . . . . . .4H 29
Woodbourne Cl. GU46: Yate 9C 48
SW16 . . . . .4J 29
Woodbourne Dr. KT10: Clay 3F 58
Woodbourne Gdns.
SM6: W'ton 4F 62
Woodbridge Av. KT22: Leat 5G 79
Woodbridge Bus. Pk.
GU1: Guil 1A 202 (2M 113)
Woodbridge Cnr. KT22: Leat . . .5G 78
Woodbridge Ct.
RH12: Hors 3N 197

Woodbridge Dr.—Woolsack Ct.

Woodbridge Dr.
GU15: Camb ... 8B 50
Woodbridge Gro. KT22: Leat ... 5G 79
WOODBRIDGE HILL ... 2L 113
Woodbridge Hill GU2: Guil ... 2L 113
Woodbridge Hill Gdns.
GU2: Guil ... 2K 113
Woodbridge Mdws.
GU1: Guil ... 1A 202 (2M 113)
Woodbridge Rd.
GU1: Guil ... 1A 202 (2M 113)
GU17: B'water ... 1G 69
Woodbridge Trade & Retail Pk.
GU1: Guil ... 1A 202
Woodbury Av.
RH19: E Grin ... 8D 166
Woodbury Cl. CR0: Croy ... 8C 46
RH19: E Grin ... 1C 186
TN16: B Hil ... 5H 87
Woodbury Dr. SM2: Sut ... 6A 62
Woodbury St. SW17 ... 6C 28
Woodby Dr. SL5: S'dale ... 6C 34
Wood Cl. RH1: Salf ... 3E 142
SL4: W'sor ... 7F 4
Woodcock Bottom & Whitmore Vale ... 4N 169
Woodcock Chase RG12: Brac ... 3J 31
Woodcock Dr. GU24: Chob ... 4F 52
Woodcock Hill RH19: Felb ... 4J 165
Woodcock La. GU24: Chob ... 4E 52
Woodcock Rd. TW6: Lon A ... 7K 7
WOODCOTE
CR8 ... 8H 63
KT18 ... 2B 80
Woodcote GU2: Guil ... 7L 113
GU6: Cranl ... 6K 155
GU7: Godal ... 5G 133
RH6: Horl ... 7F 142
Woodcote Av. CR7: T Hea ... 3M 45
SM6: W'ton ... 5F 62
Woodcote Cl. KT2: K Tham ... 6M 25
KT18: Eps ... 8J 201 (1C 80)
Woodcote Dr. CR8: Pur ... 6H 63
Woodcote End KT18: Eps ... 2C 80
WOODCOTE GREEN ... 5G 62
Woodcote Grn. SM6: W'ton ... 5G 62
Woodcote Grn. Rd.
KT18: Eps ... 2B 80
WOODCOTE GROVE ... 9F 62
Woodcote Gro. Rd.
CR5: Coul ... 9H 63
Woodcote Hall
KT18: Eps ... 8J 201 (1C 80)
Woodcote Ho. KT18: Eps ... 2B 80
Woodcote Ho. Ct. KT18: Eps ... 2C 80
Woodcote Hurst KT18: Eps ... 3B 80
Woodcote La. CR8: Pur ... 7H 63
Woodcote Lodge KT18: Eps ... 2B 80
Woodcote M. SM6: W'ton ... 3F 62
WOODCOTE PARK ... 4B 80
Woodcote Pk. Av. CR8: Pur ... 8G 63
Woodcote Pk. Golf Course ... 1F 82
Woodcote Pk. Rd.
KT18: Eps ... 3B 80
Woodcote Pl. SE27 ... 6M 29
SL5: Asc ... 9K 17
Woodcote Rd. CR8: Pur ... 3F 62
KT18: Eps ... 8J 201 (1C 80)
RH18: F Row ... 7G 187
SM6: W'ton ... 3F 62
Woodcote Side KT18: Eps ... 2A 80
Woodcote Valley Rd.
CR8: Pur ... 9H 63
Woodcote Vs. *SE27* ... *6N 29*
(off Woodcote Pl.)
Woodcot Gdns. GU14: Cove ... 1J 89
Woodcott Ter. GU12: Alde ... 4B 110
Wood Ct. GU2: Guil ... 1L 113
Woodcourt RH11: Craw ... 8A 182
Woodcray La. RG40: W'ham ... 6A 30
Wood Crest *SM2: Sut* ... *4A 62*
(off Christchurch Pk.)
Woodcrest Rd. CR8: Pur ... 9J 63
Woodcrest Wlk. RH2: Reig ... 1C 122
Woodcroft Rd. CR7: T Hea ... 4M 45
RH11: Ifield ... 5J 181
Woodcut Rd. GU10: Wrec ... 5E 128
WOOD END ... 7M 17
Wood End GU14: Farnb ... 2B 90
RG45: Crowt ... 3E 48
RH12: Hors ... 3B 198
Wood End, The SM6: W'ton ... 5F 62
Woodend KT10: Esh ... 8C 40
KT22: Leat ... 3J 99
SE19 ... 7N 29
SM1: Sut ... 8A 44
Wood End Cl. SL5: Asc ... 9J 17
Woodend Cl. GU21: Wok ... 6K 73
RH10: Craw ... 1E 182
Woodend Dr. SL5: S'hill ... 4M 33
Woodend Pk. KT11: Cob ... 2L 77
Woodend Ride SL4: Wink ... 8L 17
SL5: Asc ... 8L 17
Woodend Rd. GU16: Deep ... 7G 71
Woodenhill RG12: Brac ... 6K 31
Wooderson Cl. SE25 ... 3B 46
Woodfield KT21: Asht ... 4K 79
Woodfield Av. SM5: Cars ... 3E 62
SW16 ... 4H 29
Woodfield Cl. CR5: Coul ... 6G 82
KT21: Asht ... 4K 79
RH1: Red ... 1C 122
RH10: Craw ... 2C 182
SE19 ... 8N 29
Woodfield Gdns. KT3: N Mal ... 4E 42
Woodfield Gro. SW16 ... 4H 29
Woodfield Hill CR5: Coul ... 6F 82
Woodfield Ho. *KT7: T Dit* ... *8F 40*
(off Woodfield Rd.)
Woodfield La. KT21: Asht ... 4L 79
SW16 ... 4H 29
Woodfield Lodge
RH10: Craw ... 1E 182
Woodfield Rd. KT7: T Dit ... 8F 40
KT21: Asht ... 4K 79
RH10: Craw ... 2C 182
RH12: Rudg ... 1E 194
TW4: C'ford ... 5J 9
Woodfields, The
CR2: Sande ... 7C 64
Woodfield Way RH1: Red ... 1C 122
Woodforde Ct. UB3: Harl ... 1E 8
Woodford Grn. RG12: Brac ... 3D 32
Woodgate GU51: Fleet ... 2D 88
Woodgate Av. KT9: Ches ... 2K 59
Woodgate Cl. KT11: Cob ... 9J 57
Woodgate Dr. SW16 ... 8H 29
Woodgates Cl.
RH13: Hors ... 5M 197
Woodgavil SM7: Ban ... 3L 81
Woodger Cl. GU4: Guil ... 1E 114
Woodhall La. SL5: S'dale ... 8B 34
WOODHAM ... 7H 55
Woodham Ga. GU21: Wok ... 9E 54
Woodham Hall Est.
GU21: Wok ... 1D 74
Woodham La. GU21: Wok ... 1D 74
KT15: Wood, N Haw ... 8G 55
Woodham Lock
KT14: W By ... 8H 55
Woodham Pk. Rd.
KT15: Wood ... 5H 55
Woodham Pk. Way
KT15: Wood ... 7H 55
Woodham Pl. GU21: Wok ... 1B 74
Woodham Ri. GU21: Wok ... 1B 74
Woodham Rd. GU21: Wok ... 2A 74
Woodham Waye GU21: Wok ... 9D 54
WOODHATCH ... 6N 121
Woodhatch Rd. RH1: Red ... 6N 121
RH2: Reig ... 6N 121
Woodhatch Spinney
CR5: Coul ... 3J 83
Woodhaven M. KT12: Wal T ... 1H 57
Woodhaw TW20: Egh ... 5D 20
Woodhayes RH6: Horl ... 7F 142
Woodhayes Rd. SW19 ... 8H 27
Woodhill GU23: Send ... 4F 94
Woodhill Ct. GU23: Send ... 3F 94
Woodhill La. GU5: Sha G ... 7G 135
GU10: Fren ... 2D 148
Woodhouse La.
RH5: Holm M ... 3H 137
Woodhouse St. RG42: Bin ... 8K 15
Woodhurst La. RH8: Oxt ... 8A 106
Woodhurst Pk. RH8: Oxt ... 8A 106
Woodhyrst Gdns. CR8: Ken ... 2M 83
Woodies Cl. RG42: Bin ... 8H 15
Woodies La. KT3: N Mal ... 5C 42
Wooding Gro. RH11: Craw ... 8N 181
Woodland Av. GU6: Cranl ... 7A 156
SL4: W'sor ... 7C 4
Woodland Cl. KT13: Weybr ... 1E 56
KT19: Ewe ... 3D 60
KT24: E Hor ... 5G 97
RH13: Hors ... 4A 198
Woodland Copse RH14: Ifo ... 6F 192
Woodland Ct. KT17: Eps ... 8E 60
RH8: Oxt ... 6N 105
Woodland Cres.
GU14: Farnb ... 8A 70
RG42: Brac ... 8A 16
Woodland Dr. GU10: Wrec ... 5G 128
KT11: Cob ... 7N 57
KT24: E Hor ... 5G 96
RH5: Ockl ... 5G 159
RH10: Craw D ... 1E 184
TN8: Eden ... 9M 127
Woodland Gdns. CR2: Sels ... 7F 64
TW7: Isle ... 6E 10
Woodland Gro. KT13: Weybr ... 1E 56
Woodland La. RH13: Colg ... 6G 198
Woodland M. SW16 ... 4J 29
Woodland Ri. GU52: Chu C ... 8A 88
RH8: Oxt ... 8A 106
Woodland Rd. CR7: T Hea ... 3L 45
WOODLANDS ... 6E 10
Woodlands GU22: Wok ... 5B 74
GU23: Send ... 3H 95
GU46: Yate ... 3C 68
GU51: Fleet ... 3A 88
KT15: Addl ... 9N 37
KT21: Asht ... 5L 79
RH6: Horl ... 7G 143
RH10: Craw ... 1H 183
SW20 ... 3H 43
Woodlands, The GU1: Guil ... 2E 114
KT10: Esh ... 8C 40
RH6: Smallf ... 8M 143
SE19 ... 8N 29
SM6: W'ton ... 5F 62
TW7: Isle ... 5F 10
Woodlands Av.
GU9: Weybo ... 5L 109
KT3: N Mal ... 9B 26
KT4: W Pk ... 8E 42
KT14: W By ... 9H 55
RH1: Red ... 4D 122
Woodlands Caravan Pk.
GU12: Ash ... 3D 110
Woodlands Cl. GU1: Guil ... 8A 94
GU6: Cranl ... 7A 156
GU12: Ash V ... 8E 90
GU17: Haw ... 5K 69
KT10: Clay ... 4F 58
KT16: Otter ... 6D 54
RH10: Craw D ... 2E 184
SL5: Asc ... 5K 33
Woodlands Copse
KT21: Asht ... 3K 79
Woodlands Cotts.
RH5: Newd ... 7B 160
Woodlands Ct. GU21: Wok ... 5K 73
GU22: Wok ... 6A 74
GU47: Owls ... 6L 49
KT12: Wal T ... 7J 39
RH1: Red ... 5D 122
Woodlands Dr.
RH9: S Gods ... 6H 125
TW16: Sunb ... 1K 39
Woodlands Gdns.
KT18: Tat C ... 4H 81
Woodlands Ga. *SW15* ... *8L 13*
(off Woodlands Way)
Woodlands Gro. CR5: Coul ... 4E 82
TW7: Isle ... 5E 10
Woodlands Ho. GU21: Wok ... 1E 74
Woodlands La. GU20: Windl ... 3A 52
GU27: Hasl ... 1D 188
KT11: Leat, Sto D ... 4A 78
Woodlands Pde.
TW15: Ashf ... 7D 22
Woodlands Pk. GU1: Guil ... 2D 114
GU21: Wok ... 1E 74
KT15: Addl ... 2H 55
KT20: Box H ... 9A 100
Woodlands Pl. CR3: Cate ... 4E 104
Woodlands Ride SL5: Asc ... 5K 33
Woodlands Rd. GU1: Guil ... 8N 93
GU8: Hamb ... 9G 152
GU14: Cove ... 8J 69
GU15: Camb ... 1N 69
GU25: V Wat ... 3M 35
KT6: Surb ... 6K 41
KT14: W By ... 1H 75
KT18: Eps ... 2N 79
KT22: Leat ... 4D 78
KT23: Book ... 6M 97
RH1: Red ... 5D 122
RH19: E Grin ... 6C 166
SW13 ... 6E 12
TW7: Isle ... 6D 10
Woodlands Rd. E.
GU25: V Wat ... 3M 35
Woodlands Rd. W.
GU25: V Wat ... 3M 35
Woodlands Vw.
RH5: Mid H ... 2H 139
Woodlands Wlk. GU17: Haw ... 5K 69
Woodlands Way KT21: Asht ... 3N 79
SW15 ... 8L 13
Woodland Vw. GU7: Godal ... 2H 133
Woodland Wlk. GU12: Alde ... 1B 110
KT19: Ewe ... 3N 59
Woodland Way BR4: W Wick ... 1L 65
CR0: Croy ... 7H 47
CR3: Cate ... 6B 104
CR4: Mit ... 8E 28
CR8: Pur ... 9L 63
KT5: Surb ... 8A 42
KT13: Weybr ... 2E 56
KT20: Box H ... 8B 100
KT20: K'wood ... 9K 81
RH13: Hors ... 4N 197
SM4: Mord ... 3L 43
Wood La. CR3: Cate ... 2A 104
GU10: Seal ... 8F 110
GU14: Cove ... 2M 89
GU21: Knap ... 5G 72
GU51: Fleet ... 4D 88
KT13: Weybr ... 5D 56
KT20: Tad ... 4L 81
RG42: Bin ... 6J 15
TW7: Isle ... 2E 10
Woodlark Ct. KT10: Clay ... 3F 58
Woodlark Glade
GU15: Camb ... 8B 50
Woodlawn Cl. SW15 ... 8L 13
Woodlawn Cres. TW2: Whitt ... 3B 24
Woodlawn Dr. TW13: Felt ... 3L 23
Woodlawn Gro. GU21: Wok ... 2B 74
Woodlawn Rd. SW6 ... 3J 13
Woodlawns KT19: Ewe ... 4C 60
Wood Lea Cotts.
RH12: Broadb H ... 1N 195
Woodlee Cl. GU25: V Wat ... 1M 35
Woodleigh GU51: Fleet ... 5B 88
Woodleigh Gdns. SW16 ... 4J 29
Woodley Cl. SW17 ... 8D 28
Woodley Ho. GU7: Godal ... 3H 133
Woodley La. SM5: Cars ... 9C 44
Woodlodge KT21: Asht ... 4L 79
Wood Lodge La.
BR4: W Wick ... 9M 47
Woodmancote Ct.
RH12: Hors ... *3K 197*
(off Blenheim Rd.)
Woodmancote Gdns.
KT14: W By ... 9J 55
Woodmancott Cl.
RG12: Brac ... 5D 32
Woodman Ct. GU51: Fleet ... 5A 88
Woodmancourt GU7: Godal ... 3F 132
Woodman M. TW9: Kew ... 4A 12
Woodman Rd. CR5: Coul ... 2G 83
Woodmans Hill
RH11: Craw ... 8A 182
WOODMANSTERNE ... 2D 82
Woodmansterne La.
SM5: Cars ... 8D 62
SM6: W'ton ... 7F 62
SM7: Ban ... 2N 81
Woodmansterne Rd.
CR5: Coul ... 2G 83
SM5: Cars ... 8D 62
SW16 ... 8G 29
Woodmansterne Station (Rail) ... 3F 82
Woodmansterne St.
SM7: Ban ... 2C 82
Woodman Way RH6: Horl ... 6G 143
Woodmere RG12: Brac ... 3C 32
Woodmere Av. CR0: Croy ... 6F 46
Woodmere Cl. CR0: Croy ... 6G 47
Woodmere Gdns.
CR0: Croy ... 6G 46
Woodmere Way BR3: Beck ... 4N 47
Woodmill Cl. SW15 ... 9F 12
Woodmill Ct. SL5: Asc ... 2H 33
Woodnook Rd. SW16 ... 6F 28
Woodpecker Cl. GU10: Ews ... 4C 108
KT11: Cob ... 8M 57
TN8: Eden ... 9M 127
Woodpecker La.
RH5: Newd ... 9B 140
Woodpecker Mt. CR0: Sels ... 5H 65
Woodpecker Pl. RG12: Brac ... 3J 31
Woodpeckers GU8: Mil ... 3B 152
RG12: Brac ... *3N 31*
(off Crowthorne Rd.)
Woodpecker Way
GU22: Wok ... 2N 93
RH10: Turn H ... 4F 184
Woodplace Cl. CR5: Coul ... 6G 83
Woodplace La. CR5: Coul ... 5G 83
Woodridge Cl. RG12: Brac ... 2A 32
Wood Riding GU22: Pyr ... 2G 75
Woodridings KT13: Weybr ... 3B 56
Wood Ri. GU3: Guil ... 1H 113
Wood Rd. GU7: Godal ... 4J 133
GU9: Up Hale ... 5H 109
GU15: Camb ... 5N 69
GU26: Hind ... 3B 170
TN16: B Hil ... 5E 86
TW17: Shep ... 3B 38
Woodroffe Benton Ho.
RH11: Craw ... *3L 181*
(off Rusper Rd.)
Woodrough Copse
GU5: Braml ... 6C 134
Woodrough La. *GU5: Braml* ... *5B 134*
(off High St.)
Woodrow Dr.
RG40: W'ham ... 2D 30
Woodroyd Av. RH6: Horl ... 9D 142
Woodroyd Gdns. RH6: Horl ... 1D 162
Woodruff Av. GU1: Guil ... 9D 94
Woods Cl. *TW3: Houn* ... *6B 10*
(off High St.)
Woods Hill Cl.
RH19: Ash W ... 3F 186
Woods Hill La.
RH19: Ash W ... 3F 186
Woodshore Cl. GU25: V Wat ... 5L 35
WOODSIDE
SE25 ... 5D 46
SL4 ... 6N 17
Woodside GU14: Farnb ... 7N 69
GU15: Camb ... 8L 49
GU17: Haw ... 4H 69
KT12: Wal T ... 7H 39
KT15: N Haw ... 5L 55
KT20: Lwr K ... 6L 101
KT22: Fetc ... 9B 78
KT24: W Hors ... 4D 96
RH13: Hors ... 4A 198
SW19 ... 7L 27
Woodside Av. KT10: Esh ... 6E 40
KT12: Hers ... 1J 57
SE25 ... 5E 46
Woodside Cl. CR3: Cate ... 2B 104
GU8: Chid ... 5E 172
GU21: Knap ... 4G 73
KT5: Surb ... 6B 42
Woodside Cotts.
CR3: Wold ... 1K 105
GU8: Els ... 8G 131
Woodside Ct. *GU14: Cove* ... *9J 69*
(off Guillemont Flds.)
Woodside Ct. Rd.
CR0: Croy ... 6D 46
Woodside Cres.
RH6: Smallf ... 8L 143
Woodside Gdns.
GU51: Fleet ... 4D 88
Woodside Grn. SE25 ... 5D 46
Woodside Ho. SW19 ... 7L 27
Woodside La. SL4: Wink ... 6N 17
Woodside Pk. SE25 ... 5E 46
Woodside Pk. Ind. Est.
GU7: Godal ... 7J 133
Woodside Rd. CR8: Pur ... 9H 63
GU2: Guil ... 2J 113
GU8: Chid ... 4C 172
GU9: Weybo ... 5K 109
GU14: Farnb ... 6L 89
KT2: K Tham ... 8L 25
KT3: N Mal ... 1C 42
KT11: Cob ... 9A 58
RH5: B Grn ... 8K 139
Woodside Rd. RH10: Craw ... 1D 182
SE25 ... 5E 46
SL4: Wink ... 6M 17
SM1: Sut ... 9A 44
Woodside Rd. Flats
GU8: Chid ... *5E 172*
(off Woodside Rd.)
Woodside Stop
(London Tramlink) ... 5E 46
Woodside Way CR0: Croy ... 5F 46
CR4: Mit ... 9F 28
GU25: V Wat ... 2L 35
RH1: Red ... 4E 122
(Redstone Hollow)
RH1: Red ... 9E 122
(West Av.)
Woodsome Lodge
KT13: Weybr ... 3D 56
Woodspring Rd. SW19 ... 3K 27
WOODSTOCK, THE ... 6L 43
Woodstock GU4: W Cla ... 6K 95
RG40: W'ham ... *2B 30*
(off Palmer School Rd.)
RH19: E Grin ... 8M 165
Woodstock Av. SL3: Lang ... 1N 5
SM3: Sut ... 6L 43
TW7: Isle ... 8G 10
Woodstock Cl. GU6: Cranl ... 9A 156
GU21: Wok ... 3A 74
RH12: Hors ... 3K 197
Woodstock Ct.
KT19: Eps ... 5K 201 (9C 60)
Woodstock Gro.
GU7: Godal ... 4G 133
Woodstock La. KT9: Ches ... 1H 59
Woodstock La. Nth.
KT6: Surb ... 8J 41
Woodstock La. Sth.
KT9: Ches ... 2H 59
KT10: Clay ... 2H 59
Woodstock Ri. SM3: Sut ... 6L 43
Woodstock Rd.
CR0: Croy ... 5D 200 (9A 46)
CR5: Coul ... 3F 82
SM5: Cars ... 2E 62
Woodstocks GU14: Farnb ... 8A 70
Woodstock Way CR4: Mit ... 1F 44
Woodstone Av. KT17: Ewe ... 2F 60
Wood St. CR4: Mit ... 6E 44
GU12: Ash V ... 7E 90
KT1: K Tham ... 3H 203 (1K 41)
RH1: Mers ... 7G 103
RH19: E Grin ... 9N 165
W4 ... 1D 12
Wood St. Grn.
GU3: Wood V ... 1D 112
WOOD STREET VILLAGE ... 1E 112
Woodsway KT22: Oxs ... 1E 78
Woodthorpe Rd. SW15 ... 7G 13
TW15: Ashf ... 7M 21
Woodvale Av. SE25 ... 2C 46
Woodvale Rd. GU14: Farnb ... 5N 89
Woodvale Wlk. SE27 ... 6N 29
Woodview KT9: Ches ... 7J 59
Woodview Cl. CR2: Sande ... 1E 84
KT21: Asht ... 3N 79
SW15 ... 5C 26
Woodview Ct. KT13: Weybr ... 2D 56
Woodville Cl. GU17: B'water ... 1G 68
TW11: Tedd ... 5G 24
Woodville Ct. KT22: Leat ... 7H 79
Woodville Gdns. KT6: Surb ... 6K 41
Woodville Rd. CR7: T Hea ... 3N 45
SM4: Mord ... 3M 43
TW10: Ham ... 4H 25
Woodvill Rd. KT22: Leat ... 7H 79
Woodward Cl. KT10: Clay ... 3F 58
Woodwards RH11: Craw ... 8N 181
Woodward's Footpath
TW2: Whitt ... 9C 10
Woodway GU1: Guil ... 2D 114
GU15: Camb ... 1N 69
Woodyers Cl. GU5: Wone ... 4D 134
Woolacombe Way UB3: Harl ... 1G 8
Wooland Ct. GU52: Chu C ... 9A 88
Woolborough Cl.
RH10: Craw ... 2C 182
Woolborough La. RH1: Out ... 3K 143
RH10: Craw ... 9D 162
Woolborough Rd.
RH10: Craw ... 2B 182
Wooldridge Cl. TW14: Bedf ... 2D 22
Woolf Dr. RG40: W'ham ... 1A 30
Woolford Cl. RG42: Wink R ... 8F 16
Woolfords La. GU8: Els ... 3E 150
Woolhampton Way
RG12: Brac ... 4B 32
Woolhams CR3: Cate ... 4D 104
Woollards Rd. GU12: Ash V ... 9F 90
Woolmead, The
GU9: Farnh ... 9H 109
Woolmead Rd. GU9: Farnh ... 9H 109
Woolmead Wlk.
GU9: Farnh ... *9H 109*
(off Woolmead Rd.)
WOOLMER HILL ... 1A 188
Woolmer Hill Rd.
GU27: Hasl ... 9A 170
Woolmer La.
GU30: Brams
... 8F 168 & 9H 169
Woolmer Vw. GU26: G'hott ... 6B 170
Woolneigh St. SW6 ... 6N 13
Wool Rd. SW20 ... 7G 27
Woolsack Ct. GU2: Guil ... 9K 93

Woolsack Way—Zodiac Ct.

Woolsack Way GU7: Godal 7H 133
Wootton Cl. KT18: Eps 3E 80
Wootton Grange GU22: Wok 6A 74
(off Langley Wlk.)
Wootton Pl. KT10: Esh 1C 58
Worbeck Rd. SE20 1E 46
Worcester Cl. CR0: Croy 8K 47
CR4: Mit 1E 44
GU14: Farnb 7N 69
Worcester Ct. GU51: Fleet 2A 88
(off King John St.)
KT4: W Pk 9D 42
KT12: Wal T 8K 39
RH1: Red 1C 122
(off Timperley Gdns.)
Worcester Dr. TW15: Ashf 6C 22
Worcester Gdns. KT4: W Pk 9D 42
WORCESTER PARK 7F 42
Worcester Pk. Rd.
KT4: W Pk 9C 42
Worcester Park Station (Rail) 7F 42
Worcester Rd. GU2: Guil 1J 113
RH2: Reig 2L 121
RH10: Craw 7C 182
SM2: Sut 4M 61
SW19 6L 27
Worcestershire Lea
RG42: Warf 8D 16
Wordsworth RG12: Brac 4K 31
Wordsworth Av. CR8: Ken 2A 84
GU46: Yate 1A 68
Wordsworth Cl. RH10: Craw 1F 182
Wordsworth Dr. SM3: Chea 1H 61
Wordsworth Mans. W14 2L 13
(off Queens Club Gdns.)
Wordsworth Mead
RH1: Red 1E 122
Wordsworth Pl.
RH12: Hors 1L 197
Wordsworth Ri.
RH19: E Grin 9M 165
Wordsworth Rd. KT15: Addl 1M 55
SM6: W'ton 3G 63
TW12: Hamp 5N 23
Wordsworth Way
UB7: W Dray 1N 7
Workshop Gym
Guildford 1D 202 (2N 113)
World Bus. Cen. TW6: Lon A 4D 8
World of Golf Driving Range 2F 42
World Rugby Mus. 9E 10
Worlds End KT11: Cob 1H 77
KT18: Eps 3C 80
Worlds End Hill RG12: Brac 5D 32
Worleys Dr. BR6: Orp 1M 67
Worlidge St. W6 1H 13
WORMLEY 9C 152
Wormley La. GU8: Worm 9D 152
Worple, The TW19: Wray 9B 6
Worple Av. SW19 8J 27
TW7: Isle 8G 10
TW18: Stain 7K 21
Worple Rd.
KT18: Eps 8K 201 (2C 80)
KT22: Leat 9H 79
(not continuous)
SW19 9J 27
SW20 1H 43
TW7: Isle 7G 10
TW18: Stain 7K 21
(not continuous)
Worple Rd. M. SW19 7L 27
WORPLESDON 5H 93
Worplesdon Golf Course 9H 73
Worplesdon Hill GU22: Wok 9F 72
Worplesdon Hill Ho.
GU22: Wok 9G 73
Worplesdon Rd. GU2: Guil 6H 93
GU3: Guil, Worp 3F 92
Worplesdon Station (Rail) 2L 93
Worple St. SW14 6C 12
Worple Way TW10: Rich 8L 11
Worsfold Cl. GU23: Send 1D 94
Worslade Rd. SW17 5B 28
Worsley Rd. GU16: Frim 6C 70
Worsted Grn. RH1: Mers 7G 103
Worsted La. RH19: E Grin 1D 186
WORTH 3J 183
WORTH ABBEY 8M 183
Worth Cl. BR6: Orp 1N 67
Worth Ct. RH10: Turn H 8M 183
Worthfield Cl. KT19: Ewe 4C 60
Worthing Rd. RH12: Hors 6H 197
RH13: Hors 9G 197
TW5: Hest 2N 9
Worthington Cl. CR4: Mit 3F 44
Worthington Rd. KT6: Surb 7M 41
Worth Pk. Av. RH10: Craw 2F 182
Worth Rd. RH10: Craw 2G 182
Worth Way
RH10: Craw D, Rowf 2C 184
RH10: E Grin 1G 185
RH10: Rowf, Worth 3M 183
RH10: Worth 4J 183
RH19: E Grin 1G 185
Wortley Rd. CR0: Croy 6L 45
Worton Ct. TW7: Isle 7E 10
Worton Gdns. TW7: Isle 5D 10
Worton Hall Ind. Est.
TW7: Isle 7E 10
Worton Rd. TW7: Isle 7D 10
Worton Way TW3: Houn 5D 10
TW7: Houn, Isle 5D 10
WOTTON 8N 117
Wotton Dr. RH5: Wott 9N 117
Wotton Ho. SL4: Eton 1G 4
(off Common La.)
Wotton Way SM2: Chea 6H 61
Wrabness Way TW18: Stain 9K 21
Wrangthorn Wlk.
CR0: Wad 1L 63
Wray Cl. RH19: Ash W 3F 186
WRAY COMMON 2B 122
Wray Comn. Rd. RH2: Reig 2A 122
Wrayfield Av. RH2: Reig 2A 122
Wrayfield Rd. SM3: Chea 9J 43
Wraylands Dr. RH2: Reig 1B 122
Wray La. RH2: Reig 8A 102
Wraymead Pl. RH2: Reig 2N 121
Wraymill Ct. RH2: Reig 3B 122
(off Wray Comn. Rd.)
Wray Mill Pk. RH2: Reig 1B 122
Wray Pk. Rd. RH2: Reig 2N 121
Wray Rd. SM2: Chea 5L 61
WRAYS 7M 141
WRAYSBURY 9B 6
Wraysbury Cl. TW4: Houn 8M 9
Wraysbury Dive Cen. 9B 6
Wraysbury Gdns.
TW18: Stain 5G 21
Wraysbury Lake Sailing Club 8A 6
Wraysbury Rd. TW18: Stain 4E 20
TW19: Stain 3D 20
Wraysbury Station (Rail) 9C 6
WRECCLESHAM 4E 128
Wrecclesham Hill
GU10: Wrec 6C 128
Wrecclesham Rd.
GU9: Farnh 4E 128
GU10: Wrec 4E 128
Wrekin, The GU14: Farnb 4C 90
Wren Cl. CR2: Sels 5G 65
GU46: Yate 9A 48
RH12: Hors 1K 197
TW6: Lon A 6K 7
Wren Ct. CR0: Croy 6E 200
GU12: Ash 1F 110
RH10: Craw 6C 182
Wren Cres. KT15: Addl 2M 55
Wren Gdns. RG12: Brac 3J 31
Wren Ho. KT1: H Wic 3G 203
(off High St.)
Wrenn Ho. SW13 2H 13
Wren's Av. TW15: Ashf 5D 22
Wrens Hill KT22: Oxs 2C 78
Wren St. RH10: Turn H 4F 184
Wren Way GU14: Farnb 7L 69
Wright SL4: W'sor 6A 4
Wright Cl. RH10: Craw 7F 182
Wright Gdns. TW17: Shep 4B 38
Wright Rd. TW5: Hest 3K 9
Wrights All. SW19 7H 27
Wright Sq. SL4: W'sor 6A 4
Wrights Rd. SE25 2B 46
Wrights Row SM6: W'ton 1F 62
Wrights Wlk. SW14 6C 12
Wright Way SL4: W'sor 6A 4
TW6: Lon A 5K 7
Wriotsley Way KT15: Addl 3J 55
Writers Cl. GU26: Hind 3A 170
Wrotham Hill GU8: Duns 6A 174
Wroxham RG12: Brac 4L 31
Wroxham Wlk. RH10: Craw 5F 182
WRYTHE, THE 9D 44
Wrythe Grn. SM5: Cars 9D 44
Wrythe Grn. Rd. SM5: Cars 9D 44
Wrythe La. SM5: Cars 7A 44
Wulwyn Ct. RG45: Crowt 2E 48
Wulwyn Side RG45: Crowt 2E 48
Wyatt Cl. TW13: Felt 2L 23
Wyatt Ct. GU47: Coll T 8J 49
Wyatt Dr. SW13 2G 13
Wyatt Ho. TW1: Twick 9K 11
Wyatt Pk. Rd. SW2 3J 29
Wyatt Rd. SL4: W'sor 6A 4
TW18: Stain 6J 21
Wyatts Almshouses
GU7: Godal 5K 133
(off Wyatt's Cl.)
Wyatt's Cl. GU7: Godal 5K 133
Wyche Gro. CR2: S Croy 4N 63
Wych Elm Cl.
KT2: K Tham 1L 203 (8M 25)
Wych Elm Pas.
KT2: K Tham 1L 203 (8M 25)
Wych Elm Ri.
GU1: Guil 8F 202 (6A 114)
Wychelm Rd. GU18: Ligh 7N 51
Wych Hill GU22: Wok 6M 73
Wych Hill La. GU22: Wok 6N 73
Wych Hill Pk. GU22: Wok 6N 73
Wych Hill Ri. GU22: Wok 6M 73
Wych Hill Way GU22: Wok 7N 73
Wych Warren RH18: F Row 9G 186
Wychwood RH14: Ifo 5F 192
Wychwood Av. CR7: T Hea 2N 45
RG12: Brac 3D 32
Wychwood Cl. GU12: Ash 2D 110
KT22: Oxs 1D 78
TW16: Sunb 7H 23
Wychwood Pl. GU15: Camb 6F 50
Wyckham Ho. RH8: Oxt 7A 106
(off Station App.)
Wycliffe Bldgs. GU2: Guil 6B 202
Wycliffe Ct. RH11: Craw 6K 181
Wycliffe Rd. SW19 7N 27
Wycombe Pl. SW18 9N 13
Wydehurst Rd. CR0: Croy 6D 46
Wydell Cl. SM4: Mord 5J 43
Wyecliffe Gdns. RH1: Mers 8G 103
Wye Cl. RH11: Craw 9A 182
TW15: Ashf 5C 22
Wyeths M. KT17: Eps 9E 60
Wyeths Rd.
KT17: Eps 6M 201 (9E 60)
Wyfold Rd. SW6 3K 13
WYKE 1L 111
Wyke Av. GU12: Ash 1H 111
Wyke Bungs. GU12: Ash 1H 111
Wyke Cl. TW7: Isle 2F 10
Wyke Cross GU3: Norm 1L 111
Wyke Green Golf Course 2F 10
Wykeham Cl. UB7: Sip 2B 8
Wykeham Rd. GU1: Guil 2F 114
GU9: Farnh 9H 109
Wykehurst La. GU6: Ewh 4C 156
Wyke La. GU12: Ash 1H 111
Wyke Rd. SW20 1H 43
Wylam RG12: Brac 4L 31
Wylands Rd. SL3: Lang 1C 6
Wyldewoods SL5: S'hill 5A 34
Wymering Ct. GU14: Farnb 2B 90
Wymond St. SW15 6H 13
Wynash Gdns. SM5: Cars 2C 62
Wyncote Way CR2: Sels 5G 64
Wyndham Av. KT11: Cob 9H 57
Wyndham Cl. GU46: Yate 8C 48
SM2: Sut 4M 61
Wyndham Cres. GU6: Cranl 7J 155
TW4: Houn 9A 10
Wyndham Rd. GU21: Wok 5L 73
KT2: K Tham 8M 25
Wyndham St. GU12: Alde 3A 110
Wyndhurst Cl. CR2: S Croy 4M 63
Wynfields GU16: Mytc 2D 90
Wyngates RH10: Copt 6M 163
Wynlea Cl. RH10: Craw D 1D 184
Wynne Gdns. GU52: Chu C 8C 88
Wynnstow Pk. RH8: Oxt 9B 106
Wynsham Way GU20: Windl 2M 51
Wynton Gdns. SE25 4C 46
Wynton Gro. KT12: Wal T 9H 39
Wyphurst Rd. GU6: Cranl 6M 155
Wyresdale RG12: Brac 6C 32
Wysemead RH6: Horl 7G 143
Wythegate TW18: Stain 8H 21
Wythemede RG42: Bin 7G 15
Wyvern Cl. GU12: Ash V 8D 90
RG12: Brac 3N 31
Wyvern Est. KT3: N Mal 3F 42
Wyvern Pl. KT15: Addl 1K 55
RH12: Warnh 9F 178
Wyvern Rd. CR8: Pur 6M 63

X

Xylon Ho. KT4: W Pk 8G 42

Y

Yaffle Rd. KT13: Weybr 6D 56
Yale Cl. GU47: Owls 5L 49
TW4: Houn 8N 9
Yarborough Rd. SW19 9B 28
Yarbridge Cl. SM2: Sut 6N 61
Yardley RG12: Brac 4L 31
Yardley Cl. RH2: Reig 1N 121
Yardley Ct. SM3: Chea 1H 61
Yard Mead TW20: Egh 4C 20
Yarm Cl. KT22: Leat 1J 99
Yarm Ct. Rd. KT22: Leat 1J 99
Yarm Holt KT22: Leat 2J 99
Yarmouth Cl. RH10: Craw 5E 182
Yarm Way KT22: Leat 1K 99
Yarnold Cl. RG40: W'ham 1E 30
Yarrell Mans. W14 2L 13
(off Queen's Club Gdns.)
Yarrow Cl. RH12: Hors 3L 197
YATELEY 9C 48
Yateley Cen. GU46: Yate 1B 68
Yateley Common Country Pk. 3D 68
Yateley Ct. CR8: Ken 1N 83
Yateley Dr. GU17: Min 5A 68
Yateley Health & Fitness Cen. 1A 68
Yateley Rd. GU47: Sandh 7E 48
Yatesbury Cl. GU9: Farnh 4E 128
Yattendon Rd. RH6: Horl 8F 142
Yaverland Dr. GU19: Bag 5H 51
Yeats Cl. RH1: Red 6A 122
Yeend Cl. KT8: W Mole 3A 40
Yehudi Menuhin Hall 6A 78
Yeldham Ho. W6 1J 13
(off Yeldham Rd.)
Yeldham Rd. W6 1J 13
Yeldham Vs. W6 1J 13
(off Yeldham Rd.)
Yellowcress Dr. GU24: Bis 3D 72
Yelverton Lodge TW1: Twick 1J 25
(off Richmond Rd.)
Ye Market CR2: S Croy 8D 200
Yenston Cl. SM4: Mord 5M 43
Yeoman Cl. SE27 4M 29
Yeoman Ct. TW5: Hest 3N 9
Yeoman Dr. TW19: Stan 2N 21
Yeomanry Cl. KT17: Eps 8E 60
Yeomans Cl. GU10: Tong 4D 110
GU14: Cove 9M 69
Yeomans Cft. KT23: Book 3A 98
Yeomans M. TW7: Isle 9D 10
Yeomans Pl. GU35: Head 4D 168
Yeomans Way GU15: Camb 1C 70
Yeoman Way RH1: Red 8F 122
Yeoveney Cl. TW19: Stain 3F 20
Yeovil Cl. GU14: Farnb 4B 90
Yeovil Rd. GU14: Farnb 4C 90
GU47: Coll T, Owls 6J 49
Yeovilton Pl. KT2: K Tham 6J 25
Yetminster Rd. GU14: Farnb 4B 90
Yewbank Cl. CR8: Ken 2A 84
Yew Barton Ct. GU52: Chu C 9B 88
Yew Cl. RG42: Warf 8E 16
Yew Cnr. RG12: Brac 2A 32
Yew Ct. RH11: Craw 4B 182
(off Springfield Rd.)
RH19: E Grin 8M 165
Yewdells Cl. RH3: Buckl 2F 120
Yewens GU8: Chid 4E 172
Yewlands Cl. SM7: Ban 2A 82
Yewlands Wlk. RH11: Ifield 5J 181
Yew La. RH19: E Grin 7L 165
Yew Pl. KT13: Weybr 1G 56
Yews, The KT14: Byf 8N 55
TW15: Ashf 5C 22
Yew Tree Bottom Rd.
KT17: Eps D 3G 81
KT18: Tat C 3G 81
Yew Tree Cl. CR5: Chip 6D 82
GU14: Cove 2H 89
KT4: W Pk 7D 42
RH6: Horl 6D 142
Yew Tree Cotts.
RH11: Hand 5N 199
RH13: Itch 8B 196
Yew Tree Ct. RH6: Horl 7E 142
SM2: Sut 4A 62
(off Walnut M.)
Yew Tree Dr. CR3: Cate 3C 104
GU1: Guil 8M 93
Yew Tree Gdns. KT18: Eps 2B 80
Yew Tree La. RH2: Reig 9N 101
Yewtree La. RH5: Ran C 9A 98
Yew Tree Lodge SW16 5G 28
Yew Tree M. TN16: Weste 5M 107
(off Market Sq.)
Yew Tree Rd. BR3: Beck 2J 47
GU8: Wit 4A 152
RH4: Dork 3G 119
RH6: Charlw 3K 161
Yew Trees TW17: Shep 3A 38
TW20: Thor 2E 36
Yew Tree Wlk. CR8: Pur 6N 63
GU16: Frim 5D 70
KT24: Eff 5L 97
TW4: Houn 8N 9
Yew Tree Way CR0: Sels 6H 65
Yew Wlk. KT24: E Hor 1F 116
YMCA Hawker Cen. 6K 25
YMCA Sports Cen.
Earlswood 6E 122
Yockley Cl. GU15: Camb 2H 71
Yoga Way KT4: W Pk 8F 42
Yolland Cl. GU9: Up Hale 5H 109
York Av. RH19: E Grin 1B 186
SL4: W'sor 5E 4
SW14 8B 12
York Cl. KT14: Byf 8N 55
RH13: Hors 5M 197
SM4: Mord 3N 43
TW18: Stain 7N 21
York Ct. KT19: Eps 8N 59
York Cres. GU11: Alde 3L 109
Yorke Gdns. RH2: Reig 2M 121
Yorke Ga. CR3: Cate 9A 84
Yorke Rd. RH2: Reig 2L 121
York Gdns. KT12: Wal T 8L 39
York Hill SE27 4M 29
York Ho. KT2: K Tham 1M 203
KT20: Lwr K 5L 101
RG42: Brac 9L 15
York Mans. SW5 1N 13
(off Earls Ct. Rd.)
York Pde. TW8: Brent 1K 11
York Pl. GU15: Camb 8B 50
York Rd. CR0: Croy 6L 45
CR2: Sels 6G 64
GU1: Guil 4C 202 (4N 113)
GU9: Farnh 3H 129
GU11: Alde 3L 109
GU12: Ash 1E 110
GU14: Farnb 4A 90
GU15: Camb 8B 50
GU22: Wok 6N 73
KT2: K Tham 1M 203 (8M 25)
KT13: Weybr 2D 56
KT14: Byf 8N 55
RG42: Bin 6J 15
RH10: Craw 7C 182
SL4: W'sor 5E 4
SM1: Sut 3M 61
SM2: Sut 3M 61
SW19 7A 28
TN16: B Hil 6D 86
TW3: Houn 6B 10
TW8: Brent 1K 11
TW10: Rich 8M 11
TW11: Tedd 5E 24
Yorkshire Pl. RG42: Warf 8C 16
Yorkshire Rd. CR4: Mit 4J 45
York St. CR4: Mit 6E 44
TW1: Twick 2G 25
York Ter. La. GU15: Camb 1M 69
YORK TOWN 1M 69
York Town Ind. Est.
GU15: Camb 2M 69
Yorktown Rd.
GU47: Coll T, Sandh 7F 48
Yorktown Way GU15: Camb 1L 69
York Way GU47: Sandh 7G 48
KT9: Ches 4L 59
TW13: Hanw 4N 23
(not continuous)
Youlden Cl. GU15: Camb 1E 70
Youlden Dr. GU15: Camb 1E 70
Youngs Dr. GU12: Ash 2D 110
Young St. KT22: Fetc, Leat 3E 98
Youngstroat La.
GU24: Chob 6A 54
Yoxall M. RH1: Red 1F 122
Yukon Rd. SW12 1F 28
Yvonne Arnaud Theatre
Guildford 6C 202 (5N 113)

Z

Zealand Av. UB7: Harm 3M 7
Zennor Rd. SW12 2G 28
Zennor Rd. Ind. Est.
SW12 2G 28
Zenobia Mans. W14 2L 13
(off Queen's Club Gdns.)
Zermatt Rd. CR7: T Hea 3N 45
Zigzag, The KT20: Box H 1K 119
RH5: Mick 8J 99
Zig Zag Rd. CR8: Ken 3N 83
Zinnia Dr. GU24: Bis 3D 72
Zion Pl. CR7: T Hea 3A 46
Zion Rd. CR7: T Hea 3A 46
Zodiac Ct. CR0: Croy 7M 45

HOSPITALS, HOSPICES and selected HEALTHCARE FACILITIES covered by this atlas.

N.B. Where it is not possible to name these facilities on the map, the reference given is for the road in which they are situated.

ABRAHAM COWLEY UNIT 9F 36
  Holloway Hill
  Lyne
  CHERTSEY
  KT16 0QE
  Tel: 01932 722471

ALPHA HOSPITAL, WOKING 5G 72
  Redding Way
  Knaphill
  WOKING
  GU21 2QS
  Tel: 01483 795100

ASHFORD HOSPITAL 3N 21
  London Road
  ASHFORD
  TW15 3AA
  Tel: 01784 884488

ASHTEAD PRIVATE HOSPITAL 6L 79
  The Warren
  ASHTEAD
  KT21 2SB
  Tel: 01372 221400

BARNES HOSPITAL 6D 12
  South Worple Way
  LONDON
  SW14 8SU
  Tel: 0203513 3600

BECKENHAM BEACON 1J 47
  379 Croydon Road
  BECKENHAM
  BR3 3QL
  Tel: 01689 866667

BETHLEM ROYAL HOSPITAL 6K 47
  Monks Orchard Road
  BECKENHAM
  BR3 3BX
  Tel: 020 32286000

BROADMOOR HOSPITAL 2K 49
  Kentigern Drive
  CROWTHORNE
  RG45 7EG
  Tel: 01344 773111

CASSEL HOSPITAL 5K 25
  1 Ham Common
  RICHMOND
  TW10 7JF
  Tel: 020 84832 900

CATERHAM DENE HOSPITAL 1C 104
  Church Road
  CATERHAM
  CR3 5RA
  Tel: 01883 837500

CHARING CROSS HOSPITAL 2J 13
  Fulham Palace Road
  LONDON
  W6 8RF
  Tel: 0203311 1234

CHILDREN'S TRUST 8J 81
  Tadworth Court
  TADWORTH
  KT20 5RU
  Tel: 01737 365000

CHRISTOPHER'S CHILDREN'S HOSPICE
  (SHOOTING STAR CHASE) 8M 113
  Old Portsmouth Road
  Artington
  GUILDFORD
  GU3 1LP
  Tel: 01483 230960

CLARE PARK SPIRE HOSPITAL 8A 108
  Crondall Lane
  FARNHAM
  GU10 5XX
  Tel: 01252 850216

CRAWLEY HOSPITAL 3A 182
  West Green Drive
  CRAWLEY
  RH11 7DH
  Tel: 01293 600300

CROYDON UNIVERSITY HOSPITAL 5M 45
  530 London Road
  THORNTON HEATH
  CR7 7YE
  Tel: 020 8401 3000

DORKING COMMUNITY HOSPITAL
  . . . . .4J 201 (6H 119)
  Horsham Road
  DORKING
  RH4 2AA
  Tel: 01306 646200

EAST SURREY HOSPITAL 7F 122
  Canada Avenue
  REDHILL
  RH1 5RH
  Tel: 01737 768511

EDENBRIDGE WAR MEMORIAL HOSPITAL
  . . . . .4L 147
  Mill Hill
  EDENBRIDGE
  TN8 5DA
  Tel: 01732 863164

EDRIDGE ROAD COMMUNITY HEALTH CENTRE
  . . . . .5C 200 (9N 45)
  Impact House
  Edridge Road
  CROYDON
  CR9 1PJ
  Tel: 020 8714 2888

EPSOM DAY SURGERY CENTRE 9E 60
  Alexandra Road
  The Old Cottage Hospital
  EPSOM
  KT17 4BL
  Tel: 01372 739002

EPSOM GENERAL HOSPITAL 2B 80
  Dorking Road
  EPSOM
  KT18 7EG
  Tel: 01372 735735

FARNHAM HOSPITAL & CENTRE FOR HEALTH
  . . . . .9J 109
  Hale Road
  FARNHAM
  GU9 9QL
  Tel: 01483 782000

FARNHAM ROAD HOSPITAL 6A 202 (5L 113)
  Farnham Road
  GUILDFORD
  GU2 7LX
  Tel: 01483 443535

FLEET COMMUNITY HOSPITAL 3A 88
  Church Road
  FLEET
  GU51 4LZ
  Tel: 01252 813800

FRIMLEY PARK HOSPITAL 4B 70
  Portsmouth Road
  Frimley
  CAMBERLEY
  GU16 7UJ
  Tel: 01276 604604

GATWICK PARK SPIRE HOSPITAL 9C 142
  Povey Cross Road
  HORLEY
  RH6 0BB
  Tel: 01293 785511

GUILDFORD NUFFIELD HEALTH HOSPITAL
  . . . . .3H 113
  Stirling Road
  GUILDFORD
  GU2 7RF
  Tel: 01483 378684

HARLINGTON HOSPICE
  (REG HOPKINS DAY CARE HOSPICE)
  . . . . .1E 8
  St Peters Way
  HAYES
  UB3 5AB
  Tel: 020 8759 0453

HASLEMERE COMMUNITY HOSPITAL . . .1H 189
  Church Lane
  HASLEMERE
  GU27 2BJ
  Tel: 01483 782334

HEATHERWOOD HOSPITAL 2J 33
  London Road
  ASCOT
  SL5 8AA
  Tel: 01344 623333

HOLY CROSS HOSPITAL 1D 188
  Hindhead Road
  HASLEMERE
  GU27 1NQ
  Tel: 01428 643311

HORSHAM HOSPITAL 5J 197
  Hurst Road
  HORSHAM
  RH12 2DR
  Tel: 01403 227000

KING EDWARD VII HOSPITAL 6F 4
  St Leonard's Road
  WINDSOR
  SL4 3DP
  Tel: 01753 860 441

KINGSTON HOSPITAL 9A 26
  Galsworthy Road
  KINGSTON UPON THAMES
  KT2 7QB
  Tel: 020 8546 7711

LANGLEY GREEN HOSPITAL 8B 162
  Martyrs Avenue
  CRAWLEY
  RH11 7EJ
  Tel: 01293 590400

LEATHERHEAD COMMUNITY HOSPITAL . . .9J 79
  Poplar Road
  LEATHERHEAD
  KT22 8SD
  Tel: 01372 384384

MACMILLAN HOUSE BA HOSPICE 3A 30
  Wokingham Community Hospital
  Barkham Road
  WOKINGHAM
  RG41 2RE
  Tel: 0118 949 5030

MCINDOE SURGICAL CENTRE 7B 166
  Holtye Road
  EAST GRINSTEAD
  RH19 3EB
  Tel: 01342 330300

MILFORD SPECIALIST REHABILITATION
  HOSPITAL 2F 152
  Tuesley Lane
  GODALMING
  GU7 1UF
  Tel: 01483 782500

MOLESEY HOSPITAL 4A 40
  High Street
  WEST MOLESEY
  KT8 2LU
  Tel: 020 87833092

MOUNT ALVERNIA BMI HOSPITAL
  . . . . .6F 202 (5A 114)
  46 Harvey Road
  GUILDFORD
  GU1 3LX
  Tel: 01483 570122

NELSON HOSPITAL 1L 43
  Kingston Road
  LONDON
  SW20 8DB
  Tel: 020 8296 3795

NEW EPSOM & EWELL COTTAGE HOSPITAL
  . . . . .7L 59
  West Park Road
  Horton Lane
  EPSOM
  KT19 8PB
  Tel: 01372 7348555

NEW VICTORIA HOSPITAL 9D 26
  184 Coombe Lane West
  KINGSTON UPON THAMES
  KT2 7EG
  Tel: 020 8949 9000

NHS WALK-IN CENTRE (ASHFORD) 3N 21
  Ashford Hospital
  London Road
  ASHFORD
  TW15 3AA
  Tel: 01784 884000

NHS WALK-IN CENTRE (CHARING CROSS)
  . . . . .1J 13
  Charing Cross Hospital
  Fulham Palace Road
  LONDON
  W6 8RF
  Tel: 020 3311105

NHS WALK-IN CENTRE (CRAWLEY) 3A 182
  Crawley Hospital
  West Green Drive
  CRAWLEY
  RH11 7DH
  Tel: 01293 600300

NHS WALK-IN CENTRE (PARSONS GREEN)
  . . . . .4M 13
  5-7 Parsons Green
  LONDON
  SW6 4UL
  Tel: 020 8846 6758

NHS WALK-IN CENTRE (REDHILL) 7F 122
  East Surrey Hospital
  Canada Avenue
  REDHILL
  RH1 5RH
  Tel: 01737 768511

NHS WALK-IN CENTRE (TEDDINGTON) . . .7E 24
  Teddington Memorial Hospital
  Hampton Road
  TEDDINGTON
  TW11 0JL
  Tel: 020 8714 4004

NHS WALK-IN CENTRE (TOOTING) 6C 28
  St George's Hospital
  Blackshaw Road
  LONDON
  SW17 0QT
  Tel: 020 8700 0505

NHS WALK-IN CENTRE (WEYBRIDGE) 1B 56
  Weybridge Community Hospital
  22 Church Street
  WEYBRIDGE
  KT13 8DY
  Tel: 01932 826013

NHS WALK-IN CENTRE (WOKING) 5B 74
  Woking Community Hospital
  Heathside Road
  WOKING
  GU22 7HS
  Tel: 01483 846209

NORTH DOWNS PRIVATE HOSPITAL 3C 104
  46 Tupwood Lane
  CATERHAM
  CR3 6DP
  Tel: 01883 348981

PARKSIDE HOSPITAL 4J 27
  53 Parkside
  LONDON
  SW19 5NX
  Tel: 020 8971 8000

PAUL BEVAN HOUSE (THAMES HOSPICECARE)
  . . . . .2J 33
  King's Ride
  ASCOT
  SL5 7RD
  Tel: 01344 875555

PHYLLIS TUCKWELL HOSPICE 2K 129
  Waverley Lane
  FARNHAM
  GU9 8BL
  Tel: 01252 729400

PRINCESS ALICE HOSPICE 2A 58
  West End Lane
  ESHER
  KT10 8NA
  Tel: 01372 468811

PRINCESS MARGARET BMI HOSPITAL 5G 4
  Osborne Road
  WINDSOR
  SL4 3SJ
  Tel: 01753 743434

PRINCESS ROYAL UNIVERSITY HOSPITAL
  . . . . .1J 67
  Farnborough Common
  ORPINGTON
  BR6 8ND
  Tel: 01689 863000

PRIORY GRANGE STURT HOUSE 5F 100
  Sturts Lane
  Walton on the Hill
  TADWORTH
  KT20 7RQ
  Tel: 01737 817610

PURLEY WAR MEMORIAL HOSPITAL 7L **63**
856 Brighton Road
PURLEY
CR8 2YL
Tel: 020 8401 3000

QUEEN MARY'S HOSPITAL FOR CHILDREN
.....7A **44**
Wrythe Lane
CARSHALTON
SM5 1AA
Tel: 020 8296 2000

QUEEN MARY'S HOSPITAL, ROEHAMPTON
.....9F **12**
Roehampton Lane
LONDON
SW15 5PN
Tel: 020 8487 6000

QUEEN VICTORIA HOSPITAL 7B **166**
Holtye Road
EAST GRINSTEAD
RH19 3DZ
Tel: 01342 414000

RICHMOND ROYAL HOSPITAL 6L **11**
Kew Foot Road
RICHMOND
TW9 2TE
Tel: 020 3513 3200

RIDGEWOOD CENTRE 3G **71**
Old Bisley Road
CAMBERLEY
GU16 9QE
Tel: 01276 692919

ROEHAMPTON HUNTERCOMBE HOSPITAL
.....1F **26**
Holybourne Avenue
LONDON
SW15 4JD
Tel: 020 8780 6155

ROEHAMPTON PRIORY HOSPITAL 7E **12**
Priory Lane
LONDON
SW15 5JJ
Tel: 020 8876 8261

ROYAL HOSPITAL FOR NEURO-DISABILITY
.....9K **13**
West Hill
LONDON
SW15 3SW
Tel: 020 8780 4500

ROYAL MARSDEN HOSPITAL (SUTTON)
.....6A **62**
Downs Road
SUTTON
SM2 5PT
Tel: 020 8642 6011

ROYAL SURREY COUNTY HOSPITAL
.....3H **113**
Egerton Road
GUILDFORD
GU2 7XX
Tel: 01483 571122

RUNNYMEDE BMI HOSPITAL 9F **36**
Guildford Road
Ottershaw
CHERTSEY
KT16 0RQ
Tel: 01932 877800

ST ANTHONY'S HOSPITAL 7J **43**
801 London Road
SUTTON
SM3 9DW
Tel: 020 8337 6691

ST CATHERINE'S HOSPICE (CATERHAM)
.....8B **84**
Foxon Lane
Dormers
CATERHAM
CR3 5SG
Tel: 01293 447387

ST CATHERINE'S HOSPICE (CRAWLEY)
.....5B **182**
Malthouse Road
CRAWLEY
RH10 6BH
Tel: 01293 447333

ST EBBA'S 5B **60**
Hook Road
EPSOM
KT19 8QJ
Tel: 01883 388300

ST GEORGE'S HOSPITAL (TOOTING) 6B **28**
Blackshaw Road
LONDON
SW17 0QT
Tel: 020 8672 1255

ST HELIER HOSPITAL 7A **44**
Wrythe Lane
CARSHALTON
SM5 1AA
Tel: 020 8296 2000

ST PETER'S HOSPITAL 9F **36**
Guildford Road
CHERTSEY
KT16 0PZ
Tel: 01932 872000

ST RAPHAEL'S HOSPICE 8J **43**
London Road
SUTTON
SM3 9DX
Tel: 020 8335 4575

SAM BEARE HOSPICE 1B **56**
22 Church Street
WEYBRIDGE
KT13 8DY
Tel: 01932 826095

SHIRLEY OAKS BMI HOSPITAL 6F **46**
Poppy Lane
CROYDON
CR9 8AB
Tel: 020 8655 5500

SHOOTING STAR HOUSE, CHILDREN'S HOSPICE
.....7N **23**
The Avenue
HAMPTON
TW12 3RA
Tel: 020 8783 2000

SLOANE BMI HOSPITAL 1N **47**
125 Albemarle Road
BECKENHAM
BR3 5HS
Tel: 020 8466 4000

SOUTH WEST LONDON ELECTIVE
ORTHOPAEDIC CENTRE 2B **80**
Epsom General Hospital
Dorking Road
EPSOM
KT18 7EG
Tel: 01372 735800

SPRINGFIELD UNIVERSITY HOSPITAL
.....3C **28**
61 Glenburnie Road
LONDON
SW17 7DJ
Tel: 020 3513 5000

SUTTON HOSPITAL 6N **61**
Cotswold Road
SUTTON
SM2 5NF
Tel: 020 8296 2000

TEDDINGTON MEMORIAL HOSPITAL 7E **24**
Hampton Road
TEDDINGTON
TW11 0JL
Tel: 020 8714 4000

THAMES HOSPICECARE (WINDSOR) 6D **4**
Hatch Lane
Pine Lodge
WINDSOR
SL4 3RW
Tel: 08456 128812

TOLWORTH HOSPITAL 8N **41**
Red Lion Road
SURBITON
KT6 7QU
Tel: 020 3513 5000

WALTON COMMUNITY HOSPITAL
.....8J **39**
Rodney Road
WALTON-ON-THAMES
KT12 3LD
Tel: 01932 414205

WEST MIDDLESEX UNIVERSITY HOSPITAL
.....5G **11**
Twickenham Road
ISLEWORTH
TW7 6AF
Tel: 020 8560 2121

WEYBRIDGE COMMUNITY HOSPITAL
.....1B **56**
22 Church Street
WEYBRIDGE
KT13 8DY
Tel: 01932 852931

WOKING COMMUNITY HOSPITAL 5B **74**
Heathside Road
WOKING
GU22 7HS
Tel: 01483 715911

WOKINGHAM COMMUNITY HOSPITAL
.....2A **30**
41 Barkham Road
WOKINGHAM
RG41 2RE
Tel: 0118 949 5000

WOKING HOSPICE 5B **74**
5 Hill View Road
WOKING
GU22 7HW
Tel: 01483 881750

WOKING NUFFIELD HEALTH HOSPITAL
.....1A **74**
Shores Road
WOKING
GU21 4BY
Tel: 01483 3604071

WOKING PRIORY HOSPITAL 3F **72**
Chobham Road
Knaphill
WOKING
GU21 2QF
Tel: 01483 489211

The representation on the maps of a road, track or footpath is no evidence of the existence of a right of way.

The Grid on this map is the National Grid taken from Ordnance Survey® mapping with the permission of the Controller of Her Majesty's Stationery Office.

Copyright of Geographers' A-Z Map Company Ltd.

SAFETY CAMERA INFORMATION

PocketGPSWorld.com's CamerAlert is a self-contained speed and red light camera warning system for SatNavs and Android or Apple iOS smartphones/tablets. Visit www.cameralert.co.uk to download.

Safety camera locations are publicised by the Safer Roads Partnership which operates them in order to encourage drivers to comply with speed limits at these sites. It is the driver's absolute responsibility to be aware of and to adhere to speed limits at all times.

By showing this safety camera information it is the intention of Geographers' A-Z Map Company Ltd., to encourage safe driving and greater awareness of speed limits and vehicle speed. Data accurate at time of printing.